THIRD EDITION
VOLUME ONE

Worlds Together, WORLDS APART

GLOBAL SATELLITE MOSAIC

The beauty and complexity of Earth's landscape and below the oceans is revealed with the Global Satellite Mosaic. The mosaic was produced for the National Geographic Society by NASA's Jet Propulsion Laboratory, from more than 500 satellite images from the National Oceanic and Atmospheric Administration. The cloud-free images show Earth in its natural colors as it would be seen from space. One can easily identify the world's major glaciers, deserts, mountain ranges, and rain forests. For example, follow the green ribbon of lush vegetation along the Nile into the stark, dry Sahara. The mountain ranges seem to rise off the map thanks to digital elevation data from the Department of Defense. The deepest areas of the ocean realm are colored dark blue in contrast to the light blue areas highlighting continental shelves, submarine ridges, and underwater mountains.

BIOSPHERE

Thousands of satellite images combined to show a picture of biological productivity. In the oceans, red, yellow, and green indicate waters rich in phytoplankton. On land, green areas show high potential plant productivity; tan areas suffer from productivity limitations due to aridity and temperature.

THE W

SATELLI

NORTH POLAR REGION

SOUTH POLAR REGION

THE NEED FOR SATELLITES

SURFACE TEMPERATURE
Reddish colors vividly show average high temperatures on the two largest continents, Africa and Asia, from the Sahara to Central Asia. Latitude, mountains, and oceans influence land temperatures.

WORLD
TE MAP

WORLD · POLITICAL

NATIONAL BOUNDARIES

While man's impact is quite evident, and even striking, on many remotely sensed scenes, sometimes, as in the case with most political boundaries, it is invisible. State, provincial, and national boundaries can follow natural features, such as mountain ridges, rivers, or coastlines. Artificial constructs that possess no physical reality—for example, lines of latitude and longitude—can also determine political borders. The world political map (right) represents man's imaginary lines as they slice and divide Earth.

The National Geographic Society recognizes 192 independent states in the world as represented here. Of those nations, 185 are members of the United Nations.

Winkel Tripel Projection

ROBERT TIGNOR

JEREMY ADELMAN

PETER BROWN

BENJAMIN ELMAN

XINRU LIU

HOLLY PITTMAN

BRENT SHAW

THIRD EDITION
VOLUME ONE
BEGINNINGS THROUGH THE FIFTEENTH CENTURY

Worlds Together, WORLDS APART

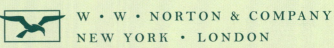

W · W · NORTON & COMPANY
NEW YORK · LONDON

W. W. Norton & Company has been independent since its founding in 1923, when William Warder Norton and Mary D. Herter Norton first published lectures delivered at the People's Institute, the adult education division of New York City's Cooper Union. The firm soon expanded its program beyond the Institute, publishing books by celebrated academics from America and abroad. By mid-century, the two major pillars of Norton's publishing program—trade books and college texts— were firmly established. In the 1950s, the Norton family transferred control of the company to its employees, and today—with a staff of four hundred and a comparable number of trade, college, and professional titles published each year—W. W. Norton & Company stands as the largest and oldest publishing house owned wholly by its employees.

Editor: Jon Durbin
Developmental Editor: Alice Vigliani
Copy Editor: Ellen Lohman
Project Editor: Rebecca Homiski
Photo Editor: Stephanie Romeo
Production Manager: Benjamin Reynolds
Managing Editor, College: Marian Johnson
Marketing Manager: Tamara McNeill
Emedia Editor: Steve Hoge
Design Director: Rubina Yeh
Ancillary Editor: Lorraine Klimowich
Editorial Assistant: Jason Spears
Layout Artist: Brad Walrod
Composition: TexTech, Inc.
Cartographer: Carto-Graphics/Alice Thiede

The Library of Congress has cataloged the one-volume edition as follows:

Worlds together, worlds apart : a history of the world from the beginnings of humankind to the present / Robert Tignor . . . [et al.]. — 3rd ed.
    p. cm.
  Includes bibliographical references and index.
  ISBN 978-0-393-93492-2 (hardcover)
1. World history. I. Tignor, Robert L.
  D21.W94 2011
  909—dc22

2010036837

This edition:
ISBN: 978-0-393-93493-9 (pbk.)

W. W. Norton & Company, Inc., 500 Fifth Avenue, New York, NY 10110
wwnorton.com

W. W. Norton & Company Ltd., Castle House, 75/76 Wells Street, London W1T 3QT

1 2 3 4 5 6 7 8 9

Contents in Brief

Contents

CHAPTER 2   RIVERS, CITIES, AND FIRST STATES, 4000–2000 BCE   43

CHAPTER 3   NOMADS, TERRITORIAL STATES, AND MICROSOCIETIES, 2000–1200 BCE   85

CHAPTER 6   SHRINKING THE AFRO-EURASIAN WORLD, 350 BCE–250 CE   203

CHAPTER 10   BECOMING "THE WORLD," 1000–1300 CE   363

CHAPTER 11   CRISES AND RECOVERY IN AFRO-EURASIA, 1300–1500   411

Global Connections & Disconnections Features

Primary Sources

Maps

Preface

The New Edition

Worlds Together, Worlds Apart has set the standard for two editions for those instructors who want to teach a globally integrated world history survey course. Just as the dynamic field of world history evolves, so has *Worlds Together, Worlds Apart* with each edition. With the Third Edition, *Worlds Together, Worlds Apart* continues to offer a highly coherent, cutting-edge survey of the field, while becoming more streamlined and accessible for a wider range of students. The Third Edition offers a number of improvements over the first two. First, the chapters are shorter. We cut the narrative by 50,000 words, reducing its length by nearly 20 percent. We shrank the text to highlight even more clearly the distinctive world history stories and themes that each chapter is built around. Readers should be in little doubt now about what truly counted globally in each of the time periods that the chapters cover. The new edition should also be a good page turner for students for while we reduced the length of the book to just over 840 pages, we did not dramatically cut back on the map, illustration, and primary-source programs. By shortening the text, we also wanted to allow instructors to make greater use of outside reading materials, especially primary sources, so vital to understanding the life and thought of people living in different time periods and which are locations. Second, pedagogically, we have re-written the chapter introductions to emphasize the themes even more strongly. We have also added a new pedagogy feature called "Storylines," which is designed to provide the reader with a snapshot of the main chapter themes and show how they relate to each major region of the world. We also went through all the pedagogical features with great care to make sure that the prose and questions were pitched at a good level for a wide range of students. Third, we are pleased to announce the publication of *Worlds Together, Worlds Apart: A Companion Reader*. Long-time users of the book have been asking for a primary-source reader designed to accompany *Worlds Together, Worlds Apart* since its First Edition. The companion reader has been carefully assembled by Ken Pomeranz, Laura Mitchell, and James Given, all of whom teach the world history survey course at the University of California, Irvine, and all of whom have been teaching with *Worlds Together, Worlds Apart* for many years. The companion reader contains nearly 150 primary sources (both visual and textual) and will greatly enhance an instructor's ability to teach students how to analyze primary sources, while building off the key themes and topics of *Worlds Together, Worlds Apart*. Finally, Norton StudySpace offers an exciting new feature called World History Tours powered by Google Maps. These digitally based tours trace global developments over time, touching down on locations to launch documents and images for analysis. For example, the Silk Road tour follows the bubonic plague from its eastern origins to Europe, chronicling this movement through journals and images from the Muslim world, Italy, and England.

Since work began on *Worlds Together, Worlds Apart*, world history has gained even more prominence in college classrooms and historical studies. Courses in the history of the world now abound, often replacing the standard surveys of European history and western civilization overviews. Graduate history students receive training in world history, and journals routinely publish studies in this field. A new generation of textbooks was needed to help students and instructors make sense of this vast, complex, and rapidly evolving field.

We believe that *Worlds Together, Worlds Apart* remains the most cutting-edge, engaging, readable, and useful text available for all students of world history. We also believe that this text, one that has advanced the teaching of this field, could have only grown out of the highly collaborative effort of a team of scholars and teachers rather than the more typical single- or two-author efforts. Indeed, the idea to build each chapter around stories of world history significance and the execution of this model grew out of our monthly team meetings and our joint writing efforts during the development stage. As a team-driven text, *Worlds Together, Worlds Apart* also has the advantage of area experts to make sure the material is presented accurately, which is always a challenge for the single- or two-author texts, especially in world history. Finally, our book also reads with a single voice due to the extraordinary efforts of our general editor, and leader, Robert Tignor, who with every edition makes the final major sweep through the text to make sure that the voice, style, and level of detail are consistent throughout. Building on these distinctive strengths, we have worked hard and thoughtfully to make the Third Edition of *Worlds Together, Worlds Apart* the best one so far. While there are many exciting additions to the main text and support package, we have made every effort to remain true to our original vision.

OUR GUIDING PRINCIPLES

Five principles inform this book, guiding its framework and the organization of its individual chapters. The first is that **world history is global history**. There are many fine histories of the individual regions of the world, which we have endeavored to make good use of. But unlike the authors of many other so-called world histories, we have chosen not to deal with the great regions and cultures of the world as separate units, reserving individual chapters to East Asia, South Asia, Southwest Asia, Europe, Africa, and the Americas. Our goal is to place each of these regions in its largest geographical context. Accordingly, we have written chapters that are truly global in that most major regions of the world are discussed in each one. We achieved these globally integrated chapters

by building each around a significant world history story or theme. There are a number of wonderful examples throughout the book, including the peopling of the earth (Chapter 1), the building of the Silk Road (Chapter 6), the rise of universal religions (Chapters 8 and 9), the Black Death (Chapter 11), the effects of New World silver on the economies of the world (Chapter 13), alternative visions to nineteenth-century capitalism (Chapter 15), the rise of nation states and empires (Chapter 16), and so on. It would be misleading, of course, to say that the context is the world, because none of these regions, even the most highly developed commercially, enjoyed commercial or cultural contact with peoples all over the globe before Columbus's voyage to the Americas and the sixteenth century. But the peoples living in the Afro-Eurasian landmass, probably the single most important building block for our study, were deeply influenced by one another, as were the more scattered peoples living in the Americas and in Africa below the Sahara. Products, ideas, and persons traveled widely across the large land units of Eurasia, Africa, and the Americas. Indeed, Afro-Eurasia was not divided or thought of as divided into separate landmasses until recent times. It is in this sense that our world history is global.

The second principle informing this work is **the importance of chronology in framing world history**. Rather than telling the story of world history by analyzing separate geographical areas, we have elected to frame the chapters around significant world history themes and periods that transcended regional and cultural boundaries—moments or periods of meaningful change in the way that human beings organized their lives. Some of these changes were dramatic and affected many people. Environments changed; the earth became drier and warmer; humans learned to domesticate plants and animals; technological innovations in warfare, political organization, and commercial activities occurred; and new religious and cultural beliefs spread far and wide. These changes swept across large landmasses, paying scant heed to preexisting cultural and geographical unity. They affected peoples living in widely dispersed societies. In other cases, changes occurred in only one locality while other places retained their traditions or took alternative routes. Chronology helps us understand the ways in which the world has, and has not, shared a common history.

The third principle is **historical and geographical balance**. Ours is not a history focused on the rise of the West. We seek to pay attention to the global histories of all peoples and not to privilege those developments that led directly into European history as if the rest of the history of the world was but a prelude to the rise of western civilization. We deal with peoples living outside Europe on their own terms and try to see world history from their perspective. Even more significantly, while we describe societies that obviously influenced Europe's historical development, we do so in a context very different from that which western historians have stressed. Rather than simply viewing these cultures in terms of their role in western development, we seek to understand them in their own terms and to illuminate the ways they influenced other parts of the world. From our perspective, it is historically inaccurate to annex Mesopotamia and Egypt to western civilization, because these territories lay well outside Europe and had a large influence on Africa, South Asia, and East Asia as well as on Europe. Indeed, our presentation of Europe in the period leading up to and including the founding of the Roman Empire is different from many of the standard treatments. The Europeans we describe are rather rough, wild-living, warring peoples living on the fringes of the settled parts of the world and looked down on by more politically stable communities. They hardly seem to be made of the stuff that will catapult Europeans to world leadership a millennium later—indeed, they were very different people from those who, as the result of myriad intervening and contingent events, founded the nineteenth- and twentieth-century empires whose ruins are still all around us.

Our fourth principle is **an emphasis on connections and what we call disconnections across societal and cultural boundaries.** World history is not the history of separate regions of the world at different periods of time. It is the history of the connections among peoples living often at great distances from one another, and it is also the history of the resistances of peoples living within and outside societies to connections that threatened to put them in subordinate positions or to rob them of their independence.

A stress on connections inevitably foregrounds those elements within societies that promoted long-distance ties. Merchants are important, as are military men and political potentates seeking to expand their polities. So are scholars and religious leaders, particularly those who believed that they had universalistic messages with which to convert others to their visions. Perhaps most important of all in pre-modern world history, certainly the most understudied, are the nomadic pastoral peoples, who were often the agents for the transmission of products, peoples, and ideas across long and harsh distances. They exploded onto the scene of settled societies at critical junctures, erasing old cultural and geographical barriers and producing new unities, as the Arabs did in the seventh century CE and the Mongols in the thirteenth century. *Worlds Together, Worlds Apart* is not intended to convey the message that the history of the world is a story of increasing integration. What for one ruling group brought benefits in the form of increased workforces, material prosperity, and political stability often meant enslavement, political subordination, and loss of territory for other groups. The historian's task, then, is not only to represent the different experiences of increased connectedness, describing worlds that came together, but also to be attentive to the opposite trends, describing peoples and communities that remained apart.

The fifth and final principle is that **world history is a narrative of big themes and high-level comparisons.** *Worlds Together, Worlds Apart* is not a book of record. Indeed, in a work that covers the whole of the historical record of humankind from the beginnings of history to the present, the notion that no event or individual worthy of attention would be excluded is the height of folly. We have sought to offer clear themes and interpretations in order to synthesize the vast body of data that often overwhelms histories of the world. Our aspiration is to identify the main historical forces that have moved history, to highlight those monumental innovations that have changed the way humans lived, and to describe the creation and evolution of those bedrock institutions, many of which, of course, endure. In this regard, self-conscious cross-cultural comparisons of developments, institutions, and even founding figures receive attention to make students aware that some common institutions, such as slavery, did not have the same features in every society. Or, in the opposite fashion, the seemingly diverse terms that were used, say, to describe learned and religious men in different parts of the world—monks in Europe, ulama in Islam, Brahmans in India, and scholar-gentries in China—often meant much the same thing in very different settings. We have constructed *Worlds Together, Worlds Apart* around big ideas, stories, and themes rather than filling the book with names and dates that encourage students only to memorize rather than understand world history concepts.

OUR MAJOR THEMES

The primary organizing framework of *Worlds Together, Worlds Apart*—one that runs through the chapters and connects the different parts of the volume—is the theme of **interconnection and divergence.** While describing movements that facilitated global connectedness, this book also shows how different regions developed their own ways of handling or resisting connections and change. Throughout history, different regions and different population groups often stood apart from the rest of the world until touched by traders or explorers or missionaries or soldiers. Some of these regions welcomed global connections. Others sought to change the nature of their connections with the outside world, and yet others resisted efforts to bring them into the larger world. All, however, were somehow affected by their experience of connection. Yet, the history of the world is not simply one of increasing globalization, in which all societies eventually join a common path to the present. Rather, it is a history of the ways in which, as people became linked, their experience of these global connections diverged.

Besides the central theme of interconnection and divergence, other themes also stand out in *Worlds Together, Worlds Apart*. First, the book discusses **how the recurring efforts of people to cross religious, political, and cultural borders brought the world together.** Merchants and educated men and women traded goods and ideas. Whole communities, in addition to select groups, moved to safer or more promising environments. **The transregional crossings of ideas, goods, and peoples produced transformations and conflicts**—a second important theme. Finally, the movement of ideas, peoples, products, and germs over long distances upset the balance of power across the world and within individual societies. Such movements changed the relationship of different population groups with other peoples and areas of the world and led over time to dramatic shifts in the ascendancy of regions. **Changes in power arrangements within and between regions explain which parts of the world and regional groups benefited from integration and which resisted it.** These three themes (exchange and migration, conflict and resistance, and alterations in the balance of power) weave themselves through every chapter of this work. While we highlight major themes throughout, we tell the stories of the people caught in these currents of exchange, conflict, and changing power relations, paying particular attention to the role that gender and the environment play in shaping the evolution of societies.

The history of the world is not a single, sweeping narrative. On the contrary, the last 5,000 years have produced multiple histories, moving along many paths and trajectories. Sometimes these histories merge, intertwining themselves in substantial ways. Sometimes they disentangle themselves and simply stand apart. Much of the time, however, they are simultaneously together and apart. In place of a single narrative, the usual one being the rise of the West, this book maps the many forks in the road that confronted the world's societies at different times and the surprising turns and unintended consequences that marked the choices that peoples and societies made, including the unanticipated and dramatic rise of the West in the nineteenth century. Formulated in this way, world history is the unfolding of many possible histories, and readers of this book should come away with a reinforced sense of the unpredictability of the past, the instability of the present, and the uncertainty of the future.

OVERVIEW OF VOLUME ONE

Volume One of *Worlds Together, Worlds Apart* deals with the period from the beginnings of human history through the Mongol invasions of the thirteenth century and the spread of the Black Death across Afro-Eurasia. It is divided into eleven chapters, each of which marks a distinct historical period. Hence, each chapter has an overarching theme or small set of themes that hold otherwise highly diverse material together.

Chapter 1, "Becoming Human," presents biological and cultural perspectives on the way that early hominoids became truly human. We believe that this chapter is important in establishing the global context of world history. We believe too that our chapter is unique in its focus on how humans became humans, so we discuss how early humans became bipedal and how they developed complex cognitive processes such as language and artistic abilities. Recent research indicates that *Homo sapiens* originated in Africa, probably no more than 200,000 years ago. These early men and women walked out of the African landmass sometime between 120,000 and 50,000 years ago, gradually populating all regions of the world. What is significant in this story is that the different population groups around the world, the so-called races of humankind, have only recently broken off from one another. Also in this chapter, we describe the domestication of plants and animals and the founding of the first village settlements around the globe.

NEW: Discussions of the role that dogs played in human evolution and the latest findings on the origins of humans.

Chapter 2, "Rivers, Cities, and First States, 4000–2000 BCE," covers the period during which five of the great river basins experienced extraordinary breakthroughs in human activity. On the flood plains of the Tigris and Euphrates in Mesopotamia, the Nile in Egypt, the Indus valley in modern-day northern India and Pakistan, and the Yellow and Yangzi rivers in China, men and women mastered annual floods and became expert in seeding and cultivating foodstuffs. In these areas, populations became dense. Riverine cultures had much in common. They had highly developed hierarchical political, social, and cultural systems, priestly and bureaucratic classes, and organized religious and cultural systems. But they also differed greatly, and these differences were passed from generation to generation. The development of these major complex societies certainly is a turning point in world history.

Extensive climatic and technological changes serve as major turning points for **Chapter 3, "Nomads, Territorial States, and Microsocieties, 2000–1200 BCE."** Drought, environmental degradation, and political instability brought the first riverine societies to a crashing end around 2000 BCE. When aridity forced tribal and nomadic peoples living on the fringes of the settled populations to move closer to settled areas, they brought with them an insurmountable military advantage. They had become adept at yoking horses to war chariots, and hence they were in a position to subjugate or intermarry with the peoples in the settled polities in the river basins. Around 2000 BCE these peoples established new territorial kingdoms in Mesopotamia, Egypt, the Indus valley, and China, which gave way a millennium later (1000 BCE) to even larger, militarily and politically more powerful states. In the Americas, the Mediterranean, sub-Saharan Africa, and the

Pacific worlds, microsocieties arose as an alternative form of polity in which peoples lived in much smaller-scale societies that showcased their own unique and compelling features.

NEW: Expanded discussions of how the Egyptian pyramids were built and their role in Egyptian cosmology and fuller integration of material on the environmental catastrophe that shaped the third millennium BCE.

Chapter 4, "First Empires and Common Cultures in Afro-Eurasia, 1200–350 BCE," describes the different ways in which larger-scale societies grew and became unified. In the case of the world's first empires, the neo-Assyrian and Persian, political power was the main unifying element. Both states established different models that future empires would emulate. The Assyrians used brutal force to intimidate and subjugate different groups within their societies and neighboring states. The Persians followed a pattern that relied less on coercion and more on tributary relationships, while reveling in cultural diversity. The Zhou state in China offered yet a third way of political unity, basing its rule on the doctrine of the mandate of heaven, which legitimated its rulers' succession as long as they were able to maintain stability and order. Vedic society in South Asia offers a dramatically different model in which religion and culture were the main unifying forces. Religion moves to the forefront of the narrative in other ways in this chapter. The birth of monotheism occurred in the Zoroastrian and Hebrew faiths and the beginnings of Buddhism. All three religions endure today.

NEW: Revised and expanded discussion of the origins of Judaism.

The last millennium before the common era witnessed some of the most monumental developments in human history. In the six and half centuries discussed in **Chapter 5, "Worlds Turned Inside Out, 1000–350 BCE,"** teachers and thinkers, rather than kings, priests, and warriors, came to the fore. Men like Confucius, the Buddha, Plato, and Aristotle, to name only the best known of this brilliant group, offered new insights into the natural world and provided new guidelines for how to govern justly and live ethically. In this era, small-scale societies, benefiting from more intimate relationships, took the place of the first great empires, now in decline. These highly individualistic cultures developed new strategies for political organization, even including experimenting with a democratic polity. In Africa, the Bantu peoples spread across sub-Saharan Africa, and the Sudanic peoples of Meroe created a society that blended Egyptian and sub-Saharan influences. These were all dynamic hybrid societies building on existing knowledge. Equally dramatic transformations occurred in the Americas, where the Olmec and Chavín peoples were creating hierarchical societies of the like never before seen in their part of the world.

NEW: Increased discussion of the first millennium as an "axial age."

Chapter 6, "Shrinking the Afro-Eurasian World, 350 BCE–250 CE," describes three major forces that simultaneously integrated large segments of the Afro-Eurasian landmass culturally and economically. First, Alexander and his armies changed the political and cultural landscape of North Africa and Southwest and South Asia. Culturally, Alexander spread Hellenism through North Africa and Southwest and central Asia, making it the first cultural system to achieve a transregional scope. Second, it was in the post-Alexander world that these commercial roads were stabilized and intensified. For the first time, a trading network, known as the Silk Road, stretching from Palmyra in the West to central Asia in the East, came into being. Buddhism was the first religion to seize on the Silk Road's more formal existence as its followers moved quickly with the support of the Mauryan Empire to spread their ideas into central Asia. Finally, we witness the growth of a "silk road of the seas" as new technologies and bigger ships allowed for a dramatic expansion in maritime trade from South Asia all the way to Egypt and East Africa.

Chapter 7, "Han Dynasty China and Imperial Rome, 300 BCE–300 CE," compares Han China and the Roman Empire, the two political, economic, and cultural systems that dominated much of the Afro-Eurasian landmass from 200 BCE to 200 CE. Both the Han Dynasty and the Roman Empire ruled effectively in their own way, providing an instructive comparative case study. Both left their imprint on Afro-Eurasia, and rulers for centuries afterward tried to revive these glorious polities and use them as models of greatness. This chapter also discusses the effect of state sponsorship on religion, as Christianity came into existence in the context of the late Roman Empire and Buddhism was introduced to China during the decline of the Han.

Out of the crumbling Roman Empire new polities and a new religion emerged, the major topic of **Chapter 8, "The Rise of Universal Religions, 300–600 CE."** The Byzantine Empire, claiming to be the successor state to the Roman Empire, embraced Christianity as its state religion. The Tang rulers patronized Buddhism to such a degree that Confucian statesmen feared it had become the state religion. Both Buddhism and Christianity enjoyed spectacular success in the politically fragmented post-Han era in China and in the feudal world of western Europe. These dynamic religions represent a decisive transformation in world history. Christianity enjoyed its eventual successes through state sponsorship via the Roman and Byzantine empires and by providing spiritual comfort and hope during the chaotic years of Rome's decline. Buddhism grew through imperial sponsorship and significant changes to its fundamental beliefs, when adherents to the faith deified Buddha and created notions of an afterlife. In Africa a wide range of significant developments and a myriad of cultural practices existed; yet large common cultures also arose. The Bantu peoples spread throughout the southern half of the landmass, spoke closely related languages, and developed similar political institutions based on the prestige of individuals of high achievement. In the Americas the Olmecs established their own form of the city-state, while the Mayans owed their success to a decentralized common culture built around a strong religious belief system and a series of spiritual centers.

NEW: Revised discussions of what enables a religion to become "universal."

In **Chapter 9, "New Empires and Common Cultures, 600–1000 CE,"** in a relatively remote corner of the Arabian Peninsula another world religion, Islam, exploded with world-changing consequences. The rise of Islam provides a contrast to the way in which universalizing religions and political empires interacted. Islam and empire arose in a fashion quite different from Christianity and the Roman Empire. Christianity took over an already existing empire—the Roman—after suffering persecution at its hands for several centuries. In contrast, Islam created an empire almost at the moment of its emergence. By the time the Abbasid Empire came into being in the middle of the eighth century, Islamic armies, political leaders, and clerics exercised power over much of the Afro-Eurasian landmass from southern Spain, across North Africa, all the way to Central Asia. The Tang Empire in China, however, served as a counterweight to Islam's power both politically and intellectually. Confucianism enjoyed a spectacular recovery in this period. With the Tang rulers, Confucianism slowed the spread of Buddhism and further reinforced China's development along different, more secular pathways. Japan and Korea also enter world history at this time, as tributary states to Tang China and as hybrid cultures that mixed Chinese customs and practices with their own. The Christian world split in this period between the western Latin church and the eastern Byzantine church. Both branches of Christianity played a role in unifying societies, especially in western Europe, which lacked strong political rule.

NEW: Reorganized to integrate material on the agricultural revolutions that spread across Afro-Eurasia as a result of the rise of Islam between 600 and 1000 BCE.

In the three centuries from 1000 to 1300 (**Chapter 10, "Becoming 'the World,' 1000–1300 CE"**) Afro-Eurasia experienced an unprecedented rise in prosperity and population that even spread into West and East Africa. Just as importantly, the world in this period divided into regional zones that are recognizable today. And trade grew rapidly.

A view of the major trading cities of this time demonstrates how commerce transformed cultures. Sub-Saharan Africa also underwent intense regional integration via the spread of the Mande-speaking peoples and the Mali Empire.

The Americas witnessed their first empire in the form of the Chimu peoples in the Andes. This chapter ends with the Mongol conquests of the twelfth and thirteenth centuries, which brought massive destruction. The Mongol Empire, however, once in place, promoted long-distance commerce, scholarly exchange, and travel on an unprecedented scale. The Mongols brought Eurasia, North Africa, and many parts of sub-Saharan Africa into a new connectedness. The Mongol story also underscores the important role that nomads played throughout the history of the early world.

NEW: Expanded discussion of the Crusades.

The Black Death brought Afro-Eurasia's prosperity and population growth to a catastrophic end as discussed in **Chapter 11, "Crises and Recovery in Afro-Eurasia, 1300s–1500s."** The dying and destruction of the fourteenth century saw traditional institutions give way and forced peoples to rebuild their cultures. The polities that came into being at this time and the intense religious experimentation that took place effected a sharp break with the past. The bubonic plague wiped out as much as two-thirds of the population in many of the densely settled locations of Afro-Eurasia. Societies were brought to their knees by the Mongols' depredations as well as by biological pathogens. In the face of one of humanity's grimmest periods, peoples and societies demonstrated tremendous resilience as they looked for new ways to rebuild their communities, some turning inward and others seeking inspiration, conquests, and riches elsewhere. Volume One concludes on the eve of the "Columbian Exchange," the moment when "old" worlds discovered "new" ones and a vast series of global interconnections and divergences commenced.

NEW: Expanded discussion of the Renaissance.

OVERVIEW OF VOLUME TWO

The organizational structure for Volume Two reaffirms the commitment to write a decentered, global history of the world. Christopher Columbus is not the starting point, as he is in so many modern world histories. Rather, we begin in the eleventh and twelfth centuries with two major developments in world history: the Mongols and the Black Death. The first, set forth in **Chapter 10, "Becoming 'the World,' 1000–1300 CE,"** describes a world that was divided for the first time into regions that are recognizable today. This world experienced rapid population growth, as is shown by a simple look at the major trading cities from Asia in the East to the Mediterranean in the West. Yet nomadic peoples remain a force as revealed in the Mongol invasions of Afro-Eurasia.

NEW: Expanded discussion of the Crusades.

Chapter 11, "Crises and Recovery in Afro-Eurasia, 1300s–1500s," describes how the Mongol warriors, through their conquests and the integration of the Afro-Eurasian world, spread the bubonic plague, which brought death and depopulation to much of Afro-Eurasia. Both these stories set the stage for the modern world and are clear-cut turning points in world history. The primary agents of world connection described in this chapter were dynasts, soldiers, clerics, merchants, and adventurers who rebuilt the societies that disease and political collapse had destroyed.

NEW: Expanded discussion of the Renaissance.

The Mongols joined the two hemispheres, as we describe in **Chapter 12, "Contact, Commerce, and Colonization, 1450s–1600,"** bringing the peoples and products of the Western Hemisphere into contact and conflict with Eurasia and Africa. It is the collision between the Eastern and Western Hemispheres that sets in motion modern world history and marks a distinct divide or turning point between the premodern and the modern. Here, too, disease and increasing trade linkages were vital. Unprepared for the advanced military technology and the disease pool of European and African peoples, the Amerindian population experienced a population decline even more devastating than that caused by the Black Death.

NEW: Expanded discussion of the Protestant Reformation.

Europeans sailed across the Atlantic Ocean to find a more direct, less encumbered route to Asia and came upon lands, peoples, and products that they had not expected. One item, however, that they had sought in every part of the world and that they found in abundance in the Americas was precious metal. In **Chapter 13, "Worlds Entangled, 1600–1750,"** we discuss how New World silver from Mexico and Peru became the major currency of global commerce, oiling the long-distance trading networks that had been revived after the Black Death. The effect of New World silver on the world economy was so great that it, even more than the Iberian explorations of the New World, brought the hemispheres together and marks the true genesis of modern world history. Sugar also linked the economies and polities of western Europe, Africa, and the Americas and was a powerful force in a triangular trade centered on the Atlantic Ocean. This trade involved the shipment of vast numbers of African captives to the Americas, where they toiled on sugar, tobacco, cotton, and rice slave plantations.

Chapter 14, "Cultures of Splendor and Power, 1500–1780," discusses the Ottoman scientists, Safavid and Mughal artists, and Chinese literati, as well as European thinkers, whose notable achievements were rooted in their own cultures but tempered by awareness of the intellectual activities of others. In this chapter, we look closely at how culture is created as a historical process and describe how the massive increase in wealth during this period, growing out of global trade, led to one of the great periods of cultural flourishing in world history.

NEW: Discussions of the Seven Years' War as the first global war.

Around 1800, transformations reverberated outward from the Atlantic world and altered economic and political relationships in the rest of the world. In **Chapter 15, "Reordering the World, 1750–1850,"** we discuss how political revolutions in the Americas and Europe, new ideas about how to trade and organize labor, and a powerful rhetoric of freedom and universal rights underlay the beginning of "a great divide" between peoples of European descent and those who were not. These forces of laissez-faire capitalism, industrialization, the nation-state, and republicanism not only attracted diverse groups around the world; they also threatened groups that put forth alternative visions. Ideas of freedom, as manifested in trading relations, labor, and political activities, clashed with a traditional world based on inherited rights and statuses and further challenged the way men and women had lived in earlier times. These political, intellectual, and economic reorderings changed the way people around the world saw themselves and thus represent something quite novel in world history.

NEW: Discussions of "industriousness" and how the work habits of westerners were changing in the period before the Industrial Revolution.

These new ways of envisioning the world did not go unchallenged, as **Chapter 16, "Alternative Visions of the Nineteenth Century,"** makes clear. Here, intense resistance to evolving modernity reflected the diversity of peoples and their hopes for the future. Wahabbism in Islam, the strongman movement in Africa, Indian resistance in America and Mexico, socialism and communism in Europe, the Taiping Rebellion in China, and the Indian Mutiny in South Asia catapulted to historical prominence prophets and leaders whose visions often drew on earlier traditions and led these individuals to resist rapid change.

NEW: Streamlined discussions comparing the alternative visions of the nineteenth century.

Chapter 17, "Nations and Empires, 1850–1914," discusses the political, economic, military, and ideological power that thrust Europe and North America to the fore of global events and led to an era of nationalism and modern imperialism, new forces in world history. Yet this period of seeming European supremacy was to prove short-lived.

As **Chapter 18, "An Unsettled World, 1890–1914,"** demonstrates, even before World War I shattered Europe's moral certitude, many groups at home (feminists, Marxists, and unfulfilled nationalists) and abroad (anti-colonial nationalists) had raised a chorus of complaints about European and North American dominance. As in Chapter 14, we look at the processes by which specific cultural movements rose and reflected the concerns of individual societies. Yet here, too, syncretistic movements emerged in many cultures and reflected the sway of global imperialism, which by then had become a dominant force.

NEW: Revised discussions of cultural modernism.

Chapter 19, "Of Masses and Visions of the Modern, 1910–1939," briefly covers World War I and then discusses how, from the end of World War I until World War II, different visions of being modern competed around the world. It is the development of modernism and its effects on multiple cultures that integrate the diverse developments discussed in this chapter. In the decades between the world wars, proponents of liberal democracy struggled to defend their views and often to impose their will on authoritarian rulers and anticolonial nationalists.

NEW: Discussions of the Spanish Civil War as a global phenomenon.

Chapter 20, "The Three-World Order, 1940–1975," presents World War II and describes how new adversaries arose after the war. A three-world order came into being—the First World, led by the United States and extolling capitalism, the nation-state, and democratic government; the Second World, led by the Soviet Union and favoring authoritarian polities and economies; and the Third World, made up of former colonies seeking an independent status for themselves in world affairs. The rise of this three-world order dominates the second half of the twentieth century and constitutes another major theme of world history.

NEW: Expanded discussions of the Holocaust.

In **Chapter 21, "Globalization, 1970–2000,"** we explain that, at the end of the cold war, the modern world, while clearly more unified than before, still had profound cultural differences and political divisions. At the beginning of the twenty-first century, capital, commodities, peoples, and ideas move rapidly over long distances. But cultural tensions and political impasses continue to exist. It is the rise of this form of globalism that represents a vital new element as humankind heads into a new century and millennium.

We close with an **Epilogue**, which tracks developments since the turn of the millennium. These last few years have brought profound changes to the world order, yet we hope readers of *Worlds Together, Worlds Apart* will see more clearly how this most recent history is, in fact, entwined with trends of much longer duration that are the chief focus of this book.

NEW: Fully up-to-date on the global financial collapse, wars in the Middle East, and the Obama presidency.

INNOVATIVE PEDAGOGICAL PROGRAM, MADE BETTER

Worlds Together, Worlds Apart is designed for maximum readability. The crisp, clear, and succinct narrative, built around memorable world history stories and themes, is reinforced through a highly innovative pedagogical program designed to help students think critically and master the core content. All the pedagogical elements have been carefully revised for the Third Edition to ensure that students will find them highly useful. Highlights of this innovative program are described below.

NEW "STORYLINES" FEATURE

New "Storylines" features provide a thematic snapshot of the chapter and appear right after the chapter introduction. Each "Storylines" feature highlights the chapter themes and shows how they apply to each region of the world.

STELLAR MAP PROGRAM WITH NEW GUIDING QUESTIONS

The book's more than 120 beautiful maps are designed to reinforce the main stories and themes in each chapter. Most chapters open with a beautiful two-page map of the world to highlight the main storyline of the chapter. Within the chapter are four to five more maps that focus on the regions covered. Enhanced captions with new guiding questions help students learn how to read historical maps and to understand the relationship between geography and history.

REVISED FOCUS-QUESTION SYSTEM

The focus-question system has been fully revised and now contains more manageable questions in order to help the reader remain alert to key concepts and questions on every page of the text. Focus questions guide students' reading in three ways: (1) a focus question box at the beginning of the chapter previews the chapter's contents, (2) relevant questions reappear at the start of the section where they are discussed, and (3) running heads on right-hand pages keep these questions in view throughout the chapter.

PRIMARY-SOURCE DOCUMENTS WITH NEW QUESTIONS FOR ANALYSIS

The authors have selected three to five primary-source documents for each chapter that reinforce the chapter's main themes and help students learn how to analyze primary sources. Many of them challenge students to see world history through the eyes of others and from different perspectives. The questions for analysis after each document have been carefully revised to draw students into the document, moving from simpler to more complex. Additional primary sources are available in *Worlds Together, Worlds Apart: A Companion Reader* and in the Digital History Reader, which is part of the Norton StudySpace website.

GLOBAL CONNECTIONS & DISCONNECTIONS

Each chapter contains one thematic feature built around key individuals or phenomena that exemplify the main emphasis of the text. Among the many topics are how historians use technology to date bones and objects from early history, the use of ritual funeral objects in the contexts of religion and trade, the role of libraries in early world history, the travels of Marco Polo and Ibn Battuta, coffee drinking and coffeehouses in different parts of the world, cartography and maps as expressions of different worldviews, the growth of universities around the world, and Che Guevera as a radical visionary who tried to export revolution throughout the Third World.

STREAMLINED CHAPTER CHRONOLOGIES

Chapter chronologies appear at the end of each chapter, and they are organized regionally rather than temporally. The chapter chronologies have been streamlined for the Third Edition to make it easier for students to identify the most important events, to track unifying concepts, and to see influences across cultures and societies within a given time period.

REVISED STUDY QUESTIONS

New Study Questions appear at the end of each chapter. Each question has been carefully crafted to ensure that students can identify chapter themes, master core content, and identify the most important comparisons and connections from the reading.

FURTHER READINGS

A section at the back of the book includes an ample list of up-to-date suggestions for further reading, broken down by chapter and annotated so that students can see what each work covers.

RESOURCES FOR INSTRUCTORS

INSTRUCTOR'S MANUAL

Amy Hudnall and Neva Specht
Appalachian State University
Includes chapter outlines, lecture ideas, classroom activities, recommended books, recommended film lists with annotations, and recommended websites.

TEST BANK/COMPUTERIZED TEST BANK

Sara Jorgensen and Andrea Becksvoort
University of Tennessee, Chattanooga
The Test Bank has been revised in accordance with the Norton Assessment Guidelines. Questions are organized around a Concept Map and are ranked by knowledge type, difficulty, and section reference.

All Norton test banks are available with Exam View Test Generator software, allowing instructors to effortlessly create, administer, and manage assessments. The convenient and intuitive testmaking wizard makes it easy to create customized exams with no software learning curve. Other key features include the ability to create paper exams with algorithmically generated variables and to export files directly to Blackboard, WebCT, and Angel.

INSTRUCTOR'S RESOURCE DISC

This helpful classroom presentation tool features:
- Lecture PowerPoint slides that include a suggested classroom-lecture script in the notes field. These are particularly helpful to first-time teachers of the course.
- A separate set of art PowerPoints featuring photographs and maps, retouched for in-class projection.

DOWNLOADABLE INSTRUCTOR'S RESOURCES

wwnorton.com/instructors
Instructional content for use in lecture and distance education, including coursepacks, test banks, PowerPoint lecture slides, images, figures, and more.

COURSEPACKS

Available at no cost to professors or students, Norton coursepacks for online or hybrid courses are available in a variety of formats, including all versions of Blackboard and WebCT. With just a simple download from our instructor's website, an instructor can bring high-quality Norton digital media into a new or existing online course (no extra student passwords required), and it's theirs to keep forever. Content includes chapter-based assignments, test banks and quizzes, interactive learning tools, and selected content from the StudySpace website.

NORTON GRADEBOOK

With the free, easy-to-use Norton Gradebook, instructors can easily access StudySpace student quiz results and avoid email inbox clutter. No course setup required. For more information and an audio tour of the Gradebook, visit wwnorton.com/college/nrl/gradebook.

NORTON ONLINE

Norton Online provides a seamless and flexible online learning environment featuring proven resources that help students succeed. By integrating Norton's market-leading textbooks with interactive tools in an easy-to-use learning-management system, Norton Online provides a high-quality online course that can be used right away or customized to suit an instructor's specific needs.

RESOURCES FOR STUDENTS

STUDYSPACE: YOUR PLACE FOR A BETTER GRADE

StudySpace tells students what they know, shows them what they need to review, and then gives them an organized study plan to master the material.

Students rely on effective and well-designed online resources to help them succeed in their courses—StudySpace is unmatched in providing a one-stop solution that's closely aligned with their textbook. This free and easy-to-navigate website offers students an impressive range of exercises, interactive-learning tools, assessment, and review materials, including:

Quiz+ Quiz+ doesn't just tell students how they did; it shows them how they can do better. With Quiz+, students are presented with a targeted study plan that offers specific page references and links to the ebook and other online learning tools.

NEW: World History Tours powered by Google Maps. These tours trace global developments over time, touching down on locations to launch documents and images for analysis.

NEW: Nearly 100 new documents increase the collection of readings to 350 sources. Each source is accompanied by a media analysis worksheet that offers students a simple guided method to *Observe* a document's primary themes, *Express* an opinion or respond to the author's objective, and *Connect* the document to broader historical relevance.

Engaging Review Materials include chapter summaries and outlines, focus questions, flashcards with audio pronunciations, and diagnostic quizzes.

More Help with Geography: iMaps offer students tools to view maps one layer of information at a time, focusing on specific geographic sections.

Map Review Worksheets provide each map in the textbook as a label-less image; students are given a list of labels to connect to the map. These worksheets can be printed out so that the exercises can be completed off line.

Chrono-Sequencers: These interactive chapter chronologies challenge students to reassemble sequences of events and reinforce their understanding of the flow of history.

Research Topics and Documents: Each chapter clusters primary sources around a topic, complete with an opening question and introduction to help students focus on the connections between the documents.

EBOOK AND CUSTOM VERSIONS

Ebook: Same great book, *one-third* the price!
An affordable and convenient alternative, Norton ebooks retain the content and design of the print book and allow students to highlight and take notes with ease, print chapters as needed, and search the text. Norton ebooks are available online and as downloadable PDFs. They can be purchased directly from our website or with a registration folder that can be sold in the bookstore.

Chapter Select
With Chapter Select instructors can create a custom ebook that contains only the chapters they want to assign. For more information, go to nortonebooks.com: includes pricing and purchasing details as well as instructions about how to create a custom ebook using Chapter Select.

ACKNOWLEDGMENTS

Worlds Together, Worlds Apart would never have happened without the full support of Princeton University. In a highly unusual move, and one for which we are truly grateful, the university helped underwrite this project with financial support from its 250th Anniversary Fund for undergraduate teaching and by allowing release time for the authors from campus commitments.

The history department's support of the effort over many years has been exceptional. Four chairs made funds and departmental support available, including the department's incomparable administrative talents. We would be remiss if we did not single out the department manager, Judith Hanson, who provided us with assistance whenever we needed it. We also thank Eileen Kane, who provided help in tracking down references and illustrations and in integrating changes into the manuscript. We also would like to thank Pamela Long, who made all of the complicated arrangements for ensuring that we were able to discuss matters in a leisurely and attractive setting. Sometimes that meant arranging for long-distance conference calls. She went even further and proofread the entire manuscript, finding many errors that we had all overlooked.

We drew shamelessly on the expertise of the departmental faculty, and although it might be wise simply to include a roster of the Princeton history department, that would do an injustice to those of whom we took most advantage. So here they are: Mariana Candido, Robert Darnton, Sheldon Garon, Anthony Grafton, Molly Greene, David Howell, Harold James, William Jordan, Emmanuel Kreike, Michael Mahoney, Arno Mayer, Kenneth Mills, John Murrin, Susan Naquin,

Willard Peterson, Theodore Rabb, Bhavani Raman, Stanley Stein, and Richard Turits. When necessary, we went outside the history department, getting help from L. Carl Brown, Michael Cook, Norman Itzkowitz, Martin Kern, Thomas Leisten, Heath Lowry, and Peter Schaefer. Two departmental colleagues—Natalie Z. Davis and Elizabeth Lunbeck—were part of the original team but had to withdraw because of other commitments. Their contributions were vital, and we want to express our thanks to them. David Gordon, now at Bowdoin College, used portions of the text while teaching an undergraduate course at the University of Durban in South Africa and shared comments with us. Shamil Jeppie, like David Gordon a graduate of the Princeton history department, now teaching at the University of Cape Town in South Africa, read and commented on various chapters.

Beyond Princeton, we have also benefited from exceptionally gifted and giving colleagues who have assisted this book in many ways. Colleagues at Louisiana State University, the University of Florida, the University of North Carolina, the University of Pennsylvania, and the University of California at Los Angeles, where Suzanne Marchand, Michael Tsin, Holly Pittman, and Stephen Aron, respectively, are now teaching, pitched in whenever we turned to them. Especially helpful have been the contributions of James Gelvin, Naomi Lamoreaux, Gary Nash, and Joyce Appleby at UCLA; Michael Bernstein at Tulane University; and Maribel Dietz, John Henderson, Christine Kooi, David Lindenfeld, Reza Pirbhai, and Victor Stater at Louisiana State University. It goes without saying that none of these individuals bears any responsibility for factual or interpretive errors that the text may contain. Xinru Liu would like to thank her Indian mentor, Romila Thapar, who changed the way we think about Indian history.

The quality and range of reviews on this project were truly exceptional. The final version of the manuscript was greatly influenced by the thoughts and ideas of numerous instructors. We wish to particularly thank our consulting reviewers, who read multiple versions of the manuscript from start to finish.

First Edition Consultants
Hugh Clark, Ursinus College
Jonathan Lee, San Antonio College
Pamela McVay, Ursuline College
Tom Sanders, United States Naval Academy

Second Edition Consultants
Jonathan Lee, San Antonio College
Pamela McVay, Ursuline College
Steve Rapp, Georgia State University
Cliff Rosenberg, City University of New York

First Edition Reviewers
Lauren Benton, New Jersey Institute of Technology
Ida Blom, University of Bergen, Norway

Ricardo Duchesne, University of New Brunswick
Major Bradley T. Gericke, United States Military Academy
John Gillis, Rutgers University
David Kenley, Marshall University
John Kicza, Washington State University
Matthew Levinger, Lewis and Clark College
James Long, Colorado State University
Adam McKeown, Columbia University
Mark McLeod, University of Delaware
John Mears, Southern Methodist University
Michael Murdock, Brigham Young University
David Newberry, University of North Carolina, Chapel Hill
Tom Pearcy, Slippery Rock State University
Oliver B. Pollak, University of Nebraska, Omaha
Ken Pomeranz, University of California, Irvine
Major David L. Ruffley, United States Air Force Academy
William Schell, Murray State University
Major Deborah Schmitt, United States Air Force Academy
Sarah Shields, University of North Carolina, Chapel Hill
Mary Watrous-Schlesinger, Washington State University

Second Edition Reviewers
William Atwell, Hobart and William Smith Colleges
Susan Besse, City University of New York
Tithi Bhattacharya, Purdue University
Mauricio Borrerero, St. John's University
Charlie Briggs, Georgia Southern University
Antoinne Burton, University of Illinois, Urbana-Champaign
Jim Cameron, St. Francis Xavier University
Kathleen Comerford, Georgia Southern University
Duane Corpis, Georgia State University
Denise Davidson, Georgia State University
Ross Doughty, Ursinus College
Alison Fletcher, Kent State University
Phillip Gavitt, Saint Louis University
Brent Geary, Ohio University
Henda Gilli-Elewy, California State Polytechnic University, Pomona
Fritz Gumbach, John Jay College
William Hagen, University of California, Davis
Laura Hilton, Muskingum College
Jeff Johnson, Villanova University
David Kammerling-Smith, Eastern Illinois University
Jonathan Lee, San Antonio College
Dorothea Martin, Appalachian State University
Don McGuire, State University of New York, Buffalo
Pamela McVay, Ursuline College
Joel Migdal, University of Washington
Anthony Parent, Wake Forest University
Sandra Peacock, Georgia Southern University
David Pietz, Washington State University
Jared Poley, Georgia State University

John Quist, Shippensburg State University
Steve Rapp, Georgia State University
Paul Rodell, Georgia Southern University
Ariel Salzman, Queen's University
Bill Schell, Murray State University
Claire Schen, State University of New York, Buffalo
Jonathan Skaff, Shippensburg State University
David Smith, California State Polytechnic University, Pomona
Neva Specht, Appalachian State University
Ramya Sreeniva, State University of New York, Buffalo
Charles Stewart, University of Illinois, Urbana-Champaign
Rachel Stocking, Southern Illinois University, Carbondale
Heather Streets, Washington State University
Tim Teeter, Georgia Southern University
Charlie Wheeler, University of California, Irvine
Owen White, University of Delaware
James Wilson, Wake Forest University

Third Edition Reviewers
Henry Antkiewicz, Eastern Tennessee State University
Anthony Barbieri-Lowi, University of California, Santa Barbara
Andrea Becksvoort, University of Tennessee, Chattanooga
Hayden Bellonoit, United States Naval Academy
John Bloom, Shippensburg University
Kathryn Braund, Auburn University
Catherine Candy, University of New Orleans
Karen Carter, Brigham Young University
Stephen Chappell, James Madison University
Jessey Choo, University of Missouri, Kansas City
Timothy Coates, College of Charleston
Gregory Crider, Wingate University
Denise Davidson, Georgia State University
Jessica Davidson, James Madison University
Sal Diaz, Santa Rosa Junior College
Todd Dozier, Baton Rouge Community College
Richard Eaton, University of Arizona
Lee Farrow, Auburn University, Montgomery
Bei Gao, College of Charleston
Behrooz Ghamari-Tabrizi, University of Illinois, Urbana-Champaign
Steven Gish, Auburn University, Montgomery
Jeffrey Hamilton, Baylor University
Barry Hankins, Baylor University
Brian Harding, Mott Community College
Tim Henderson, Auburn University, Montgomery
Marjorie Hilton, University of Redlands
Richard Hines, Washington State University
Lisa Holliday, Appalachian State University
Jonathan Lee, San Antonio College
David Kalivas, University of Massachusetts, Lowell

Christopher Kelley, Miami University, Ohio
Kenneth Koons, Virginia Military Institute
Michael Kulikowski, Pennsylvania State University
Benjamin Lawrence, University of California, Davis
Lu Liu, University of Tennessee, Knoxville
David Longfellow, Baylor University
Harold Marcuse, University of California, Santa Barbara
Dorothea Martin, Appalachian State University
David Mayes, Sam Houston State University
James Mokhiber, University of New Orleans
Mark Munzinger, Radford College
David Murphree, Virginia Tech University
Joshua Nadel, North Carolina Central University
Wing Chung Nq, University of Texas, San Antonio
Robert Norrell, University of Tennessee, Knoxville
Chandrika Paul, Shippensburg University
Beth Pollard, San Diego State University
Timothy Pytell, California State University, San Bernardino
Stephen Rapp, Professional Historian
Alice Roberti, Santa Rosa Junior College
Aviel Roshwald, Georgetown University
James Sanders, Utah State University
Lynn Sargeant, California State University, Fullerton
William Schell, Murray State University
Michael Seth, James Madison University
Barry Stentiford, Grambling State University
Gabrielle Sutherland, Baylor University
Lisa Tran, California State University, Fullerton
Michael Vann, California State University, Sacramento
Peter Von Sivers, University of Utah
Andrew Wackerfuss, Georgetown University
Ted Weeks, Southern Illinois University, Carbondale
Angela White, Indiana University of Pennsylvania
Jennifer Williams, Nichols State University
Andrew Wise, State University of New York, Buffalo
Eloy Zarate, Pasadena City College
William Zogby, Mohawk Valley Community College

We also want to thank Nancy Khalek (Ph.D. Princeton University), who now teaches at Brown University. Nancy was our jack-of-all-trades who helped in any way she could. She attended all the monthly meetings during the development of the early volume. She provided critiques of the manuscript, helped with primary research, worked on the photo program and the Global Connections & Disconnections features, and contributed content to the student website. She was invaluable. For the Third Edition, Nancy has authored a number of the new digital World History Tours powered by Google Maps. We would also like to thank Neva Specht and Amy Hudnall (both from Appalachian State University), who have authored the Instructor's Manual for the last two editions. They have filled the manual with many wonderful classroom exercises and a highly useful annotated suggested films list. Finally, we'd like to thank our two newcomers, Sara Jorgensen and Andrea Becksvoort (both from the University of Tennessee, Chattanooga) for thoroughly revising the test bank.

Our association with the publisher of this volume, W. W. Norton & Company, has been everything we could have asked for. Jon Durbin took us under the wing of the Norton firm. He attended all of our monthly meetings for the first two editions spanning the better part of four years across the creation of both volumes. How he put up with some of our interminable discussions will always be a mystery, but his enthusiasm for the endeavor never flagged, even when we seemed to grow weary. He has brought the same energy and determination to the Third Edition. Sandy Lifland was the ever-watchful and ever-careful development editor for each volume for the First Edition and a good portion of the Second Edition. She let us know when we were making sense and when we needed to explain ourselves more fully. Alice Falk was our talented and insightful co-developmental editor for the Second Edition. Between the efforts of Sandy and Alice, our vision became a reality. For the Third Edition, Alice Vigliani was an unimaginably superb development editor. She took a book that we were all very proud of, and she has helped bring it closest to our original vision. She responded immediately to all queries, kept everyone on an even keel, shrank the text where it was too wordy, and demanded that we add color and vitality where the writing flagged. If the Third Edition showcases the big world history stories better than ever, and it is easier to read and more accessible than the first two (and we believe that this is the case), we owe these improvements to her. Rebecca

Homiski did a fabulous job as our project editor on the Second and Third editions, coordinating the responses of up to twelve authors on both volumes combined and locking down all the details on the project. We also want to thank Ellen Lohman for copyediting the manuscript ably and with just the right touch for the Second and Third Editions. Stephanie Romeo led the charge again, finding all the new photos we requested, and Rubina Yeh integrated the new "Storylines" features and the new chapter chronologies into her already gorgeous design. Debra Morton-Hoyt has provided us again with what have to be the most distinctive and appealing world history book covers in the field. Ben Reynolds guided the manuscript through the production process, and Jason Spears capably pulled together all the important loose ends to get the manuscript ready for copyediting, working on the photo captions, glossary, and art manuscript, among other tasks. On the media front, we want to thank Steve Hoge for creating the Norton StudySpace website, which includes the impressive Norton Digital History Reader and the exciting new Norton World History Tours powered by Google Maps. On the print ancillary front, we'd like to thank Lorraine Klimowich and Rachel Comerford for finding an excellent group of authors to create the instructor's manual and test bank. Carla Zimowsk, the information officer for the history department at Princeton University, simplified the multiple transmission of revised chapters among all twelve of the authors, no easy task. She made what is a very complicated set of procedures easy to understand and workable.

Finally, we must recognize that while this project often kept us apart from family members, their support held our personal worlds together.

About the Authors

ROBERT TIGNOR (Ph.D. Yale University) is Professor Emeritus and the Rosengarten Professor of Modern and Contemporary History at Princeton University and the three-time chair of the history department. With Gyan Prakash, he introduced Princeton's first course in world history nearly twenty years ago. Professor Tignor has taught graduate and undergraduate courses in African history and world history and written extensively on the history of twentieth-century Egypt, Nigeria, and Kenya. Besides his many research trips to Africa, Professor Tignor has taught at the University of Ibadan in Nigeria and the University of Nairobi in Kenya.

JEREMY ADELMAN (D.Phil. Oxford University) is currently the Director of the Council for International Teaching and Research at Princeton University and the Walter S. Carpenter III Professor of Spanish Civilization and Culture. He has written and edited five books, including *Republic of Capital: Buenos Aires and the Legal Transformation of the Atlantic World*, which won the best book prize in Atlantic history from the American Historical Association, and most recently *Sovereignty and Revolution in the Iberian Atlantic*. Professor Adelman is the recent recipient of a Guggenheim Memorial Foundation Fellowship and the Frederick Burkhardt Award from the American Council of Learned Societies.

STEPHEN ARON (Ph.D. University of California, Berkeley) is professor of history at the University of California, Los Angeles, and executive director of the Institute for the Study of the American West, Autry National Center. A specialist in frontier and Western American history, Aron is the author of *How the West Was Lost: The Transformation of Kentucky from Daniel Boone to Henry Clay* and *American Confluence: The Missouri Frontier from Borderland to Border State*. He is currently editing the multi-volume *Autry History of the American West* and writing a book with the tentative title *Can We All Just Get Along: An Alternative History of the American West*.

PETER BROWN (Ph.D. Oxford University) is the Rollins Professor of History at Princeton University. He previously taught at London University and the University of California, Berkeley. He has written on the rise of Christianity and the end of the Roman Empire. His works include *Augustine of Hippo, The World of Late Antiquity, The Cult of the Saints, Body and Society, The Rise of Western Christendom*, and *Poverty and Leadership in the Later Roman Empire*. He is presently working on issues of wealth and poverty in the late Roman and early medieval Christian worlds.

BENJAMIN ELMAN (Ph.D. University of Pennsylvania) is professor of East Asian studies and history at Princeton University. He is currently serving as the chair of the Princeton East Asian Studies Department. He taught at the University of California, Los Angeles, for over fifteen years. His teaching and research fields include Chinese intellectual and cultural history, 1000–1900; the history of science in China, 1600–1930; the history of education in late imperial China; and Sino-Japanese cultural history, 1600–1850. He is the author of five books: *From Philosophy to Philology: Intellectual and Social Aspects of Change in Late Imperial China; Classicism, Politics, and Kinship: The Ch'ang-chou School of New Text Confucianism in Late Imperial China; A Cultural History of Civil Examinations in Late Imperial China; On Their Own Terms: Science in China, 1550–1900*; and *A Cultural History of Modern Science in China*. He is the creator of Classical Historiography for Chinese History at www.princeton.edu/~classbib/, a bibliography and teaching website published since 1996.

xlv

STEPHEN KOTKIN (Ph.D. University of California, Berkeley) is professor of European and Asian history as well as international affairs at Princeton University. He formerly directed Princeton's program in Russian and Eurasian studies (1996–2009). He is the author of *Magnetic Mountain: Stalinism as a Civilization, Uncivil Society: 1989 and the Implosion of the Communist Establishment,* and *Armageddon Averted: The Soviet Collapse, 1970–2000.* He is a coeditor of *Mongolia in the Twentieth Century: Landlocked Cosmopolitan.* Professor Kotkin has twice been a visiting professor in Japan.

XINRU LIU (Ph.D. University of Pennsylvania) is associate professor of early Indian history and world history at the College of New Jersey. She is associated with the Institute of World History and the Chinese Academy of Social Sciences. She is the author of *Ancient India and Ancient China, Trade and Religious Exchanges,* AD 1–600; *Silk and Religion, an Exploration of Material Life and the Thought of People,* AD 600–1200; *Connections across Eurasia, Transportation, Communication, and Cultural Exchange on the Silk Roads,* co-authored with Lynda Norene Shaffer; and *A Social History of Ancient India* (in Chinese). Professor Liu promotes South Asian studies and world history studies in both the United States and the People's Republic of China.

SUZANNE MARCHAND (Ph.D. University of Chicago) is professor of European and intellectual history at Louisiana State University, Baton Rouge. Professor Marchand also spent a number of years teaching at Princeton University. She is the author of *Down from Olympus: Archaeology and Philhellenism in Germany, 1750–1970* and *German Orientalism in the Age of Empire: Religion, Race and Scholarship.*

HOLLY PITTMAN (Ph.D. Columbia University) is professor of art history at the University of Pennsylvania, where she teaches art and archaeology of Mesopotamia and the Iranian Plateau. She also serves as curator in the Near East Section of the University of Pennsylvania Museum of Archaeology and Anthropology. Previously she served as a curator in the Ancient Near Eastern Art Department of the Metropolitan Museum of Art. She has written extensively on the art and culture of the Bronze Age in the Middle East and has participated in excavations in Cyprus, Turkey, Syria, Iraq, and Iran, where she currently works. Her research investigates works of art as media through which patterns of thought, cultural development, and historical interactions of ancient cultures of the Near East are reconstructed.

GYAN PRAKASH (Ph.D. University of Pennsylvania) is professor of modern Indian history at Princeton University and a member of the Subaltern Studies Editorial Collective. He is the author of *Bonded Histories: Genealogies of Labor Servitude in Colonial India, Another Reason: Science and the Imagination of Modern India,* and *Mumbai Fables.* Professor Prakash edited *After Colonialism: Imperial Histories and Postcolonial Displacements* and *Noir Urbanisms,* coedited *The Space of the Modern City* and *Utopia/Dystopia,* and has written a number of articles on colonialism and history writing. He is currently working on a history of the city of Bombay. With Robert Tignor, he introduced the modern world history course at Princeton University.

BRENT SHAW (Ph.D. Cambridge University) is the Andrew Fleming West Professor of Classics at Princeton University, where he is director of the Program in the Ancient World. He was previously at the University of Pennsylvania, where he chaired the Graduate Group in Ancient History. His principal areas of specialization as a Roman historian are Roman family history and demography, sectarian violence and conflict in Late Antiquity, and the regional history of Africa as part of the Roman Empire. He has published *Spartacus and the Slaves Wars*; edited the papers of Sir Moses Finley, *Economy and Society in Ancient Greece*; and published in a variety of books and journals, including the *Journal of Roman Studies,* the *American Historical Review,* the *Journal of Early Christian Studies,* and *Past & Present.*

MICHAEL TSIN (Ph.D. Princeton) is associate professor of history and international studies at the University of North Carolina at Chapel Hill. He previously taught at the University of Illinois at Chicago, Princeton University, Columbia University, and the University of Florida. Professor Tsin's primary interests include the histories of modern China and colonialism. He is the author of *Nation, Governance, and Modernity in China: Canton, 1900–1927.* He is currently writing a social history of the reconfiguration of Chinese identity in the twentieth century.

NORTH
AMERICA

ATLANTIC
OCEAN

SAHARA

Niger R.

PACIFIC
OCEAN

SOUTH
AMERICA

| 0 | 1000 | 2000 Miles |
| 0 | 1000 | 2000 Kilometers |

The Geography of the Ancient and Modern Worlds

Today, we believe the world to be divided into continents, and most of us think that it was always so. Geographers usually identify six inhabited continents: Africa, North America, South America, Europe, Asia, and Australia. Inside these continents they locate a vast number of subcontinental units, such as East Asia, South Asia, Southeast Asia, the Middle East, North Africa, and sub-Saharan Africa. Yet this geographical understanding would have been completely alien to premodern men and women, who did not think that they inhabited continents bounded by large bodies of water. Lacking a firm command of the seas,

they saw themselves living on contiguous landmasses, and they thought these territorial bodies were the main geographical units of their lives. Hence, in this volume we have chosen to use a set of geographical terms, the main one being *Afro-Eurasia*, that more accurately reflect the world that the premoderns believed that they inhabited.

The most interconnected and populous landmass of premodern times was Afro-Eurasia. The term *Eurasia* is widely used in general histories, but we think it is in its own ways inadequate. The preferred term from our perspective must be *Afro-Eurasia*, for the interconnected

ARCTIC OCEAN

A F R O - E U R A S I A

EUROPE

INNER EURASIA

Danube R.

BLACK SEA

ARAL SEA

CENTRAL ASIA

TAKLAMAKAN DESERT

AEGEAN SEA

MEDITERRANEAN SEA

TAURUS MTS.

CASPIAN SEA

Tigris R.

IRANIAN PLATEAU

SOUTHWEST ASIA

Yellow R.

HIMALAYA MTS.

Yangzi R.

EAST ASIA

YELLOW SEA

DESERT

Euphrates R.

RED SEA

Indus R.

Pearl R.

Lake Chad

ARABIAN SEA

SOUTH ASIA

PACIFIC OCEAN

SOUTHEAST ASIA

SOUTH CHINA SEA

Nile R.

SUB-SAHARAN AFRICA

Congo R.

Lake Victoria

INDIAN OCEAN

AUSTRALIA

landmass of premodern and indeed much of modern times included large parts of Europe and Asia and significant regions in Africa. The major African territories that were regularly joined to Europe and Asia were Egypt, North Africa, and even parts of sub-Saharan Africa.

Only gradually and fitfully did the divisions of the world that we take for granted today take shape. The peoples inhabiting the north-western part of the Afro-Eurasian landmass did not see themselves as European Christians, and hence as a distinctive cultural entity, until the Middle Ages drew to a close in the twelfth and thirteenth centuries. Islam did not arise and extend its influence throughout the middle zone of the Afro-Eurasian landmass until the eighth and ninth

centuries. And, finally, the peoples living in what we today term the *Indian subcontinent* did not feel a strong sense of their own cultural and political unity until the Delhi Sultanate of the thirteenth and fourteenth centuries and the Mughal Empire, which emerged at the beginning of the sixteenth century, brought political unity to that vast region. As a result, we use the terms *South Asia, Vedic society,* and *India* in place of *Indian subcontinent* for the premodern part of our narrative, and we use *Southwest Asia* and *North Africa* to refer to what today is designated as the *Middle East*. In fact, it is only in the period from 1000 to 1300 that some of the major cultural areas that are familiar to us today truly crystallized.

THIRD EDITION
VOLUME ONE
BEGINNINGS THROUGH THE FIFTEENTH CENTURY

Worlds Together, WORLDS APART

Chapter 1

BECOMING HUMAN

In 2003, in a remote corner of the Ethiopian highlands of Africa, a team of evolutionary biologists came upon a remarkable cache of fossil remains lodged in volcanic rock. Identifying and reassembling these remains took six years, but the researchers eventually reconstructed one of the most revealing sets of human fossils ever found: a nearly complete skeleton of an adult male, and the partial remains of another adult and a juvenile. By dating the volcanic rock, the team determined that the bones were about 160,000 years old. Although the skeletal remains were not identical to those of modern men and women (who are technically *Homo sapiens sapiens*, the sole surviving subspecies of *Homo sapiens*), they were close enough to form part of the family of modern humans. In short, the bones represented the oldest record of *Homo sapiens*. The fossil finds confirmed what earlier studies had suggested: *Homo sapiens*, or modern humans, originated in a small region of Africa about 200,000 years ago and migrated out of Africa about 100,000 years ago. As the team leader proclaimed, "We are all Africans."

Not everyone agrees with the "Out of Africa" thesis, which contends that modern human beings are all descendants of recent migrants out of Africa. Doubters claim that the world's "races" evolved separately in different regions for up to one million years after migrating out of Africa. These doubters argue that as the early descendants of modern men and women evolved in widely dispersed geographical settings, they took on diverse personality traits and distinctive physical appearances, with the result that they appear today as different "races." In this view, the story of humanity was about fundamental differences. Now the opposite is becoming clear: all humans share a common heritage, and our differences are not genetic or crudely physical, but mainly cultural. We are also much newer than scholars once imagined.

As a species we have been living apart for a comparatively short amount of time, and as a result the world's "races" have much in common. Most of the common traits of human beings—the abilities to make tools, engage in family life, use language, and refine cognitive abilities—evolved over many millennia and crystallized on the eve of the exodus from Africa. Only with the advent of settled agriculture did significant cultural divergences occur, as artifacts such as tools, cooking devices, and storage containers reveal. The differences in humankind's cultures are less than 15,000 or 20,000 years old.

This chapter lays out the origins of humanity from its common source. It shows how many different hominids (erect bipedal mammals, represented today by humans, chimpanzees, gorillas, and orangutans) preceded modern humans, and that humans came from only one—very recent—stock of migrants out of Africa. Fanning out across the world, our ancestors adapted to environmental constraints and opportunities. They created languages, families, and clan systems, often innovating to defend themselves against predators. One of the biggest breakthroughs was the domestication of animals and plants—the creation of agrarian settlements. With this development,

humans could cease following food and begin producing it in their own backyards.

Before we begin our exploration, it will be useful to clarify two terms that occur frequently in this chapter's discussion: *evolution*, and *modern humans*. **Evolution** is the process by which the different species of the world—its plants and animals—made changes in response to their environment that enabled them to survive and increase in numbers. Biological evolution does not imply progress to higher and more exalted forms of life, only adaptation to environmental surroundings. The term *modern humans* refers to members of the *Homo sapiens* subspecies that evolved about 200,000 years ago. So when we say "modern" (and "recent") we are speaking in relative terms; compared to the life of the universe and even to the earliest hominids, the ancient creatures we call modern humans were indeed "modern." This chapter's discussion will show that as modern humans evolved, they passed through successive waves of migration, adaptation, and innovation.

PRECURSORS TO MODERN HUMANS

> → *What traits made early hominids different from other animal species?*

To understand the origins of modern humans (*Homo sapiens*), we must consider what is common to all humans and what distinguishes them from one another. We must also come to terms with time. Though the hominids that evolved into modern humans lived millions of years ago, our tools for analyzing them are relatively new. What we now know about the origins of human existence and the evolution into modern humans would have been unimaginable a century ago.

Focus Questions

→ *What traits made early hominids different from other animal species?*

→ *How did* Homo sapiens *become the only hominid species?*

→ *How did art and language increase* Homo sapiens' *chances of survival?*

→ *What factors contributed to the domestication of plants and animals?*

→ *What factors contributed to innovation, as opposed to borrowing, in agriculture?*

→ *How did agricultural revolutions change human relations?*

MAIN THEMES

↔ *Hominids are ancestors to modern humans.*
↔ *All humans share a common heritage "out of Africa."*
↔ *Early humans populate the earth, adapting to changes in environment and diet, innovating, and accumulating knowledge.*
↔ *People domesticate plants and animals and settle in agrarian villages.*

FOCUS ON *What Makes Us Human*

◆ *Bipedalism:* Hominids come down from the trees in Africa, become upright, and walk on two legs.
◆ *Big brains:* Ancestors to modern humans make tools and fire and acquire larger brains.
◆ *Language: Homo sapiens* learn to communicate with one another, develop a sense of self, and produce art.

◆ *Writing:* In a few places on the globe, humans invent systems of writing.
◆ *Village life:* People domesticate plants and animals and settle in villages.

CREATION MYTHS AND BELIEFS

Only 350 years ago, English clerics claimed on the basis of biblical calculations and Christian tradition that the first day of creation was Sunday, October 23, 4004 BCE. One scholar even specified that creation happened at 9:00 A.M. on the morning of that day. Now we see things differently. The origin of the universe dates back some 15 billion years, and the hominid separation from African pongids (members of the ape family) began some 6 or 7 million years ago. These discoveries have proved as mind-boggling to Hindus and Muslims as to Christians and Jews—all of whom believed, in different ways, in a creationist account of humanity's origins. (See Primary Source: A Hindu Creation Myth.) The Judaic-Christian belief in creation was based on the first book of the Old Testament, Genesis, which portrayed God creating the universe from nothingness, all of its plants and animals and the first set of human beings (Adam and Eve), over a period of seven days. This story became foundational for Western societies and also for the Islamic world, which accepted the Old and New Testaments—though not the divinity of Jesus—as the word of God.

Modern discoveries about humanity's origins have also challenged other major cultural traditions, because no tradition conceived that creatures evolved into new kinds of life, that humans were related to apes, and that all of humanity originated in a remote corner of Africa. The Yoruba peoples of West Africa, whose creation story is centuries old and is representative of many African creation accounts, believed that God descended from the heavens in human form. He became the godlike king Oduduwa, who established the Yoruba kingdom and the rules by which his subjects were to live. According to the Brahmanical Vedas and the Upanishads, which date to the seventh or sixth century BCE and remain fundamental to Hindu faith today, the world is millions, not billions, of years old. The Chinese from East Asia, who do not appear to have their own creation story, and the Buddhists believed in a continuous reappearance of human and animal souls. Chinese Han dynasty (202 BCE–220 CE) astronomers also believed that at the world's beginning the planets were conjoined and that they would merge again at the end of time. The Buddhists' cosmos comprised millions of worlds, each consisting of a mountain encircled by four continents, its seas surrounded by a wall of iron.

Even the million-year time frames and multiple planetary systems that ancient Asian thinkers endorsed did not prepare their communities for the idea that humans are related to apes. In all traditional cosmologies, humans came into existence fully formed, at a single moment, as did the other beings that populated the world.

A HINDU CREATION MYTH

Around 1500 BCE a migrant people speaking an Indo-European language settled in South Asia. These Vedic people sang hymns while making sacrifices to their gods, and the hymns were later collected in the Rig-Veda—the earliest Hindu sacred text. This hymn describes the creation of the universe by the gods' sacrifice ("oblation") of a creature—Purusha, or "Man." From Purusha's body come four different kinds of people: the Brahman, the Rajanya, the Vaishya, and the Shudra. They represent the forefathers of the four castes, or hereditary social classes, of India.

Thousand-headed Purusha, thousand-eyed, thousand-footed—he, having pervaded the earth on all sides, extends ten fingers beyond it.

Purusha alone is all this—whatever has been and whatever is going to be. Further, he is the lord of immortality and also of what grows on account of food.

Such is his greatness; greater, indeed than this is Purusha. All creatures constitute but one-quarter of him, his three-quarters are the immortal in the heaven.

With his three-quarters did Purusha rise up; one-quarter of him again remains here. With it did he variously spread out on all sides over what eats and what eats not. . . . When the gods performed the sacrifice with Purusha as the oblation, then the spring was its clarified butter, the summer the sacrificial fuel, and the autumn the oblation.

The sacrificial victim, namely, Purusha born at the very beginning, they sprinkled with sacred water upon the sacrificial grass. With him as oblation, the gods performed the sacrifice, and also the Sādhyas [a class of semidivine beings] and the rishis [ancient seers].

From that wholly offered sacrificial oblation were born the verses and the sacred chants; from it were born the meters [*chandas*]; the sacrificial formula was born from it.

From it horses were born and also those animals who have double rows [i.e., upper and lower] of teeth; cows were born from it, from it were born goats and sheep.

When they divided Purusha, in how many different portions did they arrange him? What became of his mouth, what of his two arms? What were his two thighs and his two feet called?

His mouth became the brāhman; his two arms were made into the rājanya; his two thighs the vaishyas; from his two feet the shūdra was born.

The moon was born from the mind, from the eye the sun was born; from the mouth Indra and Agni, from the breath [*prāna*] the wind [*vāyu*] was born.

From the navel was the atmosphere created, from the head the heaven issued forth; from two feet was born the earth and the quarters (the cardinal directions) from the ear. Thus did they fashion the worlds.

→ *In early Vedic society the Brahman (priest) was the highest caste, and the Shudra (outsider/laborer) was the lowest. What parts of Purusha's body did these two castes come from, and what is the significance of each?*

→ *According to this myth, what other beings came into existence fully formed?*

SOURCE: *Sources of Indian Tradition*, vol. 1, *From the Beginning to 1800*, edited and revised by Ainslie T. Embree, 2nd ed. (New York: Columbia University Press, 1988), pp. 18–19.

EVOLUTIONARY FINDINGS AND RESEARCH METHODS

Revisions in the time frame of the universe and human existence have occurred over a long period of time. Geologists made early breakthroughs in the eighteenth century when their research into the layers of the earth's surface revealed a world much older than biblical time implied. Evolutionary biologists, most notably Charles Darwin (1809–1882), concluded that all life had evolved over long periods from simple forms of matter. In the twentieth century astronomers, evolutionary biologists, and archaeologists (scholars of ancient cultures whose information comes mainly from nonliterary sources such as fossils, monuments, and artifacts) have employed sophisticated dating techniques to pinpoint the chronology of the universe's creation and the evolution of all forms of life on earth. (See Global Connections & Disconnections: Determining the Age of Fossils and Sediments.) Their discoveries have radically transformed humanity's understanding of its own history, a shift comparable to the

DETERMINING THE AGE OF FOSSILS AND SEDIMENTS

Our knowledge of human origins has been the result of several remarkable scientific breakthroughs. Only recently have scholars been able to date fossil remains and to use biological research to understand the relationships among the world's early peoples.

The first major advance in the study of prehistory (the time before written historical records) occurred after World War II, and it involved the use of *radiocarbon dating*. All living things contain the radiocarbon isotope C^{14}, which plants acquire directly from the atmosphere and animals acquire indirectly when they consume plants or other animals. When these living things die, the C^{14} isotope begins to decay into a stable nonradioactive element, C^{12}. Because the rate of decay is regular and measurable, it is possible to determine the age of fossils that leave organic remains for up to 40,000 years.

A second major dating technique, the *potassium-argon method*, also involves analysis of the changing chemical structure of objects over time. Scientists can calculate the age of nonliving objects by measuring the ratio of potassium to argon in them, since potassium decays into argon. This method allows scientists to calculate the age of objects up to a million years old. It also enables them to date the sediments in which researchers find fossils—as a gauge of the age of the fossils themselves.

DNA (deoxyribonucleic acid) analysis is a third crucial tool for unraveling the beginnings of modern humans. DNA, which determines biological inheritances, exists in two places within the cells of all living organisms—including the human body. *Nuclear DNA* occurs in the nucleus of every cell, where it controls most aspects of physical appearance and makeup. *Mitochondrial DNA* occurs outside the nucleus of cells, where its structures within cell bodies convert the energy from food into a form that cells can use. While nuclear DNA exists in males and females, mitochondrial DNA exists only in females and passes from mothers to female offspring. By examining mitochondrial DNA, researchers can measure the genetic variation among living objects—including human beings. Such analysis has enabled researchers to pinpoint human descent from an original African population to other, genetically related populations that lived approximately 100,000 years ago.

The genetic similarity of modern humans suggests that the population from which all *Homo sapiens* descended originated in Africa about 200,000 years ago. When these humans moved out of Africa around 100,000 years ago, they spread eastward into Southwest Asia and then throughout the rest of Afro-Eurasia. One group migrated to Australia about 50,000 years ago. Another group moved into the area of Europe about 40,000 years ago. When the scientific journal *Nature* published these findings in 1987, it inspired a groundswell of public interest—and a contentious scientific debate that continues today.

Neanderthal DNA Extraction. This sample of fossilized Neanderthal bone will have its genetic material extracted and sequenced as part of the Neanderthal Genome Project.

sixteenth-century realization that the earth rotates around the sun. Understanding the sweep of human history, calculated in millions of years, requires us to revise our sense of time. Moreover, the scientists' findings have important, if unsettling, implications concerning who we are as human beings.

A mere century ago, who would have accepted the fact that the universe came into being 15 billion years ago, that the earth appeared about 4.5 billion years ago, and that the earliest life forms began to exist about 3.8 billion years ago? The great cultural traditions would not have considered that human beings are part of a long evolutionary chain stretching from microscopic bacteria to African apes that appeared about 23 million years ago. And they would not have accepted the findings that Africa's ape population separated into three distinct groups: one becoming present-day gorillas; the second becoming chimpanzees; and the third group, **hominids**, becoming modern-day humans only after following a long and complicated evolutionary process.

At what stage did the first hominids appear? What traits distinguished them from other animals? No single variable separated these humanlike beings from other creatures; instead, a combination of distinguishing traits evolved over several million years. These include (1) lifting the torso and walking on two legs (bipedalism), thereby freeing hands and arms to carry objects and hurl weapons; (2) controlling and then making fire; (3) fashioning and using tools; (4) developing cognitive skills and an enlarged brain and therefore the capacity for language; and (5) acquiring a consciousness of "self." Together, these traits began to differentiate hominids from other animal species and in the long (long!) run enabled humans to become the dominant species on the globe. All these traits were in place at least 150,000 years ago.

Yet this was just a beginning in human development. It was only about 12,000 years ago that modern humans were ready to make another spectacular advance: domesticating plants and animals, and living in village communities.

EARLY HOMINIDS AND ADAPTATION

What was it like to be a hominid in the millions of years before the emergence of modern humans? The first clue came from a discovery made in 1924 at Taung, not far from the present-day city of Johannesburg, South Africa. A scientist named Raymond Dart happened upon a skull and bones that appeared to be partly human and partly ape. Believing the creature to be "an extinct race of apes intermediate between living anthropoids (apes) and man," Dart labeled the creature the "Southern Ape of Africa," or *Australopithecus africanus*. This individual had a brain capacity of approximately one pint, or a little less than one-third that of a modern man and about the same as that of modern-day African apes. Yet these **australopithecines** were different from other animals, for they walked on two legs. Because Dart also found animal bones in the same vicinity, he mistakenly concluded that our early ancestors were bloodthirsty creatures who carried their prey to slaughtering grounds. It turns out that early hominids were only about five feet tall and weighed at most 110 pounds, so they were no match for big, muscular, and swift animal predators; the hominids were the hunted, not the hunters.

The fact that the hominids survived at all in such a hostile environment is a miracle. But they did, and over the first million years of their existence in Africa the australopithecines developed into more than six species. (A **species** is a group of animals or plants possessing one or more distinctive characteristics.) It is important to emphasize that these australopithecines were not humans but that they carried the genetic and biological material out of which modern humans would later emerge. These precursors to modern humans had a key trait for evolutionary survival: they were remarkably good adapters. They could deal with dynamic environmental shifts, and they were intelligent.

LUCY Australopithecines existed not only in southern Africa but in the north as well. In 1974, an archaeological team working at a site in present-day Ethiopia unearthed a relatively intact skeleton of a young adult female australopithecine in the valley of the Awash River. The researchers gave the skeleton a nickname, Lucy, based on the popular Beatles song "Lucy in the Sky with Diamonds."

Lucy was remarkable. She stood a little over three feet tall, she walked upright, her skull contained a brain within the ape size range, and her jaw and teeth were humanlike. Her arms were long, hanging halfway from her hips to her knees—suggesting that she might not have been bipedal at all

Fossil Bones of Lucy. Archaeologist Donald Johanson discovered the fossilized bones of this young female in the Afar region of Ethiopia. They are believed to date from approximately 3.2 million years ago and provide evidence of some of the first hominids to appear in Africa. This find was of great importance because the bones were so fully and completely preserved.

TABLE 1-1   Human Evolution

Australopithecus anamensis	4.2 million years ago
Australopithecus afarensis (including Lucy)	3.4 million years ago
Australopithecus africanus	3.0 million years ago
Homo habilis (including Dear Boy)	2.5 million years ago
Homo erectus (including Java and Peking Man)	1.8 million years ago
Neanderthals	200,000 years ago
Homo sapiens	200,000 years ago
Homo sapiens sapiens (modern humans)	35,000 years ago

times and sometimes resorted to arms for locomotion, in the fashion of a modern baboon. Above all, Lucy's skeleton was relatively complete and was very, very old—half a million years older than any other complete hominid skeleton found up to that time. Lucy showed us that human precursors were walking around as early as 3 million years ago. (See Table 1-1.) But it also raised some significant questions: Was Lucy a precursor to modern-day humans? If so, what kind of a precursor? What species did she represent? Or was she a modern human?

ADAPTATION   To survive, hominids had to adapt and evolve as their environments altered. During the first millions of years of hominid existence, these changes were slow. They involved far more physical adaptations to the environment than cultural transformations. Hominids, like the rest of the plant and animal world, had to keep pace with rapidly changing physical environments—for if they did not, they would die out. Many of the early hominid groups did just that. In fact, no straight-line descent tree exists from the first hominids to modern men and women. The places where researchers have found early hominid remains in southern and eastern Africa had environments that changed from being heavily forested and well watered to being arid and desert-like, and then back again. (See Map 1-1.) Survival required constant **adaptation** (the ability to alter behavior and to innovate, finding new ways of doing things), and some of the hominid groups were better at it than others.

In adapting, early hominids began to distinguish themselves from other mammals that were physically similar to themselves. It was not their hunting prowess that made the hominids stand out, because plenty of other species chased their prey with skill and dexterity. The single trait that gave

early hominids a real advantage for survival was **bipedalism**: they became "two-footed" creatures that stood upright. At some point, the first hominids were able to remain upright and move about, leaving their arms and hands free for other useful tasks, like carrying food over long distances. Once they ventured into open savannas (grassy plains with a few scattered trees), about 1.7 million years ago, hominids had a tremendous advantage. They were the only primates (an order of mammals consisting of man, apes, and monkeys) to move consistently on two legs. Because they could move continuously and over great distances, they were able to migrate out of hostile environments and into more hospitable locations as needed.

Explaining why and how hominids began to walk on two legs is critical to understanding our human origins. Along with the other primates, the first hominids enjoyed the advantages of being long-limbed, tree-loving animals with good vision and dexterous digits. Why did these primates, in contrast to their closest relatives (gorillas and chimpanzees), leave the shelter of trees and venture out into the open grasslands, where they were vulnerable to attack? The answer is not self-evident. Explaining how and why some apes took these first steps also sheds light on why humanity's origins lie in Africa. Fifteen million years ago there were apes all over the world, so why did a small number of them evolve new traits in Africa?

ENVIRONMENTAL CHANGES   What eastern and southern Africa offered was a climate conducive to the development of diverse plant and animal species. At a critical moment, the environment in this region changed dramatically. The world had entered its fourth great ice age approximately 40 million years ago, during which the earth's temperatures diminished and its continental ice sheets, polar ice sheets, and mountain glaciers increased. This ice age lasted until 10,000 years ago. Like all ice ages, it had alternating warming and cooling phases that lasted between 40,000 and 100,000 years each. Between 10 and 15 million years ago, the climate in Africa went through one such cooling and drying phase. To the east of Africa's Rift Valley, stretching from South Africa north to the Ethiopian highlands, the cooling and drying forced forests to contract and savannas to spread. It was in this region that some apes came down from trees, stood up, and learned to walk, to run, and to live in savanna lands—thus becoming the precursors to humans, and distinctive as a new species.

Using two feet for locomotion did more than augment the means of survival for creatures whose environments were changing. It also increased their options for subsistence and led to the acquisition of **cognitive skills** (such as thought, memory, problem-solving, and—ultimately—language) to obtain food and avoid predators. Cognition itself became the basis for further developments. Thus, as hands no longer had to pull bodies around, they were free for carrying other things

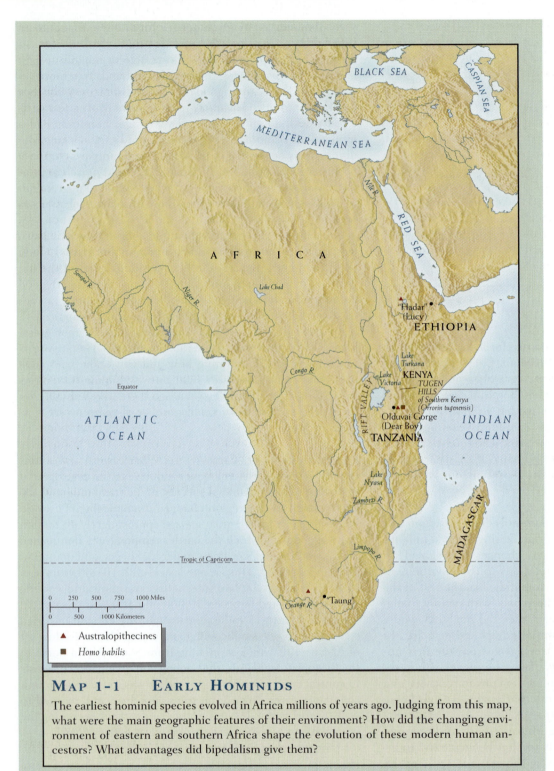

MAP 1-1   EARLY HOMINIDS

The earliest hominid species evolved in Africa millions of years ago. Judging from this map, what were the main geographic features of their environment? How did the changing environment of eastern and southern Africa shape the evolution of these modern human ancestors? What advantages did bipedalism give them?

alter materials found in nature. Manual dexterity and standing upright also enabled them to carry young family members if they needed to relocate, or to throw missiles (such as rocks and sticks) with deadly accuracy to protect themselves or to obtain food. They used their increased powers of observation and memory to gather wild berries and grains and to scavenge the meat and marrow of animals that had died of natural causes or as the prey of predators. All primates are good at these activities, but hominids came to excel at them.

The early hominids were highly social. They lived in bands of about twenty-five individuals, trying to survive by hunting small game and gathering wild plants. Not yet a match for large predators, they had to find safe hiding places. They also sought ecological niches where a diverse supply of wild grains and fruits and abundant wildlife ensured a secure, comfortable existence. In such locations, small hunting bands of twenty-five could swell through alliances with others to as many as 500 individuals. Like other primates, hominids communicated through gestures, but they also may have developed an early form of spoken language that led (among other things) to the establishment of cultural codes such as common rules and customs.

The early hominids lived in this manner for up to 3 million years, changing their way of life very little except for moving around the African landmass in their never-ending search for more favorable environments. Even so, their survival is surprising. There were not many of them, and they struggled in hostile environments surrounded by a diversity of large mammals, including predators such as lions.

and, eventually, making the first tools. A free hand could hold a spear or the ever-useful digging stick.

In addition to being bipedal, hominids had another trait that helped them to survive and create and use tools—opposable thumbs. This trait, shared with other primates, gave hominids great physical dexterity, enhancing their ability to explore and to

As the environment changed over the millennia, these early hominids gradually altered in appearance. Fossils from 3 million years ago reveal that their brains almost doubled in size; their foreheads became more elongated; their jaws became less massive; and they took on a much more modern look. Adaptation to environmental changes also created new skills and aptitudes, which expanded the ability to store and analyze information. With larger brains, hominids could form mental maps of their worlds—they could learn, remember what they learned, and convey these lessons to their neighbors and offspring. In this fashion, larger groups of hominids created communities with shared understandings of their environments. This process enhanced the advantages of those with larger brains as they underwent natural selection—the process whereby offspring inherit traits that improve the probability of survival and reproduction.

DIVERSITY We know that hominids were much older than we thought, but it turns out that they were also much more diverse. Consider some startling finds from Ethiopia and Kenya. In southern Kenya, researchers have discovered bone remains, at least 6 million years old, of a chimpanzee-sized hominid (named *Orrorin tugenensis*) that walked upright on two feet. This discovery indicates that bipedalism must be millions of years older than we used to think. Moreover, these hominids' teeth indicate that they were closer to modern humans than to australopithecines. In their arms and hands, though, which show characteristics needed for tree climbing, the *Orrorin* hominids seemed more apelike than the australopithecines. So *Orrorin* hominids were still somewhat tied to an environment in the trees. Also, recent discoveries of the bones of five individuals in the Afar depression in Ethiopia (an area just south of Lucy's discovery) have revealed a different kind of bipedal hominid dating back at least 5 million years. Yet another recent discovery, this one in northern Kenya, has revealed yet another species of early hominid.

The fact that different kinds of early hominids were living side by side in the same environment in eastern Africa between 3 and 4 million years ago indicates much greater diversity and development among their populations than scholars previously imagined. The environment in eastern Africa was generating a fair number of different hominid populations, a few of which would provide our genetic base, but most of which would not survive in the long run. In fact, the survival of any of these hominid lines was no certain thing.

THE FIRST HUMANS: *HOMO HABILIS*

One million years after Lucy, the first examples of human beings, to whom we give the name *homo,* or "true human," appeared. They, too, were bipedal, possessing a smooth walk based on upright posture. And they had an even more important advantage over other hominids: large brains. Big brains were like little motors of **innovation**: learning and storing lessons so that humans could pass those lessons on to later generations, especially in the making of tools and the

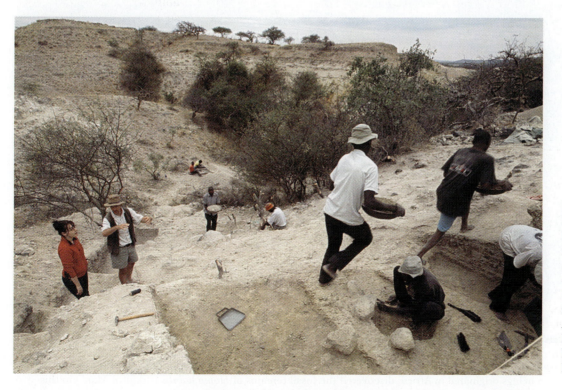

Searching for Hominid Fossils. Olorgasalie in Kenya has proved to be one of the most important archaeological sites for uncovering evidence of early hominid development. Rick Potts, a leader in the field, is shown here on-site. Among his discoveries were hand axes and indications that hominids in this area had learned to use fire.

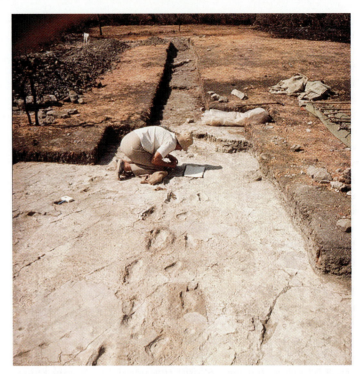

The Leakeys. Louis Leakey and his wife, Mary, were dedicated archaeologists whose work in East Africa established the area as one of the starting points of human development. Mary Leakey (*right*) was among the most successful archaeologists studying hominids in Africa. Her finds, including the one in this photograph from Laetoli, Tanzania, highlight the activities of early men and women in Africa. The footprints, believed to be those of an *Australopithecus afarensis*, date from 3.7 to 3 million years ago.

Olduvai Gorge, Tanzania. Olduvai Gorge is arguably the most famous archaeological site containing hominid finds. Mary and Louis Leakey, convinced that early human beings originated in Africa, discovered the fossil remains of *Homo habilis* ("Skillful Man") in this area between 1960 and 1963. They argued that these findings represent a direct link to *Homo erectus*.

efficient use of resources (and, we suspect, in defending themselves). Mary and Louis Leakey, who made astonishing fossil discoveries in the 1950s at Olduvai Gorge (part of the Great Rift Valley) in present-day northeastern Tanzania, identified these important traits. The Leakeys' finds are the most significant discoveries of early humans in Africa—in particular, an intact skull that was 1.8 million years old.

The Olduvai Gorge is a thirty-mile-long canyon in which a winding stream has exposed many layers of volcanic rock containing abundant fossil remains. Louis S. B. Leakey was a paleontologist (a scientist studying fossil remains from past geological periods) educated at the University of Cambridge. In 1931, Leakey began a research project in Olduvai along with his wife, Mary Nicol Leakey, an archaeologist. Although their Cambridge mentors had rejected the notion of humanity's African origins, the Leakeys' work would ultimately prove them wrong. After decades of frustrating work and financial troubles, Mary Leakey could hardly believe her good fortune when she stumbled upon an almost totally intact skull. The Leakeys nicknamed it Dear Boy.

Other objects discovered with Dear Boy demonstrated that by this time early humans had begun to make tools for butchering animals and, possibly, for hunting and killing smaller animals. The tools were flaked stones with sharpened edges for cutting apart animal flesh and scooping out the marrow from bones. To mimic the slicing teeth of lions, leopards, and other carnivores, the Oldowans had devised these tools through careful chipping. Dear Boy and his companions had carried usable rocks to distant places where they made their implements with special hammer stones—tools to make tools. Unlike other tool-using animals (for example, chimpanzees), early humans were now intentionally fashioning implements, not simply finding them when needed. More important, they were passing on knowledge of these tools to their offspring and, in the process, gradually improving the tools. Because the Leakeys believed that making and using tools represented a new stage in the evolution of human beings, they gave these creatures a new name: **Homo habilis**, or "Skillful Man." Their tool-making ability made them the forerunners, though very distant, of modern men and women.

EARLY HUMANS ON THE MOVE: MIGRATIONS OF *HOMO ERECTUS*

All the different species of hominids flourished together in Africa between 1 and 2.5 million years ago. By 1 million years ago, however, many had died out. One surviving species, which emerged about 1.8 million years ago, had a large brain capacity and walked truly upright; it therefore gained the name **Homo erectus,** or "Standing Man." Even though this species was more able to cope with environmental changes than other hominids had been, its story was not a predictable triumph. Only with the hindsight of millions of years can we understand the decisive advantage of intelligence over brawn—larger brains over larger teeth. Indeed, there were many more failures than successes in the gradual changes that led *Homo erectus* to be one of the few hominid species that would survive until the arrival of *Homo sapiens*.

One of the traits that contributed to the survival of *Homo erectus* was the development of extended periods of caring for their young. Although their enlarged brain gave these hominids advantages over the rest of the animal world, it also brought one significant problem: their heads were too large to pass through the females' pelvises at birth. Their pelvises were only big enough to deliver an infant with a cranial capacity that was about a third an adult's size. As a result, offspring required a long period of protection by adults as they matured and their brain size tripled.

This difference from other species also affected family dynamics. For example, the long maturing process gave adult members of hunting and gathering bands time to train their children in those activities. In addition, maturation and brain growth required mothers to spend years attending to their infants, via lactation as well as food preparation for children after weaning. This investment of time and energy was so critical to survival that mothers devised means to share the burden of childrearing. They figured out how to reduce the risks of accidents or attacks, sometimes even fending off assaults by predatory fathers and other males. Mothers relied on other women (their own mothers, sisters, and friends) and girls (often their own daughters) to help in the nurturing and protecting, a process known as allomothering (literally, "other mothering").

Two main features of *Homo erectus* distinguished them from their competitors: bipedalism and their attempts to control the environment. Being bipedal, they could move with a smooth and rapid gait, so they could cover large distances quickly. They were the world's first long-distance travelers, forming the first mobile human communities. In addition, they began to make rudimentary attempts to control their environment. Not only did these early human ancestors make stone tools for hunting and food preparation, but they also began to control fire—another significant marker in the development of human culture. It is hard to tell from fossils when humans learned to use fire. The most reliable evidence comes from cave sites, less than 250,000 years old, where early humans apparently cooked some of their food. Less conservative estimates suggest that human mastery of fire occurred as early as 500,000 years ago. Fire provided heat, protection, a gathering point for small communities, and a way to cook food. It was also symbolically powerful: here was a source of energy that humans could extinguish and revive at will. The uses of fire had enormous long-term effects on human evolution. Because they were able to boil, steam, and fry wild plants, as well as otherwise undigestible foods (especially raw muscle fiber), early humans could expand their diets and their potential food base. Mastery of fire also enabled early humans to survive in colder regions. Without fire, hominids might not have ventured out of Africa.

The populating of the world by hominids proceeded in waves. Around 1 or 2 million years ago, *Homo erectus* individuals migrated first into the lands of Southwest Asia. From there, according to some scholars, they traveled along the Indian Ocean shoreline, moving into South Asia and Southeast Asia and later northward into what is now China. Their **migration** was a response in part to the environmental changes that were transforming the world. The Northern Hemisphere experienced thirty major cold phases during this period, marked by glaciers (huge sheets of ice) spreading over vast expanses of the northern parts of Eurasia and the Americas. The glaciers formed as a result of intense cold that froze much of the world's oceans, lowering them some 325 feet below present-day levels. So it was possible for the migrants to travel across land bridges into Southeast Asia and from East Asia to Japan, as well as from New Guinea to Australia. The last parts of the Afro-Eurasian landmass to be occupied were in Europe. The geological record indicates that ice mantles blanketed the areas of present-day Scotland, Ireland, Wales, Scandinavia, and the whole of northern Europe (including the areas of present-day Berlin, Warsaw, Moscow, and Kiev). Here, too, a lowered ocean level enabled human predecessors to cross by foot from areas in Europe into what is now England.

It is astonishing how far *Homo erectus* hominids traveled. Discoveries of the bone remains of "Java Man" and "Peking Man" (named according to the places where archaeologists first unearthed their remains) confirmed early settlements of *Homo erectus* in Southeast and Eastern Asia. The remains of Java Man, found in 1891 in central Java, turned out to be those of an early *Homo erectus* that had dispersed into Asia nearly 2 million years ago. In 1969, at Sangiran (also on the island of Java), archaeologists uncovered remains with a fuller cranium that was very thick, indicating that the individual's brain was about half the size of a modern human's. Because this discovery dates from about 800,000 years ago, scientists realized that African hominids were moving northward and eastward into Asia at least a million years ago and had reached Java, which was then connected by land to the rest of the Afro-Eurasian landmass.

Similar twentieth-century finds in China give a clearer picture of the daily lives of these pioneering hominids. Peking Man was a cave dweller, toolmaker, and hunter and gatherer who settled in the warmer climate in northern China perhaps 400,000 years ago. Peking Man's brain was larger than that of his Javan cousins, and there is evidence that he controlled fire and cooked meat in addition to hunting large animals. He made tools of vein quartz, quartz crystals, flint, and sandstone. These *Homo erectus* hominids were more adept at toolmaking than their predecessors. Their major innovation was the double-faced axe, a stone instrument whittled down to sharp edges on both sides to serve as a hand axe, a cleaver, a pick, and probably a weapon to hurl against foes or animals. Even so, and in spite of their enlarged brains, these early predecessors still had a long way to go before becoming modern humans.

Rather than seeing human evolution as a single, gradual development, increasingly scientists view our origins as shaped by a series of progressions and regressions as hominids adapted or failed to adapt and went extinct (died out). As the climate changed, especially with the cyclical warming and cooling of the ice ages, weather conditions altered the course of *speciation*, or species formation. Several species could exist simultaneously, but some were more suited to changing environmental

Skulls of Ancestors of *Homo sapiens*. Shown here are seven skulls of ancestors of modern-day men and women, arranged to highlight brain growth over time. The skulls represent (left to right): *Adapis*, a lemur-like animal that lived 50 million years ago; *Proconsul*, a primate that lived about 23 million years ago; *Australopithecus africanus*; *Homo habilis*; *Homo erectus*; *Homo sapiens* from the Qafzeh site in Israel, about 90,000 years old; and Cro-Magnon *Homo sapiens sapiens* from France, about 22,000 years old.

conditions—and thus more likely to survive—than others. Although those in the *Homo habilis* and *Homo erectus* species were among some of the world's first humanlike inhabitants, they probably were not direct ancestors of modern man and woman. The early settlers of Afro-Eurasia from the *Homo erectus* group went extinct. Later waves of hominids followed them, walking out of the African landmass just as their predecessors had done. By 500,000 years ago, caves in many areas of Afro-Eurasia housed residents who made fire, flaked stones into implements, and formed settlements. Yet we are not their descendants. Although the existence of *Homo erectus* may have been necessary for the evolution into *Homo sapiens*, it was not, in itself, sufficient.

THE FIRST MODERN HUMANS

> ↑ *How did* Homo sapiens *become the only hominid species?*

Homo sapiens moved out of Africa sometime between 120,000 and 50,000 years ago. If we consider the 5 million years of hominid life as a single hour of our time today, then the history of *Homo sapiens* is slightly less than two minutes.

The early hominids could not form large communities, as they had limited communication skills. They could utter simple commands and communicate with hand signals, but complex linguistic expression eluded them. This achievement was one of the last in the evolutionary process of becoming human; it did not occur until between 100,000 and 50,000 years ago. Many scholars view it as the critical ingredient in distinguishing human beings from other animals. It is this skill that made *Homo sapiens* "sapiens," which is to say "wise" or "intelligent"—humans who could create culture. Creating language enabled humans to become modern humans.

HOMO SAPIENS AND THEIR MIGRATION

About 200,000 years ago, large-scale shifts in Africa's climate and environment put huge pressures on all types of mammals, including hominids. In these extremely warm and dry environments, the smaller, quicker, and more adaptable mammals survived. What counted now was no longer large size and brute strength, but the ability to respond quickly, with agility, and with great speed.

Caught up in these environmental transformations, early humans were no different from other mammals. It is therefore no surprise that a bigger-brained, more dexterous, and more agile species of humans appeared in the highlands of eastern Africa. Referred to as **Homo sapiens**, they differed notably from their precursors. The eclipse of *Homo erectus* by *Homo sapiens* was not inevitable. After all, *Homo erectus* was already scattered around Africa and Eurasia; in contrast, current thinking suggests that even as late as 100,000 years ago there were only about 10,000 *Homo sapiens* adults living in a small part of the African landmass. But when *Homo sapiens* moved out of Africa and the two species encountered each other in the same places across the globe, *Homo sapiens* individuals were better suited to survive—in part because of their greater cognitive and language skills.

The *Homo sapiens* newcomers followed the trails blazed by earlier migrants from Africa. (See Map 1-2.) In many places, they moved into the same areas as their genetic cousins, migrating by way of the Levant (the area encompassing modern-day Lebanon, Israel, Palestine, Jordan, and Syria), moving across Southwest Asia and from there into central Asia—but not into the area of Europe. They flourished and reproduced. By 30,000 years ago, the population of *Homo sapiens* had grown to about 300,000. Between 60,000

The Physical Evolution of Hominids. These three figures show the femur bones of Lucy, *Orronin tugenensis* (one of the earliest of the hominids, who may have existed as many as 6 million years ago), and *Homo sapiens*. *Homo sapiens* has a larger femur bone and was bigger than Lucy—a representative of the hominid species *Australopithecus afarensis*—but has the same bone structure.

ARCTIC OCEAN

INNER ASIA

by 25,000 BCE

AFRO – EURASIA

NORTH
SEA

EUROPE

CASPIAN
SEA

ARAL
SEA

CENTRAL ASIA

BLACK SEA

50-40,000
BCE

MEDITERRANEAN SEA

SOUTHWEST ASIA

by 60,000 BCE

EAST ASIA

100,000
BCE

100,000
BCE

SOUTH
ASIA

ARABIAN
SEA

Bay
of
Bengal

SOUTH
CHINA
SEA

AFRICA

SOUTHEAST ASIA

ATLANTIC
OCEAN

INDIAN
OCEAN

60-50,000 BCE

120,000 BCE

AUSTRALIA

→ Spread of *Homo erectus* before 200,000 years ago
→ Colonization of *Homo sapiens*
▢ Area occupied by *Homo neanderthalensis*
▢ Area occupied by *Homo erectus*
⋯ Coastline at time of glacial maximum
▢ Maximum extent of ice sheets c.16,000 BCE
▢ Land exposed by lower sea level c. 16,000 BCE

0   1000   2000 Miles
0   1000   2000 Kilometers

MAP 1-2   EARLY MIGRATIONS: OUT OF AFRICA

Hominid species began migrating out of Africa hundreds of thousands of years ago, but only *Homo sapiens* went to all major inhabitable regions. According to this map, what regions did *Homo sapiens* spread to, and in what order? How did geography shape each species' migration patterns? Why do you think *Homo sapiens* migrated to more distant lands than *Homo erectus* did?

ARCTIC OCEAN

From Asia
16,000 BCE

NORTH
AMERICA

ATLANTIC
OCEAN

Tropic of Cancer

12,000 BCE

PACIFIC
OCEAN

Equator

SOUTH
AMERICA

Tropic of Capricorn

9000 BCE

and 12,000 years ago, these modern humans were surging into areas tens of thousands of miles from the Rift Valley and the Ethiopian highlands of Africa. In the area of present-day China, they were thriving and creating distinct regional cultures. Consider Shandingdong Man, a *Homo sapiens* whose fossil remains and relics date to about 18,000 years ago. His physical characteristics were closer to those of modern humans, and he had a similar brain size. His stone tools, which included choppers and scrapers for preparing food, were similar to those of the *Homo erectus* Peking Man. His bone needles, however, were the first stitching tools of their kind found in China, and they indicated the making of garments. Some of the needles measured a little over an inch in length and had small holes drilled in them. Shandingdong Man also buried his dead. In fact, a tomb of grave goods includes ornaments suggesting the development of aesthetic tastes and religious beliefs. The social unit of these hominids may have been some sort of clan descended from a common ancestor and thus linked by genealogy.

Homo sapiens were also migrating into the northeastern fringe of East Asia. In the frigid climate there, they learned to follow herds of large Siberian grazing animals. The bones and dung of Mastodons, large-tusked mammals, for instance, made decent fuel and good building material. Pursuing their prey eastward as the herds sought pastures in the steppes (treeless grasslands) and marshes, these groups migrated across the ice to Japan. Archaeologists have discovered a mammoth fossil in the colder north of Japan, for example, and an elephant fossil in the warmer south. Elephants in particular roamed the warmer parts of inner Eurasia. The hunters and gatherers who moved into Japan gathered wild plants for sustenance, and they dried, smoked, or broiled meat by using fire. They refined these practices once the seas separated the islands from Asia and limited the supplies of game and plants.

About 16,000 years ago, *Homo sapiens* began edging into the weedy landmass that linked Siberia and North America (which hominids had not populated). This thousand-mile-long land bridge, later called Beringia, must have seemed like an extension of familiar steppeland terrain. For thousands of years, modern humans poured eastward and southward into the uninhabited terrain of North America. The oldest known location of human settlement in the Americas is Broken Mammoth, a 14,000-year-old site in central Alaska. A final migration occurred about 8,000 years ago by boat, since by then the land bridge had disappeared under the sea. (See Table 1-2.)

Using their ability to adapt to new environments and to innovate, these expansionist migrants, who were the first discoverers of America, began to fill up the landmasses. They found ample prey in the herds of woolly mammoths, caribou, giant sloths (weighing nearly three tons), and 200-pound beavers. But the explorers could also themselves be prey—

TABLE 1-2	Migrations of *Homo sapiens*
Homo erectus leave Africa	c. 1.5 million years ago
Homo sapiens leave Africa	c. 100,000 years ago
Homo sapiens migrate into Asia	c. 60,000 years ago
migrate into Europe	c. 40–50,000 years ago
migrate into Australia	c. 40,000 years ago
migrate into the Americas	c. 11–16,000 years ago

for they encountered saber-toothed tigers, long-legged eagles, and giant bears that moved faster than horses. The melting of the glaciers about 8,000 years ago and the resulting disappearance of the land bridge eventually cut off the first Americans from their Afro-Eurasian origins. Thereafter, the Americas became a world apart from Afro-Eurasia.

CRO-MAGNON *HOMO SAPIENS* REPLACE NEANDERTHALS

Homo sapiens spread out and occupied habitats where earlier hominid migrants had dwelled. From the time that they left Africa, approximately 100,000 years ago, they migrated over the whole globe. By 25,000 years ago, as DNA analysis reveals, all genetic cousins to *Homo sapiens* were extinct, leaving only modern humans' ancestors to populate the world.

Skulls of a Neanderthal Man (left) and Cro-Magnon (right). These two skulls show that Neanderthals had a large brain capacity and a larger head than modern man. However, Neanderthals lost out to *Homo sapiens* in the struggle to survive as *Homo sapiens* spread across the globe.

Neanderthals, members of an early wave of hominids from Africa, had settled in western Afro-Eurasia (ranging from present-day Uzbekistan and Iraq to Spain) perhaps 150,000 years ago. They were there well before *Homo sapiens*. Therein lies a tale, for Western scholars have had a long fascination with these hominids.

For a long time, many scholars believed that Neanderthals were the primary precursors of modern-day Europeans. We now know that this is not true. The first knowledge of Neanderthals came with the discovery in 1856 of a skull in the Neander Valley of present-day Germany (the *thal* or *tal* in their name is the German word for "valley"). Some authorities wondered if the skull represented the so-called missing link between apes and humans. Not only did Neanderthals have big brains, but they also used tools, buried their dead, hunted, and lived in caves. To judge from their behavior, their brain structure was not as complex as that of modern humans, so their cognitive abilities were far more limited than those of *Homo sapiens*, especially in their perception and creation of symbols.

Neanderthals eventually gave way to Cro-Magnon peoples, a group of *Homo sapiens* named after fossil discoveries from 1868 in Cro-Magnon, France. Although Neanderthal and Cro-Magnon communities overlapped in Europe for thousands of years, the Neanderthals were not as well equipped to survive as the Cro-Magnons, who were truly modern humans. The Neanderthals' short arms and legs and bulky torso may have made them stronger than Cro-Magnon men and women, but the Neanderthals were awkward and clumsy. The Cro-Magnons had the advantages of physical dexterity and high intelligence; the latter attribute gave them cognitive and language abilities not available to Neanderthals to the same degree.

Neanderthals and other advanced hominids in China and Java represented the culmination of a long evolutionary process that made individuals more specialized and better adapted to specific environmental conditions. When the environment began to change, these descendants from Africa had difficulty coping. They lacked the range and adaptive fluidity of *Homo sapiens*. In the scramble for food and shelter, *Homo sapiens* had an edge. From their last refuge around Zafarraya in Spain, the Neanderthals vanished, leaving only a small trace in the gene pool that evolved into modern humanity somewhere between 1 and 4 percent. Like the *Homo erectus* species in Java and China, this particular trajectory of hominid development came to a dead end.

EARLY *HOMO SAPIENS* AS HUNTERS AND GATHERERS

Like their hominid predecessors, modern humans were hunters and gatherers, and they subsisted in this way until

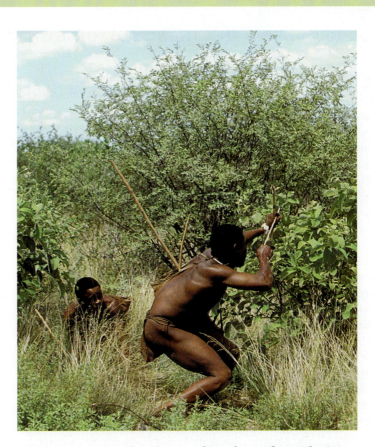

The San Hunters and Gatherers of Southern Africa. The San, who live in the Kalahari Desert in present-day Botswana, continue to follow a hunting and gathering existence that has died out in many parts of the world. Hunting and gathering was the way that most humans lived for millennia.

around 12,000 years ago. They hunted animals, fished, and foraged for wild berries, nuts, fruit, and grains, rather than planting crops, vines, or trees. Even today hunting and gathering societies endure, although only in the most marginal locations—often at the edge of deserts. For example, researchers consider the present-day San peoples of southern Africa as an isolated remnant continuing their traditional hunting and gathering modes of life. On the basis of analogy, modern scholars use the San to reveal how men and women must have lived hundreds of thousands of years ago. (See Primary Source: Problems in the Study of Hunters and Gatherers.) As late as 1500 CE, as much as 15 percent of the world's population still lived by **hunting and gathering**.

The fact that hominid men and women survived as hunters and gatherers for millions of years, that early *Homo sapiens* also lived this way, and that a few contemporary communities still forage for food suggests the powerful attractions of this way of life. Hunters and gatherers could find enough food in about three hours of foraging each day, thus affording time for other pursuits such as relaxation, interaction, and friendly competitions with other members of their

PROBLEMS IN THE STUDY OF HUNTERS AND GATHERERS

One of the challenges in studying the origins of humanity is that the evidence is incomplete. Archaeologists and anthropologists have to theorize on the basis of what they can lay their hands on. In the case of archaeologists, these include fossil records. In the case of anthropologists, their subjects are tribal peoples—such as the San of southern Africa—whose lifeways today may resemble those of their ancestors tens of thousands of years ago.

To date, the hunting way of life has been the most successful and persistent adaptation man has ever achieved.

. . . It is appropriate that anthropologists take stock of the much older way of life of the hunters. This is not simply a study of biological evolution, since zoologists have come to regard behavior as central to the adaptation and evolution of all species. The emergence of economic, social, and ideological forms are as much a part of human evolution as are the developments in human anatomy and physiology. . . .

. . . Ever since the origin of agriculture, Neolithic (new stone age) peoples have been steadily expanding at the expense of the hunters. Today the latter are often found in unattractive environments, in lands which are of no use to their neighbors and which pose difficult and dramatic problems of survival. The more favorable habitats have long ago been appropriated by peoples with stronger, more aggressive social systems.

. . . Taking hunters as they are found, anthropologists have naturally been led to the conclusion that their life (and by implication the life of our ancestors) was a constant struggle for survival.

At the dawn of agriculture 12,000 years ago, hunters covered most of the habitable globe, and appeared to be generally most successful in those areas which later supported the densest populations of agricultural peoples. By 1500 CE the area left to hunters had shrunk drastically and their distribution fell largely at the peripheries of the continents and in the inaccessible interiors. However, even at this late date, hunting peoples occupied all of Australia, most of western and northern North America, and large portions of South America and Africa. This situation rapidly changed with the era of colonial expansion, and by 1900, when serious ethnographic research got under way,

much of this way of life had been destroyed. As a result, our notion of unacculturated hunter-gatherer life has been largely drawn from peoples no longer living in the optimum portion of their traditional range.

To mention a few examples, the Netsilik Eskimos, the Arunta, and the Kung Bushmen are now classic cases in ethnography. However, the majority of the precontact Eskimos, Australian aborigines, and Bushmen lived in much better environments. Two-thirds of the Eskimos, according to Laughlin, lived *south* of the Arctic circle, and the populations in the Australian and Kalahari deserts were but a fraction of the populations living in the well-watered regions of southeast Australia and the Cape Province of Africa. Thus, within a given region the "classic cases" may, in fact, be precisely the opposite: namely, the most isolated peoples who managed to avoid contact until the arrival of the ethnographers. In order to understand hunters better it may be more profitable to consider the few hunters in rich environments, since it is likely that these peoples will be more representative of the ecological conditions under which man evolved than are the dramatic and unusual cases that illustrate extreme environmental pressure. Such a perspective may better help us to understand the extraordinary persistence and success of the human adaptation.

→ *Why is it important to study hunting and gathering communities?*

→ *Why are the "classic cases" not necessarily the most representative of this early lifeway?*

SOURCE: Richard B. Lee and Irven De Vore, "Problems in the Study of Hunters and Gatherers" from *Man the Hunter*, pp. 3 and 5. Copyright © 1968 by Aldine Publishers. Reprinted by permission of Aldine Transaction, a division of Transaction Publishers.

bands. Scholars believe that these small bands were relatively egalitarian. They speculate that men specialized in hunting and women specialized in gathering and child rearing but that men and women contributed equally to the bands' welfare.

Scholars also believe that women made a larger contribution and had high status because the dietary staples were cereals and fruits, whose harvesting and preparation were likely women's responsibility.

ART AND LANGUAGE

> → *How did art and language increase* Homo sapiens' *chances of survival?*

Despite the remorselessly nature-bound quality of life for early humans, the first *Homo sapiens* made an evolutionary breakthrough. They developed cultural forms that reflected a consciousness of self, a drive to survive, an appreciation of beauty, and an ability to engage dynamically with their environments.

ART

Few of the cultural achievements of early *Homo sapiens* communities have engaged modern-day observers more than their artistic endeavors. Accomplished drawings have come to light in areas in Europe, probably as a response to the harsher environment there and also because of intense competition with the Neanderthals. The ability to draw allowed *Homo sapiens* to understand their environment, to bond among their kin groups (groups related by blood ties), and to articulate important mythologies. In times of stress, such behaviors gave these individuals an adaptive advantage to survive in extremely challenging circumstances.

"Look, Daddy, oxen!" That is what the daughter of Marcelino Sanz de Sauruola cried to her father as she looked at the ceiling of a deep cave on his property at Altamira, Spain, that he was exploring one summer afternoon. As he looked up, Sauruola could not believe what he saw. Arranged across the ceiling of the huge chamber were more than two dozen life-size figures of bison, horses, and wild bulls, all painted in vivid red, black, yellow, and brown. He did not think that anyone would believe these fabulous images were tens of thousands of years old, but he knew in his heart that they were. That was in 1879. Only in 1906 did the world accept that the Altamira paintings, and those later discovered in other caves, were the work of early humans. Even today, with researchers having found more than 50,000 works of art by early humans in Europe, these paintings compel wonder and awe at the innate artistic abilities unique to humans. (See Primary Source: The Art of Chauvet Cave.)

The images on cave walls accumulated over a period of 25,000 years, and they changed very little in that time. The subjects are most often large game—animals that early humans would have considered powerful symbols. The artists rendered these animals with a striking economy of line, frequently painted in such a way that the natural contours of the cave wall defined a bulging belly or an eye socket. Many appear more than once, suggesting that they are the works from several occasions or by several artists. The remarkably few human images show naked females or dancing males.

There are also many handprints made by blowing paint around a hand placed on the cave wall, or by dipping hands in paint and then pressing them to the wall. There are even abstract symbols such as circles, wavy lines, and checkerboards; often these appear at places of transition in the caves.

We can only speculate what the images meant to ancient humans. Scholars have rejected an initial explanation that they were decorative, for the deep caves were not the ancients' homes and had no natural light to render the images visible. Perhaps the images had a social function, helping the early humans to define themselves as separate from other parts of nature. Among other interpretations is a theory that they were the work of powerful shamans, individuals believed to hold special powers to understand and control the tremendous forces of the cosmos. The subjects and the style of the paintings are similar to images engraved or painted on rocks by some hunter and gatherer societies living today, especially the San and the !Kung peoples of southern Africa. In those societies, paintings mark important places of ritual: shamans make them during trances while interceding with the spirit world on behalf of their communities.

Paintings were not the only form of artistic expression for early humans. Archaeologists also have unearthed small sculptures of animals shaped out of bone and stone that are even older than the paintings. Most famous are figurines of enormously fat and pregnant females. Statuettes like the so-called Venus of Willendorf, found in Austria, demonstrate that successful reproduction was a very important theme. Among the most exquisite sculptures are those of animals carved in postures of movement or at rest.

The caves of early men and women also resounded to the strains of music. In 2008 archaeologists working in southwestern Germany discovered a hollowed-out bone flute with five openings that they dated to approximately 35,000 years ago, roughly the same time that humans began to occupy this

Willendorf Venus. This squat limestone statuette—only about six inches in height—was discovered in 1908 near the village of Willendorf, Austria, and dates back about 25,000 years. As one of the earliest representations of a female figure found in Europe, it is a famous icon of prehistoric art. The emphasis on the woman's breasts and reproductive organs—to the exclusion, for example, of her facial features—and the presence of a red ochre dye on her genitalia suggest the maker's concern with the woman's fertility and procreative functions.

THE ART OF CHAUVET CAVE

A spectacular discovery at Chauvet Cave in southwestern France in 1994 overturned all previous ideas about the development of prehistoric art. Dating to about 35,000 years ago (much older than the 20,000-year-old paintings from Lascaux in southeastern France, or the 17,000-year-old paintings from Altamira in northwestern Spain), they are the oldest prehistoric cave paintings known in Europe. The hundreds of representations found at Chauvet Cave are more detailed and more brilliant than the ones at Altamira and Lascaux. There are drawings of mammoths, musk oxen, horses, lions, bears, and even rhinoceroses, as well as human palm prints (and footprints on the cave's floor) and "Venus" figures with exaggerated female genitalia—

the latter apparently signifying a preoccupation with human fertility. These amazing engravings and paintings shocked scholars because they were produced only a few thousand years after the first modern humans appeared in Europe.

→ *These drawings show horses, a musk ox, and a rhinoceros. What characteristics of these animals might have inspired the early* Homo sapiens *artists, and why?*
→ *What does their decision to portray certain animals but not others tell us?*

Almost as soon as their first appearance in western Europe, modern humans seemed to have rapidly developed a sense, ability, and desire to portray other living beings in their environment. This brilliant drawing shows the detail in a depiction of horses' heads.

This image uses a doubling effect—drawing additional hindquarters and legs—to give the bison the appearance of motion and speed. The ability to portray dynamic movement was once thought to be a skill that humans developed much later.

region. When researchers put the flute to musical tests, they also concluded that this seemingly primitive instrument was capable of making harmonic sounds comparable to those of modern-day flutes, no small achievement for these early humans whose artistic prowess must have provided much enjoyment to listeners and viewers.

Sculpture and drawing are the oldest forms of visual representation, which was a fundamental part of early human life; yet with the possible exception of the Neanderthals, hominid lines produced very few extant examples. Only members of *Homo sapiens* developed and used this cognitive capacity for symbolic expression by leaving a permanent mark

on the landscape. Such visual expressions marked the dawn of human culture and of a consciousness of men and women's place in the world. Symbolic activity of this sort helped early humans to make sense of themselves, nature, and the relationships between humanity and nature.

LANGUAGE

Few things set humans off from the rest of the animal world more starkly than their use of language, whose genesis and evolution spark heated controversies. Scholars do agree, however, that the cognitive abilities involved in language development marked an evolutionary milestone.

It is important to distinguish between vocal-utterance speech, possessed by many precursor hominids (such as the Neanderthals), and natural **language** (the use of sounds to make words that convey meaning to others), which is unique to modern humans. The development of language necessitated a large brain and complex cognitive organization to create word groups that would convey symbolic meaning. Verbal communication thus required an ability to think abstractly and to communicate abstractions. Language was a huge breakthrough, because individuals could teach words to neighbors and offspring and could use them to integrate communities for survival. Language also enhanced the ability to accumulate knowledge that could be transmitted across both space and time.

Biological research has demonstrated that humans can make and process many more primary and distinctive sounds, called phonemes, than other animals can. Whereas a human being can utter fifty phonemes, an ape can form only twelve. Also, humans can process sounds more quickly than other primates can. With fifty phonemes it is possible to create more than 100,000 words; by arranging those words in different sequences and developing syntax in language, individuals can express countless subtle and complex meanings. Recent research suggests that use of complex languages occurred about 100,000 years ago and that the nearest approximation to humanity's proto-language (earliest language) existing today belongs to two African peoples, the !Kung of southern Africa and the Hadza of Tanzania. These peoples make a clicking sound by dropping the tongue down from the roof of the mouth and exhaling—a sound similar to vervet monkeys' warnings of impending danger. As humans moved out of Africa and dispersed around the globe, they expanded their original language into nineteen language families, from which all of the world's languages then evolved. (See Map 1-3.) It was the development of cultural forms and language that allowed *Homo sapiens* to engage dynamically with their environments.

MAP 1-3   ORIGINAL LANGUAGE FAMILY GROUPS

The use of complex language developed 100,000 years ago among *Homo sapiens* in Africa. As humans dispersed throughout the globe, nineteen language families evolved from which all modern languages originate. How many different landmasses did language evolve on? On the basis of this map, what geographic features kept emerging language families distinct from one another? Why do you think separate languages emerged over time?

THE BEGINNINGS OF FOOD PRODUCTION

> → *What factors contributed to the domestication of plants and animals?*

About 12,000 years ago, a fundamental change occurred in human behavior. It involved a shift in the way humans controlled and produced food for themselves—what some scholars have called a revolution in agriculture and ecology. In this era of major change, humans established greater control over nature, especially over plants and animals. This new wave of innovation and adaptation changed human modes of life. The transformation consisted of the cultivation of wild grasses and cereals and the **domestication** (the bringing under human control) of wild animals. For the first time, human intelligence refashioned nature to meet human needs. Five locations that scholars acknowledge to be independent centers of this agricultural revolution were Southwest Asia, East Asia, Southeast Asia, Mesoamerica, and northeastern America. (See Map 1-4.) Four others may also have been independent regions for this revolution, although the evidence suggests some borrowing. These were East Africa, inland West Africa, southeastern Europe, and South America.

Many factors triggered the move to settled agriculture. Population pressure was a precipitant, as hunting and gathering alone could not sustain the growth in numbers of people. Some regions may have hit the ceiling of natural food supply without the cultivation of crops or the domestication of animals. An agricultural revolution shattered this ceiling—and led to a vast population expansion because men and women could now produce more calories per unit of land than in the past. To be sure, learning to control environments and domesticate resources did not liberate humans from the risks of natural disasters. Without food storage systems, for example, a sharp drought could wipe out or uproot entire communities.

EARLY DOMESTICATION OF PLANTS AND ANIMALS

Settled agriculture, the application of human labor and tools to a fixed plot of land for more than one growing cycle, entails the changeover from a hunting and gathering lifestyle to one based on agriculture, which requires staying in one place until the soil has been exhausted. Around 9000 BCE, abundant rainfall and mild winters created optimal conditions in Southwest Asia for settled life. Once hunters and gatherers could meet their subsistence needs in one diverse ecological niche, they could afford to settle in a single location. They did so throughout Southwest Asia in greater numbers than before, learning to exploit mountainous areas covered with forest vegetation and home to wild sheep, wild goats, and long-horned wild oxen. In attractive locations such as the valleys of the Taurus Mountains in Upper Mesopotamia (present-day Iraq) and the Anatolian plateau (in modern-day Turkey), the early humans established permanent settlements.

The formation of settled communities enabled humans to take advantage of favorable regions and to take risks, spurring agricultural innovation. In areas with abundant wild game and edible plants, people began to observe and experiment with the most adaptable plants. For ages, people gathered grains by collecting seeds that fell freely from their stalks. At some point, observant collectors perceived that they could obtain larger harvests if they pulled grain seeds directly from plants. The process of plant domestication probably began when people noticed that certain edible plants retained their nutritious grains longer than others, so they collected these seeds and scattered them across fertile soils. When ripe, these plants produced bigger and more concentrated crops. It took time to understand this process, but ultimately a community supporting this kind of innovation realized that it could sustain a larger population than its neighbors. Plant domestication occurred when the plant retained its ripe, mature seeds, allowing an easy harvest. People used most seeds for food but saved some for planting in the next growing cycle, to ensure a food supply for the next year. The gradual domestication of plants began in the southern Levant and spread from there into the rest of Southwest Asia.

DOMESTICATION OF ANIMALS If dogs are a man's best friend, we are now beginning to learn how long and important that friendship has been. Dogs were the first animals to be domesticated (although in fact they may have adopted humans, rather than the other way around). About 12,000 years ago in the area of present-day Iraq, dogs became an essential part of human society. They did more than comfort humans, however, for they provided a vital example of how to achieve the domestication of other animals. Moreover, dogs with herding instincts aided humans in controlling sheep once they had been domesticated.

Wild sheep and wild goats were the next animals to come under human control. This process took place in the central Zagros Mountains region, where wild sheep and wild goats were abundant. A favored explanation is that hunters returned home with young wild sheep, which then grew up within the human community. They reproduced, and their offspring never returned to the wild. The animals accepted their dependence because the humans fed them. As it became clear that controlling animal reproduction was more reliable than hunting, domesticated herds became the primary source of protein in the early humans' diet. This shift probably happened first with the wild sheep living in herds on the mountain slopes.

When the number of animals under human control and living close to the settlement outstripped the supply of food needed to feed them, community members could move the animals to grassy steppes for grazing. Later this lifestyle, called **pastoralism** (the herding of domesticated animals), became an important subsistence strategy that complemented settled farming. Pastoralists herded domesticated animals, moving them to new pastures on a seasonal basis. Goats, the other main domesticated animal of Southwest Asia, are smarter than sheep but more difficult to control. The pastoralists may have introduced goats into herds of sheep to better control herd movement. Pigs and cattle also came under human control at this time.

PASTORALISTS AND AGRICULTURALISTS

The domestication of plants and animals offered new and powerful subsistence strategies that at first augmented and then replaced hunting, gathering, and foraging. Both of these new sources of food and raw materials required radically different ways to use the land which in turn led to different modes of social, political, and economic organization.

Pastoralism, which involved the herding of sheep and goats but also cattle, appeared as a way of life around 5500 BCE, essentially at the same time that full-time farmers appeared. The first pastoralists were closely affiliated with agricultural villages whose inhabitants grew grains, especially wheat and barley, which required large parcels of land. Pastoralists produced both meat and dairy products, as well as wool for textiles, and exchanged these products with the agriculturalists for grain, pottery, and other staples. In the fertile crescent surrounding the Mesopotamian alluvium, many extended families farmed and herded at the same time, growing crops on large estates and grazing their herds in the foothills and mountains nearby. These herders moved their livestock seasonally, usually pasturing their flocks in higher lands during summer and in valleys in winter. This movement over short distances is called transhumance and did not require herders to vacate their primary locations, which were generally in the mountain valleys.

A quite different form of pastoralism, often called nomadic pastoralism, also based on the herding of cattle and other livestock, came to flourish in other settings, notably in the steppe lands north of the agricultural zone of southern Eurasia. This way of life was characterized by horse-riding herders of livestock. These herders often had no fixed home, unlike the transhumant herders of Southwestern Asia, though they often returned to their traditional locations, but moved in response to the size and needs of their herds. The

northern areas of the Eurasian landmass stretching from present-day Ukraine across Siberia and Mongolia to the Pacific Ocean became the preserve of these horse-riding pastoral peoples in a region unable to support the extensive agriculture necessary for large settled populations.

Historians know much less about these horse-riding pastoral peoples than about the agriculturalists and their transhumant cousins, as their numbers were small and they left fewer archaeological traces or historical records. Their role in world history, however, is as important as that of the settled societies. In Afro-Eurasia, they domesticated horses and developed weapons and techniques that at certain points in history enabled them to conquer sedentary societies. They also transmitted ideas, products, and people across long distances, maintaining the linkages that connected east and west.

The archaeological record indicates that full-fledged pastoralism had crystallized in the steppe lands of northern Eurasia by 3000 BCE. By this time, the peoples living there had learned to yoke and ride animals, to milk them, and to use their hair for clothing, as well as to slaughter them for food. Of all the domesticated animals in the steppe lands, the horse became the most important. Because horses provided decisive advantages in transportation and warfare, they gained more value than other domesticated animals. Thus, horses soon became the measure of household wealth and prestige. The domestication of plants and animals and the move to settled agriculture led to a global agricultural revolution.

EMERGENCE OF AGRICULTURE IN OTHER AREAS

Agricultural revolutions occurred worldwide between 9000 and 2000 BCE. They had much in common: the same factors of climatic change; increased knowledge about plants and animals; and the need for more efficient ways to feed, house, and promote the survival of larger numbers. These concerns led peoples in Eurasia, Africa, and the Americas to see the advantages of cultivating plants and domesticating wildlife.

The following sections examine early agriculture in five key regions: (1) Southwest Asia; (2) the southern part of China in East Asia, where water and rice were critical; (3) western Europe, where the new cultivators borrowed from Southwest Asia; (4) the Americas, which had the disadvantage of offering few animals that humans could domesticate; and (5) Africa,

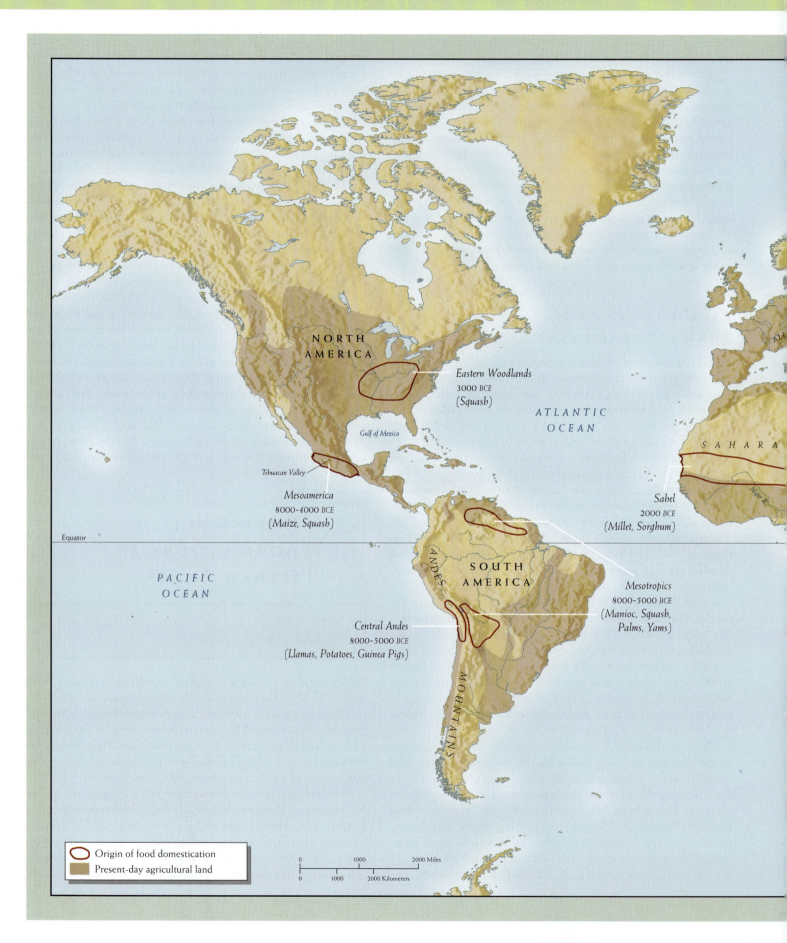

NORTH AMERICA

Eastern Woodlands
3000 BCE
(Squash)

ATLANTIC OCEAN

SAHARA

Gulf of Mexico

Tehuacan Valley

Mesoamerica
8000–4000 BCE
(Maize, Squash)

Sahel
2000 BCE
(Millet, Sorghum)

Niger R.

ANDES

SOUTH AMERICA

PACIFIC OCEAN

Equator

Mesotropics
8000–5000 BCE
(Manioc, Squash, Palms, Yams)

Central Andes
8000–5000 BCE
(Llamas, Potatoes, Guinea Pigs)

MOUNTAINS

◯ Origin of food domestication
▨ Present-day agricultural land

0   1000   2000 Miles
0   1000   2000 Kilometers

→ *What factors contributed to innovation, as opposed to borrowing, in agriculture?*

Southeastern Europe
7000 BCE
(Pigs, Cattle, Wheat,
Barley, Sheep, Goats)

Fertile Crescent
8000 BCE
(Barley, Cattle,
Goats, Pigs,
Sheep, Wheat)

Yellow River
6000 BCE (Millet)

Yangzi River
6000 BCE (Rice)

MAP 1-4   THE ORIGINS OF FOOD PRODUCTION

Agricultural production emerged in many regions at different times. The variety of patterns reflected local resources and conditions. How many different locations did agricultural production emerge in? Are there any common geographic features among these early food-producing areas? Why do you think agriculture emerged in certain areas and not in others? How did the domestication of plants and animals affect kinship systems, political organization, and social relations?

Large Two-handled Yangshao Pot. This pot comes from the village of Yangshao in Henan Province, along the Yellow River in Northwest China, where remains were first found in 1921 of a people who lived more than 6,000 years ago. The Yangshao lived in small, rammed-earth fortresses and, without the use of pottery wheels, created fine white, red, and black painted pottery with human faces and animal and geometric designs. This jar dates back to the third or second millennium BCE.

prerequisites for large-scale millet planting in the drier north and the rice-cultivated areas of the wetter south. Each crop depended on ecological suitability and the human knowledge of how to manipulate plants.

EUROPE: BORROWING ALONG TWO PATHWAYS

At the western fringe of Afro-Eurasia, in Europe, domestication occurred through the diffusion of ideas and peoples from centers elsewhere. As in East Asia, once the new techniques arrived, they spread rapidly. By 6000–5000 BCE, people in regions of Europe close to the societies of Southwest Asia, such as Greece and the Balkans, were abandoning their hunting and gathering lifeways to become agriculturists who exerted control over plants and animals. (See Map 1-7.) Places like the Franchthi Cave in Greece reveal that around 6000 BCE the inhabitants borrowed innovations from their neighbors in Southwest Asia, such as how to herd domesticated animals and to plant wheat and barley. From the Aegean and Greece, settled agriculture and domesticated animals expanded westward throughout Europe, accompanied by the development of settled communities.

The emergence of agriculture and village life occurred in Europe along two separate paths. The first and most rapid trajectory followed the northern rim of the Mediterranean Sea. Domestication of crops and animals moved westward, following the prevailing currents of the Mediterranean, from what is now Turkey through the islands of the Aegean Sea to mainland Greece, and from there to southern and central Italy and Sicily. Whether the process involved the actual migration of individuals or the abstract spread of ideas, connections by sea quickened the pace of the transition. Once the basic elements of domestication had arrived in the Mediterranean region from Southwest Asia, the speed and ease of seaborne communications aided astonishingly rapid changes. Almost overnight, hunting and gathering gave way to domesticated agriculture and herding.

Pottery in Banpo Village (c. 4800–4200 BCE). This remarkable, intact village, one of the best-known ditch-enclosed settlements of Yangshao culture, provides us with clear evidence of a sophisticated agriculture based on millet and Chinese cabbage. One of China's first farming cultures, the people of Banpo interacted directly with other villages on the North China Plain and were indirectly in contact with peoples from as far away as Southeast Asia.

MAP 1-7   THE SPREAD OF AGRICULTURE IN EUROPE

The spread of agricultural production into Europe after 7000 BCE represents geographic diffusion. Europeans borrowed agricultural techniques and technology from other groups, adapting those innovations to their own situations. Where did the ideas and techniques originate? Through what two pathways did agriculture spread across Europe? Did Europe's settled agricultural communities have different features from those that appeared in Southwest Asia, East Asia, and Africa?

The second trajectory took an overland route: from Anatolia, across northern Greece into the Balkans, then northwestward along the Danube River into the Hungarian plain, and from there farther north and west into the Rhine River valley in modern-day Germany. Change here likely resulted from the transmission of ideas rather than from population migrations, for community after community adopted domesticated plants and animals and the new mode of life. This route of agricultural development was slower than the Mediterranean route for two reasons. First, domesticated crops, or individuals who

"Long House." The people who opened up the whole of central Europe to agriculture typically lived in communities of six to twelve "long houses." Although large in size (varying between 60 and 120 feet in length), long houses were built on simple principles: a framework of wooden beams and posts with walls made of mud and woven branches beneath a thatched roof. These dwellings probably sheltered large extended family or kinship units that cooperated to provide the hard work needed to carve out pioneer farming settlements along river valleys. This cutaway reconstruction of a long house shows the placement of wall timbers and internal support posts.

knew about them, had to travel by land, as there were few large rivers like the Danube. Second, it was necessary to find new groups of domesticated plants and animals that could flourish in the colder and more forested lands of central Europe. Agriculturalists here had to plant their crops in the spring and harvest in the autumn, rather than the other way around. Cattle rather than sheep became the dominant herd animals.

In Europe, the main cereal crops were wheat and barley, and the main herd animals were sheep, goats, and cattle—all of which had been domesticated in Southwest Asia. (Residents domesticated additional plants, such as olives and grape-producing vines, later.) These fundamental changes did not bring dramatic material progress, however. The normal settlement in Europe at this time consisted of a few dozen mud huts. These settlements, although few, often comprised large "long houses" built of timber and mud, designed to store produce and to shelter animals during the long winters. Some settlements had sixty to seventy huts—in rare cases, up to a hundred. Hunting, gathering, and fishing still supplemented the new settled agriculture and the herding of domesticated animals. The innovators were dynamic in blending the new ways with the old. Consider that around 6000 BCE, hunter-gatherers in southern France adopted the herding of domesticated sheep, but not the planting of domesticated crops—*that* would have conflicted with their

preference for a life of hunting, which was a traditional part of their economy.

By about 5000–4000 BCE, communities living in areas around rivers and in the large plains had embraced the new food-producing economy. Elsewhere (notably in the rugged mountain lands that still predominate in Europe's landscape), hunting and foraging remained humans' primary way of relating to nature. The transition to settled farming and herding brought an enormous rise in population, however. As agricultural communities supported more and more people, such communities became the dominant social organization.

THE AMERICAS: A SLOWER TRANSITION TO AGRICULTURE

When people crossed Beringia and trekked southward through the Americas, they set off an ecological transformation but also adapted to unfamiliar habitats. The flora and fauna of the Americas were different enough to induce the early settlers to devise ways of living that distinguished them from their ancestors in Afro-Eurasia. Then, when the glaciers began to melt around 12,500 BCE and water began to cover the land bridge between East Asia and America, the Americas and their peoples truly became a whole world apart.

Early humans in America used chipped blades and pointed spears to pursue their prey, which included mastodons, woolly mammoths, and bison. In doing so, they extended the hunting traditions they had learned in Afro-Eurasia, establishing campsites and moving with their herds. Researchers have named these hunters "Clovis people" because a site near Clovis, New Mexico, first yielded their typical arrowhead point. Their archaeological sites located all over North America contain the remains of their weaponry.

CLIMATIC CHANGE AND ADAPTATION For many years, scientists thought that the Clovis communities had wiped out the large Ice Age mammals they found in America. Recent research suggests, though, that climatic change destroyed the indigenous plants and trees—the feeding grounds of large prehistoric mammals—and that abundant forage became scarce. The vast spruce forests that had fed the great mastodons, for instance, shrank into isolated pockets, leaving undernourished mastodons vulnerable to human and animal predators until they vanished. The tall grassland prairies gave way to areas with short grass; where short grass once flourished, cacti took over. As in Afro-Eurasia, the arrival of a long warming cycle compelled those living in the Americas to adapt to different ecological niches and to create new subsistence strategies. Thus, in the woodland area of the present-day northeastern United States, hunters learned to trap smaller wild animals for food and furs. To supplement the protein from meat and fish, these people also dug for roots and gathered berries. What is important is that even as most communities adapted to the settled agricultural economy, they did not abandon basic survival strategies of hunting and gathering.

Food-producing changes in the Americas were different from those in Afro-Eurasia because this area did not undergo the sudden cluster of innovations that revolutionized agriculture in Southwest Asia and elsewhere. Tools ground from stone, rather than chipped implements, appeared in the Tehuacán Valley by 6700 BCE, and evidence of plant domestication there dates back to 5000 BCE. But villages, pottery making, and sustained population growth came later. For many early American inhabitants, the life of hunting, trapping, and fishing went on as it had for millennia. Indeed, researchers have found the remains of ancient shellfishing throughout the coastal Americas from Alaska to Chile on the Pacific Ocean side. Along the Pacific coast, communities formed around fishing cultures, many relying on dugout canoes and spears to obtain food.

On the coast of what is now Peru, people found food by fishing and gathering shellfish from the Pacific. Archaeological remains include the remnants of fishnets, bags, baskets, and textile implements; gourds for carrying water; and stone knives, choppers, scrapers, bone awls, and thorn needles. Oddly enough, there is no evidence of watercraft even though thousands of villages likely dotted the seashores and riverbanks of the Americas. Some made breakthroughs in the management of fire that enabled them to manufacture pottery; others devised irrigation and water sluices in floodplains. And some even began to send their fish catches inland in return for agricultural produce.

DOMESTICATION OF PLANTS AND ANIMALS The earliest evidence of plant experimentation in Mesoamerica dates from around 7000 BCE, and it went on for a long time. Maize, squash, and beans (first found in what is now central Mexico) became dietary staples. The early settlers foraged small seeds of maize, peeled them from ears only a few inches long, and planted them. Maize offered real advantages because it was easy to store, relatively imperishable, nutritious, and easy to cultivate alongside other plants. Nonetheless, it took 5,000 years for farmers to complete its domestication—that is, to settle in one place, live there year-round, plant maize, and stay beyond a single growing and harvesting cycle. Over the years, farmers had to mix and breed different strains of maize for it to evolve from thin spikes of seeds to cobs rich with kernels, with a single plant yielding big, thick ears to feed a growing permanent population. (See Primary Source: A Mesoamerican Creation Myth.) Thus the agricultural changes afoot in Mesoamerica were slow and late in maturing. The pace was even more gradual in South America, where early settlers clung to their hunting and gathering traditions.

Head of Mayan Corn God. Corn, or maize, was a revered crop in Mesoamerica, where people ritually prayed to their deities for good harvests. Notice the crown made not of precious metals and stones but of corn husks as an example of the cultural emphasis on maize.

Across the Americas, the settled, agrarian communities found that legumes (beans), grains (maize), and tubers (potatoes) complemented one another in keeping the soil fertile and offering a balanced diet. Unlike the Afro-Eurasians, however, the settlers did not use domesticated animals as an alternative source of protein. In only a few pockets of the Andean highlands is there evidence of the domestication of tiny guinea pigs, which may have been tasty but unfulfilling meals. Nor did people in the Americas tame animals that could protect villages (as dogs did in Afro-Eurasia) or carry heavy loads over long distances (as camels did in Afro-Eurasia). Although llamas could haul heavy loads, their patience and cooperation were limited. Considered at best semi-domesticates, llamas were mainly useful for clothing.

Nonetheless, the domestication of plants and animals in the Americas, as well as the presence of villages and clans, suggests significant diversification and refinement of technique. At the same time, the centers of such activity were

Primary Source

MOTHERING AND LACTATION

One of the dividing lines among all animals, humans included, involves child rearing and the division of labor between mothers and fathers. This text argues that lactation (milk production) became a major factor shaping the social roles of primate mothers.

"Is sex destiny?" When this question is posed, it's a safe bet that the underlying agenda has to do with what women *should* be doing. Should they be home caring for their children or off pursuing other interests? A comparative look at other creatures that (like humans) breed cooperatively and share responsibilities for rearing young with other group members reveals that sex *per se* is not the issue. Lactation is.

Caretakers of both sexes, wet-nurses, even "daycare"—none of these are uniquely human, nor particularly new. They are standard features of many cooperatively breeding species. As we saw, cooperative breeding is exquisitely well developed in insects such as honeybees and wasps. Shared provisioning is also common among birds such as acorn woodpeckers, bee-eaters, dunnocks, and scrub jays. Although cooperative breeding is uncommon among mammals generally, it is richly developed in species such as wolves, wild dogs, dwarf mongooses, elephants, tamarins, marmosets, and humans. In all these animals, individuals other than the mother ("allomothers") help her provision or otherwise care for her young. Typically, allomothers will include the mother's mate (often but not necessarily the genetic progenitor). Individuals other than either parent ("alloparents") also help. These helpers are most often recruited from kin who are not yet ready to reproduce themselves, or from subordinates who do not currently—or may never have—better options. In the human case, the most important alloparents are often older, post-reproductive relatives who have already reproduced.

Among mammals, the trend toward having young who require costly long-term care began modestly enough. It probably began with an egg-laying brooding reptile that started to secrete something milklike. Such egg-layers gradually developed glands especially equipped for milk production. Only among mammals did one sex come to specialize in manufacturing custom-made baby formula, to provide something critical for infant survival that the other sex could not. This peculiarity has had many ramifications, especially as infants became dependent for longer periods in the primate line.

The ante was upped substantially when primate mothers, instead of bearing litters, began focusing care on one baby at a time. These singletons were born mature enough to cling to their mother's fur, to be carried by her right from birth and for months thereafter. Whether or not this intimate and prolonged association is the mother's destiny, *sex* is not the issue. Lactation is.

→ *How does lactation affect mothers' child-rearing roles differently from fathers'?*

→ *Why is the difference more marked among humans than among other species?*

SOURCE: From *Mother Nature* by Sarah Blaffer Hrdy, copyright © 1999 by Sarah Blaffer Hrdy. Used by permission of Pantheon Books, a division of Random House, Inc.

fields. Perhaps because of the increased demands for community work to maintain the irrigation systems, the communities in southern Mesopotamia became stratified, with some people having more power than others. We can see from the burial sites and myriad public buildings uncovered by archaeologists that for the first time, some people had higher status derived from birth rather than through the merits of their work. A class of people who had access to more luxury goods, and who lived in bigger and better houses, now became part of the social organization.

It is important to emphasize that changes arising from agriculture enabled larger numbers of people to live in denser concentrations, and the household with its dominant male replaced the small, relatively egalitarian band as the primary social unit.

MEN, WOMEN, AND EVOLVING GENDER RELATIONS

One of the fundamental divisions evident in the fossil remains of early hominids and humans is the division between males and females. This observation raises questions about the relationships between the sexes in prehistoric times.

For millions of years, biological differences—the fact that females give birth to offspring and that males do not—determined female and male behaviors and attitudes toward each other. Thus it is incorrect to think of these biologically based sexual relations as "gender" (social and cultural) relations. One can speak of the emergence of "gender" relations and roles only with the appearance of modern humans (*Homo sapiens*) and, perhaps, Neanderthals. Only when humans began to think in complex symbolic ways and give voice to these perceptions in a spoken language did true gender categories as *man* and *woman* crystallize. As these cultural aspects of human life took shape, the distinction between "men" and "women," rather than between "males" and "females," arose. At that point, around 150,000 years ago, culture joined biology in governing human interactions. (See Primary Source: Mothering and Lactation.)

Gender roles became more pronounced during the gradual transition to an agriculturally based way of life. As human communities became larger, more hierarchical, and more powerful, the rough gender egalitarianism of hunting and gathering societies eroded. However, an enhanced human power over the environment did not bring equal power to everyone, and it is possible to say that women were the net losers of the agricultural revolution. Although their knowledge of wild plants had contributed to early settled agriculture, they did not necessarily benefit from that transition. One observer of primate behavior, Sarah Hrdy, has called the settled agricultural transformation a "Great Leap Sideways" because advances for some people meant losses for others.

Advances in agrarian tools introduced a harsh working life that undermined women's traditional status as farmers. Men, no longer so involved in hunting and gathering, now took on the heavy work of yoking animals to plows. This left to women the backbreaking and repetitive tasks of planting, weeding, harvesting, and grinding the grain into flour. Thus, although agricultural innovations increased productivity, they also increased the drudgery of work, especially for women. Consider the evidence from fossils found in Abu Hureyra, Syria: damage to the vertebrae, osteoarthritis in the toes, and curved and arched femurs suggest that the work of bending over and kneeling in the fields took its toll on female agriculturalists. These maladies do not usually appear among the bone remains of (male) hunters and gatherers.

The increasing differentiation of the roles of men and women also affected power relations within households and communities. The senior male figure became dominant in these households, and males became dominant over females in leadership positions. The agricultural revolution marked a greater division among men, and particularly between men and women. Where the agricultural transformation was most widespread, and where population densities began to grow, the social and political differences created inequalities. As these inequalities affected gender relations, patriarchy (the rule of senior males within households) began to spread around the globe.

CONCLUSION

Over thousands of generations, African hominids evolved from other primates into *Homo erectus* hominids, who migrated far from their native habitats to fill other landmasses. They did so in waves, responding to worldwide cycles of glaciation and melting. These human predecessors had some features in common with modern humans (*Homo sapiens*): they stood erect on two feet, made stone tools, lived in extended families, and, to a certain extent, communicated with one another (by means other than language).

What separated humans from other animal species was their ability to adapt to environmental change, to innovate, and to accumulate their breakthroughs. *Homo sapiens*, who had greater cognitive skills than other hominids had, also emerged in Africa and migrated out of Africa about 100,000 years ago. Since *Homo sapiens* had greater adaptive skills, they were better prepared to face the elements when a cooling cycle returned, and eventually they eclipsed their genetic cousins. One critical variable was their ability to use language—to engage in abstract, representational thought, and to convey the lessons of experience to their neighbors and descendants. As modern humans stored and shared knowledge, their adaptive abilities increased. Another remarkable development was the use of art to portray the world around them and to locate themselves within it.

Although modern men and women shared an African heritage, these individuals adapted over many millennia to the environments they encountered as they began to fill the earth's corners. Some settled near lakes and took to fishing, while others roamed the northern steppes hunting large mammals. No matter where they went, their dependence on nature yielded broadly similar social and cultural structures.

It took another warming cycle for people ranging from Africa to the Americas to begin putting down their hunting weapons and start domesticating animals and plants.

The changeover to settled agriculture was not uniform worldwide, although there were some common features. These included reliance on wood, stone, and natural fibers to make tools, shelter, and cultural items; and increasing social hierarchies—especially an unequal status between men and women. As communities became more settled, though, the world's regions began to vary as humans learned to modify nature to fit their needs. The varieties of animals that they could domesticate and the differing climatic conditions and topography that they encountered shaped the ways in which people drifted apart in spite of their common origins.

One important commonality remained: there was a limit to the scale and complexity of settlements and communities. As a result, most people continued a life of foraging for food. Villages grew—but they did not become cities. Peoples moved across mountains or deserts to find fresh pastures for their animals, richer lands for their crops, or new waters where fish were spawning. The remains of rudimentary pottery, tools, and dwellings reflect worlds that were rural, socially egalitarian, and dependent on the natural flow of fresh water and the natural fertility of soils. As we will see in Chapter 2, another round of technical advances was necessary before humans could further change their relationship to nature and create the foundations for complex societies.

Chronology

5 mya*		1 mya

♦ 3 mya *Australopithecus africanus hominid species appears*

2.5 mya Homo habilus *appears* ♦

2.5–1 mya Homo erectus *appears and migrates* ♦-------------------------------♦

Beginnings of Ice Age across the Northern Hemisphere ♦

Review and research materials are available
at StudySpace: ⊚ WWNORTON.COM/STUDYSPACE

KEY TERMS

adaptation (p. 9)
australopithecines (p. 8)
bipedalism (p. 9)
cognitive skills (p. 9)
domestication (p. 24)
evolution (p. 4)
hominid (p. 7)
Homo erectus (p. 13)
Homo habilis (p. 13)

Homo sapiens (p. 15)
hunting and gathering (p. 19)
innovation (p. 11)
language (p. 23)
migration (p. 14)
pastoralism (p. 25)
settled agriculture (p. 24)
species (p. 8)

STUDY QUESTIONS

1. Explain how evolutionary biologists and archaeologists working in recent decades have transformed our understanding of human origins. What tools and discoveries led them to their conclusions?
2. Describe the evolutionary process through which *Homo sapiens* emerged. Was it a linear progression?
3. Identify the advantages that language and symbolic art gave *Homo sapiens* over other species. What can modern observers learn about early humans by studying their artistic expressions?
4. List the nine regions where agricultural production first emerged. What common factors in all these places facilitated the domestication of plants and animals?
5. Why did the first agricultural breakthrough occur in Southwest Asia?
6. Analyze the advantages and disadvantages of agricultural production versus nomadic foraging. How were agricultural or pastoral communities different from those of hunters and gatherers?

200,000 ya**	150,000 ya		100,000 ya	50,000 ya		10,000 ya	1 CE

30,000 ya Cave art develops in Europe ◆
◆ 200,000 ya Neanderthal evident in Europe   18,000 ya Human migration from Afro-Eurasia to Americas begins ◆
120,000–50,000 ya Homo sapiens emerges in Africa and migrates   16,000–10,000 BCE Ice age ◆-----◆
◆------------------◆   9000 BCE Beginnings of agricultural revolution in Southwest Asia ◆
6500 BCE Millet cultivation in Yellow River valley develops ◆
5500 BCE Rice cultivation in Yangzi River valley develops ◆
6700–2000 BCE Domestication of plants and animals begins ◆-----◆
6000–5000 BCE Agricultural settlements using Southwest Asian domesticants emerges ◆
3000 BCE Pastoralism begins in Inner Asia ◆
2000 BCE Maize cultivation emerges in central Mexico ◆

**years ago

2

RIVERS, CITIES, AND FIRST STATES, 4000–2000 BCE

One of the first urban centers in the world was the ancient city of Uruk. Located in southern Mesopotamia on a branch of the Euphrates River, it was home to more than 10,000 people by the late fourth millennium BCE and boasted many large public structures and temples. One temple had stood there since before 3000 BCE; with a lime-plastered surface of niched mud-brick walls that formed stepped indentations, it perched high above the plain. In another sacred precinct, administrative buildings and temples adorned with elaborate façades stood in courtyards defined by tall columns. Colored stone cones arranged in elaborate geometric patterns covered parts of these buildings, making Uruk the "shining city" of the epic devoted to its later king, Gilgamesh.

Over the years Uruk became an immense commercial and administrative center. A huge wall with seven massive gates surrounded the metropolis, and down the middle ran a canal carrying

Desert

Pastoral belt – steppe lands

Tropical rain forest

Agricultural society 3000 BCE

Riverine societies (early cities)

Widespread village culture

NORTH AMERICA

ATLANTIC OCEAN

SAHARA

SAHEL

TEHUACAN VALLEY

PACIFIC OCEAN

CHICAMA VALLEY

ANDES MOUNTAINS

SOUTH AMERICA

0   1000   2000 Miles

0   1000   2000 Kilometers

MAP 2-1   THE WORLD IN THE THIRD MILLENNIUM BCE
Human societies became increasingly diversified as agricultural, urban, and pastoral nomadic communities expanded. In what different regions did pastoralism and riverine societies emerge? Considering the geographic features highlighted on this map, why do you think cities appeared in the regions that they did? How did geographic and environmental factors promote interaction between nomadic pastoral and sedentary agricultural societies?

technological breakthroughs required to produce pottery; others devised irrigation systems and water sluices in flood-plains (areas where rivers overflowed and deposited fertile soil). Some even began to send their fish catches inland in return for agricultural produce. In the remains of these villages, archaeologists have recovered temples, fire-pit chambers, and tombs that reveal an elaborate religious life. These ceremonial structures highlighted communal devotion and homage to deities, and rituals to celebrate birth, death, and the memory of ancestors.

In the Americas, the largest population center was in the valley of Tehuacán (near modern-day Mexico City). Here the domestication of corn created a subsistence base that enabled people to migrate from caves to a cluster of pit-house villages that supported a growing population. By 3500 BCE the valley held nothing resembling a large city, although it teemed with inhabitants. People lived in clusters of interdependent villages, especially on the lakeshores: here was a case of high population density, but not urbanization.

SUB-SAHARAN AFRICA   The same pattern occurred in sub-Saharan Africa, where the population grew but did not concentrate in urban communities. About 12,000 years ago, when rainfall and temperatures increased, small encampments of hunting, gathering, and fishing communities congregated around the large lakes and rivers flowing through the region that would later become the Sahara Desert. Elephants, rhinoceroses, gazelles, antelopes, lions, and panthers roamed, posing a threat but also providing a source of food. Over the millennia, in the wetter and more temperate locations of this vast region—particularly the upland massifs (mountains) and their foothills—permanent villages emerged.

As the Sahara region became drier, people moved to the desert's edges, to areas along the Niger River and the Sudan. Here they grew yams, oil palms (a tree whose fruit and seeds produce oil), and plantains (a fruit similar to bananas). In the savannah lands that stretched all the way from the Atlantic Ocean in West Africa to the Nile River basin in present-day Sudan, settlers grew grains such as millet and sorghum, which spread from their places of origin to areas along the lands surrounding the Niger River basin. Residents constructed stone dwellings and dug underground wells and food storage areas. As an increasing population strained resources, groups migrated south toward the Congo River and east toward Lake Nyanza, where they established new farms and villages. Although population centers were often hundreds or thousands of miles apart and were smaller than the urban centers in Egypt and Mesopotamia, they maintained trading and cultural contacts. We know of their connection because villagers from the area spanning present-day Mali in the west to present-day Kenya in the southeast used the same style of pottery, characterized by bowls with rounded bottoms and wavy decorations.

PASTORAL NOMADIC COMMUNITIES

Around 3500 BCE, Afro-Eurasia witnessed the growth and spread of pastoral nomadic communities. The transhumant herder communities that had appeared in Southwest Asia around 5500 BCE (see Chapter 1) continued to be small and their settlements impermanent. They lacked substantial public buildings or infrastructure, but their seasonal moves were stable. Across the vast expanse of Afro-Eurasia's great mountains and its desert barriers, and from its steppe lands ranging across inner and central Eurasia to the Pacific Ocean, these transhumant herders lived alongside settled agrarian people, especially when occupying their lowland pastures. They traded meat and animal products for grains, pottery, and tools produced in the agrarian communities.

In the arid environments of Inner Mongolia and central Asia transhumant herding and agrarian communities initially followed the same combination of herding animals and cultivating crops that had proved so successful in Southwest Asia. However, because the steppe environment could not support large-scale farming, these communities came to focus on animal breeding and herding. As secondary pursuits they continued to fish, hunt, and farm small plots in their winter pastures. Their economy centered on domesticated cattle, sheep, and horses. As their herds increased, these horse-riding nomads had to move often to new pastures, driving their herds across vast expanses of land. By the second millennium BCE, they had become full-scale nomadic pastoral communities, and they dominated the steppes. In these pastoral nomadic economies of the arid zones of central Eurasia, horses became crucial to survival.

THE RISE OF TRADE

When the earliest farming villages developed around 7000 BCE, trade patterns across Afro-Eurasia were already well established. Much of this trade was in exotic materials such as obsidian, a black volcanic glass that made superb chipped-stone tools.

Vitally important to the cities of southern Mesopotamia was long-distance trade. Lacking many raw materials that developed settlements require, they needed to find sources of wood, stones, and metal to augment local building materials of mud and reeds. Thus these communities established outposts near the raw materials' sources to coordinate their import. In exchange the cities offered manufactured goods, especially luxury textiles made from the finest quality wool and embroidery. This trade began around 5000 BCE, carried out by boats along the shores of the Persian Gulf. By 3000 BCE there was extensive interaction between southern Mesopotamia and the highlands of Anatolia, the forests of the Levant bordering the eastern Mediterranean, and the rich mountains and vast plateau of Iran. (See Map 2-2.)

MAIN THEMES

→ *Complex societies form around five great river basins.*
→ *The world's first cities arise from the river-basin societies, transforming human life.*
→ *Most people around the globe still live in interdependent villages.*
→ *Pastoral nomadic peoples appear, herding animals and trading animal products for grains, pottery, and tools.*

FOCUS ON *Societies in the Great River Basins*

Mesopotamia

+ Peoples living along the **Tigris River** and **Euphrates River** control floodwaters and refine irrigation techniques.
+ Mesopotamians establish the world's first large cities, featuring powerful rulers, social hierarchies, and monumental architecture.
+ Mesopotamia is the birthplace of writing.

Indus Valley

+ South Asian peoples harness the **Indus River** and create cities like Harappa and Mohenjo Daro.

Egypt

+ Peoples of Egypt use **Nile River** waters to irrigate their lands and create a bountiful agriculture.
+ Egyptian rulers known as pharaohs unify their territory, establish a powerful state, and develop a vibrant economy.
+ Egyptians build magnificent burial chambers (pyramids) and worship a pantheon of gods.

East Asia

+ Peoples dwelling in the basins of the **Yellow River** and the **Yangzi River** control the waters' flow and expand agriculture.
+ These people develop an elaborate culture, which scholars later label Yangshao and Longshan.

Over thousands of years, trade increased. By the mid-third millennium BCE, flourishing communities populated the oases (fertile areas with water in the midst of arid regions) dotting the deserts of western Syria, the Iranian plateau, northern Afghanistan, and Turkmenistan. As these communities actively traded with their neighbors, trading stations at the borders facilitated exchanges among many partners. Here in these "borderlands," although far from big cities, the urbanites exchanged cultural information. Their caravans of pack animals—first donkeys and wild asses; much later, camels—transported goods through deserts, steppes, and forests. Stopping at oasis communities to exchange their wares for water and supplies, these caravans carried ideas across Afro-Eurasia. In this way, borderlands and borderlanders—along with the cities they connected—played a vital role in world history.

BETWEEN THE TIGRIS AND EUPHRATES RIVERS: MESOPOTAMIA

→ *What role did cities play in Mesopotamian society?*

In 3500 BCE, in a world where people had been living close to the land in small clans and settlements, a radical breakthrough occurred in one place: the Mesopotamian river basin. Here the world's first complex society arose. Here the city and the river changed how people lived.

MAP 2-2   TRADE AND EXCHANGE IN SOUTHWEST ASIA AND THE EASTERN MEDITERRANEAN—THIRD MILLENNIUM BCE

Extensive commercial networks linked the urban cores of Southwest Asia. Of the traded raw materials shown on the map, which ones were used for building materials, and which ones for luxury items? Why were there more extensive trade connections between Mesopotamians and people to their northwest and east than with Egypt to the west? According to the map, in what ways did Mesopotamia become the crossroads of Afro-Eurasia?

TAPPING THE WATERS

Mesopotamia, whose name is a Greek word meaning "[country] between two rivers," is not at first glance a hospitable place. From their headwaters in the mountains to the north and east to their destination in the Persian Gulf, the Tigris and Euphrates rivers are wild and unpredictable, flooding in periods of heavy rainfall and snow, and drying up during the parched summer months. Thus water was both scourge and blessing for those who migrated to the Tigris and Euphrates river basin. Unpredictable floodwaters could wipe out years of hard work, but when managed properly they could

transform the landscape into verdant and productive fields. In retrospect, the irrigation systems that the earliest Mesopotamians created were revolutionary. A landmass that includes all of modern-day Iraq and parts of Syria and southeastern Turkey, Mesopotamia embraces a rich variety of topography and cultures—all unified by natural drainage basins. Both rivers provided water for irrigation and, although hardly navigable, were important routes for transportation and communication by pack animal and by foot.

The first advances occurred in the foothills of the Zagros Mountains along the banks of the smaller rivers that feed the Tigris. Here, settlers discovered that rudimentary irrigation techniques enabled them to achieve higher agricultural yields and greater surpluses than the rain-fed areas to the north could provide. Over time they ventured out of the foothills onto the southern alluvial plain of the Tigris and Euphrates basin. (An **alluvium** is an area of land created by river deposits.) Although floods were more severe there and the water harder to harness, the land held greater promise of abundant harvests.

Converting the floodplain of the Euphrates River into a breadbasket required mastering the unpredictable waters. Both the Euphrates and the Tigris, unless controlled by waterworks, were profoundly unfavorable to cultivators because the annual floods and low-water seasons came at the wrong times in the farming sequence. Floods occurred at the height of the growing season, when crops were most vulnerable. Low water levels occurred when crops required abundant irrigation. To prevent the river from overflowing during its flood stage, farmers built levees (barriers to the waters) along the banks and dug ditches and canals to drain away the floodwaters. Their solution was ingenious. Since the bed of the Euphrates is higher than that of the Tigris, and the Euphrates floods sometimes drained toward the Tigris, engineers devised extensive irrigation systems contoured to the shallow gradient between the rivers. Under this scheme the Euphrates served as the supply and the Tigris as the drain of the southern alluvium. Storing and channeling water year after year required constant maintenance and innovation by a corps of engineers.

The Mesopotamians' technological breakthrough was in irrigation, not in agrarian methods. Because the soils were fine, rich, and constantly replenished by the floodwaters' silt,

Early Mesopotamian Waterworks. From the sixth millennium BCE, irrigation was necessary for successful farming in southern Mesopotamia. By the first millennium BCE, sophisticated feats of engineering allowed the Assyrians to redirect water through constructed aqueducts, like the one illustrated here on a relief from the palace of the Assyrian king Sennacherib at Nineveh.

soil tillage was light work. Farmers sowed a combination of wheat, millet, sesame, and barley (the basis for beer, a staple of their diet). Their yields may have been as high as those afforded by modern-day wheat fields in Canada.

CROSSROADS OF SOUTHWEST ASIA

Though its soil was rich and water was abundant, southern Mesopotamia had few other natural resources apart from the mud, marsh reeds, spindly trees, and low-quality limestone that served as basic building materials. To obtain high-quality, dense wood, stone, metal, and other materials for constructing and embellishing their cities (notably their temples and palaces), Mesopotamians had to interact with the inhabitants of surrounding regions. In return for textiles, oils, and other commodities, they imported cedar wood from Lebanon, copper and stones from Oman, more copper from Turkey and Iran, and the precious blue gemstone called lapis lazuli, as well as the ever-useful tin, from faraway Afghanistan. Maintaining trading contacts was easy, given Mesopotamia's open boundaries on all sides. (In this crucial respect Mesopotamia contrasted with Egypt, whose land was cut off by impassable deserts to the east and west, and by the Nile River rapids to the south.)

Mesopotamia's natural advantages—its rich agricultural land and water, combined with easy access to neighboring regions—favored the growth of cities. The area became a magnet for waves of newcomers from the deserts and the mountains (an early version of migration from the countryside to cities), and thus a crossroads for the peoples of Southwest Asia, the meeting grounds for distinct cultural and linguistic groups. Among the dominant groups were Sumerians, who concentrated in the south; Hurrians, who lived in the north; and Akkadians, who populated western and central Mesopotamia.

THE WORLD'S FIRST CITIES

During the first half of the fourth millennium BCE, a demographic transformation occurred in the Tigris-Euphrates river basin. The population expanded as a result of the region's agricultural bounty, and swelling ranks of Mesopotamians migrated from country villages to centers that eventually became cities. (A **city** is a large, well-defined urban area with a dense population.) The earliest cities—Eridu, Nippur, and Uruk—developed over about 1,000 years, dominating the southern part of the floodplain by 3500 BCE. Here archaeologists have found buildings of mud brick marking successive layers of urban development. Consider Eridu, a village dating back to 6000 BCE. Home to the Sumerian water god, Ea, Eridu was a sacred site where temples piled up on top of one another for over 4,000 years. Throughout more than twenty

The Royal Tombs of Ur. The Royal Tombs of Ur, excavated in the 1930s, contained thousands of objects in gold, silver, lapis lazuli, and shell that were buried along with elites of the First Dynasty of Ur. In one grave, along with the skeletons of more than sixty members of a royal household, were musical instruments, including this large harp with a golden bull's head. Such instruments would have been played at the ritual meal associated with these fabulously rich burials. Pu-Abi, identified as a queen by the cylinder near her body, was buried in a separate chamber. She was interred in full regalia, including the elaborate headdress shown here.

who joined their masters in the graves. Honoring the royal dead by including their followers and possessions in their tombs reinforced the social hierarchies—including the vertical ties between humans and gods—that were the cornerstone of these early city-states.

SOCIAL HIERARCHY AND FAMILIES

Social hierarchies were an important part of the fabric of Sumerian city-states. Mesopotamia's city-states at first had assemblies of elders and young men who made collective decisions for the community. At times, certain effective individuals took charge of emergencies, and over time these people surrounding the leaders acquired more durable political power. The social hierarchy set off the rulers from the ruled. Ruling groups secured their privileged access to economic and political resources by erecting systems of bureaucracies, priesthoods, and laws. Priests and bureaucrats served their rulers well, championing rules and norms that legitimized the political leadership.

Occupations within the cities were highly specialized, and a list of professions circulated across the land so that everyone could know his or her place in the social order. The king and priest in Sumer were at the top of the list, followed by bureaucrats (scribes and household accountants), supervisors, and craftworkers. The latter included cooks, jewelers, gardeners, potters, metalsmiths, and traders. The biggest group, which was at the bottom of the hierarchy, comprised workers who were not slaves but who were dependent on their employers' households. Movement among economic classes was not impossible but, as in many traditional societies, it was

rare. There were also independent merchants who risked long-distance trading ventures, hoping for a generous return on their investment.

The family and the household provided the bedrock for Sumerian society, and its organization reflected the balance between women and men, children and parents. The Sumerian family was hierarchical, so the senior male dominated as the patriarch. Most households were composed of a single extended family, all of whose members lived under the same roof. The family consisted of the husband and wife bound by a contract: she would provide children, preferably male, while he provided support and protection. Monogamy was the norm unless there was no son, in which case a second wife or a slave girl would bear male children to serve as the married couple's offspring. Adoption was another way to gain a male heir. Sons would inherit the family's property in equal shares, while daughters would receive dowries necessary for successful marriage into other families. Most women lived inside the contract of marriage, but a special class of women joined the temple staff as priestesses. By the second millennium BCE, they gained economic autonomy that included ownership of estates and productive enterprises. Even in this case, though, their fathers and brothers remained responsible for their well-being.

FIRST WRITING AND EARLY TEXTS

Mesopotamia was the birthplace of the first recorded words of history, inscribed to promote the power of the temples and kings in the expanding city-states. Small-scale hunter-gatherer societies and village-farming communities had

Cylinder Seal of Adad Carved from Green Stone. Many people in Mesopotamia involved with administration and public life had one or more cylinder seals. Cylinder seals were carved with imagery and inscriptions and were impressed into clay tablets and other documents while they were still malleable in order to guarantee the authenticity of a transaction. The cylinder seal shown here carries the inscription of the scribe Adda. The imagery includes representations of important gods of the Akkadian pantheon. The sun god Shamash rises from between the mountains in the center. Ishtar as a warrior goddess stands to the left. To the right is Ea, the god of wisdom, who is associated with flowing water and fish. Behind him is the servant Usmu, whose double face allows him to see everything. At the far left is a god of hunting.

developed rituals of oral celebrations based on collective memories transmitted by families across generations. But as societies grew larger and more complex, and their members more anonymous, oral traditions provided inadequate "glue" to hold the centers together.

Those who wielded new writing tools were **scribes**; from the very beginning they were at the top of the social ladder, under the major power brokers—the big man and the priests. As the writing of texts became more important to the social fabric of cities, and facilitated information sharing across wider spans of distance and time, scribes consolidated their grip on the upper rungs of the social ladder.

Mesopotamians became the world's first record keepers and readers. The precursors to writing appeared in Mesopotamian societies when farming peoples and officials who had been using clay tokens and images carved on stones to seal off storage areas began to use them to convey messages. These images, when combined with numbers drawn on clay tablets, could record the distribution of goods and services.

In a flash of human genius, someone, probably in Uruk, understood that the marks (most were pictures of objects) could also represent words or sounds. A representation that transfers meaning from the name of a thing to the sound of that name is a *rebus*. Before long, scribes connected visual symbols with sounds, and sounds with meanings. As people combined rebus symbols with other visual marks, they discovered they could record messages by using abstract symbols or signs to denote concepts. Such signs later came to represent syllables, the building blocks of words. (See Primary Source: The Origins of Writing According to the Sumerians.)

By impressing signs into wet clay with the cut end of a reed, scribes pioneered a form of wedge-shaped writing that we call *cuneiform*; it filled tablets with information that was intelligible to anyone who could decipher it, even in faraway

locations or in future generations. This Sumerian innovation enhanced the urban elites' ability to produce and trade goods, to control property, and to transmit ideas through literature, historical records, and sacred texts. The result was a profound change in human experience, because representing symbols of spoken language facilitated an extension of communication and memory. Although these gradual steps toward literacy were fundamental to the innovative process occurring in cities, only a tiny but influential scribal elite mastered writing at first.

Much of what we know about Mesopotamia rests on our ability to decipher cuneiform script. Rebus writing appeared around 3200 BCE, but not until 700 years later could the script record spoken utterances completely. By around 2400 BCE, texts began to describe the political makeup of southern Mesopotamia, giving details of its history and economy. Northern cities borrowed cuneiform to record economic transactions and political events, but in their own Semitic tongue. In fact, cuneiform's adaptability to different languages was a main reason its use spread widely.

As city life and literacy expanded, they gave rise not only to documents but also to written narratives, the stories of a "people" and their origins. One famous set of texts written around 2100 BCE, "The Temple Hymns," describes thirty-five divine sanctuaries. The magnificent Sumerian King List, known from texts written around 2000 BCE, recounts the reigns of kings by dynasty, one city at a time. It narrates the fabulously long reigns of legendary kings before the so-called Great Flood, which, in turn, is one of many traditional stories that people transmitted orally for generations (and it later evolved into the book of Genesis as part of the Bible's creation story). The Great Flood, a crucial event in Sumerian identity, explained Uruk's demise as the gods' doing. Flooding was the most riveting of natural forces in the lives of a riverine folk, and it helped shape the material and symbolic foundations of Mesopotamian societies.

THE MYSTERY OF HARAPPAN WRITING

No one has deciphered the writing system of the Harappa culture in the Indus Valley. The Indus script appeared on seals and tablets—and in a recently discovered site, on a board for public display. Although no one is sure which language it represents, some of its characteristics provide scholars with fuel for speculation.

As for verbal communication through writing, it needs to be understood that no one has as yet succeeded in deciphering the Harappan script and that this will remain an unlikely eventuality unless a bilingual inscription—in Harappan and a known form of writing—is found, that incorporates the names of people or places. The Harappan script is logographic: there are 375 to 400 signs, which rules out an alphabet (where one sign stands for one vowel or consonant) because alphabets usually have no more than thirty-six signs. Often Harappan bangles or metal tools are inscribed with just one sign. Harappan writing goes from right to left, as can be made out from close examination of overlapping signs scratched on pots. Short strokes indicate numbers, and numerals precede other signs, which could mean that in the Harappan language adjectives preceded the nouns they qualified. Certain signs, computer concordances reveal, tend to occur frequently at the end of inscriptions, which points to a language using a set of phonetic suffixes.

The Harappan language was probably agglutinative, or a language which added suffixes to an unchanging root. This feature is characteristic of the Dravidian language family rather than the Indo-Aryan languages. This, and the fact that the earliest Indo-Aryan text, the *Rigveda*, shows Dravidian influence (indicating that the early Indo-Aryans in the northwest had some contact with Dravidian speakers), make it likely that the language of the Harappans was a Dravidian one. (Note, also, that Brahui, spoken in the hills of southern Baluchistan today, is a Dravidian language.)

The inscriptions on the seals being brief, on average five to six signs long, they probably gave little more than the owner's name and designation. Perhaps it was the pictorial (often solo animal) emblem, rendered with great skill, that indicated the lineage, ancestry or social origins of the owner. There is no geographic pattern to the occurrence of the various seal animals (unicorn, bull, rhinoceros, antelope, tiger or elephant), so the animal could not possibly have signified the place of origin of the seal owner. Perhaps it was this pictorial image that lent authority to any spoken message that accompanied a seal or an object stamped with one. It may be noted that so far it is Harappa and Mohenjo-daro—and mound E rather than the 'citadel mound' AB at Harappa—that have yielded the evidence for the most intensive writing activity. These were probably centres of administration.

Harappan writing occurs on pots, seals, terracotta (stoneware) and shell bangles, copper tablets and tools, and ivory rods. Large numbers of scored goblets with pointed bases that occur at Harappa and Mohenjo-daro are important as they are one of the very few pottery forms that can occasionally carry seal impressions (as distinct from scratched signs)—their use remains a mystery. We get the impression that writing was for humdrum purposes. A striking exception to this is the occurrence of a huge "public" inscription that seems to have been set up on a street at Dholavira in Kutch, with letters about thirty-seven centimetres high cut out of stones and, R. S. Bisht suggests, fastened on a wooden board.

The most important point, however, is the enormous intellectual advance that the emergence of writing signifies. When we speak we utter sounds in one or other language using a series of sound sequences that carry specific meanings in that language. What writing does is to encode in visual form, that is, through a set of distinct symbols or signs, those sounds and sound sequences—thereby conveying meaning or information. Further, writing makes possible the storage of information or the maintenance of records for future reference. It makes communication at a distance possible. It requires of the writer knowledge of the signs and some amount of manual dexterity, and of the reader, knowledge of how the visual signs are vocalized and of course familiarity with the relevant language. Writing has been termed the most momentous invention human beings have ever made.

→ *Even though we cannot read Harappan script, why is the knowledge that the Harappans wrote in script important?*
→ *Judging from the information above about Harappan writing, what language do you think the script most likely represents?*

SOURCE: Shereen Ratnagar, "The Mystery of Harappan Writing" from *Understanding Harappa Civilization in the Greater Indus Valley* (New Delhi: Tulika Publishers, 2001), pp. 60–62.

Mohenjo Daro. Mohenjo Daro, the "mound of dead," is a large urban site of the Harappan culture. The view of the city demonstrates a neat layout of houses and civic facilities such as sewer draining.

drained into municipal sewers, also made of bricks. Houses in small towns and villages were made of less durable and less costly sun-baked bricks, which are used throughout southern Eurasia even today.

TRADE

The Harappans engaged in trade along the Indus River, through the mountain passes to the Iranian plateau, and along the coast of the Arabian Sea as far as the Persian Gulf and Mesopotamia. They traded copper, flint, shells, and ivory, as well as pottery, flint blades, and jewelry created by their craftworkers, in exchange for gold, silver, gemstones, and textiles.

Some of the Harappan trading towns nestled in remote but strategically important places. Consider Lothal, a well-fortified port at the head of the Gulf of Khambhat (Cambay). Although distant from the center of Harappan society, it provided vital access to the sea and to valuable raw materials. Its many workshops processed precious stones, both local and foreign. Because the demand for gemstones was high on the Iranian plateau and in Mesopotamia, the Harappans knew that controlling their extraction and trade was essential to maintaining economic power. Carnelian, a precious red stone, was a local resource, but lapis lazuli had to come from what is now northern Afghanistan. So the Harappans built fortifications and settlements near its sources. Extending their frontier did not stop at gemstones, however. Because metals such as copper and silver also had strategic commercial

Harappan Gemstone Necklace. Beadmakers perforated lapis lazuli and other semi-precious stones using a bow drill to make tiny holes for suspension.

Harappan Seal Stamps. The stamp seals of the Indus Valley culture are distinctive. Cut from the soft stone steatite and fired to a white color to make them hard, they have a rounded boss pierced for suspension on the back. The images carved on their surface are usually animals: elephants, tigers, bulls. Occasionally human figures, perhaps deities, perhaps rulers, are depicted seated on a platform, or dancing, or surrounded by animals. Many of the stamp seals have inscriptions across the top edge. The script of the Harappan people has not been deciphered, nor has its underlying language been identified.

importance, the Harappans established settlements near their copper mines as well.

Through a complex and vibrant trading system, the Harappans maintained access to mineral and agrarian resources. To facilitate trade, rulers relied not just on Harappan script but also on a system of weights and measures that they devised and standardized. Archaeologists have found Harappan seals, used to stamp commodities with the names of their owners or the nature of the goods, at sites as far away as the Persian Gulf, Mesopotamia, and the Iranian plateau (see Global Connections & Disconnections on p. 78).

The general uniformity in Harappan sites suggests a centralized and structured state. Unlike the Mesopotamians and the Egyptians, however, the Harappans apparently built neither palaces, nor grand royal tombs, nor impressive monumental structures. The elites expressed their elaborate urban culture in ways that did not proclaim their high standing. The Harappans were as unassuming as the Egyptians and Mesopotamians were boastful. This quality has puzzled scholars, but it underscores the profound differences in ancient societies: they did not all value the same things. The advent of writing, urban culture, long-distance trade, and large cities did not always produce the same social hierarchies and the

same ethos (a set of principles governing social and political relations). What the Indus River people show us is how much the urbanized parts of the world were diverging from one another, even as they borrowed from and imitated their neighbors.

"THE GIFT OF THE NILE": EGYPT

> → *How did the Nile River shape early Egyptian society?*

The earliest inhabitants along the banks of the Nile River were a mixed people. Some had migrated from the eastern and western deserts in Sinai and Libya as these areas grew barren from climate change. Others came from the Mediterranean. Equally important were peoples who trekked northward from Nubia and central Africa. Ancient Egypt was a melting pot where immigrants blended cultural practices and technologies.

Egypt had much in common with Mesopotamia and the Indus Valley. Like them, it had densely populated areas whose inhabitants depended on irrigation, built monumental architecture, gave their rulers immense authority, and created a complex social order. Tapping the Nile waters gave rise to agrarian wealth, commercial and devotional centers, early states, and new techniques of communication.

Yet the ancient Egyptian culture was profoundly distinct from its contemporaries in Mesopotamia and the Indus Valley. To understand its unique qualities, we must begin with its geography. The environment and the natural boundaries of deserts, river rapids, and sea dominated the country and its inhabitants. The core area of ancient Egypt covered 386,560 square miles, of which only 11,720 square miles (7.5 million acres) were cultivable. Of this total, roughly 6 million acres were in the Nile delta—the rich alluvial land lying between the river's two main branches as it flows north of modern-day Cairo into the Mediterranean Sea.

THE NILE RIVER AND ITS FLOODWATERS

Knowing Egypt requires appreciating the pulses of the Nile. The world's longest river, it stretches 4,238 miles from its sources in the highlands of central Africa to its destination in the Mediterranean Sea. In this way (and many others), Egypt was deeply attached to sub-Saharan Africa. Not only did its life-giving irrigation waters and rich silt deposits come from the African highlands, but much of its original population had migrated into the Nile valley from the west and the south many millennia earlier.

The Upper Nile is a sluggish river that cuts through the Sahara Desert. Rising out of central Africa and Ethiopia, its two main branches—the White and Blue Niles—meet at present-day Khartoum and then scour out a single riverbed 1,500 miles long to the Mediterranean. The annual floods gave the basin regular moisture and alluvial richness. Although the Nile's floodwaters did not fertilize or irrigate fields as broad as those in Mesopotamia or Harappa, they created green belts flanking the broad waterway. These gave rise to a society whose culture stretched along the navigable river and its carefully preserved banks. Away from the riverbanks, on both sides, lay a desert rich in raw materials but largely uninhabited. Egypt had no fertile hinterland like the sprawling plains of Mesopotamia and the Indus Valley. In a sense, Egypt was the most "riverine" of the riverine cultures.

The Nile's predictability as the source of life and abundance shaped the character of the people and their culture. In contrast to the wild and uncertain Euphrates and Tigris rivers, the Nile was gentle and bountiful, leading Egyptians to view the world as beneficent. During the summer as the Nile swelled, local villagers built earthen walls that divided the floodplain into basins. By trapping the floodwaters, these basins captured the rich silt washing down from the Ethiopian highlands. Annual flooding meant that the land received a new layer of topsoil every year.

The light, fertile soils made planting simple. Peasants cast seeds into the alluvial soil and then had their livestock trample them to the proper depth. The never-failing sun, which the Egyptians worshipped, ensured an abundant harvest. In the early spring, when the Nile's waters were at their lowest and no crops were under cultivation, the sun dried out the soil.

EGYPT'S UNIQUE RIVERINE CULTURE

The peculiarities of the Nile region distinguished it from Mesopotamia and the Indus Valley. Some 2,500 years ago, the Greek historian and geographer Herodotus noted that Egypt was the gift of the Nile and that the entire length of its basin was one of the world's most self-contained geographical entities. Bounded on the north by the Mediterranean Sea, on the east and west by deserts, and on the south by cataracts (large waterfalls), Egypt was destined to achieve a common culture. The region was far less open to outsiders than were Mesopotamia and the Indus River basin.

Like the other pioneering societies, Egypt created a common culture by balancing regional tensions and reconciling regional rivalries. Ancient Egyptian history is a struggle of opposing forces: the north or Lower Egypt versus the south or

Nile Agriculture. The Nile is fed by the Blue Nile, which has its source in the Ethiopian highlands, and the White Nile in southern Sudan. It rises and falls according to a regular pattern that was the basis for the ancient Egyptian agricultural cycle. Flooding the valley in August and September, the Nile recedes, depositing a rich layer of silt in which the crops were planted in the fall and harvested in April and May.

Upper Egypt; the sand, the so-called red part of the earth, versus the rich soil, described as black; life versus death; heaven versus earth; order versus disorder. For Egypt's ruling groups—notably the kings—the primary task was to bring stability or order, known as *ma'at*, out of these antagonistic impulses. The Egyptians believed that keeping chaos, personified by the desert and its marauders, at bay through attention to *ma'at* would allow all that was good and right to occur.

THE RISE OF THE EGYPTIAN STATE AND DYNASTIES

Once the early Egyptians harnessed the Nile to agriculture, the area changed from being scarcely inhabited to socially complex. Whereas Mesopotamia and Harappa developed gradually, Egypt seemed to grow overnight. It quickly became a powerhouse state, projecting its splendor along the full length of the river valley.

A king, called pharaoh, was at the center of Egyptian life. His primary responsibility was to ensure that the forces of nature, in particular the regular flooding of the Nile, continued without interruption. This task had more to do with appeasing the gods than with running a complex hydraulic

TABLE 2-1 Dynasties of Ancient Egypt	
Pre-dynastic Period	
dynasties I and II	3100–2686 BCE
Old Kingdom	
dynasties III–VI	2686–2181 BCE
First Intermediate Period	
dynasties VII–X	2181–2055 BCE
Middle Kingdom	
dynasties XI–XIII	2055–1650 BCE
Second Intermediate Period	
dynasties XIV–XVII	1650–1550 BCE
New Kingdom	
dynasties XVIII–XX	1550–1069 BCE
Third Intermediate Period	
dynasties XXI–XXV	1069–747 BCE
Late Period	
dynasties XXVI–XXXI	747–332 BCE

SOURCE: Compiled from Ian Shaw and Paul Nicholson, eds., *The Dictionary of Ancient Egypt* (1995), pp. 310–11.

system—hence, Egypt's large clerical class. The king also had to protect his people from invaders from the eastern desert, as well as from Nubians on the southern borders. These groups threatened Egypt with social chaos. As guarantors of the social and political order, the early kings depicted themselves as shepherds. In wall carvings, artists portrayed them carrying the crook and the flail, indicating their responsibility for the welfare of their flocks (the people) and of the land. Moreover, under the king an elaborate bureaucracy organized labor and produced public works, sustaining both his vast holdings and general order throughout the realm.

The narrative of ancient Egyptian history follows its dynasties—a structure that gives a sense of deep continuity. According to a third-century BCE Egyptian cleric named Manetho, Egypt saw no fewer than thirty-one dynasties, spanning three millennia from 3100 BCE down to its conquest by Alexander the Great in 332 BCE. (See Table 2-1.) Since the nineteenth century, however, scholars have recast the story around three periods of dynastic achievement: the Old Kingdom, the Middle Kingdom, and the New Kingdom. At the end of each era, cultural flourishing suffered a breakdown in central authority, known respectively as the First, Second, and Third Intermediate Periods. No other region of the world has charted a history of such extraordinary length and durability.

RITUALS, PYRAMIDS, AND COSMIC ORDER

The Third Dynasty (2686–2613 BCE) launched the foundational period known as the Old Kingdom, the golden age of ancient Egypt. (See Map 2-5.) By the time it began, the basic institutions of the Egyptian state were in place, as were the ideology and ritual life that legitimized the dynastic rulers.

The king as god presented himself to the population by means of impressive architectural spaces, and the priestly class performed rituals reinforcing his supreme status within the universe's natural order. The most important ceremony was the Sed festival, which renewed the king's vitality after he had ruled for thirty years. Although it focused on the king's vitality, its origins lay in ensuring the perpetual presence of water.

King Djoser, the second king of the Third Dynasty, celebrated the Sed festival in his tomb complex at Saqqara. This magnificent complex, the world's oldest stone structure (rather than the mud-brick temples and palaces of Mesopotamia), took shape during his reign. It began as a huge flat structure identical to earlier royal tombs. However, the architect, Imhotep, was not satisfied with the modest shape of earlier burial chambers. Throughout six renovations he transformed the structure into a step pyramid that ultimately rose some 200 feet above the plain, dominating the landscape like the later Mesopotamian ziggurats did (see p. 53). This mountainlike

MAP 2-5   OLD KINGDOM EGYPT, 2686–2181 BCE

Old Kingdom Egyptian society reflected a strong influence from its unique geographical location. What geographical features contributed to Egypt's isolation from the outside world and the people's sense of their unity? What natural resource enabled the Egyptians to build the Great Pyramids? Based on the map, why do you think it was important for upper and lower Egypt to be united?

structure stood at the center of an enormous walled precinct housing five courts where the king performed rituals emphasizing the divinity of kingship and the unity of Upper and Lower Egypt. Because most of the structures were facades, the whole complex became a stage for state rituals. The symbolism of the unity of Upper and Lower Egypt was pervasive, embodied in the entwined lotus and papyrus—symbols of each region. The step pyramid complex incorporated artistic and architectural forms that would characterize Egyptian culture for millennia.

The Egyptian pharaoh—the king as god—used the royal tomb to embody the state's ideology and the principles of the Egyptian cosmos. The ritual of death, leading to everlasting life, became part of the cultural myth. So did a common ideology stressing the unity of the long river valley's distinct regions. The pharaoh also employed symbols (for example, the dual crown representing Upper and Lower Egypt), throne names, and descriptive titles for himself and his advisers to represent his own power and that of his administrators, the priests, and the landed elite. The Egyptian cosmic order was one of inequality and stark hierarchy. Established at the time of creation, the universe was the king's responsibility to maintain for eternity. The belief that the king was a god compelled him to behave like one: serene, orderly, merciful, and perfect. He always had to wear an expression of divine peace, not the angry snarl of mere human power.

Pyramid building evolved rapidly from the step version of Djoser to the grand pyramids of the Fourth Dynasty (2613–2494 BCE). These kings erected their

The Pyramids of Giza. The Pyramid Fields of Giza lie on the western side of the Nile just south of the modern city of Cairo. The Old Kingdom pharaohs built their eternal resting places there, surrounded by the smaller pyramids and bench tombs of their relatives and courtiers. The largest pyramid of Khufu is to the north. Khafra's is linked to the Nile by a causeway flanked by the famous Sphinx. The smallest is that of Menkaure, the penultimate king of the glorious Fourth Dynasty.

magnificent structures at Giza, just outside modern-day Cairo and not far from the early royal cemetery site of Saqqara. The pyramid of Khufu, rising 481 feet above ground, is the largest stone structure in the world, and its corners are almost perfectly aligned to due north, west, south, and east. Khafra's pyramid, though smaller, is even more alluring because it retains some of its original limestone casing and because it enjoys the protective presence of the sphinx. Surrounding these royal tombs were those of high officials, almost all members of the royal family. The enormous amount of labor involved in constructing these monuments provides another measure of the degree of centralization and the surpluses in Egyptian society at this time. The manpower came from peasants and workers who labored for the state at certain times of year, slaves brought from Nubia, and captured Mediterranean peoples.

Through their majesty and architectural complexity, the Giza pyramids reflect the peak of Old Kingdom culture and the remarkable feats that its bureaucracy could accomplish. Construction of these monuments entailed the back-breaking work of quarrying the massive stones (some weighed over two tons), digging a canal so barges could bring them from the Nile to the base of the Giza plateau, building a harbor there, and then constructing sturdy brick ramps that could withstand the stones' weight as workers hauled them ever higher along the pyramids' faces. Most likely a permanent work force of up to 21,000 laborers endured 10-hour workdays, 300 days per year, for approximately 14 years just to complete the great pyramid of Khufu.

RELIGION

Religion stood at the center of this ancient world, so all aspects of the culture reflected spiritual expression. Egyptians understood their world as inhabited by three groups: gods, kings, and the rest of humanity. Official records only showed representations of gods and kings. Yet the people did not confuse their kings with gods—at least during the kings' lifetimes. Mortality was the bar between rulers and deities; after death, kings joined the gods whom they had represented while alive.

CULTS OF THE GODS As in Mesopotamia, every region in Egypt had its resident god. The fate of each deity found expression in the history of its region. Some gods, such as Amun (believed to be physically present in Thebes, the political center of Upper Egypt), transcended regional status because of the importance of their hometown. Over the centuries the Egyptian gods evolved, combining often-contradictory aspects into single deities represented by symbols: animals and human figures that often had animal as well as divine attributes. They included Horus, the hawk god; Osiris, the god of regeneration and the underworld; Hathor, the goddess of childbirth and love; Ra, the sun god; and Amun, a creator considered to be the hidden god.

Official religious practices took place in the main temples, the heart of ceremonial events. The king and his agents cared for the gods in their temples, giving them respect, adoration, and thanks. In return the gods, embodied

Egyptian Gods. Osiris (*top left*) is the dying god who rules over the netherworld. Most frequently he is depicted as a mummy wearing a white crown with plumes and holding the scepter across his chest. The god Horus (*top right and bottom*), who was also rendered as Ra-Horakhty, is the falcon-headed Egyptian sky god. Horus is the earliest state god of Egypt and is always closely associated with the king. Horus is a member of the nine deities of Heliopolis and is the son of Osiris and Isis.

Primary Source

THE ADMONITIONS OF IPUWER

In order to maintain power during a period of increasing drought, Pepy II (r. 2278–2184 BCE) gave many advantages and tax exemptions to provincial nobles. At the end of his long reign, no successors were capable of maintaining centralized power. The collapse of the central state was traumatic, and Egyptian society fell into chaos. A number of poignant texts written by prophets and wise men captured this situation. One of the most moving was the text known as the Ipuwer Papyrus, written by an Egyptian sage.

Behold, the fire has gone up on high, and its burning goes forth against the enemies of the land.

Behold, things have been done which have not happened for a long time past; the king has been deposed by the rabble.

Behold, he who was buried as a falcon [is devoid] of biers, and what the pyramid concealed has become empty.

Behold, it has befallen that the land has been deprived of the kingship by a few lawless men.

Behold, men have fallen into rebellion against the Uraeus, the [. . .] of Re, even she who makes the Two Lands content.

Behold, the secret of the land whose limits were unknown is divulged, and the Residence is thrown down in a moment.

Behold, Egypt is fallen to pouring of water, and he who poured water on the ground has carried off the strong man in misery.

Behold, the Serpent is taken from its hole, and the secrets of the Kings of Upper and Lower Egypt are divulged.

Behold, the Residence is afraid because of want, and [men go about] unopposed to stir up strife.

Behold, the land has knotted itself up with confederacies, and the coward takes the brave man's property.

Behold, the Serpent [. . .] the dead: he who could not make a sarcophagus for himself is now the possessor of a tomb.

Behold, the possessors of tombs are ejected on to the high ground, while he who could not make a coffin for himself is now [the possessor] of a treasury.

Behold, this has happened [to] men; he who could not build a room for himself is now a possessor of walls.

Behold, the magistrates of the land are driven out throughout the land: [. . .] are driven out from the palaces.

Behold, noble ladies are now on rafts, and magnates are in the labor establishment, while he who could not sleep even on walls is now the possessor of a bed.

Behold, the possessor of wealth now spends the night thirsty, while he who once begged his dregs for himself is now the possessor of overflowing bowls.

Behold, the possessors of robes are now in rags, while he who could not weave for himself is now a possessor of fine linen.

Behold, he who could not build a boat for himself is now the possessor of a fleet; their erstwhile owner looks at them, but they are not his.

Behold, he who had no shade is now the possessor of shade, while the erstwhile possessors of shade are now in the full blast of the storm.

Behold, he who was ignorant of the lyre is now the possessor of a harp, while he who never sang for himself now vaunts the Songstress-goddess.

→ *In this reading, the "Residence" is the palace and the "Two Lands" are Upper and Lower Egypt. Who do you think "he who was buried as a falcon" is?*

→ *What were the effects of the collapse of Egypt's Old Kingdom?*

→ *How can we use such a document as "The Admonitions of Ipuwer" to understand conditions in Egypt at this time?*

SOURCE: James B. Pritchard, ed., "The Admonitions of Ipuwer" from *Ancient Near Eastern Texts Relating to the Old Testament*, Third Edition with Supplement. Copyright © 1950, 1955, 1969, renewed 1978 by Princeton University Press. Reprinted by permission of Princeton University Press.

THE YELLOW AND YANGZI RIVER BASINS: EAST ASIA

> → *What hallmarks of urban life emerged in China during this period?*

Like the Mesopotamians and Egyptians, East Asian peoples clustered in river basins. Their settlements along the Yellow River in the north and the Yangzi River in the south became the foundation of the future Chinese state. By 5000 BCE, both millet in the north and rice in the south were under widespread cultivation.

Yet in the following three millennia (when Mesopotamia, Egypt, and the Indus Valley were creating complex, city-based cultures) the Chinese moved slowly. China's great riverine cultures did not arise until the second millennium BCE. (See Map 2-6.) Like the other regions' waterways, the Yellow and Yangzi rivers had annual floods and extensive floodplains suitable for producing high agricultural yields and supporting dense populations. In China, however, the evolution of hydraulic works, big cities, priestly and bureaucratic classes, and a new writing system took longer.

Living conditions and the environment played a key role in ancient Chinese society, just as they did in the riverine cultures of Mesopotamia, Harappa, and Egypt. In the river basins of China, abundant food and the fact that communities were widely dispersed encouraged the development of localized agrarian cultures. Complex cities would come later. Also contributing to their different development were a lack of easily domesticated animals and plants and an abundance of geographic barriers. Geography isolated China, for the Himalayan Mountains and the Taklamakan and Gobi deserts prevented large-scale migrations between East Asia and central Asia and hindered the diffusion of cultural breakthroughs occurring elsewhere in Afro-Eurasia.

FROM YANGSHAO TO LONGSHAN CULTURE

China's classical histories place the beginnings of Chinese culture at the Xia dynasty, dating from 2200 BCE. Archaeological studies of riverine environments in East Asia tell a different story. Whether or not the Xia existed as a historical dynasty, archaeological evidence suggests our study of the Yellow River basin and Yangzi delta should begin earlier—in the two millennia from 4000 to 2000 BCE.

China was never completely free of outside influences. Unlike the Americas, East Asia was not separated from the rest of Afro-Eurasia by great oceans. Some travelers did arrive via the ocean, but more came via the Mongolian steppe, through which nomads introduced important technologies such as metalworks. Nomads were drawn to the agricultural settlements (as they were in Mesopotamia), and they brought innovations, bronze (an alloy of copper and tin), and other goods from afar. Through trade and migration, nomadic cultures and technologies filtered from the steppes to settled communities on the rivers.

The combination of agrarian settlements and increasing contact with neighbors promoted greater cultural complexity. The evidence includes breakthroughs in communication. Although the Chinese did not create a graphic writing system until the middle of the second millennium BCE, archaeologists have found preliterate signs and marks on pottery at Jiahu, on the Yellow River. These date as early as the seventh millennium BCE—long before similar signs appeared in Mesopotamia and Egypt.

Markings on red pottery, found near the village of Yangshao along the Yellow River in northwestern China, are another pioneering system of signs and symbols from as early as 5000 BCE. Archaeologists have also discovered analogous signs on early pottery in southern China. A complex society that required writing (such as that of the Sumerians) did not develop until much later. Nevertheless, shamans in the emerging villages of the fourth and third millennia BCE may have used signs in performing rituals, music, and healing, as well as in divination.

China's early riverine societies produced stone and pottery storage vessels that reflected increasingly urban settlements. Near the village of Longshan in Shandong province on the North China plain, for example, archaeologists discovered

Yangshao Bowl with Dancing Figures, c. 5000–1700 BCE. The Yangshao, also referred to as the "painted pottery" culture, produced gray or red pottery painted with black geometric designs and occasionally with pictures of fish or human faces and figures. Because the potter's wheel was unknown at the time, the vessels were probably fashioned with strips of clay.

Legend:
- Mongolian steppe lands
- Desert lands
- Extent of Longshan culture
- Extent of Yangshao culture
- Extent of Liangzhu culture
- Longshan migration
- Rice
- Millet
- Spread of rice farming
- Initial farming settlement before 3000 BCE
- Farming settlement after 3000 BCE

MAP 2-6   RIVERINE PEOPLES IN EAST ASIA, 5000–2000 BCE

Complex agricultural societies emerged in East Asia during the third millennium BCE. What were the regional cultures that flourished here during this time? What are the major geographic differences between the northern and southern regions of China in this period? Based on geographic differences among the areas, how were these cultures different, and how were they similar?

polished black pottery and a complete town enclosure of compacted earth. Such finds contrast with the simpler artifacts of the Yangshao sites. Furthermore, Longshan residents burned deer scapulas (shoulder blades) so that diviners could

interpret the cracks that formed. This ritual probably gave rise to the inscribed oracle bones introduced later during the Shang dynasty (1600–1045 BCE), which diviners consulted for advice from ancestors when making important decisions.

Longshan Beaker, c. 2500 BCE. Longshan has been called the "black pottery" culture, and its exquisite black pottery was not painted but rather decorated with rings, either raised or grooved. Longshan culture was more advanced than the Yangshao culture, and its distinctive pottery was likely formed on a potter's wheel.

The Longshan people likely migrated in waves from the peripheries of East Asia to the eastern China seashore. Their achievements, compared to those of the Yangshao, suggest marked development between 5000 and 2000 BCE. Several independent regional cultures in northern and southern China began to produce similar pottery and tools and to plant the same crops, probably reflecting contact. They did not yet produce city-states, but agriculture and small settlements flourished in the increasingly populated Yellow River valley.

Some of the hallmarks of early urban life are evident. For example, the Longshan buried their dead in cemeteries outside their villages. Of several thousand graves uncovered in southern Shanxi province, the largest ones contain ritual pottery vessels, wooden musical instruments, copper bells, and painted murals. Shamans performed rituals using jade axes. Jade quarrying in particular indicated technical sophistication, as skilled craftworkers incised jade tablets with powerful expressions of ritual and military authority. The recent discovery of a Longshan household whose members were scalped demonstrates the danger of organized violence. Attackers filled the water wells with five layers of human skeletons, some decapitated. Clearly, the villages' defensive walls were essential.

As communities became more centralized, contact between regions increased. Links between northern and southern China arose when Longshan peoples began to migrate along the East Asian coast to Taiwan and the Pearl River delta in the far south. Similarities in artifacts found along the coast and at Longshan sites in northern China, such as the form and decoration of pottery and jade items, also point to a shared sphere of culture and trade. (See Primary Source: Archaeological Evidence for Longshan Culture.)

Archaeologists also have found evidence of short-lived political organizations. Although they were nothing like the dynastic systems in Egypt, Mesopotamia, and the Indus Valley, they were wealthy—if localized—polities. They constituted what scholars call the era of Ten Thousand States (*Wan'guo*). One of them, the Liangzhu, has drawn particular interest for its remarkable jade objects.

Oracle Bone Artifact. The Shang dynasty use of oracle bones (such as the one above) may have grown out of the Longshan people's ritual of interpreting the cracks in burned deer scapulas.

ARCHAEOLOGICAL EVIDENCE FOR LONGSHAN CULTURE

Over the course of a millennium, multiple cultures with strong similarities emerged in north and northwest China. Some scholars argue that a single Longshan culture grew out of these close-knit groups. While these were not fully integrated spheres interacting with one another, the changes that Longshan represented were remarkable.

Let us take a quick look at the kind of innovations that sprouted everywhere and that, because of the similarities of style, must be interrelated:

1. Archaeologically acceptable evidence of copper objects, mostly trinkets and small tools of no agricultural value, has been unearthed in Shantung, western Honan, southern Shansi, and Ch'i-chia from archaeological horizons comparable in age. The finds do not suffice to point to a major metal industry as yet, but in light of what happened later on one must regard the Lung-shan metallurgy as worthy of note. . . .

2. Industrially much more important is the extremely widespread use of potter's wheels for the manufacture of ceramics. There was tremendous variation in the pottery wares of the various Lung-shan Cultures, but the overwhelming change from red to gray and the general decline of painted decoration must have been the result of a conscious choice on the part of the potters, who, armed with improved kilns and the wheel, must have represented a specialized profession in the Lung-shan society.

3. The stamped-earth construction technology and the construction of town walls using that technology are separate issues, but the town walls in Shantung, east Honan, north Honan, and west Honan indicate both the transmission of a technology and the rise of the necessity for defensive public works.

4. Related to the rise of defensive ramparts is the archaeological evidence of institutionalized violence. This takes two forms—evidence of raids or wars, such as the Chien-kou-ts'un finds of skulls and bodies in the water well; and burials of possible ritual victims relating to the construction of chiefly or royal monuments.

5. There are several manifestations of rituals, especially ones closely tied to persons of high political status. The first is the role of some animals and birds in ritual art, such as those found or identified recently in Liang-ch'eng, Shantung; the Liang-chu sites, in Kiangsu and Chekiang; and T'ao-ssu, Shansi.

6. The *ts'ung* tube, especially if associated with animals and birds, is a very distinctive ritual object manifesting a unique cosmology. Its discovery in Liang-chu on the coast and T'ao-ssu in the interior cannot be accidental; it indicates

without question an interregional transmission of cosmology or even a spherewide substratum featuring that cosmology. If we include jade rings (*pi*) in this cosmological bag, the Ch'i-chia Culture also becomes involved.

7. The virtually universal occurrence of scapulimancy among the Lung-shan Cultures is another manifestation of the spherewide communication or substratum of cosmology.

8. The archaeological evidence for violence and for ritual on an institutional basis almost inevitably means a society featuring sharp political and economic divisions, and that is exactly what we find in the mortuary remains of many of the Lung-shan Cultures. We have already seen archaeological indications of social ranking in the mortuary remains of the Neolithic sites of the fifth and fourth centuries B.C. . . . These trends accelerated and further intensified in the Lung-shan cemeteries. Furthermore, as the Ch'eng-tzu (Shantung) and T'ao-ssu (Shansi) cemeteries show, the economic and political polarization appears to have taken place within the framework of the unilinear clans and lineages.

All of the above happenings are plainly indicated by archaeological evidence, but they do not point to a single Lung-shan Culture. Instead, they indicate a series of interrelated changes in culture and society that took place within each of the regional cultures in the Chinese interaction sphere. From the point of view of each of the regional sequences, both the external interaction network and internal changes during a period of two thousand years were essential for its readiness, toward the end of the third millennium B.C., to step over the next threshold into the state society, urbanism, and civilization.

→ *What were the key features of Longshan culture?*
→ *What does* scapulimancy *mean, and how widespread was its use?*
→ *What does the evidence of violence reveal about Longshan society?*

SOURCE: Kwang-chih Chang, *The Archaeology of Ancient China*, 4th ed. (New Haven: Yale University Press, 1986), pp. 287–88.

LIFE ON THE MARGINS OF AFRO-EURASIA | **75**

→ *How did the growth of urban societies in river basins affect people living in the Aegean region, Anatolia, and Europe?*

LIANGZHU CULTURE

The Liangzhu people were sophisticated agriculturalists, growing rice and fruits along the Qiantang River where it flows into Hangzhou Bay. Among their implements were flat and perforated spades, as well as rectangular and curved sickle-like knives with holes. They raised domesticated water buffalo, pigs, dogs, and sheep. Archaeologists have discovered the remains of net sinkers, wooden floats, and wooden paddles, which demonstrate a familiarity with watercraft and fishing. Other wood artifacts are pieces of boats, house foundations, tools, and utensils. Stone and bone artifacts were sophisticated as well. Liangzhu artisans produced a black pottery from soft paste thrown on a wheel, and like the Longshan they created ritual objects from several varieties of jade. They mined it in the Great Lake (Taihu) area of the Yangzi delta, close to the Liangzhu tombs. Animal masks and bird designs adorned many pieces, revealing a shared cosmology that informed the rituals of the Liangzhu elite.

In the late third millennium BCE, a long drought hit China (as it did Egypt, Mesopotamia, and India). Although the climate change limited progress and forced migrations to more dependable habitats, the Chinese recovered early in the second millennium BCE. Now they created elaborate agrarian systems along the Yellow and Yangzi rivers that were similar to earlier irrigation systems along the Euphrates, Indus, and

Liangzhu Jade Axe Blade, c. 3400–2250 BCE. The Liangzhu represented the last new Stone Age culture in the Yangzi River delta. Their culture was highly stratified, and jade, silk, ivory, and lacquer artifacts were found exclusively in elite burial sites.

Nile. Extensive trading networks and a stratified social hierarchy emerged; like the other river basin complexes of Asia and North Africa, China became a centralized polity. Here, too, a powerful monarchy eventually united the independent communities. But what developed in China was a social and political system that emphasized an idealized past and a tradition represented by sage-kings. In this and other ways, China diverged from the rest of Afro-Eurasia.

LIFE ON THE MARGINS OF AFRO-EURASIA

> → *How did the growth of urban societies in river basins affect people living in the Aegean region, Anatolia, and Europe?*

Those dwelling in river basins and established cities with hierarchies, bureaucracies, and strong militaries were inclined to see outsiders—particularly nomads—as "barbarians." Actually, the city people's imagery and narratives that depict nomads as uncivilized are not objective, because they were more concerned with promoting themselves than with portraying the nomads accurately. The nomads surely would not have recognized themselves as savages lacking culture, faith, and organized life. In fact, they had frequent contact with the urbanites and became skilled users of their technologies. (See Map 2-7.) Despite being less urbanized and stratified than city dwellers, they fashioned institutions and belief systems that were as durable as those of the metropolitan centers.

The people living outside the river basins had a distinctive warrior-based ethos, such that the top tiers of the social ladder held chiefs and military men instead of priests and scribes. This feature was especially evident in Europe and Anatolia, where weaponry rather than writing, palisades (defensive walls and turrets) rather than palaces, and conquest rather than commerce dominated everyday life. Here, too, the inhabitants moved beyond stone implements and hunting and gathering, but they remained more egalitarian than riverine folk and did not evolve much beyond small societies led by chiefs.

AEGEAN WORLDS

Contact with Egypt and Mesopotamia affected the Aegean worlds, but it did not transform them. Geography stood in the way of significant urban development on the mountainous islands, on the Anatolian plateau, and in Europe. Even though people from Anatolia, Greece, and the Levant had

MAP 2-7   SETTLEMENTS ON THE MARGINS: THE EASTERN MEDITERRANEAN AND EUROPE, 5000–2000 BCE

Urban societies in Southwest Asia had profound influences on peripheral societies. What three peripheral worlds did the urban societies of Southwest Asia influence? In what ways did the spread of flint and copper tools and weapons transform Aegean and European societies? How did agriculture spread from Southwest Asia to these worlds?

populated the Aegean islands in the sixth millennium BCE, their small villages endured for 2,000 years before becoming more complex.

On mainland Greece and on the Cycladic islands in the Aegean, fortified settlements housed local rulers who controlled a small area of agriculturally productive countryside. Metallurgy developed in both Crete and the Cyclades. There

is evidence of more formal administration and organizations in some communities by 2500 BCE, but the norm was scattered settlements separated by natural obstacles. Consider rocky and mountainous Crete, the largest island in the Aegean, where seafaring peoples occupied settlements sprinkled throughout its rugged interior. By the early third millennium BCE, Crete had made occasional contact with Egypt

LIFE ON THE MARGINS OF AFRO-EURASIA | 77

→ *How did the growth of urban societies in river basins affect people living in the Aegean region, Anatolia, and Europe?*

and the coastal towns of the Levant, encountering new ideas, technologies, and materials as foreigners arrived on its shores. People coming by ship from the coasts of Anatolia and the Levant, as well as from Egypt, traded stone vessels and other luxury objects for the island's abundant copper.

Lacking a rich agrarian base, most communities remained small at fewer than 100 inhabitants, and only a few grew over time. By the middle of the third millennium BCE, a more complex society was emerging in eastern Crete. During the second millennium BCE, Knossos, located in a rich agricultural plain, became the primary palace-town in an extended network of palaces. Evidence from burial sites suggests that some households belonged to an elite class, for they took gold jewelry and other exotic objects with them to their graves. (For a discussion of objects buried with the dead in several cultures, see Global Connections & Disconnections: Ritual Objects in the Iranian Plateau, China, and Egypt.) Aegean elites did not reject the niceties of cultured life, but they knew that their power rested as much on their rugged landscape's resources as on self-defense and trade with others.

ANATOLIA

The highland plateau of Anatolia shows clear evidence of regional cultures focused on the control of trade routes and mining outposts. This area had been populated almost from the time that humans walked out of Africa, and the pace of change was slow because people clung to their village ways and stone tools. True cities did not develop here until the third millennium BCE, and even then they were not the sprawling population centers typical of the Mesopotamian plain. Instead, small communities emerged around fortified citadels housing local rulers who competed with one another. Two impressively fortified centers were Horoz Tepe and Alaça Hüyük, which have yielded more than a dozen graves—apparently royal—full of gold jewelry, ceremonial standards, and elaborate weapons.

Another important site in Anatolia was Troy to the far west. It is legendary as the place of the famous war launched by the Greeks (the Achaeans) and recounted by Homer in the *Iliad*. Troy developed around 3000 BCE on the Mediterranean coast in a fertile plain. In the 1870s the German archaeologist Heinrich Schliemann identified Troy level I as a third-millennium BCE fortified settlement with monumental stone gateways and stone-paved ramps. The extremely rich Troy level II had five large buildings called *megarons*, forerunners of the classic Greek temple. Here, Schliemann found gold and silver objects, vessels, jewelry, and other artifacts. Many are similar to the ones found in graves at Alaça Hüyük. Moreover, since they parallel finds on Crete and on the Greek mainland, they indicate that Troy participated in the trading system linking the Aegean and Southwest Asian worlds. At the same time, Troy faced predatory neighbors and pirates who attacked from the sea—an observation that explains its impressive fortifications.

EUROPE: THE WESTERN FRONTIER

At the western reaches of the Eurasian landmass was a region featuring more temperate and also more frigid climates with smaller population densities. Its peoples—forerunners of present-day Europeans—began to make objects out of metal, formed permanent settlements, and started to create complex societies. Here, too, hierarchies replaced egalitarian ways. Yet, as in the Aegean worlds, population density and social complexity had limits.

More than in the Mediterranean or Anatolia, warfare dominated social development in Europe. Two contributing factors were the persistent fragmentation of the region's peoples and the type of agrarian development they pursued. The introduction of the plow and the clearing of woodlands expanded agriculture. Agrarian development here was not the result of city-states or dynasties organizing irrigation and settlement (as in Mesopotamia and Egypt), but rather the result of households and communities wielding axes for defense and for cutting down trees. Compared to the riverine societies, Europe was a wild frontier where violent conflicts over resources were common.

The gradual expansion of agricultural communities eventually reached a critical point. The growth of flint mining to an industrial level (as evident in the thousand shafts sunk at Krzemionki in Poland and the flint-mining complex of Grimes Graves in England) indicates a social and economic transformation. Most important, mining output slashed the cost and increased the availability of raw materials needed to make tools for clearing forested lands and tilling them into arable fields. As agricultural communities proliferated, some became villages that dominated their regions. But nowhere did these folk create large cities and corresponding states.

By 4000 BCE the more developed agrarian peoples had coalesced into large communities, constructing impressive monuments that remain visible today. In western Europe, large ceremonial centers shared the same model: enormous shaped stones, some weighing several tons each, set in common patterns—in alleyways, troughs, or circles—known as *megalithic* ("great stone") constructions. These daunting projects required cooperative planning and work. In the British Isles, where such developments occurred later, the famous megalithic complexes at Avebury and Stonehenge probably reached their highest stages of development just before 2000 BCE. No matter how forbidding the ecology of Europe was in this period, in the centuries after 3000 BCE, culminating in new developments around 2000 BCE, the whole of the northern European plain came to share a common

Global Connections & Disconnections

RITUAL OBJECTS IN THE IRANIAN PLATEAU, CHINA, AND EGYPT

An important aspect of religious practice is the interaction between the worldly and the divine, between the living and the dead. Thousands of years ago ritual objects, such as amulets, statues, or carved objects representing the gods, were tangible representations of the connection between the earthly and the sacred. Other objects carrying images of important myths and stories were useful in ceremonies marking major events, such as birth or death. They may also have acted as more permanent signs of the divine, in shrines or temples. In both cases, ritual objects represented the sacred in everyday life.

IRANIAN PLATEAU   Ancient humans deposited symbolic objects with the dead to ease the journey to the world beyond and to provide necessities in the afterlife. Excavated graves in the Jiroft region of south-central Iran contain thousands of symbolic objects as well as utilitarian vessels. Most numerous are cylindrical vessels made of soft green stone (locally available steatite or chlorite) carved with elaborate designs that carried symbolic meaning. Also carved from the green stone and featuring similar designs are furniture inlays and rectangular slabs with handles.

While many of the designs show a repeating grid pattern or curls or scorpions, some represent gods in human form wearing bull horns on their heads as a sign of divinity. A common motif portrays a bird of prey grasping a snake in its talons; a leopard confronts the snake. Both the body of the bird and the snake have holes for holding multihued stones, making the overall pattern colorful and lively. The confrontation of the snake and the leopard represents the struggle between forces of nature. Neither wins; rather, they are always in equilibrium.

Vessels from Jiroft have come to light in the Persian Gulf and in Mesopotamia. Some historians argue that they were objects of trade, just like semiprecious lapis lazuli and carnelian were. However, the centrality of these

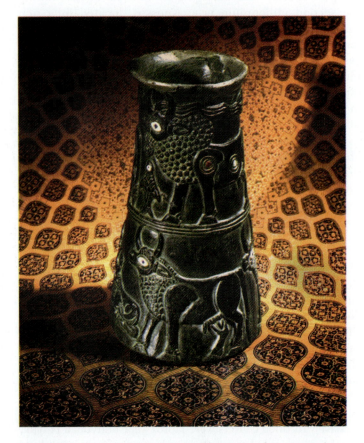

Jiroft Vase. Persians looked to the distant past for universal imagery. Bull icons appear on a chlorite vase from near Jiroft, where such items were crafted in about 2500 BCE.

vessels to the home society's funerary customs suggests that they were personal effects carried by traders and craftsmen who traveled to the large cities of the distant river valleys. There is no evidence that the objects were exchanged in trade.

CHINA   The Liangzhu people of ancient China crafted ritual objects from several varieties of jade that they mined in the Yangzi delta. The Liangzhu decorated many of these pieces with animal masks or bird designs. Especially important were circular jade objects called *bi* discs (found in tomb sites) and square *cong* tubes. The *cong* jades, used in divination practices, were round in their hollow interior. The rounded portion represented heaven and the square portion the earth; the jade tubes thus signified interaction between heaven and earth, the dead and the living. Both heaven and earth were penetrated by a central axis running through the jade's shaft, which symbolized the sacred mountains dividing the land of the living from the place of the dead.

Jade was the most important precious substance in East Asia. Associated with qualities of goodness, purity, luck, and virtue, it was carved into ceremonial knives, blade handles, religious objects, and elaborate jewelry. Because jade is extremely hard, its intricate carving required much time and great skill. Smaller objects, such as blades and amulets, could also serve a ceremonial purpose. Jade objects used in burials might sit in the mouths and on the eyes of the deceased, or jade ornaments, jewelry, and ritual objects might accompany them. Men and women had different ornaments, including necklaces and head-dresses, swords and seals.

EGYPT   In ancient Egypt, precious stones and metals shaped into jewelry and ritual objects were important, especially in burying the dead. Archaeologists often find amulets and funerary jewelry placed in specific positions on the bodies of mummies. The system of preparing a body for mummification was so specialized that it required special jewelry distinct from what ordinary people wore during their lives. Scholars think that funerary amulets served to protect mummies from suffering in the afterlife. The Egyptian *Book of the Dead* contains

Egyptian Funeral Amulet. This winged scarab is a symbol of rebirth and would have been placed in the wrapping of the mummy along with other amulets to assure the successful passage of the deceased into the afterlife. The Egyptians understood the dung-beetle that pushes a ball of dung as Khepri, the divine protector of the daily solar cycle.

drawings, paintings, and spells explaining how to use certain amulets.

Nearly every mummy that archaeologists have discovered has had one such amulet, made of stone, glass, or wood in the shape of a pillar with cross bars at its top, perhaps mimicking the form of a tree (see Carol Andrews, *Egyptian Mummies*). Other types of amulets resemble parts of the body, particularly an arm or a foot, indicating that the person had suffered in that body part or that a limb was missing, and the amulet could serve as its substitute. In either case, embalmers apparently desired to make the deceased person as whole as possible for the journey into the afterlife. Amulets of this sort often complemented the features of the person whom they accompanied.

Whether they expressed religious or social status in this world or fended off evil spirits in the next, ritual objects were key in the practice of religion. Amulets and ritual jewelry personalized the divine, representing a connection to heaven that could belong to an individual. In this way, ritual objects stressed the interconnectedness of worldly and spiritual life.

Stonehenge. This spectacular site, located in the Salisbury Plain in Wiltshire in southwestern England, is one of several such megalithic structures found in the region. Constructed by many generations of builders, the arrangement of the large stone uprights enabled people to determine precise times in the year through the position of the sun. Events such as the spring and autumn equinoxes were connected with agricultural and religious activities.

material culture based on agriculture, the herding of cattle for meat and milk, the use of the plough, and the use of wheeled vehicles and metal tools and weapons, mainly of copper. The most characteristic objects associated with this shared culture are the Corded Ware pots—so-called from the cords used to impress lines on their surfaces (see Map 2-7). The fact that this new economy was found from Ukraine in the east to the Low Countries in the west is evidence of the much improved communications that linked and united previous disparate and widely separated regions.

Increasing communication, exchange, and mobility among the European communities led to increasing wealth but also sparked organized warfare over frontier lands and valuable resources. In an ironic twist, the integration of local communities led to greater friction and produced regional social stratification. The first sign of an emerging warrior culture was the appearance of drinking cups. (See Primary Source: The Male Warrior Burials of Varna and Nett Down.) The violent men who now protected their communities received ceremonial burials complete with their own drinking cups and weapons. Archaeologists have found these warrior burials in a swath of European lands extending from present-day France and Switzerland to present-day central Russia. Because the agricultural communities now were producing surpluses that they could store, residents had to defend their land and resources from encroaching neighbors.

An aggressive culture was taking shape based on violent confrontations between adult males organized in "tribal" groups. War cultures arose in all western European societies,

THE MALE WARRIOR BURIALS OF VARNA AND NETT DOWN

Burials of elite individuals across the region stretching from the Black Sea to the Atlantic reveal precious objects and weapons associated with a competitive warrior culture. At Varna, on the Black Sea coast of Bulgaria, the lifestyle of the "big men" associated with a farming village from around 4000 BCE came to light in 1972 when a farmer driving a tractor uncovered an ancient cemetery. The burials at Varna may represent a powerful and well-connected settlement, since most other contemporary sites do not display such high levels of wealth. The grave of a man who died at about age forty-five (pictured here), large pots used for drinking and storage were found. More striking were the 990 gold objects: most were decorative devices sewn onto his clothing, but others included bracelets on both arms, a necklace, and small gold-handled axe. The weapons buried with him—daggers, axes, and spearheads, and points—were made of flint.

Another burial—from Nett Down in Wiltshire, England, and dating to around 2500 BCE—reveals a less developed culture. In this case, a small tomb cut into the chalk ground and covered with a small mound of earth contained a young male warrior. He was buried with the two most significant objects connected with his life: a bronze dagger and, by his hands, a large bell beaker. No gold or precious metal ornaments accompanied the man, who was clearly part of a poorer society than Varna's. As one scholar has remarked, "the grave neatly encapsulates the ideal male image of drinking and fighting."

→ *Most individual burials contain male bodies. What does this fact tell us about men's roles in these evolving patriarchal societies?*

→ *When we compare these sites to those in Egypt and China, what can we learn about the importance of burying the dead across these societies?*

marked by the universal presence of a new drinking instrument, the "bell beaker"—so named by archaeologists because it resembled an inverted bell. Armed groups carried these cups across Europe, using them to swig beer and mead distilled from grains, honey, herbs, and nuts. As beer drinking spread, many local variations on beer mugs appeared, again illustrating the constant interplay between external communication and local forces.

As new tools and weapons spread across Europe, the region adopted similar cultural practices. The twin pillars of agriculture and metalworking, initially in copper, became the supports of daily life almost everywhere. At the same time, though, a split between Europe's eastern and western flanks occurred: in the millennium following 2500 BCE, warriors in

western Europe became more combative in battling for territory and resources.

Warfare had the ironic effect of accentuating the borrowing among the region's competing peoples. After all, the violent struggles and emerging kinship groups fueled a massive demand for weapons, alcohol, and horses. Warrior elites borrowed from Anatolia the technique of combining copper with tin to produce harder-edged weapons made of the alloy bronze. Soon smiths were producing them in bulk—as evidenced by hoards of copper and bronze tools and weapons from the period found in central Europe. Traders used the rivers of central and northern Europe to exchange their prized metal products, creating one of the first commercial networks that covered the landmass.

Constant warfare propelled Europe to become an innovative frontier society. The culture of violence and conflict that now drove a basic agricultural economy had two significant effects: it integrated European kinship-based oral societies in a realm of their own, and it separated them from the Mediterranean societies—an ordered world of palaces, scribes, and well-disciplined commoners.

CONCLUSION

Over the fourth and third millennia BCE, the world's social landscape changed in significant ways. In a few key locations, where giant rivers irrigated fertile lands, complex human cultures began to emerge. These areas experienced all the advantages and difficulties of expanding populations: occupational specialization; social hierarchy; rising standards of living; sophisticated systems of art and science; and centralized production and distribution of food, clothing, and other goods. Ceremonial sites and trading crossroads became cities that developed centralized religious and political systems. As scribes, priests, and rulers labored to keep complex societies together, the differences between country folk and city dwellers sharpened. In effect, urbanization was an example of the many ways in which societies were becoming more complex and stratified. Social distinctions also affected the roles of men and women, as urban families began to differ from kinship groups in the countryside.

Although the riverine cultures shared basic features, each one's evolution followed a distinctive path. Where there was a single river—the Nile or the Indus—the agrarian hinterlands that fed the cities lay along the banks of the mighty waterway. In these areas cities were small; thus the Egyptian and Harappan worlds enjoyed more political stability and less rivalry. In contrast, cities in the immense floodplain of the Tigris and Euphrates needed large hinterlands to sustain their populations. Because of their growing power and need for resources, Mesopotamian cities vied for preeminence, and their competition often became violent. (As we will see in Chapter 3, a similar pattern emerged after 1500 BCE in China, where the Yellow and Yangzi river environments facilitated the rapid expansion of Chinese settlements into cities.)

Cities stood at one end of the spectrum of social complexity. At the other end, in most areas of the world, people still lived in simple, egalitarian societies based on hunting, gathering, and basic agriculture—as in the Americas and sub-Saharan Africa. In between were worlds such as Anatolia, Europe, and large parts of China, where towns emerged and agriculture advanced—but not with the leaps and bounds of the great riverine cultures. Beyond these frontiers, farmers and nomads survived as they had for many centuries. Some of them, as in the Aegean, forged warrior societies. Elsewhere, as in the borderlands between Mesopotamian city-states, people created thriving trading networks.

In spite of these global differences, changes in climate affected everyone and could slow or even reverse development.

Chronology

	5000 BCE	4000 BCE
SOUTHWEST ASIA AND NORTH AFRICA		3500 BCE *Earliest Sumerian cities in southern Mesopotamia appear* ✦
SOUTH ASIA		
EAST ASIA	✦ 5000 BCE *Yangshao culture thrives in northwest China along Yellow River* ✦ 5000–2000 BCE *Longshan culture emerges in northeast Yellow River valley* - - - - - - ✦ 5000–2500 BCE *Jomon culture in Japan* - - - - - -	
THE EASTERN MEDITERRANEAN AND EUROPE	4000 BCE *Megalithic stone constructions begin in western Europe* ✦	
THE AMERICAS		3500 BCE *Chicama Valley along Pacific Ocean coast in modern-day Peru thrives* ✦ 3500 BCE *Tehuacán Valley in modern-day Mexico thrives* ✦
SUB-SAHARAN AFRICA	3500 BCE *Dense village life by Lake Chad and Niger River, Congo River, and Lake Victoria* ✦	
INNER AND CENTRAL EURASIA		3500 BCE *Growth and spread of nomadic pastoralism begins* ✦

How—and whether—cultures adapted depended on local circumstances. As the next chapter will show, the human agents of change often came from the fringes of larger settlements and urban areas.

Review and research materials are available at StudySpace: ⊙ WWNORTON.COM/STUDYSPACE

KEY TERMS

alluvium (p. 51)

bronze (p. 45)

city (p. 51)

city-state (p. 52)

cult (p. 53)

palace (p. 53)

river basin (p. 44)

scribes (p. 55)

social hierarchies (p. 52)

temple (p. 52)

territorial state (p. 57)

urban-rural divide (p. 45)

STUDY QUESTIONS

1. Describe how cities in Mesopotamia, the Indus Valley, and Egypt differed from small village communities across the globe. Why did cities emerge in relatively few places between 4000 and 2000 BCE?

2. Define *pastoralism*. Where in Afro-Eurasia did this form of social organization develop and thrive?

3. Identify shared characteristics among urbanites in Mesopotamia, the Indus Valley, and Egypt. What features distinguished each from the others?

4. Compare and contrast city-state structures in Egypt and Mesopotamia. Why was Egypt more politically unified than Mesopotamia?

5. Analyze the influence of long-distance trade on the political and economic development of urban societies in Egypt, Mesopotamia, and the Indus Valley. How did contacts with other people influence each society?

6. Compare and contrast the ways in which early writing emerged in the urban societies between 4000 and 2000 BCE. How did each use this new technology? How common was literacy?

7. Explain how the rise of cities represented a leap forward in complexity in human history. How did urban dwellers shape political, economic, and cultural developments in their region?

8. Explain East Asia's relative physical isolation from other Afro-Eurasian societies during this period. To what extent did this isolation shape social development in this region between 4000 and 2000 BCE?

9. Identify shared characteristics of European, Anatolian, and Aegean settlements between 5000 and 2000 BCE. How did settlements in these regions on the margins differ from urban settlements in river basins?

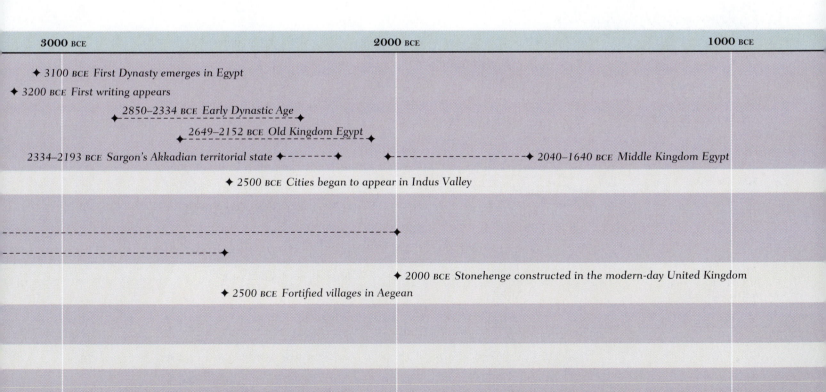

3000 BCE   **2000 BCE**   **1000 BCE**

◆ 3100 BCE First Dynasty emerges in Egypt

◆ 3200 BCE First writing appears

2850–2334 BCE Early Dynastic Age

2649–2152 BCE Old Kingdom Egypt

2334–2193 BCE Sargon's Akkadian territorial state ◆- - - - - - - ◆   ◆- - - - - - - - - - - - - - - ◆ 2040–1640 BCE Middle Kingdom Egypt

◆ 2500 BCE Cities began to appear in Indus Valley

◆ 2000 BCE Stonehenge constructed in the modern-day United Kingdom

◆ 2500 BCE Fortified villages in Aegean

殷代车马坑
编号:(AGM5146)
坑内葬1车、2
马,1人,2000
年发现于孝民屯
东地

Chariot Pit of the Shang Dynasty
(No. AGM5146)
One chariot, 2
horses and one per-
son were buried in
this pit, which were
discovered and un-
earthed in the east-
ern land of Xiaomi-
ntun Village in 2000.

3

NOMADS, TERRITORIAL STATES, AND MICROSOCIETIES, 2000–1200 BCE

Around 2200 BCE, the Old Kingdom of Egypt collapsed. Evidence for its ruin includes a history of numerous ineffective rulers in Memphis, imprecise workmanship on pyramids, and many incomplete funerary and temple structures. Yet the collapse did not occur because of incompetent rulers or a decline in the arts and sciences. The Old Kingdom fell because of radical changes in climate—namely, a powerful warming and drying trend that blanketed Afro-Eurasia between 2200 and 2150. The Mesopotamians and Harappans were as hard hit as the Egyptians. In Egypt the environmental disaster yielded a series of low Niles because the usual monsoon rains did not arrive to feed the river's upper regions, particularly the Blue Nile arising in the mountains of Ethiopia.

Documents from this period reveal widespread suffering and despair. Indeed, people who had enjoyed prosperity and good government for centuries now lived in utter disbelief that the world had been turned upside down and that the wicked triumphed over the virtuous. Consider the following tomb inscription: "All of Egypt was dying of hunger to such a degree that everyone had come to eating his children." Or another: "The tribes of the desert have become Egyptians everywhere. . . . The plunderer is everywhere, and the servant takes what he finds."

Settled societies were not alone in their losses. Herders and pastoral nomads also felt the pinch. As these outsiders pressed upon permanent settlements in search of sustenance, the governing structures in Egypt, Mesopotamia, and the Indus Valley collapsed. The pioneering city-states may have created unprecedented differences between elites and commoners, between urbanites and rural folk, but everyone felt the effects of this disaster.

This chapter focuses on the impact of climate change on the peoples of Afro-Eurasia. At first, the consequences were decisively negative: famines occurred, followed by political and economic turmoil; the old order gave way; river-basin states in Egypt, Mesopotamia, and the Indus Valley collapsed. Herders and pastoral nomads, driven from grazing areas that were drying up, forced their way into the heartlands of these great states in pursuit of better-watered lands. Once there, they challenged the traditional ruling elites. They also brought with them an awesome new military weapon—the horse-drawn chariot, which would dominate warfare for a half a millennium. Yet the nomads' advantage was temporary. Soon the Egyptians, Mesopotamians, Chinese, and many others learned from their conquerors: they assimilated some of their foes into their own societies and drove others away, adopting the invaders' most useful techniques.

We must note that the rise of highly centralized polities does not tell the entire story of this period; thus the chapter also examines worlds apart from the expanding centers of population and politics. The islanders of the Pacific and the Aegean, as well as peoples living in the Americas, did not interact with one another with such intensity—and therefore their political systems evolved differently. In these locales, microsocieties were the norm.

NOMADIC MOVEMENT AND THE EMERGENCE OF TERRITORIAL STATES

> → *How did nomadic groups change the cultural landscape of Afro-Eurasia during the second millennium BCE?*

At the end of the third millennium BCE, drought and food shortages led to the overthrow of ruling elites throughout central and western Afro-Eurasia. Walled cities could not defend their hinterlands. Trade routes lay open to predators, and pillaging became a lucrative enterprise. Clans of pastoral nomads from the Inner Eurasian steppes swept across vast distances on horseback. Later, they threatened settled people in the mighty cities. More immediately threatening were the **transhumant migrants** from the borderlands of the Iranian plateau and the Arabian Desert who advanced on the populated areas, searching for food and resources. Similar migratory patterns occurred in the Indus River valley and the Yellow River valley. (See Map 3-1.)

Environmental changes compelled humans across Afro-Eurasia to adapt or perish. When and where the pastoral

Focus Questions

→ *How did nomadic groups change the cultural landscape of Afro-Eurasia during the second millennium BCE?*

→ *What were the direct and indirect effects of drought on the organization of societies?*

→ *How did Vedic migrations influence South Asia?*

→ *What methods did the Shang state use to maintain its rule?*

→ *How did Austronesian migrations affect the emergence of microsocieties in the South Pacific?*

→ *How did long-distance trade influence the Aegean world?*

→ *Why did polities remain small-scale in Europe?*

→ *How did the environment influence early state systems in the Central Andes?*

nomads and transhumant herders managed to adjust to the dry conditions, they prompted the rise of new territorial states from pharaonic Egypt and Mesopotamia to Vedic South Asia and Shang China. Using **chariots** (a two-wheeled horse-drawn vehicle used in warfare and later in processions and races), the horse-mounted nomads introduced technologies that led to new forms of warfare whose spread transformed the Afro-Eurasian world. Moreover, the new rulers' efforts at state building altered society and government so that people could survive and flourish in the changed climate.

NOMADIC AND TRANSHUMANT MIGRATIONS

Desperate for secure water sources and pastures, many transhumant herders and pastoralists migrated onto the highland plateaus bordering the Inner Eurasian steppes. From there, some continued into the more populated river valleys and soon were competing with the farming communities over space and resources. They also streamed in from the western and southern deserts in Southwest Asia in modern-day Turkey.

These migrants settled in the agrarian heartlands of Mesopotamia, the Indus River valley, the highlands of Anatolia, Iran, China, and Europe. After the first wave of newcomers, more migrants arrived by foot or in wagons pulled by draft animals. Some sought temporary work; others settled permanently. They brought horses and new technologies that were useful in warfare; religious practices and languages; and new pressures to feed, house, and clothe an ever-growing population.

HORSES AND CHARIOTS Although the hard-riding pastoral nomads contributed much to settled societies (they

War Chariots. *Bottom left*: A large vase typical of Mycenaean art on the mainland areas of Greece. The regular banding and presentation of scenes reflect a society that is more formally ordered and rigidly hierarchical than that on Minoan Crete. Note the presence of the horse-drawn chariot. Possessing this more elaborate means of transport and warfare characterized the warrior elites of Mycenaean society and linked them to developments over wide expanses of Afro-Eurasia at the time. *Upper left*: This wooden chest covered with stucco and painted on all sides with images of the Egyptian pharoah in his war chariot was found in the fabulously wealthy tomb of Tutankhamun in the Valley of the Kings in Egypt. The war chariot was introduced into Egypt by the Hyksos. By the reign of Tutankhamun in the New Kingdom, depictions of the pharaoh single-handedly smiting the enemy from a war chariot drawn by two powerful horses were common. *Upper right*: The Shang fought with neighboring pastoral nomads from the central Asian steppes. To do this, they imported horses from central Asia and copied the chariots of nomads they had encountered. This gave Shang warriors devastating range and speed for further conquest.

Transhumant migrations
Spread of wheeled vehicles
Spread of war chariots
Dispersal of nomads
Pastoral nomads c. 2000 – 1500 BCE

Southwest Asian Society
Zone of urban civilization

MAP 3-1   NOMADIC MIGRATIONS IN AFRO-EURASIA, 2000-1000 BCE

According to this map, what parts of the world did pastoral peoples migrate from? What areas did they move into? What regions did they bring into closer connection? How did nomadic pastoral migrations affect settled, agriculture-based societies?

linked cities in South Asia and China for the first time, enhanced trade, and maintained peace), they could not control what the elites whom they conquered wrote about them. Those who lost power described the nomadic warriors as "barbaric," portraying them as cruel enemies of "civilization." Yet what we know of these nomads today suggests that they were anything but barbaric.

Perhaps the most vital breakthroughs that nomadic pastoralists transmitted to settled societies were the harnessing of horses and the invention of the chariot. On the vast steppe lands north of the Caucasus Mountains, during the late fourth millennium BCE, settled people had domesticated horses in their native habitat. Elsewhere, as on the northern steppes of what is now Russia, horses were a food source. Only during the late third millennium BCE did people harness them with cheek pieces and mouth bits, signaling their use for transportation. Horses can outrun other draft animals, but harnessing them for pulling is complicated. Unlike cattle or donkeys, which stretch their necks ahead when walking, a horse raises its head. So the drivers needed headgear to control their steeds' speed and direction. In tombs scattered around the steppe, archaeologists have found parts of horse harnesses made from wood, bone, bronze, and iron. These reveal the evolution of headgear from simple mouth bits to full bridles with headpiece, mouthpiece, and reins.

Sometime around 2000 BCE, pastoral nomads beyond the Mesopotamian plain to the north in the mountains of the Caucasus joined the harnessed horse to the chariot. Pastoralists lightened chariots so their war horses could pull them faster. They were so light that an empty one could be lifted by one hand. Such techniques included spoked wheels made of special wood and bent into circular shapes, wheel covers, axles, and bearings—all produced by settled people. But there was even more adaptation: durable metal went into the chariot's moving parts, first bronze and later iron. A cluster of more than twenty settlements of steppe nomads, based in the area to the east of the Ural Mountains, led the way in making bronze weapons and chariot parts. Farther south, artisans working out of urban settlements fashioned true tin-bronze weapons and utensils and imported horses and chariots from the steppe peoples.

The next innovation in the chariot was the use of iron. Initially iron was a decorative and experimental metal, and all tools and weapons were bronze. Iron's hardness and flexibility, however, eventually made it more desirable for reinforcing moving parts and protecting wheels. Similarly, solid wood wheels that were prone to shatter ceded to spokes and hooped bronze (and, later, iron) rims. Thus the horse chariots were the result of a creative combination of innovations by both nomadic and agrarian peoples. These innovations—combining new engineering skills, metallurgy, and animal domestication—and their ultimate diffusion revolutionized the way humans made war.

The horse chariot slashed travel time between capitals and overturned the machinery of war. Slow-moving infantry now ceded to battalions of chariots. Each vehicle carried a driver and an archer, and it charged into battle with lethal precision and ravaging speed. In fact, the mobility, accuracy, and shooting power of warriors in horse-drawn chariots tilted the political balance. For after the nomads perfected this type of warfare (by 1600 BCE), they challenged the political systems of Mesopotamia and Egypt and soon were affecting war-making in distant regions such as present-day Greece, India, China, and Sweden. Only with the arrival of cheaper armor made of iron (after 1000 BCE) could foot soldiers (in China, armed with crossbows) recover their military importance. For much of the second millennium BCE, then, charioteer elites prevailed in Afro-Eurasia.

For city dwellers in the river basins the first sight of horse-drawn chariots must have been terrifying, but they knew that war-making had changed and they scrambled to adapt. The Shang kings of China and the pharaohs in Egypt probably copied chariots from nomads or neighbors, and they came to value them highly. For example, the young pharaoh Tutankhamun (c. 1350) was a chariot archer who made sure his war vehicle and other gear accompanied him in his tomb. A century later the Shang kings of the Yellow River valley, in the heartland of agricultural China, likewise were entombed with their horse chariots.

THE EMERGENCE OF TERRITORIAL STATES

While nomad and transhumant populations toppled the riverine cities in Mesopotamia, Egypt, and China, the turmoil that ensued sowed seeds for a new type of regime: the territorial state. (See Map 3-2.) Breaking out of the urban confines of its predecessors, the **territorial state** exerted power over distant hinterlands. In this way, it represented the chief political innovation of this new era. Centralized kingdoms, organized around charismatic rulers, now emerged. In so doing they stabilized political systems, by devising rituals for passing the torch of command from one generation to the next. People no longer identified themselves as residents of cities; instead, they felt allegiance to large territories, rulers, and broad linguistic and ethnic communities. These territories for the first time had identifiable borders, and their residents felt a shared identity.

Territorial states differed from the city-states that preceded them. The city-states of the riverine societies, organized around the temple and palace, were autonomous **polities** (politically organized communities or states) without clearly defined borders. In contrast, the new territorial states in Egypt, Mesopotamia, and China based their authority on monarchs, widespread bureaucracies, elaborate legal codes,

MAIN THEMES

→ *Dramatic warming and drying of the world's climate leads to the collapse of river-basin societies.*

→ *Herders and pastoral nomads migrate into riverine societies, utilizing horse-drawn chariot warfare to challenge traditional ruling elites and conquer surrounding states.*

→ *Large territorial states arise, led by charismatic rulers who expand boundaries, create more competition and trade, and wage warfare.*

→ *Microsocieties emerge in other parts of the world based on expanding populations and increased trade.*

FOCUS ON *The Emergence of Territorial States*

Egypt and Southwest Asia

◆ Invasions by nomads and transhumant herders lead to the creation of larger territorial states: New Kingdom Egypt, Hittites, Babylonia, and Kassites.

◆ A centuries-long peaceful era, "The Community of Major Powers," emerges among the major states as the result of shrewd statecraft and diplomacy.

Indus River Valley

◆ Migratory Vedic peoples from the steppes of inner Eurasia use charioteer technology and rely on domesticated animals to spread out and begin integrating the northern half of South Asia.

Shang State (China)

◆ Shang dynasts promote improvements in metalworking, agriculture, and the development of writing, leading to the growth of China's first major state.

Microsocieties

◆ Substantial increases in population, migrations, and trade lead to the emergence of microsocieties among peoples in the South Pacific (Austronesians), the Aegean world (Minoans and Mycenaeans), and the Americas, while Europe remains a land of warmaking small chieftanships.

---

large territorial expanses, definable borders, and ambitions for continuous expansion. Although power still emanated from central cities, some new ruling groups had appeared: the once-marginalized peoples of the Syrian Desert (the Amorites) and of the northern steppe lands and Anatolia (the Hittites) now held power. Their drive to conquer and expand replaced the earlier models of competition and coexistence. Territorial states also emerged in Greece and the Aegean where the newcomers who took power adopted local ways more completely. Other regions went through similar processes, but more slowly; they would not see state formation for a few more centuries. In one fundamental way, the South Pacific, the Aegean, Europe, and the Americas were different from the lands stretching from North Africa to South Asia: because they were less densely populated, they experienced less rivalry and less conflict over borders.

THE RISE OF TERRITORIAL STATES IN EGYPT AND SOUTHWEST ASIA

→ *What were the direct and indirect effects of drought on the organization of societies?*

Climatic change, invasions by pastoral nomads, and the use of war chariots transformed the city-states of Egypt and Southwest Asia. They brought an end to regimes like Old Kingdom Egypt and the many states occupying the

MAP 3-2

TERRITORIAL STATES AND TRADE ROUTES IN SOUTHWEST ASIA, NORTH AFRICA, AND THE EASTERN MEDITERRANEAN, 1500–1350 BCE

What were the major trade routes and the major trading states in Southwest Asia, North Africa, and the Eastern Mediterranean during this time? What were the major trade goods? Did trade enhance peaceful interactions among the territorial states?

Mesopotamian floodplain. But, as inhabitants of these areas assimilated the newcomers or drove out those who resisted assimilation, new states came to the fore. Thus the second millennium BCE divides into two distinct phases. The first phase, roughly 2000 to 1600 BCE, resembled what had gone before: small kingdoms, organized by territorial and ethnic identities, dominated the landscape from the Aegean Sea through Mesopotamia and Iran. The most powerful kingdoms were Babylonia in Mesopotamia and the Middle Kingdom in Egypt. A more radical phase occurred after 1600 BCE, when a renewed wave of nomadic migrations and conquests undermined these earlier fledgling but unstable territorial kingdoms. After an agonizing century of turmoil, the balance of power shifted and a new group of expansionist, territorial states emerged. From their urban capitals, these new states commanded vast hinterlands, claimed definable boundaries, and consolidated common cultures. The most powerful states of the second period were New Kingdom Egypt, the Hittites of Anatolia, and Babylonia and the Kassites of Mesopotamia.

In this second period the entire region was marked by competition between well-balanced military kingdoms. Although there was much quarreling and some warfare, shrewd statecraft and international diplomacy kept the peace for many centuries. Not so fortunate were the smaller kingdoms, such as the Syro-Palestinian states, squeezed between the major powers. They served as buffer zones between the regions that the territorial powers dominated.

EGYPT

The first of the great territorial kingdoms of this era arose from the ashes of chaos in Egypt. There the pharaohs of the Middle Kingdom and, later, the New Kingdom reunified the river valley and expanded south and north. The long era of prosperity associated with the Old Kingdom had ended when drought brought catastrophe to the area. For several decades the Nile did not overflow its banks, and Egyptian harvests withered. As the pharaohs lost legitimacy and fell prey to feuding among rivals for the throne, regional notables replaced the authority of the centralized state. Egypt, which had been one of the most stable corners of Afro-Eurasia, would endure more than a century of tumult before a new order emerged.

MIDDLE KINGDOM EGYPT (2040–1640 BCE) Around 2050 BCE, after a century of drought, the Nile's floodwaters returned to normal. Crops grew again. But who would restore order and reunite the kingdom? From about 2061 to 1991 BCE, two rulers at Thebes (far south of the Old Kingdom's seat of power in Memphis) both named Mentuhotep consolidated power in Upper Egypt and began new state-building activity. They ushered in a new phase of stability that historians call the Middle Kingdom. For 350 years, the new pharaonic line built on earlier foundations to increase the

Amun. This sculpture of the head of the god Amun was carved from quartzite during the Eighteenth Dynasty, around 1335 BCE. At Thebes in Upper Egypt, a huge temple complex was dedicated to the combined god Amun-Re. The powerful kings of the Middle and New Kingdoms each added a courtyard or a pylon, making this one of the largest religious structures in the ancient world.

state's power and to develop religious and political institutions far beyond their original forms.

GODS AND KINGS Spiritual and worldly powers reinforced each other in Egypt. Just as rulers of this new phase came from the margins, so did its gods. The Twelfth Dynasty (1985–1795 BCE), with its long list of kings, dominated the Middle Kingdom partly because its sacred order replaced the chaos that people believed had brought drought and despair. Amenemhet I (1985–1955 BCE) elevated a formerly insignificant god, Amun, to prominence. The king capitalized on the god's name, which means "hidden," to convey a sense of his own invisible omnipresence throughout the realm.

Because Amun's attributes were largely hidden, believers in other gods were able to embrace his cult. Amun's cosmic power appealed to those in areas that had recently been impoverished. As the pharaoh elevated the cult of Amun he unified the disparate parts of his kingdom, further empowering Amun—as well as his worldly sponsor, the pharaoh. In this way Amun eclipsed all the other gods of Thebes. Merging with the formerly omnipotent sun god Re, the deity now was called Amun-Re: the king of the gods. Because the power of the gods and kings was intertwined, Amun's earthly champion (the king) enjoyed enhanced legitimacy as the supreme ruler. The cult was more than a tool of political power, however: it also

had a strong spiritual impact on the pharaoh and on Egyptian society.

ROYAL SPLENDOR AND ROYAL CARE While gods and kings allied, Middle Kingdom rulers tapped into their kingdom's bounty, their subjects' loyalty, and the work of untold slaves and commoners to build the largest, longest-lasting public works project ever undertaken. For 2,000 years, Egyptians and slaves toiled to erect monumental gates, enormous courtyards, and other structures in a massive temple complex at Thebes. Dedicated to Amun-Re, it demonstrated the glorious power of the pharaohs and the gods.

Unlike the spiritually perfect and remote rulers of the Old Kingdom, the Middle Kingdom rulers nurtured a cult of the pharaoh as the good shepherd whose prime responsibility was to fulfill the needs of his human flock. By instituting charities, offering homage to gods at the palace to ensure regular floodwaters, and performing ceremonies to honor their own generosity, the pharaohs portrayed themselves as the stewards of their people.

MERCHANTS AND TRADE NETWORKS Prosperity gave rise to an urban class of merchants and professionals who used their wealth and skills to carve out places for their own leisure and pastimes. Indoors they indulged in formal banquets with professional dancers and singers, and outdoors they honed their skills in hunting, fowling, and fishing. What was new was that they did not depend on the kings for such benefits. In a sign of their upward mobility and autonomy, some members of the middle class constructed tombs filled with representations of the material goods they would use in the afterlife as well as the occupations that would engage them for eternity. During the Old Kingdom, this privilege had been the exclusive right of the royal family and a few powerful nobles.

Centralized and reforming kingdoms also expanded their trade networks. Because the floodplains had long since been deforested, the Egyptians needed to import massive quantities of wood by ship. Most prized were the cedars from Byblos (a city in the land soon known as Phoenicia, roughly present-day Lebanon), which artisans crafted into furniture for the living and coffins for the dead. Superb examples remain from the tombs of nobles and pharaohs. Commercial networks extended south through the Red Sea as far as present-day Ethiopia; traders brought back precious metals, ivory, livestock, slaves, and exotic animals such as panthers and monkeys to enhance the pharaoh's palace. Expeditions to the Sinai Peninsula searched for copper and turquoise. Egyptians looked south for gold, which they prized for personal and architectural ornamentation. To acquire it they crossed into Nubia, where they met stiff resistance; eventually the Egyptians colonized Nubia to broaden their trade routes and secure these coveted resources. As part of their colonization, a series of forts extended as far south as the second cataract of the Nile River. (See Map 2-5 in Chapter 2.)

HYKSOS INVADERS AND NEW FOUNDATIONS Pharaonic peace brought prosperity, but it did not ensure uninterrupted pharaonic rule. Now Egypt found itself open to migration and foreign invasion, coming once again from the margins. First, the very success of the new commercial networks lured pastoral nomads who were searching for work. Later, a new people from Southwest Asia attacked Egypt, initially destabilizing the kingdom but ultimately putting it on stronger foundations.

Sometime around 1640 BCE a western Semitic-speaking people, whom the Egyptians called the Hyksos ("Rulers of Foreign Lands"), overthrew the unstable Thirteenth Dynasty. The Hyksos had mastered the art of horse chariots. Thundering into battle with their war chariots and their superior bronze axes and composite bows (made of wood, horn, and sinew), they easily defeated the pharaoh's foot soldiers. Yet the victors did not destroy the conquered land; instead, they ruled over it. By adopting Egyptian ways, they also reinforced them. The Hyksos settled down and ruled as the Fifteenth Dynasty, asserting control over the northern part of the country and transforming the Egyptian military force.

After a century of political conflict, an Egyptian who ruled the southern part of the country, Ahmosis (r. 1550–1525 BCE), successfully used the Hyksos weaponry—horse chariots—against the invaders themselves and became pharaoh. The Egyptian rulers had learned an important lesson from the invasion: they had to vigilantly monitor their frontiers, for they could no longer rely on deserts as buffers. Ahmosis assembled large, mobile armies and drove the "foreigners" back. Diplomats followed in the army's path, as the pharaoh initiated a strategy of interference in the affairs of southwest Asian states. Such policies laid the groundwork for statecraft and an international diplomatic system that future Egyptian kings would use to dominate the eastern Mediterranean world.

The migrants and invaders from the west introduced new techniques that the Egyptians adopted to consolidate their power. These included bronze working (which the Egyptians had not perfected), an improved potter's wheel, and a vertical loom. In addition, South Asian animals such as humped zebu cattle, as well as vegetable and fruit crops, now appeared on the banks of the Nile for the first time.

Of course, the most significant innovations pertained to war: the horse and chariot, the composite bow, the scimitar (a sword with a curved blade), and other weapons from western Eurasia. These weapons transformed the Egyptian army from a standing infantry to a high-speed, mobile, and deadly fighting force. As Egyptian troops extended the military frontier as far south as the fourth cataract of the Nile River, the kingdom now stretched from the Mediterranean shores to Ethiopia.

NEW KINGDOM EGYPT By the beginning of the New Kingdom (1550–1069 BCE), Egypt was projecting its interests outward: it defined itself as a superior, cosmopolitan society with an efficient bureaucracy run by competent and socially mobile individuals. For 100 years Egypt expanded its control southward into Nubia, a source of gold, exotic raw materials, and manpower. Historians identify this expansion most strongly with the reign of Egypt's most powerful woman ruler, Hatshepsut. She served as regent for her young son, Thutmosis III, who came to the throne in 1479 BCE. When he was seven years old she proclaimed herself "king," ruling as co-regent until she died. During her reign there was little military activity, but trade contacts into the Levant and Mediterranean and southward into Nubia flourished.

Thutmosis III (r. 1479–1425 BCE) launched another expansionary phase that lasted for 200 years. Spreading northeastward into the Levant, under his rule the Egyptians collided with the Mitanni and the Hittite kingdoms. At the Battle of Megiddo (1469 BCE), the first recorded chariot battle in history, Thutmosis III defeated vassals of the Mitanni and established an Egyptian presence in Palestine. Egypt was now poised to engage in commercial, political, and cultural exchanges with the rest of the region (see "The Community of Major Powers" on p. 100).

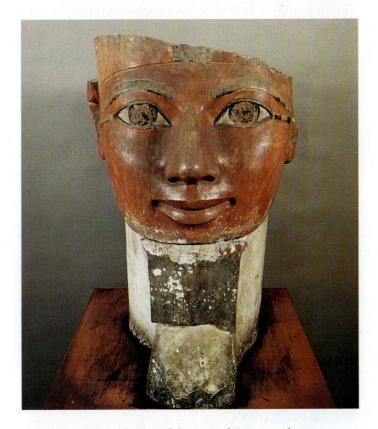

Hatshepsut. The only powerful queen of Egyptian pharaonic history was Hatshepsut, seen here in a portrait head created during her reign. Because a woman on the throne of Egypt would offend the basic principles of order (*ma'at*), Hatshepsut usually portrayed herself as a man, especially late in her reign. This was reinforced by the use of male determinatives in the hieroglyphic renditions of her name.

ANATOLIA AND THE RISE OF THE HITTITES

Anatolia was an overland crossroads that linked the Black and Mediterranean seas. Like other plateaus of Afro-Eurasia it had high tablelands, was easy to traverse, and was hospitable to large herding communities. Thus during the third millennium BCE Anatolia had become home to numerous polities run by indigenous elites. These societies combined pastoral lifeways, agriculture, and urban commercial centers. Before 2000 BCE, peoples speaking Indo-European languages began to enter the plateau, probably coming from the steppe lands north and west of the Black Sea. The newcomers lived in fortified settlements and often engaged in regional warfare, and their numbers grew. Splintered into competing clans, they fought for regional supremacy. They also borrowed extensively from the cultural developments of the Southwest Asian urban cultures, especially those of Mesopotamia.

THE OLD AND NEW HITTITE KINGDOMS (1800–1200 BCE)   In the early second millennium BCE chariot warrior groups, which were the most powerful of the competing communities in Anatolia, grew even more powerful on the commercial activity that passed through Anatolia. Chief among them were the Hittites. Their chariots carried lancers and archers across vast expanses to plunder their neighbors and demand taxes and tribute. The chariot aristocracies finally became unified during the seventeenth century BCE under Hattusilis I.

After securing his base in Anatolia, Hattusilis turned his attention to the east, crossed the Taurus Mountains, and defeated the kingdom that controlled all of northern Syria. In 1595 BCE, Hattusilis and his son Mursilis I marched even farther, campaigning along the Euphrates River as far as the city of Babylon, which they sacked. The Hittites enjoyed another period of political and military success two centuries later under the great king Suppilulimua I (r. 1380–1345 BCE), who restored Hittite glory in Southwest Asia from the Euphrates in the east to Syria in the south. At Qadesh they met the Egyptians in what some experts regard as the greatest battle in ancient times, one that involved a vast number of chariots. Because the Hittites controlled much of the territory between Mesopotamia and the Nile, their rulers were crucial in maintaining the region's balance of power.

MESOPOTAMIA

In Mesopotamia, as in Egypt and Anatolia, the intervention of pastoral peoples led to the emergence of new states. Here, too, drought was devastating. Harvests shrank, the price of basic goods rose, and the social order broke down. Already short of agricultural produce, the towns of southern Mesopotamia suffered invasions by transhumant migrants from two directions: the Zagros Mountains and the Syrian Desert. These herders, who did not use horses or chariots, were seeking grazing lands to replace those swallowed up by the expanding deserts. As elsewhere in Afro-Eurasia, environmental changes were altering the human landscape.

A millennium of intense cultivation, combined with severe drought, had ruined the land's productivity. The rich alluvial soil lost more and more nutrients, while at the same time salt water from the Persian Gulf seeped into the marshy deltas and contaminated the water table (the underground level at which water can reliably be found). As the main branch of the Euphrates River shifted to the west, large areas of previously arable land no longer received sufficient water for cultivation. As a result, many of the ancient cities lost access to their fertile agrarian hinterlands and withered away. All these alterations pushed Mesopotamia's center of political and economic gravity northward, away from the silted, marshy deltas of the southern heartland.

NOMADIC AND TRANSHUMANT MIGRATION TO MESOPOTAMIAN CITIES   The conquerors of Mesopotamian cities were the Amorites, a name given them by their vanquished urban dwellers and taken from the Akkadian word for "west," *Amurru*. City dwellers were scornful of these rustic folk, as the following poetry makes clear. It states that the Amorite is

> a tent-dweller, [buffeted] by wind and rain, [who offers no] prayer,
> He who dwells in the mountains, [knows not] the places [of the gods];
> A man who digs up mushrooms at the foot of the mountain, who knows no submission,
> He eats uncooked meat,
> In his lifetime has no house,
> When he dies, he will not be buried;
> My girlfriend—why would you marry Martu?!
> (Klein, "The Marriage of Martu," 89)

Transhumant herders may have been "foreigners" in the cities of Mesopotamia, but they were not strangers to them. They had always played an important role in Mesopotamian urban life and knew the culture of its city-states. These rural folk wintered in villages close to the river to water their animals, which grazed on fallow fields. In the scorching summer, they retreated to the cooler highlands. Their flocks provided wools for the vast textile industries of Mesopotamia, as well as leather, bones, and tendons for other crafted products. In return, the herders purchased crafted products and agricultural goods. They also paid taxes, served as warriors, and labored on public works projects. Yet despite being part of the urban fabric, they had few political rights within city-states.

As scarcities mounted, transhumant peoples began to press in upon settled communities more closely. Finally, in

2004 BCE, Amorites from the western desert joined allies from the Iranian plateau to bring down the Third Dynasty of Ur (which had controlled all of Mesopotamia and southwestern Iran for more than a century). As in Egypt, a century of political instability followed the demise of the old city-state models. Here, too, it was pastoral folk who finally restored order, taking the wealth of the regions they conquered and helping the cultural realm to flourish. They founded the Old Babylonian kingdom around 2000 BCE; they also expanded trade and founded new kinds of political communities: territorial states with dynastic ruling families and well-defined frontiers. This was yet another example of the contribution of mobile communities to settled societies.

RESTORED ORDER AND CULTURE   Restored order and prosperity enabled the new kings of Babylonia to nourish a vibrant intellectual and cultural milieu. They commissioned public art and works projects, and institutions of learning thrived. The court supported workshops for skilled artisans such as jewelers and sculptors, and it established schools for scribes, the transmitters of an expanding literary culture.

Now the Babylonians and their successors, the Kassites (1475–1125 BCE), reproduced the cultural achievements of earlier Mesopotamia. To dispel their image as rustic foreigners and to demonstrate their familiarity with the region's core values, they studied the oral tales and written records of the earlier Sumerians and Akkadians. Scribes copied the ancient texts and preserved their tradition. Royal hymns, for instance, continued the Sumerian language that had not been spoken for centuries. These hymns portrayed the king as a legendary hero of quasi-divine status.

Heroic narratives about legendary founders, based on traditional stories about the rulers of ancient Uruk, served to legitimize the new rulers. These great poems constituted the first epic narratives of human—as opposed to godly—achievement. Written in the Old Babylonian dialect of the Semitic Akkadian language, they identified the history of a people with their king, and their wide circulation helped to unify the kingdom. The most famous was the *Epic of Gilgamesh* (see Primary Source: *The Epic of Gilgamesh*). This story (composed more than a millennium earlier in the Sumerian language) narrated the heroism of the legendary king of early Uruk, Gilgamesh. Throughout the ages, scribes of royal courts preserved the tradition for future generations to venerate the idea of the benevolent king. It stands out as an example of how the Mesopotamian kings continually invested in cultural production in order to explain important political relations, unify their people, and distinguish their subjects from those of other kingdoms.

TRADE AND THE RISE OF A PRIVATE ECONOMY   With restored prosperity came a shift away from economic activity dominated by the city-state and toward independent private ventures. The new rulers designated private entrepreneurs rather than state bureaucrats to collect taxes. People paid taxes in the form of commodities such as grain, vegetables, and wool, which the entrepreneurs exchanged for silver. They, in turn, passed on the silver to the state after pocketing a percentage for their profit. This process generated more private activity and wealth, and more revenues for the state.

Mesopotamia at this time was a crossroads for caravans leading east and west. When the region was peaceful and well

Gilgamesh. This terra-cotta plaque in the Berlin Museum is one of the very few depictions of Gilgamesh (on the left wielding the knife) and his sidekick, Enkidu. It illustrates one of the episodes in their shared adventures, the killing of Ḫumwawa, the monster of the Cedar Forest. The style of the plaque indicates that it was made during the Old Babylonian period, between 2000 and 1600 BCE.

THE EPIC OF GILGAMESH

Gilgamesh, an early ruler of ancient Uruk, was the supreme hero of Mesopotamian legend. He was a successful ruler, boastful and vain, as well as a courageous adventurer and a devoted friend to his companion Enkidu. The Gilgamesh epic, constructed in the early second millennium BCE from numerous stories, is the oldest piece of world literature. It portrays a tragic hero who is obsessed with glory and whose quest for immortality ends in failure. The following excerpt tells of his anguish on his fruitless journey to gain immortal life. He is speaking to an alewife (a woman who keeps an alehouse) as he continues to deny his humanity and the inevitability of death.

The alewife spoke to him, to Gilgamesh,
"If you are truly Gilgamesh, that struck down the
   Guardian,
Destroyed Humbaba, who lived in the Pine Forest,
Killed lions at the mountain passes,
Seized the Bull of Heaven who came down from the sky,
   struck him down,
Why are your cheeks wasted, your face dejected,
Your heart so wretched, your appearance worn out,
And grief in your innermost being?
Your face is like that of a long-distance traveler,
Your face is weathered by cold and heat . . .
Clad only in a lion skin you roam open country."
Gilgamesh spoke to her, to Siduri the alewife,
"How could my cheeks not be wasted, my face not
   dejected.
Nor my heart wretched, nor my appearance worn out,
Nor grief in my innermost being,
Nor my face like that of a long-distance traveler,
My friend whom I love so much, who
Experienced every hardship with me,
Enkidu, whom I love so much, who experienced every
   hardship with me—
The fate of mortals conquered him! Six days and seven
   nights I wept over him,

I did not allow him to be buried, until a worm fell out of
   his nose.
I was frightened and . . .
I am afraid of Death, and so I roam open country.
The words of my friend weigh upon me.
I roam open country for long distances; the words of my
   friend
Enkidu weigh upon me.
I roam open country on long journeys.
How, O how, could I stay silent, how O how could I keep
   quiet
My friend whom I love has turned to clay:
Enkidu my friend whom I love has turned to clay.
Am I not like him? Must I lie down too,
Never to rise, ever again?"

➤ *What lines of the passage reveal how Gilgamesh feels about the death of Enkidu? Why does he feel that way?*

➤ *What does this passage tell us about human relationships and human nature during this period? What does it tell us about rulers and their relationship with their gods?*

SOURCE: "The Epic of Gilgamesh" from *Myths from Mesopotamia: Creation, The Flood, Gilgamesh and Others*, pp. 100–101, trans. Stephanie Dalley. © Stephanie Dalley 1989. Reprinted with permission of Oxford University Press.

governed, the trading community flourished. The ability to move exotic foodstuffs, valuable minerals, textiles, and luxury goods across Southwest Asia won Mesopotamian merchants and entrepreneurs a privileged position as they connected producers with distant consumers. Merchants also used sea routes for trade with the Indus Valley. Before 2000 BCE, mariners had charted the waters of the Red Sea, the Gulf of Aden, the Persian Gulf, and much of the Arabian Sea. Now, during the second millennium BCE, shipbuilders figured out how to construct larger vessels and to rig them with towering masts and woven sails—creating truly seaworthy craft that could carry bulkier loads. Of course, shipbuilding required wood (particularly cedar from Phoenicia) as well as wool and other fibers (from the pastoral hinterlands) for sails. Such reliance on imported materials reflected a growing regional economic specialization and an expanding sphere of interaction across western Afro-Eurasia.

Doing business in Mesopotamia was profitable but also risky. If harvests were poor, cultivators and merchants could not meet their tax obligations and thus incurred heavy debts. The frequency of such misfortune is evident from the many royal edicts that annulled certain debts as a gesture of tax relief. Moreover, traders and goods had to pass through lands where some hostile rulers refused to protect the caravans. Thus taxes, duties, and bribes flowed out along the entire route. If goods reached their final destination, they yielded large profits; if disaster struck, investors and traders had nothing to show for their efforts. As a result, merchant households sought to lower their risks by formalizing commercial rules, establishing insurance schemes, and cultivating extended kinship networks in cities along trade routes to ensure strong commercial alliances and to gather intelligence. They also cemented their ties with local political authorities. Indeed, the merchants who dominated the ancient city of Assur on the Tigris pumped revenues into the coffers of the local kingdom in the hope that its wealthy dynasts would protect their interests.

MESOPOTAMIAN KINGDOMS The new rulers of Mesopotamia also changed the organization of the state. Where city-states had once prevailed, rulers from nomadic stock now fashioned kingdoms that covered large territories. These herders-turned-urbanites mixed their own social organization with that of the city-states to create the structures necessary to support territorial states.

The basic social organization of the Amorites was tribal, dominated by a ruling chief. Tribal polities, even those extending over wide areas, comprised clans; each claimed descent from a common ancestor and thus drew a line between itself and all who were not kin. (However, the clans did allow intermarriage and adoption.) Even the many Amorites who had given up their nomadic ways and settled in the cities remained conscious of their genealogical roots. The new territorial polities honored identification with the clan and tribe.

The emergence of ruling cliques from among the nomadic chieftains led to a new model of statecraft. This process occurred in three stages. First, chieftains became kings. Second, the new kings turned their authority—which in the tribe had depended on personal charisma and battlefield prowess—into an alliance with wealthy merchants in exchange for revenues and political support. Third, royal status became hereditary. This practice of hereditary succession replaced the tribal system under which influential community leaders had elected the leaders. Even in the new system, though, kings could not rule without the support of nobles and merchants.

Over the centuries, powerful Mesopotamian kings continued to expand their territories. They subdued weaker neighbors, coaxing or forcing them to become **vassal states**— that is, allies who had to pay tribute in luxury goods, raw materials, and manpower as part of a broad confederation of polities under the kings' protection. Control over military resources (access to metals for weaponry and, later, to herds of horses for pulling chariots) was necessary to gain dominance, but it was no guarantee of success. The ruler's charisma also mattered. This emphasis on personality explains why Mesopotamian kingdoms were strong for certain periods under certain rulers, but vulnerable to rivals and neighbors under other rulers. It also distinguished them from Middle Kingdom Egypt and Hittite Anatolia, territorial states where power was more institutionalized and durable.

The most famous Mesopotamian ruler of this period was Hammurapi (or Hammurabi) (r. 1792–1750), who ascended the throne as the sixth king of Old Babylonia's First Dynasty. Continuously struggling with powerful neighbors, he sought to centralize state authority and to create a new legal order. Using diplomatic and military skills to become the strongest king in Mesopotamia, he made Babylon his capital and declared himself "the king who made the four quarters of the earth obedient." He implemented a new system to secure his power, appointing regional governors to manage outlying provinces and to deal with local elites.

Hammurapi's image as ruler imitated that of the Egyptian pharaohs of the Middle Kingdom. The king was shepherd and patriarch of his people, responsible for proper preparation of the fields and irrigation canals and for his followers' well-being. Such an ideal recognized that being king was a delicate balancing act. While he had to curry favor among powerful merchants and elites, he also had to meet the needs of the poor and disadvantaged—in part to avoid a reputation for cruelty, and in part to gain a key base of support should the elites become dissatisfied with his rule.

Hammurapi elevated this balancing act into an art form, encapsulated in a grand legal code—**Hammurapi's Code**. It began and concluded with the rhetoric of paternal justice. For example, he concluded by describing himself as "the shepherd who brings peace, whose scepter is just. My benevolent shade was spread over my city, I held the people of the lands of Sumer and Akkad safely on my lap."

Hammurapi's Code was in fact a compilation of more than 300 edicts addressing crimes and their punishments. One theme rings loud and clear: governing public matters was man's work, and upholding a just order was the supreme charge of rulers. Whereas the gods' role in ordering the world was distant, the king was directly in command of ordering relations among people. Accordingly, the code elaborated in exhaustive detail the social rules that would ensure the kingdom's peace through its primary instrument—the family. The code outlined the rights and privileges of fathers, wives, and children. The father's duty was to treat his kin as the ruler would treat his subjects, with strict authority and care. Adultery, which represented the supreme violation of this moral code, was a female crime. Any woman found with a man who

Hammurapi's Code. The inscription on the shaft of Hammurapi's Code is carved in a beautiful rendition of the cuneiform script. Because none of the laws on the code were recorded in the thousands of judicial texts of the period, it is uncertain if Hammurapi's Code presented actual laws or only norms for the proper behavior of Babylonian citizens.

was not her husband would be bound and thrown into the river, and likewise her lover.

Hammurapi's Code also divided the Babylonian kingdom into three classes: each member was a free person (*awilum*), a dependent (*mushkenum*), or a slave (*wardum*). Each had an assigned value and distinct rights and responsibilities. In this way, Hammurapi's order stratified society while also pacifying the region. By the end of his reign, Hammurapi had established Babylon as the single great power in Mesopotamia and had reduced competitor kingdoms to mere vassals. Following his death, his sons and successors struggled to maintain control over a shrinking domain for another 155 years in the face of internal rebellions and foreign invasions. In 1595 BCE, Babylon fell to the Hittite king Hattusilis I.

KASSITE RULE As a crossroads for Afro-Eurasia, Mesopotamia continued both to benefit from and be threatened by the arrival of nomadic and transhumant migrants. The

Kassites, for instance, who came from the Zagros Mountains, had entered southern Mesopotamia from the Iranian plateau. Arriving in the river valley as agricultural laborers as early as 2000 BCE, they integrated themselves into Babylonian society by becoming bureaucrats associated with the temple. Once entrenched, they were well placed to fill the power vacuum when the Hittites destroyed the First Dynasty of Babylon. By 1475 BCE, Kassite rulers had reestablished order in the region. Over the next 350 years they brought all of southern Mesopotamia under their control, creating one of the great territorial states within an emerging network of states from North Africa to Southwest Asia.

The Kassites presided over a golden age based on trade in such precious commodities as horses, chariots, and lapis lazuli, which they exchanged for gold, wood, and ivory. Like earlier immigrant communities to this ancient land, the Kassites absorbed the traditions and institutions of Mesopotamia. Even more than their predecessors, they strove to preserve the past and transmit its institutions to posterity. Although very little remains of their own language and customs (apart from their personal names), with thoroughness and dedication the Kassite scribes translated much of the older Sumerian literature into Akkadian. They revised and compiled texts into standard editions, from which scholars have recovered a Babylonian creation myth called the Enuma Elish. In their determination to become even more Babylonian than the Babylonians, the Kassites saved a treasure trove of historical literature and artifacts for later generations. During the subsequent period of the Community of Major Powers the Kassites served as the crucial link between Egypt, Anatolia, and southwestern Iran.

THE COMMUNITY OF MAJOR POWERS (1400–1200 BCE)

Between 1400 and 1200 BCE, the major territorial states of Southwest Asia and Egypt perfected instruments of international diplomacy that have stood the test of time and inspired later leaders. The leaders of these powers learned to settle their differences through treaties and diplomatic negotiations rather than on the battlefield. Each state knew its place in the political pecking order. It was an order that depended on constant communication—the foundation of what we now call diplomacy. In fact, a remarkable cache of 300 letters discovered at the present-day village of Amarna, beneath which Egyptologists discovered the remains of the capital city of the New Kingdom pharaoh Akhenaten, offers intimate views of these complex interactions. Most are letters from the Egyptian king to his subordinates in the vassal states of Palestine, but others are from Akhenaten and his father to the Babylonian, Mitanni, Middle Assyrian, Kassite, and Hittite kings. Many of these letters are in a dialect of Akkadian (used by the Babylonian bureaucrats) that served as the diplomatic

Akhenaten. The pharaoh Amenhotep IV changed his name to Akhenaten to reflect his deep devotion to Aten, the god of the sun disk. The art of the period of his reign, like his religion, challenged conventions. In it, the faces of the king and queen, as well as their bodies, were extremely elongated and distorted. Some scholars think that this distortion reflects a condition that the king himself suffered from.

language of the era. This correspondence reveals a delicate balance, constantly shifting, among competing kings who were intent on maintaining their status and who knew that winning the loyalty of the small buffer kingdoms was crucial to political success.

Formal treaties brought an end to military eruptions and replaced them with diplomatic contacts. In its more common form, diplomacy involved strategic marriages and the exchange of specialized personnel to reside at the court of foreign territorial states. Gifts also strengthened relations among the major powers and signaled a ruler's respect for his neighbors. Rulers had to acknowledge the gesture by reciprocating with gifts of equal value.

The foundations of power were not always durable, however. Building the state system was ultimately the task of those at the bottom of the social pyramid, and the ruling classes' reliance on them for power and political authority was a weakness of these regimes. Commoners remained tied to the land, which sometimes belonged to communities or institutions, not individual families. They paid taxes to the state, performed labor required by the state for public works (such as irrigation or building projects), and served as foot soldiers. The collapse of the international age had many

causes, but one factor was the disintegration of the social fabric as workers could not pay their taxes or fled their communities rather than fight in the rulers' armies.

NOMADS AND THE INDUS RIVER VALLEY

→ *How did Vedic migrations influence South Asia?*

Late in the third millennium BCE, drought ravaged the Indus River valley as it did other regions. By 1700 BCE, the population of the old Harappan heartland had plummeted. Here, too, around 1500 BCE, yet another group of nomadic peoples calling themselves Aryans ("respected ones") wandered out of their homelands in the steppes of inner Eurasia. But in contrast to Egypt, Anatolia, and Mesopotamia, these pastoral nomads did not immediately establish large territorial states. Crossing the northern highlands of central Asia through the Hindu Kush, they were a sight to behold. They descended into the fertile Indus River basin (see Map 3-3) with large flocks of cattle and horses, singing chants called Rig Veda as they sacrificed some of their livestock to their gods. Known collectively as the Veda ("knowledge"), these hymns served as the most sacred texts for the newcomers, who have been known ever since as the **Vedic people**. They also arrived with an extraordinary language, Sanskrit (perhaps prophetically labeled "perfectly made"). It was one of the earliest known Indo-European languages and a source for virtually all of the European languages, including Greek, Latin, English, French, and German. (See Global Connections & Disconnections: How Languages Spread— The Case of Nomadic Indo-European Languages.)

Like other nomads from the northern steppe, they brought domesticated animals—especially horses, which pulled their chariots and established their military superiority. Not only were the Vedic people superb horse charioteers, but they were also masters of copper and bronze metallurgy and wheel making. Their expertise in these areas allowed them to produce the very chariots that transported them into their new lands.

Like other Indo-European-speaking groups, the Vedic peoples were deeply religious. They worshipped a host of natural and supernatural deities, the most powerful of which were the sky god and the gods that represented horses. They were confident that their chief god, Indra (the deity of war), was on their side. The Vedic people also brought elaborate rituals of worship, which set them apart from the indigenous populations. (See Primary Source: Vedic Hymns to the Chariot Race of the Gods.) But, as with many Afro-Eurasian migrations, the outsiders' arrival led to fusion as well as to conflict. While the native-born peoples eventually adopted

MAP 3-3 INDO-EUROPEAN MIGRATIONS, 2ND MILLENNIUM BCE
Where did the Indo-European migration originate? Where did Indo-European migrations spread to during this time? How did widespread drought push or draw the migrants into more settled agricultural regions, such as the Indus Valley?

the newcomers' language, the newcomers themselves took up the techniques and rhythms of agrarian life.

The Vedic people used the Indus Valley as a staging area for migrations throughout the northern plain of South Asia. As they mixed agrarian and pastoral ways and borrowed technologies (such as ironworking) from farther west, their population expanded and they began to look for new resources. With horses, chariots, and iron tools and weapons, they marched south and east. By 1000 BCE, they reached the southern foothills of the Himalayas and began to settle in the Ganges River valley. Five hundred years later, they had settlements as far south as the Deccan plateau.

Each wave of occupation involved violence, but the invaders did not simply dominate the indigenous peoples. Instead, the confrontations led them to embrace many of the ways of the vanquished. Although the Vedic people despised

Primary Source

VEDIC HYMNS TO THE CHARIOT RACE OF THE GODS

There are no extant accounts of the Vedic people's chariot races and festivals, despite the centrality of these events to their culture. However, scholars have translated Vedic hymns praising the chariot races of gods. The following hymn portrays the Maruts—the storm gods under the direction of Indra—as skilled charioteers.

1. The Maruts charged with rain, endowed with fierce force, terrible like wild beasts, blazing in their strength, brilliant like fires, and impetuous, have uncovered the (rain-giving) cows by blowing away the cloud.

2. The [Maruts] with their rings appeared like the heavens with their stars, they shone wide like streams from clouds as soon as Rudra, the strong man, was born for you, O golden-breasted Maruts, in the bright lap of Prisni.

3. They wash their horses like racers in the courses, they hasten with the points of the reed on their quick steeds. O golden-jawed Maruts, violently shaking [your jaws], you go quick with your spotted deer, being friends of one mind.

4. Those Maruts have grown to feed all these beings, or, it may be, [they have come] hither for the sake of a friend, they who always bring quickening rain. They have spotted horses, their bounties cannot be taken away, they are like headlong charioteers on their ways.

5. O Maruts, wielding your brilliant spears, come hither on smooth roads with your fiery cows [clouds] whose udders are swelling; [come hither], being of one mind, like swans toward their nests, to enjoy the sweet offering.

6. O one-minded Maruts, come to our prayers, come to our libations like [Indra] praised by men! Fulfil [our prayer] like the udder of a barren cow, and make the prayer glorious by booty to the singer.

7. Grant us this strong horse for our chariot, a draught that rouses our prayers, from day to day, food to the singers, and to the poet in our homesteads luck, wisdom, inviolable and invincible strength.

8. When the gold-breasted Maruts harness the horses to their chariots, bounteous in wealth, then it is as if a cow in the folds poured out to her calf copious food, to every man who has offered libations.

→ *What parts of the hymn give clues about how the charioteers' horses looked and were cared for?*

→ *How do the images relating rain-filled clouds to cows reflect the pastoral roots of the Vedic nomads?*

→ *What kinds of gods were the Maruts, and what was their heavenly job when racing on horse chariots?*

SOURCE: Mandala II, Hymn 34, in Vedic Hymns, translated by Hermann Oldenberg, in vol. 32 of *Sacred Books of the East*, edited by F. Max Müller (1897; reprint, New Delhi: Motilal Banarsidass, 1979), pp. 295–96.

the local rituals, they were in awe of the inhabitants' farming skills and knowledge of seasonal weather. So they adapted even as they continued to expand their territory. They moved into huts constructed from mud, bamboo, and reeds. They refined the already sophisticated production of beautiful carnelian stone beads, and they further aided commerce by devising standardized weights. In addition to raising domesticated animals, they sowed wheat and rye on the Indus plain, and they learned to plant rice in the marshy lands of the Ganges River valley. Later they mastered the use of plows with iron blades, an innovation that transformed the agrarian base of South Asia.

The turn to settled agriculture was a major shift for the pastoral Vedic people. After all, their staple foods had always been dairy products and meat, and they were used to measuring their wealth in livestock (horses were most valuable, and cows were more valuable than sheep). Moreover, because they could not breed their prized horses in South Asia's semi-tropical climate, they initiated a brisk import trade from central and Southwestern Asia.

As the Vedic people adapted to their new environment and fanned out across uncharted agrarian frontiers, their initial political organization took a somewhat different course from those of Southwest Asia. Whereas competitive kingdoms dominated the landscape there, in South Asia competitive, balanced regimes were slower to emerge. The result was a slower process of political integration.

Global Connections & Disconnections

HOW LANGUAGES SPREAD: THE CASE OF NOMADIC INDO-EUROPEAN LANGUAGES

Language arose independently in a number of places around the world. All languages change with time, and scholars call related tongues with a common origin "language families." Even though members of the same language family diverged over time, they all share grammatical features and root vocabularies.

While technically there are more than a hundred language families, a much smaller number have influenced vast geographic areas. For example, the *Altaic* languages spread from Europe to central Asia. The *Sino-Tibetan* language family includes Mandarin, the most widely spoken language in the world. The *Uralic* family, which includes Hungarian and Finnish, occurs mainly in Europe. The *Afro-Asiatic* language family contains several hundred languages spoken in North Africa, sub-Saharan Africa, and Southeast Asia, Hebrew and Arabic among them.

One language family that linguists have studied extensively, and the one with the largest number of speakers, is *Indo-European*. It was identified by scholars who recognized similarities in grammar and vocabulary among classical Sanskrit, Persian, Greek, and Latin. Living languages in this family include English, Irish, German, Norwegian, Portuguese, French, Russian, Persian, Hindi, and Bengali. For the past 200 years, comparative linguists have sought to reconstruct Proto-Indo-European, the parent of all the languages in the family. They have drawn conclusions about its grammar, hypothesizing a highly inflected language with different endings on nouns and verbs according to their use. They have also made suggestions about its vocabulary. For example, after analyzing patterns of linguistic change, scholars have proposed that the basic Indo-European root that means "horse"—in Sanskrit, *aśva*; Persian, *aspa*; Latin, *equus*; and Greek, *hippos* (ἵππος)—is *ekwo-.

Table 3-1 demonstrates the similarity of words in some of the major Indo-European languages. We have emphasized numbers, which are especially stable in language systems because people do not like to change the way they count. We have also provided the equivalents in two Semitic languages (Arabic and Hebrew) to show how different these basic words are in another language family (the Afro-Asiatic).

Attempts to locate the homeland of the original speakers of Proto-Indo-European involve mapping the reconstructed vocabulary onto a matching geography. For example, some of the vocabulary contains words for "snow," "mountain," and "swift river," as well as for animals that are not native to Europe, such as "lion," "monkey," and "elephant." Other words describe agricultural practices and farming tools that date back as far as 5000 BCE. Many linguists believe that nomadic and pastoral peoples of the Eurasian steppes took this language—along with their precious horses and chariots—as far as the borderlands of what is now Afghanistan and eastern Iran.

We know that the early speakers of Indo-European languages used chariots and had words for "wheel," "yoke," and "axle." In fact, the earliest pictures of horse-drawn chariots, used in battle, came from the steppe region east of the Ural Mountains. Indo-European-speaking nomads inhabited this area and subsequently migrated to South Asia and the Iranian plateau. Thus the chariot was literally the vehicle for cultural mingling and, ultimately, the spread of the people's language.

Migration is only one of the possible reasons that languages move and change over vast areas and periods of time. Other influential factors are invasions, climatic conditions, natural resources, and ways of life. Even within one language, words can change through generations of

TABLE 3-1   Similarity of Words in Some Major Indo-European Languages

	WORDS OF COMMON ORIGIN IN INDO-EUROPEAN LANGUAGES							SEMITIC LANGUAGES	
	Sanskrit	Hindi	Greek	Latin	French	German	Spanish	Arabic	Hebrew
Numbers									
one	eka	ek	hen	unus	un	ein	uno	wahid	ehad
two	dva	do	duo	duo	deux	zwei	dos	ithnin	shnayim
three	tri	teen	treis	tres	trois	drei	tres	thalatha	shlasha
four	catur	chār	tessara	quattuor	quatre	vier	cuatro	arba'a	arba'a
five	pañca	pānch	penta	quinque	cinq	fünf	cinco	khamsa	hamisha
ten	daśa	das	deka	decem	dix	zehn	diez	ashra	asara
hundred	śata	sau	hekaton	centum	cent	hundert	cien	mi'a	me'a
Other common words									
father	pitṛ	pitā	pater	pater	père	vater	padre	abu	aba
mother	mātṛ	mātā	mêter	mater	mère	mutter	madre	umm	em
son	sūnu	betā	huios	filius	fils	sohn	hijo	ibn	ben
heart	hṛdaya	dil	kardia	cor	coeur	herz	corazón	qalb	lev
foot	pada	pair	pous	pes	pied	fuss	pie	qadam	regel
god	deva	dev	theos	deus	dieu	gott	dios	Allah	yahweh

use. And words from a common root can sometimes take on very different meanings while remaining similar phonetically. (To use an Indo-European root as an example, the Sanskrit *aśura* means "demonic creature" whereas the Persian *ahura* means "Supreme God.")

Linguistic analysis sheds light on the geographic and demographic details of language penetration into different regions. Part of its allure is the fact that some issues defy resolution (for example, in some cases whether a given language was the dialect of the conquerors or the conquered). Nonetheless, the study of language families and their history underscores the key role of language in the intermingling of cultures throughout time.

Indra with Buddha. The Vedic people worshipped their gods by sacrificing and burning cows and horses and by singing hymns and songs, but they never built temples or sculptured idols. Therefore we do not know how they envisioned Indra and their other gods. However, when Buddhists started to make images of Buddha in the early centuries CE, they also sculpted Indra and Brahma as attendants of the Buddha. Indra in Buddhist iconography evolved into Vajrapani, the Diamond Lord. In this plate, the one on the left holding a stick with diamond-shaped heads is Indra/Vajrapani.

RISE OF THE SHANG STATE (1600–1045 BCE)

→ *What methods did the Shang state use to maintain its rule?*

Climatic change affected East Asia much as it had central and Southwestern Asia. As Chapter 2 detailed, this was a time of cultural integration among agricultural communities along the Yellow and Yangzi rivers. Chinese lore says that during this era a mythological Yu the Great founded the Xia dynasty. While evidence for such a kingdom is sketchy, archaeological and other evidence confirms the emergence, around 1600 BCE, of a territorial state called Shang, located in northeastern China. (See Map 3-4.)

Like the ruling families in Southwest Asian societies, the Shang handed down their own foundation myths to unify the state. Stories supposedly written on bamboo strips and later collected into what historians call the "Bamboo Annals" tell of a time at the end of the Xia dynasty when the sun dimmed, frost and ice appeared in summer, and a long drought followed heavy rainfall and flooding. According to Chinese mythology, Tang, the first ruler of the Shang dynasty, defeated a despotic Xia king and then offered to sacrifice himself so that the drought would end. Tang survived, however, and proved to be a just and moral ruler who strengthened his state and unified his people.

As in South Asia, the Shang political system did not become highly centralized. The Shang state did not have clearly established borders like those of the territorial kingdoms of Southwest Asia. To be sure, it faced threats—but not in the form of rival territorial states encroaching on its peripheries. Thus it had little need for a strongly defended permanent capital, though its heartland was called Zhong Shang, or "center Shang." Its capital moved as its frontier expanded and contracted. This relative security is evident in the Shang kings' personalized style of rule, as they made regular trips around the country to meet, hunt, and conduct military campaigns with those who owed allegiance to them. Yet, like the territorial kingdoms of Southwest Asia, the Shang state had a ruling lineage (a line of male sovereigns descended from a common ancestor) that was eventually set down in a written record. (See Primary Source: Sima Qian on the Ruler's Mandate from Heaven to Rule.)

Shang rulers used metallurgy and writing to reinforce their rule, as well as ancestor worship, divination, and other rituals. At the heart of their power was their keen awareness of the importance of promoting agricultural growth and controlling the precious metals used to finance war.

STATE FORMATION

The Shang state built on the agricultural and riverine village cultures of the Longshan peoples, who had set the stage for a centralized state, urban life, and a cohesive culture (see Chapter 2). The Shang territorial state did not evolve out of city-states as occurred in Mesopotamia and Egypt. Rather, as the population increased and the number of village conflicts grew, it became necessary to have larger and more centralized forms of control. The Shang state emerged to play that governmental role.

The Longshan peoples had already introduced four elements that were instrumental in forming the Shang state: a

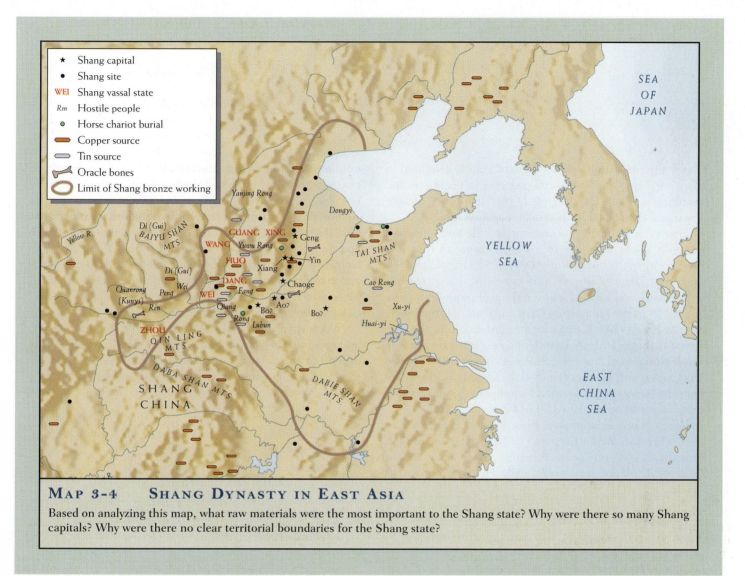

MAP 3-4 SHANG DYNASTY IN EAST ASIA

Based on analyzing this map, what raw materials were the most important to the Shang state? Why were there so many Shang capitals? Why were there no clear territorial boundaries for the Shang state?

metal industry based on copper; pottery making; walled towns; and divination using animal bones. To these foundations the Shang dynasty added a lineage of hereditary rulers whose power derived from their relation to ancestors and gods; written records; tribute; and rituals that enabled them to commune with ancestors and foretell the future. In particular, the Shang promoted large-scale metallurgy and the development of writing. These were major elements in the advance of Chinese society in the second millennium BCE.

To expand and protect their borders, the Shang fought with neighboring states and with pastoral nomads from the central Asian steppes. Horses imported from central Asia helped the Shang dominate northern and central China. Moreover, the Shang copied the chariots of the nomads they

encountered, improving them by adding bronze fittings and harnesses; this new technology gave the warriors devastating range and speed. Here too, as in Southwest Asia, chariot aristocracies emerged. But here, it is important to recall, chariot aristocracies did not produce centralized kingdoms.

Instead, East Asia became a patchwork of regimes that did not rise to the level of military-diplomatic jostling of Southwest Asia. Several other large states also developed in East Asia at this time. These included relatively urban and wealthy peoples in the southeast and more rustic peoples bordering the Shang. The latter traded with the former, whom they knew as the Fang—their label for those who lived in non-Shang areas. Other kingdoms in the south and southwest also had independent bronze industries, with casting technologies comparable to those of the Shang.

SIMA QIAN ON THE RULER'S MANDATE FROM HEAVEN TO RULE

Sima Qian was the first great historian in ancient China. He later had as much influence in East Asia as Herodotus, the first Greek historian, had in Greece and Rome. The excerpt below presents the transition from Xia ("Hsia") dynasty to Shang ("T'ang") dynasty as an example of the transfer of the ruler's heavenly mandate.

After Emperor K'ung-chia was enthroned, he delighted in following ghosts and spirits and engaging in licentious and disorderly actions. The prestige of the Hsia-hou Clan declined and the feudal lords rebelled against him.

Heaven sent down two dragons, a male and a female. K'ung-chia was not able to care for them and he lost the support of the Huan-lung (Dragon Raising) Clan. The Yao-t'ang Clan was already in decline, [but] among their descendants one Liu Lei learned the technique of taming dragons from the Huan-lung Clan and thus obtained service with K'ung-chia. K'ung-chia bestowed on him the *cognomen* Yü-lung (Dragon Tamer) and conferred on him the people descended from the Shih-wei [Clan]. The female dragon died and Liu Lei fed it to the Hsia-hou, the Hsia-hou sent [someone] to demand [more of it], and, fearing [that he would be punished], Liu Lei moved on.

When K'ung-chia passed away, his son Emperor Kao was enthroned. When Emperor Kao passed away his son Emperor Fa was enthroned. When Fa passed away, his son Emperor Lu-k'uei was enthroned. He was known as Chieh.

From K'ung-chia's time to the time of Emperor Chieh, the feudal lords had revolted many times against the Hsia. Chieh did not engage in virtuous [government] but in military power and [this] hurt the families of the hundred cognomens. The families of the hundred cognomens were not able to bear him.

Chieh then summoned T'ang and jailed him in Hsia-t'ai. After a while he freed him. T'ang cultivated his virtue and the feudal lords all submitted to T'ang. T'ang then led troops to attack Chieh of Hsia. Chieh fled to Ming-t'iao and subsequently was exiled and died there. Before he died he said to someone, "I regret failing to kill T'ang in Hsia-t'ai; that is what has brought me to this."

T'ang then ascended the throne of the Son of Heaven and received the world's homage in the Hsia's place. T'ang enfeoffed [made vassals or subjects] the descendants of the Hsia. In the Chou dynasty they were enfeoffed at Ch'i.

→ *What role did morality play in Sima Qian's description of the transfer of the Xia ruler's mandate from heaven to the Shang dynasty?*

→ *How do the references to feuding illustrate the type of society that China had at this time?*

SOURCE: Ssu-ma Ch'ien, "Sima Qian on the Ruler's Mandate," from *The Grand Scribe's Records*, ed. William H. Nienhauser Jr. Reprinted with permission of Indiana University Press.

The Shang state reached its peak around 1200 BCE. At Yin, the Shang erected massive palaces, royal neighborhoods, and bronze foundries. In workshops surrounding the palace, craftworkers decorated jade, stone, and ivory objects; wove silk on special looms; and produced bronze weapons as well as bronze ritual objects and ceremonial drinking vessels. Taking advantage of the local abundance of metal ores, artisans organized workshops to mass-produce the large bronze vessels. The levels of urbanization reached at Yin indicate that the Shang also collected tribute from the agrarian heartlands to support the city's nobles, priests, and dependent artisans and metalworkers. The Shang state simultaneously promoted the writings of elite scribes and the productions of common artisans.

METALWORKING, AGRICULTURE, AND TRIBUTE

Small-scale metalworking, which first emerged in northwestern China, was a critical element in the power of the Shang state. Pre-Shang sites reveal that casting techniques were in use as early as 1800 BCE. Because copper and tin were available from the North China plain, only short-distance trade was necessary to obtain the resources that a bronze culture needed. Access to copper and tin, and to new metallurgy technology, gave the Shang a huge advantage and unprecedented power over their neighbors.

The Shang used copper, lead, and tin to produce bronze, from which they made weapons, fittings for chariots, and

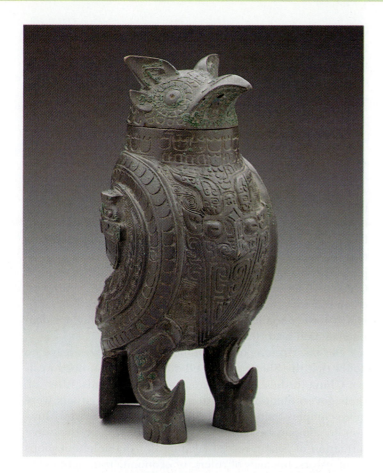

Bronze. At the height of the Shang state, circa 1200 BCE, its rulers erected massive palaces at the capital of Yin, which required bronze foundries for its wine and food vessels. In these foundries, skilled workers produced bronze weapons and ritual objects and elaborate ceremonial drinking and eating vessels, like the one pictured.

ritual vessels. They created hollow clay molds to hold the molten metal alloy, and then they removed the bronze objects after the liquid had cooled and solidified. The casting of modular components that artisans could assemble later promoted increased production and fueled the elites' extravagant uses of bronze vessels for burials. For example, archaeologists have unearthed a tomb at Anyang containing an enormous 1,925-pound bronze vessel; the Shang workshops had produced it around 1200 BCE. Another Anyang tomb from the same period contained 3,500 pounds of cast bronze.

The bronze industry of this period shows the high level not only of material culture (the physical objects produced) but also of cultural development. The Shang metalworking required extensive mining (and thus a large labor force), efficient casting, and a reproducible artistic style. The extraction of the resources was distinct from their conversion into goods: although the Shang state highly valued its artisans, it treated its copper miners as lowly tribute laborers.

By controlling access to tin and copper and to the production of bronze, the Shang kings prevented their rivals from forging bronze weapons and thus increased their own power and legitimacy. With their superior weapons, Shang armies could easily destroy armies wielding wooden clubs and stone-tipped spears. Moreover, the ruler enhanced his power by hiring artisans to record his feats for posterity. Shang workers produced large and small bronze vessels on which they delicately inscribed images of important events—particularly those showing the ruler in a significant role, such as a battle, a wedding, the birth of an heir, or an astrological sighting.

The Shang dynasts also understood the importance of agriculture for winning and maintaining power, so they did much to promote its development. In fact, the activities of local governors and the masses revolved around agriculture. The rulers controlled their own farms, which supplied food to the royal family, craftworkers, and army. New technologies led to increased food production. Farmers drained low-lying fields and cleared forested areas to expand the cultivation of millet, wheat, barley, and possibly rice. Their implements included stone plows, spades, and sickles. In addition, farmers cultivated silkworms and raised pigs, dogs, sheep, and oxen. To best use the land and increase production, they tracked the growing season. And to record the seasons, the Shang developed a twelve-month, 360-day lunar calendar; it contained leap months to maintain the proper relationship between months and seasons. The calendar also relieved fears about events such as solar and lunar eclipses by making them predictable.

As in other Afro-Eurasian states, the ruler's wealth and power depended on tribute from elites and allies. Elites supplied warriors and laborers, horses and cattle. Allies sent foodstuffs, soldiers, and workers and "assisted in the king's affairs"—perhaps by hunting, burning brush, or clearing land—in return for his help in defending against invaders and making predictions about the harvest. Commoners sent their tribute to the elites, who held the land as fiefs from the king. (Fiefs were grants, usually of land and occasionally of office, by kings and lords to subordinates.) Farmers transferred their surplus crops to the elite landholders (or to the ruler if they worked on his personal landholdings) on a regular schedule. Commoners also made payments in labor: some worked in the royal workshops producing bronze ritual vessels and armaments, such as dagger-axes, arrowheads, spearheads, helmets, shields, and chariot fittings; others labored to drain fields, clear land, build palaces, excavate tombs, or construct walls to protect towns or the capital.

Tribute could also take the form of turtle shells and cattle scapulas (shoulder blades), which the Shang used for divination (see below). Divining the future was a powerful way to legitimate royal power—and then to justify the right to collect more tribute. By placing themselves symbolically and literally at the center of all exchanges, the Shang kings reinforced their power over others.

SHANG SOCIETY AND BELIEFS

Both metalworking and agriculture contributed to the state's wealth and supported a complex society. The organizing principle of Shang society was a patrilineal ideal that traced descent back through the generations to a common male ancestor. Grandparents, parents, sons, and daughters lived and worked together. They held property in common, and male family elders took precedence. Women from other patrilines married into the family and won honor when they became mothers, particularly of sons.

The death ritual, which involved sacrificing humans to accompany the deceased in the next life, also reflected the social hierarchy. A member of the royal elite was often buried with his full entourage, including his wife, consorts, servants, chariots, horses, and drivers. The inclusion of personal slaves and servants indicates a belief that the familiar social hierarchy would continue in the afterlife. Modern Chinese historians have described the Shang as a "slave society," but the basis of its economy was not slave labor. Instead, the driving force was the tribute labor (in particular, metalworking and farming) of the commoners who constituted most of society.

The Shang state was a patrimonial theocracy: it claimed that the ruler at the top of the hierarchy derived his authority through guidance from ancestors and gods. Rulers therefore had to find ways to communicate with ancestors and foretell the future, and they relied on **divination**, much as did the rulers in Greece and Mesopotamia at this time. When diviners applied intense heat to the shoulder bones of cattle or to turtle shells, the bones or shells cracked. Diviners would interpret those cracks as an auspicious or inauspicious sign from the ancestors regarding royal plans and actions. (See Primary Source: The Oracle Bone.) On these bones, scribes subsequently inscribed the queries asked of the ancestors to confirm the diviners' interpretations. Thus, Shang writing began as a dramatic ritual performance in which the living responded to their ancestors' oracular signs.

In Shang theocracy, the ruler was also the head of a unified clergy. Because the ruler embodied both religious and political power, no independent priesthood emerged to challenge the royal family. Diviners and scribes were subordinate to the ruler and the royal pantheon of ancestors he represented. (Unlike in Mesopotamia and Egypt, rulers never entrusted diviners with independent action.) Ancestor worship sanctified Shang control and legitimized the rulers' lineage, ensuring that the ruling family kept all political and religious power.

Because the Shang gods were ancestral deities, all the rulers were deified when they died and ranked in descending chronological order. Thus, the primary Shang deity was Di, the High God (Shangdi), who was the founding ancestor of the Shang royal family. The Shang ruler who became a god was closer to the world of humans than the supreme Egyptian and Mesopotamian gods were, and he served to unite the world of the living with the world of the dead. Much as the Egyptians believed their pharaohs (supposedly born of human mothers and godlike fathers) ascended into heaven after their deaths, so the Shang believed their kings moved into a parallel other world when they died.

THE DEVELOPMENT OF WRITING IN CHINA

Although Shang scholars did not invent writing in East Asia, they perfected it. Oracle bones, so central to political and religious authority, are the primary evidence of early writing in China. Other written records may have been on materials that did not survive. Thus accidents of preservation may explain the major differences between the ancient texts in China (primarily divinations on bones) and in the Southwest Asian societies that impressed cuneiform on clay tablets (primarily for economic transactions, literary and religious documents, and historical records).

The inscriptions on oracle bones and bronzes leave no doubt that the Shang surpassed other peoples in northwestern China in their determination to leave records. After all, their governmental institutions and religious rituals were more complex than those of the peoples living nearby. However, in comparison with Mesopotamia and Egypt, the transformation of Shang record keeping (for example, questions to ancestors, lineages of rulers, or economic transactions) to literature (for example, myths about the founding of states) was slower.

As noted, Shang kings used writing to reinforce their position at the top of the hierarchy of royal families. And priests used it on oracle bones to address the other world and gain information about the future. Because the North China climate entered a warmer and wetter phase in the twelfth and eleventh centuries BCE, many divinations aimed at predicting rainfall for the sustenance of crops—in particular the staple crop, millet. Priests presented the living Shang ruler as the religious pivot among Di, the High God (who controlled the ever-important rain cycles), the ancestors, and their royal descendants.

In addition, like the Babylonian dynasts, later Shang rulers used an enlarged and increasingly powerful bureaucracy to promote their authority over tributary states and peoples. Imperial records of foods, wines, bronze vessels, and livestock are evidence of a centralized "royal household." During this period, the original archaic script evolved into the preclassical script seen on many bronze vessels. The preclassical script preceded the formal character-based system that has endured among elites to the present. The latter system sets apart the later Chinese, Japanese, Korean, and Vietnamese societies from the cultures in Mesopotamia and the Mediterranean that rely on syllable- and alphabet-based writing. (See Global Connections & Disconnections on p. 104.)

Primary Source

THE ORACLE BONE

About 3,000 years old, the oracle bone below dates from the Shang dynasty reign of King Wu Ding (c. 1200 BCE). Oracle bones enabled diviners to access the other world and provided the ruler with important information about the future. Shang kings often used divination to make political or military decisions and to predict the weather.

A partial translation of the left-hand side of this oracle bone reads

[Preface:] Crack making on *gui-si* day, Que divined:

[Charge:] In the next ten days there will be no disaster.

[Prognostication:] The king, reading the cracks, said, "There will be no harm; there will perhaps be the coming of alarming news."

[Verification:] When it came to the fifth day, *ding-you*, there really was the coming of alarming news from the west. Zhi Guo, reporting, said, "The Du Fang [a border people] are besieging in our eastern borders and have harmed two settlements." The Gong-fang also raided the fields of our western borders.

→ *What political or military decision do you think King Wu Ding might have made in response to the "alarming news"?*

→ *Why did Shang kings rely on oracle bones?*

SOURCE: This translation follows, with slight modifications by Bryan W. Van Norden, David N. Keightley, *Sources of Shang History* (Berkeley: University of California Press, 1978), p. 44.

THE SOUTH PACIFIC (2500 BCE–400 CE)

→ *How did Austronesian migrations affect the emergence of microsocieties in the South Pacific?*

As Afro-Eurasian populations grew, and migration and trade brought cultures together, some peoples took to the waters in search of opportunities or refuge. By comparing the vocabularies and grammatical similarities of languages spoken today by the tribal peoples in Taiwan, the Philippines, and Indonesia, we can trace the ancient Austronesian-speaking peoples back to coastal South China in the fourth millennium BCE. Their first wave of migrants reached the islands of Polynesia. A second wave from Taiwan around 2500 BCE again reached Polynesia and then went beyond into the South Pacific. By 2000 BCE these peoples had replaced the earlier inhabitants of the East Asian coastal islands, the hunter-gatherers known as the Negritos. They had migrated south from the Asian landmass around 28,000 BCE, during an ice age when the coastal Pacific islands were connected to the Asian mainland.

Austronesian Canoe. Early Austronesians crossed the Taiwan Straits and colonized key islands in the Pacific using double-outrigger canoes from sixty to one hundred feet long equipped with triangular sails. In good weather, such canoes could cover more than 120 miles in a day.

SEAFARING SKILLS

Using their remarkable double-outrigger canoes, which were 60 to 100 feet long and bore huge triangular sails, the early Austronesians crossed the Taiwan Straits and colonized key islands in the Pacific. Their vessels were much more advanced than the simple dugout canoes used in inland waterways. In good weather, double-outrigger canoes could cover more than 120 miles in a day. The invention of a stabilization device for deep-sea sailing sometime after 2500 BCE triggered further Austronesian expansion into the Pacific. By 400 CE, these nomads of the sea had reached most of the South Pacific except for Australia and New Zealand.

Their seafaring skills enabled the Austronesians to monopolize trade wherever they went (as the Phoenicians did during the first half of the first millennium BCE). Among their craftworkers were potters, who produced distinctive Lapita ware (bowls and vessels) on offshore islets or in coastal villages. Archaeological finds reveal that these canoe-building people also conducted inter-island trade in New Guinea after 1600 BCE. By four hundred years later they had reached Fiji, Samoa, and Tonga, according to the evidence from pottery fragments and the remains of domesticated animals.

ENVIRONMENT AND CULTURE

Pottery, stone tools, and domesticated crops and pigs characterized Austronesian settlements throughout the coastal islands and in the South Pacific. These cultural markers reached the Philippines from Taiwan. By 2500 BCE, according to archaeologists, the same cultural features had spread to the islands of Java, Sumatra, Celebes, Borneo, and Timor.

Austronesians arrived in Java and Sumatra in 2000 BCE; by 1600 BCE they were in Australia and New Guinea, although they failed to penetrate the interior, where descendants of the indigenous peoples still live. The Austronesians then ventured farther eastward into the South Pacific, apparently arriving in Samoa and Fiji in 1200 BCE and on mainland Southeast Asia in 1000 BCE. (See Map 3-5.)

Equatorial lands in the South Pacific have a tropical or subtropical climate and, in many places, fertile soils containing nutrient-rich volcanic ash. In this environment the Austronesians cultivated dry-land crops (yams and sweet potatoes), irrigated crops (more yams, which grew better in paddy fields or in rainy areas), and tree crops (breadfruit, bananas, and coconuts). In addition, colonized areas beyond the landmass, such as the islands of Indonesia, had labyrinthine coastlines rich in maritime resources, including coral reefs and mangrove swamps teeming with wildlife. Island hopping led the adventurers to encounter new food sources, but the shallow waters and reefs offered sufficient fish and shellfish for their needs.

In the South Pacific, the Polynesian descendants of the early Austronesians shared a common culture, language, technology, and stores of domesticated plants and animals. These later seafarers came from many different island communities (hence the name *Polynesian,* "belonging to many islands"), and after they settled down, their numbers grew. Their crop surpluses allowed more densely populated communities to support craft specialists and soldiers. Most settlements boasted ceremonial buildings to promote local solidarity and forts to provide defense. On larger islands, communities often cooperated and organized workforces to enclose ponds for fish production and to build and maintain large irrigation works for agriculture. In terms of

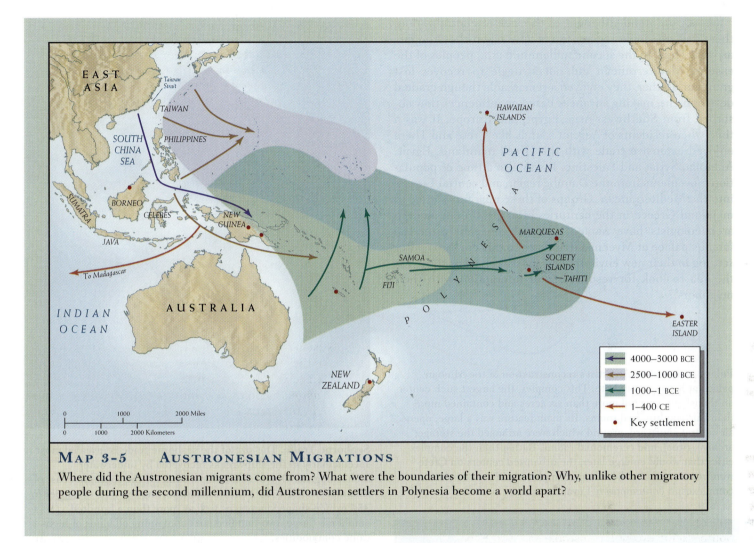

MAP 3-5   AUSTRONESIAN MIGRATIONS

Where did the Austronesian migrants come from? What were the boundaries of their migration? Why, unlike other migratory people during the second millennium, did Austronesian settlers in Polynesia become a world apart?

political structure, Polynesian communities ranged from tribal or village units to multi-island alliances that sometimes invaded other areas.

The Austronesians reached the Marquesas Islands, strategically located for northern and southern exploration, in the central Pacific around 200 CE. Over the next few centuries, some moved on to Easter Island to the south and Hawaii to the north. The immense thirty-ton stone structures on Easter Island represent the monumental Polynesian architecture produced after their arrival. In separate migrations they traversed the Indian Ocean westward and arrived at the island of Madagascar by the sixth century CE. Along the way, they transmitted crops such as the banana to East Africa.

The expansion of East Asian peoples throughout the South Pacific and their trade back and forth did not, however, integrate the islands into the mainland culture. Expansion could not overcome the tendency of these **microsocieties**, dispersed across a huge ocean, toward fragmentation and isolation.

MICROSOCIETIES IN THE AEGEAN WORLD

→ *How did long-distance trade influence the Aegean world?*

In the region around the Aegean Sea, the islands and the mainland of present-day Greece, no single power emerged before the second millennium BCE. Settled agrarian communities developed into local polities linked only by trade and culture. Fragmentation was the norm—in part because the landscape had no great riverine systems or large common plain. In terms of its fragmentation, the island world of the eastern Mediterranean initially resembled that of the South Pacific.

Cerro Sechin Artifact. This stela of a warrior brandishing a club was discovered in the Casma Valley in present-day Peru and is a good example of the many striking stone sculptures found in this area.

fish; this was a staple that, when dried, was hardly perishable and easy to transport. The rivers flowing down from the Andean mountains fanned out through the desert, often carving out basins suitable for agriculture. And where the mountains rose from the Pacific, rainfall and higher altitudes favored extensive pasturelands. Here roamed wild llamas and alpacas—difficult as beasts of burden, but valued for their wool in textile production. Such ecological diversity within a limited area promoted greater trade among subregions and towns. Indeed, the interchange of manioc (root of the cassava plant), chili peppers, dried fish, and wool gave rise to the commercial networks that could support political ones.

Communities on the coast, in the riverbeds, or in the mountain valleys were small but numerous. They took shape around central plazas, most of which had large platforms with special burial chambers for elders and persons of importance. Clusters of dwellings surrounded these centers. Much of what we know about political and economic transactions among these communities—as well as long-distance trade and statecraft—comes from the offerings and ornaments left in the burial chambers. Painted gourds, pottery, and fine textiles illustrate the increasing contact among cultures, often bound in alliances. For instance, marriage between noble families could strengthen a pact or confederation.

One early site known as Aspero reveals how a local community evolved into a form of chiefship, with a political elite and diplomatic and trading ties with neighbors. Temples straddled the top of the central platform, and the large structure at the center boasted lavish ornamentation. Also, there is evidence that smaller communities around Aspero sent

Chronology

	MAJOR TRENDS	2000 BCE	1500 BCE
NORTHERN AFRICA	Global warming and drying cycle beginning 2000 BCE	2010–1640 BCE Middle Kingdom in Egypt — ◆ 2000 BCE Development of chariot technology	
SOUTHWEST ASIA		1800–1600 BCE Old Hittite Kingdom in Anatolia / ◆----◆1792–1750 BCE Hammurapi's Babylonia	
SOUTH ASIA		1500 BCE Vedic migration into Indus River valley begins ◆	
EAST ASIA		1600 BCE Shang State emerges ◆	
THE AEGEAN		2000–1600 BCE Minoan culture / 1850–1200 BCE Mycenaean culture	
SOUTH PACIFIC		2500–1000 BCE Austronesian migration to East Asian coastal islands	
EUROPE			Rise of small chieftains ◆
CENTRAL ANDES		Emergence of small-scale political confederations 1700 BCE ◆	

crops (fruits) and fish (anchovies) as part of an intercommunity system of mutual dependence.

Not all politics among the valley peoples of Peru consisted of trade and diplomacy, however. In the Casma Valley near the Pacific coast, a clay and stone architectural complex at Cerro Sechín has revealed a much larger sprawl of dwellings and plazas dating back to 1700 BCE. Around the community's central structure stood a wall composed of hundreds of massive stone tablets, carved with ornate etchings of warriors, battles, prisoners, executions, and human body parts. The warriors' clothing is simple and rustic, and the main weapon resembles a club. Clearly, warfare accompanied the first expressions of statecraft in the Americas.

CONCLUSION

The second millennium BCE was an era of migrations, warfare, and kingdom building in Afro-Eurasia. Whereas riverine societies had flourished in the fourth and third millennia BCE in Mesopotamia, Egypt, and the Indus Valley, now droughts and deserts shook the agrarian foundations of their economies. Old states crumbled; from the steppes and plateaus nomadic pastoralists and transhumant herders descended in search of food, grazing lands, and plunder. As transhumant herders pressed into the riverine societies, the social and political fabric of these communities changed. Likewise, horse-riding nomads from steppe communities in inner Eurasia conquered and settled in the agrarian states, bringing key innovations. Foremost were the horse chariots, which became a military catalyst sparking the evolution from smaller states to large kingdoms encompassing crowded cities and vast hinterlands. The nomads and herders also adopted many of the settled peoples' beliefs and customs. On land and sea, migrating peoples created zones of long-distance trade that linked agrarian societies.

The Nile Delta, the basin of the Tigris and Euphrates rivers, the Indus Valley, and the Yellow River basin were worlds apart before 2000 BCE. Now trade and conquest brought many of these societies into closer contact, especially those in Southwest Asia and the Nile River basin. Here, the interaction even led to an elaborate system of diplomatic relations. The first territorial states appeared in this millennium, composed of communities living under common laws and customs. An alliance of farmers and warriors united agrarian wealth and production with political power to create and defend territorial boundaries. The new arrangements overshadowed the nomads' historic role as predators and enabled them to become military elites. Through taxes and drafted labor, villagers repaid their rulers for local security and state-run diplomacy.

The rhythms of state formation differed where regimes were not closely packed together. In East Asia, the absence of strong rivals allowed the emerging Shang dynasty to develop more gradually. Where landscapes had sharper divisions— as in the island archipelagos of the South China Sea, or in Europe—small-scale, decentralized microsocieties emerged. This was true above all in the Americas, where the lack of

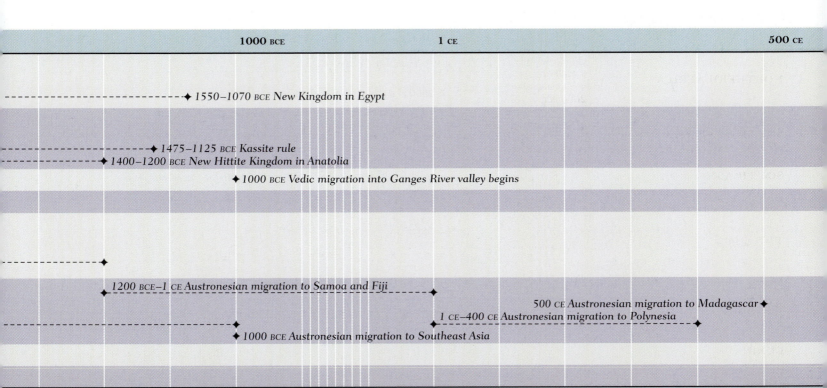

1000 BCE   1 CE   500 CE

◆ 1550–1070 BCE *New Kingdom in Egypt*

◆ 1475–1125 BCE *Kassite rule*
◆ 1400–1200 BCE *New Hittite Kingdom in Anatolia*
◆ 1000 BCE *Vedic migration into Ganges River valley begins*

1200 BCE–1 CE *Austronesian migration to Samoa and Fiji*

500 CE *Austronesian migration to Madagascar* ◆
1 CE–400 CE *Austronesian migration to Polynesia*

◆ 1000 BCE *Austronesian migration to Southeast Asia*

wheeled vehicles and horses made long-distance communication much more challenging—and inhibited rulers' territorial ambitions. Here, too, microsocieties were the norm. But fragmentation is not the same as isolation. Even peoples on the fringes and the subjects of microsocieties were not entirely secluded from the increasing flows of technologies, languages, goods, and migrants.

Review and research materials are available at StudySpace: Ⓢ WWNORTON.COM/STUDYSPACE

KEY TERMS

chariots (p. 87)

divination (p. 110)

Hammurapi's Code (p. 99)

microsocieties (p. 113)

polities (p. 90)

territorial state (p. 90)

transhumant migrants (p. 86)

vassal states (p. 99)

Vedic people (p. 101)

STUDY QUESTIONS

1. Explain the differences between nomadic pastoral and transhumant migrations. How did each shape Afro-Eurasian history during the second millennium BCE?

2. Analyze the impact of the domestication of horses on Afro-Eurasia during this period. How did this development affect both nomadic and settled societies?

3. Define the term *territorial state*. In what areas of Afro-Eurasia did this new form of political organization emerge and thrive?

4. Compare and contrast political developments in Mesopotamia and Egypt during this period. To what extent did outside groups influence each region?

5. Identify the great territorial states of western Asia and North Africa during the second half of the second millennium BCE, and describe their relationships with one another. How did they pioneer international diplomacy?

6. Compare and contrast Austronesian and Indo-European migrations. What impact did each people have on the regions it settled?

7. Describe the Shang state in East Asia. How was it similar to and different from the territorial states of western Afro-Eurasia?

8. Compare and contrast the islands of the South Pacific to those in the eastern Mediterranean. Why were societies in the South Pacific more fragmented and isolated than those in the eastern Mediterranean?

9. Explain why early state structures were smaller and less integrated in Europe and the Central Andes than the territorial states that arose elsewhere. How similar and different were the early state structures in Europe and the Central Andes?

4

FIRST EMPIRES AND COMMON CULTURES IN AFRO-EURASIA, 1250–325 BCE

Sennacherib—ruler of the Assyrian Empire, which spanned much of Southwest Asia early in the seventh century BCE—writes that at the end of one successful campaign he took "200,150 people, great and small, male and female, horses, mules, asses, camels, and sheep without number. I brought away from them and counted them my spoil." Those who resisted were dragged back to Assyria and forced to labor on Sennacherib's expanding, magnificent capital, Nineveh, and toiled on the immense irrigation works to open up new agricultural frontiers.

The booty that Sennacherib took away was unheard of in earlier ages, even within the great territorial states of ancient Egypt and Mesopotamia. The immensity of the conquest highlights the arrival of a new era that involved states with even larger geographical, political, economic, and cultural ambitions and achievements. In fact, the prosperity and bounty of the first millennium BCE were the fruits of a spasm of disorder across Afro-Eurasia. As the states of the previous millennium collapsed, their successors were replacements—not descendants. The key factor

125

shaping human development now was warfare spurred by military innovation.

Some of the warrior/political leaders of this era came from the fringes of formerly powerful empires and city-states, driven to challenge these centers of power when radical changes in climate made their home territories less viable. They established hybrid societies in Assyria, Persia, Vedic parts of South Asia, and Zhou China where new imperial ideologies and religious beliefs were elaborated in support of the new states. Under the protection of fierce warriors, cities and hinterlands came together under a single ruler. Farming yields again increased, and populations grew. The expansion of territorial power via conquest contributed to the integration of increasingly larger states, some of which became the first empires. Also, on the fringes of formerly great empires microsocieties arose and made significant contributions to human development: the seafaring Phoenicians provided Afro-Eurasia a simplified alphabet, the Israelites espoused a strict monotheism, and Greek city-states came to the fore and even began to challenge the power of the Persian Empire.

FORCES OF UPHEAVAL AND THE RISE OF EARLY EMPIRES

→ *What were the factors that led to the rise of early empires?*

Although the new, bigger states built on the existing achievements of earlier complex societies, they also developed in response to new forces. The first factor was *climate change*. Beginning around 1200 BCE another warming phase gripped Afro-Eurasia, with varying effects across the landmass. In some areas prolonged drought caused social upheavals and migrations: it led nomadic and seminomadic populations that had lived at the edge of settled societies to leave their home territories and move into the lands of the settled communities. In other regions the warming produced rapid population growth and led to soil depletion, forcing peoples to leave their homes in search of food and fertile land. (See Map 4-1.) Renewed migrations overturned urban societies and destroyed the administrative centers of kings, priests, and dynasties, leaving the way open for new states to develop.

A second factor was the large-scale and violent *movement of peoples*, often connected with climate change. Invaders moved out of loosely organized peripheral societies and assaulted the urban centers and territorial kingdoms of mainland Greece, Crete, Anatolia, Mesopotamia, and Egypt. Marauders from the Mediterranean basin and the Syrian desert upset the diplomatic relations and the elaborate system of international trade that had linked Southwestern Asia and North Africa. In East Asia, nomads from the steppes of Inner Eurasia tangled with the Shang authorities in the Yellow River valley and eventually overwhelmed the regime. In the Indus Valley, waves of nomads pressed down from the northwest, lured by fertile lands to the south. Once there, they became an agrarian folk. The process of settling down took centuries, but by the time of Alexander the Great (see Chapter 6) the splendor of India had become legendary.

The mingling of nomadic and settled societies provided opportunities for ambitious men to expand the old territorial kingdoms or to create new states that went on to conquer other kingdoms. Gradually, a new political organization came into being: the empire. (An **empire** is a group of states or different ethnic groups under a single sovereign power.)

Focus Questions

◎ WWNORTON.COM/STUDYSPACE

→ *What were the factors that led to the rise of early empires?*

→ *How was the Neo-Assyrian Empire different from earlier territorial kingdoms?*

→ *In what ways was the Persian Empire similar to the Neo-Assyrian Empire, and in what ways was it different?*

→ *How did the growth of the first empires in Southwest Asia affect the broader region?*

→ *How did South Asia become more integrated despite the absence of an imperial state?*

→ *To what extent was the Zhou state similar to contemporary Southwest Asian empires?*

Empires connected distant regions through common languages (or through individuals fluent in multiple languages), unifying political systems, and shared religious beliefs. Some regions did not experience the rise of empire. The peoples of South Asia were united less through shared political systems than through shared cultures and religious beliefs. Trade also united regions. For example, the commercial activities of coastal cities such as Byblos and Tyre reached as far as—and sometimes farther than—the empires' military conquests. There were great variations within and across Afro-Eurasia.

A third factor was *technological change*. Pack camels, seaworthy vessels, iron tools for cultivation, and iron weapons for warfare were vital new ingredients in the rise of imperial institutions. The first-millennium empires were centralized and militarized states that used force to expand their boundaries, and the role of changing technology was significant in this process.

PACK CAMELS

The camel became the chief overland agent of change during this period, helping to open up trade routes across the Syrian and Arabian deserts. The fat stored in camels' humps allows them to survive long journeys and harsh desert conditions, and thick pads under their hoofs enable them to walk smoothly over sand. First to be domesticated was the one-humped camel called the *dromedary,* or Arab camel native to the Sahara Desert. Other peoples, probably in central Asia, later domesticated the bigger, two-humped Bactrian camel. A stockier and hardier animal, it was better able than the dromedary to survive the scorching heat of northern Iran and the frozen winters along the route from China that later

became the Silk Road (so named because silk was a major product carried along this route).

NEW SHIPS

New shipbuilding technologies had been developing rapidly since 1600 BCE and now were making a significant impact. Boats that had once been designed for limited transport on rivers and lakes and along shorelines could now be built stronger and bigger for sailing on seas. These new, truly seafaring ships boasted larger and better-reinforced hulls, and stronger masts and rigging that allowed billowing sails to harness wind power effectively. These innovations, along with smaller ones in steering and ballast (among others), propelled bold mariners to venture out across large bodies of open water like the Mediterranean Sea.

IRON

Although far more abundant than the tin and copper used to make bronze, iron is a harder substance to mold and hammer into shape. (**Iron** is a malleable metal found in combined forms almost everywhere in the world; it became the most important and widely used metal in world history after the Bronze Age.) To make iron implements, metalworkers learned to apply intense heat to soften the ore and remove its impurities. Subsequently they discovered that by adding carbon to the iron they could make an early form of steel. When the technology to smelt and harden iron advanced, iron tools and weapons replaced those made of bronze. The ability to use iron was a staggering breakthrough that leaped across territorial and cultural borders.

Camels. Dromedary camels (*left*) are good draft animals for travel and domestic work in the deserts of Arabia, Afghanistan, and India. Two-hump camels (*right*) are much bigger than dromedary camels. They are more suited to the extreme dry and cold weather in Iran and central Asia.

NORTH SEA

BALTIC SEA

EUROPE

URAL MOUNTAINS

Dnieper R.

Dniester R.

Volga R.

ARAL SEA

BLACK SEA

CASPIAN SEA

Danube R.

CENTR

A F R O

MYCENAEANS • Troy
AEGEAN
SEA
Tiryns

ANATOLIA

Tigris R.

HITTITES • Nineveh
MITANNI • Ashur

CRETE

CYPRUS

SYRIAN
DESERT

Euphrates R.

ELAMITES

ZAGROS MTS.

IRANIAN PLATEAU

MEDITERRANEAN SEA

LEVANT

Tyre •
Jericho •
Jerusalem

Babylon •

SOUTHWEST ASIA

Persian Gulf

NORTH AFRICA

A F R I C A

Amarna •
EGYPT
• Thebes

ARABIAN
PENINSULA

S A H A R A

Sub-Saharan periphery:
Increased population
and gradual adoption
of agriculture

Nile R.

RED SEA

NUBIA

S U B - S A H A R A N   A F R I C A

Niger R.

Tropical woodlands:
Yams and palm nuts
cultivated

ATLANTIC
OCEAN

Congo R.

Lake
Victoria

▮	Urban cores
▮	Vedic settlement by 900 BCE
←	Nomadic incursions (sea peoples)
←	Nomadic incursions (pastoralists)
▪	Destroyed site
•	City

MAP 4-1   AFRO-EURASIA, 1200 BCE—URBAN CORES AND NOMADIC INVADERS

Nomadic incursions shattered the social and political status quo in Afro-Eurasia at this time. While destroying old polities, these migrations fostered a new social and political order in a variety of regions. Where did nomadic groups originate, and to where did they migrate? What is a major difference between the invasions of the Sea Peoples in this period versus pastoral invasions? Why do you think historians' knowledge of these nomadic incursions is limited and sketchy?

A S I A

INNER ASIA

Lake Baikal

Lake Balkas

ALTAI MOUNTAINS

GOBI DESERT

TIEN SHAN

AL ASIA

TAKLAMAKAN DESERT

EAST ASIA

Yellow R.

SHANG CHINA

PAMIR MTS.

HINDU KUSH MTS.

HIMALAYA MOUNTAINS

Indus R.

Mithila

Ganges R.

Yangzi R.

THAR DESERT

SOUTH ASIA

DECCAN PLATEAU

Dantapura

Ganges Valley: Rice-farming villages

Bay of Bengal

SOUTHEAST ASIA

SOUTH CHINA SEA

Maritime Southeast Asia: Slow transition from hunting and gathering to agriculture

ARABIAN SEA

Mainland Southeast Asia: Rice-farming villages, bronze tools and ornaments

INDIAN   OCEAN

0   500   1000 Miles

0   500   1000 Kilometers

MAIN THEMES

→ *Climate change, nomadic migrations, and invasions from neighboring states lead to the collapse of territorial states across Afro-Eurasia.*
→ *The first great empires emerge, based on innovations in warfare, administration, commerce, metallurgy (iron), and agricultural production.*
→ *South Asia and smaller borderland states like the Greeks, Phoenicians, and Israelites innovate and build common cultures in nonpolitical ways.*

FOCUS ON *First Empires and Smaller States*

Ancient Near East
◆ Neo-Assyrians use raw military power and massive population relocations to build and maintain the world's first empire.
◆ Persians rely on persuasion and tolerance to build a cosmopolitan empire.

Mediterranean World
◆ Greeks, Phoenicians, and Israelites show the advantages of small-scale states with innovations in writing, trading, and religious thought.

South Asia
◆ Vedic peoples build a unified common culture through religious and economic ties.

China
◆ Zhou dynasty constructs a powerful tributary state and legitimates its rule via the mandate of heaven doctrine (good governance and upright behavior = legitimate rule).

Iron also helped cause a revolutionary shift in agrarian techniques. Innovators learned to tip their plowshares with forged-iron edges that they could easily shape and resharpen. With the iron-tipped plow, for instance, cultivators could clear the dense jungle of the Ganges plain and repeatedly till the topsoil to keep it weed-free and to enhance its quality. Increasingly, farmers did not have to rely on floods to restore layers of rich soil to their fields; instead, they could break the sod and turn it over to bring up fertile subsoils. The effects of this transformation drove the agrarian frontier far beyond the traditional floodplains of riverbank settings. Agricultural developments thus provided the technological basis for supporting larger, more integrated societies linked by roads and canals.

The final developments driving change were *innovations in military and administrative control.* Indeed, the expansion of the first empires depended on military might. For example, with an army wielding the most advanced weapons and armor, the Assyrian king led annual campaigns to establish and reinforce his control over the countryside. Deportations were another strategy to break resisters' unity, to provide slave labor in parts of the empire that needed manpower, and to integrate the realm. Throughout the 300 years of their rule, the Assyrians constructed an infrastructure of roads, garrisons,

and relay stations throughout the entire territory, making it easier to transfer information and move troops. Moreover, they made subject peoples send tribute in the form of grains, animals, raw materials and people, which they used to build imperial cities and to enrich the royal coffers. In later centuries these practices would become common among empires, with varying degrees of brutality as a method of control.

THE NEO-ASSYRIAN EMPIRE

→ *How was the Neo-Assyrian Empire different from earlier territorial kingdoms?*

The narrative of the rise of empires begins in Southwest Asia with the Neo-Assyrian Empire (911–612 BCE), successor to the "Old" and "Middle" Assyrian states of the second millennium. The Neo-Assyrians perfected techniques of imperial rule that others imitated (not only their successors but also

Greeks and Romans) and that ultimately became standard in many ancient and modern empires. In particular the Neo-Assyrian state revealed the raw military side of imperial rule: constant and harsh warfare, brutal exploitation of subjects, and an ideology that glorified imperial masters and justified the subjugation and harsh treatment of subjects. In this regard the Neo-Assyrians were legendary for their ruthless efficiency, reliance on terror (such as cutting off ears, lips, and fingers; castration; and mass executions), deportations, and intimidation to crush their adversaries.

Neo-Assyrian rulers had ambitions beyond governing their own people: they also wanted to subordinate peoples in distant lands and control those areas' resources, trading cities, and trade routes. By the time that the state's full-scale expansion was under way, all institutions of the Neo-Assyrian state were focused on becoming an empire. They succeeded by the mid-seventh century BCE with the conquest of Southwest Asia and parts of North Africa, including Egypt (see Map 4-2).

EXPANSION INTO AN EMPIRE

The heartland of Assyria cradled the ancient cities of Ashur and Nineveh on the upper reaches of the Tigris River. By the ninth century BCE the Assyrian state had become strong enough to expand westward; by 824 BCE it dominated the lands and peoples all the way to the Mediterranean, controlling trade and tribute from the entire area.

The Assyrians had several advantages. First, their armies were hardened and disciplined professional troops led by officers who rose high in the ranks because of their merit, not their birth. In addition, they perfected the combined deployment of infantry and cavalry (horse-mounted

warriors equipped with iron weapons) together with horse-drawn chariots armored with iron plates and carrying expert archers. The Assyrians were also skilled siege warriors, using iron to build massive wheeled siege towers and to cap their battering rams. No city walls could stand against them for long. Finally, the Assyrian armies were massive. At the height of their power in the ninth century BCE, the rulers sent 120,000 soldiers on the annual campaign to the west. (In contrast, Chinese armies would not reach this scale for another 500 years.)

Assyrian expansion provoked fierce but ultimately futile opposition, particularly from the small independent states in the west. Resisting populations were devastated—they were

MAP 4-2   THE NEO-ASSYRIAN EMPIRE

The Neo-Assyrians built the first strong regional empire in Afro-Eurasia. In the process, they faced the challenge of promoting order and stability throughout their diverse realm. Where did the Neo-Assyrian Empire expand? Which parts of the empire were "the Land of Ashur," and which were "the Land under the Yoke of Ashur"? Why do you think expansion after 720 BCE led to the empire's destruction?

Tiglath Pileser III. The walls of the Assyrian palaces were lined with stone slabs carved with images of the victories of the king. This fragmentary slab from the palace of Tiglath Pileser III originally decorated the wall of his palace at Nimrud. It shows the inhabitants and their herds being forced to leave after the defeat of their town by the Assyrians. Below is Tiglath Pileser III, shaded by his royal umbrella, in his war chariot.

relocated through forced deportations, and their lands were annexed. The Assyrian state grew even more ambitious when a talented military leader usurped the throne. Naming himself Tiglath Pileser III (r. 745–728 BCE) after an earlier reform-minded Assyrian king, he reorganized the Assyrian state to centralize power in royal hands and thus prepare for a second phase of imperial expansion and consolidation. He took away the nobles' rights to own and inherit land and other wealth, and he replaced hereditary provincial governors with appointed officials whom the center of the empire controlled. He also reinstated aggressive, expansionary annual military campaigns. But the destruction and mass deportations carried out by his armies intensified the conquered peoples' hatred of the Assyrians.

INTEGRATION AND CONTROL OF THE EMPIRE

A unique imperial structure, deportations, and the labors of subjugated peoples, and an imperial ideology were the defining features of the Neo-Assyrian Empire. While they were hugely important to the success of the empire, they also contributed to its ultimate failure.

STRUCTURE OF THE EMPIRE The Assyrian rulers divided their empire into two parts and ruled them in different ways. The core, which the Assyrians called the "Land of Ashur," included the lands between the Zagros Mountains and the Euphrates River. The king's appointees governed these interior lands, whose inhabitants had to supply food for the temple of the national god Ashur, manpower for the god's residence in the city of Ashur, and officials to carry out the state's business.

The other area, known as "the Land under the Yoke of Ashur," lay outside of Assyria proper. Its inhabitants were not considered Assyrians; rather, their local rulers held power as vassals of Assyria. Instead of supplying agricultural goods and manpower, these vassal states had the greater burden of delivering massive amounts of tribute in the form of gold and silver. This wealth went directly to the king, who used it to pay for his extravagant court and ever-increasing military costs. After the reforms of Tiglath Pileser III, even more lands came into the Land of Ashur proper. While such incorporation eliminated the oppressive need to pay tribute, the empire continued to harshly administer its programs of forced Assyrianization. (Many empires in later centuries, including the Persian, Roman, and even the modern-day British and French empires, would use this strategy as well.)

DEPORTATION AND FORCED LABOR In the empire's early years, the army comprised Assyrians who went to war on annual summer campaigns. Later, when campaigning became year-round, the army grew to several hundred thousand men mobilized to protect and extend the imperial holdings. These forces included not only Assyrians but also men from the conquered peoples. By the seventh century BCE, the Assyrians

Capture of an Egyptian City. This stone panel from the palace in Nineveh shows warriors scaling walls with ladders during Ashurbanipal's campaign against Egypt (mid-seventh century BCE).

assigned different ethnic groups to specialized military functions: Phoenicians from the Levant provided ships and sailors for battle in the Mediterranean, Medes from the Iranian plateau served as the king's bodyguards, and charioteers from Israel subdued rebellious western provinces.

To accomplish its goals, the Assyrian state needed huge labor forces for agricultural work and for enormous building projects. Since so many Assyrians served in the army, the state recruited most agricultural and construction workers from conquered peoples. Over three centuries the Neo-Assyrian state relocated more than 4 million people—a practice that not only supported its stupendous work projects but also undermined local resistance efforts.

ASSYRIAN IDEOLOGY AND PROPAGANDA   The Neo-Assyrian Empire put forth an imperial ideology to support and justify its system of expansion, exploitation, and inequality. (An **ideology** is the dominant set of ideas of a widespread culture or movement.) Even in the early stages of expansion, Assyrian inscriptions and art expressed a divinely determined destiny that drove the regime to expand westward toward the Mediterranean Sea. According to the ideology, the national god Ashur commanded all Assyrians to support the forcible growth of the empire, whose goal was to establish and maintain order and keep an ever-threatening cosmic chaos at bay. Only the god Ashur and his agent, the king, could bring universal order. The king conducted holy war to transform the known world into the well-regulated Land of Ashur, intensifying his campaign of terror and expansion with elaborate propaganda. This propaganda, based on a detailed historical record of countless military and political victories, proclaimed that Assyria's triumph was inevitable. Its main focus was the nobles, whom the king and the empire relied on for support.

The rulers devised three mutually reinforcing types of propaganda campaigns. First, they used elaborate architectural complexes to stage ceremonial displays of pomp and power (as in Egypt and China). Second, they made sure that different types of texts glorified the king and the empire. These texts were recited at state occasions, inscribed on monuments, written in annals about the kings' military campaigns and achievements, and buried at propitious places in public buildings, where only the eyes of Ashur could view them. (See Primary Source: The Banquet Stele of Assurnasirpal II.) Third, state officials placed images glorifying the king and the Assyrian army on palace walls. These images depicted the army's force, showing all who resisted being smashed into submission—their towns burned; their men killed, impaled on stakes, or flayed; and their women and children deported along with any male survivors.

The commitment to "accurately" depict the regime's triumphal events was evident not only on palace walls but also in a uniquely Assyrian literary form called **annals** (historical records, usually arranged chronologically). Constituting a milestone in human history, these documents illustrate how communication and writing promoted the formation of organized

The Annals of Ashurbanipal. This baked clay faceted cylinder carries a portion of the annals of Ashurbanipal. It was found at Nineveh along with thousands of other tablets preserved in his famous library. The annals of Ashurbanipal were detailed, almost novelistic accounts of his military and civic achievements. Unlike earlier annals, there is first-person discourse, indirect discourse, flashbacks, and lively description of events and places.

states. Court scribes inscribed the annals in cuneiform on stone slabs, tablets, and clay cylinders, detailing each campaign in the yearly report of the king's achievements. These written compositions, like the images, never gave any indication that the Assyrians did or could lose a battle.

ASSYRIAN SOCIAL STRUCTURE AND POPULATION

The Assyrians' iron-fisted rule rested on a rigid social hierarchy. Alone at the top was the king, who as the sole agent of the god Ashur conducted war to expand the Land of Ashur. Below were the state's military elites, handsomely rewarded through gifts of land, silver, and exemptions from royal taxes. Over time, they became the noble class and intimates of the king, replacing the older landed elites who lost their resources after Tiglath Pileser III reorganized the empire's landholdings. Elites often controlled vast estates that included both the land and the local people who worked it. The throne and the elites owned the most populous part of the society, the peasantry, in which various

Primary Source

THE BANQUET STELE OF ASSURNASIRPAL II

Starting in the third millennium BCE, the rulers of Mesopotamia used architecture to signal their power to their subjects. When a change of dynasty or other reorganization of power occurred, rulers would build new palaces or even move their capital city. In the ninth century, Assurnasirpal II established Assyria as an imperial power that intended to expand and consolidate its economic and political control of surrounding peoples. After moving the capital and building a new palace and royal precinct, he called all of the empire's peoples to a ten-day celebration. This remarkable event was commemorated by an inscribed stele (an inscribed stone pillar) that he erected next to the throne room.

(102) When Ashur-nasir-apli, king of Assyria, consecrated the joyful palace, the palace full of wisdom, in Kalach [and] invited inside Ashur, the great lord, and the gods of the entire land; 1,000 fat oxen, 1,000 calves [and] sheep of the stable, 14,000 . . . -sheep which belonged to the goddess Ishtar my mistress, 200 oxen which belonged to the goddess Ishtar my mistress, 1,000 . . . -sheep, 1,000 spring lambs, 500 *ayalu*-deer, 500 deer, 1,000 ducks [*iṣṣū rū rabûtu*], 500 ducks [*usū*], 500 geese, 1,000 wild geese, 1,000 *qaribu*-birds, 10,000 pigeons, 10,000 wild pigeons, 10,000 small birds, 10,000 fish, 10,000 jerboa, 10,000 eggs, 10,000 loaves of bread, 10,000 jugs of beer, 10,000 skins of wine, 10,000 containers of grain [and] sesame, 10,000 pots of hot . . . , 1,000 boxes of greens, 300 [containers of] oil, 300 [containers of] malt, 300 [containers of] mixed *raqqatu*-plants, 100 [containers of] *kudimmus*, 100 [containers of] . . . , 100 [containers of] parched barley, 100 [containers of] *ubuḫšennu*-grain, 100 [containers of] fine *billatu*, 100 [containers of] pomegranates, 100 [containers of] grapes, 100 [containers of] mixed *zamrus*, 100 [containers of] pistachios, 100 [containers of] . . . , 100 [containers of] *ionions*, 100 [containers of] garlic, 100 [containers of] *kunipḫus*, 100 *bunches* of turnips, 100 [containers of] *ḫinḫinu*-seeds, 100 [containers of] *giddū*, 100 [containers of] honey, 100 [containers of] ghee, 100 [containers of] roasted *abšu*-seeds, 100 [containers of] roasted *šu'u*-seeds, 100 [containers of] *karkartu*-plants, 100 [containers of] *tiatu*-plants, 100 [containers of] mustard, 100 [containers of] milk, 100 [containers of] cheese, 100 bowls of *mīzu*-drink, 100 stuffed oxen, 10 homers of shelled *dukdu*-nuts, 10 homers of shelled pistachios, 10 homers of . . . , 10 homers of *ḫabbaququ*, 10 homers of dates, 10 homers of *titip*, 10 homers of cumin, 10 homers of *saḫūnu*, 10 homers of . . . , 10 homers of *andaḫšu*, 10 homers of *šišanibu*, 10 homers of *simberu*-fruit, 10 homers of *ḫašū*, 10 homers of fine oil, 10 homers of fine aromatics, 10 homers of . . . , 10 homers of *naṣṣabu*-gourds, 10 homers of *zinzimmu*-onions, 10 homers of olives; when I consecrated the palace of Kalach, 47,074 men [and] women who were invited from every part of my land, 5,000 dignitaries [and] envoys of the people of the lands Suhu, Hindanu, Patinu, Hatti, Tyre, Sidon, Gurgumu, Malidu, Hubushkia, Gilzanu, Kumu, [and] Musasiru, 16,000 people of Kalach, [and] 1,500 *zarīqū* of my palace, all of them—altogether 69,574 [including] those summoned from all lands and the people of Kalach—for ten days I gave them food, I gave them drink, I had them bathed, I had them anointed. [Thus] did I honour them [and] send them back to their lands in peace and joy.

→ *What does the extensive list of food and drink listed in the text tell the reader about the size and geographical reach of the empire and the role of trade in it?*

→ *What techniques, as reflected in the text of the Banquet Stele, did Assurnasirpal use to build loyalty among his subjects?*

SOURCE: *Assyrian Royal Inscriptions, Part 2: From Tiglath-pileser I to Ashur-nasir-apli II*, compiled and translated by Albert Kirk Grayson, vol. 2 of *Records of the Ancient Near East*, edited by Hans Goedicke (Wiesbaden: Otto Harrassowitz, 1976), pp. 175–76.

categories of workers had differing privileges. Those who were enslaved because they could not pay their debts were allowed to marry nonslave partners, conduct financial transactions, and even own property with other slaves attached. In contrast, foreigners who were enslaved after being captured had no rights—they were forced to do hard manual labor on the state's monumental building projects. Those who were forcibly relocated were not slaves but became attached to the lands that they had to work. Families were small and lived on modest plots of land, where they raised vegetables and planted vineyards.

Women in Assyria were far more restricted than their counterparts in the earlier periods of Sumerian and Old Babylonian Mesopotamia (see Chapter 3). Under the Assyrians' patriarchal social system, women had almost no control over their lives. Because all inheritance passed through the male line, it was crucial that a man be certain of the paternity of the children borne by his wives. As a result, all interactions between men and women outside of the family were highly restricted. The Middle Assyrians introduced the practice of veiling in the thirteenth century BCE, requiring it of all respectable women. Indeed, prostitutes who serviced the men of the army and worked in the taverns were forbidden to wear the veil, so that their revealed faces and hair could signal their disreputable status. Any prostitute found wearing the veil would be dragged to the top of the city wall, stripped of her clothing, flogged, and sometimes even killed.

The queens of Assyria obeyed the same social norms, but their lives were more comfortable and varied than the commoners'. They lived in a separate part of the palace with servants who were either women slaves or eunuchs (castrated males). Though Assyrian queens rarely wielded genuine power, they enjoyed respect and recognition, especially in the role of mother of the king. In fact, a queen could serve as regent for her son if the king died while his heir was still a child. Such was the case of Sammuramat, who served as regent from 810 to 806 BCE, successfully ruling the empire until her son came of age.

THE INSTABILITY OF THE ASSYRIAN EMPIRE

At their peak, the Assyrians controlled most of the lands stretching from Persia to Egypt. This was an awesome feat, but the empire was unstable nonetheless. Assyrian commanders had to position occupying armies far and wide to keep subjects in line; and as the propaganda machine ramped up, so did discontent among the nobility. When subject peoples rose up, they often used the same types of iron weapons on which their tormentors had relied. Once a successful rebellion challenged the Assyrian worldview of invincibility, the empire's fall was inevitable. Although successor states temporarily filled the Assyrian political vacuum, the three-millennia-long culture of Mesopotamia was dead. In 612 BCE, the Neo-Assyrian Empire collapsed as Nineveh was conquered.

THE PERSIAN EMPIRE

> → *In what ways was the Persian Empire similar to the Neo-Assyrian Empire, and in what ways was it different?*

The Persians were successors to the Neo-Assyrians. They created a gentler form of imperial rule, based more on persuasion and mutual benefit than on raw power. A nomadic group speaking an Indo-Iranian language, the Persians had arrived on the Iranian plateau from central Asia during the second millennium and gradually spread to the plateau's southwestern part. These expert horsemen shot arrows with deadly

Cyrus the Great. This great Genius with four wings was preserved in the doorjamb of Gate R at the palace of Cyrus the Great at Pasargadae. When Cyrus forged the Persian Empire from Media, Assyria, Babylonia, and Egypt, there was no coherent imperial imagery to represent the new political entity. His court artists borrowed freely from the realms that he had brought into his empire. The image is a combination of features borrowed from Egypt (the headdress), Assyria (low-relief representation on a stone slab and the four wings), and Babylonia (the long garment).

accuracy while whirling on horseback in the midst of battle. After Cyrus the Great (r. 559–529 BCE) united the Persian tribes, his armies defeated the Lydians in southwestern Anatolia and took over their gold mines, land, and trading routes. He next overpowered the Greek city-states on the Aegean coast of Anatolia.

Further conquests set the stage for a vast multicultural empire that spread from Europe to South Asia. Because their ancestors were pastoralists, the Persians had no urban tradition to draw on. Instead, they adapted the ideologies and institutions of the Babylonians (see Chapter 3) and the Assyrians, modifying them to fit their own customs and political aims. This process gave rise to uniquely Persian institutions that undergirded the new empire, which would last until the arrival of Alexander the Great in 331 BCE.

THE INTEGRATION OF A MULTICULTURAL EMPIRE

Cyrus, the founder of the Persian Empire, traced his ancestry back to a legendary king and used that heritage to legitimate his empire-building. From their base on the Iranian plateau, over the next 200 years the Persian rulers developed an enormous empire that reached from the Indus Valley to northern Greece and from central Asia to the south of Egypt. (See Map 4-3.)

Cyrus presented himself as a benevolent ruler who claimed to have liberated his subjects from the oppression of their own kings. He pointed to his victory in Babylon as a sign that the city's gods had turned against its king as a heretic. According to the cuneiform text known as the Cyrus cylinder, the Babylonians greeted him "with shining faces." At the same

Persian core territory before 550 BCE
Persian expansion by 550 BCE
Persian expansion by 547 BCE
Persian expansion by 539 BCE
Persian expansion by 525 BCE
Persian expansion by 512 BCE

XVI Satrap
✳ Clashes between Persians and Greeks
— Royal road
— Major trade route

MAP 4-3   THE PERSIAN EMPIRE, 550–479 BCE

Starting in the sixth century BCE, the Persians succeeded the Assyrians as rulers of the large regional empire of Southwest Asia and North Africa. Compare the Persian Empire's territorial domains to those of the Neo-Assyrian Empire in Map 4-2. Geographically, how did the Persian Empire differ from the Neo-Assyrian state? Analyzing the map, how many Persian satrapies existed, and what role do you think they played in the success of the Persian Empire? How does geography help explain why the Greeks were able to defeat the Persians twice?

time, Cyrus released the Jews from their fifty-year captivity in Babylon. They, too, considered him a savior who, having freed them on the orders of their God, allowed them to return to Jerusalem and rebuild their temple. Even the Greeks, who later defeated the Persians, saw Cyrus as a model ruler.

Following Cyrus's death on the battlefield, Darius I (r. 521–486 BCE) put the nascent empire on a solid footing. First he suppressed revolts across the lands, recording this feat on a monumental rock relief overhanging the road to his capital, Persepolis. (See Primary Source: Beisitun Inscription.) Then he conquered territories held by seventy different ethnic groups, stretching from the Indus River in the east to the Aegean and Mediterranean seas in the west, and from the Black, Caspian, and Aral seas in the north to the Nile River in the south. To manage this huge domain, Darius introduced dynamic administrative systems that enabled the empire to flourish for another two centuries. Its new bureaucracy combined central and local administration to make best use of the strengths of local tradition, economy, and rule—rather than forcing Persian customs on subject people via rigid central control (as the Assyrians had done).

This empire was both centralized and multicultural. The Persians believed that all subject peoples were equal; the only requirement was to give the king their loyalty and pay tribute—which was considered an honor, not a burden. Although local Persian administrators used local languages, in time Aramaic (a dialect of a Semitic language long spoken in Southwest Asia) became the empire's official language because many of its literate scribes came from Mesopotamia. They wrote Aramaic on parchment or papyrus in an alphabetic script, and its use spread quickly.

Much like Tiglath Pileser III of Assyria, Darius understood that he could not expand the empire without reorganizing and centralizing. To bring the wealth of the provinces to the imperial center he established a system of provinces, or satrapies, each ruled by a satrap (a governor) who was a relative or a close associate of the king. The local bureaucrats and officials who administered the government worked under close monitoring by military officers, central tax collectors, and spies (the so-called eyes of the king) who enforced the satraps' loyalty. Further, Darius established a system of fixed taxation and formal tribute allocations; when needed, he also instituted economic reforms. Moreover, he promoted trade throughout the empire by building roads, establishing a standardized currency including coinage, and introducing standard weights and measures.

ZOROASTRIANISM, IDEOLOGY, AND SOCIAL STRUCTURE

Like the Assyrians, the Persians established their ideology of kingship on religious foundations. They believed that the supreme god, Ahura Mazda, appointed the monarch as ruler over all people and lands of the earth and charged him with maintaining a perfect order from which all would benefit. Unlike their Mesopotamian neighbors, the Persians drew their religious ideas from their pastoral and tribal roots (which reflected the same traditions of warrior and priestly classes as those preserved in the Vedic texts of the Indus Valley; see Chapter 3).

Zoroaster (also known as Zarathustra), who most likely taught sometime after 1000 BCE in eastern Iran, was responsible for crystallizing the region's traditional beliefs into a formal religious system. The eastern tribes of the Iranian plateau spread the ideas of **Zoroastrianism** to the Iranian peoples living in the west, and Zoroastrianism ultimately became the religion of the entire empire. The main source for the teachings of Zoroaster is the Avesta, a collection of holy works initially transmitted orally by priests and then written down in the sixth century CE. (It has much in common linguistically with the Vedic texts of the people of the Indus Valley.)

Zoroaster's teachings tried to wean the Iranian faithful away from their earlier animistic beliefs that led them to see all objects, alive and dead, as possessing life and vitality. In a radical change, Zoroaster promoted belief in the god Ahura Mazda, who had created the world and all that was good. (Though rare, monotheism also existed during this time in Judah; it had briefly been the official religion of Egypt, when Akhenaten imposed worship of Aten, the sun.) Persians came to believe that the universe was dualistic: Ahura Mazda was good and capable only of good, whereas his adversary, Ahiram, was deceitful and wicked. The Persians saw these two forces as engaging in a cosmic struggle for control of the universe.

Unlike the fatalistic religions of Mesopotamia, Zoroastrianism treated humans as capable of choosing between good and evil. Their choices had consequences—rewards or punishments in the afterlife. Strict rules of behavior determined the fate of each individual. For example, because animals were good, they deserved to be treated well. Intoxicants, widely used in tribal religions, were forbidden. Also, there were strict rules for treatment of the dead. For example, to prevent death from contaminating the sacred elements of earth, fire, and water, it was forbidden to bury, burn, or drown the deceased. Instead, people left corpses out for beasts and birds of prey to devour.

Persian kings enjoyed absolute authority. In return, they were expected to follow moral and political guidelines that reflected Zoroastrian notions of ethical behavior. As the embodiment of the positive virtues that made them fit to hold power, they were to display insight and the ability to distinguish right from wrong so that they could preserve justice and maintain social order. In addition, kings had to show physical superiority that matched their moral standing. They had to be awe-inspiring horsemen and peerless in wielding bows and spears—qualities valued by all Persian nobles, who revered the virtues of their nomadic ancestors. Indeed, the ancient Greek historian Herodotus tells us that Persian boys were taught three things only: "to ride, to shoot with the bow, and to tell the truth."

The Persian social order included four diverse groups: a ruling class of priests, nobles, and warriors; an administrative

BEISITUN INSCRIPTION

To commemorate his consolidation of power over the Persian state, Darius I commissioned a pictorial relief of himself as victor high above the main road leading from Mesopotamia to Ecbatana (the modern city of Hamadan) in western Iran. The images are surrounded by a long text inscribed in three languages—Old Persian, Akkadian, and Elamite. This is the earliest Old Persian inscription; it is a version of cuneiform script that Darius devised especially for this occasion.

4.31–2. Saith Darius the King: These IX kings I took prisoner within these battles.

4.33–6. Saith Darius the King: These are the provinces which became rebellious. The Lie made them rebellious, so that these [men] deceived the people. Afterwards Ahuramazda put them into my hand; as was my desire, so I did unto them.

4.36–40. Saith Darius the King: Thou who shalt be king hereafter, protect thyself vigorously from the Lie; the man who shall be a Lie-follower, him do thou punish well, if thus thou shalt think, "May my country be secure!"

4.40–3. Saith Darius the King: This is what I did; by the favor of Ahuramazda, in one and the same year I did [it]. Thou who shalt hereafter read this inscription, let that which has been done by me convince thee; do not thou think it a lie.

Darius's Relief at Beisitun. At Beisitun, high above the Royal Road through the Zagros Mountains, Darius carved a relief commemorating his victories over Gaumata (the false Smerdis) and nine rebel kings. The kings are roped together at the neck, and Gaumata lies under Darius's feet. Above the rebels is a winged disk, probably representing the god Ahura Mazda. Darius had his scribes develop a version of cuneiform script to represent Old Persian. In a trilingual inscription (Old Persian, Elamite, and Akkadian) he recorded this victory, which consolidated and expanded the empire founded by Cyrus. This inscription provided the key for deciphering Babylonian cuneiform.

4.43–5. Saith Darius the King: I turn myself quickly to Ahuramazda, that this [is] true, not false, [which] I did in one and the same year. . . .

4.52–6. Saith Darius the King: Now let that which has been done by me convince thee; thus to the people impart, do not conceal it: if this record thou shalt not conceal, [but] tell it to the people, may Ahuramazda be a friend unto thee, and may family be unto thee in abundance, and may thou live long!

4.57–9. Saith Darius the King: If this record thou shalt conceal, [and] not tell it to the people, may Ahuramazda be a smiter unto thee, and may family not be to thee!

4.59–61. Saith Darius the King: This which I did, in one and the same year by the favor of Ahuramazda I did; Ahuramazda bore me aid, and the other gods who are.

4.61–7. Saith Darius the King: For this reason Ahuramazda bore aid, and the other gods who are, because I was not hostile, I was not a Lie-follower, I was not a doer of wrong—neither I nor my family. According to righteousness I conducted myself. Neither to the weak nor to the powerful did I do wrong. The man who cooperated with my house, him I rewarded well; whoso did injury, him I punished well.

4.67–9. Saith Darius the King: Thou who shalt be king hereafter, the man who shall be a Lie-follower or who shall be a doer of wrong—unto them do thou not be a friend, [but] punish them well.

4.69–72. Saith Darius the King: Thou who shalt hereafter behold this inscription which I have inscribed, or these sculptures, do thou not destroy them, [but] thence onward protect them; as long as thou shalt be in good strength!

→ *Throughout the millennia, local and imperial rulers on the Iranian plateau used rock reliefs such as the Beisitun inscription to project their power and to mark boundaries. Who would see these monuments, and what messages would they receive?*

SOURCE: Roland G. Kent, *Old Persian: Grammar, Texts, Lexicon*, 2nd rev. ed. (New Haven: American Oriental Society, 1953), pp. 131–32.

Panel from the Palace of Darius. The Palace of Darius at Susa was elaborately decorated with glazed bricks. This panel shows human-headed winged lions in a heraldic seated posture. Above them is a winged disk with tendrils and a human bust. This symbol, which borrows from Assyrian and Egyptian imagery, is thought to represent the Zoroastrian god Ahura Mazda.

and commercial class consisting of scribes, bureaucrats, and merchants; and two laboring groups of artisans and peasants. Each group had a well-defined role. Priests maintained the ritual fire in temples, nobles administered the state by paying taxes and performing appropriate duties, warriors protected and expanded the empire, bureaucrats kept records, merchants secured goods from distant lands, artisans rendered raw materials into symbolic form, and peasants grew the crops and tended the flocks that fed the imperial machine.

Surrounding the king was the powerful Persian hereditary nobility, whose support was crucial. These men had vast land-holdings and often served the king as satraps or advisers. Also close to the king were wealthy merchants who directed trade across the vast empire. The king's obligations to them involved taking his wives only from their families and exempting them from certain taxes. To consolidate his hold on the throne, though, Darius reduced the aristocrats' political power. By controlling all appointments, he essentially made the nobles his puppets. However, he let them keep their high status in a society in which birth and royal favor counted for everything.

Royal gifts solidified the relations between king and nobles, reinforcing the king's place at the top of the political pyramid. In public ceremonies he presented gold vessels, elaborate textiles, and jewelry to reward each recipient's loyalty and demonstrate dependence on the crown. Most gifts were made from gold and silver obtained through tribute, and they reminded the recipients of their continual obligation to the ruler. Any kind of failure would result in the withdrawal of royal favor. Should such failures be serious or treasonous, the offenders faced torture and death.

PUBLIC WORKS AND IMPERIAL IDENTITY

Persian power begat large-scale road building and a system of rapid and dependable communication. A key unifying element was the Royal Road, which followed age-old trade

Persian Water-Moving Technique. The Persians perfected the channeling of water over long distances through underground channels called *qanats*. This technique, an efficient way to move water without evaporation, is still used today in hot, arid regions. In this example near Yazd, in central Iran, the domed structure leading to the underground tunnel is flanked by two brick towers called "badgir," an ancient form of air conditioning that cools the water using wind (*bad* in Persian).

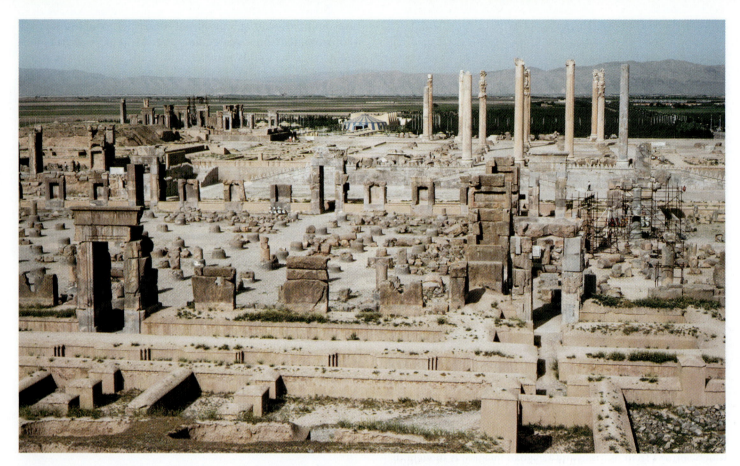

Persepolis. In the highland valley of Fars, the homeland of the Persians, Darius and his successors built a capital city and ceremonial center at the site of Persepolis. On top of a huge platform, there were audience halls, a massive treasury, the harem, and residential spaces. The building was constructed of mudbrick. The roof was supported by enormous columns projecting the images of bulls.

The King and His Courtiers. Leading to the Apadana (reception hall) are two monumental staircases that are faced with low-relief representations of the king and his courtiers, as well as all of the delegations bringing tribute to the center of the empire. The lion attacking the bull is a symbolic rendering of the forces of nature. Above the central plane is the winged disk of Ahura Mazda and the human-headed lion griffins.

routes some 1,600 miles from western Anatolia to the heart of the empire in southwestern Iran, continuing eastward across the northern Iranian plateau and into central Asia. Traders used the Royal Road, as did the Persian army (and, later, other warriors); subjects took tribute to the king, and royal couriers carried messages to the satraps and imperial armies. As the Assyrians had done, the Persians placed way stations with fresh mounts and provisions along the route.

In addition to the Royal Road, the Persians devised other ways to connect the far reaches of the empire with its center. Darius oversaw the construction of a canal more than 50 miles long linking the Red Sea to the Nile River. One of the Persians' most ingenious contributions was the invention of qanats, underground tunnels through which water flowed over long distances without evaporating or being contaminated. (Later adopted by many cultures, this type of system moves water across arid lands even today.) Laborers from the local populations toiled to build these feats of engineering as part of their civic obligation.

Until Cyrus's time, the Persians had been pastoral nomads who lacked traditions of monumental architecture, visual arts, or written literature or history. Cyrus began to define a Persian court style, but Darius was most responsible for promoting visual and physical expressions that were uniquely Persian. The vast capital at Persepolis expressed this new imperial identity. On the highland plain near Cyrus's capital at Pasargadae, Darius built an immense complex that complemented the administrative center at Susa in the lowlands. Skilled craftsmen from all over the empire labored on the complex, blending their distinct cultural influences into a new Persian architectural style. Darius erected his city, designed for celebrations and ceremonies, on a monumental terrace covering more than thirty acres. Into the cliffs behind it, he and his successors cut their eternal resting places from the rock. Persepolis was also an important administrative hub, where archaeologists have found more than 30,000 cuneiform tablets detailing the workings of the bureaucracy of the great empire.

The Persians used monumental architecture with grand columned halls and huge open spaces to provide reception rooms for thousands of representatives bringing tribute from all over the empire and as a way to help integrate subject peoples by connecting them to one central, imperial authority. In the royal palace, three of the columned halls stood on raised platforms accessed via processional stairways that were lined with elaborate images of subjects bringing gifts and tribute to the king. This was a highly refined program of visual propaganda, with the carved images showing the Persian Empire as a diverse society of obedient peoples. The carvings on the great stairway of Persepolis offer a veritable ethnographic museum frozen in stone. Each group brings distinctive tribute—the Armenians present precious metal vessels, the Lydians from Anatolia carry gold armlets and bowls, the Egyptians offer exotic animals, and the Sogdians from central Asia lead proud horses. Gateway figures and protective relief images copied from the palaces of Assyria represent the grandeur of the occasion and the power of the king.

IMPERIAL FRINGES IN WESTERN AFRO-EURASIA

→ *How did the growth of the first empires in Southwest Asia affect the broader region?*

A very different world emerged on Afro-Eurasia's western edges, well beyond the reach of the Neo-Assyrian and Persian empires. Although their powerful neighbors affected them, these western people retained their own languages, beliefs, and systems of rule. Their communities were smaller than those in Southwest Asia, and their compactness and intimacy enabled them to project a unique kind of power and influence.

MIGRATIONS AND UPHEAVAL

Beginning around 1200 BCE, demographic upheavals and migrations propelled new waves of Indo-European-speaking peoples inhabiting the Danube River basin in Central Europe to become dynamic historical actors. Previously this area's dynamism had come from the outside (from the imperial centers of Southwest Asia and Egypt), but two key factors reversed this trend. These were a rapid rise in population and the development of local natural resources—including metallurgy in a new metal, iron. By the end of the second millennium BCE, this surplus population, armed with its new metal weapons, moved in large groups back down the Danube into southeastern Europe, the Aegean, and the eastern Mediterranean. Advancing even into Southwest Asia, the invaders brought turmoil to the peoples living there. These huge movements weakened the power of empires and regimes in the region, increased the value of mobility and communication as peoples vied for resources, and opened new frontiers for the development of smaller, more innovative communities.

The ultimate blow to imperial states from the fringe was military: armed invasions caused the collapse of even the most highly developed societies in the region. The first to fall were the Hittites, who had once dominated the central lands of what is today Turkey (see Chapter 3), because they could not retain power in the face of violence and social chaos. The

Mycenaean Arms and Armor. A Mycenaean vase that illustrates the central role of arms and war to the societies on mainland Greece in the period down to 1200 BCE. The men bear common suits of armor and weapons—helmets, corsets, spears, and shields—most likely supplied to them by the palace-centered organizations to which they belonged. Despite these advantages, they were not able to mount a successful defense against the land incursions that destroyed the Mycenaean palaces toward the end of the thirteenth century BCE.

result was general upheaval as the center of political, military, and technological power moved to the fringes.

Once the invaders reached the Mediterranean, they mainly used boats for transportation. These dynamic communities are sometimes known as the Sea Peoples. The Egyptians knew them as the Peleset, and only by marshalling all the resources of their land did the pharaohs manage to repel them. Outside Egypt, states and kingdoms suffered heavily from their ravages. The Sea Peoples settled along the southern coast of the Levant, where they became known as the Philistines.

From 1100 to 900 BCE, a long economic downturn further unsettled the major kingdoms as well as the coastal cities of the eastern Mediterranean and the Aegean islands. During this time societies began to decline: artistic representation and large-scale construction declined, urban centers ceased to develop, trading and shipping ebbed, and writing, record keeping, and much else disappeared. Societies now comprised smaller, technically simpler, impoverished, illiterate, and more violent rural communities.

In the Mediterranean, the Sea Peoples' intrusion shook the social order of the Minoans on the island of Crete and of the Mycenaeans in mainland Greece (see Chapter 3). Agricultural production declined, and local populations moved to other islands in the Aegean and to southwestern Anatolia. As the palace-centered bureaucracies and priesthoods of the second millennium BCE vanished, more violent societies

emerged that relied on the newcomers' iron weapons. This was the culture of warrior-heroes described in the *Iliad*, an epic poem about the Trojan War composed centuries after the events it relates. It was based on oral tales passed down and embellished for generations. The Greeks told these stories about a hazily recalled war that may have occurred around 1200 BCE at Troy, a city in Anatolia, during a time of seismic political and social upheaval. (See Primary Source: War in Homer's *Iliad*.)

For the long-established kingdoms and states of Southwest Asia and the Mediterranean, these rapid transformations were destructive and traumatic. But they were also creative because they shattered traditional ways of doing things, wiping the social slate clean. In fact, violent change and the emergence of new powers at the margins were the first steps toward completely new patterns of human relations.

PERSIA AND THE GREEKS

Of the different small-scale societies that emerged in Persia's shadow, the Greeks offer the best example of the energy and dynamism of these communities. In areas of contact with the Persian Empire, Greek-speaking people in different cities sometimes cooperated with the Persians, even borrowing their ideas, but sometimes strongly resisted them.

In 499 BCE, some Greek city-states and others in the eastern Mediterranean revolted against the Persians, who claimed control over the Greek islands and mainland from their base in Anatolia. During the five-year struggle, some Greek communities sided with the Persians and suffered condemnation by other Greeks for doing so. On the mainland, farther away from the contact zone, most Greek cities resisted the Persian king's authority. So, in 492 BCE, Darius sent his fleet to subdue Athens and Sparta on the mainland, but the ships were destroyed in a storm. Two years later, Darius and his vast army invaded mainland Greece but suffered a humiliating defeat at the hands of the much smaller force of Athenians at Marathon, near Athens. The Persians retreated and waited another decade before challenging their western foe again. Meanwhile, however, Athens was becoming a major sea power.

Under the leadership of Themistocles in the 480s BCE and exploiting newfound silver mines, Athens became a naval power whose strength was its fleet of triremes (battleships). This shift in power had a significant effect on the subsequent relationship between Greeks and Persians. When the two forces met again in 480 BCE, the Persians lost the pivotal naval battle at Salamis. A year later, they suffered a decisive defeat on land and eventually lost the war. (But in a way that was typical of the intertwined relationships between the two cultures, Themistocles, the hero of Salamis, later finished his career in the service of the Persian king.)

Persian military defeats changed the balance of power. For the next 150 years Persia lost ground to the Greeks,

Primary Source

WAR IN HOMER'S *ILIAD*

The great epic poem called the Iliad—*about the war that took place at Ilium, a Greek name for the city of Troy—was attributed by the later Greeks to a poet named Homer. However, the written text is actually the result of generations of oral singers who composed different versions of this story in the ninth and eighth centuries* BCE. *The story takes place on the plains in front of Troy, and it focuses on a few prominent warriors—such as Achilles and Odysseus on the side of the Achaeans (the Greeks, also called Akhaians), and Hector and Paris (the son of Priam, king of Troy) on the Trojans' side. Historians debate the historical reality of the story, but almost all agree on the site of the ancient city it describes.*

The son of Priam wearing a gleaming breastplate
let fly through the lines but his sharp spear missed
and he hit Leucus instead, Odysseus' loyal comrade,
gouging his groin as the man hauled off a corpse—
it dropped from his hands and Leucus sprawled across it.
Enraged at his friend's death Odysseus sprang in fury,
helmed in fiery bronze he plowed through the front
and charging the enemy, glaring left and right
he hurled his spear—a glinting brazen streak—
and the Trojans gave ground, scattering back,
panicking there before his whirling shaft—
a direct hit! Odysseus struck Democoon,
. . . speared him straight through one temple
and out the other punched the sharp bronze point
and the dark came swirling thick across his eyes—
down he crashed, armor clanging against his chest.
And the Trojan front shrank back, glorious Hector too
as the Argives yelled and dragged away the corpses,
pushing on, breakneck on. But lord god Apollo,
gazing down now from the heights of Pergamus,
rose in outrage, crying down at the Trojans,
"Up and at them, you stallion-breaking Trojans!
Never give up your lust for war against these Argives!
What are their bodies made of, rock or iron to block
your tearing bronze? Stab them, slash their flesh!

* * *

Now Amarinceus' son
Diores . . . . a jagged rock
struck him against his right shin, beside the ankle.
Pirous son of Imbrasus winged it hard and true,
the Thracian chief who had sailed across from Aenus . . .
the ruthless rock striking the bones and tendons

crushed them to pulp—he landed flat on his back,
slamming the dust, both arms flung out to his comrades,
gasping out his life. Pirous who heaved the rock
came rushing in and speared him up the navel—
his bowels uncoiled, spilling loose on the ground
and the dark came swirling down across his eyes.

But Pirous—
Aetolian Thoas speared *him* as he swerved and sprang away,
the lancehead piercing his chest above the nipple
plunged deep in his lung, and Thoas, running up,
wrenched the heavy spear from the man's chest,
drew his blade, ripped him across the belly,
took his life but he could not strip his armor.

And now . . .
no man who waded into that work could scorn it any longer,
anyone still not speared or stabbed by tearing bronze
who whirled into the heart of all that slaughter—
not even if great Athena led him by the hand,
flicking away the weapons hailing down against him.
That day ranks of Trojans, ranks of Achaean fighters
sprawled there side-by-side, facedown in the dust.

→ *What does this selection reveal about the style of combat and the weapons used in this period?*

→ *More important, what do the poet's words tell us about how violence connects gods, humans, social identity, and personal relationships?*

→ *What can we surmise about the cultures from which these soldiers come?*

SOURCE: "The Truce Erupts in War" from *The Iliad* by Homer, translated by Robert Fagles, copyright © 1990 by Robert Fagles. Used by permission of Viking Penguin, a division of Penguin Group (USA), Inc.

MAP 4-5   SOUTH ASIA, 1500–400 BCE
Where did the Indo-Europeans originally come from? What enabled Vedic culture to spread so rapidly? What kept it from spreading further?

lineage through blood ties, alliances via marriage, and, in many cases, invented family relations. The earliest Vedic society had two main lineages: the lunar lineage and the solar lineage. Each had its own creation myth, ancestors, language, and rituals. The lineages included many clans (a **clan** is a social group comprising many households, claiming descent from a common ancestor) in which seniority determined one's power and importance. The Vedic people absorbed many of the indigenous people's clans into their own lineages. Clans that adopted the Vedic culture became part of the lineage (through marriage or made-up ties) and were considered insiders. In contrast, clans that had other languages and rituals were considered uncivilized outsiders.

As the Vedic society expanded, the clans of the solar lineage usually stayed together in the same area. In contrast, the clans of the lunar lineage split into many branches; some migrated east to the Ganges River valley and others south to the northern Deccan plain. Though separated by distance, the clans maintained their relationship through marriage. Within kin-bound clan structures, each member had a well-defined place in the political and social order.

Once urban society and states arose, these lineages no longer underpinned the social structure, but they lived on in two major epics that recounted tales of the Vedic people. The *Mahabharata* relates the last phase of the lunar lineage, and the *Ramayana* focuses on a hero of the solar lineage. Later rulers continued to draw on the memory of these two ancient lineages, legitimizing their regimes by claiming blood links with them.

SPLINTERED STATES

The region's social and economic integration offered a stark contrast to its continuing political disintegration. In the process of fanning out from the Punjab (the region of the five tributaries of the Indus River) and settling along the Ganges River, the Vedic peoples created small regional governments and chieftainships. And as much as they fought with the indigenous peoples, they fought even more fiercely among themselves. Such aggression reinforced the importance of warriors and of the gods of war (Indra) and fire (Agni). The elite warriors battled one another and the farmers for land and other resources (just as in the Mycenaean societies, the tribal societies of the Iranian plateau, and Zhou China).

Their chieftainships eventually became small kingdoms with inhabitants bound to each other through lines of descent from a common ancestor. They traced their family descent or

CASTES IN A STRATIFIED SOCIETY

When the Vedic peoples first spread out across South Asia, their herding societies were all quite similar. But as they settled down and created state structures, they became more complex and varied. Thus, the rise of settled agriculture after 1000 BCE led to a greater divide between those who controlled land and those who worked it. As these divisions hardened, the Vedic peoples created a unique social system based on rigid class distinctions. Later, in the fourteenth century, the Portuguese called these rigid class differences **castes**—a term that has served ever since to describe the specific lineages representing social, political, and economic differences in South Asia. (See Chapter 5 for more discussion.) Dominant clan members became Kshatriyas. Originally the warrior class,

Primary Source

BECOMING A BRAHMAN PRIEST

When the Vedic people became farmers, many of them started to question the validity of sacrificing cows, the draft animals valued for their use in cultivation. Around the seventh century BCE, some thinkers abandoned Vedic rituals and chose to live simply in forests as they debated the meaning of life and the structure of the universe. Those sages were Brahman rishi, highly respected priests. However, not every one of the famous Brahmans was born a Brahman.

1. Satyakâma, the son of Gabâlâ, addressed his mother and said: 'I wish to become a Brahmakârin [religious student], mother. Of what family am I?'

2. She said to him: 'I do not know, my child, of what family thou art. In my youth when I had to move about much as a servant [waiting on the guests in my father's house] I conceived thee. I do not know of what family thou art. I am Gabâlâ by name, thou art Satyakâma [Philalethes]. Say that thou art Satyakâma Gâbâla.'

3. He going to Gautama Hâridrumata said to him, 'I wish to become a Brahmakârin with you, Sir. May I come to you, Sir?'

4. He said to him: 'Of what family are you, my friend?' He replied: 'I do not know, Sir, of what family I am. I asked my mother, and she answered: "In my youth when I had to move about much as a servant, I conceived thee. I do not know of what family thou art. I am Gabâlâ by name, thou art Satyakâma," I am therefore Satyakâma Gâbâla, Sir.'

5. He said to him: 'No one but a true Bráhmana would thus speak out. Go and fetch fuel, friend, I shall initiate you. You have not swerved from the truth.'

Having initiated him, he chose four hundred lean and weak cows, and said: 'Tend these friend.'

He drove them out and said to himself. 'I shall not return unless I bring back a thousand.' He dwelt a number of years [in the forest], until the cows became a thousand.

→ *Satyakama became a well-known Brahman teacher after his study. Judging from this story, was he born a Brahman?*

→ *At that time, how did the rishis and their disciples survive in the forest areas when thinking and studying?*

SOURCE: *The Upanishads,* translated by F. Max Müller, vol. 1 of *Sacred Books of the East,* edited by F. Max Müller (1900; reprint, New Delhi: Motilal Banarsidass, 1981), pp. 60–61.

---

they had power and controlled the land. Meanwhile, lesser clan members became Vaishya, householders who worked the land and tended livestock. As rice production expanded and labor-intensive paddy cultivation took hold, many households hired laborers and used slaves. These people came from outside the Vedic lineages and were known as Shudras ("the small ones"). They constituted the lowest caste.

In time, the Vedic social system gave rise to four castes, known as *varna*. The Kshatriyas controlled the land and were the ruling caste, the Vaishyas were agrarian commoners, and the Shudras were servants and laborers. A fourth caste, the priests or Brahmans who performed rituals and communicated with gods, was above the Kshatriyas. Some of them still functioned as priests for the chiefs, and some were sages who lived as ascetics (individuals who deny themselves comforts) in forests, where they discussed philosophical questions with

their students. Their ability to communicate with the heavens, the most coveted of skills, placed them at the top of the social pyramid. Indeed, the Brahmans guided a society in which the proper relationship with the forces of nature as represented by the deities constituted the basis of prosperity. As agriculture became ever more important, Brahmans acted as agents of Agni, the god of fire, to purify the new land for cultivation. (See Primary Source: Becoming a Brahman Priest.)

Thus, as the Vedic peoples settled down, they created stratified societies that bore little resemblance to those of their egalitarian, pastoral ancestors. In time, powerful monarchies arose around hereditary kings who ruled with councils of elders. Kings also had help from the Brahmans, who transformed social rules and practices into formal legal codes. Much later (c. 100 BCE–100 CE) one or several sages, using the name Manu (Sanskrit for "human being"),

FOUNDING TEXTS—
COMPARING JEWISH AND VEDIC SOURCES

One of the defining traits of religious movements is a reliance on sacred texts. Their stories, historical material, and parables contributed to belief systems that have become the backbone of religious identity. In many faiths we find one immutable core text, such as the Bible, for Jews and Christians; the Vedas, for Hindus; and the Koran, for Muslims. Additional supplementary texts clarify or expand on the core texts.

Like many religions, Judaism is based on a revealed scripture, thought to have been transmitted directly from God to his prophets. Rabbis argued for centuries over the interpretation of these works, and their students passed on the discussions orally. Judaism is thus built on a series of texts that include debates about the Bible by generations of scholars.

Biblical texts from a Hebrew Bible. Written around 3,000 years ago, these texts served as the primary source of the religion of the Israelites—Judaism.

The Jews did not originally use the name *Bible*; instead, a common term was *Tanakh*, an acronym derived from the Hebrew titles of the text's three major parts: (1) Torah (literally, "Instruction")—the law of the Jewish people whose authorship was traditionally ascribed to Moses; (2) Nevi'im (Prophets)—texts ascribed to prophets who preached about how to live in accordance with the law; (3) Ketuvim (Writings)—texts that include the Psalms and Proverbs.

According to Jewish tradition, the Tanakh consists of twenty-four books that took their canonical written form gradually, beginning with the Torah in the sixth century BCE. Determined to ensure their religion's survival, priests in exile in Babylon combined and finalized writings that others had begun to record in the tenth century BCE. The entire canon was not closed until the first or second century CE, when the Jewish religion was imperiled by social and religious upheaval following the Romans' destruction of the second temple in Jerusalem in 70 CE. The huge compilation of oral law, the Talmud, was finally written down (in two versions) around the fifth and sixth centuries BCE. Taken together, these texts express the Jewish community's ability to adapt and persevere when historical conditions changed.

We have already discussed the four foundational Vedic texts and their use in religious rituals. Brahmans, the priests and intellectuals of Vedic society, composed other works— the Brahmanas and Aranyakas—to explain how and when to recite the hymns and chants of the Vedas during ritual performances. However, as Vedic peoples embraced settled agriculture and abandoned their former nomadic lifeways, some thinkers doubted the validity of sacrificial rituals based on gods driving chariots and began to reflect on the meaning of life and the universe. Scholars then composed the Upanishads, mystic speculative works whose concepts of

gathered these laws into a single text (see Chapter 8). These legal books both guided the king and regulated the behavior of his subjects.

VEDIC WORLDS

A Vedic culture, transmitted from generation to generation by the Brahman caste, unified what political rivalries had divided. Belief in Indra and other gods, a common language

(Sanskrit), and shared cultural symbols linked the dispersed communities and gave the Vedic peoples a collective sense of destiny. Though Sanskrit was a language imported from central Asia, the people used it to transmit the Vedas orally. By expressing the people's sacred knowledge in the beautiful rhythms and rhymes of Sanskrit, the Vedas effectively passed on their culture from one age to the next.

As the priests of Vedic society, the Brahmans were responsible for memorizing every syllable and tone of the Vedic

The Bodhisattva Manjusri. This text was written in 967 at one of the great monasteries of northeastern India. It is an example of how Buddhists copied foundational texts onto palm leaves.

life and death, time and space, geography and the cosmos laid the foundations for most, if not all, of South Asia's later schools of thought, including Buddhism and Jainism.

Vedic literature, both hymns and rules for rituals, long remained an oral tradition. Even after Buddhists started to write down texts in the late first millennium BCE, Brahmans resisted the temptation to make copies of the Vedas, fearing they would lose exclusive control of their sacred works. Sometime after the beginning of the Common Era, they may have started copying Vedic passages onto palm leaves to aid their memory. When Brahmanism was reborn as Hinduism during the first millennium CE, a host of new

deities became objects of cults of worship and gave rise to new genres of Sanskrit literature, such as Puranas (stories of the past) and epics. The Vedas are still the final authority of Hinduism, though most Hindus find their contents incomprehensible and of little relevance.

In both Jewish and Vedic traditions, the pressures of a changing world created a new relationship among oral culture, texts, and interpretation. Though they abandoned their old systems of religious practice, Jewish and Vedic worshippers continued to interpret sacred texts as they made sense of their lives, passing from religions of oral tradition to those of the written word.

works. These included commentaries on sacred works from early nomadic times, as well as new rules and rituals explaining the settled, farming way of life. The Vedas promoted cultural unity and pride through common ritual practices and support for hereditary *raja* kingdoms. The main body of Vedic literature includes the four Vedas: Rig-Veda, Sama-Veda, Yajur-Veda, and Atharva-Veda. The Rig-Veda, the earliest text, is a collection of hymns praising the gods, including Indra (god of war), Agni (god of fire), and Varuna (god of water).

Indra stands out as the most powerful and important, as he is the one who set the order of the universe and made life possible. The Sama-Veda is a textbook of songs for priests to perform when making ritual sacrifices; most of their stanzas also appear in the Rig-Veda. The Yajur-Veda is a prayerbook for the priest who conducted rituals for chariot races, horse sacrifices, or the king's coronation. The Atharva-Veda includes charms and remedies; many address problems related to agriculture, a central aspect of life.

Although the Vedic period left no impressive buildings and artifacts, it created a wealth of thinking about cosmology and human society. In this way, it laid the religious foundations for coming generations. (See Global Connections & Disconnections: Founding Texts—Comparing Jewish and Vedic Sources.)

During the middle of the first millennium BCE, thinkers (mostly Brahman ascetics dwelling in forests) felt that the Vedic rituals no longer provided satisfactory answers to the many questions of a rapidly changing society. The result was a collection of works known as the Upanishads, or the supreme knowledge, which expanded the Vedic cultural system. Taking the form of dialogues between disciples and a sage, the Upanishads explored questions of deep concern at that time. Out of these dialogues came a set of lessons that offered insights into the ideal social order, and a script and eventually a canon to be shared beyond local communities.

The Upanishads teach that people are not separate from each other but belong to a cosmic universe called Brahma. While the physical world is always changing and is filled with chaos and illusion, *atman*, the eternal being, exists in all people and all creatures. Atman's presence in each living being makes all creatures part of a universal soul. While all living beings must die, the atman guarantees eternal life, ensuring that souls are reborn and transmigrate into new lives. This cycle continues with humans as they are either reborn as humans or as other living creatures, like cows, insects, or plants. Only when humans reach a permanent union with Brahma, which is the highest level of achievement, are they able to break this cycle of birth and rebirth. Living an ascetic life, separated from the pleasures and comforts of this world, and engaging in meditation enable individuals to transcend the physical world, merge their souls with Brahma, and experience eternal life and happiness.

These unique Vedic views of life and the universe were passed along as principles of faith, bringing spiritual unity to the northern half of South Asia. Unlike the societies of Southwest Asia and North Africa, here in the kingdoms of the Indus Valley and the Ganges plain the common Vedic culture—rather than larger political units—was the unifying bond.

Zhou Chariots. After swearing allegiance to the Shang, the Zhou assembled superior military forces in the northwest, in part by emulating Shang chariots. The Zhou subsequently used their own chariots and archers to defeat the Shang in about 1045 BCE. The regional lords who owed allegiance to the Zhou king distinguished themselves in the aristocratic hierarchy by using chariots for travel and battle.

THE EARLY ZHOU EMPIRE IN EAST ASIA (1045–771 BCE)

> → *To what extent was the Zhou state similar to contemporary Southwest Asian empires?*

Around the same time that western Afro-Eurasian societies experienced periods of upheaval and reconsolidation, the political and social map of East Asia featured invasion and warfare. The small Zhou state, based in the Shanxi region, initially swore allegiance to the Shang and allied with them in their fight against nomadic incursions on the western borderlands. But the Zhou eventually turned against the Shang, assembling superior military forces to defeat them in about 1045 BCE. (See Map 4-6.)

INTEGRATION THROUGH DYNASTIC INSTITUTIONS

When the Zhou took over from the Shang, China was not yet a fully integrated empire. Like Vedic South Asia, China under the Zhou dynasty was initially split into regional powers. As we will see, though, China's local administration, first developed in the Shang Dynasty, gave it greater unity. Moreover, the Zhou copied the Shang's unifying dynastic structure: a patrimonial state centered on ancestor worship in which the rulers' power passed down through genealogies of

MAP 4-6   THE ZHOU DYNASTY, 2200–256 BCE

Toward the end of the second millennium BCE, the Zhou state supplanted the Shang dynasty as the most powerful political force in East Asia. Using the map above, compare and contrast the territorial reach of the Zhou state with that of the Shang. In what direction did the Zhou state expand the most dramatically? Why do you think this was the case? How did the Zhou integrate their geographically large and diverse state?

male ancestors reaching back to the gods. (A **genealogy** is a history of the descent of a person or family from a distant ancestor.) On such a foundation (notably absent in Vedic South Asia) an integrated and remarkably lasting dynasty structure developed.

As the Zhou adopted the local political organization of the Shang, they began an extended process of integration. Bit by bit, regional aristocracies subordinated themselves to a single ruler. It was a balancing act between a dynastic central ruler and powerful local lords, however. Using cultural symbols and the art of statecraft rather than religion, the Zhou peoples established a dynasty that had broad geographic influence but limited power over its regional states. This was integration, but not quite unification.

ZHOU SUCCESSION AND POLITICAL FOUNDATIONS

The nature of early Chinese political successions differed from that of Southwest Asia, where outsiders invaded and took power. Instead, in China, the northwestern Zhou peoples gradually took over from the Shang. For many years, the Zhou and the Shang lived side by side, trading and often allying to fend off raiders from the far west. Though initially less advanced in writing and technology than the Shang, the Zhou learned and borrowed from them. And when the Zhou became strong enough, they overcame the Shang.

Evidence from this period indicates that a powerful King Wu established Zhou control in northwestern China and expanded north toward what is now Beijing and south toward the Yangzi River valley. (See Primary Source: Zhou Succession Story.) This king held the allegiance of the lords of older states and of new lords whom he appointed in annexed areas. Rewarding his relatives and key followers with lands that they could pass on to their descendants was an important means of controlling strategic areas. Often, the new colonies consisted of a garrison town (where the Zhou colonizers lived) surrounded by fields containing the local inhabitants (the farmers). As under the Shang, Zhou regional lords had to supply military forces as needed, pay tribute, and appear at the imperial court to pledge their continuing allegiance to the king.

THE ZHOU "MANDATE OF HEAVEN" AND THE JUSTIFICATION OF POWER

The Zhou rulers justified their takeover of Shang wealth and territories by claiming moral superiority. To accomplish this, they developed an ideology that supported a morally correct transfer of power, which they called the **mandate of heaven**. At first the mandate was a religious compact between the Zhou people and their supreme god in heaven (literally, the "sky god"), but it evolved into a fundamental Chinese political doctrine. The Zhou argued that since worldly affairs were supposed to align with those of the heavens, heavenly powers conferred legitimate rights to rule on their chosen representative. The ruler was then duty-bound to uphold heaven's principles of harmony and honor. Any ruler who failed in this duty, who let instability creep into earthly affairs, or who let his people suffer would lose his mandate. Under this system, it was the prerogative of spiritual authority to withdraw support from any wayward dynasts and find another, more worthy agent. Thus the Zhou sky god legitimated regime change.

In using this creed to justify their takeover, the Zhou rulers had to acknowledge that any group of rulers, themselves included, could be ousted if they lost the mandate of heaven because of improper practices. After the Zhou overturned the Shang line of succession, rulers were no longer considered gods. From that point on, dynastic legitimacy depended on ruling in accordance with the principles of good governance and upright behavior. China's rulers (unlike the theocracies of Southwest Asia and the later emperor system of Japan) created an empire based more on politics, military power, and morality than on religious legitimacy.

The early Zhou kings contended that heaven favored their triumph because the last Shang kings had been evil men whose policies brought pain to the people through waste and corruption. Thereafter, the mandate became a political tool. It was a compelling way to defend continuity of political institutions, if not rulers, in the name of preserving a natural order. It also helps explain why the change in power did not bring about an abrupt overhaul of political and cultural institutions.

The Shang had used writing to communicate with the divine world, and the Zhou continued this practice. But the Zhou also expanded its use, recording matters ranging from royal divinations (omens, predictions, and questions for the gods) to a variety of political practices, such as kingly speeches, grants of official offices, and rewards. Other texts described the organization and administration of government. These were reportedly the work of the Duke of Zhou, but they were actually from a much later period.

Writing became even more essential when King Mu (r. 956–918 BCE) established a more formal system of bureaucratic governance. He restructured the court and military by appointing officials, supervisors, and military captains who were not related to him, and he instituted a formal legal code. These changes created a need for bureaucratic records, including archives of appointments and legal verdicts. Increasingly, a pool of scribes and scholars joined the entourage of royal diviners, using their mastery of writing to find patrons at court and among regional powers. Through their powerful rhetoric, they tied many of the new changes to the early Zhou founding myth.

One of the duties and privileges of the king was to create a royal calendar. This official document defined times for undertaking agricultural activities and celebrating rituals, and it was an impartial measure of the ruler's success or failure. In fact, unexpected events such as solar eclipses or natural calamities threw into question the ruling house's authority. Since rulers claimed that their authority came from heaven, the Zhou made great efforts to gain accurate knowledge of the stars and to perfect the astronomical system on which they based their calendar. By creating a calendar that improved on the Shang's version, they enhanced their public legitimacy. Advances in astronomy and mathematics enabled Zhou astronomers to precisely calculate the length of a lunar month (29.53 days) and measure the length of the solar year (365.25 days). But a year of twelve lunar months is 354.36 days long, so to resolve the discrepancy the Zhou occasionally inserted a leap month. Scribes dated the reigns of kings by days and years within a repeating sixty-year cycle, which was said to match the cosmological interaction between heaven and earth.

Zhou legitimacy also derived indirectly from Shang material culture—that is, the use of bronze ritual vessels, statues,

Primary Source

ZHOU SUCCESSION STORY

Chinese lore often glamorized the early Zhou dynasty as an era of sage rulers such as King Wu and the Duke of Zhou (Chou). The Shangshu (Book of History) *account, however, shows that the transition of power from the founder, King Wu, to the Duke of Zhou was fraught with difficulty— as was often the case in early states. It reveals how the Duke of Zhou tried simultaneously to protect his reputation as regent to King Wu's young son and to preserve Zhou rule. This document also represents one of the first major efforts in Chinese history to provide a historical narrative of events.*

After he had completed the conquest of the Shang people, in the second year, King Wu fell ill and was despondent. The two lords, the duke of Shao and Tai-kung Wang, said, "For the king's sake let us solemnly consult the tortoise oracle." But the duke of Chou [King Wu's younger brother, named Tan] said, "We must not distress the ancestors, the former kings."

The duke of Chou then offered himself to the ancestors, constructing three altars within a single compound. . . . Then he made this announcement to the Great King, to King Chi, and to King Wen, his great grandfather, grandfather, and father, and the scribe copied down the words of his prayer on tablets:

"Your chief descendant So-and-so [King Wu's personal name is tabooed] has met with a fearful disease and is violently ill. If you three kings are obliged to render to Heaven the life of an illustrious son, then substitute me, Tan, for So-and-so's person. I am good and compliant, clever and capable. I have much talent and much skill and can serve the spirits. . . ."

Then he divined with three tortoises, and all were auspicious. He opened the bamboo receptacles and consulted the documents, and they too indicated an auspicious answer. The duke of Chou said to the king, "According to the indications of the oracle, you will suffer no harm."

[The king said,] "I, the little child, have obtained a new life from the three kings. I shall plan for a distant end. I hope that they will think of me, the solitary man."

After the duke of Chou returned, he placed the tablets containing the prayer in a metal-bound casket. The next day the king began to recover.

[Later, King Wu died and was succeeded by his infant son, King Ch'eng. The duke of Chou acted as regent and was slandered by King Wu's younger brothers, whom he was eventually forced to punish.]

In the autumn, when a plentiful crop had ripened but had not yet been harvested, Heaven sent great thunder and lightning accompanied by wind. The grain was completely flattened and even large trees were uprooted. The people of the land were in great fear. The king and his high ministers donned their ceremonial caps and opened the documents of the metal-bound casket and thus discovered the record of how the duke of Chou had offered himself as a substitute for King Wu. . . .

The king grasped the document and wept. "There is no need for us to make solemn divination about what has happened," he said. "In former times the duke of Chou toiled diligently for the royal house, but I, the youthful one, had no way of knowing it. Now Heaven has displayed its terror in order to make clear the virtue of the duke of Chou. I, the little child, will go in person to greet him, for the rites of our royal house approve such action."

When the king came out to the suburbs to meet the duke of Chou, Heaven sent down rain and reversed the wind, so that the grain all stood up once more. The two lords ordered the people of the land to right all the large trees that had been blown over and to earth them up. Then the year was plentiful. (*Chin t'eng.*)

→ *How does the passage demonstrate the Zhou's reliance on male ancestor worship?*
→ *What do the direct speeches tell us about the place of divination in Zhou politics?*

SOURCE: Translated in Burton Watson, *Early Chinese Literature* (New York: Columbia University Press, 1962), pp. 35–36.

Zhou Wine Vessel and Sword. Under the Zhou, bronze metallurgy depended on a large labor force. Many workers initially came from Shang labor groups, who were superior to the Zhou in technology. The use of bronze, such as for this wine vessel and sword, exemplified dynastic continuity between the Shang and Zhou.

ornaments, and weapons. As the Zhou emulated the Shang's large-scale production of ceremonial bronzes, they developed an extensive system of bronze metalworking that required a large force of tribute labor. Many of its members were Shang, who were sometimes forcibly transported to new Zhou towns to produce the bronze ritual objects.

Such continuity with old ways was very useful to the Zhou, who revered their predecessors and conducted elaborate rituals to underscore the importance of inheritance and thereby justify their power. Ancestor worship was a critical component of political life, which celebrated the resilient influence of the past on the present.

SOCIAL AND ECONOMIC TRANSFORMATION

As the Chinese social order became more integrated, it also became more class-based. Directly under the Zhou ruler and his royal ministers were the hereditary nobles, divided into five ranks. These regional lords had landholdings of different sizes. They all owed allegiance to the Zhou king, and they all supplied warriors to fight in the king's army and laborers to clear land, drain fields, and do other work. They periodically appeared at court and took part in complex rituals to reaffirm their allegiance to the king. Below the regional lords were high officers at the Zhou court, as well as ministers and administrators who supervised the people's work. A military caste of aristocratic warriors stood at the bottom of the noble hierarchy.

OCCUPATIONAL GROUPS AND FAMILY STRUCTURES

Initially, most of the population worked as farmers on fields owned by great landholding families. Some commoners were artisans, such as those who produced valuable bronze ritual vessels, or weavers who spun delicate silk textiles. Over time, an elaborate ladder of occupational strata arose. This system divided people by function: landholders who produced grain, growers of plants and fruit trees, woodsmen, breeders of cattle and chickens, artisans, merchants, weavers, servants, and those with no fixed occupation. The central government apparently controlled how each group did its work—for example, telling landholders what crops to plant, when to harvest, and when to irrigate. Although reports of these efforts may overstate the government's reach, the Chinese state clearly played a major role in uniting the region's diverse peoples—in ways that none of Eurasia's other great regimes did.

One important method of integration was the political and legal use of family structures. In their patrilineal society, the Zhou established strict hierarchies for both men and women. Both art and literature celebrated the son who honored his parents. Men and women had different roles in family and ceremonial life. On landholdings, men farmed and hunted, while women produced silk and other textiles and fashioned them into clothing. Wealth increasingly trumped gender and class distinctions, however. In particular, rich women high in the Zhou aristocracy enjoyed a greater range of actions than other women. And wealthy merchants in emerging cities challenged the authority of local lords.

TECHNOLOGICAL DEVELOPMENT What has been remarkable about China throughout history is how its integration progressed in small steps, not in a single, triumphal bound. Zhou achievements likewise were incremental, rooted in a transformation of the countryside as both princes and peasants began expanding the agrarian frontier inland. Wooden and, much later, iron plows enabled farmers to break the hard sod of lands beyond the river basins, and over time cultivators learned the practice of field rotation to prevent soil nutrients from being exhausted. A great advance occurred in the middle of the first millennium BCE as regional states organized local efforts to regulate the flow of the main rivers. They built long canals to promote communication and trade, and they dug impressive irrigation networks to convert arid lands into fertile belts. (Some of these systems remain in use today.) This slow agrarian revolution enabled the Chinese population to soar—reaching perhaps 20 million by the late Zhou era.

Under the Zhou dynasty, landowners and rulers organized the construction of dikes and irrigation systems to control the floodplain of the Yellow River and Wei River valley surrounding the capital at Xianyang (present-day Xi'an). For centuries, peasants labored over this floodplain and its tributaries—building dikes, digging canals, and raising levees as the waters flowed to the sea. When their work was done, the bottom of the floodplain was a latticework of rich, well-watered fields, with carefully manicured terraces rising in gradual steps to higher ground. This enormous undertaking was the work of many generations. Eventually, irrigation works grew to such a scale that they required management by powerful territorial rulers, the Zhou dynasts centered in the Wei River valley, and their skilled engineers. The engineers also designed canals that connected rivers and supported commerce and other internal exchanges. Tens of thousands of workers spent countless days digging these canals, paying tribute in the form of labor. (As we have seen, other dynasties in Afro-Eurasia also produced massive building works through forced labor.)

Increasingly, the canals linked China's two breadbaskets: the wheat and millet fields in the north, and the rice fields in the south. And as with the Yellow River in the north, engineers controlled the Yangzi River in the south. So wealthy was China that its influence even reached the distant steppe lands to the north and west. Nomads in mountainous areas or on the Zhou frontiers, who often fought with the Zhou ruler and his regional lords, now depended on trade with the fertile heartlands. In return for their pastoral produce the Zhou received textiles, metal tools and weapons, and luxury items.

LIMITS AND DECLINE OF ZHOU POWER

At its center the Zhou state had great influence, but its power elsewhere was limited. Unlike Assyria and Persia, it never evolved into a regional power. The dynasty relied instead on culture (its bronzes) and statecraft (the mandate of heaven) to maintain its leadership among competing powers and lesser principalities. Rather than having absolute control of an empire, the Zhou state was first among many regional economic and political allies.

The Zhou dynasty ruled over a much larger territory than the Shang did, but it was not highly centralized. Instead, it expected regional lords (who in this regard resembled Persian satraps) to hold provinces in line. Military campaigns continued to press into new lands or to defend Zhou holdings from enemies. Rulers attempted to keep neighbors and allies in line by giving them power, protecting them from aggression, and continuing the tried-and-true method of intermarriage between dynastic family members and local nobles. However, as a result of the Zhou's ruling methods, their subordinates had more than autonomy; they also had genuine resources that they could turn against the dynasts at opportune moments.

The power of the Zhou royal house over its regional lords declined in the ninth and eighth centuries BCE. In response, the Zhou court at its impressive capital at Xianyang introduced ritual reforms with grandiose ceremonies featuring larger, standardized bronze vessels. Yet even this move could not reverse the regime's growing political weakness in dealing with its steppe neighbors and internal regional lords. For the most part, the Zhou court became a theater state, hoping that impressive rituals would conceal its lack of military might.

The facade began to crumble as wars, social dislocations, and changes in landholding shook the system's social and political foundations. The Zhou dynasts managed to cling to their authority until 771 BCE, when northern steppe invaders forced them to flee their western capital. The Zhou dynastic period, like the Shang, was later idealized by Chinese historians as a golden age of wise kings and officials. In fact, the Zhou model of government, culture, and society became the standard for later generations. As a result, a tradition emerged in China of upholding political continuity and social stability. The regime's legitimacy was seen as resting on the moral bonds between ruling families, who were at the top of a carefully managed social pyramid, and those in the orderly layers beneath them. Though the Mesopotamian and Persian superpowers were capable of greater expansion during this period, China was sowing the seeds of a more durable state.

CONCLUSION

Upheavals in the territorial states of Afro-Eurasia led to the emergence of more extensive political powers—in Mesopotamia, Persia, and China—during the first half of the first millennium BCE. For seven centuries, both the Assyrian Empire based in Mesopotamia and the Persian Empire based in Iran were superpowers whose reach continued to grow. These first empires expanded territorial states far beyond their "ethnic" or linguistic homelands and, in so doing, brought more extensive interactions and exchanges to parts of Afro-Eurasia. Driving these events were changes in climate, invasions by nomadic people, new weaponry, trade, and new administrative strategies and institutions.

The Assyrian and Persian empires differed in fundamental ways from the earlier city-states and territorial states of this area. Assyrians and Persians created ideologies, political institutions, economic ties, and cultural ways that extended their power across vast regions. Indeed, their strong imperial institutions enabled them to exploit human and material resources at great distances from the imperial centers.

But there were other models of expansion that did not yield political empires—at least at first. In the Vedic world of the Indus Valley and Ganges plain, shared values and revered texts did not lead even to a single state. The unparalleled degree of integration across northern South Asia was cultural and economic rather than political. Centuries would pass before a regime would layer a state over this shared cultural world.

In China as well, a core of cultural and political beliefs developed. As in Persia and the Indus Valley and Ganges plain, shared ideas and values spanned a wide geographic area. But unlike in Vedic South Asia, a powerful dynastic political system emerged in China when the Zhou rulers began integrating diverse peoples and territories. Their rule could not last, however. Although the Zhou transformed China, they could not overcome the power of local nobles or fully protect the western frontier from nomadic attacks. Thus the regime never developed military and fiscal powers as great as those of the Southwest Asian empires. Nevertheless, Zhou efforts did implant the foundations of a political and ruling culture that enabled later imperial rulers to achieve success.

Empire building did not occur everywhere; the majority of the world's people still lived in smaller political groupings. Even within Afro-Eurasia, some areas were completely untouched. And even where the Assyrian and Persian rulers,

Chronology

	1100 BCE	1000 BCE	900 BCE
SOUTHWEST ASIA AND NORTH AFRICA			◆ *950–612 BCE Neo-Assyrian Empire* - - - - -
THE MEDITERRANEAN			
SOUTH ASIA		◆ *1000 BCE New Vedic migrations into the Ganges River valley begin* ◆ *1000 BCE Development of settled agriculture* ◆ *1000 BCE Emergence of caste system*	
EAST ASIA		*1045–771 BCE Zhou state* ◆ - - - - - - - - - - -	

soldiers, and traders came into contact with certain groups, they did not necessarily crush them. For example, the nomadic peoples of the northern steppes and the southern desert locations throughout Eurasia continued to be autonomous. But fewer and fewer were untouched by the technological, cultural, and political pulses of empires.

The peoples living on the eastern Mediterranean shore, in the Vedic society of South Asia, and in the Zhou kingdom of China made lasting contributions to the cultural and religious history of humanity. The Phoenician Sea Peoples traversed the whole of the Mediterranean basin and spread their simplified alphabet. From the land of Judah, a budding monotheism sprouted. Late Vedic South Asia spun out the concept of cyclic universal time in the form of reincarnation. And in late Zhou China, an ideal of statecraft and social order took shape. All evolved into powerful cultural forms that in time spread their influences far beyond their sites of origin.

Review and research materials are available at StudySpace: ⑥ WWNORTON.COM/STUDYSPACE

KEY TERMS

annals (p. 133)	iron (p. 127)
caste (p. 148)	mandate of heaven (p. 154)
clan (p. 148)	prophets (p. 146)
empire (p. 126)	Vedas (p. 147)
genealogy (p. 153)	Zoroastrianism (p. 137)
ideology (p. 133)	

STUDY QUESTIONS

1. Migrating populations paved the way for greater cultural integration across Afro-Eurasia after 1200 BCE. Where did the migrants come from, and where did they invade? In South Asia, for example, how much of the original culture did the migrants incorporate into their own way of life?

2. Compare and contrast the statecraft of the Neo-Assyrian and Persian empires. How did each try to integrate their multicultural empires?

3. Analyze the role of the fringe societies in the Aegean and Levant in western Afro-Eurasia during the first millennium BCE. How did they contribute to cultural integration and expansion during this time?

4. Explain the role of clans and castes in Vedic society in South Asia during the first millennium BCE. To what extent did they maintain a culturally integrated and distinct world in the absence of political unity?

5. Compare and contrast the Zhou state to the regional empires in western Afro-Eurasia in the second millennium BCE. What legacies did each leave?

6. Compare and contrast the role of the state in facilitating regional integration in East Asia, South Asia, and western Afro-Eurasia.

800 BCE	700 BCE	600 BCE	500 BCE

550–479 BCE Persian Empire

◆- ◆

◆- - - - - - - - - - - - - - - - - ◆ 800–700 BCE Phoenician colonization

◆ 700–600 BCE Greek colonization

499–480 BCE Greek/Persian battles ◆- - - - ◆

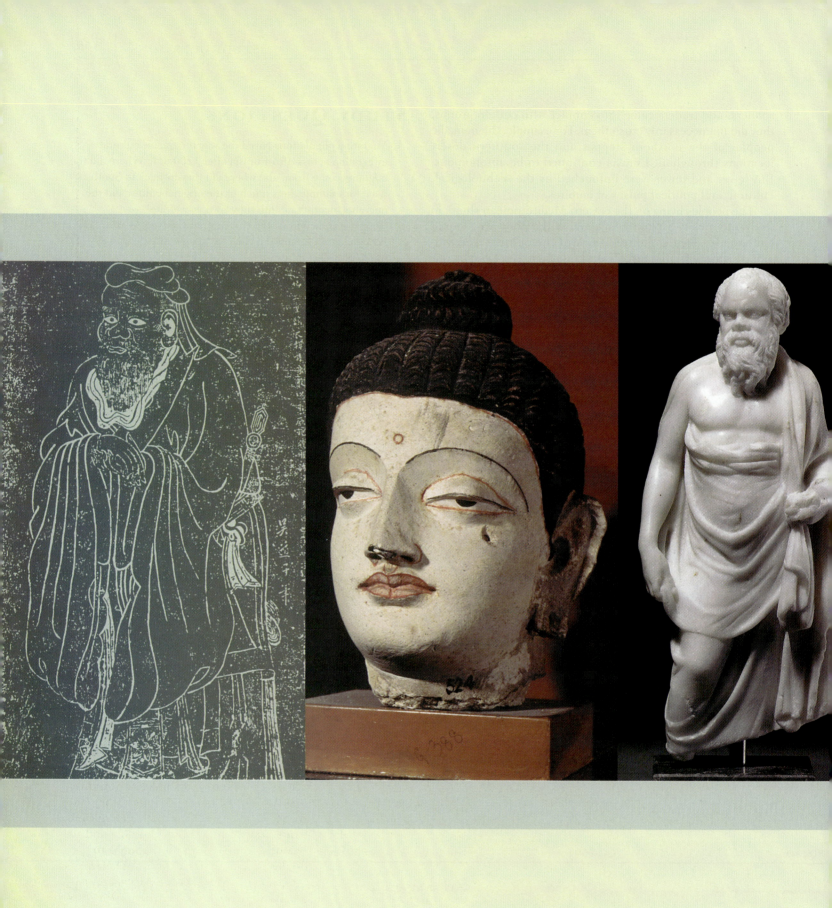

5

WORLDS TURNED INSIDE OUT, 1000–350 BCE

A struggle for power and territory gripped societies from China to Africa. It turned the sixth century BCE into an age of violent upheaval. In the midst of this mayhem, Master Kong Fuzi of China instructed his disciples on how to govern, saying: "Guide them by edicts, keep them in line with punishments, and the people will stay out of trouble but will have no sense of shame. Guide them by virtue, keep them in line with the rites, and they will, besides having a sense of shame, reform themselves" (Confucius, *The Analects*, II, 3).

Master Kong, also known as Confucius, represented a new breed of influential leaders—teachers and thinkers; not kings, priests, or warriors. Instead of fighting wars of conquest, they conducted wars of ideas. At the same time, it was the convulsions around them that motivated the search for new insights and solutions. By viewing the world in new ways, they sought to lead societies out of that turbulence. Their arsenal: words. Their strategy: instruction. These teachers strove to instruct rulers on how to govern justly, and to show ordinary individuals how to live ethically. In doing so, they began to integrate regional worlds with shared beliefs.

Teachers and prophets are a primary focus of this chapter, for the period's thinkers were some of the most influential in history. In China, Confucius elaborated a set of principles for ethical living that has guided the Chinese population up to modern times. In South Asia, Siddhartha Gautama (the Buddha) laid out social and spiritual tenets that challenged the traditional caste system and the privileged warrior and priestly classes. In Greece, Socrates, Plato, and Aristotle described a world that conformed to natural and intelligible laws. New thinking also led to new institutions, most notably in the city-states of the eastern Mediterranean where political, economic, and cultural innovations led to new political institutions, including experiments in democratic forms of government, and vigorous economic activity. Some modern thinkers call these centuries "the axial age," to emphasize it as a pivotal period between the declining empires of ancient Egypt, Northern India, and Zhou China, and the successor empires of Alexander the Great, Rome, and the Han Chinese (see Chapters 6 and 7). This intellectually and institutionally dynamic period gave rise to the ethical, philosophical, and religious foundations of cultures in India, China, and what later became western Europe. Even distant worlds saw major breakthroughs in belief systems that created more culturally integrated regions. In Mesoamerica, the Olmecs established the first complex, urban-based society, with artistic and religious reverberations well beyond their homelands. In Africa, distinct regional identities spread in the Upper Nile (in Nubia) and West Africa.

The philosophers, theologians, poets, political leaders, and merchants of the axial age founded literary traditions, articulated new belief systems, and established new political and economic institutions that spread well beyond the places that inspired them. While wars and havoc occurred within their societies and long-distance trade and travel linked societies, these centuries were dominated by a search for order and an appetite for new thinking. This created opportunities for texts and their authors to create cultural systems that re-imagined entire regions integrated by more than trade or conquest, but by common values and shared beliefs. The axial age involved powerful impulses for cultural integration.

ALTERNATIVE PATHWAYS AND IDEAS

> → *How did "second-generation" cultures expand social, political, and cultural options?*

During the first millennium BCE, societies on the edges of regional empires or within declining empires started to follow innovative paths. (See Map 5-1.) They tinkered with new types of political and social organization, and new ways of fighting and expanding borders. Such innovation occurred, for example, in Eastern Zhou China, where nearly constant warfare and power struggles ultimately led to the formation of several large and powerful territorial states and led to ethical and political formulas for ordering human behavior. Radical changes also occurred in Greece and the Levant, where the chaos and economic decline caused by the Sea Peoples' onslaught culminated in the emergence of dynamic city-states and new ideas about good governance.

Along the great river valleys of East and South Asia, the Caribbean coast of Mexico, and the coasts of the Mediterranean, complex societies arose with cultural and political ideas that differed radically from those of the regional empires

Focus Questions

Ⓖ WWNORTON.COM/STUDYSPACE

→ *How did "second-generation" cultures expand social, political, and cultural options?*

→ *In what ways did scholars propose ending the warfare and chaos of China's Spring and Autumn and Warring States periods?*

→ *How did political and social transformations encourage new beliefs and dissident thinkers in South Asia?*

→ *How did cultural integration occur in the Andes and Mesoamerica in the absence of political unity?*

→ *How did the spread of iron smelting shape the social landscape of sub-Saharan Africa?*

→ *In what ways did city-states integrate the dispersed settlements of the Mediterranean?*

MAIN THEMES

→ *Age of violent warfare spreads across Afro-Eurasia.*
→ *Innovative societies arise worldwide.*
→ *Teachers and prophets reshape peoples' views of the world.*

FOCUS ON *Innovative Societies*

China

+ Multistate system emerges from warfare, revolutionizing society and thought.
+ Confucius and the hundred masters outline the ideals of governing and living.

South Asia

+ Small monarchies and urban oligarchies emerge after the Vedic peoples' migrations and rule over societies organized around the caste system.
+ Dissident thinkers like Mahavira and the Buddha challenge Brahman priests and the caste system.

The Americas

+ Olmecs and Chavín peoples produce increasingly hierarchical societies and connect villages via trade.
+ Large-scale common cultures emerge.

Sub-Saharan Africa

+ Expansion of the Sahara Desert and population explosion cause people to coalesce in a few locations.
+ Early signs of a Sudanic common culture appear across the region.

The Mediterranean World

+ Independent city-states emerge from social destruction and facilitate revolutionary principles in rulership, commerce, and thought.
+ Thinkers like Democritus, Plato, and Aristotle challenge conventions and encourage public discourse about the role of the individual in society and the way the universe works.

---

of Southwest Asia. In the Indus Valley, such societies emphasized sacred categories (especially caste, which determined every individual's status and occupation) and new religious experiences. These communities revolved around small-scale monarchies and urban oligarchies (societies led by small cliques) dominated by elite families. In China, small polities held by regional lords under the Zhou king gave way to increasingly centralized and belligerent states. In the Americas, the dispersed settlements of the Olmecs in Mesoamerica and the Chavín peoples of the Andes produced increasingly hierarchical social orders despite a continued reliance on simple agricultural technology. Around the Mediterranean Sea, new social forms were taking shape in independent cities. These communities borrowed some elements from older societies, but more often they developed in place to match their environments.

The new communities were not just extensions of old lifeways. In each, dramatic innovations in cultural and religious beliefs expanded people's social, political, and cultural options.

Although the cultures were clearly different from one another, we might call them all **second-generation societies**, simultaneously building on their predecessors and representing a departure from ancient legacies.

New ideas by no means bred consensus. In fact, the age of great ideas witnessed magnificent disputes over what was best for humanity, and over the very political and moral status of the individual. In Greece, philosophers questioned the possibility of gaining and transmitting true or reliable knowledge of the world. They began to doubt the permanence of the social order and pondered the relationship between humans and the cosmos. In Eastern Zhou China, beset by constant warfare, sages debated how best to restore order; some advocated engagement while others urged withdrawal from government. In the Ganges Valley, thinkers questioned the traditional Brahmanic rituals and sought new ways of behaving morally and attaining enlightenment. Whereas many Greek philosophers endorsed skepticism for its own sake, thinkers in Eastern Zhou China and in the Ganges Valley at

NORTH AMERICA

ROCKY MOUNTAINS

NOMADIC HUNTERS

Great Lakes

Mississippi R.

St. Lawrence R.

ATLANTIC OCEAN

Gulf of Mexico

OLMEC

MESOAMERICA

La Venta

Monte Alban

WEST INDIES

PACIFIC OCEAN

CHAVÍN

ANDES MOUNTAINS

NOMADIC HUNTERS

Amazon R.

SOUTH AMERICA

CELTIC PEOPLES

Rhine R.

IBERIANS

Latin cities

Carthage

SAHARA

SAHARAN PEOPLES

SAHEL

Niger R.

NOK

	Persian Empire
	Zhou China
	South Asian states
	Nubia
	Kush
	Nok
	Olmec
	Chavín
	Mediterranean colonies
•	City
NOK	State
SLAVS	People

0   1000   2000 Miles

0   1000   2000 Kilometers

→ *How did "second-generation" cultures expand social, political, and cultural options?*

MAP 5-1   THE WORLD, C. 500 BCE

By the middle of the first millennium BCE, complex agriculture-based societies beyond the regional empires of Southwest Asia and North Africa contributed to the flowering of new cultural pathways and ideas. According to this map, where did these "second-generation" societies appear? Which societies had greater opportunities for cultural mixing, and which ones were more isolated? How did proximity to others or relative isolation shape these societies' development?

the time of the Buddha sought ultimate truths that would yield a unitary vision of state and society.

EASTERN ZHOU CHINA

> ❧ *In what ways did scholars propose ending the warfare and chaos of China's Spring and Autumn and Warring States periods?*

Altogether critical for the appearance of new ideas, radical thinkers like Confucius, and the notion of starting anew in China was the utter destruction of the old political order. In short, political degeneration preceded widespread political and intellectual innovation. Thus, to understand the circumstances that led to Confucian thought and China's cultural flourishing, one must begin with the political arena. The starting point is the emergence of the Eastern Zhou dynasty, centered on Luoyang, a period in Chinese history known as the Spring and Autumn period (722–481 BCE), which in turn ended with the Warring States period (403–221 BCE) when seven major regional states consolidated their power into territorial states. The result was a multistate system that fostered revolutionary developments in agriculture, government, politics, and society and during which scholar-officials assumed great political and social importance.

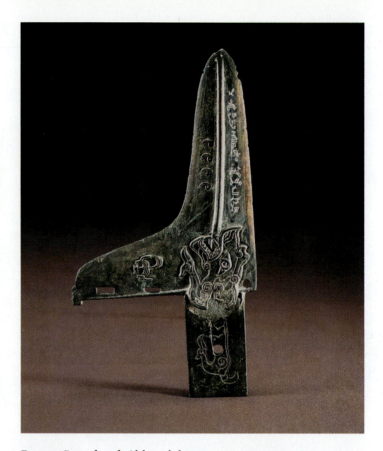

Bronze Spearhead. Although bronze weaponry gave way to stronger iron swords and armor during the Warring States era, stylized bronze spearheads were still prized by Zhou kings and regional lords.

THE SPRING AND AUTUMN PERIOD

From the outset of the Spring and Autumn period, China witnessed levels of anarchic violence previously unseen for centuries. Regional states possessed more power than the central Zhou ruler; they forged alliances and created new administrative units in the countryside to conscript men and to collect taxes. Even though the major states competed for power and land, they still nominally accepted the Zhou ruler's authority. In effect, China's fractured political system inverted the normal pattern. Here, strong central states did not dominate weaker satellites. Instead, the central states were a buffer zone between the large peripheral states to which they were forced to swear allegiance. They became the battlefields on which larger states fought for dominance.

Growing political anarchy coincided with technological breakthroughs. As new smelting techniques to remove impurities from iron spread across China, bronze weaponry gave way to stronger iron swords and armor. Zhou kings tried hard to monopolize iron production and stockpile weapons, but to no avail. The spread of cheaper and more lethal weaponry shifted influence from the central government to local authorities.

In fact, the regional states became so powerful that they undertook large-scale projects that earlier had been feasible only for empires. While constructing dikes and drainage and irrigation systems, they brought greater areas of land under cultivation. New canals linked rivers, and the networks spurred transformation. For example, in 486 BCE the lord of the Wu state began to build what would eventually become the 1,000-mile-long Grand Canal, linking the Yellow River in the north with the Yangzi River in the south. Stretching several hundred miles, Wu's canal functioned as an artificial Nile, promoting greater integration of the various states' economies. Like all the grand infrastructure projects of this era, it owed its existence to the back-breaking labor of peasants working off their tax obligations to regional lords.

THE WARRING STATES PERIOD

At the beginning of the Warring States period, seven large territorial states dominated the Zhou world, and several smaller states on the Central Plain remained within the major powers'

MAP 5-2   ZHOU CHINA IN THE WARRING STATES PERIOD

The Warring States period witnessed a fracturing of the Zhou dynasty into a myriad of states. Find the Zhou capital of Luoyang on the map. Where was it located relative to the other key states? What about this map tells us why diplomacy was so important during this period? What does this map tell us about the relationships between "civilized" and "barbarian" peoples in East Asia? How do you think so many smaller polities could survive when they were surrounded first by seven and then by three even larger and more powerful states (Qin, Qi, and Chu)?

sphere of influence. (See Map 5-2.) Their wars and shifting political alliances involved the mobilization of armies and resources on an unprecedented scale (far surpassing the Assyrian armies at the height of their power). Qin, the greatest state, ultimately replaced the Zhou dynasty in 221 BCE. Its armies in particular combined huge infantries in the tens of thousands with lethal cavalries and even more lethal legions of skilled archers using state-of-the-art crossbows. To ensure the Qin war machine could match all threats, the preparation

to defend the Chinese heartland even crossed into the other-world. Some 7,000 artisans and workers prepared thousands of ornate, carefully made terra-cotta warriors and horses, which the Qin buried in precise military formations within the tomb of the first Qin emperor to help him in the expected wars he would face in the next life.

The Warring States alternately engaged in diplomacy or battle, depending on which furthered their interests at the moment. Thus statecraft emerged (similar to that among

Primary Source

WARRING IDEAS: CONFUCIANISM VERSUS DAOISM—ON THE FOUNDATIONS OF GOVERNMENT

Though both Confucians and Daoists viewed the world of political power as perilous, their competing teachings offered regional Chinese rulers a choice in political philosophies.

Confucius wanted to end the chaos of the times and restore order by promoting education, moral behavior, and the performance of ritual. He thought that cooperation rather than conflict, ethical behavior rather than reckless actions, merit rather than heredity, and concern with the welfare of others rather than self-aggrandizement should be the basis of society and government. Not as interventionist as the Legalists, the Confucians opposed autocracy and appealed to the mandate of heaven as the "voice of the people." Not as laissez-faire as the Daoists, the Confucians prioritized strict ritual as a philosophy of behavior that would lead to cultural solidarity even in times of political chaos. The Daoists' rejoinder charged that the Confucians were, in effect, shutting the barn door after the horses had already escaped. A natural morality had once been the rule in small villages; a true morality was now the social exception, betrayed in practice by the moral hypocrisy of Confucian officials in the capital.

Initially, Confucius's call for moral rigor had little appeal to those in power. But some saw the attractions of his beliefs after they realized that a tyrannical government that punished its citizens harshly could be brought down by a peasant rebellion. In one exchange with a student, Confucius described the core foundations of government:

> Zigong asked about government. The Master said, "Sufficient food, sufficient military force, the confidence of the people." Zigong said, "If one had, unavoidably, to dispense with one of these, which of them should go first?" The Master said, "Get rid of the military." Zigong said, "If one had, unavoidably, to dispense with one of the remaining two, which should go first?" The Master said, "Dispense with food: Since ancient times there has always been death, but without confidence a people cannot stand." (*Analects* 12.7)

Many individuals who sought power were drawn more to Daoism, whose teachings warned that overly assertive rulers could ruin the state. Thus, the Daodejing (*The Book of the Way and Its Power*), a famous Daoist work attributed to Master Lao (Laozi), argued that political and social intervention was futile and that long-term rule should be based on "doing nothing" (*wuwei*); that is, letting everything take its natural course without premeditated human intervention:

> If one desires to take the empire and act on it,
> I say that he will not succeed.
> The empire is a sacred vessel,
> That cannot be acted upon.
> In being acted upon, it is harmed;
> And in being grasped, it is lost.
> Thus the sage rejects the excessive, the extravagant,
>   the extreme.
> (*The Book of the Way and Its Power*, Vol. 1, p. 86)

→ *What elements of Confucius's teaching emphasized moral rigor and, when applied to government, would enable it to win "the confidence of the people"?*

→ *Why did Confucius believe that a cruel tyrant could not remain in power for very long?*

→ *Why did the Legalists find Daoism more appealing than Confucianism as a practical and moral philosophy?*

SOURCE: Excerpts from *Analects* and *The Book of the Way and Its Power* from *Sources of Chinese Tradition*, Volume 1, eds. William Theodore de Bary and Irene Bloom, © 1999 Columbia University Press. Reprinted with the permission of the publisher.

recruit men for their armies, and to oversee conquered areas. This trend continued in the Warring States period, as the major states created administrative districts with stewards, sheriffs, and judges and a system of registering peasant households to facilitate tax collection and army conscription. The officials were drawn from the *shi,* who under the Western Zhou had been knights but were now bureaucrats in direct service to the ruler. Confucius and other classical masters called them "gentlemen" or "superior men" (*junzi*) and considered them partners of the ruler in state affairs. Officials were paid in grain and sometimes received gifts of gold and silver, as well as titles and seals of office, from the ruler.

Of all the ministers who sought to enhance the central government, none was more successful than Shang Yang of Qin. His reforms positioned the Qin domain to become the dominant state of its time. Dividing the state into administrative districts and appointing their magistrates, vice magistrates, military commanders, and overseers, he extended the ruler's authority into the hinterland and used the districts for universal military recruitment. He divided the land into blocks for individual households to farm, and he introduced a head tax, ensuring that households having two or more adult sons would pay more taxes than families with only one. Those who distinguished themselves in war (as determined by the number of enemy killed in battle) earned titles and land; conversely, nobles who failed to distinguish themselves in war were stripped of

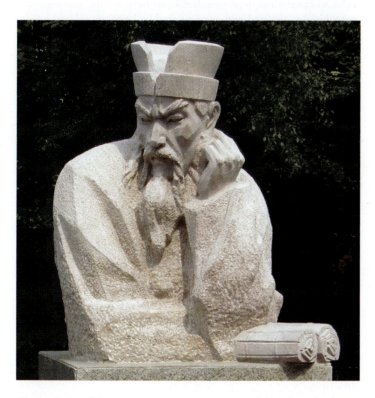

Shang Yang of Qin. An important statesman of Qin during the Warring States period, Shang Yang introduced administrative reforms that enhanced the power of the central government.

status and honors. Shang Yang introduced a harsh penal code that stressed collective responsibility (for example, those who harbored criminals had their bodies cut in two). The legal code applied equally to government officials and peasants, with severe punishments for violent crimes, theft, use of nonstandard weights and measures, and wrongdoing in office.

INNOVATIONS IN WARFARE

The most successful states in China ruled over millions of people, and by 221 BCE they boasted million-man armies. (Contrast this with Athens, the most powerful city-state in the Mediterranean: with a population of 250,000, it could field an army of just 20,000 men. Only Rome, later to become a mega-state, could ultimately match China's scale.) With administrative reform came reforms in military recruitment and warfare. As noted above, one purpose of registering the rural population was to guarantee their military service. During the Spring and Autumn period, rulers relied on men from the countryside to expand their armies and to serve as personal bodyguards. During the Warring States period, as such practices persisted, the conscription of peasants guaranteed ever-larger military organizations.

In earlier battles, nobles had let fly their arrows from chariots while conscripted peasants fought beside them on the blood-stained ground. Now the Warring States relied on massed infantries of peasants bearing iron lances who fought fiercely and to the death, unconstrained by their relationships with nobles. War now involved huge state armies containing as many as 1,000,000 commoners in the infantry, supported by 1,000 chariots and 10,000 bow-wielding cavalrymen. During the Spring and Autumn period, one state's entire army would face another state's; now armies could divide into separate forces and wage several battles simultaneously.

Armies also boasted elite professional troops wearing heavy iron armor and helmets, brandishing iron weapons, and wielding the recently invented crossbow. The crossbow's tremendous power, range, and accuracy, with its ingenious trigger mechanism, enabled archers to easily kill lightly armored cavalrymen or charioteers at a distance. The technology of siege warfare also advanced in response to the growing presence of defensive walls along frontiers and around towns. Enemy armies used counterweighted siege ladders (the Chinese called them "cloud ladders") to scale urban walls or dug tunnels under them; defenders often pumped smoke into the tunnels to thwart the attackers. The rhythms of warfare also changed. Rather than lasting through an agricultural season, campaigns now stretched over a year or longer. As commanders strategized over which troops to place where, which terrain was best suited for battle, and how to outmaneuver opposing armies, military action and thought became increasingly sophisticated.

ECONOMIC, SOCIAL, AND CULTURAL CHANGES

Rather than draining the economy, the incessant warfare of both the Spring and Autumn period and the Warring States period spurred China's economic growth to remarkable heights. As an agricultural revolution on the North China plain along the Yellow River led to rapid population growth, the inhabitants of the Eastern Zhou reached approximately 20 million. Demographic changes also affected the environment. As more people required more fuel, deforestation—particularly on the North China plain—led to erosion of the fields. In addition, many animals were hunted to extinction; others, like the elephant, found their open range sharply curtailed. Many inhabitants migrated south to domesticate the marshes, lakes, and rivers of the Yangzi River delta; here they created new arable frontiers out of former wetlands, thus averting the ecological disaster that swept through northern China.

Eventually, such population pressures on arable land set in motion a vicious and tragic economic cycle for Chinese peasants. The shortage of cultivable land eventually pushed agricultural technology, based largely on peasant manual labor, to its limits. The agrarian methods of the time could produce only so much food. With historical hindsight, we know that population growth typically outpaces agricultural productivity—that is, until some kind of technological breakthrough raises productivity. Agricultural growth was the result of ever-attentive peasant farmers tilling the fields of North and South China. From the late Zhou forward, they produced more rice and wheat than anyone else on earth, but they also created families with an unprecedented number of mouths to feed. The long-term economic result was a declining standard of living for the massive numbers of Chinese peasants, unless new land or new "miracle" rice came under cultivation. In the meantime, the search for food propelled farmers into new frontiers at the expense of the wetlands, its flora and its fauna. When this frontier hit its limits—which it did, invariably—Chinese families faced terrible food shortages and famines.

Knife Coin. Zhou dynasty coins, like the later Han coin shown here, were made of bronze and produced in a variety of shapes, some resembling spades and knives, depending on the region. Each of the Warring States had its own currency.

Pendant. Gender relations became more inflexible because of male-centered kinship groups. Relations between the sexes were increasingly ritualized and were marked by heavy moral and legal sanctions against any behavior that appeared to threaten the purity of powerful lineages. This pendant depicts two women who formed a close relationship with each other in the "inner chambers" of their homes.

Nevertheless, in the short term, economic changes began in the Spring and Autumn period when some rulers gave peasants the right to own their land in exchange for taxes and military service. Because the peasants now could enjoy the benefits of their own labor, their productivity increased. Innovations in agricultural technologies also raised productivity, through crop rotation (millet and wheat in the north, rice and millet in the south) and the use of iron plowshares harnessed to oxen to prepare fields.

With larger harvests and advances in bronze and iron casting came trade in surplus grain, pottery, and ritual objects—the beginning of a market economy. Grain and goods traveled along roads, rivers, and canals. Peasants continued to barter, but elites and rulers used minted coins. Early bronze coins had a variety of shapes, some resembling spades. Private traders and merchants also emerged during this time.

During the Warring States period, these changes continued. The new bargain with the peasants (private ownership of land in exchange for taxes and military service) undergirded the economies of all the Warring States, as did a strong emphasis on the military. Infrastructure benefited directly, as roads and walls, forts and towers rose to defend against invading armies. In addition, rulers and administrators applied their keen military organizational skills to public projects, undertaking irrigation projects, building canals and dikes, and draining low-lying lands to open more acreage for agriculture. Military conscripts worked on these municipal projects when they were not needed for fighting.

Economic growth helped the rulers attain a high level of cultural sophistication, as reflected in their magnificent palaces and burial sites. At the same time, social relations became more fluid as commoners gained power and aristocrats lost it. In Qin, for example, peasants who served in the ruler's army were rewarded for killing enemy soldiers; their military success could win them land, houses, slaves, and a change in status. Officials also received lands and gifts that enhanced their status and wealth. Officials, ministers, and diplomats traveled far and wide during this period, but peasants had to keep toiling in their fields and villages, leaving them only to fight in the ruler's army.

While class relations had a revolutionary fluidity, gender relations became more rigid for elites and nonelites alike as male-centered kinship groups grew. The resulting separation of the sexes and male domination within the family affected women's position. An emphasis on monogamy, or at least the primacy of the first wife over additional wives and concubines, also emerged. Relations between the sexes became increasingly ritualized and constrained by moral and legal sanctions against any behavior that appeared to threaten the purity of authoritarian male lineages.

Archaeological evidence reveals that commoners and elites alike tried to restore stability in their lives through religion, medicine, and statecraft. The elites' rites of divination to predict the future and medical recipes to heal the body found parallels in the commoners' use of ghost stories and astrological almanacs to understand the meaning of their lives and the significance of their deaths. Elites recorded their political discourses on wood and bamboo slips, tied together to form scrolls. They also prepared military treatises, arts of persuasion, ritual texts, geographic works, and poetry in this way. Social changes were evident as well, as in commoners purchasing bronze metalwork whereas previously only Zhou rulers and aristocrats could afford to do so.

Even with the endless cycles of warfare and chaos—or perhaps because of them—many foundational beliefs, values, and philosophies for later dynasties sprang forth during the Spring and Autumn and Warring States periods. By the middle of the first millennium BCE, China's political activities and innovations were affecting larger numbers of people, spread over a much broader area, than comparable developments in South Asia and the Mediterranean.

Chinese Calendar. This Han-period calendar for 63 BCE is formed from sixteen slips of wood with handwritten characters; each begins with day one, day two, and so on; the calendar is to be read from right to left.

THE NEW WORLDS OF SOUTH ASIA

→ *How did political and social transformations encourage new beliefs and dissident thinkers in South Asia?*

As in China, violence and warfare in South Asia provided the setting for vibrant cultural and intellectual insight. Following their migration into the Indus River Valley around 1500 BCE, the Vedic peoples fought with the indigenous population and with each other as they established and enlarged new states. Around 1000 BCE, they expanded eastward into the mid-Ganges plain, where they created new polities. At the same time that scholar-officials in Zhou China were theorizing about how to govern and make economic and social innovations, the Vedic peoples were also forging new political institutions, economic activities, and ways of viewing the natural and supernatural worlds. Vedic warriors and upper-class intellectuals drove these transformations.

THE RISE OF NEW POLITIES

Political and social transformations began around 600 BCE, after the Vedic peoples had spread into the mid-Ganges plain. This was a monsoon region where abundant rainfall made the land suitable for cultivating rice (whereas the best Indus Valley crops were wheat and barley). The migrants cleared land by setting fire to the forests and using iron tools—fashioned from ore mined locally—to remove what was left of the jungle.

Between 1000 and 600 BCE, settlements and towns evolved into small territorial states; as in China, it was a time of constant feuding. (See Map 5-3.) It was also a time of new thinking—especially Buddhism and its challenge to the authority of Vedic sacrifices and Brahmanical leadership.

Two major kinds of states appeared in the mid- and lower Ganges plain: those ruled by hereditary monarchs, and those ruled by an elected elite, or oligarchies. (An **oligarchy** is a clique of privileged rulers.) As described in Chapter 4, the South Asian oligarchies were led by warriors and officials called collectively as a class the Kshatriya. Both the rulers of the kingdoms and citizens of the Kshatriya republics assumed the title *raja*, usually translated as "king." But in the oligarchic communities, which were ruled collectively, each adult freeborn male head of a family was called a *raja*. Still, the Kshatriya oligarchy alone controlled the land and other resources. While there were ties between rulers and ruled, it was

MAP 5-3   SIXTEEN STATES IN THE TIME OF THE BUDDHA IN SOUTH ASIA

South Asia underwent profound transformations in the first millennium BCE that reflected growing urbanization, increased commerce, and the emergence of two types of states: monarchies and oligarchies. Where did the new states and cities appear? What geographic and environmental features encouraged social and cultural integration? According to this map, what other regions had influence on South Asia, and where might South Asian culture spread?

clear that a small minority oversaw the large majority. How did the potentates get their power? There were a number of social ladders: upward through military ranks, marriage upward, and accumulation of land. Rulers often blended all three strategies, carefully sequencing them as they accumulated power. For instance, the *rajas* in kingdoms often came from low-status clans that gained power through military strength. Such *rajas* would elevate their status by marrying women from high-status clans.

EXPANSION OF THE CASTE SYSTEM

Though the kingdoms and oligarchic cities had different political structures, they shared many social features, including the caste system—one of increasing stratification in which each caste rank defined an individual's political power, economic activity, and social status. The traditional vertical scheme of Brahmans first (scholars and priests), followed by Kshatriyas second (warriors), Vaishyas third (commoners), and Shudras fourth (laborers and servants) expanded in an economy centered on farming by extended families. But the largest group to expand was the laboring caste, as agriculture flourished. Many more Shudras, from clans outside the Vedic lineages, joined the agricultural economy as subcastes or laborers of the farming households. (The Shudra laborers planted rice seedlings and harvested crops in the watery paddies.) Cows could not work in rice paddies and therefore were replaced by water buffaloes; some plows required six or eight of the well-muscled animals to pull them. Cultivating rice paddies was highly labor-intensive, since irrigation water had to flow in from distant rivers through elaborate irrigation canals that needed constant maintenance.

As households had to rely on hired workers and slaves, Shudra peasants became a distinct social group. While men in the other castes were "twice-born," having undergone a ritual rebirth around age twelve, this ceremony was denied to the Shudras, who remained outsiders—so they invented their own social hierarchy based on kinship and religious rituals. Even when they joined the Vedic landowners' farming economy as laborers, tenants, or cultivators, they maintained their communal structure by marrying inside their group. Called *jatis*, which signified being born into the group, they became the lower orders of an expanding caste system. The four-caste system, buttressed by Brahmanical ideals, seemed right and natural; its great success was measured by its ability to bring newcomers into existing ranks. In this fashion, the caste system combined hierarchical order with absorptive strength, making the South Asian social order stable yet dynamic.

Further expansion of the caste system occurred as the booming agricultural economy generated even more labor specialization. Carpenters and ironsmiths, traders and artisans, all fell within subcastes defined not only by profession but even by product. For example, a carpenter *jatis* was more prestigious than a tradesman such as a blacksmith, and all farmers viewed all leather tanners as literally untouchable. Social hierarchies layered cities as well as countryside. In the emerging urban centers, traders were "purer" than artisans, while those making gold utensils had higher status than those making copper or iron ones. Yet, members of each group colluded to contain internal competition, and they closed ranks to preserve their status. Even these subcastes monopolized skills and resources by banning intermarriage, thereby preventing other groups from accessing their knowledge. The increasingly elaborate caste system in part reflected the growing complexity of rural and urban worlds, and the resultant specialization of social roles. The guardians of this system contrived practices to make it harder and harder to move between ranks, even as the number of members swelled within them.

Brahman Recluse. When Buddhists started to tell stories in sculptures and paintings, Brahmans were included when appropriate. This character in Gandharan Buddhist art probably represents a Brahman who lived as a recluse, instead of as a priest. He is not shaved or dressed, but his expression is passionate.

NEW CITIES AND AN EXPANDING ECONOMY

Supported by rice agriculture, cities began to emerge on the Ganges plain around 500 BCE. These cities became centers of commercial exchange. Some, such as Shravasti and Raja-griha, also thrived as artisanal centers. Others in the northwest, like Taxila (on the border between present-day Pakistan and Afghanistan), engaged in trade with Afghanistan and the Iranian plateau.

LIFE IN THE NEW CITIES   Cities in northern India grew as their commercial activities flourished, but they followed scant planning. Alleys leading from the main streets zigzagged between houses built with pebbles and clay. Although development was haphazard, civic authorities showed great interest in sanitation. The many squares dotting each city had garbage bins, and dirty water drained away in deep sink wells underground. Streets were graded so that rainfall would wash them clean. Because most cities of this period have been continuously inhabited, they are difficult sites for archaeologists to explore. Taxila, destroyed in the fifth century CE, is an exception: excavated in the twentieth century, it sheds light on urban life in early South Asia. Taxila did not have the well-planned streets and water drainage of a center like Mohenjo Daro, a rather opulent Indus city (see Chapter 2); Taxila's building materials were simpler. But civic consciousness produced a hygienic and healthy urban environment. City officials arranged to have garbage taken out of town and dirty water routed to sink wells. There is, moreover, archaeological evidence of deep ruts on the roads, from wagon wheels that plied the winding lanes and streets—revealing that bull and horse carts moved in and out of the city's open squares, which probably served as marketplaces.

The new cities offered exciting opportunities for those who were adventurous. Rural householders who moved into them prospered by importing rice and sugarcane from villages to sell in the markets; they then transported manufactured goods such as sugar, salt, and utensils back to their villages. Those who already possessed capital became bankers who financed trade and industry. The less affluent turned to craftwork, fashioning textiles, tools such as needles, fine pottery, copper plates, ivory decorations, and gold and silver utensils. Other professions included physicians, launderers, barbers, cooks, tailors, and entertainers. The elaborate division of labor suggests high degrees of specialization and commercialization in the urban hubs.

Traders and artisans formed guilds (associations of people with similar interests) to regulate competition, prices, and wages; to support destitute members and their families; and to set standards. To protect their monopolies, guilds required their members to marry within their organizations. As the guild leaders gained financial influence over the new urban communities, even kings heeded their advice on issues as important as war and peace.

Coins came into use in these cities at about the same time as they appeared in Greece and China. Traders and bankers established municipal bodies that issued the coins and vouched for their worth. Made of silver, the coins had irregular shapes but specific weights, which determined their value; they also were punch-marked, or stamped with symbols of authority on one side.

Taxila. (*Left*) Taxila became the capital of Gandhara, a kingdom located in what is today northern Pakistan and eastern Pakistan, at the time that it was occupied by the Persian Empire in the fifth century BCE. Dharmarajika was one of the most important monasteries. The walkway around the stupa, a mound-like structure containing Buddhist relics, was covered with glass tiles, and the stupa itself was decorated with jewels. (*Right*) This corner of a stupa exhibits a variety of the architectural styles that prevailed in Gandharan art at its height. Both square and round columns are covered by Corinthian capitals. The right arch gate shows the style of Sanchi, the famous stupa in central India.

UNEQUAL OPPORTUNITIES The new cities were melting pots of considerable social mobility—despite the rigid caste system. The story of the famous physician Jivika illustrates this combination of considerable mobility with persistent hierarchy. Jivika lived during the time of the Buddha, in the mid-sixth century BCE. His mother was a courtesan in the important city of Rajagriha in the lower Ganges Valley, beautiful and highly accomplished in dancing, singing, and playing the lute; her fame spread far and wide, attracting business to the city. When she discovered she was pregnant, she hid until the baby was born. Then, under cover of darkness, she had her maid carry the infant in a basket to a trash dump. The next morning, the baby's crying attracted the attention first of a crowd and then of a prince named Abhaya, who sent a servant to find out the reason for the disturbance. When he learned that the newborn boy was alive, he adopted the child as his own and named him Jivika, meaning "alive." Prince Abhaya raised the boy like a son, but after learning of his low birth Jivika decided to earn his own livelihood. From his hometown of Rajagriha, Jivika set out for Taxila. He traveled more than 800 miles along the Ganges River—a journey well worth the effort, for Taxila was an important center of learning. There, Jivika received the best training available in medicine, and after he returned to Rajagriha his knowledge and skill soon earned him a brilliant reputation throughout northern India.

The opportunities that the new cities provided for social mobility did not ensure success for everyone. Many who lost their land and livelihood entered cities in search of work, and some fared better than others. As a whole, people had more material wealth, but their lives were far more uncertain. In addition, urban life created a new social class: those who did the dirtiest jobs, such as removing garbage and sewage, and were therefore viewed as physically and ritually impure "untouchables." They were thought to be so polluting that a daughter of a decent householder was expected to wash her eyes after seeing one. Even though their work kept the cities clean, they were forced to live in shantytowns outside the city limits.

Some untouchables were dissatisfied with their fate. At a time when thinkers were questioning all types of authority, some of the outcastes joined dissident sects. As the turbulence in the new cities affected even the most abject of their inhabitants, they became receptive audiences for those challenging the Vedic rituals and Brahman priests.

BRAHMANS, THEIR CHALLENGERS, AND NEW BELIEFS

Wise men looked at the urban life around them and the increasing levels of social violence and decried what they saw. For Brahman priests, mingling was a problem: castes mixing indiscriminately, they felt, polluted society. Moreover, low-born persons grasped at higher status by acquiring wealth or skill. Even worse, as people learned to write they threatened the priests' inherited monopoly of oral traditions. When an alphabetic script appeared around 600 BCE, it undermined the Brahmans' ability to control the definition of right and wrong and thus weakened the moral legitimacy of the order they dominated. Formerly all of Vedic literature had been memorized, and only the brightest Brahmans could master the tradition. The newer, simpler writing made sacred knowledge more accessible. To the Brahmans, nothing about the cities seemed good.

Frightened by these conditions, Brahmans sought to strengthen their relationships with the *rajas* by establishing the idea of a king endowed with divine power. Kingship had been unnecessary according to Brahmanic scripts in a long-ago golden age; a moral code and priests to uphold it were enough to keep things in order. Over time, though, the world deteriorated and the pure mixed with the impure, until many inhabitants spoke of "fish eating fish" to refer to the practice of individuals killing each other for wealth. According to Brahmanic writings, the gods then decided that people on earth needed a king to maintain order. The gods selected Manu ("Man"), but Manu did not want to accept the difficult job. To win his consent, the gods promised him one-tenth of the grain harvest, one-fiftieth of the cattle, one-quarter of the merits earned by the good behavior of his subjects, and the most beautiful woman in his domain. In this Brahmanic account, royal power has a divine origin: the gods chose the king and protected him. Moreover, priests and Vedic rituals were essential to royal power, since kingly authority was validated through religious ceremonies carried out by Brahman priests. Another Brahmanic account conveys this point, relating a story in which the priests themselves magically create a king, whose "birth" wins divine celebration and approval. (See Primary Source: Warring Ideas: The Buddha versus the Brahmans—On the Origin of the King.)

This emphasis on divine kingship solved some problems but created new ones. The Brahmans' claim to moral authority caused resentment among the Kshatriyas—especially those in the oligarchic republics, whose leaders did not assert divine power. Merchants and artisans, as members of growing subcastes, also chafed at the Brahmans' claims to superiority. Such resentments provoked challenges to the Brahmans' domination. Some thinkers in South Asia (like those in China and in the Greek cities experiencing similar upheavals around this time) believed that they were in an age of acute crisis because their culture's ancient harmony had been lost. And like many scholars and philosophers elsewhere in this era, a new group of South Asian scholars and religious leaders developed their own answers to questions about human existence.

DISSIDENT THINKERS Dissident South Asian thinkers challenged the Brahmans' worldview by refusing to recognize the gods that populated the Vedic world. Some of these rebels sprang from inside the Vedic tradition; though Brahmans, they rejected the idea that sacrificial rituals pleased the gods. To them, God was a universal concept, not a superhuman

WARRING IDEAS: THE BUDDHA VERSUS THE BRAHMANS—ON THE ORIGIN OF THE KING

The Election of a King

This passage is from one of the earliest Buddhist texts, Dialogues of the Buddha. Here the Buddha explains to one of his disciples, Vāseṭṭha, how the state and king came into being. Early human beings were pure, but they became greedy and chaotic. As a result they elected one person as king to maintain order. They rewarded the chosen one, called the Great Elect, with a share of their rice. (Note that in this account the people themselves choose the king. Unlike the Brahmanic account that follows, there is no mention of priests or gods.)

When they had ceased rice appeared, ripening in open spaces, without powder, without husk, pure, fragrant and clean grained. Where we plucked and took away for the evening meal every evening, there next morning it had grown ripe again. Where we plucked and took away for the morning meal, there in the evening it had grown ripe again. There was no break visible. Enjoying this rice, feeding on it, nourished by it, we have so continued a long long while. But from evil and immoral customs becoming manifest among us, powder has enveloped the clean grain, husk too has enveloped the clean grain, and where we have reaped is no re-growth; a break has come, and the rice-stubble stands in clumps. Come now, let us divide off the rice fields and set boundaries thereto! And so they divided off the rice and set up boundaries round it.

Now some being, Vāseṭṭha, of greedy disposition, watching over his own plot, stole another plot and made use of it. They took him and holding him fast, said: Truly, good being, thou hast wrought evil in that, while watching thine own plot, thou hast stolen another plot and made use of it. See, good being, that thou do not such a thing again! Ay, sirs, he replied. And a second time he did so. And yet a third. And again they took him and admonished him. Some smote him with the hand, some with clods, some with sticks. With such a beginning, Vāseṭṭha, did stealing appear, and censure and lying and punishment became known.

Now those beings, Vāseṭṭha, gathered themselves together, and bewailed these things, saying: From our evil deeds, sirs, becoming manifest, inasmuch as stealing, censure, lying, punishment have become known, what if we were to select a certain being, who should be wrathful when indignation is right, who should censure that which should rightly be censured and should banish him who deserves to be banished? But we will give him in return a proportion of the rice.

Then, Vāseṭṭha, those beings went to the being among them who was the handsomest, the best favoured, the most attractive, the most capable and said to him: Come now, good being, be indignant at that whereat one should rightly be indignant, censure that which should rightly be censured, banish him who deserves to be banished. And we will contribute to thee a proportion of our rice.

And he consented, and did so, and they gave him a proportion of their rice.

creature. Also, they felt that the many cows that priests slaughtered for ritual sacrifices could serve more practical uses, such as plowing the land and producing milk. Their discussions and teachings about the universe and life were later collected in the Upanishads (see Chapter 4).

Other dissidents came from outside the Vedic tradition. Consider the Buddha and Mahavira (discussed below), who both came from the middle Ganges region where a pastoral economy and rituals of cattle sacrifice were nonexistent. Here people had never spoken Brahmanical Sanskrit and never had a Brahman caste in their communities. But they, too, challenged the Brahmans, though some adopted and developed ideas expressed in the Upanishads.

MAHAVIRA AND JAINISM Jainism and Buddhism were the two most influential schools outside the Vedic tradition

A King Selected by Brahmans and Endorsed by Gods

Several stories about the beginning of monarchy are preserved in Brahmanic Hindu literature. The story of Prithu tells of the mutual dependence of the king and Brahman priests, who selected the king and guaranteed the gods' endorsement of him. Initially a king named Vena refused to worship gods, so the Brahmans killed him. Then they created a new king, Prithu, who followed all the rituals.

Afterwards (after the Brahmans killed the vicious king Vena who refused to worship gods) the Munis (Brahmans) beheld a great dust arise, and they said to the people who were nigh, "What is this?" and the people answered and said, "Now that the kingdom is without a king, the dishonest men have begun to seize the property of their neighbors. The great dust that you behold, excellent Munis, is raised by troops of clustering robbers, hastening to fall upon their prey." The sages, hearing this, consulted, and together rubbed the thigh of the king, who had left no offspring, to produce a son. From the thigh, thus rubbed came forth a being of the complexion of a charred stake, with flattened features, and of dwarfish stature. "What am I to do?" cried he eagerly to the Munis. "Sit down" (Nishida), said they; and thence his name was Nishada. His descendants, the inhabitants of the Vindhya mountain, are still called Nishadas, and are characterized by the exterior tokens of depravity. By this means the wickedness of Vena was expelled; those Nishadas being born of his sins, and carrying them away. The Brahmans then proceeded to rub the right arm of the king, from which friction was engendered the illustrious son of Vena, named Prithu, resplendent in person, as if the blazing deity of Fire had been manifested.

There then fell from the sky the primitive bow (of Mahadeva) named Ajagava, and celestial arrows, and panoply from heaven. At the birth of Prithu all living creatures rejoiced; and Vena, delivered by his being born from the hell named Put, ascended to the realms above. The seas and rivers, bringing jewels from their depths, and water to perform the ablutions of his installation, appeared. The great parent of all, Brahma, with the gods and the descendants of Angiras (the fires), and with all things animate or inanimate, assembled and performed the ceremony of consecrating the son of Vena. Beholding in his right hand the (mark of the) discus of Vishnu, Brahma recognized a portion of that divinity in Prithu, and was much pleased; for the mark of Vishnu's discus is visible in the hand of one who is born to be universal emperor (chakravarti). One whose power is invincible even by the gods.

→ *After the Vedic peoples migrated into the mid-Ganges plain, rice cultivation and feuding characterized their society. How does the Buddha's story about the election of the first king reflect this social history?*

→ *How does the Brahmans' story underscore the role of the priests in upholding the monarchy? Why do you suppose the Brahman priests were so concerned that the king worship gods and follow traditional rituals?*

SOURCE: *Dialogues of the Buddha, Part iii*, vol. 4 of *Sacred Books of the Buddhists*, translated by T. W. Rhys David and C. A. F. Rhys David (London: Oxford University Press, 1921), pp. 87–88; *Vishnu Purana*, translated from Sanskrit by H. H. Wilson, 1st ed. 1840, 3rd ed. Calcutta: Punthi Pustak, 1961, pp. 83–84.

that set themselves against the Brahmans. In the sixth century BCE, Vardhamana Mahavira (c. 540–468 BCE) popularized the doctrines of **Jainism**, which had emerged in the seventh century BCE. Born a Kshatriya in an oligarchic republic, Mahavira left home at age thirty to seek the truth about life; he spent twelve years as an **ascetic** (one who rejects material possessions and physical pleasures) wandering throughout the Ganges Valley before reaching enlightenment. He taught that the universe obeys its own everlasting rules and cannot be affected by any god or other supernatural being. He also believed that the purpose of life is to purify one's soul through asceticism and to attain a state of permanent bliss. The Jains' religious doctrines emphasized asceticism over knowledge: strict self-denial enabled one to avoid harming other creatures and thereby purify the soul. Moreover, the doctrine of *ahimsa* ("no hurt") held that every living creature has a soul. Killing even an ant would lead one to an unfavorable rebirth and further away from permanent bliss. Therefore, believers had to watch every step to avoid inadvertently becoming a murderer.

Since land could not be cultivated without killing insects, the extreme nonviolence of Jainism excluded the peasants. Instead, it became a religion of traders and other city dwellers. Mahavira's followers originally transmitted his teachings orally; but a thousand years after his death they wrote them down. The strictly nonviolent doctrine, though originally intended only for followers of Jainism, has profoundly affected the inhabitants of South Asia down to modern times.

BUDDHA AND BUDDHISM The most direct challenge to traditional Brahmanic thinking came from Siddhartha Gautama (c. 563–483 BCE), usually called the **Buddha,** or the Enlightened One. He was a contemporary of Mahavira as well as of Confucius. The Buddha not only objected to

The Buddha's Footprints. Before his followers came to regard Buddha as a god, they were reluctant to make an idol of him—the footprints were an early representation of Buddha. They were carved in a limestone panel in a first-century BCE stupa in India.

Brahmanic rituals and sacrifices but also denied their elaborate **cosmology** (a branch of metaphysics devoted to understanding the order of the universe) and the preference for kingship that kept the priestly class in power. His teachings provided the peoples of South Asia and elsewhere with alternatives to established traditions. In this respect, Buddhism in South Asia functioned much like Confucianism in China. (See Global Connections & Disconnections: Prophets and the Founding Texts: Comparing Confucius and the Buddha.)

The Buddha came from a small Kshatriya, or warrior, community in the foothills of the Himalayas; in this oligarchic republic, his father was one of the *rajas.* Dismayed at the misery and political carnage of his age, Siddhartha left home at age twenty-nine in search of truth and enlightenment. Traveling through the Ganges region, he lived as a beggar and then as a hermit, and finally, according to legend, meditated for forty-nine days until he understood how to eliminate suffering from the world.

His wanderings and ascetic life led him to create a new credo, which his teachings expressed as the Four Truths: (1) life, from birth to death, is full of suffering; (2) all sufferings are caused by desires; (3) the only way to rise above suffering is to renounce desire; and (4) only through adherence to the Noble Eightfold Path can individuals rid themselves of desires and the illusion of separate identity and thus reach a state of contentment, or *nirvana.* The elements of the Eightfold Path represent wisdom (right views and right intentions), ethical behavior (right conduct, right speech, and right livelihood), and mental discipline (right effort, right thought, and right meditation). Because these principles were simple and clear, the Four Truths had a powerful appeal. This teaching also represented a dramatic shift in thinking about humanity and correct behavior. Like the teachings of Mahavira, the Buddha's doctrines left no space for the supernaturals to dictate human lives, a theme stressed in classical Brahmanic thinking. Buddha's logical explanation of human suffering and his guidelines for renouncing desire appealed to many people, for it set forth tenets by which its followers strove to live virtuously. Those who accumulated enough merits could be reborn in heaven. In contrast, wasting merits by indulging in desires could mean failing to reach heaven, or even sliding to hell.

Buddhism's appeal becomes more understandable in the context of reincarnation of the soul, a concept initiated in the Upanishads and widely accepted by the people of South Asia. If life itself is suffering, and if death leads simply to rebirth into another life, then the cycle of time brings endless suffering. Attaining nirvana, a state reached only after accumulating many merits, was the sole means of achieving liberation from life's troubles.

Like other dissident thinkers of this period, the Buddha delivered his message in a vernacular dialect of Sanskrit that all could understand. His many followers soon formed a community of monks called a *sangha* ("gathering"). The

Global Connections & Disconnections

PROPHETS AND THE FOUNDING TEXTS: COMPARING CONFUCIUS AND THE BUDDHA

Throughout history, universalizing religions have been defined not just by their sacred texts but also by central figures whose lives inspired movements and long-lasting traditions. In Confucianism and Buddhism, we find key leaders who inspired the faiths that were subsequently named for them.

 Confucius (551–479 BCE) was one of the ancient world's great innovators. Born in China, he elaborated a code of behavior that valued individual performance of traditional rituals and governmental morality based on correct social relationships, sincerity, and justice. Seeing division and war among rival states, he wished to restore order by promoting education, moral behavior, and the performance of ritual.

Over the centuries the method and substance of his teaching, with many revisions, became the mainstream value system of imperial China. His idea of modeling the state on the patriarchal family—that is, the ruler should respect the heaven as if it were his father and protect his subjects as if they were his children—became the foundation of Chinese political theory. One could summarize his philosophy of teaching in three statements: "I teach whoever wants to learn with no regard to his birth," "The best educated men should serve the government," and "Those who work with their minds should rule, and those who work with their hands should be ruled." Confucius wanted people to perform the rituals bequeathed by the early Zhou and to emulate the sages who had ordered the world according to principles of civility and culture.

Chinese philosophers did not always agree on how to interpret Confucius's ideas. Representing one school of Confucianists, Mencius (372–289 BCE) held that while recognizing the tendency of people to be led astray by worldly appetites and ambitions, Confucius believed in the inherent goodness of human nature. To recover that innate goodness required moral training. But according to Xunzi (310–237 BCE), Confucius saw humans as evil and lacking an innate moral sense. They therefore had to be controlled by education, ritual, and custom.

Nevertheless, both Mencius and Xunzi embraced Confucius's dictum that people were perfectible through education and the practice of proper conduct. All Confucians, whether pessimists or optimists, viewed moral cultivation through education as the heart of the civilizing process, and they ensured that his ideas remained a vital force throughout Chinese history.

 The teachings of the **Buddha** (c. 563–483 BCE), like those of Confucius, had far-reaching influence. The two thinkers were roughly contemporary, and both formulated their ideas in response to social chaos and degeneration. The Buddha presented a vision of society that challenged the Brahmanic order. Buddhism shaped the views of life and death and the scheme of time and space of the universe in South Asia. It also had a profound impact on peoples outside the region and even replaced Confucianism as the dominant religion in China for a few hundred years.

The Buddha offered a logical approach in the form of a unified system underlying the universe, instead of invoking divine intervention, to understand the universe and social life at a time of rapid political development. He believed that the universe and individual lives go through eternal cycles of birth, death, and rebirth, and he elaborated the concept of *karma* ("fate" or "action"), a universal principle of cause and effect. The birth of every living being, human or animal, reflects actions taken in his or her past lives. Karma embodies the sins and merits of each individual, establishing his or her status in the current life. In turn, deeds in the current life affect that karma and thus determine suffering and happiness in the next life. Buddhist believers therefore focused on the consequences of their actions: through their own behavior, they could attain better future lives.

Confucianism and Buddhism, much like the Vedic, Brahmin, and Judaic faiths discussed in Chapter 4, emerged in times of great turmoil. All the faiths were first transmitted orally; later, adherents created a written record to spread them more widely. But Buddhism and Confucianism stand out in that they have founders whose identification with their belief systems remains their most defining characteristic: the Buddha as an enlightened one, and Confucius as a sage teacher. We will see this phenomenon again with the rise of Christianity (from the teachings of Jesus) and Islam (from the teachings of Muhammad) as we continue our discussion of universalizing religions.

Buddha and his followers wandered from one city to another on the Ganges plain, where they found large audiences as well as the alms needed to sustain the expanding *sangha*. In fact, the Buddha's most influential patrons were urban merchants. And in struggles between oligarchs and kings, the Buddha sided with the oligarchs—reflecting his upbringing in an oligarchic republic. He inevitably aroused opposition from the Brahmans, who favored monarchical government. While the Buddha himself did not seek to erase the caste hierarchy, the *sangha* provided an escape from its oppressive aspects and the prestige that it afforded the Brahmans. Although Mahavira and the Buddha did not erase the Brahmans' spiritual authority or dismantle the caste hierarchy, nevertheless they established independent enclaves that carried out religious, scholarly, and social activities based on their own doctrines.

COMMON CULTURES IN THE AMERICAS

> → *How did cultural integration occur in the Andes and Mesoamerica in the absence of political unity?*

Although peoples living in the Americas during what we have termed the axial age in Eurasia and North Africa did not have immense cities, elaborate written texts, domesticated animals, and the other ingredients that underlay the radical new ideas of this era elsewhere, political and intellectual leaders among the Chavín peoples of the Andes and the Olmecs of Mesoamerica provided answers to many of the same questions that were perplexing Eurasians and North Africans Their insights also left a profound imprint on their communities and on future generations. Of course, because we do not have the impressive documentary record that exists for Eurasian and North African written texts, our knowledge of their beliefs has to be based primarily on archaeological remains. These, however, provide clues to the cultural systems that these communities embraced.

THE CHAVÍN IN THE ANDES

In a world of extreme localization and diversity, the steep mountainsides and deep fertile valleys of the Andes Mountains became the home of a distinctive people called the Chavín. In what is now northern Peru, farmers and pastoralists began to share a common belief system around 1400 BCE.

With time, their artistic influence and spiritual principles touched a broad expanse of Andean folk. Like the peoples of South Asia, the Chavín were united by culture and faith more than by any political structure.

The Chavín peoples literally organized their societies vertically. Communities and households spread their trading systems up the mountainsides: valley floors yielded tropical and subtropical produce; the mountains supported maize and other crops; and in the highlands, potatoes became a staple and llamas produced wool and dung (as fertilizer and fuel) and, eventually, served as beasts of burden. Llamas could not transport humans, however, so the Chavín migratory and political reach remained limited. No empire would emerge in the Andes for another millennium.

The ecological diversity of the Chavín societies enabled them to find all necessities close at hand, but they did undertake some long-distance trade—mainly in dyes and precious stones, such as obsidian. By 900 BCE, the Chavín were erecting elaborate stone carvings, using advanced techniques to weave fine cotton textiles, and making gold, silver, and copper metal goods. Scholars have found evidence that by 400 BCE trade in painted textiles, ceramics, and gold objects spanned the Pacific coast, the Andean highlands, and the watershed eastward to the tropical rainforests of the Amazon basin. However, these networks were not extensive and only conveyed light precious goods.

What unified the fragmented Chavín communities was a shared artistic tradition reflecting devotion to powerful deities. Their spiritual capital was the central temple complex of Chavín de Huántar, in modern Peru's northeastern highlands. The temple boasted a U-shaped platform whose opening to the east surrounded a sunken, circular plaza; from its passageways and underground galleries, priests could make dramatic entrances during ceremonies. The priests took hallucinogenic drugs, which believers felt enabled them to become jaguars—the region's most dangerous predator—and to commune with the supernatural. Pilgrims brought tribute to Chavín de Huántar, where they worshipped and feasted together.

The Chavín drew on influences from as far away as the Amazon and the Pacific coast as they created devotional cults that revered wild animals as representatives of spiritual forces. Carved stone jaguars, serpents, and hawks, baring their large fangs and claws to remind believers of nature's powers, dominated the spiritual landscape. The "Smiling God" at Chavín de Huántar, El Lanzón, shaped from a slab of white granite fifteen feet high, had a human form but a fanged, catlike face, hair of writhing snakes, feet ending with talons, and hands bristling with claws. This supernatural image dominated an awe-inspiring stage: dimly lit from above so that his face would glow from the reflection of polished mirrors, the god stood over a canal, and the vibrations and deep rumbling sounds of the rushing water below conveyed a sense of spiritual forces. Though they borrowed from

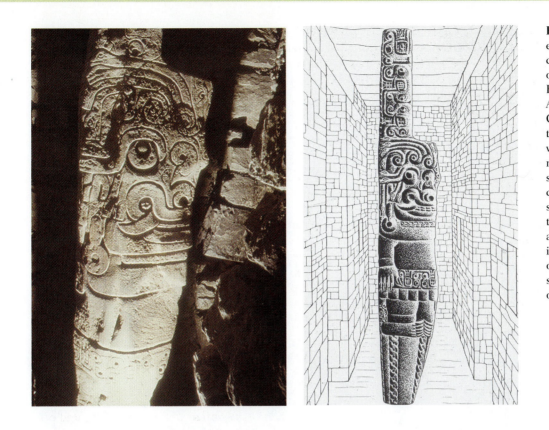

El Lanzón. The Chavín excelled at elaborate stone carvings with complex images of their deities. This image of El Lanzón is a good example. At the center of one of the Chavín peoples' greatest temples is this massive gallery with a giant monument in the middle, etched with images of snakes, felines, and humans combined into one hybrid supernatural form. Observe the hands and feet with claws and the eyebrows that turn into serpents. The rendering on the right makes it easier to see the details on the actual object.

neighbors and refined existing sculptural techniques, the Chavín created the first great art style of the Andes. Their cult gave way around 400 BCE to local cultural heirs, but some elements of it survived in successor religions adopted by stronger states to the south.

THE OLMECS IN MESOAMERICA

Further to the north, in Mesoamerica, the first complex society emerged around 1500 BCE between the highland plateaus of central Mexico and the Gulf Coast around modern-day Veracruz. (See Map 5-4.) The Olmecs are an example of a first-generation community that created new political and economic institutions while contemplating profound questions about the nature of humanity and the world beyond.

Mesoamerican cultures sprang up from local village roots. The region's peoples formed a loose confederation of villages scattered from the coast to the highlands, mainly nestling in river valleys and along the shores of swampy lakes. Their residents traded with one another, shared a common language, and worshipped the same gods. These were the **Olmecs**, a name meaning "inhabitants in the land of rubber"—one of their staples. Around 1500 BCE, the residents of hundreds of hamlets began to develop a single culture and to spread their beliefs, artistic achievements, and social structure far beyond their heartland.

At the core of Olmec culture were its decentralized villages, which housed hundreds—possibly thousands—of households apiece. In these settlements productive subsistence farmers cultivated most of the foodstuffs their communities needed (especially maize, beans, squash, and cacao), while shipping lightweight products including ceramics and precious goods (such as jade, obsidian, or quetzal feathers, used to create masks and ritual figurines) to other villages. Most of the precious objects were for religious purposes rather than everyday consumption.

CITIES AS SACRED CENTERS Despite their dispersed social landscape, the Olmec peoples created shared belief systems, a single language, and a priestly class who ensured that villagers followed highly ritualized practices. Their primary cities, including San Lorenzo, La Venta, and Tres Zapotes, were not large compared to the urban centers of Afro-Eurasia, but they were religious and secular hubs. They were built around specialized buildings that featured massive earthen mounds, platforms, palaces, and capacious plazas.

The rulers of San Lorenzo, for instance, constructed a city of terraces and ridges on a plateau high above the Chiquito River. Their vassals used baskets to haul more than 2.3 million cubic feet of soil to lay out the enormous central platform, two football fields in length, upon which palaces and workshops rose. All around the courtyards and paths were massive stone monuments—colossal heads, jaguar sculptures, and

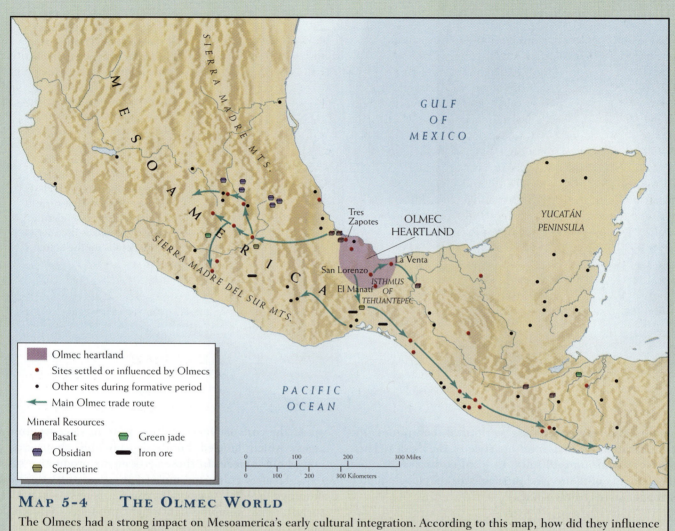

MAP 5-4   THE OLMEC WORLD

The Olmecs had a strong impact on Mesoamerica's early cultural integration. According to this map, how did they influence people living beyond the Olmec heartland? What factors limited the extent of Olmec influence? Why do you think the Olmecs never developed a politically unified regional empire?

basalt thrones—as well as clusters of large wooden busts. These vast sculpture gardens depicted the human rulers and deities to whom the Olmecs paid homage and offered sacrifice. Artificial lagoons and channels crisscrossed the precinct. Beneath these mounds archaeologists have found axes, knives of sharpened obsidian, other tools, and simple yet breathtaking figurines made most often of jade, buried as tokens for those who dwelled in the supernatural world. San Lorenzo was not a capital city with rulers and laws that controlled territorial domains. Rather, it was a devotional center whose monumental architecture and art had widespread influence reaching as far as the Olmec hinterlands.

Paying homage to their gods and rulers was part of the Olmecs' daily life. While devotional activity occurred on lakeshores, in caves, on mountaintops, and in other natural settings, it occurred above all in the primary cities. In La Venta, huge pits (one was 13 feet deep and 75 feet wide) contained massive offerings of hundreds of tons of serpentine carved blocks. Olmec art speaks to the powerful influence of devotion on creativity. (See Primary Source: Olmec Art as Ideology.) Many images featured representations of natural and supernatural entities—not just snakes, jaguars, and crocodiles, but also certain humans called **shamans**, whose powers supposedly enabled them to commune with the supernatural and to transform themselves wholly or partly into beasts (also evident in images at Chavín sites). A common figurine is the "were-jaguar," a being that was part man, part animal. Shamans representing jaguars invoked the

OLMEC ART AS IDEOLOGY

Olmec ideology emphasized ties among the natural, supernatural, and human worlds. It also sought to influence and possibly convert the Olmecs' neighbors. Known primarily for their monumental architecture and artwork, Olmec craftsworkers also made portable objects and miniature figures that unified their belief systems and could be transported over long distances to expand the spiritual frontier of Olmec belief throughout Mesoamerica.

One of the most famous surviving portable spiritual icons, called "Young Lord," combines many of the basic elements of Olmec belief into a single, beautiful jade figurine. Standing about two feet tall, Young Lord was a diplomatic artifact, intended to spread the influence of a complex belief system far and wide. His pose is rigid and tall, like that of a ruler who serves as the turning point to join earthly and supernatural worlds. Holding two scepters against his chest, and himself carved in the form of a scepter, he conveys power and influence. (A scepter is a staff or baton signifying authority.)

Young Lord is fierce. The delicate incisions around his body represent ceremonial practices—rituals that he oversees and that enable him to exercise shamanic powers over believers. His face, for instance, wears a mask that evokes classic Olmec shamanic images: a snarling mouth like a jaguar's, and a nose like an eagle's beak. The mask and its carvings suggest that this lord is capable of transforming into a jaguar or a bird of prey to conduct sacrificial rites. Extensive incisions all over his body reinforce this point.

The incisions or scars emphasize bloodletting and human sacrifice, and they underscore the importance of the scepters, which can be used to draw blood. These sacrifices were intended to please the forces of the supernatural world, which would reward believers with rain. In fact, images of ritual performers and victims cover Young Lord's arms and hands. Adorning his legs are figures of serpentlike creatures, monsters with gaping jaws, fangs, and forked tongues.

The statue as a whole is divided horizontally into three, signifying the three layers of the cosmos—the supernatural, the terrestrial, and the underworld—which Young Lord has the power to travel among as he brings messages to believers and nonbelievers alike. This is a powerful image, one meant to drive home the authority of Olmec rulers to their subjects and neighbors.

→ *What wild beings do the carvings on Young Lord represent? What characteristics of each one would have led the Olmecs to use them as symbols?*

→ *What do the symbols reveal about spiritual aspects of Olmec society?*

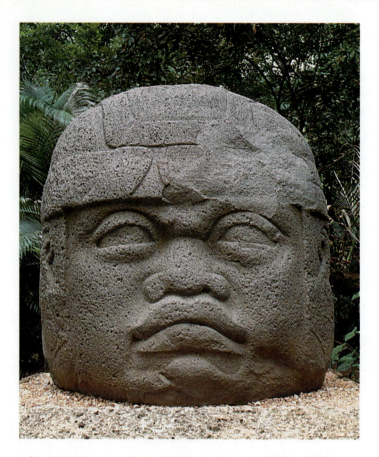

Olmec Head. At La Venta, in Tabasco State in Mexico, four colossal heads rest on the ground, remnants of a field of monumental figures that once ornamented this Olmec site. Nine feet high and weighing up to twenty tons, the heads are the source of much speculation. Carved from single boulders, they are thought to be portraits of great kings or legendary ballplayers. Each head bears distinctive elements in homage to its subject.

Olmec rain god, a jaguarlike being, to bring rainfall and secure the land's fertility. Indeed, the Olmecs' ceremonial life revolved around agricultural and rainfall cycles. Evidence of a shared iconography throughout the heartland suggests an integrated culture that transcended ecological niches.

CITIES AS ATHLETIC HUBS The Olmecs' major cities were not just devotional centers but also athletic hubs, where victorious teams paid homage to their deities. Intricate ball courts had room on the sidelines for fans to applaud and jeer at the sweating contestants, who struggled to bounce hard rubber balls off parallel sidewalls and their bodies and into a goal. Noble players, bearing helmets and heavy padding, could touch the six-pound rubber ball only with their elbows, hips, knees, and buttocks, and they were honored when they knocked the ball through the stationary stone hoop. Massive sculptures of helmeted heads carved out of volcanic basalt suggest monuments to famous ballplayers. At La Venta, a huge mosaic made out of greenstone served as an elegant ball court;

at its center was a portal that was thought to open into the otherworld. Olmec archaeological sites are filled with the remains of game equipment and trophies, some of which were entombed with dead rulers so they could play ball with the gods in the otherworld. Ritual ball games, for all their entertainment value, were integral to Olmec devotional culture. It was in honor of the powerful rain god that players struggled to win.

What added to the thrill of the ball court was that they were dangerous places associated with water and agricultural fertility, for an equally important aspect of devotional culture was human sacrifice. Indeed, it is likely that athletics and sacrifice were blended in the same rituals. Many monuments depict a victorious and costumed ballplayer (sporting a jaguar headdress or a feathered serpent helmet) atop a defeated, bound human, though scholars are not sure whether the losers were literally executed. Rainmaking rites also included human sacrifice, which involved executing and dismembering captives. At El Manatí, offering sites alongside a spring and a boggy lakeshore have yielded the bones of children slaughtered for the gods. Across the Olmecs' artistic landscape are representations of human victims fed to the gods and to the rulers who embodied them.

MAN, NATURE, AND TIME The Olmec cosmology assumed a relationship between the natural and supernatural worlds, with the latter dictating the motions of the former. Olmec culture was saturated with belief in the power of supernatural forces and with tales of shamans controlling the supernatural. But the Olmecs were hardly a simple, superstitious folk; in fact, their conviction that the supernatural pervaded the natural world drove them to systematically observe the natural world so that they could discover godly meanings. There was no hard-and-fast line between what we now call "faith" and "science." The way that rulers reckoned time reflects this belief system, for they were convinced that the gods defined calendric passages—thus the seasons and crucial rainfall patterns. Priests, charting celestial movements, devised a complex calendar that marked the passage of seasons and generations. As in China and Mesopotamia, a cultural flowering encouraged priests and scholars to study and accurately chart the rhythms of the terrestrial and celestial worlds.

A WORLD OF SOCIAL DISTINCTIONS Daily labor kept Olmecs busy. The vast majority worked the fertile lands as part of household units, with children and parents toiling in the fields with wooden tools, fishing in streams with nets, and hunting turtles and other small animals. Most Olmecs had to juggle the needs of their immediate families, their village neighbors, and the taxes imposed by rulers.

Unlike many decentralized agrarian cultures that were simple and egalitarian, the Olmecs developed an elaborate cultural system marked by many tiers of social rankings. The priestly class, raised and trained in the palaces at La Venta, San Lorenzo, and Tres Zapotes, directed the exchanges of sacred ritual objects among farming communities. Because these exchanges involved immense resources, the wealthy ruling families had to be involved—an association that buttressed their claim to be the descendants of divine ancestors. At the same time, by controlling trade in precious secular goods they added to their fortunes. As ruling families blurred the line between the everyday and the religious, they legitimized their power and gained access to vast resources.

Alongside the priestly elite, a secular one emerged composed of chieftains who supervised agrarian transactions, oversaw artisans, and accepted villagers' tribute. They set up workshops, managed by foremen, where craftsworkers created pots, painted, sculpted, and wove. Some of their work featured stones and gems imported from surrounding villages. The highest-ranking chieftains commanded villages scattered over the approximate area of a territorial state (such as current-day Veracruz in Mexico).

The combination of an integrated culture and a complex social structure gave the Olmecs a degree of cohesion unprecedented in the Americas. Ultimately their influence radiated well beyond their heartland through trade. As the Olmecs' arts expanded, so did their demand for imported obsidian and jade, seashells, plumes, and other precious goods. The Olmecs themselves exported rubber (made by combining different latexes from trees and vines into a tough but pliable material—just right for a playing ball!), cacao, pottery, ceramics, figurines, jaguar pelts, and crocodile skins all throughout Mesoamerica. Importing and exporting were probably in the hands of a merchant class, about which scholars know little. The Olmecs also conveyed their belief system to neighbors—if not to convert them, at least to influence them and reinforce a sense of superiority. Without an urge to conquer or colonize, the Olmecs nonetheless shaped the social development of much of Mesoamerica.

THE LOSS OF CENTERS The breakdown of the Olmec culture is shrouded in mystery. The decline was abrupt in some centers and drawn out in others. At La Venta, the altars and massive basalt heads were defaced and buried, indicating a dramatic shift. Yet there is little evidence of a spasm of war, a peasant uprising, a population shift, or conflict within the ruling classes. Indeed, in many parts of the heartland, the religious centers that had been the hubs of the Olmec world were abandoned but not destroyed. Much of the Olmec hinterland remained heavily populated and highly productive.

Apparently the machinery for drawing resources into Olmec capitals eventually failed. As the bonds between rulers and subjects weakened, so did the exchange of ritual objects that had enlivened the Olmec centers and made them magnets for obedience and piety. Olmec hierarchies then collapsed. Without a sacred elite to transmit the belief system, it too faded. What was left of the Olmec heritage passed on to other Mesoamericans—especially those of the central plateaus and the tropical lowlands of the Yucatán peninsula.

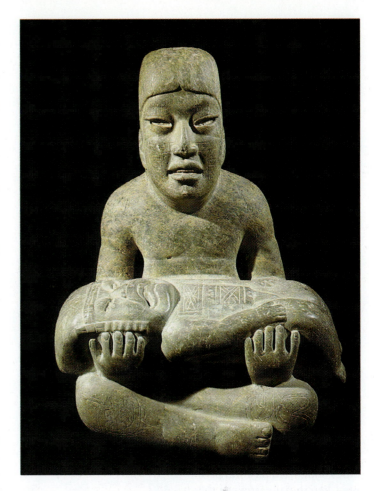

The Las Limas Monument. The were-jaguar was an important figure in the pantheon of Olmec deities. This sculpture represents a youth holding a limp were-jaguar baby. We do not know what these figures represented exactly—most likely they refer to spiritual journeys. Some have argued that this monument harkens to child sacrifice.

COMMON CULTURES IN SUB-SAHARAN AFRICA

→ *How did the spread of iron smelting shape the social landscape of sub-Saharan Africa?*

In Africa, too, widespread common cultures emerged in this era in a number of favorable locations. Yet to understand these communities it is essential first of all to describe the climate and geography of Africa because these forces played a critical role in cultural formation. Climatically, Africa's most significant historical development at this time was the continued desiccation of the northern and central landmass, and the sprawl of the great Sahara Desert as its primary geographical and population barrier. (See Map 5-5.) Large areas that had once supported abundant plant and animal life, including human settlements, now became sparsely populated. As a result, the African peoples began to coalesce in a few locations. Most important was the Nile Valley, which may have held more than half of the entire population at this time.

THE FOUR ZONES

Climatic change divided Africa from the equator northward to the Sahara Desert into four zones. The first zone was the Sahara itself, which never completely emptied out despite its extreme heat and aridity. Its oases supported pastoral peoples, like the ancestors of the modern Tuareg tribal communities, who raised livestock and promoted contacts between the northern and western parts of the landmass. South of the Sahara was the Sahel, literally the "coast" (Arabic *sahil*) of the great ocean of sand. In time, some of Africa's great commercial cities, like Timbuktu, would arise here; but in the first millennium BCE no city of great size made an appearance.

The next zone was the Sudanic savanna, an area of high grasslands stretching from present-day Senegal along the Atlantic Ocean in the west to the Nile River and the Red Sea in the east. Many of West Africa's kingdoms emerged there because the area was free of the tsetse fly, which was as lethal to animals as to humans, killing off cattle, horses, and goats. The fourth zone comprised the western and central African rain forests, a sparsely populated region characterized by small-scale societies.

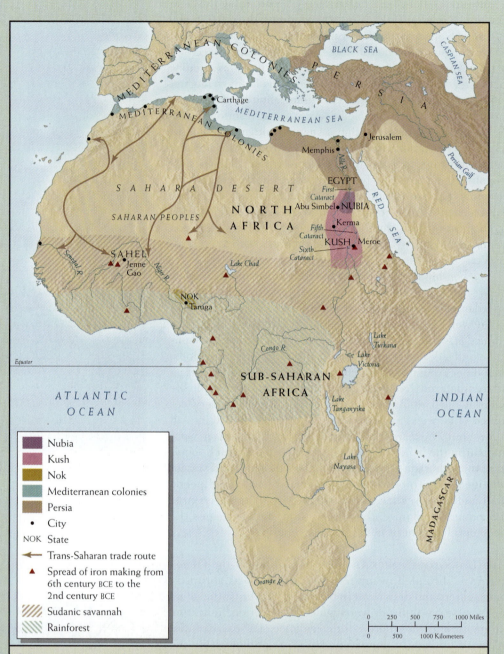

MAP 5-5   AFRICA, 500 BCE

The first millennium BCE was a period of cultural, economic, and political integration for North and sub-Saharan Africa. According to this map, what effect did the Mediterranean colonies have on Africa? What main factor integrated Kush, Nubia, and Egypt? Does the map reveal a relationship between the rise of Sudanic culture and the spread of ironworking? If so, what is it?

Although there was contact across the Sahara, Africa below the Sahara differed markedly from North Africa and Eurasia. It did not develop a plow agriculture; instead, its farmers depended on hoes. Also, except in densely populated regions, land was held communally and never carried as much value as labor. African peoples could always move into new locations. They had more difficulty finding workers to turn the soil.

Distinctive and widespread common cultures that would characterize certain parts of sub-Saharan Africa from 1000 CE onward were only beginning to emerge during the first millennium BCE. In the savanna, millet and sorghum were the primary food crops; in the rain forests, yams and other root crops predominated. Relatively large populations inhabited the Sudanic savanna, the sole area for which substantial historical records exist. Here, in fact, a way of life that we can call Sudanic began to crystallize.

These peoples were not completely dependent on their feet to get around (as were their counterparts in the Americas). They had domesticated several animals, including cattle and goats, and even possessed small horses. Although their communities were scattered widely across Africa, they had much in common. For example, they all possessed a cosmology dominated by a high god, polities led by sacred kings, and burial customs of interring servants alongside dead rulers to serve them in the afterlife. These peoples were skilled cultivators and weavers of cotton, which they had domesticated. Archaeologists and historians used to believe that the Sudanic peoples borrowed their institutions, notably their sacred kingships, from their Egyptian neighbors; but linguistic evidence and their burial customs indicate that the Sudanic communities developed these practices independently.

NUBIA: BETWEEN SUDANIC AFRICA AND PHARAONIC EGYPT

One of the most highly developed locations of common culture in sub-Saharan Africa was Nubia, a region lying between the first Nile cataract (a large waterfall) and the last (near where the Blue and White Niles come together). From at least the fourth millennium BCE onward, peoples in this region had contact with both the northern and southern parts of the African landmass. It was one of the few parts of sub-Saharan Africa known to the outside world. The Greek poet Homer described its inhabitants as "the remotest nation, the most just of men; the favorites of the gods."

The first of the important Nubian states was Kush. It flourished between 1700 and 1500 BCE between the first and third cataracts and had its capital at Kerma. Because of its close proximity to Egypt it adopted many Egyptian cultural and political practices, even though it was under constant pressure from the northern powerhouse. Its successor states had to move farther south, up the Nile, to keep free from the powerful Egyptians; the kingdom's capitals were repeatedly uprooted and relocated upriver.

Nubia's historical connection to Egypt was obvious: it was Egypt's corridor to sub-Saharan Africa; a source of ivory, gold, and slaves; and an area that Egyptian monarchs wanted to dominate. The Egyptians called the region Kush, the name that later historians gave to the various regimes that flourished there. To the Egyptians, Kush was a land and the Kushites a people to be exploited. It was not a location that the Egyptians wished to reside in. Their chroniclers best described the Egyptian view of the territory and the people, referring to it repeatedly as "miserable Kush." The best known of the Egyptian conquerors was Ramses II, who left his

The Temple of Ramses II.
The temple of Ramses II at Abu Simbel was constructed during the reign of Ramses II between 1304 and 1237 BCE. It was cut out of the rock and featured four colossal statues of the king, each of which was twenty meters high. When the Aswan High Dam was built in the 1960s, the monument had to be cut into large stone slabs and moved to higher ground so that it would not be submerged under the waters of Lake Nasser, which the High Dam formed.

imprint on Nubian culture with his magnificent monuments at Abu Simbel. Historians have long stressed such connections with Egypt, but only recently have scholars determined just how deeply the Nubian peoples were influenced by the cultures of sub-Saharan Africa.

Building on the foundations of earlier kings that had ruled Nubia, the Meroe kingdom arose in the fourth century BCE and flourished until 300 CE. Its rulers were influenced by the pharaonic culture, adapting hieroglyphs, erecting pyramids in which to bury their rulers, viewing their kings as divine, and worshipping the Egyptian god Amun. However, Meroe was equally a part of the Sudanic savanna lifeway—as evidenced by the distinctiveness of the language and the determination of its inhabitants to retain political autonomy from Egypt, including, if necessary, moving farther south out of the orbit of Egypt and more into the orbit of Sudanic polities. Although they called their kings pharaohs, the influential leaders of Meroe selected them from among the many members of the royal family, attempting to ensure that their rulers were men of proven talents. In addition, the Nubian states had close commercial contacts with other merchants and commercial hubs in Sudanic Africa.

Meroe soon became a thriving center of production and commerce. Its residents were especially skilled in iron smelting and the manufacture of textiles, and their products circulated widely throughout Africa. The capital city itself covered a square mile; at its center was a royal complex surrounded by a wall 300 yards long and half again as wide. The city featured monumental and highly decorated buildings that were constructed, according to local custom, not of stone but of mud bricks.

WEST AFRICAN KINGDOMS

Meroe was not the only sacred kingship in the Sudanic savanna lands. Similar polities thrived in West Africa, among peoples living in the Senegal River basin and among the Mande peoples living inland around the western branch of the Niger River. They established settlements at such places as Jenne and Gao, which eventually became large trading centers. Here, artisans smelted iron ore and wove textiles, and merchants engaged in long-distance trade.

Even more spectacular was the Nok culture, which arose in the sixth century BCE in an area that is today the geographical center of Nigeria. Though slightly south of the savanna lands of West Africa, it was (and still is) in regular contact with that region. At Taruga, near the present-day village of Nok, early iron smelting occurred in 600 BCE. Taruga may well have been the first place in western Africa where iron ores were smelted. Undeniably ironworking was significant for the Nok peoples, who moved from using stone materials directly to iron, bypassing bronze and copper. They made iron axes and hoes, iron knives and spears, and luxury items for trade. Ironworking had spread east toward Egypt and Nubia and south to the Congo River by 300 BCE. This region in West Africa was also home to the Bantu-speaking peoples destined to play a major role in the history of the landmass. Around 300 BCE, small Bantu groups began to migrate southward into the equatorial rain forests, where they cleared land for farming; from there, some moved on to southern Africa. (See Chapter 8 for a discussion of the Bantu peoples.)

Nok has achieved its historical fame not for its iron-smelting prowess but for its magnificent terra-cotta figurines, discovered in the 1940s in the tin-mining region of central Nigeria. These naturalistic figures, whose features bear a striking resemblance to those of the region's modern inhabitants, date to at least 500 BCE. They were altarpieces for a cult associated with the land's fertility. Placed next to new lands that were coming into cultivation, they were believed to bless the soil and enhance its productivity. (See Primary Source: Reconstructing the History of Preliterate African Peoples.)

Although most sub-Saharan African communities lived in small-scale dispersed communities, in several locations, notably Nubia and West Africa, larger, common cultures based on shared beliefs and political institutions arose. The ability of these societies to produce more food and sustain larger settled communities ultimately caused the sub-Saharan population to triple in this period. As in the Americas, these lifeways proved durable.

WARRING IDEAS IN THE MEDITERRANEAN WORLD

> → *In what ways did city-states integrate the dispersed settlements of the Mediterranean?*

The widespread migrations that convulsed southern Europe and Southwest Asia around 1200 BCE (see Chapter 4) also brought marauding armed bands into the well-settled regions of the Mediterranean. The combined impact of large population movements and social destruction radically transformed social organizations and cultures throughout the region. Thus, the first millennium BCE in the Mediterranean was a time of political, economic, and social changes, all of which stimulated new thinking and saw the creation of new political and economic institutions (just as in Eastern Zhou China and Vedic South Asia, see Map 5-6).

Primary Source

RECONSTRUCTING THE HISTORY OF PRELITERATE AFRICAN PEOPLES

Traditionally, historians have relied on written records and thus have had difficulty reconstructing the history of preliterate societies. Sources that now aid in understanding preliterate African groups include art, pottery, linguistic analysis, oral traditions, and many other elements. Here are two such vital historical sources.

The first is Nok terra-cottas. Discovered in the central region of modern-day Nigeria, the figurines probably were created in the Common Era but are part of a vibrant culture that dates back to the fifth century BCE.

The second source, Kush burial pyramids, comes from the sub-Saharan kingdom of Meroe, by no means a preliterate society but one that has many important nonwritten sources. Meroe flourished for nearly a millennium from around the fourth century BCE to the fourth century CE. Its predecessor kingdoms, referred to as the kingdoms of Kush, were located between the first and third Nile cataracts. The first kingdom of Kush existed between 1700 and 1500 BCE. A second powerful Kushitic state arose around 1000 BCE, and its most dynamic dynasty even overpowered Egypt, creating Egypt's "black pharaohs" dynasty, Egypt's twenty-fifth dynasty. Later, when Egyptian power was again ascendant, the peoples of Nubia moved even farther south to establish the kingdom of Meroe. Although Meroe continued to be deeply influenced by the culture and political forms of Egypt, its peoples spoke a different language from the Egyptians, a Nilo-Saharan language.

Nubia's close contact with Egypt led to profound and obvious influences—for example, the use of the term *pharaoh* to refer to the king, borrowed religious beliefs, and the use of hieroglyphs. Like the Egyptians, the Kushitic and Meroitic peoples buried their kings in pyramids and wrote texts on the walls of these burial chambers about what constituted an orderly and good life. The Meroitic peoples had a powerful priestly class, like the ancient Egyptians, but they retreated up the Nile to be independent of Egyptian rule. Scholars with the same archaeological and linguistic training as students of ancient Egypt (known as Egyptologists) have studied the Nubian cultures, but their studies have taken place more recently than those of ancient Egypt and have not yet yielded as much information.

Nok Figurine

→ *How do the Nok terra-cottas help scholars understand the very ancient culture of West Africa?*
→ *Do they provide insight into the artistic abilities of the people living in this region?*
→ *What can they tell us about how people dressed and how they looked?*
→ *Can you see the Egyptian influence in the photograph of the Kush burial pyramids?*

Burial Pyramids at the Royal Necropolis of the Ancient Kingdom of Kush

WARRING IDEAS: PLATO VERSUS ARISTOTLE—ON GAINING KNOWLEDGE OF THE ESSENCE OF THE WORLD

Great debates raged among Greek thinkers during the fifth and fourth centuries BCE over the essence of the world and how humans can have knowledge of it. Rejecting the existence of creator gods and goddesses, they sought explanations elsewhere. Some looked to the material world (in primary substances like water), while others turned to abstractions.

The Greek philosopher and mathematician Pythagoras suggested that numbers were the basis of everything. Some later thinkers, notably Plato, took this argument further and argued that all existence—and therefore all human knowledge—is based on absolute concepts that are like numbers, existing independent of time and place. Each of them Plato called an idea, a word whose meanings in Greek include "shape," "form," and "appearance." In a number of Plato's dialogues, his teacher, Socrates, tries to explain this theory:

> **Socrates:** I am going to try to explain to you the theory of causes that I myself have thought out. . . . I assume that you admit the existence of absolutes like "beauty" and "good" and "size" and the rest. If you admit that these absolutes exist, then I can hope with their help to show you what causes are. . . . I remain obstinately committed . . . to the explanation that the one thing that causes a thing to be "beautiful," for example, is the existence in it of "the beautiful" or its sharing in "the beautiful"[;] . . . and so, is it not also the case that things that we call "big" are big because they share the idea of "bigness" and similarly that things that we call "small" are small because they share in the idea of "smallness"? [Socrates then dismisses the claim that in calling things "tall" or "small" we are simply describing them in relation to other things.]

> **Phaedo:** I believe that Socrates has persuaded us of these matters and that we have agreed that these different ideas do exist; and he has also persuaded us that the reason why specific things in our world are named after these ideas is that they share in the existence of the specific idea. (Phaedo 99d–102b)

Still other thinkers drew on some of the first Greek philosophers of the sixth century BCE to argue that the basis of all existing things was, quite simply, other things. They rejected the proposal that all things we perceive with our senses are poor copies of permanent ideas of them that exist in a separate, unchangeable realm. Human knowledge, they argued, was in fact acquired through careful observation of existing things and through meticulous collection of data about them. Thus in the following passage Aristotle rejects Plato's concept of ideas:

> As for the followers of Plato who claim that "ideas" (or "shapes") are the causes or origins of all things, this too is objectionable. First of all, in their struggle to find causes for things that exist in our world of sense perceptions, they simply introduce as many new things into the equation as they are attempting to explain[;] . . . so their "ideas" are as many . . . as the things whose causes they are seeking to explain and for which reason they were led to invent these ideas. They must do this because they must create an idea to match every substance that exists in our real everyday world . . . and also one in the realm of the eternal heavenly entities. Not one of the arguments by which they try to demonstrate that these ideas actually exist can demonstrate or prove their claim. From some of their arguments, indeed, no real conclusions follow. From other arguments of theirs it only follows that there must be ideas of things for which they themselves hold no such ideas can exist. (*Metaphysics* 1.9, 990a–b)

In other works Aristotle put forth his own views about how to gain reliable knowledge of the world:

> All teaching and learning by means of rational argument is based on our existing knowledge and observations; . . . and I think that we have reliable knowledge of each thing . . . when we think that we have found the cause because of which that thing exists—what is the cause of that thing and of nothing else, with the result that this thing or this fact cannot be other than it is. That this is real knowledge of something is very clear. . . . We know what we do by demonstration, by showing that it is true. By demonstration I mean an argument that produces real knowledge, . . . all of which is based on a knowledge and observation of facts and things. . . . But I also say that not all real knowledge can in fact be demonstrated or proved. (*Posterior Analytics* 1.1–3, 71a–72b)

→ *Can you think of ways in which our modern attitudes toward what we can know and how we know it reflect these two approaches?*

→ *What might have provoked Plato and Aristotle to advance such different concepts of knowledge?*

→ *Might such factors be linked to other major developments of the time, occurring not just in the Greek city-states but elsewhere (in South or East Asia, for example)?*

SOURCE: Plato, *Phaedo*, 99d–102b; Aristotle, *Metaphysics*, 1.9 = 990a–b; *Posterior Analytics*, 1.1–3 = 71a–72b. All translations are by Brent Shaw.

Socrates

In the next generation, Plato's most famous pupil answered the same question differently. Deeply interested in the natural world, **Aristotle** (384–322 BCE) believed that by collecting all the facts one could about a given thing—no matter how imperfect—and studying them closely, one could achieve a better understanding. His main idea was that the interested inquirer can find out more about the world by collecting as much evidence as possible about a given thing and then making deductions from these data about general patterns. This was in stark contrast to Plato's claim that everything a person observes is in fact only a flawed copy of the "real" thing that exists in a thought-world of abstract patterns accessible only by pure mental meditation—completely the opposite of Aristotle's method. Following his approach, Aristotle collected evidence from more than 150 Greek city-states, and in *The Politics* he proposed institutional responses and codes of moral conduct that would allow urban communities to function better. But neither Plato nor Aristotle was able to preserve the city-state as the exemplary civilized society. During their lives the world of the independent city-state was to change dramatically, as new forms of bigger states emerged and became dominant.

CONCLUSION

Afro-Eurasia's great river-basin areas were still important in the first millennium BCE, but their time as centers of world cultures was passing. Now they yielded some of their leadership to regions that had been on the fringes, giving way to a generation of cultural and intellectual flourishing in search of alternative, new orders. As these borderland areas developed, the increased contacts fostered by city-states (in the Mediterranean world), smaller territorial states (in China), and smaller kingdoms and oligarchies (in Vedic South Asia) created great social dynamism.

During this period influential thinkers came to the fore with perspectives quite different from those of the river-basin civilizations. The Greek philosophers offered new views about nature, their political world, and human relations and values—all based on secular rather than religious ideas. In South Asia, dissident thinkers challenged the Brahmanic spiritual and political order, and the Buddha articulated a religious belief system that was much less hierarchical than its Vedic predecessor. In China, the political instability of the Warring States period propelled scholars such as Confucius to engage in political debate, where they stressed respect for social hierarchy.

Even where contacts with other societies were less intense, innovation occurred. In the Americas, the Olmecs developed a worldview in which mortals had to appease angry gods through human sacrifice and elaborate temples where many peoples could pay homage to the same deities. In sub-Saharan

and the Buddha in Vedic South Asia). **Plato** (427–347 BCE), a student of Socrates, presented Socrates' philosophy in a series of dialogues (much as Confucius's students had written down his thoughts). In *The Republic,* Plato envisioned a perfect city that philosopher-kings would rule. He thought that if fallible humans could imitate this model city more closely, their polities would be less susceptible to the decline that was affecting the Greek city-states of his own day. This belief was an outgrowth of his more general theory of "ideas"—eternal and perfect models of abstract concepts and material objects—that are imperfectly copied in the real world. (See Primary Source: Warring Ideas: Plato versus Aristotle—On Gaining Knowledge of the Essence of the World.)

Africa, settled pockets devised complex cultural foundations for community life. The Mediterranean and Egyptian cultures continued to expand their influence up the Nile through Nubia and into sub-Saharan Africa. A spectacular example of sub-Saharan and Egyptian synthesis was the culture of Meroe. And in West Africa, the Nok peoples promoted interregional trade and cultural contact as they expanded their horizons.

As the world was coalescing into culturally distinct regions, all the ideas newly forged in Afro-Eurasia, the Americas, and sub-Saharan Africa would endure. No matter where they were created, they had a continuing impact on societies that followed.

Review and research materials are available at StudySpace: ⑤ WWNORTON.COM/STUDYSPACE

KEY TERMS

Aristotle (p. 199)
ascetic (p. 179)
Buddha (p. 180)
chattel slavery (p. 196)
Confucius (p. 168)
cosmology (p. 180)
Daoism (p. 169)
Jainism (p. 179)

Legalism (p. 169)
oligarchy (p. 174)
Olmecs (p. 183)
Plato (p. 199)
second-generation
   societies (p. 163)
shamans (p. 184)
Socrates (p. 197)

Chronology

	1500 BCE						1000 BCE
THE AMERICAS	*1500–400 BCE Olmec culture emerges and diffuses throughout Mesoamerica*						
		1400–400 BCE Chavín culture flourishes in Central Andes of South America					
SUB-SAHARAN AFRICA							
SOUTH ASIA						*1000–600 BCE Sixteen State period* ◆-----	
						1000–600 BCE Vedic migrations ◆-----	
THE MEDITERRANEAN							
						1000–900 BCE Migration of Sea Peoples ◆-------	
EAST ASIA							

STUDY QUESTIONS

1. Explain the "war of ideas" that occurred during the first millennium BCE in China.
   How did Legalism, Confucianism, and Daoism influence political developments during the Warring States period?

2. Analyze the impact of commerce and urbanization on the Vedic belief system in South Asia at this time. Why were urban audiences more receptive to Buddhist and other challenges than to Vedic concepts?

3. Compare and contrast Buddhist and Confucian philosophies. What problems and issues did they address, and what solutions did they propose?

4. Explain the broad cultural features that characterized Olmec and Chavín societies in the Americas in the first millennium BCE. To what extent did each cultural group leave an imprint on its region?

5. Analyze the extent to which diverse sub-Saharan peoples were connected to one another and to the larger world during this period. What processes brought groups together, and what kept them apart?

6. Describe the political and economic innovations in the Mediterranean world in the first millennium BCE. What impact did these ideas have on peoples living on the periphery of that world?

7. Analyze how the use of coins shaped economic systems in Afro-Eurasia. Which regions adopted this practice?

8. Compare and contrast the Greek philosophers Socrates, Plato, and Aristotle with Confucius in China and the Buddha in South Asia. What was similar and what was different in their proposals for creating a better world?

9. Explain how small states created new cultural and social pathways and ideas in Afro-Eurasia in the first millennium BCE. What alternative approaches to philosophy, economics, and religion emerged in East Asia, South Asia, and western Afro-Eurasia?

---

500 BCE **300 BCE**

◆ 600 BCE Nok culture in West Africa (early iron smelting)

Meroe kingdom in Nubia, 4th century BCE–3rd century CE ◆ - →

◆ 500 BCE Cities emerge on Ganges plain

◆ - - - - - - - ◆ 540–468 BCE Vardhamana Mahavira popularizes Jainism

◆ - - - - - - - - ◆ c. 563–483 BCE Siddhartha Gautama develops Buddhist principles

◆ c. 800 BCE Phoenician settlements and trade networks emerge

c. 800–700 to c. 400 BCE Greek and other city-states flourish

5th and 4th centuries BCE Socrates, Plato, and Aristotle teach in Athens ◆ ◆ - - ◆ 431–404 BCE Peloponnesian War

770–221 BCE Eastern Zhou dynasty ◆ - - - - - ◆ c.479–438 BCE Mozir

722–481 BCE Spring and Autumn period of Eastern Zhou dynasty ◆ - - - - - - - ◆ c. 369–286 BCE Zhuangzi

403–221 BCE Warring State period ◆ - - - - - - - - - - - - - - - ◆

c. 605–520 BCE Laozi (founder of Daoism) ◆ - - - - - - - - ◆ 298–238 BCE Xunzi ◆ - - - - - - - ◆

c. 551–479 BCE Confucius ◆ - - - - - - - - ◆ 280–233 BCE Han Fei ◆ - - - - - ◆

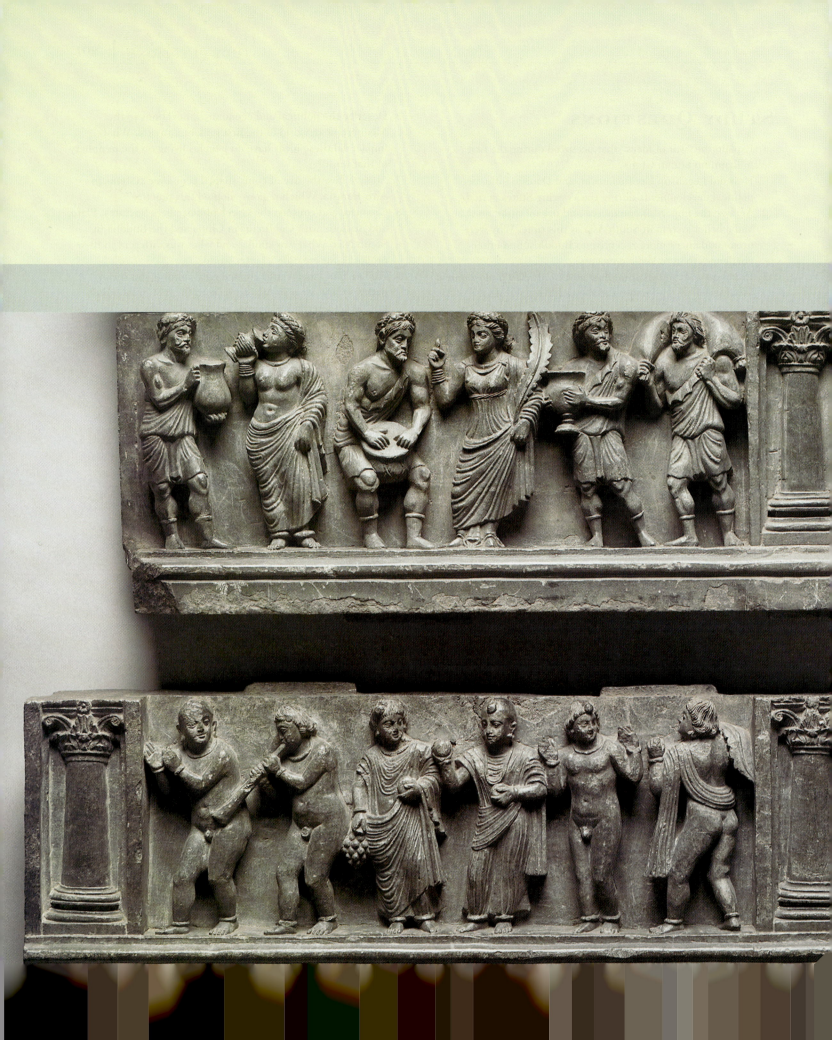

6

SHRINKING THE AFRO-EURASIAN WORLD, 350 BCE–250 CE

*I*n the blistering August heat of 324 BCE, at a town on the Euphrates River that the Greeks called Opis (not far from modern Baghdad), Alexander the Great's crack Macedonian troops declared that they had had enough. They had been fighting far from their homeland for more than a decade. They had marched eastward from the Mediterranean, forded wide rivers, traversed great deserts, trudged over high mountain passes, and slogged through rain-drenched forests. Along the way they had defeated massive armies, including those armed with fearsome war elephants. Some had taken wives from the cities and tribes they vanquished, so the army had become a giant swarm of ethnically mixed families. This was an army like no other. It did more than just defeat neighbors and rivals—it forcefully connected entire worlds, bringing together diverse peoples and lands.

Conquering in the name of building a new world, however, was not what the soldiers had bargained for. They loved their leader, but many thought he had gone too far. They had lost companions and grown weary of war. Some had mutinied at a tributary of the Indus, halting Alexander's advance into South Asia. Now they threatened to desert him altogether. Summoning up their courage, they voiced these resentments to their supreme

203

commander. Alexander's response was immediate and inspired. In persuading his troops not to desert him, he evoked the astounding military triumphs and historic achievement they had accomplished: establishing his personal rule from Macedonia to the Indus Valley. This far-reaching political vision came to a sudden end with Alexander's death a year later, when he was thirty-two years old. Even in his short lifetime, though, he set in motion cultural and economic forces that would transform Afro-Eurasia.

During this period two broad cultural movements came to link diverse populations across wide expanses of the Afro-Eurasian landmass: Hellenism and Buddhism. They constitute the central subject of this chapter. In both cases new empires and broad trade routes created the circuits through which—and beyond which—new cultures flowed. Imperial conquests and long-distance trade laid the foundations for widespread cultural systems that were far more enduring than the empires themselves. Alexander's armies forged only a fleeting political regime, though an enormous one, extending all the way from the Greek homeland to northern India enabling a Greek-based culture that we call Hellenistic to stretch over the regions of conquests, and beyond. Although this movement did not eradicate local cultures, it provoked profound shifts in them. In the process, many of the world's regions, from China to Africa, became more integrated.

One region where Hellenism had a profound impact was South Asia, where it initiated a process of gradual political integration and religious change. The result: an equally powerful cultural movement, Buddhism, spread outward from its founding in South Asia (see Chapter 5) to become the world's most expansive religious system. It, too, had a political agent: the Mauryan dynasty of South Asia, indirectly influenced by Alexander's triumphs, whose powerful armies and legions of magistrates and monks spread the religion of the Buddha throughout South Asia, laying the groundwork for its expansion beyond. Dynastic empires, therefore, created the political latticework and institutions through which cultural influences grew and extended like vines spreading into regions far from their roots.

POLITICAL EXPANSION AND CULTURAL DIFFUSION

> → *How did political expansion facilitate exchanges among different parts of the Afro-Eurasian world?*

Alexander's bloody campaigns made for legendary drama. But from a long-term perspective, it was their cultural effects that were more dramatic. His armies trampled over their victims, but they also transformed Afro-Eurasia. They promoted the establishment of culturally Greek-oriented communities across Afro-Eurasia. For at least five centuries after Alexander's short-lived rule, Hellenistic culture reverberated from Rome in the west all the way to the Ganges in the east.

Hellenism (a term derived from the Greeks' name for themselves, *Hellēnes*) was a new phenomenon. It involved the process by which the individual cultures of the Greek city-states gave way to a uniform culture stressing the common identity of all who embraced Greek ways. This culture had common features of language, art, architecture, drama, politics, philosophy, and much more, to which anyone anywhere in the Afro-Eurasian world could have access. By diffusing well beyond its homeland, it brought worlds together: its influence spread from Greece to all shores of the Mediterranean, into parts of sub-Saharan Africa, across Southwest Asia, and through the Iranian plateau into central and South Asia. It even had echoes in China.

Alexander not only conquered but also laid the foundations for state systems and introduced institutional stability for (and protection and patronage of) trading systems. Instead of plundering, governments under his rule promoted trade. With their fear of attack reduced, cities could thrive.

Focus Questions

⊚   WWNORTON.COM/STUDYSPACE

→ *How did political expansion facilitate exchanges between different parts of the Afro-Eurasian world?*

→ *How did the spread of Hellenism reshape the Mediterranean world?*

→ *How did Hellenistic and pastoral nomadic cultures influence central and South Asia?*

→ *In what ways did the transformation of Buddhism represent cultural integration in South Asia?*

→ *How did long-distance exchanges affect the cultural geography of Afro-Eurasia?*

→ *What factors promoted sea trade on the Indian Ocean?*

MAIN THEMES

→ *Two broad cultural movements, Hellenism and Buddhism, link diverse populations across Afro-Eurasia.*

→ *Conquests by Alexander the Great and the influence of his successor states spread Hellenism across southwest Asia and into South Asia, where it begins the gradual process of cultural and political integration.*

→ *The Mauryan Empire accelerates the integration of South Asia and helps Buddhism spread throughout that region and into central and East Asia via the Silk Road.*

FOCUS ON *Forces That Unify Afro-Eurasia*

The Mediterranean World

◆ The spread of Hellenism around the Mediterranean via Alexander's conquests leads to a common language, cosmopolitan cities, new types of philosophy and religion, plantation slavery, and money-based economies.

Central and South Asia

◆ Alexander's withdrawal from the Indus Valley leads to the creation of the Mauryan Empire, which integrates the northern half of India.

◆ The Seleucid and Bactrian kingdoms further solidify the spread of Hellenism into central Asia.

Transformation of Buddhism

◆ The combined influences of Hellenism, nomadism, and Arab seafaring culture transform Buddhism into a world religion.

Formation of the Silk Road

◆ Nomadic warriors from central Asia complete the final links of the overland Silk Road, strengthening the ties that joined peoples across Afro-Eurasia.

◆ Overland traders use camels to carry spices, transport precious metals, and convey Buddhist thought along the Silk Road into China.

◆ Seafaring Arab traders use new navigation techniques and larger ships called dhows to expand the transport of Silk Road commodities to the Mediterranean world via the Indian Ocean.

Increasingly, states encouraged the use of money and a common language for contracts—innovations that aided commercial transactions. In effect, major commercial arteries replaced the early passageways that had carried small bands of traders. Political expansion facilitated all kinds of exchanges within the Afro-Eurasian world. One consequence was the emergence of the **Silk Road**, an artery that for nearly a thousand years was the primary commercial network linking East Asia and the Mediterranean world. This trade route extended over 5,000 miles and took its name from the huge quantities of precious silk that passed along it.

We cannot make sense of Alexander and the Hellenistic cultural movement or the spread of Buddhism without acknowledging the important ways in which distinct parts of the Afro-Eurasian world were already in contact. Indeed, political expansion driven by military conquest followed a period of extensive migration, trade, and technological diffusion. Alexander's conquests did not take arbitrary pathways, because earlier long-distance trade and cross-cultural exchanges had laid the trails for them. Similarly, Buddhism spread along preexisting trade routes. Slowly a new idea took hold: common cultures and shared commodities could integrate the Afro-Eurasian world.

These changes created grand opportunities for expanded trade, migration, and religious conversion. Regular trade routes now supported commercial centers that crisscrossed the landmass from China to the Mediterranean. Merchants joined with monks and administrators in connecting widespread parts of Afro-Eurasia, enabling busy sea-lanes and the Silk Road to flourish. Merely a few centuries after the conquests of Alexander and Mauryan kings, the world looked very different from the realms his armies had traversed.

MAP 6-1   AFRO-EURASIA IN 250 BCE

Alexander of Macedonia did not live long enough to create one large politically unified empire, but his conquests integrated various Afro-Eurasian worlds culturally and economically. Trace the pathways that Alexander followed on his conquests. What were the names and locations of the Hellenistic successor states? What did these states have in common? Which states on the map did Greeks *not* rule? How did the spread of Hellenism affect them?

Legend:

- ← Campaigns of Alexander the Great
- ☐ Conquests of Alexander the Great
- Qin Empire
- Greek City State
- Carthage
- Area of Roman control
- Macedonia
- Ptolmaic Empire
- Seleucid Empire
- Graeco-Bactria
- Mauryan Empire
- Empire of Xiongnu

THE EMERGENCE OF A COSMOPOLITAN WORLD

→ *How did the spread of Hellenism reshape the Mediterranean world?*

The armed campaigns of a minor Greek people, the Macedonians, and their leader, Alexander the Great, began a drive for empire from the west. Alexander's novel use of new kinds of armed forces in a series of lightning attacks on the Persian Empire broke down barriers between the Mediterranean world and the rest of Southwest Asia. The massive transfers of wealth and power resulting from his conquests transformed the Mediterranean into a more unified world of economic and cultural exchange. (See Map 6-1.)

CONQUESTS OF ALEXANDER THE GREAT

Historians and biographers have filled libraries with books about **Alexander the Great** (356–323 BCE), yet he remains one of the most fascinating figures in world history. Alexander came from the frontier state of Macedonia to the north of Greece and for a dozen years commanded a highly mobile force armed with advanced military technologies that had developed during the incessant warfare among Greek city-states (see Chapter 5).

Under Alexander's predecessors—especially his father, Philip II—Macedonia had become a large ethnic and territorial state. Philip had unified Macedonia and then gone on to conquer neighboring states. Importantly, a region of Macedonia boasted gold mines that could finance his new military technology and a disciplined, full-time army. The costs of heavily armored infantry in closely arrayed phalanxes, allied with large-scale shock cavalry formations, were supported not just from the mines' substantial income but also from the enormous profits of a slave trade that passed directly through Macedonia. By the early 330s BCE, Philip had crushed the Greek city-states to the south, including Athens. After Philip's assassination, his son Alexander used this new military machine in a series of daring attacks on the apparently invincible power of the Persian Empire and its king, Darius III.

Like many other successful conquerors, Alexander owed much of his success to a readiness to take risks. In his initial forays into Southwest Asia he outpaced and outflanked his adversaries, repeatedly taking them by surprise. Through these rapid assaults he brought under the rule of his Greek-speaking elites all the lands of the former Persian Empire, which extended from Egypt and the shores of the Mediterranean to

Battle of Issus. Mosaic of the Battle of Issus between Alexander the Great of Macedon and Darius, the king of Persia (found as a wall decoration in a house at Pompeii in southern Italy). Alexander is the bareheaded figure to the far left; Darius is the figure to the right, gesturing with his right hand. The men represent two different types of warfare. On horseback, Alexander leads the cavalry-based shock forces of the Macedonian Greeks, while Darius directs his army from a chariot in the style of the great kings of Southwest Asia.

the interior of what is now Afghanistan as well as to the Indus River valley. (See Primary Source: Clash of Empires: The Battle of Gaugamela.)

The result of this violent rampage was hardly an empire, given that Alexander did not live long enough to establish institutions to hold the distant lands together. But his military campaigns continued a process that the Persians had set in motion of smashing barriers that had separated peoples on the eastern and western ends of Afro-Eurasia. Indeed, the conqueror saw himself as a new universal figure, a bridge connecting distant cultures. He demonstrated this vision in his choice of Roxana, the daughter of a Bactrian chief from central Asia, as a wife and in making Bactria, in present-day northern Afghanistan, into a center of his operations.

Alexander's conquests exposed Syria, Palestine, Egypt, and Mesopotamia to the commodities of the Mediterranean, to money-based economies (both Philip and Alexander issued gold coins to pay for their invasions), and to cultural ideas associated with the Greek city-states. Alexander founded dozens of new cities named after himself, the most famous of which was Alexandria in Egypt.

One of Alexander's most significant acts involved seizing the accumulated wealth that the Persian kings stored in their immense palaces, especially at Persepolis, and dispersing it into the money economies of the Mediterranean city-states. This massive redistribution of wealth (like the post-Columbian exploitation of the Americas; see Chapters 12 and 13) fueled a widespread economic expansion in the Mediterranean.

Primary Source

CLASH OF EMPIRES: THE BATTLE OF GAUGAMELA

The following passage, taken from the Greek historian Arrian, delineates the makeup of Darius's army as it prepared to confront Alexander and his forces in 331 BCE. In describing the size of the army—much larger than that of the largest Greek city-state, Athens—Arrian mentions the various ethnic groups of the Persian Empire that contributed troops. Contingents came from lands as far-flung as Bactria (near modern-day Afghanistan), Scythia (the broad area stretching from Ukraine to Kazakhstan), Armenia, Cappadocia (in east-central Turkey), and Caria (in southwestern Turkey), as well as from lands close to the Red Sea.

Darius's army was so large because it had been reinforced with Sogdians, with Bactrians, and with Indian peoples from the borderlands of Bactria, all under the command of Bessus, the satrap [i.e., the regional governor] of Bactria. There were also units of the Sakai—who were part of the Scythians who are found in Asia. They owed no loyalty to Bessus, but were still allies of Darius. These soldiers were mounted bowmen commanded by one Mauaces. The Arachotoi and the hillmen from India were commanded by Barsaentes, the satrap of Arachosia. The Areioi were commanded by their satrap, Satibarzanes; the Parthians, the Hyrcanians, and Tapeiroi, all cavalrymen, were commanded by Phrataphernes. The Medes, to whom were attached the Kadousioi, the Albanoi, and Sakesinai, were commanded by Atropates the Mede. All the units from the lands near the Red Sea were commanded by Orontobates, Ariobarzanes, and Orxines. The Ouxioi and Sousianoi were commanded by Oxathres, son of Aboultius. The men from Babylon, to whom were attached the Siracenioi and Carians, were commanded by Boupares—these Carians had been resettled in the empire by a mass transfer of their people. The Armenians were commanded by Orontes and Mithraustes; the Cappadocians, by Ariaces. The Syrians from Hollow Syria [i.e., the Bekáa Valley in modern Lebanon] and from Mesopotamia were commanded by Mazaeus. The total number of men in the army of Darius was reported to be 40,000 cavalry, 1,000,000 infantry, 200 scythed chariots [i.e., war chariots with blades mounted on both ends of the axle], and some war elephants—the Indians who came from this side of the Indus River had about fifteen of them.

→ *How many ethnic groups can you identify in this passage?*
→ *What does Darius's command of so many ethnic loyalties tell us about the nature of the Persian Empire?*
→ *How do you think Alexander was able to defeat such a large and talented army?*

SOURCE: Arrian, *The History of Alexander* 3.8; translated by Brent Shaw.

ALEXANDER'S SUCCESSORS AND THE TERRITORIAL KINGDOMS

Alexander died in Babylon at age thirty-two, struck down by overconsumption of alcohol and other excesses that matched his larger-than-life personality and reflected the war culture of Macedonian warriors. His death in 323 BCE brought on the collapse of the regime he had personally held together. The conquered lands fragmented into large territories over which his generals squabbled for control.

Alexander's generals became his successors. Seleucus, Ptolemy, Antigonus, Lysimachus, and others did not think of themselves as citizens, even very important ones, of a Greek city-state, but rather modeled themselves on the regional rulers they had defeated. As these men installed kingdoms in the eastern Mediterranean and Southwest and central Asia, they not only introduced Alexander's style of absolute rulership but also unified large blocks of territory under single, powerful rulers.

One effect of powerful families controlling whole kingdoms was that a few women could now hold great power, an unthinkable prospect in the democracies of the city-states. Queens in Macedonia, Syria, and Egypt—whether independent or as co-regents with their husbands—established new public roles for women. For example, Berenice of Egypt (c. 320–280 BCE) was the first in a series of powerful royal women who helped rule the kingdom of the Nile, a line that ended with the most famous of them all, Cleopatra, in the 30s BCE.

Berenice. Portrait head of Berenice, wife and consort of Ptolemy I, the first Macedonian king of Egypt after its conquest by Alexander the Great. Berenice was one of the women who, as queens of huge empires, wielded power and commanded wealth in their own right.

The old city-states of the Mediterranean, such as Athens and Corinth, still thrived, but now they functioned in a world dominated by much larger power blocs. Three large territorial states stood out in the new Hellenistic world: the Seleucid Empire (the dynasty established by Seleucus), stretching from Syria to present-day Afghanistan; Macedonia, ruled by the Antigonids (the dynasty established by Antigonus); and Egypt, ruled by the Ptolemies (the dynasty established by Ptolemy). In areas between these larger states, middle-sized kingdoms emerged. Elsewhere, polities banded together to survive; on mainland Greece, larger confederations forced previously independent city-states to join them.

In general, political states coalesced into larger units that displayed a uniformity unknown in the governments of the earlier city-states. Their impulse to standardization is evident not just in politics but in every aspect of daily life. Unlike the early empires described in Chapter 4, which subordinated neighbors as colonies or tribute states, these kingdoms integrated neighboring peoples as fellow subjects. They believed that their cultural assets merited dissemination across broader geographic areas.

Competition in war remained an unceasing fact of life, but the wars among the kingdoms of Alexander's successors were broader in scope and more complex in organization than ever before. At the same time, their relative parity in strength meant a near-constant state of wars between the new kings that never achieved very much. After all, every large state had access to essentially the same advanced military technology: rulers went into the marketplace and acquired the highly trained soldiers, mercenaries, generals, and military advisers required to run their armies. After battles that killed tens of thousands, and severely injured and wounded hundreds of thousands more, the three major kingdoms—and even the minor ones—remained largely unchanged.

The great powers therefore settled into a centuries-long game of watching one another and balancing threats with alliances. What emerged was a fierce competition that dominated international relations, in which diplomacy and treaty-making sometimes replaced actual fighting. This was an equilibrium reminiscent of the first age of international interstate relations in the second millennium BCE (see Chapter 3). Long periods of peace began to grace the intervals between the new kingdoms' violent and destructive wars.

HELLENISTIC CULTURE

Just as broad uniformity in politics and war trumped the small size and diversity of the old city-state, so the individual city-state cultures now gave way to a homogenized Hellenistic culture. Following the existing commercial networks, this uniform Greek culture spread rapidly through the entire Mediterranean basin and beyond. It was an alluring package, and ruling elites in all regions that encountered it fell under its powerful spell.

Hellenistic culture included philosophical and political thinking, secular disciplines ranging from history to biology, popular entertainment in theaters, competitive public games, and art for art's sake in all kinds of media. No other society at the time had such a complete package of high culture; hence its widespread appeal and diffusion. Archaeologists have found a Greek-style gymnasium and theater in the town of Aï Khanoum in modern Afghanistan, and adaptations of Greek sculptures made at the order of the Vedic king Sandrakottos (better known as Chandragupta; see below). We also know of Carthaginians in North Africa who became "Greek" philosophers, and Gallic and Berber chieftains, from the far west of France and North Africa, who had fine Greek-style drinking vessels buried with them.

COMMON LANGUAGE The core element of Hellenism was a common language, known as *koine*, or Greek. It replaced the city-states' numerous dialects with an everyday form that people anywhere could understand and quickly became the international language of its day.

Most peoples who came into contact with Hellenistic culture accepted the benefits that it afforded in expanding a network of communication and exchange. Peoples in Egypt, Judea, Syria, and Sicily, who all had distinct languages and cultures, could now communicate more easily with one another, and enjoy the same dramatic comedies and new forms of art and sculpture. Despite pockets of resistance, the Hellenizing movement was remarkably successful in spreading a shared Greek culture throughout the Mediterranean world and into Southwest Asia.

COSMOPOLITAN CITIES Much as Athens had been the model city of the age of the Greek city-state, Alexandria in Egypt became exemplary in the new age. Whereas fifth-century BCE Athens had zealously maintained an exclusive civic identity, Alexandria was a multiethnic city built from

THE COSMOPOLITAN CITY OF ALEXANDRIA

According to legend, Alexander selected the site of Alexandria and named the city after himself. As a result of his personal influence and its strategic location, Alexandria attracted an immense and diverse immigrant population from the entire Mediterranean world. In the following description, the Greek geographer Strabo—writing later during the time of the Roman Empire—emphasizes the city's function as an enormous entrepôt for trade and commerce across Afro-Eurasia. (Entrepôts are transshipment centers where seafaring vessels unload their cargoes and then send them elsewhere, by sea or by land.)

As for the Great Harbor at Alexandria, it is not only wonderfully well closed in and protected by artificial levees and by nature, it is also so deep that even the largest ships can be moored right at the stairs along its quayside. This Great Harbor is divided up into several minor harbors. . . . Even more exports are handled than imports. Anyone who might happen to be at Alexandria and at Dichaiarchia [the large Italian port on the Bay of Naples] would easily see for himself that the cargo ships sailing from here are bigger and more heavily laden. . . . The city itself is crisscrossed by streets that are wide enough for riding horses and driving chariots, and intersected by two main roads very much broader than the others. Its streets and avenues cut across each other at right angles. The city also boasts exceedingly beautiful public parks and its royal quarters take up a quarter, perhaps even a third of the whole city. . . . In earlier times, not even twenty ships would dare to go as far as the Arabian Gulf and manage to get a look outside its straits. But now large fleets of ships are sent out as far as India and to the furthest lands of the Ethiopians, from which the most valuable cargoes are brought to Egypt and then sent out again to other regions of the world. Double charges are collected on these shipments—both when they come in and when they go out—and the duties are especially high on luxury goods . . . for Alexandria alone does not just receive trade goods of this kind from all over the world, but it also furnishes supplies to the whole of the world outside.

→ *According to this passage, what features of the site made Alexandria well suited as a center for sea trade and a destination for immigrants?*
→ *By Strabo's time, Alexandria was the second-largest city in the Mediterranean, surpassed only by Rome. How does this passage reflect the role of trade in its development?*
→ *The passage indicates that Alexandria exported more than it imported. In what way does this indicate the city's role as a cosmopolitan entrepôt?*

SOURCE: Strabo, *Geography* 17.1.6, 7, 8, 13; translated by Brent Shaw.

scratch by immigrants, who rapidly totaled half a million as they streamed in from all over the Mediterranean and Southwest Asia seeking new opportunities. Members of its dynamic population, representing dozens of Greek and non-Greek peoples, communicated in the common language that supplanted their original dialects. Soon a new urban culture emerged to meet the needs of so diverse a population. (See Primary Source: The Cosmopolitan City of Alexandria.)

The culture of the Hellenistic movement took the place of local art forms. In the previous city-state world, comic playwrights had written plays for their individual cities and local cultures, highlighting familiar languages, foibles, problems, and politicians. In contrast, entertainment in the more widely connected world had to appeal to bigger audiences and a greater variety of people. Plays were now staged in any city touched by Greek influence, and they were understood in any environment. Distinctive regional humor and local characters gave way to dramas populated by stock characters of standard sit-coms that any audience could identify with: the miser, the old crone, the jilted lover, the golden-hearted whore, the boastful soldier, the befuddled father, the cheated husband, the rebellious son. At performances throughout the Mediterranean basin, laughter would be just as loud in Syracuse on the island of Sicily as in Scythopolis in the Jordan Valley of Judea.

Ways of thinking changed to match this unified world. The new ideas reflected the fact that individuals were no longer citizens of a particular city (*polis*); instead they were

The Theater at Syracuse. The great theater in the city-state of Syracuse in Sicily was considerably refurbished and enlarged under the Hellenistic kings. It could seat 15,000 to 20,000 persons. Here the people of Syracuse attended plays written by playwrights who lived on the far side of their world, but whose works they could understand as if the characters were from their own neighborhood. In the common culture of the Hellenistic period, plays deliberately featured typecast characters and situations, thereby broadening their audience.

the first "cosmopolitans," belonging to the whole world, or "universe" (*kosmos*). The new political style was relentlessly cosmopolitan, radiating out of cities not just into nearby hinterlands but also to distant (and often rivalrous) cities.

Kingdoms and states by now had become so enormous that individuals could relate to political style only through the personality of kings or rulers and their families. Rulership was personality, and personality and style united large numbers of subjects. For example, Demetrius Poliorcetes, the ruler of Macedonia, wore high-platform shoes and heavy makeup, and he decorated his elaborate, flowing cape with images of the sun, the stars, and the planets. In the presence of a powerful and solitary sun king like Demetrius, ordinary individuals felt small, inconsequential, and isolated. In response, an obsessive cult of the self arose, as Hellenistic religion and philosophy increasingly focused on the individual and his or her place in the larger world.

PHILOSOPHY AND RELIGION Growing concern with the individual self found expression in many ways. Consider the Athenian philosopher Diogenes (c. 412–323 BCE). He sought self-sufficiency and freedom from society's laws and customs, rejecting cultural norms as human-made inventions not in tune with nature and therefore false. He masturbated in public to "relieve himself" (it was, after all, a "natural need"), as well as to show disdain for what he considered to be the city's artificial sexual mores. He lived with no clothing in a wooden barrel in the public square, or *agora*, of Athens, with his female companion in her own barrel beside him. Other teachers also rejected the values of the city-state,

although with more finesse and less contentiousness than Diogenes. Nonetheless, all recognized the need for a new orientation now that the world of the city-state, with its face-to-face relationships, had vanished.

The teacher Epicurus (c. 341–279 BCE), founder of a school in Athens that he called The Garden, likewise emphasized the self. He envisioned an ideal community centered on The Garden and stressed the importance of sensation, saying that pleasurable sensations were good and painful sensations were bad. Epicurus taught his students to pursue a life of contemplation and ask themselves, "What is the good life?" Known as Epicureans, his followers struggled to develop a sense of "not caring" (*ataraxia*) about worries—like threats to personal health or the challenges of coping with excessive wealth—in order to find peace of mind. In Epicurus's cult, none of the social statuses of the old city-state had more value than any other: women, slaves, and others in the underclass were equally welcome in The Garden as worshippers.

Epicurus and his new ideas acquired followers throughout the Mediterranean, but they were hardly alone. Unrestrained by the controls of any one city-state, other cults and schools of philosophy emerged. Of these, Stoicism was perhaps the most widespread. A man named Zeno (c. 334–262 BCE), from the island of Cyprus, initiated it, and other cosmopolitan figures across the Hellenistic world—from Babylon in Mesopotamia to Sinope on the Black Sea—developed its beliefs. Their mission was to help individuals understand their place in the cosmos. Zeno put forth his ideas in the Stoa Poikilē, a decorated and roofed colonnade that opened onto the central marketplace in Athens and gave his followers their

The Painted Stoa. An artist's reconstruction of the Stoa Poikilē, or "Painted Stoa," in the city-state of Athens of the fourth century BCE. In the manner of a modern-day strip mall, this business and administrative center ran along the northern side of the agora, or central business and marketplace of the city. Philosophers and their students would hang out at the Stoa, lounging in the shaded areas under the colonnade as they debated the ideas flowing into Athens from all over the Hellenistic world. The painted wall decoration behind the columns (from which the Stoa received its name) depicts the Battle of Marathon.

name. For the Stoics, everything was grounded in nature itself, which they saw as the ultimate, permanent world. They regarded cities and kingdoms as human-made things, important but transient. Being in tune with nature and living a good life required understanding the rules of the natural order and being in control of one's passions, and thus indifferent to pleasure and pain.

Greek colonial control of other lands transformed long-established religions, and then re-exported them throughout the Mediterranean. For example, the Greeks in Egypt drew on the indigenous cult of Osiris and his consort, Isis (formerly a vital element in pharaonic temple rituals; see Chapter 2), to fashion a new narrative about Osiris's death and rebirth that represented personal salvation from death. Isis became a supreme goddess whose "excellencies" or "supreme virtues" encompassed the powers of dozens of other Mediterranean gods and goddesses. Believers experienced personal revelations and out-of-body experiences (*exstasis*, "ecstasy"). A ritual of dipping in water (*baptizein*, "to baptize") marked the transition of believers, "born again" into lives devoted to a "personal savior" who delivered an understanding of a new life by direct revelation. These new beliefs, like the worship of Isis, emphasized the spiritual concerns of humans as individuals, rather than the collective worries of towns or cities.

HELLENISM AND THE ELITES Once high Greek culture coalesced, its appeal to elites in widely dispersed communities along the major communication routes became almost irresistible. Social elites sought to enhance their position by adopting Hellenistic culture, the only one that had standing above the level of local values. Syrian, Jewish, and Egyptian elites in the eastern Mediterranean adopted this attitude, as well as Roman, Carthaginian, and African elites in the western Mediterranean. The later Roman high culture was itself a form of Greek culture. Of the Romans' extensive borrowings from the Greeks, not the least important was a belief in the value of a written history. The Romans, too, began writing about contemporary and past events. Secular plays, philosophy, poetry, competitive games, and art followed, all based on Greek forms or local imitations. North African kings similarly decked themselves out in Greek dress, built Greek-style theaters, imported Greek philosophers, and wrote history. Now they, too, had "culture."

The Hellenistic influences penetrated deeply into sub-Saharan Africa, where the kingdom of Meroe (see Chapter 5), already influenced by pharaonic forms, now absorbed characteristics of Greek culture as well. It is not surprising that Greek influences were extensive at Meroe, because continuous interaction with the Egyptians also exposed its people to the world of the Mediterranean. Both Meroe and its rival,

Axum, located in the Ethiopian highlands, used Greek stelae to boast of their military exploits. Moreover, the Greek historian Herodotus mentions that the citizens of Meroe "worshipped Zeus and Dionysus alone of the gods, holding them in great honor. There is an oracle of Zeus there, and they make war according to its pronouncements." The rulers of Meroe, understanding the advantages of the Greek language, employed Greek scribes to record their accomplishments on the walls of Greek-Egyptian temples. In this way, Meroe developed a remarkable mix of Greek, Egyptian, and African cultural and political elements.

JEWISH RESISTANCE TO HELLENISM

Not every community succumbed to the allure of Hellenism. The Jews in Judea, squeezed between Egypt and the superstates of Mesopotamia, offer a striking case of resistance to its universalizing forces. The Jews had a long schooling in surviving and resisting foreign rule, having been conquered by the Assyrians and the Babylonians (see Chapter 4). After the Persians defeated Babylon, a royal edict of restoration issued by the Persian monarch Cyrus led to the integration of Judea—now a province—into the Persian Empire. As the Jews who had once been forced to move to Babylon returned to Judea, the process of rebuilding Jerusalem began.

All this rebuilding of Jewish society occurred under the administration of another great Southwest Asian empire—that of the Persians, who tolerated local customs and beliefs. It took Alexander's lightning defeat of the Persian Empire in the 330s BCE to introduce a shocking new openness to the cultural innovations of the Mediterranean world. Hellenism came in the wake of Alexander's sweep through the region.

While some parts of the Jewish ruling elite began to adopt Greek ways—to wear Greek clothing, to introduce the culture of the gymnasium with its cult of male nudity, to produce images of gods as art, other rejected the push. Those who spurned assimilation rebelled against the common elements of Hellenism—its language, music, gymnasia, nudity, public art, and secularism—as being deeply immoral and threatening to their beliefs. Ultimately, this resistance led to a full-scale armed revolt, headed up by the family of the Maccabees, in 166 BCE, provoked when Syrian overlords, the Seleucids, forbade the practice of Judaism and profaned the Jews' temple. Though the Maccabees succeeded in establishing an independent Jewish state centered on the temple in Jerusalem, they did not entirely overcome the impact of the new universal culture. By the beginning of the first century BCE, descendants of the Maccabees were calling themselves kings, minting coins with Greek legends, and presiding over a largely secular kingdom. Moreover, a huge Jewish society in the Hellenistic city of Alexandria in Egypt embraced the new culture. Scholars there produced a Bible in koine Greek, and historians (such as Jason of Cyrene) and philosophers (such as Philo of Alexandria) wrote in Greek, imitating Greek models.

THE HELLENISTIC WORLD AND THE BEGINNINGS OF THE ROMAN EMPIRE

Other cities were less reluctant than Jerusalem to follow Hellenistic ways. Early on, the Romans saw the Greek model as offering opportunities to increase their own importance. In the 330s and 320s BCE, when Alexander was uniting the eastern Mediterranean, a city-state on the Tiber River in central Italy took the first critical military actions to unify Italy; eventually it would bring together the rest of the Mediterranean and parts of Southwest Asia. Rather than beginning as a kingdom like Macedonia, Rome went from being a city-state to flourishing as a large territorial state. During this transformation it adopted significant elements of Hellenistic culture: Greek-style temples, elaborately decorated Greek-style pottery and paintings, and an alphabet based on that of the Greeks.

The Roman elites saw immersion in Greek culture and language as a way to appear to the rest of the world as "civilized." Yet the Roman elites did not accept this notion without resistance, worry, and debate. Consider the Roman senator Cato the Elder (234–149 BCE), who struggled with the tensions that these changes involved. Although he was devoted to the Roman past, the Latin language, and the ideal of small-scale Roman peasant farmers and their families, he embraced many Hellenistic influences. For example, he wrote a standard manual for the new economy of slave plantation agriculture (see below), invested in shipping and trading, learned Greek rhetoric (both speaking and writing the language), added the genre of history to Latin literature, and much more. Indeed, Cato blended an extreme devotion to tradition, manifested in his public statements, with bold innovations in most aspects of his daily life.

CARTHAGE

In contrast to Rome, which assimilated Greek ways to elevate its status in the Mediterranean world, cities that were prosperous and already well integrated into the world economy welcomed Hellenistic culture because it facilitated communication and exchange. When Hellenism reached the great city of Carthage (in the area of present-day Tunisia), its residents adapted it without fanfare but with much success.

Not only did Carthaginian merchants trade with other Phoenician colonies in the western Mediterranean, but the city's ruling families took control over western Sicily and

Aerial View of Punic Carthage. Carthage was located on a promontory in the Bay of Tunis. In the lower foreground of this artist's reconstruction is a rectangular area of water and above it a circular-shaped one. These were the two major harbors of Carthage—the rectangular one was the commercial port and the circular one was the military harbor. Above these harbors are the main market square and the high central point named the Byrsa. To the left is the twenty-mile-long wall that defended the city on its land side.

Sardinia. Remains of pottery and other materials demonstrate that the Carthaginians' trading contacts extended far beyond other Phoenician settlements to towns of the Etruscans and the Romans in Italy, to the Greek trading city of Massilia (modern Marseilles) in southern France, and to Athens in the eastern Mediterranean. In addition, the Carthaginians expanded their commercial interests into the Atlantic, moving north along the coast of Iberia and south along the coast of West Africa—which, as noted in Chapter 5, the commander Hanno explored and colonized. Pushing their influence even farther, they established a trading post at the island of Mogador more than 600 miles down the Atlantic coast of Africa.

Carthaginian culture (or Punic culture, to use the Romans' name for the people with whom they would soon be at war; see Chapter 7) took on important elements of Hellenistic culture. For example, some Carthaginians went to Athens to become philosophers. Also, the design of their sanctuaries, temples, and other public buildings reveals a marriage of styles: Greek-style pediments and columns mixed with Punic designs and measurements, and local North African motifs and structures added to the mix. The splendid jewelry that Phoenician women adorned themselves with reflected styles from Egypt, such as ornate necklaces of gold and earrings of lapis-lazuli. The finest tableware and pottery were imports from Etruscans in Italy, and coinage and innovative ideas on political theory and warfare came from the Greek city-states.

ECONOMIC CHANGES: PLANTATION SLAVERY AND MONEY-BASED ECONOMIES

The main economic innovation that accompanied unification of the Mediterranean world was the use of large numbers of slaves in agricultural production—especially in Italy, Sicily, and North African regions close to Carthage. After all, Alexander's conquests and Rome's political rise produced unprecedented wealth for a small elite. These men and women used their riches to acquire huge tracts of land and to purchase slaves (either kidnapped individuals or conquered peoples) on a scale and with a degree of managerial organization never seen before.

The slave plantations, wholly devoted to producing surplus crops for profit, became one of the engines driving a new Mediterranean economy. The estates created vast wealth for their owners—though at a heavy price to others, as reliance on slave labor now left the free peasants who used to work the fields with no option but to move into overcrowded cities, where employment was hard to find. However, the sudden importation of so many slaves to work in harsh conditions had an unanticipated outcome. Between 135 and 70 BCE, authorities on Sicily and in southern Italy faced several massive slave uprisings, led by the religious seer Eunus in 130 and the slave gladiator Spartacus in the late 70s. These were among the greatest slave wars in world history. The superior

Megasthenes's *Indica* depicted a well-ordered and highly stratified society divided into seven groups: philosophers, farmers, soldiers, herdsmen, artisans, magistrates, and councilors. People respected the boundaries between groups and honored rituals that reinforced their identities; members of different groups did not intermarry or even eat together. Meanwhile, Megasthenes noted some ways in which rulers integrated the region—for example, with extensive roads connecting major cities. These arteries were lined with trees and mileage stones to beautify the realm. If these roads helped traders, they also enabled the ruler's troops to march around his dominions. According to Megasthenes, soldiers were a profession separate from the rest of the population. This surprised the Greek observer, who was more accustomed to the idea of the military closely integrated into civil society. Mauryan troops did not pretend to work when there was no war. They constituted a standing force of immense proportions, ready to obey their commander. This military force was huge, boasting cavalry divisions of mounted horses, war elephants, and scores of infantry. Most of the fighters evolved into a warrior caste of their own.

THE REGIME OF AŚOKA The Mauryan Empire reached its height during the reign of the third king, Aśoka (r. 268–231 BCE), Chandragupta's grandson. Aśoka's lands comprised almost the entirety of South Asia, including the Deccan plateau; only the southern tip of the peninsula remained

outside his control. In 261 BCE, Aśoka waged the dynasty's last campaign: the conquest of Kalinga, a kingdom on the east coast of the South Asian peninsula. It was a gruesome and despicable operation. The Mauryan army triumphed, but at a high price: about 100,000 soldiers died in battle, many more perished in its aftermath, and some 150,000 people endured forcible relocation. Aśoka himself, when he learned of the devastation, was shocked and appalled at his own handiwork, and in a fit of guilt he issued a famous edict renouncing his brutal ways.

Aśoka was a faithful follower and patron of Buddhism. In fact, the Kalinga campaign redoubled his devotion to Buddhism, which informed his peaceable edict. (See Primary Source: Aśoka's Kalinga Edict.) All over his domain he built **stupas**, or dome monuments, marking the burial sites of relics of the Buddha. In the Kalinga edict, he claimed to rule over his subjects according to **dhamma** (a vernacular form of the Sanskrit word *dharma*), a set of moral regulations that applied to all—including the priestly Brahmans, Buddhists, members of other religious sects, and even the Greeks. Dhamma or dharma became a concept that all religious schools in South Asia used, irrespective of faith; it was an encompassing moral code for all sects. Using dhamma as a unifying symbol, Aśoka wanted all people, whatever their religious practices and cultural customs, to consider themselves his subjects, to respect him as their father, and to conform to his moral code—starting with the precept that people of different religions or sects should get

Aśoka. Buddhist legend claims that Aśoka placed relics of the Buddha into the many stupas he had built. The stupa at Sarnath (*left*) is the best-preserved one from the time of Aśoka. Aśoka had his edicts carved on pillars like the one on the right all over India. The majestic lion at the top of the pillar shows the influence of Persian art, in which the lion was the symbol of royalty.

Primary Source

AŚOKA'S KALINGA EDICT

After the Kalinga war, Aśoka issued an edict to express his regret at the miseries it had caused his people. From this edict, we can tell that Aśoka ruled a country of many different cultures and religions.

Beloved of the Gods, is that those who dwell there, whether brahmans, *śramanas*, or those of other sects, or householders who show obedience to their superiors, obedience to mother and father, obedience to their teachers and behave well and devotedly towards their friends, acquaintances, colleagues, relatives, slaves, and servants suffer violence, murder, and separation from their loved ones. Even those who are fortunate to have escaped, and whose love is undiminished [by the brutalizing effect of war], suffer from the misfortunes of their friends, acquaintances, colleagues, and relatives. This participation of all men in suffering weighs heavily on the mind of the Beloved of the Gods. Except among the Greeks, there is no land where the religious orders of brahmans and *śramanas* are not to be found, and there is no land anywhere where men do not support one sect or another. Today if a hundredth or a thousandth part of those people who were killed or died or were deported when Kalinga was annexed were to suffer similarly, it would weigh heavily on the mind of the Beloved of the Gods.

The Beloved of the Gods believes that one who does wrong should be forgiven as far as it is possible to forgive him. And the Beloved of the Gods conciliates the forest tribes of his empire, but he warns them that he has power even in his remorse, and he asks them to repent, lest they be killed. For the Beloved of the Gods wishes that all beings should be unharmed, self-controlled, calm in mind, and gentle.

The Beloved of the Gods considers victory by *Dhamma* to be the foremost victory. And moreover the Beloved of the Gods has gained this victory on all his frontiers to a distance of six hundred *yojanas* [i.e., about 1,500 miles], where reigns the Greek king named Antiochus, and beyond the realm of that Antiochus in the lands of the four kings named Ptolemy, Antigonus, Magas, and Alexander; and in the south over the Colas and Pāndyas as far as Ceylon. Likewise here in the imperial territories among the Greeks and the Kambojas, Nābhakas and Nābhapanktis, Bhojas and Pitinikas, Andhras and Pārindas, everywhere the people follow the Beloved of the Gods' instructions in *Dhamma*. Even where the envoys of the Beloved of the Gods have not gone, people hear of his conduct according to *Dhamma*, his precepts and his instruction in *Dhamma*, and they follow *Dhamma* and will continue to follow it.

What is obtained by this is victory everywhere, and everywhere victory is pleasant. This pleasure has been obtained through victory by *Dhamma*—yet it is but a slight pleasure, for the Beloved of the Gods only looks upon that as important in its results which pertains to the next world.

This inscription of *Dhamma* has been engraved so that any sons or great grandsons that I may have should not think of gaining new conquests, and in whatever victories they may gain should be satisfied with patience and light punishment. They should only consider conquest by *Dhamma* to be a true conquest, and delight in *Dhamma* should be their whole delight, for this is of value in both this world and the next.

→ *Why would Aśoka refer to himself as "the Beloved of the Gods"? Whose gods might he be referring to?*

→ *Aśoka was a follower of Buddhism, which held that mortals passed through cycles of life, death, and rebirth. What parts of this passage reflect that belief?*

→ *Aśoka promises to rule his people with* Dhamma *(Dharma in Sanskrit). Whereas Buddhist doctrine considers* Dharma *to encompass religious teachings that guided the Buddha's followers, Aśoka's* Dhamma *refers to a general moral standard that applied to all religious and ethnic communities—Buddhists or not. Why do you suppose he emphasizes this broader meaning?*

SOURCE: Romila Thapar, *Aśoka and the Decline of the Maurya*, 2nd ed. (Delhi: Oxford University Press, 1973), 255–57.

along. He also lauded the benefits of agrarian progress and banned large-scale cattle sacrifice as detrimental to agriculture. Meanwhile, he warned the "forest people," the hunters and gatherers living beyond the reach of government, to avoid making trouble and be wary of his punitive wrath.

To explain and implement this dhamma Aśoka regularly issued decrees, which he displayed on stone pillars and boulders in every corner of his domain; occasionally he also issued edicts to explain his own Buddhist faith. All were inscribed in local languages. While most of his decrees were in dialects of Sanskrit, those published in northwestern regions were in Greek or Aramaic, the administrative script of old Persia. Aśoka's legal pronouncements helped legitimize the Greek-speaking population that had arrived with Alexander and now resided in Greek-style towns.

The works of art created under Aśoka's patronage celebrated the copious cultural and economic exchanges among Greeks, Persians, and Indians. The most famous monument was the edict pillar that Aśoka erected in Sarnath at the Deer Garden, where the Buddha gave his first sermon. Atop the pillar, four lions sat facing four directions. Beneath the four lions were four wheels representing universal rule; they were separated by a bull, a horse, elephants, and another lion. The majestic images of lions, animals not found in the Ganges plain, represented an Indian version of the Persian royal symbol. Its artistic technique displayed Greek influence as well, in vivid, animated style.

Elephant Cavalry. As shown by this terra-cotta statuette from 200 BCE, elephant cavalry was an important component of the Greek military. In their exchanges with India, Hellenist states demanded numerous elephants for their army.

THE SELEUCID EMPIRE AND GREEK INFLUENCES

Alexander's military thrust into Asia reached as far as the Punjab. There he defeated several rulers of Gandhara in 326 BCE. In the course of this campaign he planted many garrison towns—especially in eastern Iran, northern Afghanistan, and the Punjab, where he needed to protect his easternmost territorial acquisition. These towns were originally stations for soldiers, but they soon became centers of Hellenistic culture. Many of these outposts, such as those at Ghazni, Kandahar, Kapisi, and Bactra (modern Balkh), displayed the characteristic features of a Greek polis: a colonnaded main street lined by temples to patron gods or goddesses, a theater, a gymnasium for education, a palace administration center, a marketplace.

After Alexander's death, Seleucus Nikator (358–281 BCE), ruler of the Hellenistic successor state in this area, built more Greek garrison towns. Seleucus, who also controlled Mesopotamia, Syria, and Persia, named sixteen cities "Antioch" after his father, five "Laodiceas" after his mother, nine "Seleucia" after himself, three "Apamea" after his wife Apama, and "Stratonicea" after another wife. These towns, too, became major Hellenistic centers.

Most of the Greek invaders integrated themselves into the local societies. Once the soldiers realized they would be spending their lives far from their homeland, they married local women and started families. Bringing their native customs to the local populations, they established institutions familiar to them from the polis. Greek was the official language; but because local women used their native tongues in daily life, subsequent generations were bilingual. For centuries the traditional Greek institutions—especially Greek language and writing—survived many political changes and much cultural assimilation, providing a common basis of engagement in a long strip of land stretching from the Mediterranean to South Asia.

THE KINGDOM OF BACTRIA AND THE YAVANA KINGS

Hellenistic influences were even more pronounced in the Seleucid successor regimes of central Asia of the late third century BCE. The Seleucid state took over the entire Persian realm, including its central Asian and South Asian territory.

The Hellenistic kingdom of Bactria broke away from the Seleucids to establish a strong state, which included the Gandhara region in modern Pakistan, around 200 BCE. As Mauryan power receded from the northwestern part of India, the Bactrian rulers extended their conquests into this area. Because the cities that the Bactrian Greeks founded included many Indian residents, and thus were a mix of cultural influences, they have been called "Indo-Greek." Those in Gandhara incorporated familiar features of the Greek polis, but inhabitants still revered Indian patron gods and goddesses.

Hellenistic Bactria served as a bridge between South Asia and the Greek world of the Mediterranean. Among the goods that the Bactrians sent west were elephants, which were vital to the Greek armies. In fact, the Greeks' fascination with Indian war elephants found frequent expression in Greek art. The Greek king Demetrius, who invaded India around 200 BCE, had coins minted portraying himself wearing an elephant cap (a headdress with an elephant's trunk). In subsequent decades, Bactrian Greek invaders not only revived the cities in India left by Alexander but also founded new Hellenistic cities in the Gandhara region. Demetrius entrusted the extension of his empire in the northern region of India to his generals, many of whom became independent rulers after his death. Sanskrit literature refers to these Greek rulers as the Yavana kings—a word derived from "Ionia," a region whose name applied to all those who spoke Greek or came from the Mediterranean.

Remains of a Greek garrison town, unearthed under the site of the ancient city of Samarkand in Uzbekistan, attest to the strength of Hellenistic influences. In the 1960s, archaeologists at Aï Khanoum on the Oxus River (now the Amu) in present-day Afghanistan were stunned to find the ruins of nearly an entire Greek city. Miraculously, Aï Khanoum was able to avoid the reconstructions and devastations that befell so many other Hellenistic cities in this region. It was clearly an administrative center, if not the capital city, of the Bactrian state. The Greek-style architecture and inscriptions indicate that the original residents were soldiers from Greece. Following the typical pattern, they married local women and stayed; but they also established fundamental institutions of a Greek polis.

Aï Khanoum's characteristic Greek structures included a palace complex, a gymnasium, a theater, an arsenal, several temples, and elite residences. Featuring marble columns with Corinthian capitals, the palace contained an administrative section, storage rooms, and a library. A main road divided the city into lower and higher parts, with the palace and main religious buildings located in the lower city. Though far from Greece, the elite Greek residents read poetry and philosophy and staged Greek dramas in the theater. The palace baths had a mosaic floor of colored pebbles obtained from the nearby riverbank. Grape cultivation supported a festival of

Three Coins. *Top*: Wearing an elephant cap, Demetrius of Bactria titled himself the king of Indians as well as Greeks. On the other side of the coin is Hercules. *Middle*: The king Menander is remembered by Buddhists for his curiosity about their theology. His image appears on one side of the coin with a Greek legend of his name and title. On the other side, Athena is surrounded by Kharoshthi script, an Indian writing. *Bottom*: The Scythian king Maues used Greek to claim "King of Kings" on one side of his coin. On the other side, the goddess Nike is surrounded by Kharoshthi letters.

wine drinking, associated with the god Dionysus. The main temple housed a gigantic marble statue of an unknown deity; only its huge marble foot has survived the ravages of time. The remains of various statues indicate that the residents not only revered the Greek deity Athena and the demigod Heracles but also paid homage to the Zoroastrian religion and worshipped Mesopotamian gods.

The Hellenistic cities in the area of modern Uzbekistan, Afghanistan, and northern India maintained Greek culture, also educating young people in gymnasia and performing

MAP 6-2 NOMADIC INVASIONS 350 BCE–100 CE
Interaction between nomadic and settled societies was a major engine of change in Afro-Eurasia in the first millennium BCE. According to the map, where did most of the nomadic and settled societies come from? What were their two primary destinations? How did this interaction shape cross-cultural processes (the spread and diffusion of goods, peoples, and ideas)?

- • Permanent Hellenistic settlement
- SCYTHS Nomad confederacy
- HAN Contemporary settled culture

Greek dramas in their theaters. Because Greek religious practices were highly inclusive, temples were suitable places for cultural assimilation; there, local deities donned Greek garb to protect the city. As the Greeks planted familiar crops from their homeland, vineyards and olive orchards flourished. A material culture, such as tableware associated with wine drinking, also thrived. Cities and kings issued coins with Greek

inscriptions, or legends, in the standard weights of the Greek world. Most men and women spoke and wrote some Greek, often as a second language.

Perhaps the most adept ruler at mingling Greek and Indian influences was Menander, the best-known Yavana city-state king of the mid-second century BCE. Using images and legends on coins to promote both traditions among his subjects,

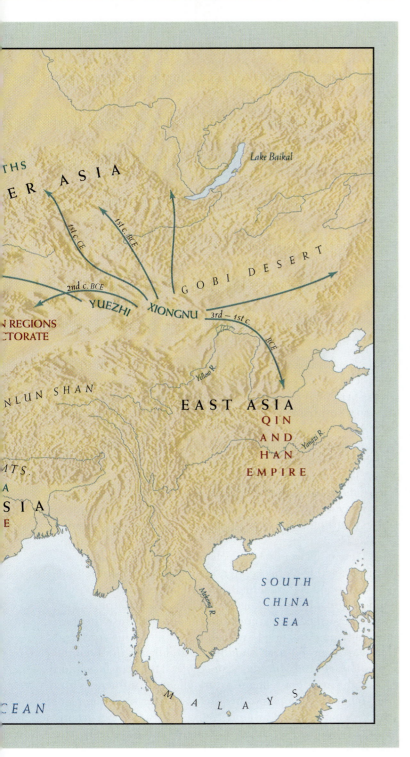

essential to communication and trade around the Indian Ocean rim.

NOMADIC INFLUENCES OF PARTHIANS AND KUSHANS

Although much of central and Southwest Asia came under the control of Alexander's successor kingdoms (and some smaller independent kingdoms), nomadic populations continued to be influential in this period. (See Map 6-2.) First to feel the impact of nomads was the Seleucid state in Iran. Having lost control of Bactria, it now came under relentless pressure from nomadic peoples living on the steppes to the north. The first to prey on them were the horse-riding Parthians, who wiped out the Greek kingdoms in Iran. The Parthians then extended their power all the way to the Mediterranean, where they would ultimately encounter the Roman Empire in Anatolia and Mesopotamia.

THE PARTHIANS The Parthian people had moved south from present-day Turkmenistan and settled in the region comprising the modern states of Iraq and Iran. Unlike the Persians before them, the Parthians had a social order founded on nomadic pastoralism and a war capability based on technical advances in mounted horseback warfare. Reliance on horses made their style of fighting highly mobile and ideal for warfare on arid plains and deserts. They perfected the so-called Parthian shot: the arrow shot from a bow with great accuracy at long distance and from horseback at a gallop. On the flat, open plains of Iran and Iraq, the Parthians had a decisive advantage over slow-moving, cumbersome mass infantry formations that had developed for war in the Mediterranean. Eventually the expansionist states of Parthia and Rome became archenemies: they confronted each other in Mesopotamia for nearly four centuries. Because the Parthians probably did not have their own writing system, their empire left no historical record. We know it only through the descriptions of Greek observers who remained in central Asia after the Greek powers retreated. According to these sources, the Hellenistic caravan cities on the Roman Empire's eastern frontier continued to trade with the east in spite of the conflicts between Romans and Parthians. From the eastern shore of the Mediterranean all the way to Afghanistan, Greek was still the essential language for commercial activities.

During a second wave of invasions, other nomadic peoples swept out of Mongolia and central Asia around 130 BCE. They filled some of the vacuum left by the disintegration of Alexander's and Aśoka's empires, infusing South Asian societies with the nomadic and equestrian values of the steppe. In the process, they blended Hellenism and Buddhist religious thought with a culture that glorified nomadic and pastoral ways and institutions. A modified Hellenistic culture

Menander claimed legitimacy as an Indian ruler but also cultivated Greek cultural forms. The face of his coins bore his regal image surrounded by the Greek words *Basileus Sōtēr Menandros* ("King, Savior, Menander"). The reverse side featured the Greek goddess Athena and the king's title in the local Pakrit language. These legacies persisted long after the Hellenistic regimes collapsed, because they remained and the Greek language now became more vital than before. Even as its connections to Greece weakened, Hellenism's influence over Buddhism and other South Asian cultures grew stronger.

The new rulers galloping down from the steppe in waves forced their predecessors to seek new tribal domains. In the second century BCE, a vast tribal confederacy called the Xiongnu became dominant in the East Asian steppe lands. While consolidating their power, the Xiongnu drove many other pastoral groups out of their homelands. Meanwhile, the Parthians (who had supplanted the Greek Seleucids in Iran) also entered the Indus Valley—from the northwest, through the mountain passes of Baluchistan.

THE KUSHANS   The most dynamic and powerful of the nomadic groups were the Yuezhi-Kushans, who appeared as a political force around 50 CE. Led by their chief, the Yuezhi unified the region's tribes and established the Kushan dynasty in Afghanistan and the Indus River basin. The Kushans' empire embraced a large and diverse territory and was critical in the formation of the Silk Road.

Like the Parthians, the Kushans had been an illiterate people, but they adopted Greek as their official language. The face of a gold coin of Wima Kadphises (the second Kushan king to rule South Asia) features the king's bust surrounded by Greek legends. The reverse side shows the Hindu god Shiva with his cow. Until the end of the Kushan Empire in the early third century CE, Greek letters continued to appear on Kushan coins. Their rulers kept alive the influence of Hellenism in an area strategically located on the Silk Road, even though by this time few Greek speakers were left in the population. Mediterranean traders arriving in the Kushan markets to purchase silks from China, as well as Indian gemstones and spices, conducted their transactions in Greek. The coins they used—struck to Roman weight standards (themselves derived from Greek coinage) and inscribed in Greek—served their needs perfectly.

These diverse nomadic groups did not undermine local cultural traditions or the Hellenistic heritage, but they introduced a powerful new cultural ingredient: equestrianism. The proud Kushans carried their horse-riding skills into India and, in spite of the hot climate, continued to wear their trademark cone-shaped leather hats, knee-length robes, trousers, and boots. Since the time of the Vedic invaders (see Chapter 3), horses had been valued imports into the region—and under the Kushans they became the most prestigious status symbol of the ruling elite. At the same time, the Kushans began consuming exotic goods that arrived from as far east as China and as far west as the Mediterranean. Their rule also stabilized the trading routes through central Asia that stretched from the steppes in the east to the Parthian Empire in the west. This would become a major segment of the Silk Road.

The Kushans also courted the local population by patronizing local religious cults. In Bactria, where they encountered the shrines of many different gods, the Kushan kings had their coins cast with images of various deities on the reverse side. They also donated generously to shrines of Zoroastrian, Vedic, and Buddhist cults. Around Kushan political centers, religious shrines mushroomed and sculptural works reached a high artistic level. Kushan kings also built royal dynastic shrines, beside which they placed statues of themselves as patrons of the local deities. Governors and generals followed their example of patronizing local religions, as did traders, artisans, and other urbanites. Wealth flowed into religious institutions, especially Buddhist monasteries later on.

THE TRANSFORMATION OF BUDDHISM

> → *In what ways did the transformation of Buddhism represent cultural integration in South Asia?*

While South Asia was undergoing noteworthy political and social change caused by encroaching nomadic tribes, it was also experiencing upheavals in the religious sphere. Perhaps the most surprising repercussion of the spread of Hellenism after Alexander was the transformation of Buddhism.

Impressed by Hellenistic thought, South Asian peoples sought to blend it with their own ethical and religious traditions. This merging began among the Yavana (that is, Greek) city-states in the northwest, where Buddhism's sway was most pronounced—and readily absorbed into the mix of cultural pulses swirling throughout the area. (See Primary Source: Sâgala: The City of the Gods.) Here, for example, the Yavana king Menander went beyond claiming that the Buddha was an inspired ethical philosopher; he held instead that the Buddha was a god. He reached this conclusion through a discussion with a Buddhist sage named Nagasena, during which Menander asked many questions about Buddhist theology and Nagasena explained away all his doubts. This conversation was recorded in a Buddhist text called *Milindapunha* (*Questions of King Milinda*). Nonetheless, the transformation of Buddhism into a religion with Hellenistic influences and wide-ranging support in other states was far from complete when Menander died around 130 BCE. It would occur only after accommodating other influences, and other gods and beliefs (see Chapter 8).

INDIA AS A SPIRITUAL CROSSROADS

Hellenism was not the sole cultural movement to affect other cultures. The nomads in India added another layer of cultural change, as did Arab and other seafarers. The latter's mastery of the monsoon trade winds opened the Indian Ocean to commerce (see below) and made India the hub for

SÂGALA: THE CITY OF THE GODS

The Indo-Greek king Menander was a famous patron of Buddhism, as described in the Questions of King Milinda. *The book, written in Pāli, a northwestern dialect of Sanskrit, begins with a description of the kingdom of Milinda (Menander) located in the country of Yonakas, the Pāli name for Greeks. This kingdom, according to the following passage, is a center of prosperous trade and people of many creeds, with a city called Sâgala whose glory rivals that of "the city of the gods."*

Thus hath it been handed down by tradition—There is in the country of the Yonakas a great centre of trade, a city that is called Sâgala, situated in a delightful country well watered and hilly, abounding in parks and gardens and groves and lakes and tanks, a paradise of rivers and mountains and woods. Wise architects have laid it out, and its people know of no oppression, since all their enemies and adversaries have been put down. Brave is its defence, with many and various strong towers and ramparts, with superb gates and entrance archways; and with the royal citadel in its midst, white walled and deeply moated. Well laid out are its streets, squares, cross roads, and market places. Well displayed are the innumerable sorts of costly merchandise with which its shops are filled. It is richly adorned with hundreds of almshalls of various kinds; and splendid with hundreds of thousands of magnificent mansions, which rise aloft like the mountain peaks of the Himâlayas. Its streets are filled with elephants, horses, carriages, and foot-passengers, frequented by groups of handsome men and beautiful women, and crowded by men of all sorts and conditions, Brahmans, nobles, artificers, and servants. They resound with cries of welcome to the teachers of every creed, and the city is the resort of the leading men of each of the differing sects. Shops are there for the sale of Benares muslin, of Kotumbara stuffs and of other cloths of various kinds; and sweet odours are exhaled from the bazaars, where all sorts of flowers and perfumes are tastefully set out. Jewels are there in plenty, such as men's hearts desire, and guilds of traders in all sorts of finery display their goods in the bazaars that face all quarters of the sky. So full is the city of money, and of gold and silver ware, of copper and stone ware, that it is a very mine of dazzling treasures. And there is laid up there much store of property and corn and things of value in warehouses—foods and drinks of every sort, syrups and sweetmeats of every kind. In wealth it rivals Uttara-kuru, and in glory it is as Âlakamandâ, the city of the gods.

→ *The city Sâgala is in the country of the Yonakas, that of the Greeks. Judging from the references to elephants, horses, and the Himalayas, where approximately would it have been located?*

→ *What kinds of people lived there?*

→ *Why do you suppose Buddhist ideas found easy acceptance there?*

SOURCE: *The Questions of King Milinda,* translated by T. W. Rhys Davis (1890; reprint, Delhi: Motilal Banarsidass, 1975), 2–3.

long-distance ocean traders and travelers. In fact, all land and sea roads seemed to lead to India. During this era the region became a melting pot of ideas and institutions, from which a powerful spiritual synthesis emerged. Indeed, the combined influences of Hellenism, nomadism, and Arab seafaring culture profoundly transformed Buddhism.

As a result, Buddhism changed dramatically from the early days when the Buddha walked from city to city preaching to his community of followers (*sangha*) and general audiences. Under the Kushans, whom we noted earlier as energetic patrons of many religions, the Buddhist *sangha* grew so rich through India's commercial prosperity that monks began to live in elegant monastic complexes. The center of each was a stupa decorated with sculptures depicting the Buddha's life and teachings. Such monasteries provided generously for the monks, with halls where they gathered and worshipped and rooms where they meditated and slept. During this age, Buddhist monasteries also opened to the public as places for worship.

THE NEW BUDDHISM: THE MAHAYANA SCHOOL

The mixing of new ways—nomadic, Hellenistic, Persian, and Mesopotamian—with traditional Buddhism produced a spectacular spiritual and religious synthesis. A new school of

Stupa Staircase. These risers from the staircase of a large stupa in the Gandhara region display scenes from Buddhist stories. The upper one shows men in nomads' clothing playing music, including the Greek-style lira. On the middle one, men and women in Greek clothing drink and make merry. The people on the lower riser wear little clothing but are as happy as those on the other two panels.

theology, **Mahayana Buddhism**, appeared at this time. For at least a hundred years, Buddhist scholars had debated whether the Buddha was a god or a wise human being. The Mahayana Buddhists resolved this dispute in the first two centuries of the Common Era with a ringing affirmation: the Buddha was, indeed, a deity. Mahayana Buddhism was worldly and accommodating, a spiritual pluralism that positioned Indian believers as a cosmopolitan people—welcoming contacts with peoples from other parts of Afro-Eurasia and laying the spiritual foundations for a region that had become a crossroads of world cultures.

As Buddhism adapted to external impulses, Mahayana Buddhism appealed especially to foreigners and immigrants who traded or settled in India. It made the Buddha as a god

easier to understand. Hitherto, the Buddha's preaching had stressed life's suffering and the renunciation of desire to end suffering and achieve nirvana. This was a tough road to a better life. As we saw in Chapter 5, those who did not believe in reincarnation found it difficult to understand the appeal of nirvana. Newcomers such as migrants or traders were unlikely to embrace the nonexistence it offered; they saw no need to escape painful cycles of birth, growth, death, and rebirth that were so ingrained in the mental worlds of local populations. This sharp dichotomy between a real world of hardship and the Buddha's abstract one of nirvana gave way to a greater variety of conditions in the Mahayana cosmos; the latter appealed to diverse peoples as a way of conceiving, and practicing, the way to a better life. In the Mahayana Buddhists'

Buddhist Cave Temple at Ajanta. Buddhists excavated cave temples along the trade routes between ports on the west coast of India and places inland. Paintings and sculptures from Ajanta became the models of Buddhist art in central Asia and China.

vision, **bodhisattvas** (enlightened demigods who were ready to reach nirvana but delayed doing so in order to help others attain it) prepared "Buddha-lands" and heavens—spiritual halfway points—to welcome deceased devotees not yet ready to release desires and enter nirvana. In this fashion the universe of the afterlife in Mahayana Buddhism was colorful and pleasant, presenting an array of alternatives to the tough real existence of worldly living.

Mahayana ("Great Vehicle") Buddhism would enable all individuals—the poor and powerless as well as the rich and powerful—to move from a life of suffering into a happy existence. Early Buddhism had left suffering devotees with little relief because of the uncertainty of achieving nirvana and the lack of a guide to lead them there, since the Buddha had already moved on to nirvana. The new Buddhist brokers—the bodhisattvas—were effective instruments for helping all classes find their way to heaven. They were the way stations, the escorts. One of these bodhisattvas, Avalokiteshvara, proclaimed his willingness to stay in this world to guide people out of trouble—especially those who traveled in caravans and had the misfortune of running into murderous robbers, or those who had to navigate unwieldy ships through violent storms. As Avalokiteshvara guided and protected the living rather than appease the deceased, lay followers, especially traveling merchants, invoked him constantly and spread the cult along the trade routes.

Just as Buddhism absorbed outside influences, became more appealing, and developed a cadre of spiritual brokers, it also inspired a new genre of literature to portray the Buddha and the bodhisattvas to audiences. This was the advent of Sanskrit Buddhist texts. Many were devoted to conveying the life of the Buddha and his message far and wide, reaching far corners of Asia. Aśvaghosa (80?–150? CE), a great Buddhist thinker and the first known Sanskrit writer, wrote a biography of the Buddha. This work, known as the Buddhacarita, set the Buddha's life story within the commercial urban environment of the Kushan Empire (instead of in the rural Shakya republic in the Himalaya foothills, where he had actually lived). Aśvaghosa said that the Buddha was born as a prince into a life of extreme luxury, becoming aware of human suffering only after experiencing heavenly revelations. To escape his mundane life, the young prince left home in the middle of the night, riding on a white horse. This largely fictive version of the Buddha's life story spread rapidly throughout India and beyond, introducing Buddha and his teachings to many new potential converts.

CULTURAL INTEGRATION

The colorful images of Sanskrit Buddhist texts of the first centuries CE gave rise to a large repertoire of Buddhist sculptural art and drama. On Buddhist stupas and shrines, artisans carved scenes of the Buddha's life, figures of bodhisattvas, and statues of patrons and donors. Buddhist sculptures from the northern Kushan territory, fashioned from gray schist rock, are called Gandharan art; those from the central region of India, created mainly from local red sandstone, are called Mathuran art. Gandharan Buddhist art shows strong Greek and Roman influences, whereas the Mathuran style evolved from the carved idols of folk gods and goddesses.

Despite their stylistic differences, the schools shared themes and cultural elements. Inspired by Hellenistic art and religious tradition, both took the bold step of sculpting the Buddha and bodhisattvas in realistic human, rather than symbolic, form (such as a bodhi tree, which symbolizes Buddha's enlightenment). Though the Buddha wore no decorations because he had cut off all links to the world, bodhisattvas were dressed as princes because they were still in this world, generously helping others. What was important was bringing the symbolic world of Buddhism closer to the people.

Buddhist art depicted a society of diverse populations, reflecting a spiritual system that appealed to people of diverse

Zoroastrianism, which had been a state religion in the Persian Empire during the fifth and fourth centuries BCE (see Chapter 4); by the time Buddhism began to spread, Zoroastrianism had long been established in Iran. Iranian Hellenism had done little to weaken the power of Zoroastrianism, whose adherents formed city-based religious communities affiliated primarily with traders. Following the Silk Road, Zoroastrian traders traveled both eastward to China and westward to the coast of the Mediterranean, impeding the westward spread of Buddhism.

TAKING TO THE SEAS: COMMERCE ON THE RED SEA AND INDIAN OCEAN

> → *What factors promoted sea trade on the Indian Ocean?*

Although land routes were the tried-and-true avenues for migrants, traders, and wayfarers, they carried only what could be borne on the backs of humans and animals. Travel on them was slow, and they were vulnerable to marauders. With time, some risk takers found ways of traversing waterways—eventually on an unprecedented scale and with an ease unimaginable to earlier merchants. These risk takers were Arabs, from the commercial middle ground of the Afro-Eurasian trading system.

Arab traders had long carried such spices as frankincense and myrrh to the Egyptians, who used them in religious and funerary rites, and later to the Greeks and Romans. Metals such as bronze, tin, and iron passed along overland routes from Anatolia, as did gold, silver, and chlorite from the Iranian plateau. Gold, ivory, and other goods from the northern part of India passed through Taxila (the capital of Gandhara) and the Hindu Kush Mountains into Persia as early as the sixth century BCE. Following the expansion of the Hellenistic world, however, ships increasingly conducted long-distance trade. They sailed down the Red Sea and across the Indian Ocean as they carried goods between the tip of the Arabian Peninsula and the ports of the Indian landmass.

Arab seafarers led the way into the Indian Ocean, forging links that joined East Africa, the eastern Mediterranean, and the Arabian Peninsula with India, Southeast Asia, and East Asia. Such voyages involved longer stays at sea and were far more dangerous than sailing in the Mediterranean. Yet by the first century CE, Arab and Indian sailors were transporting Chinese silks, central Asian furs, and fragrances from Himalayan trees across the Indian Ocean. The city of Alexandria in Egypt soon emerged as a key transit point between the Mediterranean Sea and the Indian Ocean. Boats carried Mediterranean exports of olives and olive oil, wine, drinking vessels, glassware, linen and wool textiles, and red coral up the Nile, stopping at Koptos and other port cities from which camel caravans took the goods to the Red Sea ports of Myos Hormos and Berenice. For centuries, Mediterranean merchants had considered the Arabian Peninsula to be the end of the Spice Road. But after Alexander's expedition and the establishment of colonies between Egypt and Afghanistan, they began to value the wealth and opportunities that lay along the shores of the Indian Ocean.

Arab sailors who ventured into the Indian Ocean benefited from new navigational techniques, especially celestial bearings (using the position of the stars to determine the position of the ship and the direction to sail). They used large ships called *dhows,* whose sails were rigged to easily capture the wind; these forerunners of modern cargo vessels were capable of long hauls in rough waters. Beginning about 120 BCE, mariners came to understand the seasonal rain-filled monsoon winds, which blow from the southwest between October and April and then from the northeast between April and October—knowledge that propelled the maritime trade connecting the Mediterranean with the Indian Ocean.

Mariners accumulated the new sailing knowledge in books—each called a *periplus* ("sailing around")—in which sea captains recorded the landing spots and ports between their destinations, as well as their precious cargoes. (See Global Connections & Disconnections: The Worlds of *Periplus.*) From such books, for example, we learn that trading ships left the southern Arabian coast with the monsoon winds behind them, heading for the entrepôts (trading centers) of India. Barbaricum, at the mouth of the Indus, was the first Indian port reached from the west. On their arrival, traders unloaded linen textiles, red coral, glassware, wine, and money from the Mediterranean and Egypt, as well as frankincense and storax, aromatic gum resins from Southwest Asia. These cargoes were headed to the upper Indus region of the Punjab and Gandhara. While at harbor in India, traders loaded their ships with treasures from the east: fragrances or spices from the Himalayas and India, such as costus root and bdellium, turquoise from Khorasan in Iran, lapis lazuli from Badakhshan in Afghanistan, indigo dye and cotton textiles from India, furs from central Asia, and silk textiles and yarn from China.

By now, the revolution in navigational techniques and knowledge had dramatically reduced the cost of long-distance shipping and multiplied the ports of call around large bodies of water. Some historians have argued that there were now two Silk Roads: one by land and one by sea.

CONCLUSION

Alexander's conquests were awesome in their scale and brilliant in their execution. But his empire was as transitory as it was huge. Though it crumbled upon his death, this empire

THE WORLDS OF *PERIPLUS*

Periplus Maris Erythraei, or *Periplus of the Red Sea*, was written in Greek by an Egyptian sailor and trader late in the first century CE. Its author, a shrewd businessman, keen observer, and experienced navigator, described the whole world of commerce of the Red Sea, the Mediterranean, and the Indian Ocean. He catalogued the navigable routes and listed the goods that were marketed in the ports; starting from the Red Sea, he moved southward along East Africa's coast and then eastward all the way to India. The result is the first historical record of the city-states existing along the coast of East Africa and one of the earliest accounts of Africa south of the Sahara. Throughout, he supplied data on currencies, customs, and the political regimes that controlled the ports and radiated into their hinterlands.

The author's voyage began from Berenice. After leaving this Red Sea port, he encountered tribal countries on the coastal lands of today's Sudan and Eritrea. The *Periplus* named the region Barbaria, the land of barbarians, and identified its inhabitants with such labels as "eaters of fish" and "eaters of wild animals." Farther south, the author noted the coastal area of a former Ptolemaic Egyptian colony that had fallen into decline and now exported only tortoise shells and ivory. On the other side of the Red Sea lay the coast of Arabia, where the waters were so calm that ships did not need to be anchored but where pirates from the Nabataean tribes preyed on them.

Once it sailed out of the narrow strait, the ship entered the Gulf of Aden, famed as the land of frankincense and myrrh. Beyond the territory from which incense was exported, traders brought ivory, tortoise shells, and slaves to the markets. The Somali ports received goods from India such as rice and ghee (clarified butter), sesame oil, cotton textiles, and sugar. The southernmost port along the east coast of Africa known to the author was Bhapta, nearly 3,000 miles from Berenice. This region had fallen under the influence of Arabs through intermarriage and trade.

Next the ship headed back up along the East African coast and proceeded across the Arabian Sea toward India. The most important Indian port at the time was Barygaza on the Gulf of Khambhat (Cambay), near the modern city of Broach in Gujarat, but its harbor was very difficult to navigate. The coast was rugged, the sea bottom was uneven, and the tidal waves were high and variable. Local fishermen under the king's service came out to guide foreign ships to the harbor. In fact, the entire northwestern and western parts of India were connected to the Mediterranean through Barygaza. Here the author focused on the abundance of Greek influences. For example, he noted that in the market of Barygaza old drachmas (coins) of the Indo-Greek kings Apollodotus and Menander, inscribed with Greek letters, were still circulating. Although he often garbled the names of places and people, his general point was clear: Greek culture played a critical role in the long-distance trade of India.

Map from a *Periplus*

had effects more profound than those of any military or political regime that preceded it. Alexander's armies ushered in an age of thinking and practices that transformed Greek achievements into a common culture—Hellenism—whose influences, both direct and indirect, touched far-flung societies for centuries thereafter.

This Hellenistic movement was most strongly represented by a common, simpler Greek language, which linked culture, institutions, and trade. However, many Greek-speaking peoples and their descendants in parts of Southwest and central Asia integrated local cultural practices with their own ways, creating diverse and rich cultures. Thus the influences of culture flowed both ways. The economic story is equally complex. In many respects, Alexander and his successors followed pathways established by previous kingdoms and empires. If anything, Alexander's successors helped strengthen and expand the existing trade routes and centers of commercial activity, which ultimately led to the creation of the Silk Road.

Although the effects of this Hellenistic age lasted longer than most cultural systems and had a wider appeal than previous philosophical and spiritual ideas, they did not sweep away everything before it. Indigenous cultures accommodated to this movement or fought against it with all their might, fearing the loss of their own cultural identities. Others took from it what they liked and discarded the rest. The citizens of Rome admired its achievements and steeped themselves in it while fashioning their own Latin-based culture. Eventually, they created an imperial polity that outdistanced Alexander's. In North Africa, the commercially talented Carthaginians saw some of these Greek means of expression as useful for new elites like themselves.

Of all those exposed to Hellenistic thinking, the South Asian peoples produced the most varied responses because they represented a multitude of cultures. Once opened to the influences of Macedonian invaders, steppe nomads, and Arab seafarers, South Asia became the confluence of the currents moving swiftly across Afro-Eurasia. The most telling responses were in the realm of spiritual and ethical norms, where Buddhist doctrines evolved toward a full-fledged world religious system.

Greater political integration helped fashion highways for commerce and enabled the spread of Buddhism. Nomads left their steppe lands and exchanged wares across great distances. As they found greater opportunities for business, their trade routes shifted farther south, radiating out of the oases of central Asia. Eventually merchants, rather than the trading nomads, seized the opportunities provided by new technologies, especially in sailing and navigation. These commercial transformations connected distant parts of Afro-Eurasia. Accompanying the spread of Greek ways was the opening of trade. Alexander's campaigns had followed some of the trade routes east, and his conquests opened up permanent channels of exchange. In the wake of conquests, the Silk Road and proliferating sea-lanes connected ports and caravan cities from North Africa to South China, creating new social classes, producing new urban settings, supported powerful new polities, and transported Buddhism to China, where it would ultimately proliferate on an even grander, more lasting scale than it did in South Asia.

Chronology

	400 BCE	300 BCE	200 BCE
SOUTHWEST ASIA AND NORTHERN AFRICA		◆--◆ 334–323 BCE *Conquests of Alexander the Great* ◆ 323 BCE *Emergence of Hellenistic "successor kingdoms" begins*	◆-----◆ 240 BCE–224 CE *Parthian kingdom*
THE MEDITERRANEAN		◆ 330s and 320s BCE *Roman expansion in the Italian Peninsula begins* 264–241 BCE *Roman-Carthage war* ◆------◆	
CENTRAL ASIA		◆--◆ 334–323 BCE *Conquests of Alexander the Great* 250–130 BCE *Bactrian kingdom* ◆-----------	
SOUTH ASIA		321–184 BCE *Mauryan Empire* ◆------------------------------◆ c. 200 BCE *Yavana kings emerge* ◆ c. 200 BCE *Saka invasions from central Asia* ◆	
EAST ASIA	403–221 BCE *Warring States period* ◆------------------◆	2nd or 3rd century BCE *Xiongnu Confederacy in the Mongolian steppes* ◆ 221 BCE *Unification of China under the Qin dynasty* ◆ 206 BCE *Emergence of Han Empire* ◆	*Han expands into the Silk Road* ◆

Review and research materials are available
at StudySpace: Ⓢ WWNORTON.COM/STUDYSPACE

KEY TERMS

Alexander the Great (p. 208)   Hellenism (p. 204)
bodhisattva (p. 227)   Mahayana Buddhism (p. 226)
caravan city (p. 229)   periplus (p. 236)
dhamma (p. 218)   Silk Road (p. 205)
garrison towns (p. 217)   stupa (p. 218)

STUDY QUESTIONS

1. Analyze the impact of Alexander's conquest on the Afro-Eurasian world. How did his military pursuits, and those of his successors, bring together various worlds?
2. Describe the influence of Hellenism on societies outside the Greek homeland. What aspects of Hellenistic culture held broad appeal for diverse groups?
3. Compare and contrast Judean, Roman, and Carthaginian responses to Hellenistic influences. How receptive was each society to Greek cultural influences?
4. Explain how South Asia (or India) became a melting pot for the intellectual, political, and economic currents sweeping across Afro-Eurasia between 350 BCE and 250 CE. How did this development affect Buddhist doctrine?
5. Analyze the extent to which long-distance trade routes connected societies during this period. Which societies were involved? How did commercial linkages affect them?
6. Analyze the influence of nomadic pastoral groups in Afro-Eurasia during this period. What role did they play in integrating cultures and economies?
7. Explain how interregional contacts transformed Buddhism. How did it expand across a variety of cultures?
8. Explain how art, architecture, and other forms of material culture in Afro-Eurasian societies reflected broader patterns of cultural, political, and economic integration during this period. In particular, how did caravan cities reflect new cultural configurations?

100 BCE	1 CE	100 CE	200 CE

1st–3rd centuries CE (established 60 CE) *Kushan kingdom*

◆ *1st century CE Transformation of Buddhism begins*

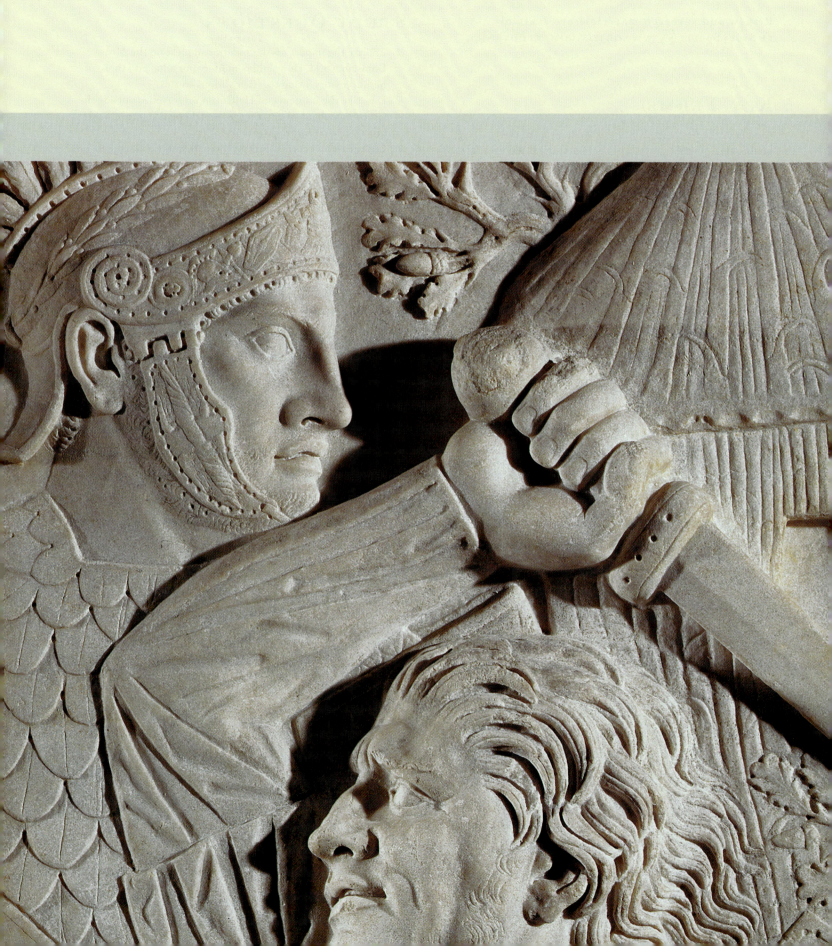

Chapter

7

HAN DYNASTY CHINA AND IMPERIAL ROME, 300 BCE–300 CE

*I*n the third century BCE, the Eastern Zhou state of Qin absorbed the remaining Warring States (see Chapter 5) and set the stage for the epic Han dynasty. The chief minister of the Qin state, Li Si, urged his king to dispense with niceties and to seize opportunities: a man who aimed at great achievements must exploit the advantages offered to him. By combining his fearsome armies and his own personal virtues, the king could sweep away his rivals as if dusting ashes from a kitchen hearth—he could eliminate them all. In this way he could establish a truly imperial rule and unify the entire world. "This is the one moment in ten thousand ages," Li Si whispered. The king listened carefully. He followed the advice. He laid the foundations for a mighty empire.

We saw in Chapter 5 how the Qin state emerged as the dominant "warring state" in Zhou China. The Qin king relied on his massive army to make himself China's First Emperor and to begin a cycle that spun out the first great land-based empire in East Asia. But the Qin Empire collapsed in 207 BCE, and soon the Han

Empire took its place. Following the Qin model, the Han defeated other regional groups and established the first long-lasting Chinese empire. Subjects of Han basked in a society whose landholding elites, free farmers, trained artisans, itinerant traders, and urban merchants were building an era that emulated the statecraft ideals of antiquity—unlike those of the cruel Qin.

At the other end of Afro-Eurasia another great state, imperial Rome, also met its rivals in war, emerged victorious, and consolidated its power into a vast empire. The Romans achieved this feat by using violent force on a scale hitherto unseen in their part of the globe. The result was a state of huge size, astonishingly unified and stable. Living in the Roman Empire in the mid-70s CE, a man of middle rank, Pliny the Elder, could write glowingly about the unity of the imperial state. In his eyes, all the benefits that flowed from its extensive reach derived from the boundless greatness of a peace that joined diverse peoples under one benevolent emperor.

The Han and the Roman states were not just new ways of organizing resources to plow them into large-scale military and administrative functions. They were not just new in the reasons rulers gave for their rulership. They were novel in laying out the political boundaries of regions we now recognize as "China" and "Christendom." Nowadays, the boundaries of both bear remarkable resemblance to those defined by these two empires at their peak. This chapter addresses how these regimes transcended the limits of previous territorial kingdoms by deploying resources and reasons of state in new ways. They concentrated military power in professionalized military elites that owed allegiance above all to the state, not to its ruler. They modernized tax collecting to support large-scale killing machines—that is, armies. They wrote laws and codes for their subjects. And they promoted the idea that the state should support schooling, the arts, architecture, and a learned society as ways to bring peace and prosperity to the realm. In this basic sense, ever since, we have

come to associate the ideal of empire with these two founders at either end of Afro-Eurasia.

Just as we see these empires as models for world history, we must understand how they were built—for they did not emerge as the inevitable consequences of destiny. They were crafted of a delicate mixture of coercion, coaxing, and convincing—and not just to prove that empires were exalted and enjoyed benefits that faraway neighbors did not. They actually had to deliver on these promises in order to endure. These were no short lasting conquerings, like Alexander the Great's. They enjoyed the institutional muscle to outlive any particular ruler.

CHINA AND ROME: HOW EMPIRES ARE BUILT

> → *How did the Roman and Han empires differ from earlier large states?*

Afro-Eurasia had seen empires come and go, emerging out of territorial kingdoms to exercise their power over neighboring states as clients, often demanding tribute in return for protection. The Romans and the Han took expansion to the next level: not content to exercise influence over neighbors, they wanted to incorporate them fully into their realm. What distinguished these two from their predecessors was their commitment to integrating conquered neighbors and rivals into the system—by extending laws, offering systems of representation, exporting belief systems, colonizing lands, and promoting trade within and beyond the empires. In effect, subject peoples became members of empires, not just the vanquished. Those who resisted not only waved away the ben-

Focus Questions

Ⓢ WWNORTON.COM/STUDYSPACE

→ *How did the Roman and Han empires differ from earlier large states?*

→ *What policies did the Qin leaders use to integrate their empire?*

→ *How did Han leaders promote peace and stability?*

→ *Were the policies and institutions that integrated the Roman Empire similar to those of Han dynasty China?*

MAIN THEMES

↝ *At both ends of Afro-Eurasia two great empires rise, flourish, and fall at roughly the same time.*

↝ *Han China and imperial Rome exercise greater power over more people and larger expanses of territory than any previous state.*

↝ *The two empires create long-lasting foundations for China and Christendom.*

FOCUS ON *Comparing the Two Empires*

◆ Han China and imperial Rome assimilate diverse peoples to their ways and regard outsiders as uncivilized.

◆ Both empires develop professional military elites, codify laws, and value the role of the state (not just the ruler) in supporting their societies.

◆ Both empires serve as models for successor states in their regions.

◆ The empires differ in their ideals and the officials they value: Han China values civilian bureaucrats and magistrates; Rome values soldiers and military governors.

efits of living under an imperial mantle but also became the targets for awesome and relentless armies.

EMPIRE AND CULTURAL IDENTITY

The mere existence of these two vast imperial states meant that at least one out of every two human beings in Afro-Eurasia now fell directly under the control of China or Rome. What did it mean to live under the imperial umbrella of these giants?

To be "Han Chinese" meant that elites shared a common written language based on the Confucian classics, which qualified them for public office. It also meant that commoners from all walks of life shared the elites' belief system based on ancestor worship, ritual practices stressing appropriate decorum and dress for each social level, and a view that the Han as an agrarian-based empire was a small-scale model of the entire cosmos. Those who lived beyond the realm of the Han were considered uncivilized.

In the fifth century BCE, being Roman meant being a citizen of the city of Rome, speaking Latin (the regional language of central Italy), and eating and dressing like Latin-speaking people. By the late second century BCE, however, the concept of citizenship expanded to include anyone who had formal membership in the larger territorial state that the Romans were building.

By the beginning of the third century CE, even this bigger view was no longer true. Now being Roman meant simply being a subject of the Roman emperors. This identity became so deeply rooted that when the western parts of the empire disintegrated two centuries later, the inhabitants of the surviving eastern parts—who had no connection with Rome, did not speak Latin, and did not dress or eat like the original Romans—still considered themselves "Romans" in this broader sense.

PATTERNS OF IMPERIAL EXPANSION

Despite their similarities, the empires reflected different patterns of development, types of public servants, and ideals for the best kind of government. For example, whereas the civilian magistrate and the bureaucrat were typical of the Han Empire, the citizen, the soldier, and the military governor stood for the Roman Empire. In China, dynastic empires fashioned themselves according to the models of past empires. The Chinese treated imperial culture as an ideal descended from the past that had to be emulated in the present. By contrast, Rome began as a collectively ruled city-state and pursued a pragmatic road to domination of its world as if creating something anew. Only by a long, sometimes violent process of trial and error did the Romans achieve a political system of one-man rule by emperors. Nonetheless, they, like the Chinese, were strongly traditional. They also idealized their ancestors. But they were less fascinated with the earlier major powers. What characterized Roman expansion and empire building was a process of continual experimentation, innovation, and adaptation.

The new empires united huge landmasses and extraordinarily diverse populations. For example, the scale of the Han dynasty was unprecedented. A land survey by the imperial government in 2 CE revealed a registered population of 12,233,062 households, or around 58 million people. These households paid taxes, provided military recruits, and supplied laborers for public works. At its height, the Han Empire covered some 3 million square miles in China proper and, for a while, another 1 million square miles in central Asia. The extent of the Yellow and Yangzi river systems that the Han dominated was also unprecedented, as each river was almost as long as the Nile. The Yellow River, nearly 3,500 miles long, drained an area of a third of a million square miles in the north, while the Yangzi River drained a basin of three-quarters of a million square miles in the south as it flowed almost 4,000 miles from central Asia to the East China Sea. The Roman Empire governed an area and a population that were as great as those of Han China.

Both empires left indelible legacies; following their collapses, both survived as models. Successor states in the Mediterranean sought to become the Second Rome, and after the Han dynasty fell, the Chinese people always identified themselves and their language simply as "Han." Both empires raised life to a new level throughout Afro-Eurasia—now people could share a common identity on a grander scale than ever before. It was a vision that would never be lost.

THE QIN DYNASTY

> → *What policies did the Qin leaders use to integrate their empire?*

The Qin dynasty's contributions to political unity and economic growth were essential to its far more powerful Han successor state. (See Map 7-1.) Together, the Qin and Han created the political, social, economic, and cultural foundations that would characterize imperial China thereafter. Through conquest and a strong bureaucracy, the Qin forged a central state whose administrative organizations, laws, and standardized measures that the Qin rulers put in place would last well beyond their own rule.

King Zheng of Qin defeated the remaining Warring States between 230 and 221 BCE, ending one of the most violent periods in Chinese history. With the help of able ministers and generals and a large conscripted army, as well as a system of taxation that financed all-out war, he assumed the mandate of heaven from the Zhou and unified the states into a centralized empire. Having accomplished this feat, he declared himself Shi Huangdi, or "First August Emperor" (much as Rome's first emperor also called himself Augustus).

He took the title of emperor (*di*) to distinguish himself from both the Zhou ruler and the rulers of the Warring States, all of whom had called themselves kings (*wang*). To further consolidate his power he forced the defeated rulers and their families to move to Xianyang, the Qin capital—where, under his watchful eye, they would be unable to gather rebel armies.

ADMINISTRATION AND CONTROL

After securing loyalty from the defeated states, the First August Emperor divided up China so that the new dynasty could rule the massive state effectively. He parceled the territory into thirty-six provinces, or **commanderies** (*jun*), which he subdivided into counties (*xian*). Each commandery had a civilian and a military governor answering to an imperial inspector. Crucial to this administrative strategy were requirements that regional and local officials answer directly to the emperor and that he could dismiss them at will. Moreover, he made sure that civilian governors did not serve in their home areas and often got reassigned to new posts—calculated moves that prevented them from building up power for themselves.

Clerks registered the common people in order to observe, control, and punish them. Registration, required of all males when they reached maturity (age sixteen or seventeen, and five feet in height), provided the basis for taxation and conscription. All able-bodied males had to serve in the army and work on public projects: building border walls, imperial roads, canals, and huge palaces in the capital. Imperial rule was harsh, and censorship was rife. These practices imposed a social order that had been lacking during nearly two and a half centuries of warfare and chaos.

To further unify varied systems surviving from the Warring States period, the Qin emperor established standard weights and measures, as well as a standard currency. Circular copper coins with square holes in the center (to string them together) replaced the coins shaped like miniature spades or knives that had characterized the different states' economies. To rule out currency forging and ensure that these coins kept their value (thus being more than mere symbols), the new Qin and later the Han "Pan Liang" copper coins bore simple

Qin Coin. After centuries of distinctive regional currencies, the Qin unified the currency as part of its general unification policy. Thereafter bronze or copper cash was the standard imperial currency in China.

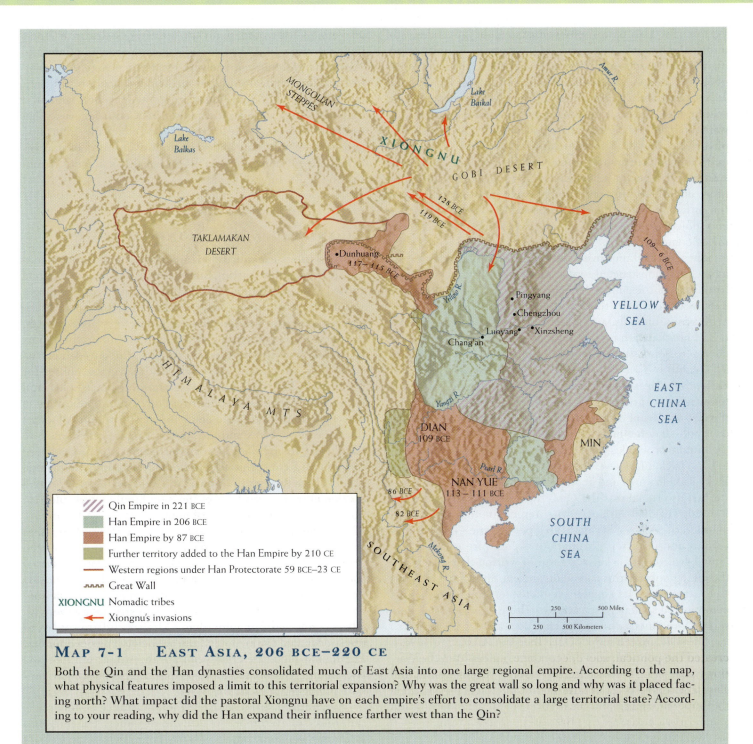

MAP 7-1 EAST ASIA, 206 BCE–220 CE

Both the Qin and the Han dynasties consolidated much of East Asia into one large regional empire. According to the map, what physical features imposed a limit to this territorial expansion? Why was the great wall so long and why was it placed facing north? What impact did the pastoral Xiongnu have on each empire's effort to consolidate a large territorial state? According to your reading, why did the Han expand their influence farther west than the Qin?

etchings that identified their value. While coins were nothing new, the Qin pioneered effective minting techniques.

The Qin extended China's boundaries in the northeast to the Korean Peninsula, in the south to present-day Vietnam, and in the west into central Asia. Han Fei, a minor official from the state of Han, introduced the notion of a "grand unity" that appealed to the Qin rulers and ministers as a guiding political idea. The chief minister of the Qin Empire, Li Si, used it to justify the harsh measures that the state enacted to unify the Central Plain states.

Both Han Fei and Li Si subscribed to the principles of Legalism developed during the Warring States period (see

Chapter 5). This philosophy valued written law codes, administrative regulations, and inflexible punishments more highly than rituals and ethics (which the Confucians emphasized) or spontaneity and the natural order (which the Daoists stressed). Determined to bring order to a turbulent society, they enacted unambiguous laws and regulations, as well as harsh punishments that applied to everyone regardless of rank or wealth. (Such punishments included beheading, mutilation by cutting off a person's nose or foot, tattooing, shaving off a person's beard or hair, hard labor, and loss of office and rank.) After registering people in groups of five and ten, officials made them all responsible for one another—and subject to punishment for any crime that any one of them might commit.

The Qin also improved communication systems. For example, they constructed roads radiating out from their capital to all parts of the empire. These immense thoroughfares were 115 feet wide, with three lanes to accommodate vehicles, pedestrians, animals, and soldiers. Their thick embankments of soil bristled with reinforcing metal poles and pine trees to check erosion. Officials required vehicles to have a standard axle length so that all wheels would fit in the same dirt ruts. Dusty in the dry seasons, the roads were often muddy and rutted when the spring rains came. Elite men and women who traveled in elegant carts with enclosed interiors would find the dust and stench almost unbearable as they journeyed along the hundreds of miles from local towns and villages to the capital and back. After several days of travel, merchants would be lucky if their wares and goods survived undamaged.

Just as crucial was the Qin effort to standardize writing. Banning regional variants in written characters, which had characterized the Warring States period, the Qin required scribes and ministers throughout the empire to adopt the "small seal script," a revised form of writing that resembled the pictographic forms carved on ancient Shang oracle bones (see Chapter 3). Its simpler characters evolved into the less complicated style of bureaucratic writing, known as "clerical script," prominent during the Han dynasty.

The standardized script helped the Qin disseminate their vision of the state and weed out competing ideas from the Warring States era. It also eased the work of regional elites and clerks, who now served as bureaucratic intermediaries between the imperial capital and local government. Standardization

also eliminated troublesome ideas that might disturb the new imperial unity. In 213 BCE, a Qin decree ordered officials to confiscate and burn all books in residents' private possession (except for technical works on medicine, divination, and agriculture). In addition, the court prosecuted teachers who used outlawed classical books, including some Confucian works that troublemakers could cite to criticize the Qin regime. Education and learning were now under the exclusive control of state officials. (See Primary Source: A Qin Legal Document: Memorial on the Burning of Books.)

ECONOMIC AND SOCIAL CHANGES

The Qin rulers expanded their agrarian empire through conquest. During the Warring States period, landownership had shifted from aristocratic clans to the peasantry, who no longer shouldered the burden of paying tribute to regional lords. An agrarian bonanza had yielded wealth that the state could tax, and increased tax revenues meant more resources for imposing order. Now, under the Qin Empire, the government issued rules on working the fields (with severe penalties for failure to follow regulations), taxed farming households, and conscripted laborers to build irrigation systems and canals so that even more land could come under cultivation. Whereas the Greek city-states and the Roman Empire relied on slave labor, the Qin and (later) the Han dynasties championed free farmers and conscripted able-bodied sons into their huge armies. Free to work their own land, and paying only a small portion of their crops in taxes, peasant families were the economic bedrock of the Chinese empire.

Consolidation of power led to major economic changes, as self-sufficient royal manors gave way to farms that produced goods for the marketplace. As production rose, landowners—some of them peasants—could enjoy profiting from their surpluses. Increasingly, public royal domains and private employers used contracts and money to strike bargains with laborers and with one another. A similar shift toward contracts occurred throughout Chinese society and government. Previously, blood ties had been all-important, but as trade and commerce boomed, farmers and traders began to dominate public and private business.

Agricultural surpluses fueled long-distance commerce—the source of even more wealth and revenues. The burgeoning money economy produced a class of merchants in China's cities, which became market centers (rather than fortresses) in the dynamic world of region-based networks. Merchants peddled foodstuffs as well as weapons, metals, horses, dogs, hides, furs, silk, and salt—all produced in different regions. Moreover, the new roads and canals not only aided soldiers' movements but also promoted commerce, carrying both goods and tax revenues from commanderies far and wide. Nonetheless, the central government continued to value the production of crops and goods over trade, and it imposed ever-higher taxes on goods in transit and in the markets.

Small Seal Script. Under the Qin, the "large seal" script of the Zhou Dynasty was unified and simplified into a smaller version "small seal" writing.

A QIN LEGAL DOCUMENT: MEMORIAL ON THE BURNING OF BOOKS

When the first Qin emperor came to power, his minister, Li Si, devised a policy to enhance state power through a unified political ideology. Any traditions of learning that differed from the Qin orthodoxy were targets for elimination. The most serious threat to Qin power came from the Five Classics (said to have been compiled by Confucius), which stressed moral rectitude, personal character, and political responsibility while holding office. Such texts were an affront to imperial power, Li thought, so he called for their destruction and the execution of scholars who defended them in public.

In earlier times the empire disintegrated and fell into disorder, and no one was capable of unifying it. Thereupon the various feudal lords rose to power. In their discourses they all praised the past in order to disparage the present and embellished empty words to confuse the truth. Everyone cherished his own favorite school of learning and criticized what had been instituted by the authorities. But at present Your Majesty possesses a unified empire, has regulated the distinctions of black and white, and has firmly established for yourself a position of sole supremacy. And yet these independent schools, joining with each other, criticize the codes of laws and instructions. Hearing of the promulgation of a decree, they criticize it, each from the standpoint of his own school. At home they disapprove of it in their hearts; going out they criticize it in the thoroughfare. They seek a reputation by discrediting their sovereign; they appear superior by expressing contrary views, and they lead the lowly multitude in the spreading of slander. If such license is not prohibited, the sovereign power will decline above and partisan factions will form below. It would be well to prohibit this.

Your servant suggests that all books in the imperial archives, save the memoirs of Qin, be burned. All persons in the empire, except members of the Academy of Learned Scholars, in possession of the *Classic of Odes*, the *Classic of Documents*, and discourses of the hundred philosophers should take them to the local governors and have them indiscriminately burned. Those who dare to talk to each other about the *Odes* and *Documents* should be executed and their bodies exposed in the marketplace. Anyone referring to the past to criticize the present should, together with all members of his family, be put to death. Officials who fail to report cases that have come under their attention are equally guilty. After thirty days from the time of issuing the decree, those who have not destroyed their books are to be branded and sent to build the Great Wall. Books not to be destroyed will be those on medicine and pharmacy, divination by the turtle and milfoil, and agriculture and arboriculture. People wishing to pursue learning should take the officials as their teachers.

➔ *According to Li Si, how would the burning of classic texts help the Qin emperor keep "a unified empire" and "sole supremacy"?*

➔ *What types of books were still acceptable? Why would the first Qin emperor want to keep these practical works alive?*

SOURCE: "A Qin Legal Document: Memorial on the Burning of the Books" from *Sources of Chinese Tradition*, Volume 1, eds. William Theodore de Bary and Irene Bloom, © 1999 Columbia University Press. Reprinted with the permission of the publisher.

NOMADS AND THE QIN ALONG THE NORTHERN FRONTIER

Both the Qin dynasty and, later, the Han dynasty grappled with the need to expand and defend their borders. During the last centuries of the Warring States period, states along the northern border had expanded by conquering nomadic frontier peoples (see Chapter 5). When the Qin united those states into an empire and then started looking beyond to the north and west, it encountered nomadic warrior peoples—especially the proud Xiongnu, who dominated the steppes. Like the Qin, the Han faced the same limits.

Relations between these nomadic peoples and the settled Chinese teetered in a precarious balance until 215 BCE, when the Qin Empire pushed north into the middle of the Yellow River basin. At that time, the First Emperor sent troops against the Xiongnu to seize their pasturelands. To secure those lands for settlement, Qin officials built roads between the frontier and the nearest cities, such as Liye in Longshan County, in Hunan. They also directed conscripts and criminals in building

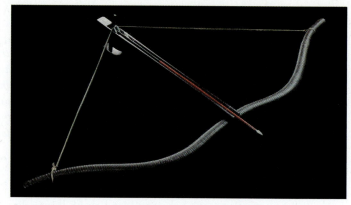

Qin Archer and Crossbow. This kneeling archer (*left*) was discovered in the tomb of the First Emperor. Notice his breastplate. The wooden bow he was holding has disintegrated, but a replica appears to the right. The bronze arrowhead and trigger mechanism in this reproduction were found with the terra-cotta army.

a massive defensive wall along the northern border (the beginnings of the Great Wall of China—though north of the current wall, which was constructed more than a millennium later). As a result of these imperial efforts, in 211 BCE the Qin settled 30,000 colonists in the steppe lands of Inner Eurasia.

THE QIN DEBACLE

Despite its military power, the Qin dynasty collapsed quickly. Its rule weighed heavily on taxpayers because of constant warfare, which consumed not just massive tax revenues but also huge numbers of laborers. Dissension at court became apparent when Chief Minister Li Si was implicated in a conspiracy and executed. When desperate conscripted workers mutinied in 211 BCE, they found allies in descendants of Warring States nobles, local military leaders, and influential merchants. The rebels swept up thousands of supporters

with their call to arms against the "tyrannical" Qin. Shortly before the First Emperor died in 210, even the educated elite joined former lords and regional vassals in revolt. The second Qin emperor committed suicide early in 207, and his weak successor surrendered to the leader of the Han forces later that year. The resurgent Xiongnu confederacy also reconquered their old pasturelands as the Qin dynasty fell.

In the aftermath of the Qin's fall, the insurgents' leader, Xiang Yu, tried to restore the Zhou system of powerful regional states—so he established nineteen feudal states. In the ensuing civil war among them, an unheralded commoner and former policeman named Liu Bang (r. 206–195 BCE) declared himself prince of his home area of Han. In 202 BCE, after Xiang Yu committed suicide, Liu proclaimed himself the first Han emperor.

Emphasizing his peasant origins, Liu demonstrated his initial disdain for intellectuals by urinating into the hat of a court scholar. But he quickly learned that power would be better served through good manners. Confucian scholars loyal to the Han soon were busy justifying Liu Bang's victory by depicting his Qin predecessors as cruel dynasts and ruthless despots. For their part, the Han court and its officials denied any link to the Qin, affirming instead Confucian ideas about the moral and cultural foundations of state power. For example, the scholar Jia Yi (c. 200–168 BCE) argued that the Qin had fallen "because the ruler lacked moral values." (See Primary Source: Jia Yi on the Faults of the Qin.) Under the cover of receiving the mandate of heaven, the Han portrayed the Qin as evil, even as they adopted the Qin's bureaucratic system.

In reality—as we can see from a cache of Qin penal codes and administrative ordinances, written on some 1,000 bamboo slips—Qin laws were no crueler than those of the later Han. Punishments suited the crimes, and the laws themselves resembled the later Han penal code.

Primary Source

JIA YI ON THE FAULTS OF THE QIN

After the Qin dynasty disintegrated, Confucians sought to explain the fall of so strong a military power that had unified China just fourteen years before. Jia Yi tied the dynasty's collapse to its autocratic rule and mean-spirited policies. Rather than blame the imperial system itself, Jia blamed the immorality of the Qin penal code and the first Qin emperor's totalitarian policies for his loss of the mandate of heaven. If the Qin had ruled according to Confucian teachings and ritual guidelines, Jia contended, the dynasty would have endured.

[Later] when the First Emperor ascended [the throne] he flourished and furthered the accomplishments of the six generations before him. Brandishing his long whip, he drove the world before him; destroying the feudal lords, he swallowed up the domains of the two Zhou dynasties. He reached the pinnacle of power and ordered all in the Six Directions, whipping the rest of the world into submission and thus spreading his might through the Four Seas. . . . He then abolished the ways of ancient sage kings and put to the torch the writings of the Hundred Schools in an attempt to keep the people in ignorance. He demolished the walls of major cities and put to death men of fame and talent, collected all the arms of the realm at Xianyang and had the spears and arrowheads melted down to form twelve huge statues in human form—all with the aim of weakening his people. Then he . . . posted capable generals and expert bowmen at important passes and placed trusted officials and well-trained soldiers in strategic array to challenge all who passed. With the empire thus pacified, the First Emperor believed that, with the capital secure within the pass and prosperous cities stretching for ten thousand *li*, he had indeed created an imperial structure to be enjoyed by his royal descendants for ten thousand generations to come.

Even after the death of the First Emperor, his reputation continued to sway the people. Chen She was a man who grew up in humble circumstances in a hut with broken pots for windows and ropes as door hinges and was a mere hired field hand and roving conscript of mediocre talent. He could neither equal the worth of Confucius and Mozi nor match the wealth of Tao Zhu or Yi Dun, yet, even stumbling as he did amidst the ranks of common soldiers and shuffling through the fields, he called forth a tired motley crowd and a mob of several hundred to turn upon the Qin. Cutting down trees to make weapons, and hoisting their flags on garden poles, they had the whole world come to them like gathering clouds, with people bringing their own food and following them like shadows. These men of courage from the East rose together, and in the end they defeated and extinguished the House of Qin.

. . . Qin, from a tiny base, had become a great power, ruling the land and receiving homage from all quarters for a hundred-odd years. Yet after they had unified the land and secured themselves within the pass, a single common rustic could nevertheless challenge this empire and cause its ancestral temples to topple and its ruler to die at the hand of others, a laughingstock in the eyes of all. Why? Because the ruler lacked humaneness and rightness; because preserving power differs fundamentally from seizing power.

→ *According to the reading, what specific steps did the Qin emperor take that were mean-spirited and autocratic?*

→ *What details in this reading help you to imagine the peasant rebellion? What did the peasants use for weapons? What was their typical dwelling like?*

→ *Why would Jia Yi want to preserve imperial government after the Qin had been so cruel?*

SOURCE: "Faults of the Qin" from *Sources of Chinese Tradition*, Volume 1, eds. William Theodore de Bary and Irene Bloom, © 1999 Columbia University Press. Reprinted with the permission of the publisher.

THE HAN DYNASTY

> → *How did Han leaders promote peace and stability?*

The Han dynasty, which lasted 400 years (206 BCE–220 CE), became China's formative empire and ultimately oversaw a blossoming of peace and prosperity. (See Map 7-2.) Its armies swelled with some 50,000 crossbowmen who brandished mass-produced weapons made from bronze and iron. Armed with the crossbow, foot soldiers and mounted archers extended Han imperial lands in all directions. Following the Qin practice, the Han also relied on a huge conscripted labor force for special projects such as building canals, roads, and defensive walls.

The first part of the dynastic cycle, known as the Western (or Former) Han dynasty (206 BCE–9 CE), brought economic prosperity and the expansion of empire. This was especially the case under Emperor Wu or Wudi, known as the "Martial Emperor" because of his many military campaigns (r. 140–87 BCE). Emperor Wu's more stringent penal code eliminated the powerful officials who got in his way. In a single year, his

Emperor Wu. This idealized representation of Emperor Wu (156–87 BCE, r. 141–87 BCE) welcoming a man of letters was one of a series of seventeenth-century silk paintings of Chinese emperors.

court system prosecuted over a thousand such cases. (See Primary Source: Han Legal Philosophy from Dong Zhongshu.) After Wu's reign, a burden of poor harvests, heavy taxes, and increased debt forced many peasants to sell their land to the wealthy, causing social tensions to simmer. A usurper who tried to introduce land reforms took power from 9 to 23 CE, but he lost control to a coalition of landowners and peasants who restored the Han dynasty to power. Thereafter Liu Xiu reconsolidated the Han Empire as the Eastern (or Later) Han dynasty (25—220 CE) and moved the capital to Luoyang on the North China plain.

Out of the experience of the Han, the Chinese produced a political narrative known as the **dynastic cycle**. In this scheme, influential families would vie for supremacy. Upon gaining power, they legitimated their authority by claiming to be the heirs of previous grand dynasts and by preserving or revitalizing the ancestors' virtuous governing ways. This continuity conferred divine support, and with it the rulers more easily united China. Dynasties rose and fell, and heaven could potentially grant its mandate to anyone who unified the empire. Indeed, the imperial continuity established by the Han was extraordinarily long-lasting, enduring more than 2,000 years until 1911.

FOUNDATIONS OF HAN POWER

The Han and Roman empires relied on political institutions, ideological supports, and control of economic assets to maintain power. Yet they differed in their use of civil bureaucracy, the military, and ideologies to ensure their subjects' consent. Undergirding the Han Empire was the tight-knit alliance between the imperial family and the new elite—the scholar-gentry class—who shared a determination to impose order on the Chinese population.

POWER AND ADMINISTRATION   The first Han emperors had no choice but to compromise with the aristocratic groups who had helped overthrow the Qin. To win their favor, Liu Bang showered land grants on military supporters as well as on his relatives. Still, all power emanated from the ruling family. Members of the Qin imperial family ruled those lands that were under their direct power, while governors appointed by the emperor administered the commanderies. A "grand counselor," chosen by the emperor, headed a civil bureaucracy of educated men who represented powerful local communities. Early in the Han dynasty, the central government was careful not to interfere with regional communities. The court followed the same flexible policy toward border peoples, using marriage alliances to gain control over their territories.

The Han had the most highly centralized bureaucracy in the world at this time, even more centralized than Rome's. That structure became the source of its enduring power. As

MAP 7-2 *PAX SINICA*: THE HAN EMPIRE IN THE FIRST CENTURY BCE

Agriculture, commerce, and industry flourished in East Asia under Han rule. According to the map, what were the main commodities that passed among the empire's regions? What type of administrative infrastructure integrated the vast domain? What Han policies contributed to this period of peace and prosperity?

under the Qin, the bureaucracy touched everyone because all males had to register, pay taxes, and serve in the military. At first, regional officials seldom intervened at the local level, simply making sure that local officials came up with the usual tax revenues and army conscripts. But the Han court was quick to tighten its grip on regional administration. First it removed powerful princes, crushed rebellions, and took over the areas controlled by regional lords. As princes lost power,

regional officials managed these aristocratic enclaves as imperial commanderies. According to arrangements instituted in 106 BCE by Emperor Wu, the empire consisted of thirteen provinces under imperial inspectors. Like the Romans' *dictator*, who was appointed in emergencies, Wu also appointed governors-general during floods or famine.

A civilian official and a commandant for military affairs shared the work of administering each commandery. These

HAN LEGAL PHILOSOPHY FROM DONG ZHONGSHU

The Qin legal system was considered brutal in its application of uniform punishments against criminals. Scholars claimed that the Qin punished all equally, regardless of the accused's motive or social status. Under the Han emperor Wu, Dong Zhongshu devised an ingenious way to humanize the Han penal code by using Confucian philosophy, so that jurists could consider the litigant's social status and personal motives behind allegedly criminal behavior. In essence, Dong as a Confucian argued that the spirit of the law took precedence over its letter when true justice was the goal.

At the time, there were those who questioned the verdict saying: "A had no son. On the side of the road, he picked up the child B and raised him as his own son. When B grew up, he committed the crime of murder. The contents of the accusation [against B] included [the fact that] A had concealed B [after the crime]. What should be the judgment regarding A?"

Tung Chung-shu passed judgment saying: "A had no son. He restored [B] to life and raised him [as his own son]. Although B was not A's natural son, who would think of seeing [B] as anyone but [A's] son? The *Poetry* [*Classic*] says: 'The mulberry-tree caterpillar has little ones, but the wasp raises them.' According to the intent of the *Annals*,

a father must cover up for his son. A accordingly concealed B. The verdict: A does not deserve to be punished."

→ *Mulberry-tree caterpillars are silkworms. What does the use of this example in a classic text indicate about the importance of that creature to Chinese culture?*

→ *Why would the Han penal code exonerate a stepfather for harboring his son even though the son had committed a serious crime?*

SOURCE: Pan Ku, *Han-shu* 3:1714 (*chüan* 30); quoted in Benjamin A. Elman, *Classicism, Politics, and Kinship: The Ch'ang-chou School of New Text Confucianism in Late Imperial China* (Berkeley: University of California Press, 1990), p. 262.

men shouldered immense responsibilities, far exceeding those of their counterparts in the Roman Empire. After all, the commanderies covered vast lands inhabited by countless ethnic groups totaling millions of people. These officials, like their Roman equivalents, had to maintain political stability and ensure the efficient collection of taxes. However, given the immense numbers under their jurisdiction and the heavy duties they bore, the local administrative staff was in many respects inadequate.

Government schools that promoted the scholar-official ideal became fertile sources for recruiting local officials. In fact, the Han established formal institutions of learning to ensure adequate numbers of well-trained bureaucrats. Emperor Wu founded a college for classical scholars in 136 BCE and soon expanded it into the Imperial University. By the second century CE it boasted 30,000 members, dwarfing the number of students in the largest Roman schools. Not only did they study the classics, but Han scholars also were naturalists and inventors. They made important medical discoveries, dealing with rational diagnoses of the body's functions and the role of wind and temperature in transmitting diseases. They also invented the magnetic compass and devel-

oped high-quality paper, which replaced silk, wood, and bamboo strips as media for communicating laws, ideas, rituals, and technical knowledge.

Increasingly, even local elites encouraged their sons to master the classical teachings of Confucianism. This practice not only guaranteed a future entrée into the ruling class but also planted the Confucian classics at the heart of the imperial state.

CONFUCIAN IDEOLOGY AND LEGITIMATE RULE

Confucian thought stood as the ideological buttress of the Han empire. According to Han political philosophy, the people's welfare was the foundation of legitimate rule. (See Primary Source: Dong Zhongshu on Responsibilities of Han Rulership.) When the Confucian scholar and official Jia Yi wrote that "the state, the ruler, and the officials all depend on the people for their mandate," he was underscoring "the primacy of the people" in affirming the mandate of heaven. Claims like these promoted classical political principles of civilizing the people and supporting local elites. However, such principles did *not* imply that the people actually chose their own leaders (as in the Greek-city states; see Chapter 5).

The Wuliang Shrine. This rubbing of a Wuliang Shrine stele depicts Han scholars sitting on mats on the floor. Chairs were not used until late medieval times.

The people's only power was the ability to reject rulers who did not promote general well-being.

By 50 BCE, three Confucian ideals reigned as the official doctrine of the Han Empire: honoring tradition, respecting the lessons of history, and emphasizing the emperor's responsibility to heaven. Confucian scholars now tutored the princes. To mark the lessons of the past, the grand historian Sima Qian provided a historical vision of good and evil Shang and Zhou rulers. By embracing Confucian political ideals, the Han rulers established a polity based on the people's mandate and crafted a careful balance between two arms of government in which the officials provided a counterweight to the emperor's autocratic strength. Of course, when the interests of the court and the bureaucracy clashed, the emperor's will was paramount.

THE NEW SOCIAL ORDER AND THE ECONOMY

Part of the Han's genius was their ability to win the support of diverse social groups that had been squabbling for centuries. They did so by forming alliances with key leaders— for example, by letting aristocratic Qin survivors reacquire some of their former power and status. They also urged enterprising peasants who had worked the nobles' lands to become local leaders in the countryside. Successful merchants won permission to extend their influence in cities, and in local areas scholars found themselves in the role of masters when their lords were removed.

Out of a massive agrarian base flowed a steady stream of tax revenues and labor for military forces and public works. The Han court also drew revenues from state-owned imperial preserves, mining, and mints; tribute from outlying domains; household taxes on the nobility; and surplus grains from wealthy merchants who were hungry for noble ranks, official appointments, or smaller tax burdens. Emperor Wu established state monopolies in salt, iron, and wine to fund his expensive military campaigns. His policies fueled silk pro-

duction and iron production—especially iron weapons and everyday tools—and controlled profiteering through price controls. He also minted standardized copper coins and imposed stiff penalties for counterfeiting. All these efforts aimed at expanding the imperial economy and supporting the emperor's ambitions.

Laid out in an orderly grid, Han cities—particularly capitals—reflected their political functions. Bustling markets south of the palace complex served as public areas. Carriages transported rich families up and down the wide avenues (and they paid dearly for the privilege, for keeping a horse required as much grain as a family of six could consume). Court palaces became forbidden inner cities, off-limits to all but those in the imperial lineage or the government. Monumental architecture in China announced the palaces and tombs of rulers rather than the sites of mass entertainment (like the Colosseum in Rome).

DAILY LIFE Wealthy families took pride in their several-story homes displaying richly carved crossbeams and rafters. They cushioned their floors with embroidered pillows, wool rugs, and mats. Fine embroideries hung as drapes, and screens in the rooms secured privacy. Families also sharply distinguished gender roles to redouble the authority of the father figure. Women and children stayed cloistered in inner quarters, preserving the sense that the family patriarch's role

Wuzhu Coin. This copper coin was issued by Emperor Xuandi during the Western Han Dynasty, 73–49 BCE. *Wuzhu*, which means "five grains," refers to the weight of the coin (1 wuzhu = 5 grains = 4 grams). The wuzhu was in circulation until 621 CE.

Primary Source

DONG ZHONGSHU ON RESPONSIBILITIES OF HAN RULERSHIP

Early Han dynasty officials sought to enhance the government's legitimacy by replacing the Legalist defense of an autocratic state with a Confucian view of the ruler as the moral and cosmological foundation of government. Thus the philosopher Dong Zhongshu offered a new theory to legitimize the Han dynasty, while criticizing the Qin's mismanagement of government. Under the guidance of Confucian officials, Dong argued, the imperial system would nourish the people and promote upright officials who would maintain the Han dynasty's mandate to govern, rather than ruling through fear and intimidation.

He who rules the people is the foundation of the state. Now in administering the state, nothing is more important for transforming [the people] than reverence for the foundation. . . . What do I mean by the foundation? Heaven, Earth, and humankind are the foundation of all living things. Heaven engenders all living things, Earth nourishes them, and humankind completes them. With filial and brotherly love, Heaven engenders them; with food and clothing, Earth nourishes them; and with rites and music, humankind completes them. These three assist one another just as the hands and feet join to complete the body. None can be dispensed with because without filial and brotherly love, people lack the means to live; without food and clothing, people lack the means to be nourished; and without rites and music, people lack the means to become complete. If all three are lost, people become like deer, each person following his own desires and each family practicing its own customs. Fathers will not be able to order their sons, and rulers will not be able to order their ministers. Although possessing inner and outer walls, [the ruler's city] will become known as "an empty settlement." Under such circumstances, the ruler will lie down with a clod of earth for his pillow. Although no one endangers him, he will naturally be endangered; although no one destroys him, he will naturally be destroyed. This is called "spontaneous punishment." When it arrives, even if he is hidden in a stone vault or barricaded in a narrow pass, the ruler will not be able to avoid "spontaneous punishment."

One who is an enlightened master and worthy ruler believes such things. For this reason he respectfully and carefully attends to the three foundations. He reverently enacts the suburban sacrifice, dutifully serves his ancestors, manifests filial and brotherly love, encourages filial conduct, and serves the foundation of Heaven in this way. He takes up the plough handle to till the soil, plucks the mulberry leaves and nourishes the silkworms, reclaims the wilds, plants grain, opens new lands to provide sufficient food and clothing, and serves the foundation of Earth in this way. He establishes academies and schools in towns and villages to teach filial piety, brotherly love, reverence, and humility, enlightens [the people] with education, moves [them] with rites and music, and serves the foundation of humanity in this way.

If these three foundations are all served, the people will resemble sons and brothers who do not dare usurp authority, while the ruler will resemble fathers and mothers. He will not rely on favors to demonstrate his love for his people nor severe measures to prompt them to act. . . . [W]hen the ruler relies on virtue to administer the state, it is sweeter than honey or sugar and firmer than glue or lacquer. This is why sages and worthies exert themselves to revere the foundation and do not dare depart from it.

➤ *Count the number of times the following words appear in this reading:* fathers, sons, brothers, filial conduct. *What do these words tell us about Han officials' view of the proper relationship between rulers and subjects?*

➤ *How does this reading reflect the gender ideology of Han China?*

➤ *Why was the emperor so important in Dong Zhongshu's vision of Han political culture after the fall of the Qin?*

SOURCE: "Responsibilities of Han Rulership" from *Sources of Chinese Tradition*, Volume 1, eds. William Theodore de Bary and Irene Bloom, © 1999 Columbia University Press. Reprinted with the permission of the publisher.

was to protect mothers, wives, and children from the harsh society. But this did not deprive women from following careers of their own. Elite women, often literate, enjoyed respect as teachers and managers within the family while their husbands served as officials away from home. Women who were commoners led less protected lives; many worked in the fields, and some joined troupes of entertainers to sing and dance for food at the open markets.

Silk was abundant and available to all classes, though in winter only the rich wrapped themselves in furs while everyone else stayed warm in woolens and ferret skins. The rich also wore distinctive slippers inlaid with leather or lined with silk. No longer were wine and meat reserved only for festivals, leading critics to decry the debauches of the well-to-do. In the cooked-meat stalls of the markets, those who could afford them pushed and shoved to buy their piglets, dog cutlets, or chopped liver. These tasty victuals came to the dinner tables of the wealthy on vessels fashioned with silver inlay or golden handles.

Entertainment for those who could afford it included performing animals, tiger fights, and foreign dancing girls. Some gambled, betting for high stakes at *liubo,* a board game that involved shaking bamboo sticks out of a cup. Live music was popular at private homes, and rich families kept their own orchestras, complete with bells and drums. Although events like these had occurred during the Zhou dynasty, they had marked only public ritual occasions. Now, Han elites called on the gods for their own spiritual and private benefits. They still took funerary rites very seriously, however: the rich ordered the finest wood for their coffins, and even the poor had at least their coffin lids painted.

SOCIAL HIERARCHY At the base of Han society was a free peasantry—farmers who owned and tilled their own land. The Han court upheld an agrarian ideal by honoring the peasants' productive labors, while subjecting merchants to a range of controls (including regulations on luxury consumption) and belittling them for not doing physical labor. Confucians and Daoists supported this hierarchy, but we will see below that the Daoists later challenged the status quo. The Confucians, for instance, envisioned scholar-officials as working hard for the ruler to enhance a moral economy in which profiteering by greedy merchants would be minimal. In reality, however, the first century of Han rule perpetuated powerful elites. At the apex were the imperial clan and nobles, followed, in order, by high-ranking officials and scholars, great merchants and manufacturers, and a regionally based class of local magnates. Below these elites, lesser clerks, medium and small landowners, free farmers, artisans, small merchants, poor tenant farmers, and hired laborers eked out a living. The more destitute became government slaves and relied on the state for food and clothing. At the bottom was a thin layer of convicts and private slaves.

Between 100 BCE and 200 CE, scholar-officials stood as the bulwark of imperial authority and legitimacy. In their official capacity, they linked the imperial center with local society. At first, their political clout and prestige complemented the power of landlords and large clans, but over time their autonomy grew as they gained wealth by acquiring private property. Following the fall of the Han, they emerged as the dominant aristocratic clans.

In the long run, the imperial court's struggle to limit the power of local lords and magnates failed. Indeed, dynasts had to rely on local officials to enforce their rule, but those officials could rarely stand up to the powerful men they were supposed to be governing. And when central rule proved too onerous for local elites, they always had the option of rebelling. Local uprisings against the Han that began in 99 BCE forced the court to relax its measures and left landlords and local magnates as dominant powers in the provinces. Below these privileged groups, powerless agrarian groups turned to Daoist religious organizations to provide the framework that crystallized into potent cells of dissent.

Model of a Han House. Elite families in Chang'an and other Han cities typically lived in two-story houses with carved crossbeams and rafters and enclosed courtyards. The floors were covered with embroidered cushions, wool rugs, and mats for sitting. Screens were used for privacy. Women and children were cloistered in the inner quarters.

Primary Source

MUNICIPAL CHARTER OF A ROMAN TOWN

Town governments in the Roman Empire followed standard rules and regulations that developed during the Roman conquest of Italy. In 1981, detailed copies of some of these regulations came to light in southern Spain at Molino del Postero (called Irni in Roman times). The Roman governor of Spain in 81 CE had the rules incised on ten plates of bronze for public display in the town's forum. By following these and other rules, the residents of a Spanish community learned how to govern themselves as the Romans did (see a Roman municipal charter on the facing page).

XIX ON AEDILES: The aediles [the two town business managers] . . . are to have the right and power of managing the grain supply, the sacred buildings, the sacred and holy places, the town and its roads and neighborhoods, the drains and sewers, the baths, the marketplace, and of checking weights and measures; and also of setting a night watch if the need arises.

XX CONCERNING THE RIGHT AND POWER OF QUAESTORS: The quaestors [the two town financial officers] . . . are to have the right and power of collecting, spending, storing, administering, and managing the common funds of the municipality at the discretion of the *duumviri* [the two town mayors]. And they are allowed to have the public slaves belonging to the municipality to help them.

XXI HOW ROMAN CITIZENSHIP IS ACQUIRED IN THE MUNICIPALITY: When those who are senators, decurions [town councillors], or conscripted town councillors who have been or are chosen as town magistrates according to the terms of this law, have completed their term of office, they are to become Roman citizens, along with their parents and wives and any children who have been born out of legal marriages and who are in the power of their parents, and likewise grandsons and granddaughters born to a son. . . .

XXVIII CONCERNING THE FREEING OF SLAVES BEFORE THE MAYORS: If any citizen of the municipality of Flavian Irni . . . in the presence of a *duumvir* [mayor] of that municipality in charge of the administration of justice sets free his male or female slave from slavery into freedom or orders him or her to be free . . . then any male slave who has been manumitted or ordered to be free in this way is to be free, any female slave who has been manumitted or ordered to be free in this way is also to be free. . . . Someone who is under twenty years of age may manumit his or her slave only if the number of town councillors necessary for decrees passed under this law to be valid decides that the grounds for said manumission are proper.

➔ *What were some of the titles of civil servants in a typical Roman town or municipality?*

➔ *According to this charter, what different types of people were part of the normal social structure?*

➔ *In what ways could certain inhabitants of towns such as Irni become Roman citizens?*

➔ *Why would making small towns uniform in design and function be important to the Roman Empire?*

SOURCE: J. González, "The *Lex Irnitana*: A New Copy of the Flavian Municipal Law," from *Journal of Roman Studies*, Vol. 76 (1986). Reprinted with permission of the Society for the Promotion of Roman Studies. Translated by Brent Shaw.

A Roman Municipal Charter. This bronze tablet inscribed in Latin is part of a group of six bronze tablets discovered in 1981 at the Roman town of Irni, near modern Molino del Postero, in southern Spain. Charters like this one, set up for public display in the forum or central open area of the town, displayed regulations for the conduct of public life in a Roman town, from rules governing family inheritance and property transfers to the election of town officials and definitions of their powers and duties. For some of these rules, see the Primary Source box on the facing page.

expensive aqueducts provided a dependable supply of water, sometimes flowing in from great distances. Most adult citizens regularly received a free, basic amount of wheat (and, later, olive oil and pork). But living conditions were often appalling, with people jammed into ramshackle high-rise apartments that threatened to collapse on their renters or go up in flames. And Romans constantly complained of crime and violence. Even worse was the lack of sanitary conditions—despite the sewage and drainage works that were wonders of their time. Rome was disease-ridden; its inhabitants died from infection at a fearsome rate—malarial infections were particularly bad—so the city required a substantial input of immigrants every year just to maintain its population.

MASS ENTERTAINMENT Every self-respecting Roman town had at least two major entertainment venues. One was an adoption from Hellenistic culture: a theater devoted to plays, dances, and other popular events. The other was a Roman innovation that combined two horseshoe-shaped theaters into a single, more elaborate structure called an amphitheater. A much larger seating capacity than in a regular theater surrounded the oval performance area at its center. The emperors Vespasian and Titus completed the Flavian

Amphitheater in Rome and dedicated it in 80 CE. It is the vast structure that we know today as the Colosseum, after the colossal statue of the emperor Nero that used to stand beside it. It was a state-of-the-art facility whose floor area, the arena, could handle elaborate hunts of exotic wild animals such as giraffes and elephants. The arena could also be flooded to stage naval battles between hostile fleets, much to the delight of the audience, or it could provide a venue for a Roman invention, gladiatorial games. In these expensive public entertainments, heavily armed and well-trained men—most of them slaves and prisoners of war, but sometimes free men who volunteered—fought each other, wounding or

Aqueduct. The Romans built aqueducts to transport to Rome the huge amounts of water needed for the city's population of over a million. The idea soon spread to the provinces, where these structures were built to bring water to Roman-style cities developing in the peripheral regions of Roman rule. This aqueduct at Segovia in modern Spain is one of the best preserved.

North African Amphitheater. This huge amphitheater is in the remains of the Roman city of Thysdrus in North Africa (the town of el-Jem in modern-day Tunisia). The wealth of the Africans under the empire enabled them to build colossal entertainment venues that competed with the one at Rome in scale and grandeur.

Roman Gladiators. In this brilliant mosaic from Rome, we see two gladiators at the end of a full combat in which Astacius has killed Astivus. The Greek letter theta, or "th" (the circle with crossbar through it), beside the names of Astivus and Rodan indicates that these men are dead—*thanatos* being the Greek word for "death."

killing for the enjoyment of the huge crowds of appreciative spectators.

Westerners tend to think of these structures for public entertainment as ordinary and normal. Seen from a contemporary Chinese perspective, however, they were strange and unusual. Among the Han, local elites and the imperial family created gigantic palace complexes complete with hunting parks to impress and amuse themselves, not the general public. In contrast, the public entertainment facilities of a Roman town reflected attitudes that stressed the importance of citizens in town life.

SOCIAL AND GENDER RELATIONS

Even more significant than political forums and game venues were the personal relations that linked the rich and powerful with the mass of average citizens. Men and women of wealth and high social status acted as **patrons**, protecting and supporting dependents or "clients" of a lower class. From the emperor at the top to the local municipal man at the bottom, these relationships were reinforced by generous distributions of food and entertainments from wealthy men to their people. The bonds between these groups in each city found formal expression in legal definitions of patrons' responsibilities to clients; at the same time, the informal social code raised expectations that the wealthy would be public benefactors. For example, a senator, Pliny the Younger, con-

structed for his hometown a public library and a bathhouse; supported a teacher of Latin; and established a fund to support the sons and daughters of former slaves. The emperors at the very top were no different. Augustus documented the scale of his gifts to the Roman people in his autobiography, gifts that exceeded hundreds of millions of sesterces (a small silver or bronze coin) in expenditures from his own pocket. A later emperor, Trajan, established a social scheme for feeding the children of poor Roman citizens in Italy—a benefaction that he advertised on coins and in pictures on arches in Beneventum and other towns in Italy.

The essence of Roman civil society, though, involved the formal relationships governed by Rome's laws and courts. Public courts heard all disputes, and decisions issued from judges and, sometimes, large juries. By the last century BCE, the Roman state's complex legal system featured not only a rich body of written law but also institutions for settling legal disputes and a growing number of highly educated men who specialized in interpreting the law. The apparatus of Roman law eventually appeared in every town and city of the empire, creating a deeply entrenched civil culture. It is no surprise that this legal infrastructure persisted long after the empire's political and military institutions had disappeared.

Municipal charters and civil laws—as well as secular philosophers and, later, Christian writers—placed the family at the very foundation of the Roman social order. The authoritarian *paterfamilias* ("father of the family") headed the family. Legally speaking, he had nearly total power over his

BIRTHDAY INVITATION OF CLAUDIA SEVERA

The ability to write in Latin became so widespread under the Roman Empire that even its frontier areas could boast basic literacy. Excavations of a Roman army base at Vindolanda, in northern England, have unearthed a cache of documents written on thin sheets of wood. These reveal the normal use of Latin writing for everyday activities late in the first century CE. Officers' wives were just as skilled in writing as the men. One of these elite women, Claudia Severa, sent a letter inviting a good friend (whom she addresses affectionately as "sister") to her birthday party. The elegant handwriting on several documents is almost certainly that of Claudia herself. The second letter is her friend's reply.

[Address on the outside:] To Sulpicia Lepidina, wife of Cerialis, from Severa.
[Claudia Severa to her Lepidina, Greetings!]

My sister, I am sending an invitation to you to attend my birthday festivities on the third day before the Ides of September [September 11 in our calendar]—just to make sure that you come to visit us. Your presence will make the day all the more enjoyable for me. Please convey my greetings to your Cerialis [i.e., Lepidina's husband]. My Aelius and our little son send him their warmest greetings.

I await your arrival, my sister.

I bid you goodbye, my sister, my dearest soul. Be well.

[Sulpicia Lepidina to Claudia Severa] Greeting.

Just as I had told you, my sister, and had promised that I would ask your Brocchus [i.e., Claudia Severa's husband, Aelius Brocchus] for permission to come to visit you, he replied to me that I was, of course, always most welcome to come. . . . [I shall try] to come to you by whatever way I can, for there are certain things that we must do . . . on which matter you will receive a letter from me so that you will know what I am going to do. . . .

Farewell, my sister, my dearest and most-desired soul . . .

→ *What does the writing of letters in Latin at this far edge of the empire tell us about Roman culture?*

→ *Sulpicia mentions asking Claudia's husband for permission to visit Claudia. Why would she do this? Do you think it indicates that the women's husbands were of different military rank, or that Sulpicia was merely following Roman social customs for women—or both? Or something else?*

→ *What does the very existence of these letters tell us about Roman women?*

SOURCE: Alan K. Bowman and J. David Thomas, with contributions by J. N. Adams, *The Vindolanda Writing-Tablets (Tabulae Vindolandenses II)* (London: British Museum Press, 1994), nos. 291 and 292, pp. 256–62. Translated by Brent Shaw.

dependents, including his wife, children, grandchildren, and the slaves whom he owned. Imperial society heightened the importance of the basic family unit of mother, father, and children in the urban centers. As in Han dynasty China, the Roman state regularly undertook a census, rigorously counting the empire's inhabitants and assessing their property for tax purposes—a process that underscored the family as the core unit of society.

This system might seem to place women under the domineering rule of fathers and husbands. That is certainly the picture presented in the repressive laws that Roman men drafted and in the histories that Roman men wrote. But compared with women in most Greek city-states, Roman women, even those of only modest wealth and status, had much greater freedom of action and much greater control of their own wealth and property. (See Primary Source: Birthday Invitation of Claudia Severa.) Thus Terentia, the wife of the Republican senator Cicero, bought and sold properties on her own, made decisions regarding her family and wealth without consulting her husband (much to his chagrin—he later divorced her), and apparently fared well following her separation from Cicero. Her behavior was normal for a woman of her status: she was well educated, literate, well connected, and in control of her own life—despite what the laws and ideas of Roman males might suggest. The daily lives of ordinary women that we know of from papyrus documents found in the Roman province of Egypt, for example, show them buying, selling, renting, and leasing with no sign that the legal constraints subjecting them to male control had any significant effect on their dealings.

Terentia reminds us of Ban Zhao, the younger sister of the historian Ban Gu (32–92 CE). She became the first female Chinese historian and lived relatively unconstrained. After marrying the local resident, Cao Shishu, at the age of fourteen, she was called Madame Cao at court. Subsequently she completed her elder brother's *History of the Former Han Dynasty* when he was imprisoned and executed. In addition to completing the first full dynastic history in China, Ban Zhao wrote *Lessons for Women*, in which she described the status of elite women and presented the ideal woman in light of her virtue, her type of work, and the words she spoke and wrote. Ban represented a conservative version of the perennial "talented woman" in China, whose virtue was never eclipsed by her literary production or lifestyle.

ECONOMY AND NEW SCALES OF PRODUCTION

Rome achieved staggering transformations in the production of agricultural, manufactured, and mined goods. Public and private demand for metals, for example, led the Romans to mine lead, silver, and copper in Spain in operations so

Coin Hoard. The use of coins for a wide spectrum of economic exchanges became common in the Roman Empire. Looking at the batches buried for safekeeping gives us an idea of the range of coins in circulation at any one time. This coin hoard was found near Didcot in Oxfordshire, England. Buried about 165 CE, it contained about 125 gold coins minted between the 50s and 160s CE and represents the equivalent of about eleven years' pay for a Roman soldier. Gold coins were used for expensive transactions or to store wealth. Most ordinary purchases or payments were made with silver or brass coins.

massive that traces of the air pollution they generated remain in ice core samples taken from Greenland today. Evidence from Mediterranean shipwrecks similarly indicates a seaborne trade on an unprecedented scale. The area of land surveyed and cultivated rose steadily throughout this period, as Romans reached into arid lands on the periphery of the Sahara Desert to the south and opened up heavily forested regions in present-day France and Germany to the north. (See Map 7-4.)

The Romans also built an unprecedented number of roads to connect far-flung parts of their empire. Although many roads did not have the high-quality flagstone paving and excellent drainage exhibited by highways in Italy, such as the Via Appia, most were systematically marked by milestones (for the first time in this part of the world) so that travelers would know their precise location and the distance to the next town. Also for the first time, complex land maps and itineraries specified all major roads and distances between towns. Adding to the roads' significance was their deliberate coordination with Mediterranean sea routes to support the smooth and safe flow of traffic, commerce, and ideas on land and at sea.

The mines produced copper, tin, silver, and gold—out of which the Roman state produced the most massive coinage known in the Western world before early modern times.

Roman Roads. Like Qin and Han China, the Roman Empire was characterized by large-scale road building, which began as early as the late fourth century BCE. Roads eventually connected most land areas and larger urban centers in the empire, considerably easing ordinary travel, as well as trade and commerce. Here we see part of the Via Appia, the great highway that connected Rome with the southern parts of Italy.

MAP 7-4 *PAX ROMANA*: **THE ROMAN EMPIRE IN THE SECOND CENTURY CE**

The Roman Empire enjoyed remarkable peace and prosperity in the second century CE. Economic production increased, and Roman culture expanded throughout the realm. According to the map, what commodities were traded most widely? With what groups did Romans trade beyond their empire, and for what commodity in particular? How did the *Pax Romana* promote the spread of Christianity?

Coinage facilitated the exchange of commodities and services, which now carried standard values. Throughout the Roman Empire, from small towns on the edge of the Sahara Desert to army towns along the northern frontiers, people appraised, purchased, and sold goods in coin denominations. Taxes were assessed and hired laborers were paid in coin. The economy in its leading sectors functioned more efficiently because of the production of coins on an immense scale (paralleled only by the coinage output of Han dynasty China and its successors).

Roman mining, as well as other sizable operations, relied on chattel slaves—human beings purchased as private property. The massive concentration of wealth and slaves at the center of the Roman world led to the first large-scale commercial plantation agriculture, along with the first technical handbooks on how to run such operations for profit. These estates specialized in products destined for the big urban markets: wheat, grapes, and olives, as well as cattle and sheep. Such developments rested on a bedrock belief that private property and its ownership were sacrosanct. In fact, the Roman senator Cicero

Primary Source

CICERO ON THE ROLE OF THE ROMAN STATE

Whereas Greek thinkers debated ethics and morals, the role of the good life, and the nature of the universe, Romans deliberated more about the nature of government and the role of the state. This focus reflects their pragmatic attitudes and their possession of a huge empire. In the following passage, Marcus Tullius Cicero, one of the leading Roman politicians from the 60s to the 40s BCE, discusses how any man who holds public office in the Roman state has a duty to defend the state's main function.

That man who undertakes responsibility for public office in the state must make it his first priority to see that every person can continue to hold what is his and that no inroads are made into the goods or property of private persons by the state. It was a bad policy when Philippus, when he was tribune of the plebs [about 104 BCE], proposed an agrarian reform law. When his law was defeated, he took the defeat well and was moderate in his response. In the debates themselves, however, he tried to curry popular favor and acted in a bad way when he said, "In our community there are not more than two thousand men who have real property."

That speech ought to be condemned outright for attempting to advocate equality of property holdings. What policy could be more dangerous? It was for this very reason—that each person should be able to keep his own property—that states and local governments were founded. Although it was by the leadership of nature herself that men gathered together in communities, it was for the hope of keeping their own property that they sought the protection of states. . . .

Some men want to become known as popular politicians and for this reason they engage in making revolutionary proposals about land, with the result that owners are driven from their homes and money lent out by creditors is simply given free to the borrowers with no need for repayment. Such men are shaking the very foundations of the state. First of all, they are destroying that goodwill and sense of trust which can no longer exist when money is simply taken from some people and given to others [by the state]. And then they take away fairness, which is totally destroyed if each person is not permitted to keep what is his own. For, as I have already said, it is the peculiar function of the state and of local government to make sure that each person should be able to keep his own things freely and without any worry.

→ *According to Cicero, what is the main function of the Roman state and the main reason men "sought the protection of states"?*

→ *How does the protection of private property rights affect the claims that citizens had on their rulers?*

→ *And how does this differ from the role of the state in contemporary Han dynasty China?*

SOURCE: *De Officiis (On Duties)*, 2.21.73, 22.78; translated by Brent Shaw.

---

argued that the defense and enjoyment of private property constituted basic reasons for the existence of the state. (See Primary Source: Cicero on the Role of the Roman State.) Roman law more clearly defined and more strictly enforced the rights of the private owner than any previous legal system had done. The extension of private ownership of land and other property to regions having little or no prior knowledge of it—Egypt in the east, Spain in the west, the lands of western Europe—was one of the most enduring effects of the Roman Empire.

RELIGIOUS CULTS AND THE RISE OF CHRISTIANITY

The political unification of the Mediterranean also suggested the possibility of uniting the beliefs of its diverse peoples. The world of gods, spirits, and demons remained hugely important, even as the region had seen the spread of new religions as part of the Hellenistic movement. Indeed, the municipal charters of Roman towns required local councilors to institute and maintain the support of official and semiofficial cults of a wide variety of gods and goddesses.

If there was any religion of empire, it was **Christianity**, although it did not achieve official recognition as the state religion until the fourth century CE. Its foundations lay in a direct confrontation with Roman imperial authority: the trial of Yeshua ben Yosef (Joshua son of Joseph). He preached the new doctrines of what was originally a sect of Judaism, and we know him today by the Greek form of his name, Jesus. A Roman governor, Pontius Pilatus, tried Jesus in a typical Roman provincial trial; he was found guilty of sedition and executed, along with two bandits, by a standard Roman penalty—crucifixion.

We know of Jesus only after his death. No reference to him survives from his own lifetime. Two years after the crucifixion, Paul of Tarsus, a Jew and a Roman citizen from southeastern Anatolia, claimed to have seen Jesus in full glory outside the city of Damascus. Paul and the communities to whom he preached between 40 and 60 CE were the first to call Yeshua "Jesus." They also referred to him as "the Christ"—*ho Christos*—or the Anointed One (i.e., the Messiah), and thought of him as a god.

Paul had not been one of Jesus's original disciples. Only much later did four of those men—Matthew, Mark, Luke, and John—write about his life and record his sayings in accounts that came to be called the Gospels. (That early English word translates their name in the original Greek, *Evangeliai*, or "Good News.") The Gospels all sought to tell the world not what Jesus had said, but who he had been. They served as answers to the question that Jesus reportedly asked his disciples a few months before he died: "Who do people say that I am?" (Mark 8:27).

Jesus's preachings could not have been more Jewish. He taught that God is the father of his people—sinners who are always liable to fall away. But God is like a good shepherd to them. Scrambling down dangerous ravines, the good shepherd seeks those who have gone astray, joyfully carrying home on his shoulders even a single lost lamb (see John 10:1–18). We have already met the image of the great king as shepherd of his people in both Egypt and Mesopotamia (see Chapter 3). With Jesus, this ancient image took on a new intimacy. Not a distant monarch but a preacher, Jesus had set out on God's behalf to gather a new, small flock. Jesus's teachings (like those of the Buddha) comforted people who lived at a distance from power, such as scholars, merchants, and farmers.

To his followers, Jesus was a man who had slowly revealed an awesome, hidden identity. He was crucified not for what he had preached but for what he (or others) claimed that he was. Through the preaching of Paul in Greek and the textual portraits painted in the Gospels, also in Greek, this image of Jesus rapidly spread beyond Palestine (where Jesus had preached only to Jews and only in the local language, Aramaic) and entered the religious bloodstream of the Mediterranean. Core elements of Jesus's message, such as the special

responsibilities of the well-off for the poor and the promised eventual empowerment of "the meek," appealed to huge numbers of ordinary persons in the wider Mediterranean world. But it was the apostle Paul who was especially responsible for recasting this message for a wider audience. While Jesus directed his teachings to villagers and peasants and cast his metaphors in that light, Paul's writing and preaching dealt with a world heavily populated by slaves. For him, God was a father figure who set converts free and embraced them as His children. His message was immediately accessible to the dwellers of the towns and cities of the Roman Empire.

Just half a century after Jesus's crucifixion, the followers of Jesus saw in his life not the wanderings of an amiable Jewish charismatic but a moment of head-on conflict between "God" and "the world." (A **charismatic** is a person who uses his personal strengths or virtues, often laced with a divine aura, to command followers.) Jesus had "overcome" the "world" and had even broken the boundaries of the human condition: God had raised him from the dead. Thus, the preaching that his followers brought to confront this world was no longer the preaching of a man. It was the message of a god—who, for thirty years half a century before, had moved (largely unrecognized) among human beings. The followers formed a church: a permanent gathering committed to the charge of leaders chosen by God and by their fellow believers. For these leaders and their followers, death—death for Jesus—was the hallmark of their faith. In dying they witnessed for the faith. Indeed, the defining experience for Christians was that of the Roman trial and the idea of "witnessing" to God. The Greek word *martus* means a witness in a trial. From this came the English term *martyr* and the concept of martyrdom.

The persecutions of Christians were sporadic and intensely local. Like imperial power itself, persecutions were responses to local concerns. Not until the emperor Decius, in the mid-third century ce, did the state direct an empire-wide attack on Christians. And that attempt failed. Decius died within the year, and Christians interpreted their persecutor's death as evidence of the hand of God in human affairs. By the last decades of the third century, Christian communities of various kinds, reflecting the different strands of their movement through the Mediterranean as well as the local cultures in which they settled, were present in every society in the empire.

THE LIMITS OF EMPIRE

The empire labeled outsiders as those whom it excluded. A crucial part of that process was the exercise of force in extending its borders. (See Map 7-5.) The limitations of that force determined who belonged in the empire and was subject to it, and who was outside it and therefore excluded. To the west the Romans pushed their authority to the shores of

MAP 7-5 POPULATION OF ROMAN WORLD IN 362 CE

Roman frontiers at the northern and eastern limits of the empire were persistent sources of anxiety and concern for imperial leaders. While not as densely populated as the Roman Empire, these regions contained large population centers as well. Name some of the major groups of peoples that lived just beyond Roman rule in the areas of eastern Europe and Southwest Asia. What were the geographical limits of the Roman Empire? According to your reading, why were Roman armies never able to subdue these neighboring peoples?

the Atlantic Ocean, and to the south they drove it to the edges of the Sahara Desert. In both cases, little farther land was available to dominate for profit. To the east and north, however, things were different.

On Rome's eastern frontiers, powerful Romans such as Marcus Licinius Crassus in the mid-50s BCE and Mark Antony in the early 30s BCE wished to imitate the achievements of Alexander the Great and conquer the arid lands beyond Judea and Syria. But they failed miserably, stopped by the Parthian Empire and their successors the Sasanian Empire (see Chapter 6 for a full discussion of the Parthians and Chapter 8 for more on the Sasanians). The Sasanians expanded the technical advances in mounted horseback warfare that the Parthians had used so successfully in open

Soldier versus Barbarian. On the frontiers of the Roman Empire, the legionary soldiers faced the non-Roman "barbarians" from the lands beyond. In this piece of a stone-carved picture from the northwestern frontier, we see a civilized and disciplined Roman soldier, to the left, facing a German "barbarian"—hair uncut and unkempt, without formal armor, his house a thatched hut. Frontier realities were never so clear-cut, of course. Roman soldiers, often recruited from the "barbarian" peoples, were a lot more like them than was convenient to admit, and the "barbarians" were influenced by and closer to Roman cultural models than this picture indicates.

desert warfare against the slow-moving Roman mass infantry formations. King Shapur I (Shabuhr), their greatest monarch, exploited the weaknesses of the Roman Empire in the mid-third century, even capturing the Roman emperor Valerian. As successful as Parthians and Sasanians were in fighting the Romans, however, they could never equal the Romans' sway, and were not a threat to expand. Their highly decentralized political structure limited their coordination and resources, and their equestrian-style warfare was ill-suited to fight around the more rocky and hilly environment of the Mediterranean world. In the lands across the Rhine and Danube, to the north, environmental conditions largely determined the limits of empire. The long and harsh winters, but excellent soil and growing conditions, produced hardy populations clustered densely across vast distances. These illiterate, kin-based agricultural societies had changed little since the first millennium BCE. And because their warrior elites still engaged in armed competitions, war and violence characterized their connections with the Roman Empire. As the empire fixed its northern frontiers along the

Rhine and Danube rivers, two factors determined its relationship with the Germans and Goths on the rivers' other side. First, these small societies had only one commodity for which the empire was willing to pay: human bodies. So the slave trade out of the land across the Rhine and Danube became immense: gold, silver, coins, wine, arms, and other luxury items flowed across the rivers in one direction in exchange for slaves in the other. Second, their wars were unremitting, as every emperor faced the expectation of dealing harshly with the "barbarians." These connections, involving arms and violence, were to enmesh the Romans ever more tightly with the tribal societies. They even overlapped, as internal conflicts within the Roman Empire ultimately prompted increasing use of "barbarians" as soldiers and officers who served the empire.

CONCLUSION

China and Rome both constructed empires of unprecedented scale and duration, yet they differed in fundamental ways. Starting out with a less numerous and less dense population than China, Rome relied on slaves and "barbarian" immigrants to expand and diversify its workforce. While about 1 percent of the Chinese population was enslaved, more than 10 percent were slaves in the Roman Empire. Also, the lifeblood of the Chinese rural economy was a huge population of free peasant farmers; this enormous labor pool, together with a remarkable bureaucracy, enabled the Han to achieve great political stability. In contrast, the millions of peasant farmers who formed the backbone of rural society in the Roman Empire were much more loosely integrated into the state structure. They never unified to revolt against their government and overthrow it, as did the raging millenarian peasant movements of Later Han China. By comparison with their counterparts in China, the peasants in the Roman Empire were not as well connected in their proximity or density, or as united by similar modes of production. Here, too, the Mediterranean environment accented separation and difference.

By Chinese standards, the Roman Empire was relatively fragmented and underadministered. Moreover, philosophy and religion never underpinned the Roman state in the way that Confucianism buttressed the dynasties of China. Both empires, however, benefited from the spread of a uniform language and imperial culture. The process was more comprehensive in China (which possessed a single language that the elites used, a literary language based on classical Chinese) than in Rome (whose empire spanned a two-language world: Latin in the western Mediterranean, Greek in the east). Both states fostered a common imperial culture across all levels of society. Once entrenched, these cultures and languages lasted well after the end of empire.

Differences in human resources, languages, and ideas led the Roman and Han states to evolve in unique ways. In both places, however, the faiths of outsiders—Christians and Buddhists—eclipsed the classical ideals that grounded their states' ideological foundations of a distinctly secular sort. Transmission of these new faiths benefited from expanded communications networks. The new religions added to the cultural mix that succeeded the Roman Empire and the Han dynasty.

At their height, both states surpassed their forebears by translating unprecedented military power into the fullest form of state-based organization. Each state's complex organization involved the systematic control, counting, and taxing of its population. In both cases, the general increase of the population, the growth of huge cities, and the success of long-distance trade contributed to the new scales of magnitude. The Han would not be superseded in East Asia as the model empire until the Tang dynasty in the seventh century. In western Afro-Eurasia, the Roman Empire would not be surpassed in scale or intensity of development until the rise of powerful European nation-states more than a millennium later.

Review and research materials are available at StudySpace: Ⓢ WWNORTON.COM/STUDYSPACE

KEY TERMS

charismatic (p. 275)
Christianity (p. 275)
commanderies (p. 244)
dynastic cycle (p. 250)
millenarian movement (p. 259)

patrons (p. 270)
Pax Romana (p. 257)
Pax Sinica (p. 257)
war ethos (p. 264)

Chronology

	400 BCE	300 BCE	200 BCE	100 BCE
THE MEDITERRANEAN		◆- - - - - - - - - - - - - - - - -◆ 350–265 BCE *Roman city-state expansion in Italian peninsula*		
				90–30 BCE *Civil wars divide Romans*
		265–146 BCE *Rome defeats Carthage in three Punic wars* ◆- - - - - - - - - - - - - -		
SOUTHWEST ASIA			129 BCE *Parthian Empire established in Southwest Asia* ◆	
EAST ASIA		221–207 BCE *Qin Empire* ◆- - -◆		
		206 BCE–220 CE *Han dynasty* ◆- -		
		206 BCE–9 CE *Western (Former) Han* ◆- -		
		140–87 BCE *Expansion of Han Empire under Emperor Wu* ◆- - - - - - - - -		

STUDY QUESTIONS

1. Analyze the impact of Xiongnu pastoralists on imperial policies of the Qin and Han dynasties. How did each dynasty counter the threat of nomadic incursions into its territorial heartlands?

2. Explain the influence of Confucian ideas during the Han dynasty. How did these ideas shape political and social hierarchies during this period?

3. Describe the process through which the Roman city-state created a vast empire in the Mediterranean world. How did Roman attitudes toward military service influence the empire's growth?

4. Explain the social and legal hierarchies that governed Roman urban life. To what extent did residents enjoy personal autonomy?

5. Explain the concepts of *Pax Sinica* and *Pax Romana*. How did Han and Roman leaders promote long periods of peace and prosperity in eastern and western Afro-Eurasia, respectively?

6. Compare and contrast the concept of emperor in the Han dynasty with that in the Roman Empire. What role did emperors play in the governing structure of their respective empires?

7. Compare and contrast the methods through which Han and Roman leaders enlisted their subjects' support. What emphasis did each state place on ideology, civil bureaucracy, and military organization?

8. Compare and contrast the labor systems in the Qin and Han dynasties with that of the Roman Empire. To what extent did each rely on forced labor?

9. Compare and contrast Roman strategies for promoting stability along its borders with those of the Han dynasty. How different were the threats that each empire faced from borderland peoples?

	1 CE	100 CE	200 CE	300 CE

27 BCE–476 CE Roman Empire

1st century CE Jesus preaches in Judea

200–300 CE Christianity expands to broader Roman Empire

27 BCE–14 CE Augustus reigns as first Roman emperor

98–117 CE Roman Empire reaches greatest territorial extent under Emperor Trajan

224 CE Sasanian Empire supplants Parthia

23 CE Red Eyebrows uprising

9–23 CE Wang Mang usurps the Han throne

184 CE Yellow Turbans uprising

25–220 CE Eastern (Later) Han

184 CE Popular rebellions against Han rule

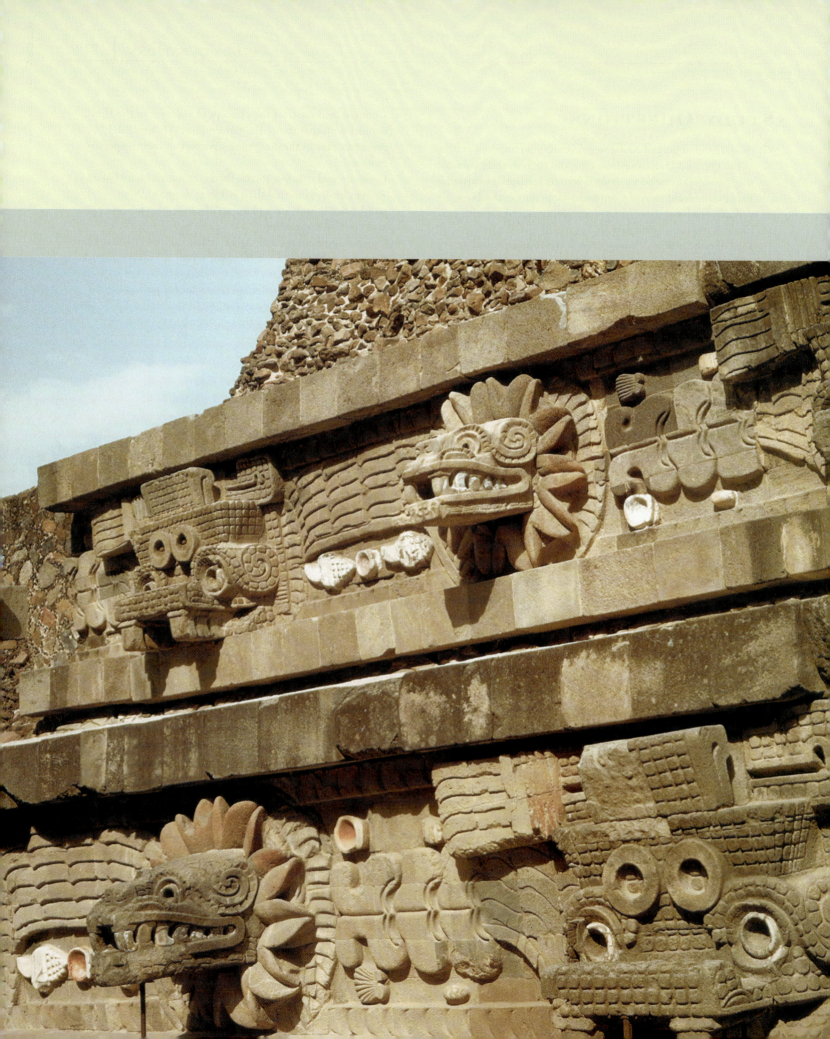

THE RISE OF UNIVERSAL RELIGIONS, 300–600 CE

Around 180 CE, a humble group of three men and three women stood trial before the provincial governor at Carthage. They claimed to be Christians, and their crime was refusal to worship the gods of the Roman Empire. The governor was unimpressed; his god was "the protecting spirit of our lord the emperor." One Christian retorted that his god was also an emperor, but that he could not be seen, for he stood "above all kings and . . . all nations." There was an unbridgeable gap between the governor and the Christians. So the governor read out a death sentence, ordering their immediate execution. "Thanks be to God!" cried the Christians, and straightaway they were beheaded.

As the centuries unfolded, the tables would turn dramatically. Old ideas of the supremacy of an emperor-lord gave way to those of the Lord God as emperor. Previously, the impulse toward universalism had come from ambitious empire builders, like Alexander the Great and the Roman emperors. Now, for the first time, religious leaders became the agents of universalist messages and worked to convert humanity to their belief systems. This period, which witnessed the bonding of religions to universal aspirations, spread religious tenets across the Afro-Eurasian landmass. What gave these religions, notably Christianity and Buddhism, their universalistic message and their widespread appeal to diverse peoples and cultures? In effect, in this era spiritual and religious fervor became an even more powerful force of integration than political ambitions, while also triggering new world divides. This advent of religion as a global influence was anything but simple. It also built on the expansive reach of the Roman and Han empires while shaping the institutions of these states. It profited from the closer commercial and intellectual connections between east and west. This chapter tells the story of how Christianity and Buddhism became universal religions forever changing world history.

UNIVERSAL RELIGIONS AND COMMON CULTURES

> → *How did religion bring worlds together and drive them apart?*

From 300 to 600 CE, the entire Afro-Eurasian landmass experienced a surge of religious ferment. In the West, Christianity became the state faith of the Roman Empire. In India, Vedic religion (Brahmanism) evolved into a more formal spiritual system called Hinduism. In northern India, central Asia, and even China, Buddhism—originally a code of ethics—became a religion. Across much of the world, spiritual concerns affected everyday life and integrated scattered communities into shared faiths.

Two faiths in particular aspired to universality in this era—Christianity and Buddhism. They were to be joined by Islam several centuries later. What made them universalistic in comparison with, say, Judaism, Hinduism, and traditional African religious beliefs was that they were not tied to a locality. Hinduism was the belief system of Hindi speakers of South Asia. Judaism was tied to a specific ethnicity, while traditional African religious beliefs varied from people to people. In contrast, Christianity and Buddhism appealed to diverse populations (men and women, freeborn and slaves, rich and poor), proved adaptable as they moved from one cultural and geographical area to another, were promoted by energetic and charismatic missionizing agents, and despite their many and insistent demands provided a deep sense of community to their converts. In the case of Christianity, though to a lesser extent Buddhism, these religions also benefited from the support of powerful empires.

The new spirituality blossomed inside and also outside empires (see Map 8-1). In western Europe, Christianity arose alongside a decaying Roman state. In the eastern Mediterranean, it inspired a revived Roman *imperium* at Byzantium. In India, Hinduism and Buddhism vied for cultural preeminence; in central Asia and China, Buddhism flourished as the old polities foundered.

The peoples living in sub-Saharan Africa and the Americas, too, reached beyond local communities and wove common spiritual worlds. In Africa, the Bantu-speaking peoples, residing in the southeastern corner of present-day Nigeria, began to spread their way of life throughout the entire southern half of the landmass. Similarly, across the Atlantic Ocean, the Mayans established political and cultural institutions over a large portion of Mesoamerica.

A wide variety of societies experienced spiritual ferment. This does not mean that people became more excitable or more otherworldly; it means that religion touched more areas of society and in more demanding ways. People felt deeply about religion because it was through religious filters that

Focus Questions

→ *How did religion bring worlds together and drive them apart?*

→ *How did empires such as the Roman and Sasanian help religions such as Christianity become universalizing?*

→ *How did central Asians influence the spread of universal religions and other cross-cultural developments during this time?*

→ *To what extent did South Asia develop a common culture despite political, religious, and social diversity?*

→ *To what extent did influences from other parts of Afro-Eurasia transform Chinese culture and politics?*

→ *How similar and different were spiritual and cultural developments in worlds apart from Afro-Eurasia during this time?*

MAIN THEMES

→ *Afro-Eurasia and the Americas witness the rise of universalizing religions and unifying cultural beliefs.*

→ *Two religions—Christianity and Buddhism—aspire to world missions and challenge the power of secular rulers and thinkers.*

→ *While undermining Roman emperors, Indian satraps, and Chinese dynasts, these new religions also win important statesmen to their cause and use the authority of the state to gain converts and spread their faiths.*

FOCUS ON *Religions and Regions*

Western and Eastern Europe and Southwest Asia

♦ **Christianity** moves from a minority, persecuted faith to a state religion in the Roman Empire.

♦ Both Christianity and South Asian religious tenets buttress the powerful Sasanian state based in Iran.

Sub-Saharan Africa and Mesoamerica

♦ Large parts of Africa and the Americas develop common cultures based on religious beliefs shared by large, widely dispersed groups.

South Asia and East Asia

♦ Brahmanism, or **Hinduism**, becomes the dominant religion among the Vedic peoples of South Asia.

♦ **Buddhism** spreads out of South Asia along the Silk Road through central Asia and into East Asia.

---

they processed the meaning of what was important to them. They discussed issues of truth, loyalty, and solidarity in terms framed by spiritual leaders who claimed to know the truth about an invisible other world.

Consider how many questions in our own world are assumed to be answerable by science. In many respects, religion functioned in that age as science does in ours. It claimed to give clear answers about the nature of human beings, why they lived in society, why they married and had children, whom they should obey, and the degree of allegiance they owed to something unseen (God, the gods, or a supernaturally guaranteed code of conduct) rather than to any ruler. Even more, as the case of the Christian martyrs showed, religion told them what they should die for.

Because religion claimed to help its followers distinguish between right and wrong, it freed people from the past. The fact that local religious practices might have existed for ages did not make the old beliefs true. As cultures shrugged off their older heritages, shared faith brought people together and enabled them to identify with people and places beyond their own local worlds. Some religious systems, such as Buddhism and Christianity, spread far and wide because they pro-

fessed universal rules and principles to guide behavior that transcended place, time, and specific cultural practices; later, Islam would follow the same pattern (see Chapter 9).

Sharp distinctions between right and wrong also drew new lines between peoples. Religion became a wedge that drove worlds apart, as absolute conviction left little room for tolerance. Centuries of harmonious interaction offered few protections to neighbors now perceived to be "wrong" in their beliefs—and their errors could get them ostracized, exiled, or killed. For wrong beliefs were considered as dangerous as today's counterfeit medicines. Like noxious drugs, they had to be removed from circulation as quickly as possible. Conflict, even violence and religious persecution, accompanied this new sense of certainty.

Moreover, religious beliefs came to apply equally from one end of Afro-Eurasia to the other. Religious leaders carrying written texts (books, scrolls, or tablets of wood or palm leaf) often traveled widely. Everywhere, universal religions were on the move. Christians from Persia went to China. Buddhists journeyed from South Asia to Afghanistan and used the caravan routes of central Asia to reach China. In 643 CE, the Chinese Buddhist Xuanzang brought back to Chang'an

FOREST NOMADIC HUNTERS

NORTH
AMERICA

ROCKY MOUNTAINS

Great Lakes

Mississippi R.

St. Lawrence R.

PLAINS NOMADIC HUNTERS

Teotihuacán •

Gulf of Mexico

MAYAN CITY STATES

WEST INDIES

ATLANTIC OCEAN

CELTIC PEOPLES

GERMANI

GOTHS

Carthage

KINGDOM OF THE VANDALS

SAHARA

SAHARA PEOPL

Niger R.

PACIFIC OCEAN

CHAVIN

ANDES MOUNTAINS

SOUTH AMERICA

Amazon R.

	Qi
	Tuoba
	Hephthalites
	Sasanian
	Gupta
	Eastern Roman
	Mayan
VANDALS	Kingdom
BANTU	People
•	City

0   1000   2000 Miles

0   1000   2000 Kilometers

MAP 8-1 EMPIRES AND COMMON CULTURES FROM 300 TO 600 CE

The period 300–600 CE was a time of tumultuous political change. Comparing this map with Map 6-3, which polities are new? Which polities have disappeared? Which ones have expanded or contracted? What historical factors are driving these changes in the political landscape?

Xuanzang. This painting c. 900 CE, which survives in the caves of Dunhuang along the Silk Road, portrays the Chinese pilgrim Xuanzang accompanied by a tiger on his epic travels to South Asia to collect important Buddhist scriptures.

(then the world's largest city) an entire library of Buddhist scriptures—527 boxes of writings and 192 birch-bark tablets—that he had collected on a pilgrimage to Buddhist holy sites in South Asia. He lodged them in the Great Wild Goose Pagoda and immediately began to translate every line into Chinese. Here was the "truth" of Buddhism for Xuanzang, similar to the way we accept information we find in a modern science textbook, and as exciting as a revelation when they reached distant China as when Buddhist thinkers had elaborated them in northern India, more than 5,000 miles away. Some Chinese Buddhists now referred to India as the "Central Kingdom."

Voyages, translations, long-distance pilgrimages, and sweeping conversion campaigns remapped the spiritual landscape of the world. New religious leaders were the brokers of more universal but also more intolerant worldviews, premised on a new relationship between gods and their subjects. Religions and their brokers profoundly integrated societies. But they also created new ways to drive them apart.

EMPIRES AND RELIGIOUS CHANGE IN WESTERN AFRO-EURASIA

> ✦ *How did empires such as the Roman and Sasanian help religions such as Christianity become universalizing?*

In western Afro-Eurasia, the Roman Empire was hardly the political and military juggernaut it had been 300 years earlier. Surrounded by peoples who coveted its wealth while resisting its power, Rome was fragmenting. Yet its endurance was a boon to the new religious ferment, which took hold in its decaying political institutions. Although so-called barbarians eventually overran the western parts of the empire, in many ways those areas still felt "Roman." They looked to the new faith of Christianity to maintain continuity with the past, eventually founding a papacy in Rome to rule the remnants of empire.

This Christian empire split almost from the start (see Map 8-2). In Rome's east, a powerful successor state appeared in the form of the Byzantine Empire based at Constantinople. Its claim to be the political arm of Christianity seemed more viable than that of the church based in Rome. But it faced a new foe still farther east. The Sasanian Empire of Persia, like the papacy at Rome and the Byzantine state, was unique. Indeed, these states represented something unprecedented: they claimed the blessing of new (or transformed) religions, and their rulers expected all subjects to worship the correct gods in the correct manner. Those who did not were treated as outsiders, in both this life and the next—where hell awaited them.

THE RISE AND SPREAD OF CHRISTIANITY

Ironically, the most crucial change ever to befall the Roman Empire had little to do with distant frontier wars. Instead, it grew from a religious war fought, from the bottom up, in the peaceful and tightly administered towns that were the nerve centers of the Roman Mediterranean.

The rise of Christianity coincided with the appearance of a new figure in matters of spiritual belief: the **martyr**. Martyrs were people whom the Roman authorities executed for

→ *How did empires such as the Roman and Sasanian help religions such as Christianity become universalizing?*

persisting in their Christian beliefs instead of submitting to pagan (polytheistic) ritual or belief. Many of them were remarkable witnesses to their faith. In 203 CE, a well-to-do mother in her early twenties, Vibia Perpetua, faced a horrible punishment for refusing to sacrifice to the Roman gods. Denied the benefit of a human executioner, she and her companions were condemned to face wild beasts in the amphitheater of Carthage. The amphitheater is still there, south of modern Tunis. It is a mean, small place—not a gigantic stadium. The condemned and the spectators would have had eye contact with one another throughout the fatal encounter.

Before her death, Perpetua dictated a prison diary that is unique in Roman literature. Here a woman speaks with a full

MAP 8-2   THE SPREAD OF UNIVERSAL RELIGIONS IN AFRO-EURASIA, 300–600 CE

The spread of universal religions and the shifting political landscape were intimately connected. Using Map 8-1, identify the major polities in Afro-Eurasia during this era. How did these political configurations differ from those in the era covered in Chapter 7? Compare and contrast Map 8-1 with Map 8-2. Where did Hinduism, Buddhism, and Christianity emerge, and where did they spread? How did the rise and fall of empires affect the expansion of universal religions?

Simurgh, the legendary dog-headed bird of Persian mythology, as shown on this seventh-century silver plate from Sasanian Persia, was a favored motif on textiles, sculptures, paintings, and architecture from the Byzantine Empire to Tang China.

jostling camel caravans, goods displaying Persian motifs (such as the legendary simurgh bird and prancing rams with fluttering ribbons that, in Iran, were the symbol of good fortune and royalty) rode side by side with Roman glass from Mediterranean cities. Along with Sasanian silver coins and gold pieces minted in Constantinople, these exotic products found eager buyers as far east as China and Japan.

BUDDHISM ON THE SILK ROAD

Unstable political systems did not hinder the flow of ideas or commodities. Instead, the civil wars marking the end of the Han Empire rendered China more open to the cultures of its far western regions. South of the Hindu Kush Mountains, in northern India, nomadic groups made the roads into central Asia safe to travel, enabling Buddhism to spread northward

and eastward via the mountainous corridor of Afghanistan into China. Here, Buddhist monks were the primary missionizing agents, the purveyors of a universal message as they traveled across the roads of central Asia, bearing holy books, offering salvation to commoners, and establishing themselves more securely in host communities than did armies, diplomats, or merchants.

Starting at Bamiyan, a valley of the Hindu Kush—where two gigantic statues of the Buddha, 121 and 180 feet in height, were hewn from the stone face of the cliff during the fourth and fifth centuries CE—travelers found welcoming cave monasteries at oases all along the way from the Taklamakan Desert to northern China. They also encountered five huge Buddhas carved from cliffs in Yungang. While those at Bamiyan stood tall with royal majesty, the Buddhas of Yungang sat in postures of meditation. Surrounding the Buddhas, over fifty caves sheltered more than 50,000 statues representing Buddhist deities and patrons. The Yungang Buddhas, seated just inside the Great Wall, welcomed travelers to the market in China and marked the eastern end of the central Asian Silk Road.

The Bamiyan and Yungang Buddhas, placed more than 2,500 miles apart, are a reminder that by now religious ideas were creating world empires of the mind. Religions such as early Christianity and Buddhism saw themselves as transcending kingdoms of this world: they were bringing a universal message contained in holy scriptures. And they enjoyed greater reach than the ponderous empires that *were* of this world—whether Roman or Chinese. Religion traveled light and traveled faster than did armies.

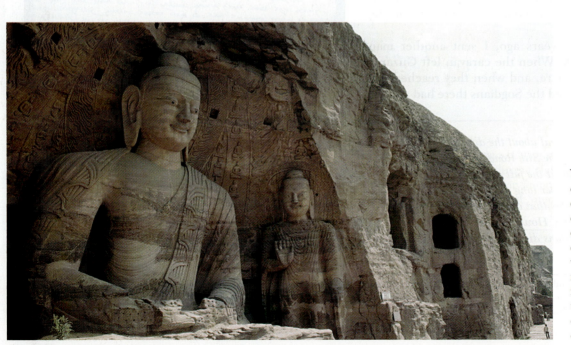

Yungang Buddha. This is one of the five giant statues of the Buddha in Yungang, created under the emperors of the Northern Wei, a dynasty built by nomads who invaded and occupied north China. Sitting at the foothills of the Great Wall, the Buddhas marked the eastern destination of the central Asian Silk Road.

POLITICAL AND RELIGIOUS CHANGE IN SOUTH ASIA

> → *To what extent did South Asia develop a common culture despite political, religious, and social diversity?*

A Gold Coin of Chandra Gupta II. The Gupta dynasty, based in the middle and lower Ganges plain, was known for its promotion of indigenous Indian culture. Here, Chandra Gupta II, the most famous king of the dynasty, is shown riding a horse in the style of the invaders from the central Asian steppes.

South Asia, especially the area of modern India, also enjoyed religious enthusiasm (see again Map 8-5). Its major cultural system, Brahmanism (Vedic religion), did not claim to be a universal faith with aspirations to reach outside India. But it did strive to meet all needs and to explain all theological problems, much as its rival, Buddhism, had done. Like Christianity in the Mediterranean and Southwest Asia and Buddhism in China, religion in India unified diverse peoples. And again, political opportunities aided its spread.

Religious change took a dramatic turn during the Gupta dynasty. The largest political entity in South Asia from the early fourth to the mid-sixth century CE, it provided stability that facilitated commercial and cultural exchange (much as the Roman Empire had done in its united territories). Chandragupta (r. c. 320–335 CE) called himself "King of Kings, Great King." His son expanded the Gupta territory to the entire northern Indian plain and made a long expedition to southern India. Even more military achievements occurred under later Gupta dynasts.

The poetry during the reign of Chandragupta, a generous patron of the arts, expressed the widespread religious yearnings and popular sentiments of the age. Kalidasa, a prolific poet and playwright, and other poets, for instance, worked with the motifs and episodes from two early epics, *Mahabharata* and *Ramayana* (see Chapter 4), to address new problems and to extol new virtues. In their hands what had once been lyric dramas and narrative poems, written to provide entertainment, now served as collective memories of the past and underscored religious commands for ideal behavior. The heroes and deeds that the poets praised served as models for kings and their subjects. Because these epics were intended to become part of the religious canon, they were rendered in classical Sanskrit and embodied religious teachings.

Nonetheless, these works preserve stories from ancient times and offer insights into those eras. Consider the original *Mahabharata* epic, which told of a king who left his court for an assertive woman of a forest society. In Kalidasa's accounting, what had been a saga of love and suffering becomes a morality play about holding to strict religious precepts. The main character, Sakuntala, now portrayed as a shy girl who had been adopted by a forest ascetic but who had neglected her religious duties, was made to suffer punishments and to live out her life in great misery. The moral of Kalidasa's story was that misfortune comes from failing to follow Brahmanical religious rules.

THE TRANSFORMATION OF THE BUDDHA

During the Gupta period, the two main schools of Buddhism acquired universalistic features. Initially regarded as a contemplative ascetic (someone who chooses a simple, hard life of self-denial), the Buddha now came to be worshipped as a god.

The doctrines of both schools—Mahayana (Greater Vehicle); and the school of elders, Hinayana (Lesser Vehicle), also referred to as Theraveda—had become quite different from what the Buddha preached centuries earlier. As we saw in Chapter 5, the historical Buddha was a sage who was believed to enter *nirvana,* ending the pain of consciousness. In the earliest Buddhist doctrine, god and supernatural powers did not exist. But by 200 CE a crucial transformation had occurred: his followers started to view the Buddha as a god (see Chapter 6). **Mahayana Buddhism** also extended worship to the many bodhisattvas who bridged the gulf between the Buddha's perfection and the world's sadly imperfect peoples.

Some Buddhists fully accepted the Buddha as god but could not accept the divinity of bodhisattvas; these adherents belonged to the more monkish school of old-fashioned **Hinayana Buddhism**, later called Theraveda in Ceylon and Southeast Asia. They rejected the Sanskrit canon on the supernatural power of bodhisattvas and cleaved to the early Buddhist texts, which were probably based on the words of Buddha himself. Hinayana temples barred all colorful idols of bodhisattvas and other heavenly beings and contained only the image of the Buddha.

It was especially in the Mahayana school that Buddhism became a universal religion, whose adherents worshipped divinities rather than simply acknowledging the worth of great men. Spreading along the Silk Road, this new religion (with claims to universality that rivaled Christianity's) eventually appealed to peoples all over East Asia.

The religion's universalizing transformation also involved rituals that recognized powerful local spirits. Consider the observations of Faxian, a Chinese pilgrim to India around 400 CE. He described the city of Sankasya, where both Mayahana and Hinayana took hold, as being home to a Buddhist *sangha* whose patron was "a white-eared dragon." Believing that it brought rain at propitious times to guarantee a good harvest, the Buddhists constructed a shrine in its honor and offered it food daily. At the end of the summer rainy period, "the dragon appears in the form of a white-eared snake. Monks recognize him and offer some cheese in a copper bowl. . . . The snake then moves from the high seats to the low seats of the sangha, as if sending his regards to everyone. Then he disappears. This happens every year." This Buddhist ritual likely reflects the local agrarian lifestyle and traditions of propitiating spirits from the natural world.

THE HINDU TRANSFORMATION

During this period, the ancient Brahmanic Vedic religion also spread widely and became the dominant religion of South Asia. Because Buddhism and Jainism (see Chapter 5) had many devotees in cities and commercial communities, conservative Brahmans turned their attention to rural India and refashioned their religion, bringing it in accord with rural life and agrarian values. As a result of these changes, the Brahmanic religion emerged as the dominant faith in Indian society as what we know today as **Hinduism**.

Hinduism is a modern word coined from *Hindu*, the people who live in Hind, the Arabic word for India. In the religion's new form, believers became vegetarians, forsaking the animal sacrifices that had been important to their earlier rituals.

Hindu Statue. This huge statue of a three-headed god in a cave on a small island near Mumbai (Bombay) represents the monotheistic theology of Hinduism. Brahma, the creator, Vishnu, the keeper, and Siva, the destroyer, are all from one *atma,* or the single soul of the universe.

They abandoned long-held customs associated with pastoralists and nomads and even absorbed Buddhist and Jain practices, as they identified themselves with agrarian culture. Their new rituals were linked to self-sacrifice—denying themselves meat rather than offering up slaughtered animals to the gods, as they had done previously. Three major deities—Brahma, Vishnu, and Siva—formed a trinity representing the three phases of the universe (birth, existence, and destruction, respectively) and the three expressions of the eternal self, or *atma*. As the universe was already born and its destruction was yet to come, the god in charge of the current world, Vishnu, was the most prominent. Next in importance was Siva, who was especially meaningful for those fearing the end of the world.

Vishnu, who embodied the present, was the most popular of the three deities. Believers thought he revealed himself to the world in various avatars (incarnations). One of these was Krishna, the dark-skinned cattle herder and charioteer of the ancient hero Arjuna in the epic poem *Mahabharata*, who also became a religious teacher to Arjuna. A vital part of this poem revolves around the final battle between two warring confederations of Vedic tribes. Arjuna, the best warrior of one of these confederations, holds back from the fray, afraid to fight against his enemies because many of them are his cousins. At a crucial moment his spiritual guide, Krishna, intervenes, commanding him to slay his foes—even those related to him. Krishna reminds Arjuna that the warrior caste, the Kshatriyas, to whom Arjuna belongs, have been put on earth to govern and to fight against the community's enemies. In the early rendition of this tale the episode takes up little space; but by the Gupta period the story had become a lengthy poem, *The Bhagavad Gita* (Song of the God). In this form it prescribed religious and ethical precepts (*dharma*) for people in all walks of life and served as a major canon of Hindu spirituality.

Hindus also absorbed other religions' deities into their pantheon, even regarding the Buddha as an avatar of Vishnu. Thus the Hindu pantheon became larger and more accessible than the Vedic one, enabling more believers to share a single faith. Hindus did not wish to approach the gods only through sacrificial rituals at which Brahmans alone could officiate. They preferred to devote their passion and faith to an individual form of each of the great gods. For example, one could be a devotee exclusively of Rama or his wife, Sita. Women, especially widows, tended to worship Krishna and kept a small idol of him in the home. Evidence from later times shows that worshippers of Krishna, Rama, Siva, or any other deity often gathered to sing, dance, and parade. This practice of personal devotion to gods was called **bhakti**. It attracted Hindus of all social strata, while the body of mythological literature wove the deities into an intriguing heavenly order presided over by the trinity of Brahma, Vishnu, and Siva. The Hindu trinity enabled believers to claim to be monotheists, since the three gods embodied a single god, Atma. The trinity also represented a divine hierarchy. In this sense the Hindu trinity may

THE LAWS OF MANU: CASTES AND OCCUPATIONS

Brahmans compiled the Laws of Manu during the first or the second century CE, when the Kushans from the northern steppes ruled over much of South Asia. It was a time of constant social upheaval. Among the many law codes that appeared throughout Indian history, that of Manu (father of the human race) holds the most authority among Hindus because it is the most comprehensive. It describes the origins of the four castes and clearly designates the occupations that provide members of each with their livelihood.

87. But in order to protect this universe He, the most resplendent one, assigned separate (duties and) occupations to those who sprang from his mouth, arms, thighs, and feet.

88. To Brâhmanas he assigned teaching and studying (the Veda), sacrificing for their own benefit and for others, giving and accepting (of alms).

89. The Kschatriya he commanded to protect the people, to bestow gifts, to offer sacrifices, to study (the Veda), and to abstain from attaching himself to sensual pleasures;

90. The Vaisya to tend cattle, to bestow gifts, to offer sacrifices, to study (the Veda), to trade, to lend money, and to cultivate land.

91. One occupation only the lord prescribed to the Sûdra, to serve meekly even these (other) three castes.

→ *According to Hindu belief, the four castes sprang from "the mouth, arms, thighs, and feet" of "the most resplendent one." In what ways is it significant that the Brahman caste sprang from the mouth?*

→ *What caste do soldiers belong to? What caste do farmers and merchants belong to? Which caste do you suppose represents the majority of the population?*

→ *How are the different caste statuses reflected in the jobs that their members can take?*

SOURCE: *The Laws of Manu*, I.87–91; translated by G. Bühler, vol. 25 of *The Sacred Books of the East* (Oxford: Clarendon Press, 1886), p. 24.

---

have taken inspiration from Christianity, as Christians had been living in India for centuries.

During this period Buddhism and Hinduism lived side by side, competing for followers by building ornate temples and sculptures of gods and by holding elaborate rituals and festivities. Hindu temples and Buddhist monasteries also developed into centers of education, as both communities learned from each other in all lines of knowledge.

A CODE OF CONDUCT
INSTEAD OF AN EMPIRE

Besides setting heaven in order, Hinduism sought to establish a "correct" social order on earth. What emerged were new ways of thinking about the bonds between rulers and subjects. Although these ideas could not transcend the region's political differences, they introduced an alternative ethic of governing—steeped in religious faith—that would eventually integrate the society.

THE LAWS OF MANU Unlike China and Rome, India did not have a centralized empire that the new governing ethic could revitalize. After the fall of the Mauryan Empire in the second century BCE (see Chapter 6), northern India came under the rule of distant rulers who had no contact with the people from whom they collected taxes and tariffs. Local populations relied on religious and social institutions such as castes and guilds to maintain order during periods of frequent warfare. But now, to maintain order, the Brahmans compiled law codes drawing on Hindu moral rules and customary law. Among them, the Laws of Manu were the most comprehensive. In Hindu mythology, Manu ("human") was the father of the human race, and the Laws of Manu applied to all persons no matter where they lived. Kingdoms might come and go, but the "true" order of society, summed up in the Laws of Manu, remained the same.

Above all, the **Laws of Manu** offered guidance for living within the caste system, whose origins lay centuries earlier. (See Primary Source: The Laws of Manu: Castes and Occupations.) Every person had to marry within his or her which pushed the arable frontier farther into the dense jungle. The result: a subsistence economy of diversified agrarian production. Villagers cultivated maize, beans, and squash, rotating them to prevent the depletion of soil nutrients. Where possible, farmers supplemented these staples with root crops such as sweet potato and cassava. Cotton was the basic fiber used for robes, dresses, and blouses; it frequently grew amid rows of other crops as part of a diversified mix.

MAYAN WRITING, MATHEMATICS, AND ARCHITECTURE   Commerce connected the dispersed Mayan worlds, as did a common set of beliefs, codes, and values that rulers supported. Villagers spoke dialects of roughly the same language. Writing developed very early, though only recently have epigraphers deciphered the Mayan script. The advent of writing created an important caste of scribes who were vital to the society's integration. Rulers rewarded them with great titles and honors, as well as material comforts, for writing grand epics about dynasties and their founders, major battles, marriages, deaths, and sacrifices. Such writings taught generations of Mayan subjects that they shared common histories, beliefs, and gods—always associated with the narratives of ruling families. The inscriptions reflected elaborate narratives that were ritually performed for commoners and rulers alike. These took the form of dances that rehearsed epic triumphs before warriors went off to battle, or acts of illusion intended to trick and humor the audiences to remind them of some devious antecedent. And there were magnificent costumes made of shells, feathers, and hides to masquerade dancers and actors as gods, enemies, or royal neighbors.

The combination of writings and performances created a historic memory to serve rulers' power and to venerate the gods whose patronage they required. The best-known surviving text is the Popol Vuh, a "Book of Community." It narrates one community's creation myth, extolling its founders (twin heroes) and trials and tribulations—wars, natural disasters, human ingenuity—that enabled a royal genealogy to rule the Quiché Kingdom. It begins, as many creation myths do, with the gods' creation of the earth, in this case the work of three water-dwelling plumed serpents. And it ends with the elaboration of rituals to which the kingdom's tribes must subscribe if they are to avoid losing their way, which had occurred several times throughout their history. After all, to be a "community" required sharing and honoring a historic memory of the gods' work. One must note, however, in the use of Mayan "written" texts like the Popol Vuh, that they comprise narratives recited to later Spanish sources. They are not texts inscribed in the Classical Mayan era.

The Mayans also were skilled mathematicians, devising a calendar and studying astronomy. They charted regular celestial movements with amazing accuracy and marked the passage of time by precise lunar and solar cycles. Keen read-

Wood Tablet. This detail of a wood-carved tablet from a temple in the city of Tikal (c. 741 CE) is a fine example of the ornate form of scribal activity, which combined images and portraits with glyphs that tell a narrative.

ers of the stars, the Mayans could map heavenly motions onto their sacred calendars and rigorously observe their rituals at the proper times. Indeed, the movement of the stars and the chronology of the calendar governed annual ritual cycles. Each change in the cycle had particular rituals, dances, performances, and offerings, including the offering of human blood to honor the gods with life's sustenance. The most sacred blood was drawn from ears, tongues, and the foreskins of penises, to open pathways to the gods through which "donors" could hear, speak, and participate in heavenly reproduction. This was one reason why the rituals took place like clockwork according to the precise angles and movements of the heavenly bodies.

Here, then, was a world characterized by political divisions and often crippling warfare, but with common religious and cultural features. A common faith provided a powerful human resource that rulers could exploit. Indeed, cities reflected a ruler's ability to summon his subjects to contribute to the kingdom's greatness. Plazas, ball courts,

POP	UO	ZIP	ZOTZ	TZEC
XUL	YAXKIN	MOL	CHEN	YAX
ZAC	CEH	MAC	KANKIN	MUAN
PAX	KAYAB	CUMHU	uayeb	

Mayan Pictograms. The Mayans were famous for keeping records of time with an elaborate calendar. Pictograms, each with a separate image, represented the months of the year. All literate Mayans would have recognized this index.

terraces, and palaces sprouted out from neighborhoods in an early form of urban sprawl. Activity revolved around grand royal palaces and massive ball courts, where competing teams treated enthusiastic audiences to contests that were more religious ritual than game (see discussion of Olmec ball courts in Chapter 5). Moreover, rulers exhorted their people to build not just outward but upward. The Mayans excelled at building skyscrapers—especially as tombs. In Tikal, for instance, surviving buildings include six steep and massive funerary pyramids featuring thick masonry walls and vaulted ceilings and chambers; the tallest temple soars above the treetops, more than 220 feet high. Embellishing the outsides are giant carvings and paintings, and deep within lie the crypts of royal family members. For example, the famous Bonampak site (in current-day southern Mexico) has a magnificent Temple of the Murals with the finest examples of Classical Mayan painting. These depict a series of events in precise detail—from an orchestra performing, to nobles discussing current affairs, to captured warriors being prepared for human sacrifice. The artwork dates from 790 CE. This kind of artwork likely adorned other Mayan centers as well.

MAYAN BLOODLETTING AND WARFARE The elites were obsessed with blood, for spilling it was a way to honor dynastic lineages as well as gods. This rite led to chronic warfare, especially among rival dynasties, the goal of which was to capture victims for the bloody rituals. Rulers also would shed their own blood at intervals set by the calendar. Royal wives drew blood from their tongues; men had their penises perforated by a stingray spine or sharpened bone. Such bloodletting was reserved for those of noble descent, with the aid of elaborately adorned and sanctified instruments; carvings and paintings portray blood cascading from rulers' mutilated bodies.

The spiral of warfare doomed the Mayans, especially after devastating confrontations between Tikal and Kalak'mul during the fourth through seventh centuries CE. With each outbreak, rulers drafted larger armies and sacrificed greater numbers of captives, and their resolve fueled the carnage. Crops perished. People fled. Food supplies dwindled. After centuries of misery, it must have seemed as if the gods themselves were abandoning the Mayan people.

As warfare engulfed the fractured Mayan communities and ruling households collapsed, entire states fell. The cycle of violence destroyed the cultural underpinnings of elite rule that had held the Mayan world together. There was no single catastrophic event, no great defeat by a rival power. The Mayan people simply abandoned their spiritual centers, and cities became ghost towns. As populations declined, jungles overtook temples. Eventually, the hallmark of Mayan unity—the ability to read a shared script—vanished.

 ## CONCLUSION

The breakdown of two imperial systems—Rome around the Mediterranean, and Han China in East Asia—introduced an era in which religion and shared culture (rather than military conquest and political institutions) linked large areas of Afro-Eurasia.

The Roman Empire gave way to a religious unity, first represented by Christian dissenters and then co-opted by the emperor Constantine. In western Europe, the sense of unity unlimited by imperial frontiers gave rise to a universal, or "Catholic," church—the "true" Christian religion that believers felt all peoples should share. In the eastern Mediterranean, where the Roman Empire survived, Christianity and empire coalesced to reinforce the feeling that true religion, high culture, and empire went hand in hand. Christians here held that beliefs about God and Jesus found their most correct expression within the eastern Roman Empire and in its capital, Constantinople.

Similarly, in East Asia, the weakening of the Han dynasty enabled Buddhism to dominate Chinese culture. Without a unified state in China, Confucian officials languished in obscurity, while Buddhist priests and monks enjoyed patronage from regional rulers, local warriors, and commoners. In India, too, a political vacuum allowed the unfolding of a new culture: the Brahman elites exploited population movements beyond the reach of traditional rulers as they established ritual forms for daily life on every level of society.

Not all regions felt the spread of universalizing religions, however. In most of sub-Saharan Africa (though not Sudan and Ethiopia, where Christianity set down deep roots) belief systems were much more localized. The same pattern emerged in the Americas, where long-distance transportation was harder and language systems had not yielded texts to share with nonbelievers. But spiritual life was no less profound. Here, it was the strong sense of a shared worldview, a shared sense of purpose, and a shared sense of faith that enabled common cultures to develop. Indeed, the Bantus and Mayans became large-scale common cultures—but ruled at the local level.

Thus, the period 300–600 CE saw the emergence of three great cultural units in Afro-Eurasia, each defined in religious terms: Christianity in the Mediterranean and Southwest Asia, Brahmanism in South Asia, and Buddhism in East Asia. They illustrated the ways in which peoples were converging under larger religious tents, while also becoming more distinct. Universal religions, whether Christian or Buddhist, and universal codes of behavior, such as the Brahmanic Laws of Manu, gave people a new way to define themselves and their loyalties.

But the pattern would soon change. As we will see, empire would return to East Asia in the form of the mighty Tang dynasty. And the zone stretching from Morocco to central Asia would find itself united in a gigantic imperial system fashioned by followers of the Prophet Muhammad.

Review and research materials are available at StudySpace: Ⓖ WWNORTON.COM/STUDYSPACE

KEY TERMS

Bantu migrations (p. 310)
bhakti (p. 304)
big men (p. 311)
conversion of Constantine (p. 290)
creed (p. 291)
Hinayana (Lesser Vehicle) Buddhism (p. 303)
Hinduism (p. 304)
Laws of Manu (p. 305)

Madhyamika (Middle Way) Buddhism (p. 307)
Mahayana (Greater Vehicle) Buddhism (p. 303)
martyr (p. 286)
Mayans (p. 315)
Northern Wei dynasty (p. 307)
Sasanian Empire (p. 297)
Sogdians (p. 299)
Teotihuacán (p. 313)

Chronology

	1 CE	100 CE	200 CE	300 CE	400 CE
THE MEDITERRANEAN AND NORTH AFRICA		313 CE Emperor Constantine legalizes Christianity in Roman Empire ◆		◆ 325 CE Nicene Creed developed	
			late 4th and 5th centuries "Barbarian" invasions of Roman Empire ◆ - - - - - - - -		
SOUTHWEST ASIA		220s Sasanians create empire in Iran, Mesopotamia ◆			
		324 CE Constantine establishes new Roman capital at Constantinople ◆			
			400 CE Jewish Talmud produced in the Levant ◆		
		◆ Buddhism spreads through central Asia			
CENTRAL ASIA		Sogdian merchant communities dominant trade routes through central Asia ◆			
		◆ Buddhism spreads through central Asia			
SOUTH ASIA	◆ 1st or 2nd centuries CE Transformation of Brahmanism to Hinduism begins				
		320–550 CE Gupta dynasty rules much of northern India ◆ - - - - - - - - - - - - - -			
EAST ASIA			c. 220 CE Han Empire collapses		
		220–589 CE Six Dynasties Period ◆ -			
		Daoism reforms and revives in popularity ◆	◆ - - - - - - - -		
		300–600 CE Buddhism spreads among Chinese society ◆ - - - - - - - - - - - - - -			
SUB-SAHARAN AFRICA	◄ 3000 BCE–1000 CE Bantu migrations from West Africa into central and southern Africa				
MESOAMERICA	250 CE Early Classic Mayan Period begins in Yucatan Peninsula ◆				
	300 CE to late 5th century City of Teotihuacán dominates valley of Mexico ◆ - - - - - - - -				

STUDY QUESTIONS

1. Describe the connections between the growing power of Christianity and the political reconfiguration of the Roman Empire. What was the appeal of Christianity in the Roman Empire?

2. Analyze the Sasanian Empire's role in facilitating the spread of universal religions and the development of common cultures in Afro-Eurasia. How did the empire's geographic location support this cross-cultural dissemination?

3. Explain the role of Sogdians and other central Asian peoples in the dispersion of universal religions. How did they influence East Asian societies in particular?

4. Describe how Brahmanism (Vedic religion) evolved into Hinduism during this era. What factors contributed to this development?

5. Identify key changes in Buddhist thought and practice in South Asia at this time. How did these refinements aid the spread of this religious outlook beyond its homeland?

6. Explain the role of written texts (such as the Laws of Manu, the Talmud, the Analects, and the New Testament) in universalizing religion. How did these texts reshape social attitudes toward spiritual behavior and identity?

7. Analyze the ways in which political decentralization affected the growing popularity of Buddhist and other religious ideas in East Asia. To what extent did they challenge Confucian ideas on social and political organization?

8. Analyze the impact of Bantu migrations on the social and cultural geography of sub-Saharan Africa. What set of beliefs helped unite societies in this region?

9. Compare and contrast Mayan society with that of Teotihuacán. To what extent did each represent a common religious and cultural outlook in Mesoamerica at different times?

10. Analyze the extent to which universal religions brought worlds together and pushed them apart. How did religion create new cultural boundaries and rivalries in Afro-Eurasia at this time?

500 CE	600 CE	700 CE	800 CE	900 CE	1000 CE

◆ 5th century CE Collapse of Roman authority in western empire

◆ 500 CE Byzantine Empire flourishes in the eastern part of former Roman Empire

◆◆ 533–540 CE Emperor Justinian attempts to revive Roman Empire

◆ 542 CE Bubonic plague begins to ravish southwest Asia

◆ Sasanian/Byzantine Wars

◆ 560 CE Turkish Confederacy begins to rule much of central Asia

◆ 5th–7th centuries CE Nestorian Christianity spreads along the Silk Road

◆◆ 630s, 640s Xuanzang, Chinese Buddhist pilgrim, visits South Asia

◆ 386–534 CE Tuoba Wei dynasty rule in northern China

◆ 8th century Mayan culture reaches its zenith

وده زوج ديكر عصبى اندكه رسته اند

Ibn Sina. Ibn Sina was a versatile scholar, most famous for his *Canon of Medicine*.

Yet the region's intellectual vitality remained strong, for young men of learning found patrons among local rulers. Consider Ibn Sina, known in the west as Avicenna (980–1037 CE). He grew to adulthood in Bukhara, practiced medicine in the courts of various Islamic rulers, and spent his later life in central Persia. Schooled in the Quran, Arabic secular literature, philosophy, geometry, and Indian and Euclidean mathematics, Ibn Sina was a master of many disciplines. His *Canon of Medicine* stood as the standard medical text in both Southwest Asia and Europe for centuries.

ISLAM IN SUB-SAHARAN AFRICA Islam also crossed the Sahara Desert and penetrated well into Africa, carried by traders and scholars (see Map 9-3). By the seventh and eighth centuries, Islamic adventurers were pouring into sub-Saharan West Africa, where they exchanged weapons and textiles for gold, salt, and slaves. Trade did more than join West Africa to North Africa. It also generated prodigious wealth, which allowed centralized political kingdoms to develop. The most celebrated was Ghana, which lay at the terminus of North Africa's major trading routes.

Of Ghana, scholars know little. The first to mention it was a Baghdadi scholar, who in the eighth century described it as "the land of gold." A century later, an Arab geographer wrote of "the kingdom of Ghana, the king of which is very powerful. In his country there are gold mines. Under his authority are other kingdoms . . . and gold is found in all of these regions" (Fage, p. 15). Although Muslim traders frequented the state, its rulers were not Muslims. Still, Ghana's pomp and power impressed visitors; in 1067–1068, a geographer from the Muslim province of Andalusia in Spain, wrote of a resplendent king who heard "grievances against officials in a domed pavilion around which stand ten horses covered with gold-embroidered materials. Behind the king stand ten pages holding shields and swords decorated with gold and on his right are the sons of the (vassal) kings of his country wearing splendid garments and their hair plaited with gold" (Levtzion and Spaulding, p. 16). (See also Primary Source: Ghana as Seen by a Muslim Observer in the Eleventh Century.)

Seafaring Muslim traders carried Islam into East Africa via the Indian Ocean. There is evidence of a small eighth-century Islamic trading community at Lamu, along the northern coast of present-day Kenya; and by the mid-ninth century other coastal trading communities had sprung up. They all exported ivory and, possibly, slaves. On the island of Pate, off the coast of Kenya, the inhabitants of Shanga constructed the region's first mosque. This simple structure was replaced 200 years later by a mosque capable of holding all adult members of the community when they gathered for their Friday prayers. By the tenth century, the East African coast featured a mixed African-Arab culture. The region's evolving Bantu language absorbed Arabic words and before long gained a new name, Swahili (derived from the Arabic plural of the word meaning "coast").

would succeed only if their rulers implemented political tenets espoused in Plato's *Republic*. He championed a virtuous "first chief" to rule over an Islamic commonwealth in the same way that Plato had favored a philosopher-king.

In the eleventh century the Abbasid caliphate began to decline, weakening under overextension and the influx of outsider groups (the same problems the Roman Empire had faced). Scholars no longer trekked to the court at Baghdad.

MAP 9-3   ISLAM AND TRADE IN SUB-SAHARAN AFRICA, 700–1000

Islamic merchants and scholars, not Islamic armies, carried Islam into sub-Saharan Africa. Trace the trade routes in Africa, being sure to follow the correct direction of trade. According to the map key and icons, what commodities were Islamic merchants seeking below the Sahara? What were the major trade routes and the direction of trade in Africa? How did trade and commerce lead to the geographic expansion of the Islamic faith?

Primary Source

GHANA AS SEEN BY A MUSLIM OBSERVER IN THE ELEVENTH CENTURY

The following excerpt is from an eleventh-century manuscript written by a Muslim serving under the Umayyads in Spain. Its author, Abdullah Abu Ubayd al-Bakri, produced a massive general geography and history of the known world, as did many Muslim scholars of the period. This manuscript has special value because it provides information about West Africa, a region in which the Spanish rulers had great interest and into which Islam had been spreading for several centuries.

Ghana is the title of the king of the people. The name of the country is Aoukar. The ruler who governs the people at the present time—the year 460 AH (after the Hijra and 1067–68 CE)—is called Tenkamein. He came to the throne in 455 AH. His predecessor, who was named Beci, began his reign at the age of 85. He was a prince worthy of great praise as much for his personal conduct as for his zeal in the pursuit of justice and his friendship to Muslims. . . .

Ghana is composed of two towns situated in a plain. The one inhabited by Muslims is large and contains twelve mosques, in which the congregants celebrate the Friday prayer. All of these mosques have their imams, their muezzins, and their salaried readers. The city possesses judges and men of great erudition. . . . The city where the king resides is six miles away and carries the name el-Ghaba, meaning "the forest." The territory separating these two locations is covered with dwellings, constructed out of rocks and the wood of the acacia tree. The dwelling of the king consists of a chateau and several surrounding huts, all of which are enclosed by a wall-like structure. In the ruler's town, close to the royal tribunal, is a mosque where Muslims come when they have business with the ruler in order to carry out their prayers. . . . The royal interpreters are chosen from the Muslim population, as was the state treasurer and the majority of the state ministers. . . .

The opening of a royal meeting is announced by the noise of a drum, which they call a *deba*, and which is formed from a long piece of dug-out wood. Upon hearing the drumming, the inhabitants assemble. When the king's coreligionists [people of the same religion] appear before him, they genuflect and throw dust on their heads. Such is the way in which they salute their sovereign. The Muslims show their respect for the king by clapping their hands. The religion of the Negroes is paganism and fetishism. . . . The land of Ghana is not healthy and has few people. Travelers who pass through the area during the height of the agricultural season are rarely able to avoid becoming sick. When the grains are at their fullest and are ready for harvesting is the time when mortality affects visitors.

The best gold in the land comes from Ghiarou, a town located eighteen days journey from the capital. All of the gold found in the mines of the empire belongs to the sovereign, but the sovereign allows the people to take gold dust. Without this precaution, the gold would become so abundant that it would lose much of its value. . . . It is claimed that the king owns a piece of gold as large as an enormous rock.

→ *From this excerpt, how much can you learn about the kingdom of Ghana? Try drawing a sketch of the region based on the description in the second paragraph.*

→ *What influence did Islam have in the empire? What aspects of the excerpt reveal the extent of Islam's acceptance?*

→ *What elements of Ghana most interested the author?*

SOURCE: Abou-Obeïd-el-Bekri, *Description de l'Afrique septentrionale*, revised and corrected edition, translated by [William] Mac Guckin de Slane (Paris: A. Maisonneuve, 1965), pp. 327–31; translated from the French by Robert Tignor.

→ *What factors created a common cultural outlook among Muslim communities in Afro-Eurasia during this era?*

Direction of trade
Trade route
Extent of the Ghana Empire, c. 1050 CE

Commodities
△ Salt
▱ Gold
⬭ Slaves
✗ Weapons
⬗ Textiles
⌒ Ivory

▨ Gold source
▲ Major salt source

MAP 9-3   ISLAM AND TRADE IN SUB-SAHARAN AFRICA, 700–1000

Islamic merchants and scholars, not Islamic armies, carried Islam into sub-Saharan Africa. Trace the trade routes in Africa, being sure to follow the correct direction of trade. According to the map key and icons, what commodities were Islamic merchants seeking below the Sahara? What were the major trade routes and the direction of trade in Africa? How did trade and commerce lead to the geographic expansion of the Islamic faith?

Primary Source

GHANA AS SEEN BY A MUSLIM OBSERVER IN THE ELEVENTH CENTURY

The following excerpt is from an eleventh-century manuscript written by a Muslim serving under the Umayyads in Spain. Its author, Abdullah Abu Ubayd al-Bakri, produced a massive general geography and history of the known world, as did many Muslim scholars of the period. This manuscript has special value because it provides information about West Africa, a region in which the Spanish rulers had great interest and into which Islam had been spreading for several centuries.

Ghana is the title of the king of the people. The name of the country is Aoukar. The ruler who governs the people at the present time—the year 460 AH (after the Hijra and 1067–68 CE)—is called Tenkamein. He came to the throne in 455 AH. His predecessor, who was named Beci, began his reign at the age of 85. He was a prince worthy of great praise as much for his personal conduct as for his zeal in the pursuit of justice and his friendship to Muslims. . . .

Ghana is composed of two towns situated in a plain. The one inhabited by Muslims is large and contains twelve mosques, in which the congregants celebrate the Friday prayer. All of these mosques have their imams, their muezzins, and their salaried readers. The city possesses judges and men of great erudition. . . . The city where the king resides is six miles away and carries the name el-Ghaba, meaning "the forest." The territory separating these two locations is covered with dwellings, constructed out of rocks and the wood of the acacia tree. The dwelling of the king consists of a chateau and several surrounding huts, all of which are enclosed by a wall-like structure. In the ruler's town, close to the royal tribunal, is a mosque where Muslims come when they have business with the ruler in order to carry out their prayers. . . . The royal interpreters are chosen from the Muslim population, as was the state treasurer and the majority of the state ministers. . . .

The opening of a royal meeting is announced by the noise of a drum, which they call a *deba*, and which is formed from a long piece of dug-out wood. Upon hearing the drumming, the inhabitants assemble. When the king's coreligionists [people of the same religion] appear before him, they genuflect and throw dust on their heads. Such is the way in which they salute their sovereign. The Muslims show their respect for the king by clapping their hands. The religion of the Negroes is paganism and fetishism. . . . The land of Ghana is not healthy and has few people. Travelers who pass through the area during the height of the agricultural season are rarely able to avoid becoming sick. When the grains are at their fullest and are ready for harvesting is the time when mortality affects visitors.

The best gold in the land comes from Ghiarou, a town located eighteen days journey from the capital. All of the gold found in the mines of the empire belongs to the sovereign, but the sovereign allows the people to take gold dust. Without this precaution, the gold would become so abundant that it would lose much of its value. . . . It is claimed that the king owns a piece of gold as large as an enormous rock.

→ *From this excerpt, how much can you learn about the kingdom of Ghana? Try drawing a sketch of the region based on the description in the second paragraph.*

→ *What influence did Islam have in the empire? What aspects of the excerpt reveal the extent of Islam's acceptance?*

→ *What elements of Ghana most interested the author?*

SOURCE: Abou-Obeïd-el-Bekri, *Description de l'Afrique septentrionale*, revised and corrected edition, translated by [William] Mac Guckin de Slane (Paris: A. Maisonneuve, 1965), pp. 327–31; translated from the French by Robert Tignor.

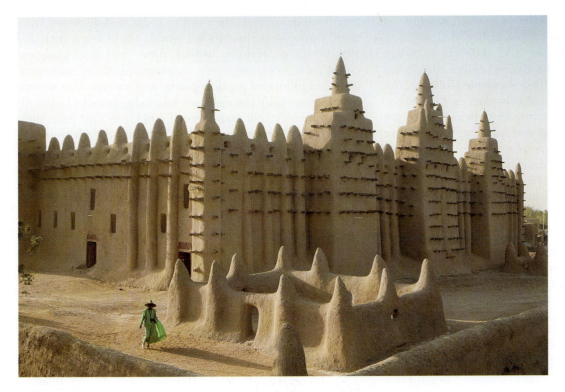

Jenne Mosque. This fabulous mosque arose in the kingdom of Mali when that kingdom was at the height of its power. The mosque speaks to the depth and importance of Islam's roots in the Malian kingdom.

OPPOSITION WITHIN ISLAM, SHIISM, AND THE RISE OF THE FATIMIDS

Islam's whirlwind rise generated internal tensions from the start. It is hardly surprising that a religion that extolled territorial conquests and created a large empire in its first decades would also spawn dissident religious movements that challenged the existing imperial structures. Muslims shared a reverence for a basic text and a single God, but little else. Religious and political divisions grew deeper as Islam spread into new corners of Afro-Eurasia. Once the charismatic prophet died, believers disagreed over who should take his place and how to preserve authority. Strains associated with selecting the first four caliphs after Muhammad's death left a legacy of protest; to this day, they represent the greatest challenge facing Islam's efforts to create a unified culture.

SUNNIS AND SHIITES The most powerful opposition movement arose in North Africa, lower Iraq, and the Iranian plateau. The questions that fueled disagreements were who should succeed the Prophet, how the succession should take place, and who should lead Islam's expansion into the wider world. The vast majority of Muslims today are **Sunnis** (from the Arabic word meaning "tradition"). They accept the political succession to the Prophet through the four rightly guided caliphs and then to the Umayyad and Abbasid dynasties was the correct one. Dissidents, like the Shiites,

contest this version. Over time the Sunnis and Shiites diverged even more than these political disputes would have indicated. Both groups had their own versions of the *sharia*, their own collections of *hadith*, and their own theological tenets.

Shiites ("members of the party of Ali"), among the earliest dissidents, felt that the proper successors should have been Ali, who had married the Prophet's daughter Fatima, and his descendants. Ali was one of the early converts to Islam and one of the band of Meccans who had migrated with the Prophet to Medina. The fourth of the rightly guided caliphs, he ruled over the Muslim community from 656 to 661 CE, dying at the hands of an assassin who struck him down as he was praying in a mosque in Kufa, Iraq. Shiites believe that Ali's descendants, whom they call *imams,* have religious and prophetic power as well as political authority—and thus should enjoy spiritual primacy. Shiism appealed to groups whom the Umayyads and Abbasids had excluded from power; it became Islam's most potent dissident force and created a permanent divide within Islam. Shiism was well established in the first century of Islam's existence.

FATIMIDS After 300 years of struggling, the Shiites finally seized power. Repressed in Iraq and Iran, Shiite activists made their way to North Africa, where they joined with dissident Berber groups to topple several rulers. In 909 CE, a Shiite religious and military leader, Abu Abdallah, overthrew the Sunni ruler there. Thus began the Fatimid regime.

After conquering Egypt in 969 CE, the Fatimids set themselves against the Abbasid caliphs of Baghdad, refusing to acknowledge their legitimacy and claiming to speak for the whole Islamic world. The Fatimid rulers established their capital in a new city that arose alongside al-Fustat, the old Umayyad capital. They called this place al-Qahira (or Cairo), "the Victorious," and promoted its beauty. Early on they founded a place of worship and learning, the al-Azhar mosque, which attracted scholars from all over Afro-Eurasia and spread Islamic learning outward; they also built other elegant mosques and centers of learning. The Fatimid regime lasted until the late twelfth century, though its rulers made little headway in persuading the Egyptian population to embrace their Shiite beliefs. Most of the population remained Sunnis.

AGRICULTURE IN THE MUSLIM WORLD

At the time Islam was spreading, the Muslim world was also experiencing significant developments in agriculture; indeed, rural bounty gave the new belief system resources to plow into its expansion.

By now, India had replaced Mesopotamia as the source of a dazzling array of new crops. Most of them originated in Southeast Asia, made their way to India, and dispersed from there throughout the Muslim world. These crops included rice, taro, sour oranges, lemons, limes, and most likely coconut palm trees, sugarcane, bananas, plantains, and mangoes. Sorghum and possibly cotton and watermelons arrived from Africa. Only the eggplant was indigenous to India. Although these staple crops spread quickly to East Asia, their westward movement was slower. Not until the Muslim conquest of Sindh in northern India in 711 CE did territories to the west fully discover the crop innovations pioneered in Southeast Asia.

India fascinated the Arabs, and they exploited its agricultural offerings to the hilt. Soon a revolution in crops and diet swept through the Muslim world. Sorghum supplanted millet and the other grains of antiquity because it was hardier, had higher yields, and required a shorter growing season. Citrus trees added flavor to the diet and provided refreshing drinks during the summer heat. Increased cotton cultivation led to a greater demand for textiles.

For over three hundred years, farmers from northwest India to Spain, Morocco, and West Africa made impressive use of the new crops. They increased agricultural output, slashed fallow periods, and grew as many as three crops on lands that formerly yielded one. (See Map 9-4.) As a result, farmers could feed larger urban communities; as cities grew, the countryside became more densely populated and even more productive.

Al-Azhar Mosque. The mosque of al-Azhar is Cairo's most important ancient mosque. Built in the tenth century by the Fatimid conquerors and rulers of Egypt, it quickly became a leading center for worship and learning, frequented by Muslim clerics and admired in Europe.

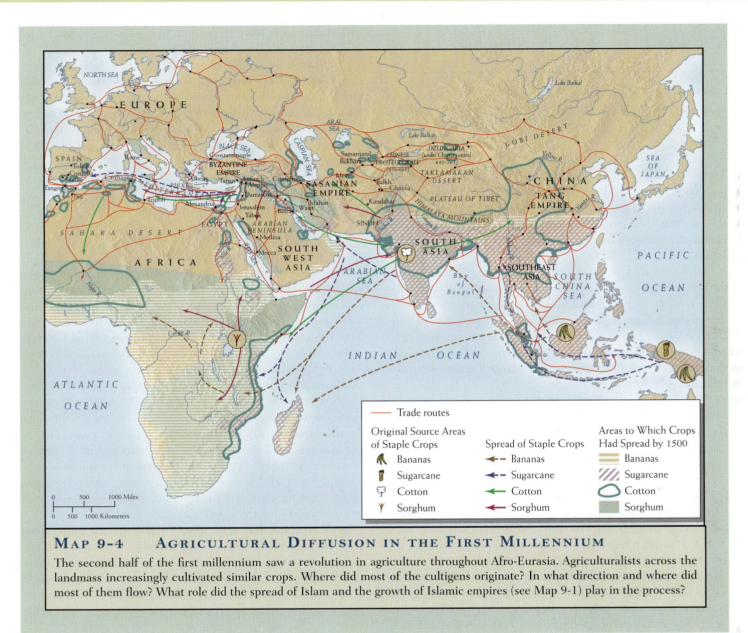

MAP 9-4   AGRICULTURAL DIFFUSION IN THE FIRST MILLENNIUM

The second half of the first millennium saw a revolution in agriculture throughout Afro-Eurasia. Agriculturalists across the landmass increasingly cultivated similar crops. Where did most of the cultigens originate? In what direction and where did most of them flow? What role did the spread of Islam and the growth of Islamic empires (see Map 9-1) play in the process?

By 1000 CE Islam, which had originated as a radical religious revolt in a small corner of the Arabian Peninsula, had grown into a vast political and religious empire. It had become the dominant political and cultural force in the middle regions of Afro-Eurasia. Like its rival in this part of the world, Christianity, it aspired to universality. But unlike Christianity, it was linked from its outset to political power. Muhammad and his early followers created an empire to facilitate the expansion of their faith while their Christian counterparts inherited an empire when Constantine embraced the new faith. A vision of a world under the jurisdiction of Muslim caliphs, adhering to the dictates of the *sharia*, drove Muslim armies, merchants, and scholars to territories thousands of miles away from Mecca and Medina. Yet the impulse to expand ran out of energy at the fringes of Islam's reach, creating political fragmentation within the Muslim world and leaving much of western Europe and China untouched. But it also had important internal consequences: Muslims were no longer the minority within their own lands, owing to the conversion of Christians, Jews, and other populations under Muslim emperors.

THE TANG STATE

> → *How did the Tang state balance its restoration of Confucian principles with the growth of new universal religions?*

The rise of the Sui and Tang empires in China, and their impact on Korea and Japan, paralleled Islam's explosion out of Arabia and its impact throughout Afro-Eurasia. Once again the landmass had two centers of power, as Islam replaced the Roman Empire in counterbalancing the power and wealth of China.

However, this bipolar world differed significantly from that of the Roman and Han empires: in the centuries since their waning, Eurasian and African worlds had drawn much closer through trade, conversion, and regular political contacts. Now the two powerhouses competed for dominance in central Asia, sharing influences and even mobile populations that weaved back and forth across porous borders between Islamic and Chinese territories.

China was both a recipient of foreign influences and a source of influences on its neighbors. Indeed, it was becoming the hub of East Asian integration. Like the Umayyads and the Abbasids, the **Tang dynasty** (608–907 CE) promoted a cosmopolitan culture. Under its rule Buddhism, medicine, and mathematics from India gave China's chief cities an international flavor. Buddhist monks from Bactria; Greeks, Armenians, and Jews from Constantinople; Muslim envoys from Samarkand and Persia; Vietnamese tributary missions from Annam; nomadic chieftains from the Siberian plains; officials and students from Korea; and monkish visitors from Japan all rubbed elbows in the streets of Chang'an and Luoyang. Ideas traveled east as well—notably to Korea and Japan, where Daoism and Buddhism made inroads. Similarly, Chinese statecraft, as expressed through the Confucian classics, struck the early Koreans and Japanese as the best model for their own state building.

AGRICULTURE IN CHINA

The agrarian transformation that swept through South Asia and the Muslim world also took East Asia by storm (see above). Indeed, China received the same crops that Islamic cultivators were carrying westward. Rice was critical. New varieties entered from the south, and groups migrating from the north (after the collapse of the Han Empire) eagerly took them up. Soon Chinese farmers became the world's most intensive wet-field rice cultivators. Early- and late-ripening seeds supported two or three plantings a year. Champa rice, introduced from central Vietnam, was especially popular for its drought resistance and rapid ripening.

Because rice needs ample water, Chinese hydraulic engineers went into the field to design water-lifting devices, which peasant farmers used to construct hillside rice paddies. They also dug more canals linking rivers and lakes (see Map 9-5) and even drained swamps, alleviating the malaria that had long troubled the region. Their efforts yielded a booming and constantly moving rice frontier.

TERRITORIAL EXPANSION UNDER THE TANG DYNASTY

After the fall of the Han, China had faced a long period of political instability (see Chapter 8). Ultimately, though, Tang rulers restored Han models of empire building. Their claims that an imperial system could outperform small states found a receptive audience in a populace fatigued by internal chaos. The Tang dynasty expanded the boundaries of the Chinese state and reestablished its dominance in East and central Asia.

A sudden change in the course of the Yellow River (not the first such environmental calamity; see Chapter 7) caused extensive flooding on the North China plain and set the stage for the emergence of the Tang dynasty. Revolts ensued as the population faced starvation. Li Yuan marched on Chang'an and took the throne for himself. He promptly established the Tang dynasty and began building a strong central government. First he increased the number of provinces and counties and expanded the bureaucracy. By doubling the number of government offices, the emperor tightened his control over individual governors. By 624 CE the initial steps of establishing the Tang dynasty were complete. But the fruits of these gains slipped into the hands of Li Yuan's ambitious son Li Shimin, who forced his father to abdicate and took the throne for himself in 627 CE.

THE ARMY AND IMPERIAL CAMPAIGNING

The Chinese empire created armies, and big armies reinforced the empire on a massive scale. An expanding Tang state required a large and professionally trained army, capable of defending far-flung frontiers and squelching rebellious populations. Toward these efforts the Tang built a military organization of aristocratic cavalry and peasant soldiers. The cavalry regularly clashed on the northern steppes with encroaching nomadic peoples, who also fought on horseback; at its height the Tang military had some 700,000 horses. At the same time, between 1 and 2 million peasant soldiers garrisoned the south and toiled on public works projects.

MAP 9-5   THE SUI DYNASTY CANALS

China, like the Islamic world, experienced a population explosion during this period. Where are the Sui dynasty canals on the map and the two areas showing population concentration? Why do you think the population concentrations are located along the canals? What other roles might the canals have played in addition to fostering population growth in this period within China?

Much like the Islamic forces, the Tang's frontier armies increasingly relied on pastoral nomadic soldiers from the Inner Eurasian steppe. Notable were the Uighurs, Turkish-speaking peoples who had moved into western China and by 750 CE constituted the empire's most potent military force. These hard-riding and hard-drinking warriors galvanized fearsome cavalries, fired longbows at distant range, and wielded steel swords and knives in hand-to-hand combat. The Tang military also pushed the state into Tibet, the Red River valley in northern Vietnam, Manchuria, and Bohai (near Korea).

By 650 CE, as Islamic armies were moving toward central Asia, the Tang were already the region's new colossus. At the empire's height, Tang armies controlled more than 4 million square miles of territory—an area as large as the entire

Islamic world in the ninth and tenth centuries. Once the Tang administrators brought South China's rich farmlands under cultivation (by draining swamps, building an intricate network of canals and channels, and connecting lakes and rivers to the rice lands), the state was able to collect taxes from roughly 10 million families, representing 57 million individuals. Most of these taxes took the form of agricultural labor, which propelled the expansion of cultivated frontiers throughout the south.

In spite of the Abbasid Empire's precocious spread, China in 750 CE was the most powerful, most advanced, and best administered empire in the world (see Map 9-6). Korea and Japan recognized its superiority in every material aspect of life. Mus-

lims were among the people who arrived at Chang'an to pay homage. Persians, Armenians, and Turks brought tribute and merchandise via the busy Silk Road or by sea, and other travelers and traders came from Southeast Asia, Korea, and Japan.

The peak of Chinese power occurred just as the Abbasids were expanding into Tang portions of central Asia. Rivalry brought these worlds together, but not peaceably. Muslim forces drove the Tang from Turkistan in 751 CE at the battle of Talas River, and their success emboldened groups such as the Sogdians and Tibetans to challenge the Tang in the west. As a result, the Tang retreated into the old heartlands along the Yellow and Yangzi rivers. They even saw their capital fall to invading Tibetans and Sogdians. Thereafter misrule, court

MAP 9-6 THE TANG STATE IN EAST ASIA, 750 CE

The Tang dynasty, at its territorial peak in 750, controlled a state that extended from central Asia to the East China Sea. What foreign areas are under Tang control? What areas were heavily influenced by Tang government and culture? How can we tell from the map that China was undergoing an economic revolution during the Tang period? How did the Tang maintain order and stability in such a large, dynamic realm?

China Trade. In this seventh-century silk painting, we see envoys from the busy Silk Road bearing tribute to gain access to the lucrative China trade.

intrigues, economic exploitation, and popular rebellions weakened the empire, but the dynasty held on for over a century more until northern invaders toppled it in 907 CE.

ORGANIZING AN EMPIRE

The Tang Empire, a worthy successor to the Han, ranks as one of China's great dynastic polities. Although its rulers emulated the Han in many ways (for example, by compiling a legal code based on the Han's), they also introduced new institutions.

CONFUCIAN ADMINISTRATORS Despite the Tang's reliance on military force, the day-to-day control of the empire required an efficient and loyal civil service. Whereas a shared spiritual commitment to Islam held together the multilingual, multiethnic, and even multireligious Islamic empire, the Tang found other ways to integrate remote territories and diverse groups. Their ingenious efforts produced an empire-wide political culture based on Confucian teachings composed in the written language of Mandarin-speaking officials and classically educated elites.

Chinese integration began at the top. Entry into the ruling group required knowledge of Confucian ideas and all of the commentaries on the Confucian classics. It also required skill in the intricate classical Chinese language, in which this literature was written. These skills were as crucial in forging a Chinese cultural and political solidarity as Islam was for the Abbasid state or Christianity was for Europe and the Byzantine Empire.

Most important in reinforcing the Tang state were the world's first fully written **civil service examinations.** These examinations, which tested sophisticated literary skills and the Confucian classics, were the only route to the top echelons of power and the ultimate means of uniting the Chinese state. Candidates for office, whom local elites recommended, gathered in the capital triennially to take qualifying exams. They had been trained since the age of three in the Classics and Histories, either by their families or in Buddhist temple schools. Most failed the grueling competition, however. Those who were successful underwent further trials to evaluate their character and determine the level of their appointments. New officials were selected from the pool of graduates on the basis of social conduct, eloquence, skill in calligraphy and mathematics, and legal knowledge. (See Primary Source: The Pressures of Maintaining Empire by Examination.) When Emperor Li Shimin observed the new officials obediently parading out of the

Tang Official. Tang officials were selected through competitive civil examinations in order to limit the power of Buddhist and Daoist clerics. This painted clay figure of a Tang official c. 717 was excavated in 1972.

THE PRESSURES OF MAINTAINING EMPIRE BY EXAMINATION

Young and old competed equally in the Tang examination halls. The rituals of success were alluring to youths, while the tortures of failure weighed heavily on older competitors still seeking an elusive degree. For all, the tensions of seeing the posted list of successful candidates—following years of preparation for young boys, and even more years of defeat for old men—were intensely personal responses to success or failure. The few who passed would look back on that day with relief and pride.

In the Southern Court they posted the list. (The Southern Court was where the Board of Rites ran the administration and accepted documents. All prescribed forms together with the stipulations for each [degree] category were usually publicized here.) The wall for hanging the list was by the eastern wall of the Southern Court. In a separate building a screen was erected which stood over ten feet tall, and it was surrounded with a fence. Before dawn they took the list from the Northern Court to the Southern Court where it was hung for display.

In the sixth year of Yuanhe [AD 811] a student at the University, Guo Dongli, broke through the thorn hedge. (The thorn hedge was below the fence. There was another outside the main gate of the Southern Court.) He then ripped up the ornamental list [*wenbang*]. It was because of this that afterwards they often came out of the gateway of the Department [of State Affairs] with a mock list. The real list was displayed a little later.

→ *Why were the stakes so high in the civil examinations? What happened to those who failed?*

→ *Was the Tang civil examination system an open system that tested talent—that is, a meritocracy?*

→ *Can you relate to the candidates' anxiety in terms of your own experiences—for example, waiting for college acceptance letters or your year-end grade point average?*

SOURCE: Wang Dingbao (870–940), quoted in Oliver J. Moore, *Rituals of Recruitment in Tang China* (Leiden: Brill, 2004), p. 175.

examination hall, he slyly noted, "The heroes of the empire are all in my pocket!" (Miyazaki, *China's Examination Hell,* 13). Overall, the civil service system gave rise in China to the perennial belief in the value of a classically trained **meritocracy** (rule by persons of talent), which lasted into modern times.

Having assumed the mandate of heaven (see Chapter 4), the Tang rulers and their supporters sought to establish a code of moral values for the whole empire. Building on Han models, they expanded the state school in the capital into an empire-wide series of select schools that accepted only fully literate candidates for the civil examinations. They also allowed the use of Daoist classics as texts for the exams, believing that the early Daoists represented an important stream of ancient wisdom. Ultimately the Tang amalgamated this range of texts, codes, and tests into a common intellectual and moral credo for the governing classes.

Although official careers were in theory open to anyone of proven talent, in practice they were closed to certain groups. Despite Empress Wu's prominence (see below), women were not permitted to serve, nor were sons of merchants, nor those who could not afford a classical education. Over time, Tang civil examinations forced aristocrats to compete with commoner southern families, whose growing wealth (from trade) and access to educational resources made them the equals of the old elites. Through examinations, this new elite eventually outdistanced the sons of the northern aristocracy in the Tang government by out-studying them.

The system also brought a few benefits to the poor by underscoring education as the primary avenue for success. Even impoverished families sought the best classical education they could afford for their sons. Although few succeeded in the civil examinations, many boys and even some girls learned the fundamentals of reading and writing. In fact, the Buddhists played a crucial role in extending education across society: as part of their charitable mission, their temple schools introduced many children to primers based on classical texts. Buddhist monks would never admit that many in their own ranks had initially hoped to become Confucian officials, but in reality quite a few entered the clergy only after not qualifying for or failing the civil examinations.

CHINA'S FEMALE EMPEROR Not all Tang power brokers were men. Women also wielded influence in the court—usually behind the scenes, but sometimes publicly. Consider Empress Wu, who dominated the court in the late seventh and early eighth centuries. She deftly exploited the examination system to check the power of aristocratic families and consolidated courtly authority by creating groups of loyal bureaucrats, who in turn preserved loyalty to the dynasty at the local level.

Born into a noble family, Wu Zhao played music and mastered the Chinese classics as a young girl. By age thirteen, because she was witty, intelligent, and beautiful, Wu was recruited to Li Shimin's court, where she became his favorite concubine. She also fell in love with his son. When Li Shimin died, his son assumed power and became the Emperor Gaozong. Wu became the new emperor's favorite concubine and gave birth to the sons he required to succeed him. As the mother of the future emperor, Wu enjoyed heightened political power. Subsequently, she took the place of Gaozong's Empress Wang by accusing her (falsely) of killing Wu's newborn daughter. Gaozong believed Wu and married her.

After Gaozong suffered a stroke, Wu became administrator of the court, a position equal to the emperor's. She created a secret police force to spy on her opposition, and she jailed or killed those who stood in her way, including Empress Wang. Upon the emperor's death Wu outmaneuvered her eldest sons, placed her youngest son in power, and named herself as his regent. Shortly thereafter she seized power in her own right as Empress Wu (r. 684–705 CE), becoming the only female ruler in Chinese history. She expanded the military and recruited her administrators from the civil examination candidates to oppose her enemies at court.

Challenging Confucian beliefs that subordinated women, Wu elevated their position. She ordered scholars to write biographies of famous women, and she empowered her mother's clan by assigning high political posts to her relatives. Later, she moved her court from Chang'an to Luoyang, where she tried to establish a new "Zhou dynasty" in imitation of the Confucian period.

Empress Wu. When she seized power in her own right as Empress Wu, Wu Zhao became the first and only female ruler in Chinese history.

Despite Wu's ruthless climb to power, her rule was relatively benign and competent. She elevated Buddhism over Daoism as the favored state religion, invited the most gifted Buddhist scholars to her capital at Luoyang, built Buddhist temples, and subsidized spectacular cave sculptures. In fact, Chinese Buddhism achieved its highest officially sponsored development in this period.

EUNUCHS Tang rulers protected themselves and their possessions, including their women, with loyal and well-compensated men. So did the Abbasids. The caliphs in Baghdad chose young male slaves as their personal guards, although males known as **eunuchs** (who were surgically castrated as youths and thus sexually impotent) also protected the harem. Similarly, Tang emperors relied on castrated males from the lower classes to protect the royal family. By the late eighth century, more than 4,500 eunuchs were fully entrenched in the Tang Empire's institutions, wielding significantly more court power than the male slaves in Baghdad.

The Chief Eunuch controlled the military. Through him, the military power of court eunuchs extended to every province and garrison station in the empire, forming an all-encompassing network. In effect, the eunuch bureaucracy mediated between the emperor and the provincial governments.

Under Emperor Xianzong (r. 806–820 CE), eunuchs acted as a third pillar of the government, working alongside the official bureaucracy and the imperial court. By establishing clear career patterns for eunuchs that paralleled those in the civil service, Xianzong sparked a striking rise in their levels of literacy and their cultural attainments. Yet by 838 CE, the delicate balance of power among throne, eunuchs, and civil officials had evaporated. Eunuchs became an unruly political force in late Tang politics, and their scheming plots equaled those of the slaves guarding the Abbasid caliph and his harem.

AN ECONOMIC REVOLUTION

In both the Abbasid caliphate and Tang China, political stability fueled remarkable economic achievements. Highlighting China's success were rising agricultural production based on an egalitarian land allotment system, an increasingly fine handicrafts industry, a diverse commodity market, and a dynamic urban life.

An earlier dynasty, the Sui, had started this economic progress by reunifying China and building canals, especially the Grand Canal linking the north and south (see again Map 9-5). The Tang continued by centering their efforts on the Grand Canal and the Yangzi River, which flows from west to east. These waterways aided communication and transport

The Tang Court. This tenth-century painting of elegant ladies of the Tang imperial court enjoying a feast and music (*left*) tells us a great deal about the aesthetic tastes of elite women in this era. It also shows the secluded "inner quarters," where court ladies passed their daily lives far from the hurly-burly of imperial politics. Castrated males, known as eunuchs (*right*), guarded the harem and protected the royal family of Tang emperors. By the late eighth century, eunuchs were fully integrated into the government and wielded a great deal of military and political power.

throughout the empire and helped raise living standards. The south grew richer, largely through the backbreaking labor of immigrants from the north. Fertile land along the Yangzi became China's new granary, and areas south of the Yangzi became its demographic center.

Chinese merchants took full advantage of the Silk Road to trade with India and the Islamic world; but when rebellions in northwest China and the rise of Islam in central Asia jeopardized the land route, the "silk road by sea" became the avenue of choice. From all over Asia and Africa, merchant ships arrived in South China ports bearing intoxicating cargoes of spices, medicines, and jewelry in exchange for Chinese silks and porcelain (see again Map 9-6). Chang'an became the richest city in the world, with its million or so residents including foreigners of every description.

In the large cities of the Yangzi delta—in some ways a nascent industrial heartland—workshops proliferated. Their reputations spread far and wide for the elegance of their wares, which included rich brocades (silk fabrics), fine paper, intricately printed woodblocks, unique iron casts, and exquisite porcelains. Art collectors especially valued Tang "tricolor pottery," fired up to 900 degrees Celsius in the Sui (1200–1300°C in Song) and decorated with brilliant hues of yellow, green, white, brown, and blue. Meanwhile, Chi-

nese artisans transformed locally grown cotton into highest-quality clothing. The textile industry prospered as painting and dyeing technology improved and superb silk products generated significant tax revenue. Such Chinese luxuries dominated the trading networks that reached Southwest Asia, Europe, and Africa via the Silk Road and the Indian Ocean.

ACCOMMODATING WORLD RELIGIONS

The early Tang emperors tolerated remarkable religious diversity, for the Confucian ideology at heart was secular. Although it posited a heaven from which the ruling dynasty claimed the authority to govern, it did not promise an afterlife or threaten nonbelievers with eternal damnation. Thus Nestorian Christianity, Zoroastrianism, and Manichaeanism (a radical Christian sect) had entered China from Persia during the time of the Sasanian Empire. Islam came later. These spiritual impulses—together with Buddhism and the indigenous teachings of Daoism and Confucianism—spread throughout the Tang Empire and at first did not conflict with state power.

THE GROWTH OF BUDDHISM Buddhism, in particular, thrived under Tang rule. In fact, many students from Korea and Japan journeyed to China in the Tang's early years to study it. Initially, Emperor Li Shimin distrusted Buddhist monks because they avoided serving the government and paying taxes. Yet after Buddhism gained acceptance as one of the "three ways" of learning—joining Daoism and Confucianism—Li endowed huge monasteries, sent emissaries to India to collect texts and relics, and commissioned Buddhist paintings and statuary. Caves along the Silk Road, such as those at Dunhuang, provided ideal venues for monks to paint the inside walls of caves where religious rites and meditation took place. Soon the caves boasted "bright" color paintings and massive statues of the Buddha and the bodhisattvas. Before long, giant carvings of the Buddha in northwestern temple sanctuaries dotted the trading routes to central Asia, and temples filled with ornate statuary offered religious refuge throughout South China.

ANTI-BUDDHIST CAMPAIGNS By the mid-ninth century, the Tang Empire contained nearly 50,000 monasteries and hundreds of thousands of Buddhist monks and nuns. (In contrast, Charlemagne's empire in France had only 700 major monasteries.) Such success by a foreign religion, in conjunction with the initial decline of the Tang dynasty, threatened China's Confucian and Daoist leaders. So they attacked Buddhism, arguing that its values conflicted with Confucian and Daoist traditions.

One of the first to attack was the scholar-official Han Yu, who represented the rising literati from the south. His Memorial of 819 protested the emperor's plan to bring a relic of the Buddha to the capital for exhibition. Striking a note that would have been inconceivable under the early Tang's cosmopolitanism, Han Yu attacked Buddhism as a foreign doctrine of barbarian peoples who were different in language, culture, and knowledge. These objections earned him exile to the southern province of Guangdong.

Yet, two decades later the state began suppressing Buddhist monasteries and confiscating their wealth, fearing that religious loyalties would undermine political ones. Increasingly intolerant Confucian scholar-administrators argued that the Buddhist monastic establishment threatened the imperial order. They accused Buddhists of undermining kinship values and traditional family relations. They claimed that members of the clergy were conspiring to destroy the state, the family, and the body.

Gradually the Tang government began challenging the power of monastic communities. Piecemeal measures against the monastic orders gave way in the 840s CE to open persecution. Emperor Wuzong, for instance, closed more than 4,600 monasteries and destroyed 40,000 temples and shrines. More than 260,000 Buddhist monks and nuns endured a forced return to secular life, after which the state parceled out monastery lands to taxpaying landlords and peasant farmers. To expunge the cultural impact of Buddhism, classically trained literati revived ancient prose styles and the teachings of Confucius and his followers. Linking classical scholarship, ancient literature, and Confucian morality, they constructed a cultural fortress that reversed the early Buddhist successes in China.

The persecution of Buddhism in this period raises two important points. First, in China, it was government (the Tang) that brought religion (the Buddhist monastic communities) under its control; in Latin Europe, in contrast, it was religion (the Christian church) that dominated government (the

One of the Four Sacred Mountains.
This monastery on Mount Song is famous because in 527 an Indian priest, Bodhidharma, arrived there to initiate the Zen school of Buddhism in China.

feudal states). Second, because the Chinese bureaucracy was steeped in the traditions of Confucianism and Daoism, it had a power base that Buddhism lacked. China's most prominent universalizing religion was thus vulnerable once Emperor Wuzong began to persecute it.

Ultimately, the Tang era represented the triumph of homegrown ideologies (Confucianism and Daoism) over universalizing religion (Buddhism). The result was persistent religious pluralism within China.

THE FALL OF TANG CHINA

China's deteriorating economic conditions in the ninth century led to peasant uprisings, some led by unsuccessful examination candidates. These revolts eventually brought down the dynasty. In the tenth century, China fragmented into regional states and entered a new era of decentralization. Even the Song dynasty that emerged in 960 CE could not overcome the disunity. Only the Mongols, invading steppe peoples, were later able to restore the glory of the Han and Tang empires.

EARLY KOREA AND JAPAN

> ⟶ *To what extent did Japanese and Korean polities imitate Tang China?*

While China was opening up to the cultures of its western regions, its own culture was reaching out to the east—to Korea and, eventually, to Japan (see Map 9-7). Being colored by Buddhism, these influences were somewhat flexible and less distinctly Chinese, although Confucianism in Japan, Korea, and Vietnam was tailored to each country's scale and needs. To comprehend Korean and Japanese history of this era, we need to explore developments that predated the Koryo kingdom of Korea and the Japanese experience of the ninth and tenth centuries.

EARLY KOREA

Scholars have documented Chinese cultural influences in Korea as early as the third century BCE. By the fourth century CE, three independent states had emerged on the peninsula. This division into the "Three Kingdoms" of Korea lasted until 668 CE, when one of these states, Silla, gained control over the entire peninsula and unified it.

UNIFICATION UNDER THE SILLA Unification enabled the Koreans to establish a government modeled on the Tang imperial state. Now Silla dispatched annual embassies to the Chinese capital and regularly sent students and monks. As a result, literary Chinese became the written language of Korean elites—not their vernacular (as Latin did among diverse populations in medieval Europe). Koreans much later in the fifteenth century devised a phonetic system for writing their own language based on simplified Chinese characters, but most official writing continued in the literary Chinese form.

In spite of Chinese influences the loyalty of most non-Chinese Koreans was to their kinship groups. These early Koreans believed that birth, not displays of learned achievement, should be the source of influence in religious and political life. Korean holy men and women (known today as shamans), who interceded with gods, demons, and ancestral spirits, remained prominent in local village life. The culture stressed small-scale agriculture for harvesting grains, fishing along the coasts, and hunting in the vast northern forests.

Silla's fortunes became entwined with the Tang's to such an extent that once the Tang declined, Silla also began to fragment. Moreover, it had never established a full-blown Tang-style government.

THE KORYO DYNASTY In 936 CE, Wang Kon, a rebel leader, absorbed Silla into the northern-based Koryo kingdom, an act that tenuously reunified the country. The Koryo dynasty (from which the country's modern name derives) began to construct a new cultural identity by enacting a bureaucratic system, which replaced the archaic tribal system that the Silla had maintained. The Koryo went beyond earlier Silla reforms and fully established Tang-style civil service examinations to select officials who would govern at court and in the provinces. Wang Kon's heirs consolidated control over the peninsula and strengthened its political and economic foundations by following the Tang's bureaucratic and land allotment systems.

During this period Korea, like Tang China itself, suffered continual harassment from northern tribes such as the Khitan. This particular group exploited the fall of the Tang dynasty to control northern Chinese lands after 907 CE, establishing themselves in what is modern-day Manchuria. Reflecting the repercussions of this troubled period, Korean artisans anxiously carved wooden printing blocks for 81,258 scriptures from the Buddhist canon as an offering to the Buddha to protect them from invading enemies—but in vain. The Korean royal family at the time was under siege, and they hoped that the woodblocks would elicit a change in fortune. The scriptures were hidden away in a single temple, and when rediscovered they represented the most comprehensive and intact version of the Buddhist canon written in the Chinese script. After being overwhelmed by the Khitan in 1010, the Koryo dynasty revived, only to be invaded by the Mongols in 1231 (see Chapter 10). Nevertheless, the dynasty managed to last until 1392.

Legend:
- ▨ Extent of Silla power, 670–935 CE
- ▨ Extent of Nara state by 600 CE
- ⊙ Capital
- • City
- ⛩ Buddhist temple
- ✺ Shinto shrine
- ▲ Holy mountain
- ▨ Bohai

MAP 9-7   BORDERLANDS: KOREA AND JAPAN, 600–1000

The Tang dynasty held great power over emerging Korean and Japanese states, although it never directly ruled either region. Based on the map, what connections do you see between Korea and Japan and the Tang Empire? To what extent did Korea and Japan adopt Tang customs during this period?

EARLY JAPAN

Like Korea, Japan also felt influences emanating from China, and it responded by thwarting and accommodating them at the same time. But Japan enjoyed added autonomy: it was an archipelago of islands, more easily separated from the main-

land although also internally more fragmented. Beginning in the Ice Age, tribal groups known as the Jomon (from 10,000 years ago to 400 BCE) and the Yayoi (400 BCE–250 CE) dominated prehistoric Japan. The early Jomon wandered into "Japan" when it was still part of the Asian mainland (see Chapter 1). Thereafter, several nomadic groups from Asia migrated to Japan via Korea. Subsequently, in the mid-third century, a warlike group also originating in Asia arrived by sea from Korea and imposed military and social power on southern Japan. These conquerors—known as the "Tomb Culture" because of their elevated burial sites—unified Japan by extolling their imperial ancestors and maintaining their social hierarchy. They also introduced a belief in the power of female shamans, who married into the imperial clans. These women became rulers of early Japanese kinship groups, combining religious and political power much like the early Korean holy men and women described above.

Chinese dynastic records describe the early Japanese, with whom imperial China had contact in this period, as a "dwarf" people who maintained a rice and fishing economy. The Japanese farmers also mastered Chinese-style sericulture: the production of raw silk by raising silkworms.

THE YAMATO EMPEROR AND THE SHINTO ORIGINS OF THE JAPANESE SACRED IDENTITY

In time, the complex aristocratic society that had developed within the Tomb Culture gave rise to a Yamato-dominated Japanese state that incorporated native Japanese as well as Korean migrants. In becoming the ruling faction, the Yamato clan elevated themselves along with their belief system, based on ancestor worship, into a national religion known as **Shinto.** (Shinto means "the way of the deities.") Shinto beliefs derived from the early Japanese groups who believed that after death a person's soul (or spirit) became a Shinto *kami*, or local deity, provided that it was nourished and purified through proper rituals and festivals. (This burial tradition continues in Japan today.) Before the imperial Yamato clan became dominant, each clan had its own ancestral deities; but after 500 CE all Japanese increasingly worshipped the Yamato ancestors. Their origins went back to the fourth-century Tomb Culture of the Yamato plain (the region now known as Nara, south of Osaka). Other regional ancestral deities later became subordinate to the Yamato deities, who claimed direct lineage from the primary Shinto deity Amaterasu, the Sun Goddess and creator of the sacred islands of Japan.

Creation Myth. Tsukioka Yoshitoshi (1839–1892) depicted Japan's creation myth in "Amaterasu Appearing from the Cave." To lure Amaterasu, the goddess of the sun, out so that light would return to the world, the other gods performed a ribald dance.

Tomb Culture. Daisenryo Kofun, in Osaka, is allegedly the tomb of Emperor Nintoku, dating from the fifth century.

PRINCE SHOTOKU AND THE TAIKA POLITICAL REFORMS After 587 CE the Soga kinship group—originally from Korea but by 500 CE a minor branch of the Yamato imperial family—became Japan's leading family and controlled the Japanese court through intermarriage. Soon, they were attributing everything that was innovative in their culture to their own Prince Shotoku (574–622 CE), a direct descendant of the Soga and thus of the Yamato imperial family as well.

Contemporary Japanese scribes claimed that Prince Shotoku, rather than Korean immigrants, introduced Buddhism to Japan and that his illustrious reign sparked Japan's rise as an exceptional island kingdom. Shotoku promoted both Buddhism and Confucianism, thus enabling Japan, like its neighbor China, to be accommodating to numerous religions. Although earlier Korean immigrants had laid the groundwork for the growth of these views, Shotoku was credited with introducing these faiths into the native religious culture, Shinto. The prince also had ties with several Buddhist temples modeled on Tang pagodas and halls; one of these, in Nara (Japan's first imperial capital), is Horyuji Temple, the oldest surviving wooden structure in the world. Its frescoes include figures derived from the art of Iran and central Asia. They are a reminder that within two centuries Buddhism had dispersed its visual culture along the full length of the Silk Road—from Afghanistan to China, and then on to Korea and the island kingdom of Japan.

Political integration under Prince Shotoku did not mean political stability, however. In 645 CE, the Nakatomi kinship group seized the throne and eliminated the Soga and their allies. Via intermarriage with the imperial clan, the Nakatomi became the new spokesmen for the Yamato tradition. Thereafter Nakatomi no Kamatari (614–669 CE) enacted a series of reforms, known as the Taika Reform, which reflected Confucian principles of government allegedly enunciated by Shotoku. These reforms enhanced the power of the ruler, no longer portrayed simply as an ancestral kinship group leader but now depicted as an exalted "emperor" (*tenno*) who ruled by the mandate of heaven, as in China, and exercised absolute authority.

MAHAYANA BUDDHISM AND THE SANCTITY OF THE JAPANESE STATE Religious influences continued to flow into Japan, contributing to spiritual pluralism while bolstering the Yamato rulers. Although Prince Shotoku and later Japanese emperors turned to Confucian models for government, they also dabbled in occult arts and Daoist purification rituals. In addition, the Taika edicts promoted Buddhism as the state religion of Japan. Although the imperial family continued to support native Shinto traditions, association with Buddhism gave the Japanese state extra status by lending it the prestige of a universal religion whose appeal stretched to Korea, China, and India.

State-sponsored spiritual diversity led native Shinto cults to formalize a creed of their own. Indeed, the introduction of Confucianism and Buddhism motivated Shinto adherents to assemble their diverse religious practices into a well-organized belief system. Shinto priests now collected ancient liturgies, and Shinto rituals (such as purification rites to ward off demons and impurities) gained recognition in the official Department of Religion.

Prince Shotoku Taishi. Shotoku was instrumental in the establishment of Buddhism in Japan, although his actual historical role was overstated. In this hanging scroll painting from the early fourteenth century (*left*), he is idealized as a sixteen-year-old son, holding an incense censer and praying for the recovery of his sick father, the Emperor Yomei (r. 585–587 CE). The main hall of the Horyuji Temple in Nara, Japan (*right*).

Although the Japanese welcomed elements of the Buddhist faith, they did not fully accept the traditional Buddhist view that the state was merely a vehicle to propagate moral and social justice for the ruler and his subjects. Instead, the Japanese saw their emperor (the embodiment of the state) as an object of worship, a sacred ruler, one in a line of luminous Shinto gods, a supreme *kami*—a divine force in his own right. Thus, Buddhism as imported from China and Korea changed in Japan to serve the interests of the state (much as Christianity served the interests of European monarchs, and Islam served the Islamic dynasties).

THE CHRISTIAN WEST

> → *How did two Christianities come to exist in western Afro-Eurasia?*

Seen from the Mediterranean and the Islamic worlds, Europe by now seemed little more than a warrior-dominated realm. In the fifth century, the mighty Roman military machine gave way to a multitude of warrior leaders whose principal allegiances were local affiliations. Yet major innovations were under way. The leading force was Christianity, and its universalizing agents were missionaries and monks. The political ideal of the Roman Empire cast a vast shadow over the western Europeans, but the inheritor of the mantle of Rome was a spiritual institution—the Roman Catholic Church—whose powerful head, the pope, was based in Rome (see Map 9-8.)

CHARLEMAGNE'S FLEDGLING EMPIRE

In 802 CE, Harun al-Rashid, the ruler of Baghdad, sent the gift of an elephant to Charlemagne, the king of the Franks, in northern Europe. The elephant caused a sensation among the Franks, who saw the gift as an acknowledgment of Charlemagne's power. In fact, Harun often sent rare beasts to distant rulers as a gracious reminder of his own formidable power. In his eyes, Charlemagne's "empire" was a minor principality.

This was an empire that Charlemagne ruled for over forty years, often traveling 2,000 miles a year on campaigns of plunder and conquest. He ultimately controlled much of western Europe, which was a significant accomplishment; yet compared with the Islamic world's rulers, he was a political lightweight. His empire had a population of less than 15 million; he rarely commanded armies larger than 5,000; and he had a rudimentary tax system. At a time when the palace quarters of the caliph at Baghdad covered nearly 250 acres,

Charlemagne's Palace and Chapel. Though not large by Byzantine or Islamic standards, Charlemagne's palace and chapel were heavy with symbolic meaning. A royal hall for banqueting in Frankish, "barbarian" style was linked by a covered walkway to the imperial domed chapel, which was meant to look like a miniature version of the Hagia Sophia of Constantinople. Outside the chapel was a courtyard, like that outside the shrine of Saint Peter at Rome.

Charlemagne's palace at Aachen was merely 330 by 655 feet. Baghdad itself was almost 40 square miles in area, whereas there was no "town" outside the palace at Aachen. It was little more than a large country house set in open countryside, close to the Ardennes woods where Charlemagne and his Franks loved to hunt wild boar on horseback.

He and his men were representatives of the warrior class that dominated post-Roman western Europe. For a time, Roman rule had imposed an alien way of life in this rough world. After that empire faded, however, war became once again the duty and joy of the aristocrat. Buoyed up by their chieftains' mead—a heavy beer made with honey, "yellow, sweet and ensnaring"—young men eagerly followed their lords into battle "among the war horses and the blood-stained armor" (Aneirin, *Y Gododdin*, ll. 102, 840).

And although the Franks vigorously engaged in trade, that trade was based on war. In fact, Europe's principal export at this time was Europeans, and the massive sale of prisoners of war financed the Frankish empire. From Venice, which grew rich from its role as middleman, captives were sent as slaves across the sea to Alexandria, Tunis, and southern Spain. The main victims of this trade were Slavic-speaking peoples, tribal hunters and cultivators from eastern Europe. Their long oppression is preserved in the English language, for the medieval Latin *sclavus* ("Slavic") replaced the classical Latin *servus* to denote "slave"; *servus*, by contrast, applied to those

MAP 9-8   CHRISTENDOM, 600–1000 CE

The end of the first millennium saw much of Europe divided between two versions of Christianity, each with different traditions. Locate Rome and Constantinople on the map, the two seats of power in Christianity. According to the map, what were the two major regions where Christianity held sway? In what directions did Latin Christianity and Orthodox Christianity spread? Why do you suppose the Catholic Church based in Rome was successful in expanding to the west, but not to the east? Why do you suppose Orthodox Christianity based in Constantinople expanded into eastern Europe, but not into the west?

who stayed at home and became "serfs"—peasants tied for life to the estates of the aristocracy.

Yet this seemingly uncivilized and inhospitable zone offered fertile ground for Christianity to sink down roots. Although its worldwide expansion did not occur for centuries, its spiritual conquest of European peoples established institutions and fired enthusiasms that would later drive believers to carry its message to faraway lands.

A CHRISTIANITY FOR THE NORTH

Charlemagne's empire was unquestionably primitive when compared with the Islamic empire or the Tang Empire of China. What made it significant was its location. Far removed from the old centers of high culture, it was a polity of the borderlands. It also featured an expansionist Christianity that drew energy from its rough frontier mentality. Indeed, Christianity now entered a world profoundly different from the Mediterranean cities in which it had taken form.

AUGUSTINE AND THE UNIVERSAL CATHOLIC CHURCH Christians of the west felt that theirs was the one truly universal religion. (See Primary Source: Christendom on the Edge: A View of Empire in Ireland.) Their goal was to bring rival groups into a single "catholic" church that was replacing a political unity lost in western Europe when the Roman Empire fell.

As far back as 410 CE, reacting to the Goths' sack of Rome, the Christian bishop Augustine of Hippo (a seaport in modern Algeria) had laid down the outlines of this belief. His book *The City of God* assured contemporary Christians that the barbarian takeover happening around them was not the end of the world. The "city of God" would take earthly shape in the form of the Catholic Church, and the Catholic Church was not just for Romans—it was for all times and for all peoples, "in a wide world which has always been inhabited by many differing peoples, that have so many different customs and languages, so many different forms of organization and so many languages, and who have had so many different religions" (Augustine, *City of God*, 14.1). Only one organization would bring them all to paradise: the Catholic Church.

Several developments gave rise to this attitude. First, the arrival of Christianity in northern Europe had provoked a cultural revolution. Preliterate societies now encountered a sacred text—the Bible—in a language that seemed utterly strange. Latin had become a sacred language, and books themselves were vehicles of the holy. The bound codex (see Chapter 8), which had replaced the clumsy scroll, was still a messy object. It had no divisions between words, no punctuation, no paragraphs, no chapter headings. Readers who knew Latin as a spoken language could understand the script. But Irishmen, Saxons, and Franks could not, for they had never spoken Latin. Hence the care lavished in the newly Christian north on the Latin scriptures. The few parchment texts that circulated there were carefully prepared with words separated, sentences correctly punctuated and introduced by uppercase letters, and chapter headings provided. They were far more like this textbook than anything available to Romans at the height of the empire.

Second, those who produced the Bibles were starkly different from ordinary men and women. They were monks and nuns. **Monasticism** had originated in Egypt, but it suited the missionary tendencies of Christianity in northern Europe particularly well. (The root of "monastic" and "monk" is the Greek *monos*, "alone": a man or a woman who chose to live alone, without the support of marriage or family.) Monasticism placed small groups of men and women in the middle of societies with which they had nothing in common. It appealed to a deep sense that the very men and women who had little in common with "normal" people were best suited to mediate between believers and God. Laypersons (common believers, not clergy) gave gifts to the monasteries and offered them protection. In return, they gained the prayers of monks and nuns and the reassurance that although they themselves were warriors and men of blood, the monks' and nuns' intercessions would keep them from going to hell.

Celtic Bible. Unlike the simple codex of early Christian times, the Bible came to be presented in Ireland and elsewhere in the northern world as a magical book. Its pages were filled with mysterious, intricate patterns, which imitated on parchment the jewelry and treasure for which early medieval warlords yearned.

CHRISTENDOM ON THE EDGE: A VIEW OF EMPIRE IN IRELAND

A young Christian Briton of Roman citizenship who lived near Hadrian's Wall experienced the pull of Christianity around 400. Captured by Irish slave raiders as a teenager, Patricius spent six years herding pigs on the Atlantic coast of Mayo. He escaped but years later returned in order to convert his former captors to Christianity. He believed that in making the fierce Irish Christians, he also made them "Romans." He thus brought Christianity to the Atlantic edge of the known world. Patricius is remembered today as Saint Patrick.

16 But after I reached Ireland, well, I pastured the flocks every day. . . . I would even stay in the forests and on the mountain and would wake to pray before dawn in all weathers, snow, frost, rain. . . .

17 And it was in fact there that one night while asleep I heard a voice saying to me: 'You do well to fast, since you will soon be going to your home country;' and again, very shortly after, I heard this prophecy: 'See, your ship is ready.' And it was not near at hand but was perhaps two hundred miles away, and I had never been there and did not know a living soul there. And then I soon ran away and abandoned the man with whom I had been for six years . . . till I reached the ship.

23 And again a few years later I was in Britain with my kinsfolk. . . . And it was there that I saw one night in a vision a man coming as it were from Ireland . . . with countless letters, and he gave me one of them, and I read the heading of the letter, 'The Voice of the Irish,' and as I read these opening words aloud, I imagined at that very instant that I heard the voice of those who were beside the forest of Foclut which is near the western sea; and thus they cried, as though with one voice: 'We beg you, holy boy, to come and walk again among us.'

→ *What does this passage reveal about life in the Celtic worlds?*

→ *How many voices or visions does Patricius experience in this passage? What other religious figure have you read about in this chapter who had a vision or a revelation?*

→ *Based on your reading, how do St. Patrick's spiritual experiences compare to those of rulers and priests in the older Christian communities of Rome and Constantinople?*

SOURCE: *St. Patrick: His Writings and Muirchu's Life*, edited and translated by A. B. E. Hood (London: Phillimore, 1978), pp. 41, 44–46, 50.

MONKS, NUNS, AND POPES With the spread of monasticism, the Christianity of the north took a decisive turn. In Muslim (as in Jewish) societies, religious leaders emphasized what they had in common with those around them: many Islamic scholars, theologians, and mystics were married men just like the public, even merchants and courtiers. In the Christian West, the opposite was true: warrior societies honored small groups of men and women (the monks and nuns) who were utterly unlike themselves: unmarried, unfit for warfare, and intensely literate in an incomprehensible tongue. Even their hair looked different. Unlike warriors, these men were close-shaven; by contrast, the Orthodox clergy of the eastern Roman empire grew long, silvery beards (signifying wisdom and maturity; not, as in the west, the warrior's masculine strength). Catholic monks and priests shaved their heads as well.

The Catholic Church of northern Europe owed its missionary zeal to the same principles that explained the spread of Buddhism: it was a religion of monks, whose communities represented an otherworldly alternative to the warrior societies of the time. By 800 CE, most regions of northern Europe held great monasteries, many of which were far larger than the local villages. Supported by thousands of serfs donated by kings and local warlords, the monasteries became powerhouses of prayer that kept the regions safe.

Northern Christianity also gained new ties to an old center: the city of Rome. The Christian bishop of Rome had always enjoyed much prestige. But being only one bishop among many, he often took second place to his peers in Carthage, Alexandria, Antioch, and Constantinople. Though people spoke of him with respect as *papa* ("the grand old man"), many others shared that title.

Monasticism. The great monasteries of the age of Charlemagne, such as the St. Gallen Monastery (*left*), were like Roman legionary settlements. Placed on the frontiers of Germany, they were vast, stone buildings, around which entire towns would gather. Their libraries, the largest in Europe, were filled with parchment volumes, carefully written out and often lavishly decorated in a "northern," Celtic style. Monasticism was also about the lonely search for God at the very end of the world, which took place in these Irish monasteries (*right*) on the Atlantic coast. The cells, made of loose stones piled in round domes, are called "beehives."

By 800 CE, this picture had changed. As believers looked down from the distant north, they saw only one *papa* left in western Europe: Rome's pope. The papacy as we know it arose because of the fervor with which the Catholic Church of western Europe united behind one symbolic center, represented by the popes at Rome and the desire of new Christians in northern borderlands to find a religious leader for their hopes.

Charlemagne recognized this desire very well. In 800 CE, he went out of his way to celebrate Christmas Day by visiting the shrine of Saint Peter at Rome. There, Pope Leo III acclaimed him as the new "emperor" of the west. The ceremony ratified the aspirations of an age. A "modern" Rome—inhabited by popes, famous for shrines of the martyrs, and protected by a "modern" Christian monarch from the north—was what his subjects wanted.

THE AGE OF THE VIKINGS

Harun's elephant died in 813 CE, one year before Charlemagne himself. The elephant's death was noteworthy because the Franks viewed it as an omen of coming disasters. The great beast keeled over when his handlers marched him out to confront a Viking army from Denmark. In the next half-century, the Vikings from Scandinavia exposed the weakness of Charlemagne's self-confident regime. His empire of bor-derland peoples met its match on the widest border of all: that between the European landmass and the mighty Atlantic (see Map 9-9).

The Vikings' motives were announced in their name, which derives from the Old Norse *vik*, "to be on the warpath." The **Vikings** sought to loot the now-wealthy Franks and replace them as the dominant warrior class of northern Europe. It was their turn to extract plunder and to sell droves of slaves across the water. They succeeded because of a deadly technological advantage: ships of unparalleled sophistication, developed by Scandinavian sailors in the Baltic Sea and the long fjords of Norway. Light and agile, with a shallow draft, they could penetrate far up the rivers of northern Europe and even be carried overland from one river system to another. Under sail, the same boats could tackle open water and cross the unexplored wastes of the North Atlantic.

In the ninth century, the Vikings set their ships on both courses. They emptied northern Europe of its treasure, sacking the great monasteries along the coasts of Ireland and Britain and overlooking the Rhine and the Seine—rivers that led into the heart of Charlemagne's empire. At the same time, Norwegian adventurers colonized the uninhabited island of Iceland, and then Greenland. By 982 CE, they had even reached the New World and established a settlement at L'Anse aux Meadows on the Labrador coast. Viking goods have been found as far west as the Inuit settlements of Baffin Island to

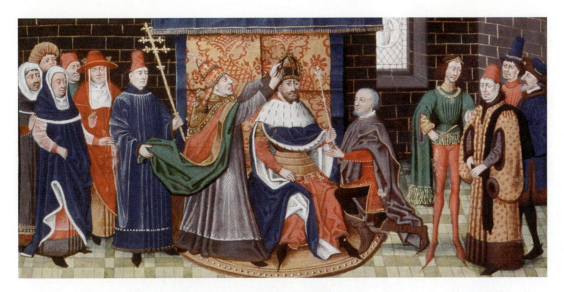

The Coronation of Charlemagne. This is how the coronation of Charlemagne at Rome in 800 CE was remembered in medieval western Europe. This painting stresses the fact that it was the pope who placed the crown on Charlemagne's head, thereby claiming him as a ruler set up by the Catholic Church for the Catholic Church. But in 800 contemporaries saw the pope as recognizing the fact that Charlemagne had already deserved to be emperor. The rise of the papacy to greater prominence and power in later medieval Europe caused this significant "re-remembering" of the event.

the north of Hudson Bay, carried there along trading routes by Native Americans.

The consequences of this spectacular reach across the ocean to America were short-lived, but the penetration of eastern Europe had lasting effects. Supremely well equipped to traverse long river systems, the Vikings sailed east along the Baltic and then turned south, edging up the rivers that

Oseberg Ship. The Viking ship was a triumph of design. It could be rowed up the great rivers of Europe, and, at the same time, its sail could take it across the Atlantic.

crossed the watershed of central Russia. Here the Dnieper, the Don, and the Volga begin to flow south into the Black Sea and the Caspian. By opening this link between the Baltic and what is now Kiev in modern Ukraine, the Vikings created an avenue of commerce that linked Scandinavia and the Baltic directly to Constantinople and Baghdad. And they added yet more slaves: Muslim geographers bluntly called this route "The Highway of the Slaves."

THE SURVIVAL OF THE CHRISTIAN EMPIRE OF THE EAST

On reaching the Black Sea, the Vikings made straight for Constantinople. In 860 CE, more than 200 Viking long ships gathered ominously in the straits of the Bosporus, beneath the walls of Constantinople. What they found was not Charlemagne's rustic Aachen, but a proud city with a population exceeding 100,000 surrounded by well-engineered late Roman walls.

The Vikings had come up against a state hardened by battle. For two centuries the empire of "East Rome," centered on Constantinople, had held Islamic armies at bay. From 640 to 840 CE they faced almost yearly campaigns launched by the Islamic empire of Damascus and Baghdad, powerhouses that grew to be ten times greater than their own. For years on end, Muslim armies and navies came within striking distance of Constantinople. Each time they failed, outmaneuvered by highly professional generals and blocked by a skillfully

MAP 9-9   THE AGE OF VIKINGS AND THE SLAVE TRADE, 800–1000

Vikings from Scandinavia dramatically altered the history of Christendom. In what directions did the Vikings carry out their voyages, trade routes, and raids? What were the geographic limits of the Viking explorations in each direction? In what direction did the slave trade move, and what role did the Vikings and the Holy Roman emperors play in expanding the slave trade?

constructed line of fortresses that controlled the roads across Anatolia. The Christian empire of East Rome fought the caliphs of Baghdad to a draw. The Viking fleet was even less well suited to assault Constantinople, as the empire of "East Rome" had a deadly technological advantage in naval warfare: Greek fire, a combination of petroleum and potassium that, when sprayed from siphons, would explode in a great sheet of flame on the water. A previous emperor had used it to destroy the Muslim fleet as it lay at anchor within sight of Constantinople. Now, a century and a half later, the experience and weaponry of East Rome were too much for the Vikings, and their raid was a spectacular failure.

GREEK ORTHODOX CHRISTIANITY   In the long run, the sense of having outlasted so many military emergencies bolstered the morale of East Roman Christianity and led to its unexpected flowering. Not just Constantinople but Justinian's

glorious church, the Hagia Sophia—its heart—had survived. That great building and the solemn Greek liturgy that reverberated within its domed spaces might not impress Catholic Franks, but upon seeing it the Scandinavian adventurers were awestruck. Here was the central church of a Christian empire that for half a millennium had represented all that was most venerable in the Christian tradition. In the tenth century, as Charlemagne's empire collapsed in western Europe, large areas of eastern Europe became Greek Orthodox, not Catholic. As a result, Greek Christianity gained a spiritual empire in Southwest Asia.

The conversion of Russian peoples and Balkan Slavs to Greek Orthodox Christianity was a complex process. It reflected a deep admiration for Constantinople on the part of Russians, Bulgarians, and other Slav princes. It was an admiration as intense as that of any Western Catholic for the Roman popes. This admiration amounted to awe, as shown by the famous story of the conversion to Greek Christianity of the rulers of Kiev (descendants of Vikings):

> The envoys reported[,] . . . "We went among the Germans [the Catholic Franks] and we saw them performing many ceremonies in their churches; but we beheld no glory there. Then we went to Greece [in fact, to Constantinople and Hagia Sophia], and the Greeks led us to the edifices where they worship their God, and we knew not whether we were in heaven or on earth. For on earth there is no such splendor or such beauty, and we are at a loss to describe it. . . . [W]e can not forget that beauty. (Cross and Sherbowitz-Westor, *The Russian Primary Chronicle*, 111)

By the year 1000, there were two Christianities: the new and confident "borderland" **Roman Catholicism** of western Europe, and an ancient **Greek Orthodoxy,** protected against extinction by the iron framework of a "Roman" state inherited from Constantine and Justinian. Together both strands of the faith constituted the realm of **Christendom:** the entire portion of the world in which Christianity prevailed. Western Catholics believed that their church was destined to expand everywhere. East Romans were less euphoric but more tenacious. They believed that their church would forever survive the regular ravages of invasion. It was a significant difference in attitude and neither side liked the other. East Romans considered the Franks barbarous and grasping; Western Catholics contemptuously called the East Romans "Greeks" and condemned them for their "Byzantine" cunning.

Thus, like Islam, the Christian world was divided. But its differences were not about the basic tenets of the faith, like those of Shiite and Sunni Islam. They were differences in heritage, customs, and levels of civilization. At that time, the orthodox world was considerably more ancient and more cultured than the world of the Catholic west. And it dealt with Islam differently. At Constantinople, eastern Christianity held off Muslim forces that constantly threatened the integrity of the great city and its Christian hinterlands. In the west, by contrast, Muslim expansionism reached all the way to the Iberian Peninsula. Western Christendom, led by the Roman papacy, did not feel the same intimidation from Islam. It set about spreading Christianity to pagan tribes in the north, and it began to contemplate retaking lands from the Muslims.

The period 600–1000 CE saw heightened movement across cultural boundaries as well as an insistence on the distinctiveness of individual societies. Commodities, technological innovations, ideas, merchants, adventurers, and scholars traveled from one end of Afro-Eurasia to the other, and up and down coastal Africa. Spreading religion into new frontiers accompanied this mercantile activity. The proximity of the period's two powerhouses—Abbasid Islam and Tang China—facilitated the dynamic movement.

Jelling Stone. Carved on the side of this great stone, Christ appears to be almost swallowed up in an intricate pattern of lines. For the Vikings, complicated interweaving like serpents or twisted gold jewelry was a sign of majesty: hence, in this, the first Christian monument in Denmark, Christ is part of an ancient pattern of carving, which brought good luck and victory to the king.

CONCLUSION

Despite the intermixing, new political and cultural boundaries were developing that would split this landmass in ways it could never have imagined. The most important dividing force was Islam, which challenged and slowed the spread of Christianity. As a consequence, Afro-Eurasia's major cultural zones began to compete in terms of religious and cultural doctrines. The Islamic Abbasid Empire pushed back the borders of the Tang Empire. But the conflict grew particularly intense between the Islamic and Christian worlds, where the clash involved faith as well as frontiers.

The Tang Empire revived Confucianism, insisting on its political and moral primacy as the foundation of a new imperial order, and it embraced the classical written language as another unifying element. By doing so the Tang counteracted universalizing foreign religions—notably Buddhism but also Islam—spreading into the Chinese state. The same adaptive strategies influenced new systems on the Korean peninsula and in Japan.

In some circumstances, faith followed empire and relied on rulers' support or tolerance to spread the word. This was the case especially in East Asia. At the opposite extreme, empire followed faith—as in the case of Islam, whose believers endeavored to spread their empire in every conceivable direction. The Islamic empire and its successors represented a new force: expanding political power backed by one God whose instructions were to spread his message. In the worlds of Christianity, a common faith absorbed elements of a common culture (shared books, a language for learned classes). But in the west, political rulers never overcame inhabitants' intense allegiance to local authority.

While universalizing religions expanded and common cultures grew, debate raged within each religion over foundational principles. In spite of the diffusion of basic texts in "official" languages, variations of Christianity, Islam, and Buddhism proliferated as each belief system spread. The period demonstrated that religion, reinforced by prosperity and imperial resources, could bring peoples together in unprecedented ways. But it could also, as the next chapter will illustrate, drive them apart in bloodcurdling confrontations.

Review and research materials are available at StudySpace: Ⓢ WWNORTON.COM/STUDYSPACE

KEY TERMS

caliphate (p. 327)
Christendom (p. 359)
civil service examinations (p. 343)
eunuchs (p. 345)
Greek Orthodoxy (p. 359)
Islam (p. 325)
jihad (p. 326)
meritocracy (p. 344)
monasticism (p. 354)

Muhammad (p. 324)
Quran (p. 324)
Roman Catholicism (p. 359)
sharia (p. 327)
Shiites (p. 337)
Shinto (p. 350)
Sunnis (p. 337)
Tang dynasty (p. 340)
ulama (p. 327)
Vikings (p. 356)

Chronology

	MAJOR TRENDS	200 CE	300 CE	400 CE	500 CE
THE ISLAMIC WORLD	Afro-Eurasian agricultural revolution begins				
EAST ASIA			3rd century–668 CE Three Kingdoms dominate Korea		500 Yamato clan becomes dominant in Japan ◆
EUROPE					

STUDY QUESTIONS

1. Analyze the impact of the spread of Islam on Afro-Asian societies. How did the large Islamic empire shape the movement of peoples, ideas, innovations, and commodities across the vast landmass?

2. Describe the process through which an expanding Islam fostered an agricultural revolution. What crops and cultivation techniques were involved?

3. Compare and contrast the spread of Islam, Christianity, and Buddhism between 600 and 1000. What was the geographic range of each religious community? Through which methods did each religion gain new converts?

4. Explain the origins and basic concepts of Islam. How similar to and different from other religions that began in Southwest Asia—such as Judaism, Christianity, and Zoroastrianism—was this new religious outlook?

5. Analyze the successes and failures of Islamic leaders in creating one large empire to govern Islamic communities. What opponents challenged this goal?

6. Describe the Tang dynasty's attempts to restore political unity to East Asia. How did Tang leaders react to the growth of universal religions within their realm?

7. Describe the state structure that emerged in Korea and Japan during this era. How did other developments in Afro-Eurasia, such as the spread of universal religions, shape these new states?

8. Compare and contrast Christian communities in western Europe to those in eastern Europe and the Byzantine Empire. What factors contributed to each region's distinctiveness?

9. Analyze the Vikings' impact on world history during this era. How did they shape developments in the Christian world especially?

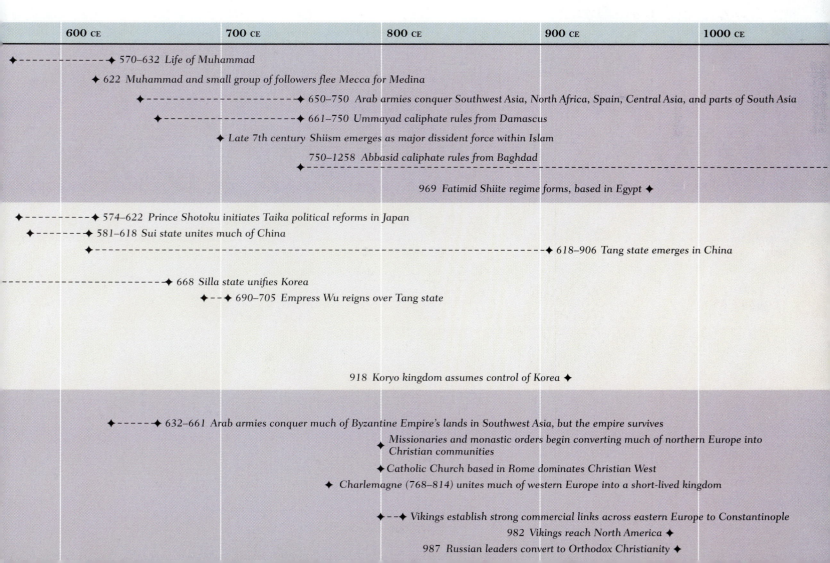

| 600 CE | 700 CE | 800 CE | 900 CE | 1000 CE |

570–632 Life of Muhammad

622 Muhammad and small group of followers flee Mecca for Medina

650–750 Arab armies conquer Southwest Asia, North Africa, Spain, Central Asia, and parts of South Asia

661–750 Ummayad caliphate rules from Damascus

Late 7th century Shiism emerges as major dissident force within Islam

750–1258 Abbasid caliphate rules from Baghdad

969 Fatimid Shiite regime forms, based in Egypt

574–622 Prince Shotoku initiates Taika political reforms in Japan

581–618 Sui state unites much of China

618–906 Tang state emerges in China

668 Silla state unifies Korea

690–705 Empress Wu reigns over Tang state

918 Koryo kingdom assumes control of Korea

632–661 Arab armies conquer much of Byzantine Empire's lands in Southwest Asia, but the empire survives

Missionaries and monastic orders begin converting much of northern Europe into Christian communities

Catholic Church based in Rome dominates Christian West

Charlemagne (768–814) unites much of western Europe into a short-lived kingdom

Vikings establish strong commercial links across eastern Europe to Constantinople

982 Vikings reach North America

987 Russian leaders convert to Orthodox Christianity

Chapter

10

BECOMING "THE WORLD,"
1000–1300 CE

*I*n the late 1270s two Christian monks, Bar Sāwmā and Markōs, voyaged into the heart of Islam. They were not Europeans. They were Uighurs, a Turkish people of central Asia, many of whom had converted to Christianity centuries earlier. Sent by the mighty Mongol ruler Kubilai Khan as he prepared to become the first emperor of China's Yuan dynasty, the monks were supposed to worship at the temple in Jerusalem. But the Great Khan also had political ambitions. He was eager to conquer Jerusalem, held by the Muslims. Accordingly, he dispatched the monks as agents to make alliances with Christian kings in the area and to gather intelligence about his potential enemy in Palestine.

By 1280, conflict and conquest had transformed many parts of the world. But friction was simply one manifestation of cultures brushing up against one another. More important was trade. Indeed, Bar Sāwmā and Markōs lingered at the magnificent trading hub of Kashgar in far western China, where caravan routes converged in a market for jade, exotic spices, and precious silks. Later, at Baghdad, the monks parted ways. Bar Sāwmā visited

363

Constantinople (where the king gave him gold and silver), Rome (where he met with the pope at the shrine of Saint Peter), and Paris (where he saw that city's vibrant university) before deciding to return to China, where the Christians of the east awaited his reports. In the end, neither monk ever returned. Yet their voyages exemplified the crisscrossing of people, money, and goods along the trade routes and sea-lanes that connected the world's regions. For just as religious conflict was a hallmark of this age, so was a surge in trade, migration, and global exchange.

The period brought to a climax many centuries of human development, and it ushered in a new, very long cycle of cultural interaction from which emerge three interrelated themes. First, trade was shifting from land-based routes to sea-based routes. Coastal trading cities began to dramatically expand. Second, intensified trade and linguistic and religious integration generated the world's four major cultural "spheres," whose inhabitants were linked by shared institutions and beliefs: China, India, Islam, and Europe. Not all cultures turned into "spheres," though. In the Americas and sub-Saharan Africa there was not the same impulse to integrate regions, which remained more fragmented but thrived nonetheless. Third, the rise of the Mongol Empire represented the peak in the long history of ties and tensions between settled and mobile peoples. From China to Persia and as far as eastern Europe, the Mongols ruled over much land in the world's major cultural spheres.

COMMERCIAL CONNECTIONS

> → *What factors led to the explosion of global trading between 1000 and 1300?*

REVOLUTIONS AT SEA

By the tenth century, sea routes were eclipsing land networks for long-distance trade. Improved navigational aids, refinements in shipbuilding, better mapmaking, and new legal arrangements and accounting practices made shipping easier and slashed the costs of seaborne trade. The numbers testify to the power of the maritime revolution: while a porter could carry about 10 pounds over long distances, and animal-drawn wagons could move 100 pounds of goods, the Arab dhows plying the Indian Ocean were capable of transporting up to 5 tons of cargo. (**Dhows** are ships with triangle-shaped sails, called lateens, that maximize the monsoon trade winds on the Arabian Sea and the Indian Ocean.) As a result some coastal ports, like Mogadishu in eastern Africa, became vast transshipment centers for a thriving trade across the Indian Ocean.

A new navigational instrument spurred this boom: the needle compass. This Chinese invention initially identified prom-

Focus Questions

ⓢ WWNORTON.COM/STUDYSPACE

- → *What factors led to the explosion of global trading between 1000 and 1300?*
- → *How did trade and migration affect sub-Saharan Africa between 1000 and 1300?*
- → *How did trade, conversion, and migration affect the Islamic world between 1000 and 1300?*
- → *In what ways did India remain a cultural mosaic?*
- → *What transformations in communication, education, and commerce promoted a distinct Chinese identity during this era?*
- → *How were Southeast Asia, Japan, and Korea influenced by sustained contact with other regions?*
- → *How did Christianity produce a distinct identity among the diverse peoples of Europe?*
- → *Where did societies in the Americas demonstrate strong commercial expansionist impulses?*
- → *How did Mongol conquests affect cross-cultural contacts and regional development in Afro-Eurasia?*

ising locations for houses and tombs, but eleventh-century sailors from Canton used it to find their way on the high seas. The device spread rapidly. Not only did it allow sailing under cloudy skies, but it also improved mapmaking. And it made all the oceans, including the Atlantic, easier to navigate.

Now shipping became less dangerous. Navigators relied on lateen-rigged dhows between the Indian Ocean and the Red Sea, heavy junks in the South China seas, and Atlantic "cogs," which linked Genoa to locations as distant as the Azores and Iceland. They also enjoyed the protection of political authorities, such as the Song dynasts in China, in guiding the trading fleets in and out of harbors. The Fatimid caliphate in Egypt, for instance, profited from maritime trade and defended merchant fleets from pirates. Armed convoys of ships escorted commercial fleets in a system called *karim* (a loose confederation of shippers banding together to protect convoys) that regularized the ocean traffic. The system soon spread to North Africa and southern Spain. Most *karimi* firms were family-based, and they sent young men of the family, sometimes servants or slaves, to work in India. Housewives in Cairo could expect gifts from their husbands to arrive with the *karimi* fleet.

Changes in navigation ushered in the demise of overland routes. Silk Road merchants eventually gave up using camel trains, caravansaries (inns for travelers), and oasis hubs as they switched to the sea-lanes. The shift took centuries, but overland routes and camels were no match for multiple-masted cargo ships.

Dhow. This modern dhow in the harbor of Zanzibar displays the characteristic triangle sail. The triangle sail can make good use of the trade monsoon and thus has guided dhows on the Arabian Sea since ancient times.

COMMERCIAL CONTACTS

The opening of the sea-lanes also tapped into changes occurring in world agriculture (see Map 10-1). By 1000 CE, major innovations in irrigation techniques, carried out over many centuries and in numerous locations, had yielded enormous returns. New strains of cereals—and in the Americas, the refinement of maize—led to grain cultivation in vast areas that had been too cold and arid to sustain them previously. Clover, alfalfa, and other newly domesticated grasses became fodder for healthier, stronger, and fatter animals. Agriculture pushed into new regions, buoying population growth and surpluses that now could be shipped over great distances.

GLOBAL COMMERCIAL HUBS

Long-distance trade spawned the growth of commercial cities. These entrepôts became cosmopolitan nerve centers of an increasingly integrated world. (**Entrepôts** are transshipment centers, located between borders or in ports, where traders exchange commodities and replenish supplies.) Beginning in the late tenth century, four places became major anchorages of the maritime trade: in the west, the Egyptian port cities of Alexandria and Cairo; in the east, the Chinese city of Quanzhou; in the Malaysian Archipelago, the city of Melaka; and near the tip of the Indian peninsula, the port of Quilon. These hubs thrived under the political stability of powerful dynasts who recognized that the free-for-all of trade and market life would generate wealth for their regimes. Yemeni rulers, for instance, offered shelter to *karimi* fleets in return for taxes collected on cargoes; so did Egyptian governments for fleets moving through the Red Sea.

Antique Chinese Compass. Chinese sailors from Canton started to use needle compasses in the eleventh century. By the thirteenth century, needle compasses were widely used on ships in the Indian Ocean and were starting to appear in the Mediterranean.

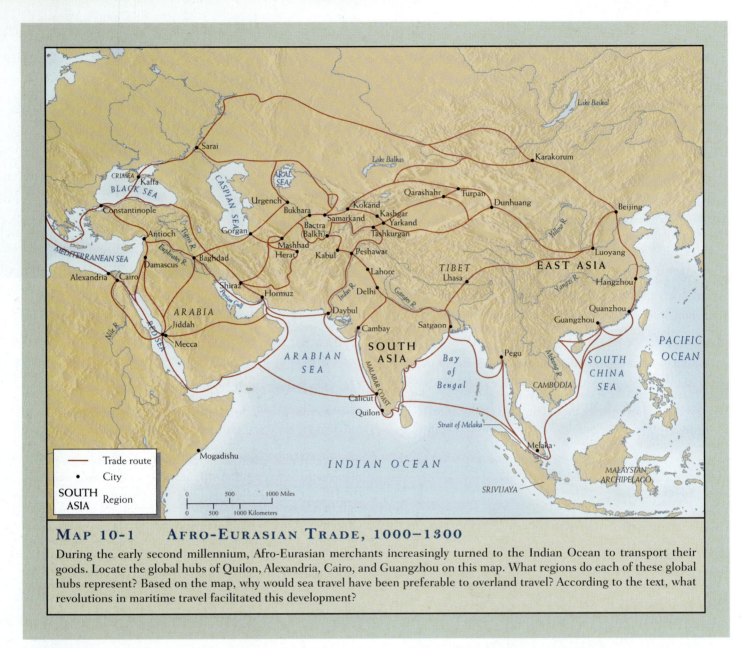

MAP 10-1   AFRO-EURASIAN TRADE, 1000–1300

During the early second millennium, Afro-Eurasian merchants increasingly turned to the Indian Ocean to transport their goods. Locate the global hubs of Quilon, Alexandria, Cairo, and Guangzhou on this map. What regions do each of these global hubs represent? Based on the map, why would sea travel have been preferable to overland travel? According to the text, what revolutions in maritime travel facilitated this development?

THE EGYPTIAN ANCHORAGE   Cairo and Alexandria were the Mediterranean's main maritime commercial centers. Cairo was home to numerous Muslim and Jewish trading firms, and Alexandria was their lookout post on the Mediterranean.

Silk yarn and textiles were the most popular commodities in the global trade involving Egypt. It was through Alexandria that Europeans acquired silks from China, especially the coveted *zaytuni* (satin) fabric from Quanzhou. Spanish silks also passed through Alexandria, heading to eastern Mediterranean markets. But the entrepôts handled much more. Goods from the Mediterranean included olive oil, glassware, flax, corals, and metals. Gemstones and aromatic perfumes poured in from India. Also changing hands were minerals and chemicals for dyeing or tanning, and raw materials such as timber and bamboo. The real novelties were paper and books. Hand-copied Bibles, Talmuds, legal and moral works, grammars in various languages, and Arabic books became the first best sellers of the Mediterranean.

Cairo and Alexandria prospered under Islamic leaders' commercial institutions. Success required states to protect merchants from predators. Armed convoys sent by Fatimid caliphs to escort commercial fleets in the Mediterranean and the Red Sea were so effective that fleets arrived on schedule and were relied on for postal service. Thus, when an Egyptian trader in Quilon (India) around 1100 was delayed on his journey home, he could send a consoling message to his wife in Cairo. He apologized for his absence but promised gifts

Mazu. Many Quanzhou sailors sought protection at the shrine of the goddess Mazu. According to legend, before assuming godhood Mazu had performed many miracles. Her temple became prominent after 1123, when Quanzhou's governor survived a storm at sea while returning from Korea. After that, sailors and their families burned incense for the goddess and prayed for her aid in keeping them safe at sea.

including pearl bracelets, red silk garments, a bronze basin, a ewer, and a slave girl: "I shall send them, if God wills it, with somebody who is traveling home in the *Karim*" (Goitein, "New Light," 179).

The Islamic legal system also promoted a favorable business environment. Consider how legal specialists got around the rule that might have brought commerce to a halt—the *sharia*'s (see Chapter 9) prohibition against earning interest on loans. With the clerics' blessing, Muslim traders formed partnerships between those who had capital to lend and those who needed money to expand their businesses. These partnerships enabled owners of capital to entrust their money or commodities to agents who, after completing their work, returned the investment and a share of the profits to the owners—and kept the rest as their reward. The English word "risk" derives from the Arabic *rizq,* the extra allowance paid to merchants in lieu of interest.

THE ANCHORAGE OF QUANZHOU   In China, Quanzhou was as busy as Cairo and Alexandria. The Song government set up offices of Seafaring Affairs in its three major ports: Canton, Quanzhou, and an area near present-day Shanghai in the Yangzi delta. In return for a portion of the taxes, these offices registered cargoes, sailors, and traders, while guards kept a keen eye on the traffic.

All foreign traders were guests of the governor, who doubled as the Chief of Seafaring Affairs. Part of his mandate was to summon favorable winds for shipping. Every year, the governor took his place on a high perch facing the harbor, in front of a rock cliff filled with inscriptions that recorded the wind-calling rituals. Traders of every origin witnessed the rite, then joined the dignitaries for a sumptuous banquet.

Ships departing from Quanzhou and other Chinese ports were junks—large, flat-bottomed ships with internal sealed bulkheads and stern-mounted rudders. Their multiple watertight compartments increased stability; the largest ones boasted four decks, six masts, and a dozen sails and could carry 500 men. Those departing Quanzhou headed for Srivijaya (Java) in the Malay Archipelago, navigating through the Strait of Melaka, a choke point between the South China Sea and the Indian Ocean. The final destination was Quilon on the coast of southwest India. Traders heading farther west in Arab-dominated seas unloaded their cargo and boarded small Arabian dhows.

Arabs, Persians, Jews, and Indians (as well as Chinese) traded at Quanzhou, and some stayed on to manage their businesses. Perhaps as many as 100,000 Muslims lived there during the Song dynasty. And traders could become power brokers in their own right. Consider the Pu family, which owned several hundred ships ferrying goods between India and Islamic countries. For generations the family made donations for public projects such as bridges, and the contributions garnered them official positions.

Although most foreign merchants did not reside apart from the rest of the city, they had their own buildings for

MAIN THEMES

→ *Trade routes shift from land to sea, transforming coastal cities into global trading hubs and elevating Afro-Eurasian trade to unprecedented levels.*
→ *Intensified trade, linguistic, and religious integration generate the foundational cultural spheres that we recognize today: China, India, Islam, and Europe.*
→ *The rise of the Mongol Empire integrates the world's foundational cultural spheres.*

FOCUS ON *Foundational Cultural Spheres*

The Islamic World

+ Islam undergoes a burst of expansion, prosperity, and cultural diversification but remains politically fractured.
+ Arab merchants and sufi mystics spread Islam over great distances and make it more appealing to other cultures, helping to transform Islam into a foundational world.
+ Islam travels across the Sahara Desert; the powerful gold- and slave-supplying empire of Mali arises in West Africa.

China

+ The Song dynasty reunites China after three centuries of fragmented rulership, reaching into the past to re-establish a sense of a "true" Chinese identity as the Han, through a widespread print culture and denigration of outsiders.
+ Breakthroughs in iron metallurgy allow agricultural expansion to support 120 million people and undergird Han commercial success.
+ China undergoes the world's first manufacturing revolution: gunpowder, porcelain, and handicrafts are produced on a large scale for widespread consumption.

India

+ India remains a mosaic under the canopy of Hinduism despite cultural interconnections and increasing prosperity.
+ The invasion of Turkish Muslims leads to the Dehli Sultanate, which rules over India for three centuries, strengthening cultural diversity and tolerance.

Christian Europe

+ Catholicism becomes a "mass" faith and helps to create a common European cultural identity.
+ An emphasis on religious education spawns numerous universities and a new intellectual elite.
+ Feudalism causes a fundamental reordering of the elite–peasant relationship, leading to agricultural and commercial expansion.
+ Europe's growing confidence is manifest in the Crusades and Reconquista, an effort to drive Islam out of Christian lands.

---

religious worship. A mosque from this period is still standing on a busy street. Hindu traders living in Quanzhou worshipped in a Buddhist shrine where statues of Hindu deities stood alongside those of Buddhist gods.

THE CROSSROADS OF AFRO-EURASIA: MELAKA Because of its strategic location and proximity to Malayan tropical produce, Melaka became a key cosmopolitan city. Indian, Javanese, and Chinese merchants and sailors spent months at a time in such ports selling their goods, purchasing return cargo, and waiting for the winds to change so they could reach their next destination. During peak season, Southeast Asian ports teemed with colorfully dressed foreign sailors,

local Javanese artisans who produced finely textured batik handicrafts (using melted wax applied to cloth before dipping it into blue and brown dyes), and money-grubbing traders. The latter converged from all over Asia to flood the markets with their merchandise and to search for pungent herbs, aromatic spices, and agrarian staples such as quick-ripening strains of rice to ship out. In a sense, each bustling port represented the cosmopolitan mosaic that Southeast Asia had become.

THE TIP OF INDIA In the tenth century, the Chola dynasty in south India supported a nerve center of maritime trade between China and the Red Sea and the Mediterranean. Although the Chola golden age lasted only about two generations, trade continued to flourish. Many Muslim traders settled in Malabar, on the southwest coast of the Indian peninsula, and Quilon became a major cosmopolitan hub. Dhows arrived, laden not only with goods from the Red Sea and Africa but also with traders, sojourners, and fugitives. Chinese junks unloaded silks and porcelain, and picked up passengers and commodities for East Asian markets. Sailors and traders strictly observed the customs of this entrepôt, for it was good business to respect others' norms and values while doing business with them.

Muslims, the largest foreign community, lived in their own neighborhoods. They shipped horses from Arab countries to India and the southeast islands, where kings viewed them as symbols of royalty. Because the animals could not survive in those climates, the demand was constant. There was even trade in elephants and cattle from tropical countries, though most goods were spices, perfumes, and textiles. Traders knew each other well, and personal relationships were key. When striking a deal with a local merchant, a Chinese trader would mention his Indian neighbor in Quanzhou and that family's residence in Quilon. Global commercial hubs relied on friendship and family to keep their businesses thriving across religious and regional divides.

SUB-SAHARAN AFRICA COMES TOGETHER

> → How did trade and migration affect sub-Saharan Africa between 1000 and 1300?

During this period sub-Saharan Africa's relationship to the rest of the world changed dramatically. Before 1000 CE sub-Saharan Africa had never been a world entirely apart, but now its integration became firmer. Africans and outsiders were determined to overcome the sea, river, and desert barriers that had blocked sub-Saharan peoples from participating in long-distance trade and intellectual exchanges (see Map 10-2). Increasingly, interior hinterlands found themselves touched by the commercial and migratory impulses emanating from the Indian Ocean and Arabian Sea transformations.

WEST AFRICA AND THE MANDE-SPEAKING PEOPLES

Once the camel bridged the Sahara Desert (see Chapter 9), the flow of commodities and ideas linked sub-Saharan Africa to the Muslim world of North Africa and Southwest Asia. As the savanna region became increasingly connected to developments in Afro-Eurasia, Mande-speaking peoples emerged as the primary agents for integration within and beyond West Africa. Exploiting their expertise in commerce and political organization, the Mande edged out rivals.

The Mande, or Mandinka, homeland was a vast area between the bend in the Senegal River to the west and the bend of the Niger River to the east (1,000 miles wide), stretching from the Senegal River in the north to the Bandama River in the south (more than 2,000 miles). This was where the kingdom of Ghana had arisen (see Chapter 9) and where Ghana's successor state—the Mandinka state of Mali, discussed below—emerged around 1100.

The Mande-speaking peoples were constantly on the go and marvelously adaptable. By the eleventh century they were spreading their cultural, commercial, and political hegemony from the high savanna grasslands southward into the woodlands and tropical rainforests stretching to the Atlantic Ocean. Those dwelling in the rainforests organized small-scale societies led by local councils, while those in the savanna lands developed centralized forms of government under sacred kingships. These peoples believed that their kings had descended from the gods and that they enjoyed the gods' blessing.

As the Mande broadened their territory to the Atlantic coast, they gained access to tradable items that residents of the interior were eager to have—notably kola nuts and malaguetta peppers, for which the Mande exchanged iron products and textile manufactures. By 1300 the Mandinka merchants had followed the Senegal River to its outlet on the coast and then pushed their commercial frontiers farther inland and down the coast. Thus, even before European explorers and traders arrived in the mid-fifteenth century, West African peoples had created dynamic networks linking the hinterlands with coastal trading hubs.

From the eleventh century to the late fifteenth century, the most vigorous businesses were those that spanned the Sahara Desert. The Mande-speaking peoples, with their far-flung commercial networks and highly dispersed populations, dominated this trade as well. Here one of the most prized commodities was salt, mined in the northern Sahel around the city of Taghaza; it was in demand on both sides of the Sahara. Another valuable commodity was gold, mined within the Mande homeland and borne by camel caravans to the far northern side of the Sahara, where traders exchanged it for various manufactures. Equally important in West African commerce were slaves, who were shipped to the settled Muslim communities of North Africa and Egypt.

THE EMPIRE OF MALI

As booming trade spawned new political organizations, the empire of Mali became the Mande successor state to the kingdom of Ghana. Founded in the twelfth century, it exercised political sway over a vast area for three centuries.

The Mali Empire represented the triumph of horse warriors, and its origins are enshrined in an epic involving the dynasty's founder, the legendary Sundiata, *The Epic of Sundiata.* Many

MAP 10-2   SUB-SAHARAN AFRICA, 1300

Increased commercial contacts influenced the religious and political dimensions of sub-Saharan Africa at this time. Compare this map to Map 9-3 (p. 335). Where had strong Islamic communities emerged by 1300? According to this map, what types of activity were affecting the Mande homeland? To what extent had sub-Saharan Africa "come together"?

Legend:
- Trans-Saharan trade routes
- Maritime trade routes
- State nucleus and sphere of influence
- Islamic areas
- Spread of Islam
- Gold deposits
- Copper deposits
- ▲ Salt
- Ivory
- Slaves

Map labels: Tunis, Fez, Marrakesh, ATLAS MOUNTAINS, Sijilmasa, MEDITERRANEAN SEA, Tripoli, Alexandria, Cairo, SAHARA DESERT, MAMLUK SULTANATE, Taghaza, Ghat, Mecca, Wadan, RED SEA, Awdaghost, Walata, Timbuktu, BORNU, Gao, MANDE HOMELAND, Lake Chad, ETHIOPIA, Aden, Gulf of Aden, MALI 12th–15th century, Jenne, Segou, HAUSA STATES, Niani, Niger R., OYO, IFE, BENIN, YORUBA STATES, Congo R., Mogadishu, ATLANTIC OCEAN, SWAHILI CITY STATES, Mombasa, ZANZIBAR, INDIAN OCEAN, KONGO, Kilwa, Zambezi R., GREAT ZIMBABWE, Sofala, KALAHARI DESERT, Limpopo R., MADAGASCAR, Orange R., Cape of Good Hope

Scale: 0 250 500 750 1000 Miles / 0 500 1000 Kilometers

West African Asante Gold. Although this gold head from the kingdom of Asante (*left*) was made in the eighteenth century, it shows the artistic abilities of the West African peoples. The head probably belonged to the Asante ruler, known as the Asantehene, and symbolized his power and wealth. This 1375 picture (*right*) shows the king of Mali on his throne, surrounded by images of gold.

historians believe that Sundiata actually existed, noting that the Arab historian Ibn Khaldun referred to him by name and reported that he was "their [Mali's] greatest king" (Levtzion and Pouwels, p. 64). His triumph, which occurred in the fourteenth century, marked the victory of new cavalry forces over traditional footsoldiers. Henceforth, horses—which had always existed in some parts of Africa—became prestige objects of the savanna peoples, symbols of state power. (See Primary Source: An African Epic.)

Under the Mali Empire, commerce was in full swing. With Mande trade routes extending to the Atlantic Ocean and spanning the Sahara Desert, West Africa was no longer an isolated periphery of the central Muslim lands. Mali's most famous sovereign, Mansa Musa (r. 1312–1332), made a celebrated hajj, or pilgrimage to Mecca, in 1325–1326, traveling through Cairo and impressing crowds with the size of his retinue and his displays of wealth, especially many dazzling items made of gold.

Mansa Musa's visit to Cairo was a sensation in its time. The stopover in one of Islam's primary cities astonished the Egyptian elite and awakened much of the world to the fact that Islam had spread far below the Sahara and that a sub-Saharan state could mount such an ostentatious display. Mansa Musa spared no expense to impress his hosts. He sent ahead an enormous gift of 50,000 dinars (a unit of money widely used in the Islamic world at this time), and his entourage included soldiers, wives, consorts, and as many as 12,000 slaves, many wearing rich brocades woven of Persian silks. And there was gold—a lot of it. He brought immense quantities and distributed it lavishly during his three-month stay. Preceding his retinue as it crossed the desert were 500 slaves, each carrying a golden staff. The caravan also included around 100 camels, each bearing two 300-pound sacks of gold.

The Mali Empire boasted two of West Africa's largest cities. Jenne, an ancient entrepôt, was a vital assembly point for caravans laden with salt, gold, and slaves preparing for journeys west to the Atlantic coast and north over the Sahara. The city had originated as an urban settlement around 200 BCE; by 1000 CE most substantial structures were made of brick. Around the city ran an impressive wall over eleven feet thick at its base and extending over a mile in length. More spectacular was the city of Timbuktu; founded around 1100 as a seasonal camp for nomads, it grew in size and importance under the patronage of various Malian kings. By the fourteenth century it was a thriving commercial and religious center famed for its two large mosques, which are still standing. Timbuktu was also renowned for its intellectual vitality. Here, West African Muslim scholars congregated to debate the tenets of Islam and to ensure that the faithful, even when distant from the Muslim heartland, practiced their religion with no taint of pagan observances. These clerics acquired treatises on Islam from all over the world for their personal libraries, remnants of which remain to this day.

Primary Source

AN AFRICAN EPIC

*The traditional story of the founding of the kingdom of Mali was passed down orally from genera-
tion to generation by griots, counselors and other official historians to the royal family. Only in
1960 was it finally written down in French. The narrative recounts the life of Sundiata, the heroic
founder of the Mali state. The following passage provides insight into the role of the narrator (the
griot) in the Malian kingdom, as well as some of the qualities of good and bad rulers.*

Griots know the history of kings and kingdoms and that is
why they are the best counsellors of kings. Every king
wants to have a singer to perpetuate his memory, for it is
the griot who rescues the memories of kings from oblivion,
as men have short memories.

Kings have prescribed destinies just like men, and seers
who probe the future know it. They have knowledge of the
future, whereas we griots are depositories of the
knowledge of the past. But whoever knows the history of
a country can read its future.

Other peoples use writing to record the past, but this
invention has killed the faculty of memory among them.
They do not feel the past any more, for writing lacks the
warmth of the human voice. . . .

I, Djeli Mamoudou Kouyaté, am the result of a long
tradition. For generations we have passed on the history of
kings from father to son. The narrative was passed on to
me without alteration and I deliver it without alteration,
for I received it free from all untruth.

Listen now to the story of Sundiata, the Na'Kamma,
the man who had a mission to accomplish.

At the time when Sundiata was preparing to assert his
claim over the kingdom of his fathers, Soumaoro was the
king of kings, the most powerful king in all the lands of
the setting sun. The fortified town of Sosso was the
bulwark of fetishism against the word of Allah. For a long
time Soumaoro defied the whole world. Since his
accession to the throne of Sosso he had defeated nine
kings whose heads served him as fetishes in his macabre
chamber. Their skins served as seats and he cut his footwear
from human skin. Soumaoro was not like other men, for the
jinn had revealed themselves to him and his power was
beyond measure. So his countless sofas [soldiers] were very
brave since they believed their king to be invincible. But
Soumaoro was an evil demon and his reign had produced
nothing but bloodshed. Nothing was taboo for him. His
greatest pleasure was publicly to flog venerable old men.
He had defiled every family and everywhere in his vast
empire there were villages populated by girls whom he had
forcibly abducted from their families without marrying
them.

➜ *Are you able to understand the function of the griot after
reading this passage?*

➜ *How reliable do you think this kind of oral history is?*

➜ *Soumaoro, the adversary of Sundiata, exemplified the
characteristics of a bad ruler. What were they? Can you
tell, indirectly, what the characteristics of a good ruler
(like Sundiata) were?*

SOURCE: *Sundiata: An Epic of Old Mali*, translated by D. T. Niane (Harlow:
Longman Group, 1965), pp. 40–41.

EAST AFRICA AND THE INDIAN OCEAN

Africa's eastern and southern regions were also integrated
into long-distance trading systems. Because of monsoon
winds, East Africa was a logical end point for much of the Indian Ocean trade. Thus Swahili peoples living along that
coast became brokers for the trade coming and going from
the Arabian Peninsula, the Persian Gulf territories, and the
western coast of India. Merchants in the city of Kilwa along
the coast of present-day Tanzania brought ivory, slaves, gold,
and other items from the interior and shipped them to destinations around the Indian Ocean.

The most valued commodity in the trade was gold. Shona-
speaking peoples grew rich by mining the ore in the highlands between the Limpopo and Zambezi rivers. By the year
1000, the Shona had founded up to fifty small religious
and political centers, each one erected from stone to display

Great Zimbabwe. These walls surrounded the city of Great Zimbabwe, which was a center of the gold trade between the East African coastal peoples and traders sailing on the Indian Ocean. Great Zimbabwe flourished during the thirteenth, fourteenth, and fifteenth centuries.

THE TRANS-SAHARAN AND INDIAN OCEAN SLAVE TRADE

African slaves were as valuable as African gold in shipments to the Mediterranean and Indian Ocean markets. There had been a lively trade in African slaves (mainly from Nubia) into pharaonic Egypt well before the Common Era. After Islam spread into Africa and sailing techniques improved, the slave trade across the Sahara Desert and Indian Ocean boomed.

Although the Quran attempted to mitigate the severity of slavery, requiring Muslim slave owners to treat their slaves kindly and praising manumission as an act of **piety** (a strong sense of religious duty and devoutness, often inspiring extraordinary actions), nonetheless the African slave trade flourished under Islam.

Slave Market. Slaves were a common commodity in the marketplaces of the Islamic world. Turkish conquests during the years from 1000 to 1300 put many prisoners into the slave market.

its power over the peasant villages surrounding it. Around 1100 one of these centers, Great Zimbabwe, stood supreme among the Shona. Built on the fortunes made from gold, its most impressive landmark was a massive elliptical building—32 feet high, 17 feet thick in parts, and extending more than 800 feet—made of stone so expertly that its fittings needed no grouting. The buildings of Great Zimbabwe probably housed the king and may also have contained smelters for melting down gold.

One of the key meeting grounds of the Indian Ocean trading system was the island of Madagascar. So intense was the interchange of peoples, plants, and animals from mainland Africa and around the rest of the Indian Ocean that Madagascar became one of the most multicultural places in the world at this time. Among the early inhabitants of the island were seafarers from Indonesia who plied the oceans with seaworthy outrigger canoes, likely picking up Bantu-speaking mainlanders from East Africa. The first evidence of human settlement there dates to the eighth century CE. Subsequently the island became a regular stopover point, as well as an import-export market, for traders crossing the Indian Ocean.

Africans became slaves during this period much as they had before: some were prisoners of war; others were considered criminals and sold into slavery as punishment. Their duties were varied. Some slaves were pressed into military service, rising in a few instances to positions of high authority. Others with seafaring skills worked as crewmen on dhows or as dockworkers. Still others, mainly women, were domestic servants, and many became concubines of Muslim political figures and businessmen. Slaves also did forced labor on plantations, the most oppressive being the agricultural estates of lower Iraq. There, slaves endured fearsome discipline and revolted in the ninth century. Yet in this era plantation-slave labor like that which later became prominent in the Americas was the exception, not the rule. Slaves were more prized as additions to family labor or as status symbols for their owners.

ISLAM IN A TIME OF POLITICAL FRAGMENTATION

> → *How did trade, conversion, and migration affect the Islamic world between 1000 and 1300?*

Islam underwent the same burst of expansion, prosperity, and cultural diversification that swept through the rest of Afro-Eurasia (see Map 10-3 and Map 10-4). However, whereas prosperity fostered greater integration in other regions, the peoples of Islam remained politically fractured. As in China, efforts to unite under a common rulership failed, giving way to defeats by marauding outsiders. The attempt to uphold centralized rule ended cataclysmically in 1258 with the Mongol sacking of Baghdad. But unlike China, Muslim leaders were unable to reunite after their collapse.

BECOMING THE "MIDDLE EAST"

Islam responded to political fragmentation by undergoing major changes, many prompted by contacts (and conflicts) with neighbors. Commercial networks, sustained by Muslim merchants, carried the word of the Quran far and wide. As Islam spread, it attracted more converts.

Decisive in the spread of Islam was a popular form of the religion, highly mystical and communal, called **Sufism.** The term *Sufi* comes from the Arabic word for wool (*suf*), which many of the early mystics wrapped themselves in to mark their penitence. Seeking closer union with God, they also performed ecstatic rituals such as repeating over and over again the name of God. In time, groups of devotees gathered to read aloud the Quran and other religious tracts. Although

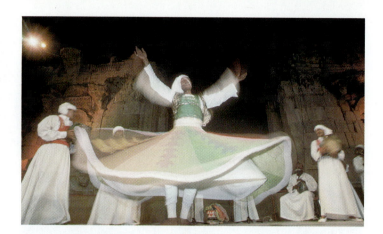

Dervishes. Today, the whirling dance of dervishes is almost a tourist attraction, as shown in this picture from the Jerash Cultural Festival in Jordan. Though Sufis in the early second millennium CE were not this neatly dressed, the whirling dance was an important means of reaching union with God.

many clerics despised the Sufis and loathed their seeming lack of theological rigor, the movement spread with astonishing speed. Sufism's emotional content and strong social bonds, sustained in Sufi brotherhoods or lodges, made its appeal to common folk irresistible. Sufi missionaries carried the universalizing faith to India, across the Sahara Desert, and to many other distant locations. It was from within these brotherhoods that Islam became truly a religion for the people.

Sufism had an intellectual and artistic dynamism that complemented its missionizing zeal. This was especially true of poetry, where the mystics' desire to experience God's love found ready expression. Most admired of Islam's mystical love poets was Jalal al-Din Rumi, spiritual founder of the Medlevi Sufi order that became famous for the ceremonial dancing of its whirling devotees, known as dervishes. Rumi, who wrote in Persian, celebrated all forms of love, spiritual and sexual, and preached a universalistic religious message:

> What is to be done of Muslims? For I do not recognize myself.
> I am neither Christian, nor Jew, nor Gabr (Zoroastrian), nor Muslim.

Another Sufi mystic and advocate of the universality of religions, the Spanish Muslim poet Ibn Arabi, wrote in Arabic:

> My heart has been of every form; it is a pasture for gazelles and a convent for Christian monks.
> And a temple for idols and the pilgrim's kaaba, and the tables of the Torah and the book of the Quran.

As trade increased and more converts appeared in the Islamic lands, urban and peasant populations came to understand the faith practiced by the political, commercial, and scholarly upper classes even while they remained attached to their

MAP 10-3   ISLAM BETWEEN 900 AND 1200

The Muslim world experienced political disintegration in the first centuries of the second millennium. According to the map key, what were the two major types of Muslim states in this period and what were the two major empires? What were the sources of instability in this period according to the map? As Islam continued to expand in this period, what challenges did it face?

Sufi brotherhood ways. Islam became even more accommodating, embracing Persian literature, Turkish ruling skills, and Arabic-language contributions in law, religion, literature, and science. In this way the world acquired a "core" region centered in what we now call the Middle East (the lands west of the "Far East" of China and Japan, and including the "Near East" of the eastern Mediterranean), united by a shared faith and pulsating with religious and commercial energies.

AFRO-EURASIAN MERCHANTS

By the thirteenth century, as the old Islamic heartland became the crossroads for commercial networks, Muslim merchants were the world's premier traders. As diverse as their businesses, these merchants were proof that a universal religion, an imagined political unity (projected by the Abbasid caliphate), the spread of the Arabic language, and Islamic law allowed entrepreneurs of varied backgrounds to flourish. The traders were not only Muslims but also Armenians, Indians, and Jews; working out of Islam's major cities; and they all had connections with families in North Africa and central Asia. (See Primary Source: The Merchants of Egypt.)

Long-distance trade surged under the protection of a sophisticated legal framework. The traders drew up elaborate contracts knowing that if breaches of contract occurred, they could take their cases to the courts. Many Jewish, Armenian, and Christian merchants went before Islamic judges, whose expertise in commercial matters they admired. Yet legal recourse was rarely necessary because the merchant community was self-policing—its members severely punished those who violated trust, sometimes ending their careers. Relying on partnerships, letters of credit, and a thorough knowledge of local trading customs and currencies, traders and their customers were confident that agreements made in India would be honored in Southeast Asia, Egypt, and North Africa.

MAP 10-4   ISLAMIC AND HINDU STATES AND THE BYZANTINE EMPIRE BETWEEN 1200 AND 1300

Islam continued to expand after the thirteenth century. Where were its largest and most important gains according to the map? How did other religions fare under Islamic rule in this period? How was Islam able to continue to expand in this period?

DIVERSITY AND UNIFORMITY IN ISLAM

Not until the ninth and tenth centuries did Muslims become a majority within their own Abbasid Empire (see Chapter 9). From the outset, Muslim rulers and clerics had to deal with large non-Muslim populations, even as these groups were converting to Islam. Rulers through the dhimma system accorded non-Muslims religious toleration as long as the non-Muslims accepted Islam's political dominion. Thus Jewish, Christian, and Zoroastrian communities were free to choose their own religious leaders and to settle internal disputes in their own religious courts. They did, however, have to pay a special tax, the *jizya,* and be deferential to their rulers. The dhimma system spared the Islamic world some of the religious conflict that afflicted other areas, and it made Islamic cities hospitable environments for traders from around the world.

While tolerant, Islam was an expansionist, universalizing faith. Intense proselytizing carried the sacred word to new frontiers and, in the process, reinforced the spread of Islamic institutions that supported commercial exchange. There were also moments of intense religious passion within Islam's frontiers, especially when Muslim rulers feared that Christian minorities would align with the Europeans pressing on their borders. Ugly incidents left some Christian churches in flames. Pressures to convert to Islam were unremitting at this time. After a surge of conversions to Islam from the ninth century onward, for example, the Christian Copts of Egypt shrank to a small community and never recovered their numbers.

POLITICAL INTEGRATION AND DISINTEGRATION

Just as the Islamic faith was increasing its reach from Africa to India and ultimately to Southeast Asia, its political institutions began to fragment. From 950 to 1050, it appeared that Shiism would be the vehicle for uniting the Islamic

THE MERCHANTS OF EGYPT

The most comprehensive collection of eleventh- and twelfth-century commercial materials from the Islamic world comes from a repository connected to the Jewish synagogue in Cairo. (It was the custom of the Jewish community to preserve, in a special storeroom, all texts that mention God.) These papers, a rich source of information about the Jewish community in Egypt at that time, touch on all manner of activities: cultural, religious, judicial, political, and commercial. The following letter is addressed to Joseph ibn 'Awkal, one of Egypt's leading merchants in the eleventh century.

Dear and beloved elder and leader, may God prolong your life, never take away your rank, and increase his favors and benefactions to you.

I inform you, my elder, that I have arrived safely. I have written you a letter before, but have seen no answer. Happy preoccupations—I hope. In that letter I provided you with all the necessary information.

I loaded nine pieces of antimony (kohl), five in baskets and four in complete pieces, on the boat of Ibn Jubār—may God keep it; these are for you personally, sent by Mūsā Ibn al-Majjānī. On this boat, I have in partnership with you—may God keep you—a load of cast copper, a basket with (copper) fragments, and two pieces of antimony. I hope God will grant their safe arrival. Kindly take delivery of everything, my lord.

I have also sent with Banāna a camel load for you from Ibn al-Majjānī and a camel load for me in partnership with you—may God keep you. He also carries another partnership of mine, namely, with 'Ammā r Ibn Yijū, four small jugs (of oil).

With Abū Zayd I have a shipload of tin in partnership with Salāma al-Mahdawī. Your share in this partnership with him is fifty pounds. I also have seventeen small jugs of s[oap]. I hope they arrive safely. They belong to a man [called . . .]r b. Salmūn, who entrusted them to me at his own risk. Also a bundle of hammered copper, belonging to [a Muslim] man from the Maghreb, called Abū Bakr Ibn

Rizq Allah. Two other bundles, on one is written Abraham, on the other M[. . .]. I agreed with the shipowner that he would transport the goods to their destination. I wish my brother Abū Nasr—may God preserve him—to take care of all the goods and carry them to his place until I shall arrive, if God wills.

Please sell the tin for me at whatever price God may grant and leave its "purse" (the money received for it) until my arrival. I am ready to travel, but must stay until I can unload the tar and oil from the ships.

Please take care of this matter and take from him the price of five skins (filled with oil). The account is with Salāma.

Al-Sabbāgh of Tripoli has bribed Bu 'l-'Alā the agent, and I shall unload my goods soon.

Kindest regards to your noble self and to my master [. . . and] Abu 'l-Fadl, may God keep them.

→ *List all the different kinds of commodities that the letter talks about.*

→ *How many different people are named as owners, partners, dealers, and agents?*

→ *What does the letter reveal about the ties among merchants and about how they conducted their business?*

SOURCE: *Letters of Medieval Jewish Traders*, translated with introductions and notes by S. D. Goitein (Princeton, NJ: Princeton University Press, 1973), pp. 85–87.

world. While the Fatimid Shiites established their authority over Egypt and much of North Africa (see Chapter 9), the Abbasid state in Baghdad fell under the sway of a Shiite family. Each group created universities (in Cairo and Baghdad, respectively), ensuring that leading centers of higher learning were Shiite. But divisions also sapped Shiism, as Sunni Muslims began to challenge Shiite power and establish their own strongholds. The last of the Shiite Fatimid rulers gave way to

a new Sunni regime in Egypt. In Baghdad, the Shiite Buyid family surrendered to a group of unrelated Sunni strongmen.

The new strongmen were mainly Turks. Their people had been migrating into the Islamic heartland from the Asian steppes since the eighth century, bringing superior military skills and an intense devotion to Sunni Islam. Once established in Baghdad, they founded outposts in Syria and Palestine, and then moved into Anatolia after defeating

Byzantine forces in 1071. But this Turkish state also crumbled, as tribesmen quarreled for preeminence. Thus by the thirteenth century the Islamic heartland had fractured into three regions. In the east (central Asia, Iran, and eastern Iraq), the remnants of the old Abbasid state persevered. Caliphs succeeded one another, still claiming to speak for all of Islam yet deferring to their Turkish military commanders. Even in the core of the Islamic world (Egypt, Syria, and the Arabian Peninsula), where Arabic was the primary tongue, military men of non-Arab origin held the reins of power. Farther west (in the Maghreb), Arab rulers prevailed—but there the influence of Berbers, some from the northern Sahara, was extensive. Islam was a vibrant faith, but its polities were splintered.

WHAT WAS ISLAM?

Buoyed by Arab dhows on the high seas and carried on the backs of camels, following commercial networks, Islam had been transformed from Muhammad's original goal of creating a religion for Arab peoples. By 1300, its influence spanned Afro-Eurasia. It attracted urbanites and rural peasants alike, as well as its original audience of desert nomads. Its extraordinary universal appeal generated an intense Islamic cultural flowering in 1000 CE.

Some people worried about the preservation of Islam's true nature as, for example, Arabic ceased to be the language of many Islamic believers when it spread beyond the Arab peoples. True, the devout read and recited the Quran in its original tongue, as the religion mandated. But Persian was now the language of Muslim philosophy and art, and Turkish was the language of law and administration. Moreover, Jerusalem and Baghdad no longer stood alone as Islamic cultural capitals. Other cities, housing universities and other centers of learning, promoted alternative, vernacular versions of Islam. In fact, some of the most dynamic thought came from Islam's fringes.

At the same time, heterogeneity fostered cultural blossoming in all fields of high learning. Arabic remained a preeminent language of science, literature, and religion in 1300. Indicative of Islam's and Arabic's prominence in thought was the legendary Ibn Rushd (1126–1198). Known as Averroës in the western world, where scholars pored over his writings, he wrestled with the same theological issues that troubled western scholars. Steeped in the writings of Aristotle, Ibn Rushd became Islam's most thoroughgoing advocate for the use of reason in understanding the universe. His knowledge of Aristotle was so great that it influenced the thinking of the Christian world's leading philosopher and theologian, Thomas of Aquino (Thomas Aquinas, 1225–1274). Above all, Ibn Rushd believed that faith and reason could be compatible. He also argued for a social hierarchy in which learned men would command influence akin to Confucian scholars in China or Greek philosophers in Athens. Ibn Rushd believed that the proper forms of reasoning had to be entrusted to the educated class—in the case of Islam, the *ulama*—which would serve the common folk.

Equally powerful works appeared in Persian, which by now was expressing the most sophisticated ideas of culture and religion. Best representing the new Persian ethnic pride was Abu al-Qasim Firdawsi (920–1020), a devout Muslim who also believed in the importance of pre-Islamic Sasanian traditions. In the epic poem *Shah Namah,* or *Book of Kings,* he celebrated the origins of Persian culture and narrated the history of the Iranian highland peoples from the dawn of time to the Muslim conquest. As part of his effort to extol a pure Persian culture, Firdawsi attempted to compose his entire poem in Persian unblemished by other languages, even avoiding Arabic words.

By the fourteenth century, Islam had achieved what early converts would have considered unthinkable. No longer a religion of a minority of peoples living amid Christian, Zoroastrian, and Jewish communities, it had become the people's faith. The agents of conversion were mainly Sufi saints and Sufi brotherhoods—not the *ulama,* whose exhortations had little impact on common people. The Sufis had carried their faith far and wide to North African Berbers, to Anatolian villagers, and to West African animists (who believed that things in nature have souls). Indeed, Ibn Rushd worried about the growing appeal of what he considered an "irrational" piety. But his message failed, because he did not appreciate that Islam's expansionist powers rested on its appeal to common folk. While the *sharia* was the core of Islam for the educated and scholarly classes, Sufism spoke to ordinary men and women.

INDIA AS A CULTURAL MOSAIC

> → *In what ways did India remain a cultural mosaic?*

Trade and migration affected India, just as it did the rest of Asia and Africa. As in the case of Islam, India's growing cultural interconnections and increasing prosperity produced little political integration. Under the canopy of Hinduism it remained a cultural mosaic; in fact, the Islamic faith now joined others to make the region even more diverse (see Map 10-5). India, in this sense, illustrates how cross-cultural integration can just as easily preserve diversity as promote internal unity.

→ *In what ways did India remain a cultural mosaic?*

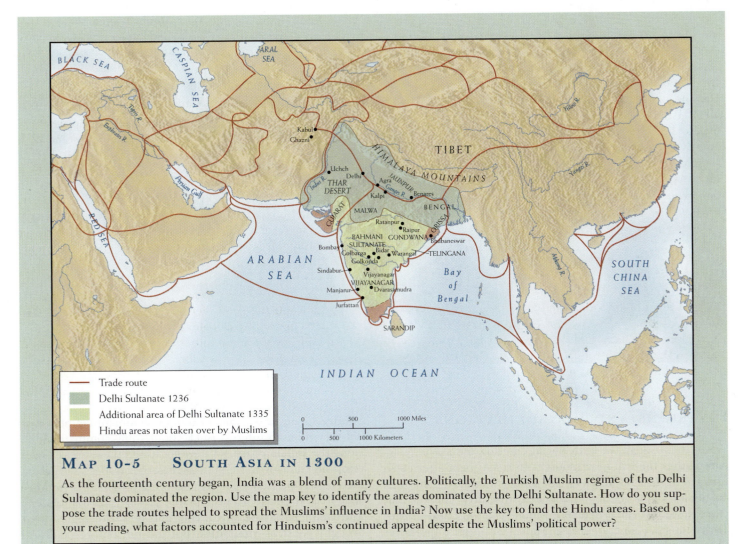

MAP 10-5   SOUTH ASIA IN 1300

As the fourteenth century began, India was a blend of many cultures. Politically, the Turkish Muslim regime of the Delhi Sultanate dominated the region. Use the map key to identify the areas dominated by the Delhi Sultanate. How do you suppose the trade routes helped to spread the Muslims' influence in India? Now use the key to find the Hindu areas. Based on your reading, what factors accounted for Hinduism's continued appeal despite the Muslims' political power?

RAJAS AND SULTANS

Turks spilled into India as they had the Islamic heartlands, bringing their newfound Islamic beliefs. But the newcomers encountered an ethnic and religious mix that they would add to without upsetting the balance. India became an intersection for the trade, migration, and culture of Afro-Eurasian peoples. Moreover, with 80 million inhabitants in 1000 CE, it had the second-largest population in the region, not far behind China's 120 million.

Before the Turks arrived, India was splintered among rival chiefs called *rajas*. (**Rajas** considered themselves kings; the term also denotes the head of a family or the person who controlled land and resources.) These leaders solicited support from high-caste Brahmans by giving them land. Much of it was uncultivated, so the Brahmans set out to make it arable: they built temples, converted the indigenous hunter-gatherer peoples to the Hindu faith, and then taught the converts how to cultivate the land. In this way the Brahmans simultaneously spread their faith and expanded the agrarian tax base for themselves and the rajas. The Brahmans reciprocated the rajas' support by compiling elaborate genealogies for them and endowing them with a lengthy (and legitimizing) ancestry. For their part, the rajas demonstrated that they were well versed in Sanskrit culture, including equestrian skills and courtly etiquette, and became the patrons of artists and poets. Ultimately, many of the warriors and their heirs became Indian rajas. However, the Turkish invaders were armed with Islam, so the conquerors remained sultans instead of becoming rajas. (Unlike rajas, **sultans** were political leaders who combined a warrior ethos with a devotion to Islam.)

Hindu Temple. When Buddhism started to decline in India, Hinduism was on the rise. Numerous Hindu temples were built, many of them adorned with ornate carvings like this small tenth-century temple in Bhubaneshwar, east India.

INVASIONS AND CONSOLIDATIONS

When the Turkish warlords began entering India, the rajas had neither the will nor resources to resist them after centuries of fighting off invaders. The Turks introduced their own customs while accepting local social structures, such as the caste system. Concerned to promote Islamic culture, the Turks constructed grandiose mosques and built impressive libraries where scholars could toil and share their wisdom with the court. Previous invaders from central Asia had reinforced the rajas' power base through intermarriage. But the Turks upset the balance of the raja kingdoms. For example, Mahmud of Ghazna (971–1030) launched many expeditions from the Afghan heartland into northern India and wanted to make his capital, Ghazni, a center of Islamic learning in order to win status within Islam. Subsequently, Muhammad Ghuri in the 1180s led another wave of Islamic Turkish invasions from Afghanistan and dispersed across the Delhi region in northern India. Wars raged between the Indus and Ganges rivers until one by one, all the way to the lower Ganges valley, the fractured kingdoms of the rajas toppled.

The most powerful and enduring of the Turkish Muslim regimes of northern India was the **Delhi Sultanate** (1206–1526), whose rulers strengthened the cultural diversity and tolerance that were already a hallmark of the Indian social order. Sultans recruited local artisans for numerous building projects, and palaces and mosques became displays of Indian architectural tastes adopted by Turkish newcomers. But the sultans did not force their subjects to convert, so that South Asia never became an Islamic-dominant country. Nor did they have an interest in the flourishing commercial life along the Indian coast. So they permitted these areas to develop on their own. Persian Zoroastrian traders settled on the coast around modern-day Mumbai (Bombay). The Malabar coast to the south became the preserve of Arab traders. The Delhi Sultanate was a rich and powerful regime that brought political integration but did not enforce cultural homogeneity.

WHAT WAS INDIA?

During the eleventh, twelfth, and thirteenth centuries India became the most diverse and, in some respects, most tolerant region in Afro-Eurasia. It is from this era that India as an impressive but fragile mosaic of cultures, religions, and ethnicities truly arises. Not even Islam's entry into the region undermined this intense cultural mixing.

When the Turks arrived, the local Hindu population, having had much experience with foreign invaders and immigrants, assimilated these intruders as they had done earlier peoples. And the Turks cooperated. Before long, they thought of themselves as Indians who, however, retained their Islamic beliefs and steppe ways. They continued to wear their distinctive trousers and robes and flaunted their horse-riding skills. At the same time, the local population embraced some of their conquerors' ways, donning the tunics and trousers that characterized Central Asian peoples.

Lodi Gardens. The Lodi Dynasty was the last Delhi sultan dynasty. Lodi Gardens, the cemetery of Lodi sultans, places central Asian Islamic architecture in the Indian landscape, thereby creating a scene of "heaven on the earth."

Diversity and cultural mixing became most visible in the multiple languages that flourished in India. Although the sultans spoke Turkish languages, they regarded Persian literature as a high cultural achievement and made Persian their courtly and administrative language. Meanwhile, most of their Hindu subjects spoke local languages (which had evolved out of Sanskrit) and followed their caste regulations. Despite living under Muslim rulers, the subject populations adhered to their local adaptations of the Hindu faith. Here the rulers did what Muslim rulers did with Christian and Jewish communities living in their midst: they collected the *jizya* tax and permitted communities to worship as they saw fit and to administer their own communal law. Ultimately, Islam proved in India that it did not have to be a conquering religion to prosper. As rulers, sultans granted lands to ulama (Islamic scholars) and Sufi saints, much as Hindu rajas had earlier granted lands to Brahmans (see Chapter 8). These scholars and saints in turn attracted followers to their large estates and forests to enjoy the benefits of membership in a community of believers.

Although newcomers and locals cleaved to separate religious traditions, nonetheless their customs began to merge.

Sultans maintained their steppe lifestyle and equestrian culture and took delight in the fact that their subjects adopted Central Asian–style clothing. Within only a few decades, once the subject peoples realized that sultans and Islam were there to stay, they embraced the fashions of the court. In turn, their Muslim rulers understood that ruling effectively meant mastering the local language. Before long, court scholars and Sufi holy men were writing and teaching proficiently in local dialects. Hindustani was the result, an Indian language incorporating Persian and Arabic words; in time, it became the root language of Hindi and Urdu.

Vishnu. With Buddhism disappearing from India, Buddha was absorbed by the cult of Vishnu and became one of the incarnations of the Hindu god. This late-twelfth-century Angkor Wat–style sculpture from Cambodia shows Vishnu asleep; from his nostril sprouts the lotus that will give birth to Buddha.

This exchange of skills among diverse communities was not confined to governance and religion. It spilled over into the economic arena as well. The foreign artisans who had arrived with their rulers brought silk textiles, rugs, and appliances to irrigate gardens that the leading families of Delhi cherished. Soon the artisans' talents were influencing local manufacturing techniques. Native-born Indians learned from Muslims how to extract long filaments from silk cocoons and were themselves weaving fine silk textiles.

Although Buddhism had been in decline in India for centuries, it, too, became part of the cultural intermixing of these centuries. As Vedic Brahmanism evolved into Hinduism (see Chapter 8), it absorbed many Buddhist doctrines and practices, such as *ahimsa* (non-killing) and vegetarianism. The two religions became so similar that Hindus simply considered the Buddha to be one of their deities—an incarnation of the great god Vishnu. Many Buddhist moral teachings mixed with and became Hindu stories. Artistic motifs reflect a similar process of adoption and adaptation. Goddesses, some beautiful and others fierce, appeared alongside Buddhas, Vishnus, and Sivas as their consorts. The Turkish invaders' destruction of major monasteries in the thirteenth century deprived Buddhism of local spiritual leaders. Lacking dynastic support, Buddhists in India were thus more easily assimilated into the Hindu population or converted to Islam.

SONG CHINA: INSIDERS VERSUS OUTSIDERS

> → *What transformations in communication, education, and commerce promoted a distinct Chinese identity during this era?*

The preeminent world power in 1000 CE was still China, despite its recent turmoil. Once dampened, that turbulence yielded to a long era of stability and splendor—a combination that made China a regional engine of Afro-Eurasian prosperity.

After the end of the Tang dynasty (907 CE), North and South China splintered into regional kingdoms, mostly led by military generals. In 960 CE one of those generals, Zhao Kuangyin, ended the fragmentation. Overthrowing the boy emperor of his own kingdom, Zhao reunified China by conquering regional kingdoms. After his death, his younger brother annexed the remaining kingdoms. Thus, the Song dynasty took over the mandate of heaven.

The following three centuries witnessed many economic and political successes, but northern nomadic tribes kept the Song from completely securing their reign (see Map 10-6 and Map 10-7). Their efforts to deter these warriors were ulti-mately unsuccessful, and in 1127 the Song lost control of northern China to the Jurchen (ancestors of the Manchu, who would rule China from the seventeenth until the twentieth century). After reconstituting their dynasty in southern China, their empire's most economically robust region, the Song enjoyed another century and a half of rule before falling to the Mongols.

CHINA'S ECONOMIC PROGRESS

China, like India and the Islamic world, participated in Afro-Eurasia's powerful long-distance trade. Indeed, Chinese merchants were as energetic as their Muslim and Indian counterparts. Yet China's commercial successes could not have occurred without the country's strong agrarian base—especially its vast rice fields, which sustained a population that reached 120 million. Agriculture benefited from breakthroughs in metalworking that yielded stronger iron plows, which the Song harnessed to sturdy water buffalo to extend the farming frontier. In 1078, for example, total Song iron production reached between 75,000 and 150,000 tons, roughly the equivalent of European iron production in the early eighteenth century. The Chinese piston bellows were a marvel, and of a size unsurpassed until the nineteenth century.

Manufacturing also flourished. In the early tenth century, Chinese alchemists mixed saltpeter with sulfur and charcoal to produce a product that would burn and could be deployed on the battlefield: gunpowder. Soon, Song entrepreneurs were inventing a remarkable array of incendiary devices that flowed from their mastery of techniques for controlling explosions. Moreover, artisans produced increasingly light, durable, and exquisitely beautiful porcelains. Before long, their porcelain (now called "china") was the envy of all Afro-Eurasia. Also flowing from the artisans' skillful hands were vast amounts of clothing and handicrafts, made from the fibers grown by Song farmers. In effect, the Song Chinese oversaw the world's first manufacturing revolution, producing finished goods on a large scale for consumption far and wide.

MONEY AND INFLATION

Expanding commerce transformed the role of money and its wide circulation. By now the Song government was annually minting nearly two million strings of currency, each containing 1,000 copper coins. In fact, the supply of metal currency could not match the demand. (The result: East Asia's thirst for gold from East Africa.) At the same time, merchant guilds in northwestern Shanxi developed the first letters of exchange, called "flying cash." These letters linked northern traders with their colleagues in the south. Before long,

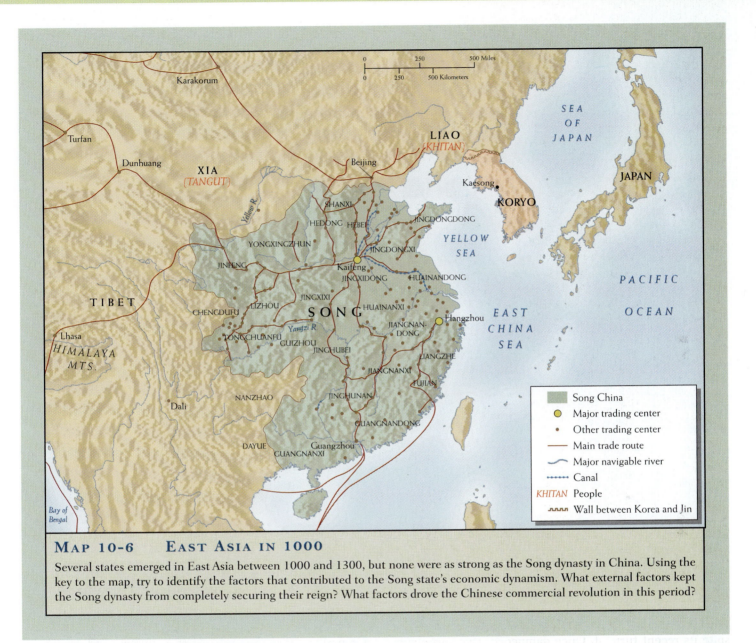

MAP 10-6   EAST ASIA IN 1000

Several states emerged in East Asia between 1000 and 1300, but none were as strong as the Song dynasty in China. Using the key to the map, try to identify the factors that contributed to the Song state's economic dynamism. What external factors kept the Song dynasty from completely securing their reign? What factors drove the Chinese commercial revolution in this period?

printed money had eclipsed coins. Even the government collected more than half its tax revenues in cash rather than grain and cloth. The government also issued more notes to pay its bills—a practice that ultimately contributed to the world's first case of runaway inflation.

NEW ELITES

Song emperors ushered in a period of social and cultural vitality. They established a central bureaucracy of scholar-officials chosen through competitive civil service examinations. Zhao Kuangyin, or Emperor Taizu (r. 960–976 CE), himself

administered the final test for all who had passed the highest-level palace examination. In subsequent dynasties, the emperor was the nation's premier examiner, symbolically demanding oaths of allegiance from successful candidates. By 1100 these ranks of learned men had accumulated sufficient power to become China's new ruling elite.

The introduction of the civil service examination system was crucial to a dramatic shift in power from a hereditary aristocracy to a less wealthy but more highly schooled class of scholar officials. Consider the career of the infamous Northern Song reformer Wang Anshi (1021–1086), who ascended to power from a commoner family outside of Hangzhou in the south. He owed his rise to power to success

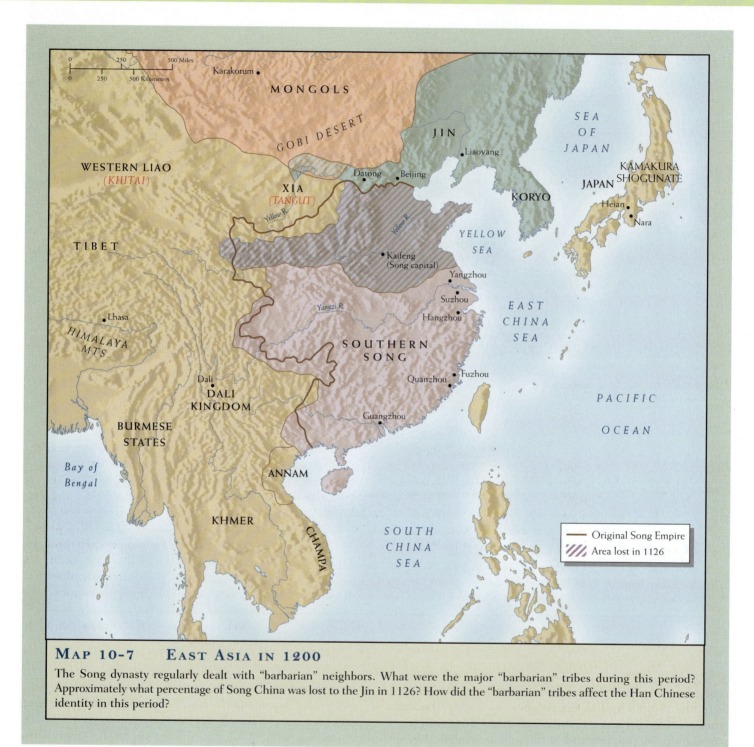

MAP 10-7 EAST ASIA IN 1200

The Song dynasty regularly dealt with "barbarian" neighbors. What were the major "barbarian" tribes during this period? Approximately what percentage of Song China was lost to the Jin in 1126? How did the "barbarian" tribes affect the Han Chinese identity in this period?

in Song state examinations—a not insignificant achievement, for in nearby Fujian province alone, of the roughly 18,000 candidates who gathered triennially to take the provincial examination, over 90 percent failed! After gaining the emperor's ear, Wang eventually challenged the political and cultural influence of the old Tang dynasty elites from the northwest.

NEGOTIATING WITH NEIGHBORS

As the Song flourished, nomads on the outskirts eyed the Chinese successes closely. To the north, Khitan, Tungusic, Tangut, and Jurchen nomadic societies formed their own dynasties and adopted Chinese techniques. Located within the "greater China" established by the Han and Tang dynasties,

Wang Anshi. He owed his rise from a commoner family to a powerful position as a reformer to the Song state examinations.

these non-Chinese nomads saw China proper as an object of conquest.

In military power the Song dynasts were relatively weak: despite their sophisticated weapons, they could not match their steppe foes when the latter united against them. Yes, steel tips improved the arrows that their soldiers shot from their crossbows, and flame throwers and "crouching tiger catapults" sent incendiary bombs streaking into their enemies' ranks; none of these breakthroughs was secret. Warrior neighbors on the steppe mastered the new arts of war more fully than did the Song dynasts themselves.

China's strength as a manufacturing powerhouse made economic diplomacy an option, so the Song relied on "gifts" and generous trade agreements with the borderlanders. For example, after losing militarily to the Khitan Liao dynasty, the Song agreed to make annual payments of 100,000 ounces of silver and 200,000 bolts of silk. The treaty allowed them to live in relative peace for more than a century. Securing peace meant emptying the state coffers and then printing more paper money. The resulting inflation added economic instability to military weakness, making the Song an easy target when Jurchen invaders made their final assault.

WHAT WAS CHINA?

Paradoxically, the increasing exchange between outsiders and insiders within China hardened the lines that divided them and gave residents of China's interior a highly developed sense of themselves as a distinctive people possessing a superior culture. Exchanges with outsiders nurtured a "Chinese" identity among those who considered themselves true insiders and referred to themselves as Han. Improvements in communications and education further intensified this Han sense that they were the authentic Chinese, and that outsiders were radically different. Driven from their ancient homeland in the eleventh century, they grew increasingly suspicious and resentful toward the outsiders living in their midst. They called these outsiders "barbarians" and treated them accordingly.

Chinese and Barbarian. After losing the north, the Han Chinese grew resentful of outsiders. They drew a dividing line between their own agrarian society and the nomadic warriors, calling them "barbarians." Such identities were not fixed, however. Chinese and so-called barbarians were mutually dependent.

Vital in crystallizing this sense of a distinct Chinese identity was print culture. In fact, of all Afro-Eurasian societies in 1300, the Chinese were the most advanced in their use of printing and book publishing and circulation. The Song government used its plentiful supply of paper to print books, especially medical texts, and to distribute calendars. The private publishing industry also expanded. Printing houses throughout the country produced Confucian classics, works on history, philosophical treatises, and literature—all of which figured in the civil examinations. Buddhist publications, too, were available everywhere. The dramatic expansion of the print culture was further emblematic of this great period of stability and splendor in China.

CHINA'S NEIGHBORS ADAPT TO CHANGE

→ *How were Southeast Asia, Japan, and Korea influenced by sustained contact with other regions?*

Feeling the pull of Chinese economic and political gravity, cultures around China's rim consolidated internal political authority to resist being swallowed up, while increasing their commercial transactions.

THE RISE OF WARRIORS IN JAPAN

In Japan, rulers sought to create a stable regime out of feuding warrior factions, so they combined the Heian court's imperial authority with the military power of provincial warriors. At first, entrenched court nobles in the new capital of Heian (today's Kyoto) dominated Japan (see Map 10-7); later, rough-and-ready warriors won possession of the throne to "protect" its sanctity as an object of popular veneration.

The most influential of these ruling groups was the Fujiwara family, ancestors of the Nakatomi kinship group (see Chapter 9). During the tenth and eleventh centuries the Fujiwara presided over Japanese society in what is known as the Heian period (794–1185). They exchanged poetry written in classical Chinese and their native language, and dressed in the elegant costumes that have influenced Japanese taste up to this day.

In time, however, power shifted to elites in the provinces. In a new hierarchy of land tenures, peasant cultivators were at the bottom, managers and estate officials in the middle, and absentee patrons at the top. Soon these large estates controlled more than half of Japan's rice land, and the state's revenue and power plummeted. In the midst of such privatization, Heian aristocrats became politically weak but culturally influential—while the hinterlands provided their economic wealth.

Heian aristocrats disdained the military and even abolished the conscription system used to raise imperial armies. In the provinces, however, trained warriors affiliated with kinship groups gathered strength. Protected by lightweight leather armor, these expert horsemen defended their private estates with remarkable long-range bowmanship and superbly crafted, single-edged long steel swords for close combat. Formidable in warfare, they formed local warrior organizations in the outlying regions and prepared the way for the rise of a warrior or samurai society.

Japan now smoldered with multiple sources of political and cultural power: an endangered aristocracy, an imperial family, and local samurai warriors. It was a combustible mix of refined high culture in the capital versus uncouth warriors in the provinces. Such a mix generated social intrigue in marriage politics and political double-dealing in the capital. Lady Murasaki Shikibu (c. 976–c. 1031), writing in native Japanese script, captured this world of elegant lives and sordid affairs of courtiers and their women in *The Tale of Genji*, Japan's—and possibly the world's—first novel. (See Primary Source: *The Tale of Genji*.)

SOUTHEAST ASIA: A MARITIME MOSAIC

Southeast Asia, like India, now became a crossroads of Afro-Eurasian influences. Its sparse population (probably around 10 million in 1000 CE—tiny compared with that of China and India) was not immune, however, to the foreign influences riding the sea-lanes into the archipelago. Indeed, the Malay Peninsula became home to many trading ports and stopovers for traders shuttling between India and China, because it connected the Bay of Bengal and the Indian Ocean with the South China Sea (see Map 10-8).

"INDO-CHINESE" INFLUENCES Indian influence had been prominent both on the Asian mainland and in island portions of Southeast Asia since 800 CE, but Islamic expansion into the islands after 1200 gradually superseded these influences. Only Bali and a few other islands far to the east of Malaya preserved their Vedic religious origins. Elsewhere in Java and Sumatra, Islam became the dominant religion. In Vietnam and northern portions of mainland Southeast Asia, Chinese cultural influences and northern schools of Mahayana Buddhism were especially prominent.

Heiji Rebellion. This illustration from the Kamakura period depicts a battle during the Heiji Rebellion, which was fought between rival subjects of the cloistered emperor Go-Shirakawa in 1159. Riding in full armor on horseback, the fighters on both sides are armed with devastating long bows.

Primary Source

THE TALE OF GENJI

Lacking a written language of their own, Heian aristocrats adopted classical Chinese as the official written language while continuing to speak Japanese. Men at the court took great pains to master the Chinese literary forms, but Japanese court ladies were not expected to do so. Lady Murasaki Shikibu, the author of The Tale of Genji, *hid her knowledge of Chinese, fearing that she would be criticized. In the meantime, the Japanese developed a native syllabary (a table of syllables) based on Chinese written graphs. Using this syllabary, Murasaki kept a diary in Japanese that gave vivid accounts of Heian court life. Her story—possibly the world's first novel—relates the adventures of a dashing young courtier named Genji. In the passage below, Genji evidently speaks for Murasaki in explaining why fiction can be as truthful as a work of history in capturing human life and its historical significance.*

Genji . . . smiled, and went on: "But I have a theory of my own about what this art of the novel is, and how it came into being. To begin with, it does not simply consist in the author's telling a story about the adventures of some other person. On the contrary, it happens because the storyteller's own experience of men and things, whether for good or ill—not only what he has passed through himself, but even events which he has only witnessed or been told of—has moved him to an emotion so passionate that he can no longer keep it shut up in his heart. Again and again something in his own life or in that around him will seem to the writer so important that he cannot bear to let it pass into oblivion. There must never come a time, he feels, when men do not know about it. That is my view of how this art arose.

"Clearly then, it is no part of the storyteller's craft to describe only what is good or beautiful. Sometimes, of course, virtue will be his theme, and he may then make such play with it as he will. But he is just as likely to have been struck by numerous examples of vice and folly in the world around him, and about them he has exactly the same feelings as about the pre-eminently good deeds which he encounters: they are more important and must all be garnered in. Thus anything whatsoever may become the subject of a novel, provided only that it happens in this mundane life and not in some fairyland beyond our human ken.

"The outward forms of this art will not of course be everywhere the same. At the court of China and in other foreign lands both the genius of the writers and their actual methods of composition are necessarily very different from ours; and even here in Japan the art of storytelling has in course of time undergone great changes. There will, too, always be a distinction between the lighter and the more serious forms of fiction. . . . So too, I think, may it be said that the art of fiction must not lose our allegiance because, in the pursuit of the main purpose to which I have alluded above, it sets virtue by the side of vice, or mingles wisdom with folly. Viewed in this light the novel is seen to be not, as is usually supposed, a mixture of useful truth with idle invention, but something which at every stage and in every part has a definite and serious purpose."

→ *According to this passage, what motivates an author to write a story (i.e., fiction)?*

→ *Genji feels it is appropriate for a writer to address not only "what is good or beautiful" but also "vice and folly." What explanation does he give? Do you agree?*

SOURCE: *Sources of Japanese Tradition*, compiled by Ryūsaku Tsunoda, Wm. Theodore de Bary, and Donald Keene (New York: Columbia University Press, 1964), vol. 1, pp. 177–79.

MAP 10-8   SOUTHEAST ASIA, 1000–1300

Cross-cultural influences affected Southeast Asian societies during this period. What makes Southeast Asia unique geographically compared to other regions of the world? Based on the map, why were the kingdoms of Southeast Asia exposed to so many cross-cultural influences? In this chapter, the term "mosaic" describes both South and Southeast Asia. Compare Map 10-5 with this map, and explain how the mosaic of Southeast Asia differed from the mosaic of India.

MAINLAND BUFFER KINGDOMS   During this period Cambodian, Burmese, and Thai peoples founded powerful mixed polities along the Mekong, Salween, Chao Phraya, and Irriwaddy river basins of the Asian mainland. Important Vedic and Buddhist kingdoms emerged here as political buffers between the strong states in China and India and brought stability and further commercial prosperity to the region.

Consider the kingdom that ruled Angkor in present-day Cambodia. With their capital in Angkor, the Khmers (889–

1431) created the most powerful and wealthy empire in Southeast Asia. Countless water reservoirs enabled them to flourish on the great plain to the west of the Mekong River after the loss of eastern territories. Public works and magnificent temples dedicated to the revived Vedic gods from India went hand in hand with the earlier influence of Indian Buddhism. Eventually the Khmer kings united adjacent kingdoms and extended Khmer influence to the Thai and Burmese states along the Chaophraya and Irriwaddy rivers.

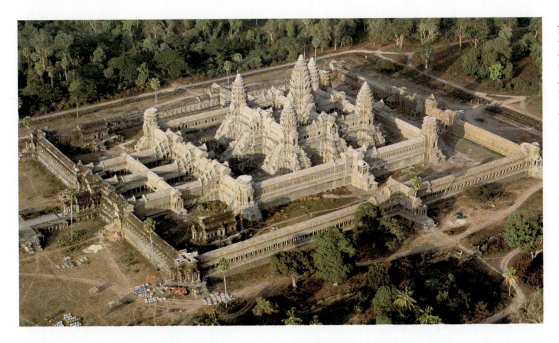

Angkor Wat. Mistaken by later European explorers as a remnant of Alexander the Great's conquests, the enormous temple complexes built by the Khmer people in Angkor borrowed their intricate layout and stupa (a moundlike structure containing religious relics) architecture from the Brahmanist Indian temples of the time. As the capital, Angkor was a microcosm of the world for the Khmer, who aspired to represent the macrocosm of the universe in the magnificence of Angkor's buildings and their geometric layout.

One of the greatest temple complexes in Angkor exemplified the Khmers' heavy borrowing from Vedic Indian architecture. Angkor aspired to represent the universe in the magnificence of its buildings. As signs of the ruler's power, the pagodas, pyramids, and terra-cotta friezes (ornamented walls) presented the life of the gods on earth. The crowning structure of the royal palace was the magnificent temple of **Angkor Wat,** possibly the largest religious structure ever built. In ornate detail and with great artistry, its buildings and statues represented the revival of the Hindu pantheon within the Khmer royal state. Far less Buddhist influence is visible.

CHRISTIAN EUROPE

> → *How did Christianity produce a distinct identity among the diverse peoples of Europe?*

In the far western corner of Afro-Eurasia, people were building a culture revealingly different. Although their numbers were small compared with the rest of Afro-Eurasia in 1000 CE (36 million in Europe, compared to 80 million in India and 120 million in China), their population would soar to 80 million before the arrival of the Black Death in the fourteenth century.

This was a region of contrasts. On the one hand, the period 1000–1300 witnessed an intense localization of politics because there was no successor to the Roman Empire or

Charlemagne's (see Chapter 9). On the other hand, the territory united under a shared sense of its place in the world. Indeed, some inhabitants even began to believe in the existence of something called "Europe" and increasingly referred to themselves as "Europeans" (see Map 10-9).

WESTERN AND NORTHERN EUROPE

The collapse of Charlemagne's empire had exposed much of northern Europe to invasion, principally from the Vikings, and left the peasantry with no central authority to protect them from local warlords. Armed with deadly weapons, these strongmen collected taxes, imposed forced labor, and became the unchallenged rulers of society. Within this growing warrior aristocracy, northern France led the way. The Franks (later called Frenchmen) were the trendsetters of eleventh- and twelfth-century western Europe.

The most important change was the peasantry's subjugation to the knightly class. Previously, well-to-do peasants had carried arms as "free" men. The moment the farmers lost the right to carry arms, they were no longer free. They slipped back to being mere agricultural laborers. Each peasant toiled under the authority of a lord, who controlled every detail of his or her life. This was the basis of a system known as **feudalism.**

Assured of control of the peasantry, feudal lords watched over an agrarian breakthrough—which fueled a commercial transformation that drew Europe into the rest of the global trading networks. Lordly protection and more advanced metal tools like axes and plows, combined with heavier livestock to pull plows through the root-infested sods of northern

MAP 10-9   LATIN CHRISTENDOM IN 1300

Catholic Europe expanded geographically and integrated culturally during this era. According to this map, into what areas did western Christendom successfully expand? What factors contributed to the growth of a widespread common culture and shared ideas? How did long-distance trade shape the history of the region during this time?

Europe, led to massive deforestation. Above this clearing activity stood the castle. Its threatening presence ensured that the peasantry stayed within range of the collector of rents for the lords and of tithes (shares of crops, earmarked as "donations") for the church. In this blunt way, "feudalism" harnessed agrarian energy to its own needs. The population of western Europe as a whole leaped forward, most spectacularly in the north. As a result, northern Europe (from England to Poland) ceased to be an underdeveloped "barbarian" appendage of the Mediterranean.

EASTERN EUROPE

Nowhere did pioneering peasants develop more land than in the wide-open spaces of eastern Europe, the region's land of opportunity. Between 1100 and 1200, some 200,000 farmers emigrated from Flanders (modern Belgium), Holland, and northern Germany into eastern frontiers. Well-watered landscapes, covered with vast forests, filled up what are now Poland, the Czech Republic, Hungary, and the Baltic states. "Little Europes," whose castles, churches, and towns echoed

The Bayeux Tapestry. This tapestry was prepared by a queen and her ladies to celebrate the victories of William, known as the Conqueror because of his successful invasion of England in 1066. It shows the fascination of the entire "feudal" class, even women, with war on which they depended—great horses, tightly meshed chain mail, long shields, and the stirrups that made such cavalry warfare possible.

the landscape of France, now replaced economies that had been based on gathering honey, hunting, and the slave trade. For a thousand miles along the Baltic Sea, forest clearings dotted with new farmsteads and small towns edged inward from the coast up the river valleys.

The social structure here was a marriage of convenience between migrating peasants and local elites. The area offered the promise of freedom from the feudal lords' arbitrary justice and imposition of forced labor. Even the harsh landscape of the eastern Baltic (where the sea froze every year and impenetrable forests blocked settlers from the coast) was preferable to life in the feudal west. For their part, the elites of eastern Europe—the nobility of Poland, Bohemia, and Hungary and the princes of the Baltic—wished to live well, in the "French"

Olavinilinna Castle. This castle in Finland was the easternmost extension of a "western," feudal style of rule through great castles. It was built at the very end of the Baltic, to keep away the Russians of Novgorod.

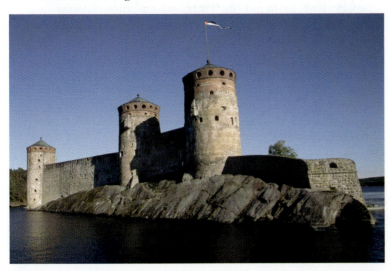

style. But they could do so only if they attracted manpower to their lands by offering newcomers a liberty that they had no hope of enjoying in the west.

THE RUSSIAN LANDS

In Russian lands, western settlers and knights met an eastern brand of Christian devotion. This world looked toward Byzantium, not Rome. Russia was a giant borderland between the steppes of Eurasia and the booming feudalisms of Europe. Its cities lay at the crossroads of overland trade and migration, and Kiev became one of the region's greatest cities. Standing on a bluff above the Dnieper River, it straddled newly opened trade routes. With a population exceeding 20,000, including merchants from eastern and western Europe and the Middle East, Kiev was larger than Paris—larger even than the much-diminished city of Rome.

Kiev looked south to the Black Sea and to Constantinople. Under Iaroslav the Wise (1016–1054), it became a small-scale Constantinople on the Dnieper. A stone church called St. Sophia stood (as in Constantinople) beside the imperial palace. Indeed, with its distinctive "Byzantine" domes, it was a miniature Hagia Sophia (see Chapter 8). Its highest dome towered a hundred feet above the floor, and its splendid mosaics depicting Byzantine saints echoed the religious art of Constantinople. But the message was political as well, for the ruler of Kiev was cast in the mold of the emperor of Constantinople. He now took the title *tsar* from the ancient Roman name given to the emperor, Caesar. From this time onward, *tsar* was the title of rulers in Russia.

The Russian form of Christianity replicated the Byzantine style of churches all along the great rivers leading to the trading cities of the north and northeast. These were not agrarian centers, but hubs of expanding long-distance trade.

Hagia Sophia, Novgorod. The cathedral of Novgorod (as that of Kiev) was called Hagia Sophia. It was a deliberate imitation of the Hagia Sophia of Constantinople, showing Russia's roots in a glorious Roman/Byzantine past that had nothing to do with western Europe.

(See Primary Source: The Birch Bark Letters of Novgorod.) Each city became a small-scale Kiev, and thus a smaller-scale echo of Constantinople. The Orthodox religion looked to Byzantium's Hagia Sophia rather than the Catholic faith associated with the popes in Rome. Russian Christianity remained the Christianity of a borderland—vivid oases of high culture set against the backdrop of vast forests and widely scattered settlements.

WHAT WAS CHRISTIAN EUROPE?

In this era Catholicism became a universalizing faith that transformed the region becoming known as "Europe." The Christianity of post-Roman Europe had been a religion of monks, and its most dynamic centers were great monasteries. Members of the laity were expected to revere and support their monks, nuns, and clergy, but not to imitate them. By 1200, all this had changed. The internal colonization of western Europe—the clearing of woods and founding of villages—ensured that parish churches arose in all but the wildest landscapes. Their spires were visible and their bells were audible from one valley to the next. Church graveyards were the only places where good Christians could be buried; criminals' and outlaws' bodies piled up in "heathen" graves outside the cemetery walls. Even the bones of the believers helped make Europe Christian.

Now the clergy reached more deeply into the private lives of the laity. Marriage and divorce, previously considered family matters, became a full-time preoccupation of the church. And sin was no longer an offense that just "happened"; it was a matter that every person could do something about. Soon, regular confession to a priest became obligatory for all Catholic, western Christians. The followers of Francis of Assisi (1182–1226) emerged as an order of preachers who brought a message of repentance. They did not tell their audiences to enter the monastery (as would have been the case in the early Middle Ages). Instead, their listeners were to weep, confess their sins to local priests, and strive to be better Christians. Franciscans instilled in the hearts of all believers a Europe-wide Catholicism based on daily remorse and daily contemplation of the sufferings of Christ and his mother, Mary. From Ireland to Riga and Budapest, Catholic Christians came to share a common piety.

UNIVERSITIES AND INTELLECTUALS Vital to the creation of Europe's Christian identity was the emergence of universities, for it was during this era that Europe acquired its first class of intellectuals. Since the late twelfth century, scholars had gathered in Paris, where they formed a *universitas*—a term borrowed from merchant communities, where it denoted a type of union. Those who belonged to the *universitas* enjoyed protection by their fellows and freedom to continue their trade. Similarly protected by their own "union," the scholars of Paris began wrestling with the new learning from Arab lands. When the bishop of Paris forbade this undertaking, they simply moved to the Left Bank of the Seine, so as to place the river between themselves and the bishop's officials, who lived around the cathedral of Notre Dame.

The scholars' ability to organize themselves gave them an advantage that their Arab contemporaries lacked. For all his

Primary Source

THE BIRCH BARK LETTERS OF NOVGOROD

The city of Novgorod was a vibrant trading center with a diverse population. From 1951 onward, Russian archaeologists in Novgorod have excavated almost a thousand letters and accounts scratched on birch bark and preserved in the sodden, frequently frozen ground. Reading them, we realize how timeless people's basic concerns can be.

First, we meet the merchants. Many letters are notes by creditors of the debts owed to them by trading partners. The sums are often expressed in precious animal furs. They contain advice to relatives or to partners in other cities:

> Giorgii sends his respects to his father and mother: Sell the house and come here to Smolensk or to Kiev: for the bread is cheap there.

Then we meet neighborhood disputes:

> From Anna to Klemiata: Help me, my lord brother, in my matter with Konstantin. . . . [For I asked him,] "Why have you been so angry with my sister and her daughter. You called her a cow and her daughter a whore. And now Fedor has thrown them both out of the house."

There are even glimpses of real love. A secret marriage is planned:

> Mikiti to Ulianitza: Come to me. I love you, and you me. Ignato will act as witness.

And a poignant note from a woman was discovered in 1993:

> I have written to you three times. What is it that you hold against me, that you did not come to see me this Sunday? I regarded you as I would my own brother. Did I really offend you by that which I sent to you? If you had been pleased you would have torn yourself away from company and come to me. Write to me. If in my clumsiness I have offended you and you should spurn me, then let God be my judge. I love you.

→ *What does the range of people writing on birch bark tell us about these people?*

→ *Think of the messages you send to friends and relatives today. Even if texting and e-mailing seem centuries distant from writing on birch bark, can you relate in any way to these ancient letter-writers?*

Source: A. V. Artsikhovskii and V. I. Borkovski, *Novgorodskie Gramoty na Bereste,* 11 vols. (Moscow: Izd-vo Akademii nauk SSSR, 1951–2004), document nos. 424, 531, 377, and 752.

genius, Ibn Rushd had to spend his life courting the favor of individual monarchs to protect him from conservative fellow Muslims, who frequently burned his books. Ironically, European scholars congregating in Paris could quietly absorb the most persuasive elements of Arabic thought, like Ibn Rushd's. Yet they endeavored to prove that Christianity was the only religion that fully met the aspirations of all rational human beings. Such was the message of the great intellectual Thomas Aquinas, who wrote *Summa contra Gentiles* (Summary of Christian Belief against Non-Christians) in 1264.

The Europe of 1300 was more culturally unified than in previous centuries. It was permeated by Catholicism, and its leading intellectuals extolled the virtues of Christian learning. Such a confident region was not, however, a tolerant place for heretics, Jews, or Muslims.

CHRISTIAN EUROPE ON THE MOVE: THE CRUSADES AND IBERIA

By the tenth and eleventh centuries, western Christianity was on the move, spreading into Scandinavia, southern Italy, the Baltic, and eastern Europe. Its ambitions to reconquer Spain and Portugal (which had been under Islamic control since the eighth century CE) demonstrated one of the effects of feudal power: the lords' self-confidence, their belief in their military capability, and their pious sense of destiny were all inflated. Besides, the wealth of the east was irresistible to those whose piety entwined with an appetite for plunder. Yet the two Christendoms formed an uneasy alliance to roll back the expanding frontiers of Islam. The result: Europeans zealously took war outside their own borders.

Global Connections & Disconnections

THE CRUSADES FROM DUAL PERSPECTIVES

In 1095, Pope Urban II called for the First Crusade in the following words:

> Oh, race of Franks, race from across the mountains, race chosen and beloved by God, as shines forth in very many of your works, set apart from all nations by the situation of your country, as well as by your Catholic faith and the honor of the Holy Church! To you our discourse is addressed, and for you our exhortation is intended. We wish you to know what a grievous cause has led us to your country, what peril, threatening you and all the faithful, has brought us.

The "grievous cause" was the occupation of the Holy City of Jerusalem by the Islamic empire. Formed within the complex relationship between the Byzantine Empire and the western Christian papacy and kingdoms of Europe, the religious motivation behind the Crusades became the subject of many literary renditions of the tumultuous events. It also generated emotionally stirring and polemical (argumentative) writing, depicting either a Muslim or Christian enemy (depending on the work's author).

Polemics are often passionate, harsh, and emotional. They also inspire and reinforce the conviction of fellow believers, with little concern for accuracy. Thus authors of polemic in the time of the Crusades were usually too biased or too misinformed to present accurate portraits of their enemies. But occasionally, firsthand accounts in the form of chronicles and histories offer us unique glimpses into Christian-Muslim relations in the age of the Crusades.

Consider Usāmah ibn Munqidh (1095–1188), the learned ruler of the city of Shaizar in western Syria. Skirmishes, truces, and the ransoming of prisoners were part of his daily life, and Usāmah socialized with his Frankish neighbors as much as he fought with them. He offers a dismissive opinion of his enemies. Basically, they struck him as "animals possessing the virtues of courage and fighting, but nothing else." In particular, their medical practice appalled him. More strange, the Franks allowed their wives to walk about freely and to talk to strangers unaccompanied by male guardians. How could men be at once so brave and yet so lacking in a proper, Arab sense of honor, which would lead a man to protect his women? Unlike other Muslim authors of his time, however, Usāmah does not refer to the Franks in derogatory terms such as "infidels" or "devils." In fact, he occasionally refers to some of them as his companions and writes of a Frank who called him "my brother" (*An Arab-Syrian Gentleman and Warrior in the Time of the Crusades*, 16).

CRUSADES In the late eleventh century, western Europeans launched a wave of attacks known as the **Crusades**. The First Crusade began in 1095, when Pope Urban II appealed to the warrior nobility of France to put their violence to good use: they should combine their role as pilgrims to Jerusalem with that of soldiers, and free Jerusalem from Muslim rule. What the clergy proposed was a novel kind of war. Whereas previously war had been a dirty business and a source of sin, now the clergy told the knights that good and just wars were possible. Such wars could cancel out the sins of those who waged them.

Starting in 1097, an armed host of around 60,000, men moved all the way from northwestern Europe to Jerusalem. This was a huge crowd. But it was divided. Knights in heavy armor led, as they did in Europe. But in the eastern Mediterranean they depended on poor masses who joined the movement to help besiege cities and construct a network of castles as the Christian knights drove their frontier forward. Later Crusaders brought their wives, especially those from the upper class. As in many colonial societies away from the homeland, these women felt freer. Eleanor of Aquitaine, for example, led her own army. Also, queens were crucial in opening up to the local populations. Consider the Armenian queen, Melisende (r. 1131–1152): regarded as wise and experienced in affairs of the state, she was popular with local Christians. As a result, the society of the Crusader states remained more open to women and the lower classes than in Europe. Above all, the Crusades could not have happened without the sailors and merchants of Italy. It was the fleets of Venice, Genoa, and Pisa that transported the later Crusaders and supplied their kingdom.

Christian authors had similar interests in documenting the customs of their enemies in battle. Jean de Joinville (1224/1225–1317) was a chronicler of medieval France. During one crusade, while in the service of the king, Joinville had occasion to note the Muslims' social behavior:

> Whenever the Sultan was in the camp, the men of the personal Guard were quartered all round his lodging, and appointed to guard his person. At the door of the Sultan's lodging there was a little tent for the Sultan's door-keepers, and for his musicians, who had Arabian horns and drums and kettledrums; and they used to make such a din at daybreak and at nightfall that people near them could not hear one another speak, and that they could be heard plainly all through the camp. The musicians never dared sound their instruments in the daytime unless by the order of the Chief of the Guard. Thus it was, that whenever the Sultan had a proclamation to make he used to send for the Chief of the Guard, and give him the order; and then the Chief would cause all the Sultan's instruments to be sounded; and thereupon all the host would come to hear the Sultan's commands.

Although scholars regard such literary renditions with caution, they are useful for gleaning personal details that other types of works omit. The colorful accounts by authors such as Usāmah ibn Munqidh and Joinville are invaluable resources for the social history of the Crusaders.

Jeane de Joinville. Joinville dictating his Memoir of St. Louis, in which he described the Seventh Crusade.

There were five Crusades in all, spread out over two centuries. None of the coalitions, in the end, created permanent Christian kingdoms in the lands they "reconquered." Only a small proportion of Crusaders remained in southwest Asia, and those who did met their match in Muslim armies. (See Global Connections & Disconnections: The Crusades from Dual Perspectives.) Part of the problem was that few Crusaders had any intention of becoming colonists. Only a small proportion remained to defend the Kingdom of Jerusalem after the First Crusade. Most knights returned home, their epic pilgrimage completed. The remaining fragile network of Crusader lordships could barely threaten the Islamic heartlands.

Muslim leaders, however, did not see the Frankish knights as a threat. For them, the Crusades were irrelevant. And as far as the average Muslim of the region was concerned, the Crusaders hardly mattered at all. Jerusalem and Palestine had always been fringe areas in the Middle East. Real prosperity and the capital cities of Muslim kingdoms lay inland, away from the coast—at Cairo, Damascus, and Baghdad. The assaults' long-term effect was to harden Muslim feelings against the Franks and the millions of non-Western Christians who had previously lived peacefully in Egypt and Syria. Muslims viewed the Crusaders as brave but uncivilized warriors. A neighboring Muslim wrote: "The Franks possess none of the virtues of men except courage. . . . Nobody counts for them except knights." Their lack of medical knowledge shocked this observer. He noted that they would rather chop off a man's leg than administer ointments, as Muslim doctors would have advised.

Other campaigns of Christian expansion were more successful. Consider the Spanish driving the Muslims out of the

Crusader. Kneeling, this Crusader promises to serve God (as he would serve a feudal lord) by going to fight on a Crusade (as he would fight for any lord to whom he had sworn loyalty). The two kinds of loyalty—to God and to one's lord—were deliberately confused in Crusader ideology. Both were about war. But fighting for God was unambiguously good, while fighting for a lord was not always so clear-cut.

Iberian Peninsula. Beginning with the capture of Toledo in 1061, the Christian kings of northern Spain (who could count on support from Christian neighbors across the Pyrenees) slowly pushed back the Muslims. Eventually they reached the heart of Andalusia and conquered Seville, adding more than 100,000 square miles of territory to Christian Europe. Another force from northern France crossed Italy to conquer Muslim-held Sicily, ensuring Christian rule in the strategically located mid-Mediterranean island. These two conquests—not the Crusaders' fragile foothold at the edge of the Middle East—turned the tide in relations between Christian and Muslim power.

THE AMERICAS

> → *Where did societies in the Americas demonstrate strong commercial expansionist impulses?*

During this period, the Americas were untouched by the connections reverberating across Afro-Eurasia. After all, navigators still could not cross the large oceans that separated the Americas from other lands. Yet, here, too, commercial and expansionist impulses fostered closer contact among peoples who lived there.

ANDEAN STATES

Growth and prosperity in the Andean region gave rise to South America's first empire. Known as the Chimú Empire, it developed early in the second millennium in the fertile Moche Valley bordering the Pacific Ocean (see Map 10-10). Ultimately the Moche people expanded their influence across numerous valleys and ecological zones, from pastoral highlands to rich valley floodplains to the fecund fishing grounds of the Pacific Coast. As their geographical reach grew, so did their wealth. The Chimú regime lasted until Incan armies invaded in the 1460s and incorporated the Pacific state into their own immense empire.

A THRIVING LOWLAND ECONOMY The Chimú economy was successful because it was highly commercialized. Agriculture was its base, and complex irrigation systems turned the arid coast into a string of fertile oases capable of feeding an increasingly dispersed population. Cotton became a lucrative export to distant markets along the Andes. Parades of llamas and porters lugged these commodities up and down the steep mountain chains that are the spine of South America. As in China, a well-trained bureaucracy oversaw the construction and maintenance of canals, with a hierarchy of provincial administrators watching over commercial hinterlands.

Between 850 and 900 CE, the Moche peoples founded their biggest city, Chan Chan, with a core population of 30,000 inhabitants. A sprawling walled metropolis, covering nearly ten square miles with extensive roads circulating through neighborhoods, it boasted ten huge palaces at its center. Protected by thick walls thirty feet high, these opulent residence halls bespoke the rulers' power. Within the compound, emperors erected mortuary monuments for storing their accumulated riches: fine cloth, gold and silver objects, splendid *Spondylus* shells, and other luxury goods. Around the compound spread neighborhoods for nobles and artisans; farther out stood rows of commoners' houses.

AN INVENTIVE HIGH-
LAND STATE   The Andes
also saw its first highland
empires during this period.
On the shores of the plateau
lake Titicaca, the people of
Tiahuanaco forged a high-
altitude state. Though neither
as large nor as wealthy as the
Chimú Empire, its residents
converted the inhospitable
highlands into an environment where farmers and
herders thrived. There is
evidence of long-distance
trade with neighbors in
semitropical valleys, and even
signs of highlanders migrating to the lowlands to produce agrarian staples for
their kin in the mountains.
Dried fish and cotton came
from the coast; fruits and
vegetables came from low-
land valleys. Trade sustained
an enormous urban popula-
tion of up to 115,000 people.
Looming over the skyline of
Tiahuanaco was an imposing
pyramid of massive sand-
stone blocks. Its advanced
engineering system conveyed
water to the summit, from
which an imitation rainfall
coursed down the carefully
carved sides—an awesome
spectacle of engineering
prowess in such an arid
region.

CONNECTIONS TO THE NORTH

Additional hubs of regional
trade developed farther north,
showing once again that even
in areas of relative geographic
isolation, cultures could flourish and interact within expanding regional spheres. The
Toltecs and the Cahokians
are superb examples.

Chimú Empire c. 1200
Tiahuanaco c. 700
Area of Tiahuanaco influence c. 700
Irrigated river valley
Underground aqueduct
Guinea pigs
Maize
Peanuts
Peppers
Potatoes
Squash
Turkeys

MAP 10-10   ANDEAN STATES

Although the Andes region of South America was isolated from Afro-Eurasian developments before 1500, it was not stagnant. Indeed, political and cultural integration
brought the peoples of this region closer together. Where are the areas of the Chimú
Empire and Tiahuanaco influence on the map? What kinds of ecological niches did they
govern? According to your reading, how did each polity encourage greater cultural and
economic integration?

Andean States. The image to the left shows what remains of Chan Chan. The city covered fifteen square miles and was divided into neighborhoods for nobles, artisans, and commoners, with the elites living closest to the hub of governmental and spiritual power. The buildings of Tiahuanaco (below) were made of giant, hand-hewn stones assembled without mortar. Engineers had not discovered the principle of curved arches and keystones and instead relied on massive slabs atop gateways. Gateways were important symbolic features, for they were places where people acknowledged the importance of sun and moon gods.

THE TOLTECS IN MESOAMERICA By 1000 CE, Mesoamerica had seen the rise and fall of several complex societies. Caravans of porters worked the intricate roads that connected the coast of the Gulf of Mexico to the Pacific, and the southern lowlands of Central America to the arid regions of modern Texas (see Map 10-11). The region's heartland was the rich valley of central Mexico. Here the Toltecs filled the political vacuum left by the decline of Teotihuacán (see Chapter 8) and tapped into the commercial network radiating from the valley.

The Toltecs were a combination of migrant groups, refugees from the south, and farmers from the north. They settled northwest of Teotihuacán as the city waned, making their capital at Tula. They relied on a maize-based economy supplemented by beans, squash, and dog, deer, and rabbit meat. Their rulers, however, made sure that enterprising merchants provided them with status goods such as ornamental pottery, rare shells and stones, and precious skins and feathers.

Tula was a commercial hub, a political capital, and a ceremonial center. While its layout differed from Teotihuacán's, many features revealed borrowings from other Mesoamerican peoples. Temples consisted of giant pyramids topped by colossal stone soldiers, and ball courts where subjects and conquered peoples alike played their ritual sport were ubiquitous. The architecture and monumental art bespoke the mixed and migratory origins of the Toltecs: a combination of Mayan and Teotihuacáno influences. At its height, the Toltec capital teemed with 60,000 people—a huge metropolis by contemporary European standards.

THE CAHOKIANS IN NORTH AMERICA Cities took shape at the hubs of trading networks all across North America. The largest was **Cahokia,** along the Mississippi River near modern-day East St. Louis. A city of about 15,000, it approximated the size of London at the time. Farmers and hunters settled in the region around 600 CE, attracted by its rich soil, its woodlands for fuel and game, and its access to the trading artery of the Mississippi. Eventually, fields of maize and other crops fanned out toward the horizon. The hoe replaced the trusty digging stick, and satellite towns erected granaries to hold the increased yields.

Now Cahokia became a commercial center for regional and long-distance trade. The hinterlands produced staples for Cahokia's urban consumers, and in return its crafts rode inland on the backs of porters and to distant markets in canoes. The city's woven fabrics and ceramics were especially desirable. In exchange, traders brought mica from the Appalachian Mountains, seashells and sharks' teeth from the Gulf of Mexico, and copper from the upper Great Lakes. Indeed, Cahokia became more than an importer and exporter:

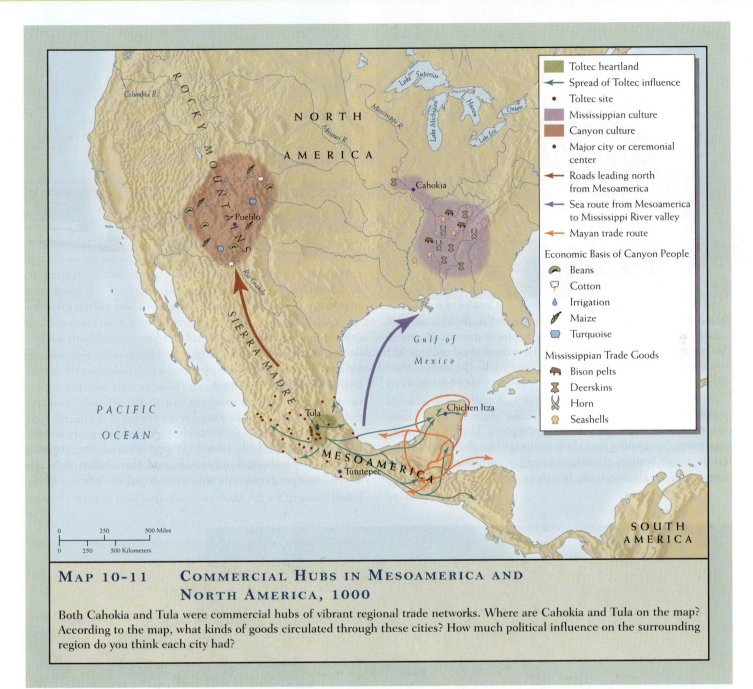

MAP 10-11   COMMERCIAL HUBS IN MESOAMERICA AND NORTH AMERICA, 1000

Both Cahokia and Tula were commercial hubs of vibrant regional trade networks. Where are Cahokia and Tula on the map? According to the map, what kinds of goods circulated through these cities? How much political influence on the surrounding region do you think each city had?

it was the entrepôt for an entire regional network trafficking in salt, tools, pottery, woven stuffs, jewelry, and ceremonial goods.

Dominating Cahokia's urban landscape were enormous mounds (thus the nickname "mound people"). These earthen monuments reveal a sophisticated design and careful maintenance: for example, their builders applied layers of sand and clay to prevent the foundations from drying and cracking. It was from these artificial hills that the people paid homage to spiritual forces. Of course, building this kind of infra-structure without draft animals, hydraulic tools, or even wheels was labor-intensive, so the Cahokians recruited neighboring people to help. A palisade around the city protected the metropolis from marauders.

Ultimately the city outgrew its environment, and its success bred its downfall. As woodlands fell to the axe and arable soil lost nutrients, timber and food became scarce. Because the city lacked a means of transportation to ship bulky items over long distances (in contrast to the sturdy dhows of the Arabian Sea and the bulky junks of the China Sea), its river

MAP 10-12 MONGOL CAMPAIGNS AND CONQUESTS, 1200–1300

Mongol campaigns and conquests brought Afro-Eurasian worlds together as never before. Trace the outline of the entire area of Mongol influence shaded on this map. What cultural groups did the Mongol armies conquer, partially conquer, or invade? How many different Khanates did the Mongols establish across Eurasia, and what were they? What role did geography play in limiting the spread of their influence?

SIBERIA

Lake Baikal

MONGOL ANCESTRAL HOMELAND

Karakorum

GOBI DESERT

GATAI

Shangdu (Xanadu)

Khanbaliq (Beijing) • Dadu

SEA OF JAPAN

KAMAKURA SHOGUNATE

KORYO

JAPAN

Kyoto •

Kaifeng

KHANATE OF THE GREAT KHAN (YUAN EMPIRE)

Yangzhou

Yangzi R.

Hangzhou

TIBET

BURMA

YUNNAN

Pagan • Guangzhou

PACIFIC OCEAN

KHMER EMPIRE

ANNAM

CHAMPA

SOUTH CHINA SEA

SUMATRA

BORNEO

| 0 | 500 | 1000 Miles |
| 0 | 500 | 1000 Kilometers |

← Mongol campaigns
▨ Mongol ancestral homeland
▨ Mongol controlled
▨ Area of loose or temporary Mongol control

THE TRAVELS OF MARCO POLO AND IBN BATTUTA

The most famous of the thirteenth- and fourteenth-century travelers were Marco Polo and Ibn Battuta. They encountered a world linked by trade routes that often had as their ultimate destination the imperial court of the Great Khan in China. These two men, and less celebrated travelers, observed worlds that were highly localized and yet culturally unified.

In 1271, Marco Polo (1254–1324), the son of an enterprising Venetian merchant, set out with his father and uncle on a journey to East Asia. Making their way along the fabled Silk Road across central Asia, the Polos arrived in Xanadu, the summer capital of the Mongol Empire, after a three-and-a-half-year journey. There they remained for more than two decades. When they returned

Marco Polo. This medieval painting shows the caravan of Marco Polo's father and uncle crossing Asia.

KINSHIP NETWORKS AND SOCIAL ROLES Mongol tribes solidified their conquests by extending kinship networks, thus building an empire out of an expanding confederation of familial tribes. The tents (households) were interrelated mostly by marriage: they were alliances sealed by the exchange of daughters. Conquering men married conquered women, and conquered men were selected to marry the conquerors' women. Chinggis Khan may have had more than 500 wives, most of them daughters of tribes that he conquered or that allied with him.

Women in Mongol society were responsible for child-rearing, shearing and milking livestock, and processing pelts for clothing. But they also took part in battles. Kubilai Khan's niece Khutulun became famous for besting men in wrestling matches and claiming their horses as spoils. Although women were often bought and sold, Mongol wives had the right to

own property and to divorce. Elite women even played important political roles. Consider Sorghaghtani Beki, Kubilai Khan's mother, who helped to engineer her sons' rule. Illiterate herself, she made sure that each son acquired a second language to aid in administering conquered lands. She gathered Confucian scholars to prepare Kubilai Khan to rule China. Chabi, Kubilai's senior wife, followed a similar pattern, offering patronage to Tibetan monks who set about converting the Mongol elite in China to Tibetan Buddhism.

CONQUEST AND EMPIRE

The nomads' need for grazing lands contributed to their desire to conquer the splendors of distant fertile belts and rich cities. Then, as they acquired new lands, they increasingly craved

Ibn Battuta. During his journey, Ibn Battuta traveled throughout Africa. In this woodcut, he is depicted in Morocco.

A half-century after Polo began his travels, the Moroccan-born scholar Muhammad ibn Abdullah ibn Battuta (1304–1369) embarked on a journey of his own. Then just twenty-one, he vowed to visit the whole of the Islamic world without traveling the same road twice. It was an ambitious goal, for Islam's domain extended from one end of the Eurasian landmass to the other and far into Africa as well. On his journey, Ibn Battuta eventually covered some 75,000 miles. Along his way, he claimed to have met at least sixty rulers, and in his book he recorded the names of more than 2,000 persons whom he knew personally.

The writings of Marco Polo and Ibn Battuta provide a wealth of information on the well-traversed lands of Africa, Europe, and Asia. What they and other travelers observed was the extreme diversity of Afro-Eurasian peoples, reflecting numerous ethnicities, political formations, and religious faiths. In addition, they observed that the vast majority of people lived deeply localized lives, primarily seeking to obtain the basic necessities of everyday life. Yet, they were also aware the same societies welcomed trade and cultural exchange. In fact, they wrote most eloquently about how each of the four major cultural systems of the landmass—Christian, Muslim, Indian, and Chinese—struggled to define itself. Interestingly, if Ibn Battuta and Marco Polo had been able to travel in the "unknown" worlds—the African hinterlands, the Americas, and Oceania—they would have witnessed to varying degrees similar phenomena and challenges.

to Venice in 1295, fellow townsmen greeted them with astonishment, believing that the Polos had perished years before. So, too, Marco Polo's published account of his travels generated an incredulous reaction. Some of his European readers considered his tales of eastern wonders to be mere fantasy, yet others found their appetites for Asian splendor whetted by his descriptions.

control of richer agricultural and urban areas nearby to increase their wealth and power through tribute. Trade disputes also likely spurred their expeditions. The Mongols depended on settled peoples for grain and manufactured goods (including iron for tools, wagons, weapons, bridles, and stirrups), and their first expansionist forays followed caravan routes.

The expansionist thrust began in 1206 under a united cluster of tribes. A gathering of clan heads acclaimed one of those present as Chinggis (Genghis) Khan, or Supreme Ruler. Chinggis (c. 1155–1227) subsequently launched a series of conquests southward across the Great Wall of China, and westward to Afghanistan and Persia. The Mongols also invaded Korea in 1231. The armies of Chinggis's son reached both the Pacific Ocean and the Adriatic Sea. His grandsons founded dynasties in China, in Persia, and on the southern Eurasian steppes. One of them, Kubilai Khan, enlisted thou-

sands of Koryo men and ships for (ill-fated) invasions of Japan. Thus, a realm took shape that touched all four of Afro-Eurasia's main worlds.

Mongol raiders ultimately built a permanent empire by incorporating conquered peoples and some of their ways. Their feat of unification was far more surprising and sudden than the ties developed incrementally by traders and travelers on ships. Now, Afro-Eurasian regions were connected by land and by sea, in historically unparalleled ways.

MONGOLS IN CHINA

Mongol forces under Chinggis Khan entered northern China at the beginning of the thirteenth century, defeating the Jin army that was no match for the Mongols' superior cavalry on the North China plain. But below the Yangzi River, where the climate and weather changed, the Mongol horsemen fell ill from diseases such as malaria, and their horses perished from the heat. To conquer the semitropical south, the Mongols took to boats and fought along rivers and canals. **Kubilai Khan** (1215–1294) seized the grandest prize of all—southern China—after 1260. His cavalries penetrated the higher plateaus of southwest China and then attacked South China's economic heartland from the west. The Southern Song army fell before his warriors brandishing the latest gunpowder-based weapons (which the Mongols had borrowed from Chinese inventors only to be used against them).

THE FALL OF HANGZHOU   Hangzhou, the last Song capital, succumbed in 1276. Rather than see the invaders pillage the city and their emperors' tombs, the Southern Song bowed to the inevitable. Kubilai Khan's most able commander, Bayan, led his crack Mongol forces in seizing town after town, ever closer to the capital. The Empress Dowager tried to buy them off, proposing substantial tribute payments, but Bayan had his eye on the prize: Hangzhou, which fell under Mongol control but survived reasonably intact. Bayan escorted the emperor and the Empress Dowager to Beijing, where Kubilai treated them with honor. Within three years, Song China's defeat was complete. With all of South China in their grip, the Mongols established the Yuan dynasty with a new capital at Dadu ("Great Capital," present-day Beijing).

Although it fell to Mongol control, Hangzhou survived reasonably intact. It was still one of the greatest cities in the world when the Venetian traveler Marco Polo visited in the 1280s and the Muslim traveler Ibn Battuta in the 1340s. Both men agreed that neither Europe nor the Islamic world had anything like it. (See Global Connections & Disconnections: The Travels of Marco Polo and Ibn Battuta.)

OUTSIDERS TAKE CONTROL   The Mongol conquest both north and south changed the political and social landscape. However, Mongol rule did not impose rough steppeland ways on the "civilized" urbanite Chinese. Outsiders, non-Chinese, took political control. They themselves were a heterogeneous group of Mongols, Tanguts, Khitan, Jurchen, Muslims, Tibetans, Persians, Turks, Nestorians, Jews, Armenians—a conquering elite that ruled over a vast Han majority. The result was a segmented ruling system in which incumbent Chinese elites governed locally, while newcomers managed the central dynastic polity and collected taxes for the Mongols.

MONGOL REVERBERATIONS IN SOUTHEAST ASIA

Southeast Asia also felt the whiplash of conquest. Circling Song defenses in southern China, the Mongols galloped southwest and conquered states in Yunnan and in Burma. From there, in the 1270s, the armies headed directly back east into

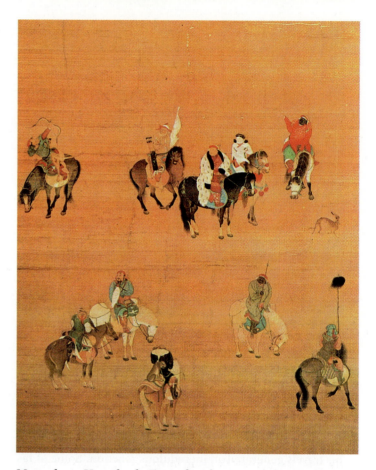

Mongols on Horseback. Even after the Mongols became the rulers of China, the emperors remembered their steppe origin and maintained the skills of horse-riding nomads. This detail from a thirteenth/fourteenth-century silk painting shows Kubilai Khan hunting.

the soft underbelly of the Song state. In this sweep, portions of mainland Southeast Asia became annexed to China for the first time. Even the distant Khmer regime felt repercussions when the Mongol fleet (which grew out of the conquered Song navy) passed by on its way to attack Java—unsuccessfully—in 1293. Kubilai Khan used the conquered Chinese fleets to push his expansionism onto the high seas—with little success during the unsuccessful 1274 and 1281 invasions of Japan from Korea. The ill-fated Javanese expedition was his last.

THE FALL OF BAGHDAD

In the thirteenth century, Mongol tribesmen streamed out of the steppes, crossing the whole of Asia and entering the eastern parts of Europe. Mongke Khan, a grandson of Chinggis, made clear the Mongol aspiration for world domination: he appointed his brother Kubilai to rule over China, Tibet, and the northern parts of India; and he commanded another brother, Hulagu, to conquer Iran, Syria, Egypt, Byzantium, and Armenia.

When Hulagu reached Baghdad in 1258, he encountered a feeble foe and a city that was a shadow of its former glorious self. Merely 10,000 horsemen faced his army of 200,000 soldiers, who were eager to acquire the booty of a wealthy city. Even before the battle had taken place, Baghdadi poets were composing elegies for their dead and mourning the defeat of Islam.

The slaughter was vast. Hulagu himself boasted of taking the lives of at least 200,000 people. The Mongols pursued their adversaries everywhere. They hunted them in wells, latrines, and sewers and followed them into the upper floors of buildings, killing them on rooftops until, as an Iraqi Arab historian observed, "blood poured from the gutters into the streets. . . . The same happened in the mosques" (Lewis, pp. 82–83). In a few weeks of sheer terror, the venerable Abbasid caliphate was demolished. Hulagu's forces showed no mercy to the caliph himself, who was rolled up in a carpet and trampled to death by horses, his blood soaked up by the rug so it would leave no mark on the ground. With Baghdad crushed, the Mongol armies pushed on to Syria, slaughtering Muslims along the way.

In the end, the Egyptian Mamluks stemmed the advancing Mongol armies and prevented Egypt from falling into their hands. The Mongol Empire had reached its outer limits. Better at conquering than governing, the Mongols struggled to rule their vast possessions in makeshift states. Bit by bit, they ceded control to local administrators and dynasts who governed as their surrogates. There was also chronic feuding among the Mongol dynasts themselves. In China and in Persia, Mongol rule collapsed in the fourteenth century.

Mongol conquest reshaped Afro-Eurasia's social landscape. Islam would never again have a unifying authority like the caliphate or a powerful center like Baghdad. China, too, was divided and changed, but in other ways. The Mongols introduced Persian, Islamic, and Byzantine influences on China's architecture, art, science, and medicine. The Yuan policy of benign tolerance also brought elements from Christianity, Judaism, Zoroastrianism, and Islam into the Chinese mix. The Mongol thrust thus led to a great opening, as fine goods, traders, and technology flowed from China to the rest of the world in ensuing centuries. Finally, the Mongol state promoted an Afro-Eurasian interconnectedness that this huge landmass had not known before and would not experience again for hundreds of years. Out of conquest and warfare would come centuries of trade, migration, and increasing contacts among Africa, Europe, and Asia.

CONCLUSION

Between 1000 and 1300, Afro-Eurasia was forming large cultural spheres. As trade and migration spanned longer distances, these spheres prospered and became more integrated. In central Afro-Eurasia, Islam was firmly established, its merchants, scholars, and travelers acting as commercial and cultural intermediaries joining the landmass together, as they spread their universalizing faith. As seaborne trade expanded, India, too, became a commercial crossroads. Merchants in its port cities welcomed traders arriving from Arab lands to the west, from China, and from Southeast Asia. China also boomed, pouring its manufactures into trading networks that reached throughout Afro-Eurasia and even into Africa. Christian Europe had two centers, both of which were at war with Islam. In the east, Byzantium was a formidable empire with a resplendent and unconquerable capital city, Constantinople, in many ways the pride of Christianity. In the west, the Catholic papacy had risen from the ashes of the Roman Empire and sought to extend its ecclesiastical authority over Rome's territories in western Europe.

Trade helped outline the parts of the world. The prosperity it brought also supported new classes of people—thinkers, writers, and naturalists—who clarified what it meant to belong to the regions of Afro-Eurasia. By 1300, learned priests and writers had begun to reimagine these regions as more than just territories: they were maturing into cultures with definable—and defensible—geographic boundaries. Increasingly these intellectuals delivered their messages to commoners as well as to rulers.

Neither the Americas nor sub-Saharan Africa saw the same degree of integration, but trade and migration in these areas did have profound effects. Certain African cultures flourished as they encountered the commercial energy of trade on the Indian Ocean. Indeed, Africans' trade with one another linked coastal and interior regions in an ever more integrated world. American peoples also built cities that dominated cultural areas and thrived through trade. American cultures shared significant features: reliance on trade, maize, and the exchange of goods such as shells and precious feathers. And larger areas honored the same spiritual centers.

By 1300, trade, migration, and conflict were connecting Afro-Eurasian worlds in unprecedented ways. When Mongol armies swept into China, into Southeast Asia, and into the heart of Islam, they applied a thin, surface-like coating of political integration to these widespread regions and built on existing trade links. At the same time, most people's lives remained quite local, driven by the need for subsistence and governed by spiritual and governmental representatives acting at the behest of distant authorities. Still, locals noticed the evidence of cross-cultural exchanges everywhere—in the clothing styles of provincial elites, such as Chinese silks in Paris or Quetzal plumes in northern Mexico; in enticements to move (and forced removals) to new frontiers; in the news of faraway conquests or advancing armies. Worlds were coming together within themselves and across territorial boundaries, while remaining apart as they sought to maintain their own identity and traditions. In Afro-Eurasia especially, as the movement of goods and peoples shifted from ancient land routes to sea-lanes, these contacts were more frequent and far-reaching. Never before had the world seen so much activity connecting its parts. Nor within them had there been so much shared cultural similarity—linguistic, religious, legal, and military. Indeed, by the time the Mongol Empire arose, the regions composing the globe were those that we now recognize as the cultural spheres of today's world. These were truly worlds together and worlds apart.

Review and research materials are available at StudySpace: Ⓢ WWNORTON.COM/STUDYSPACE

KEY TERMS

Angkor Wat (p. 389)	*karim* (p. 365)
Cahokia (p. 398)	Kubilai Khan (p. 405)
Crusades (p. 394)	Mongols (p. 401)
Delhi Sultanate (p. 380)	piety (p. 373)
dhows (p. 364)	rajas (p. 379)
entrepôts (p. 365)	Sufism (p. 374)
feudalism (p. 389)	sultans (p. 379)

Chronology

	700 CE	800 CE	900 CE	1000 CE
SUB-SAHARAN AFRICA			Mandinka merchants establish vast commercial networks linking West Africa ◆	
THE AMERICAS		c. 1000 Cahokia flourishes as a commercial hub in Mississippi River valley ◆		
		c. 900 Moche people found Chan Chan ◆		
		c. 900–1100 Toltec Empire in Mexico Valley ◆ - - - - - - - - - - - - - - - - -		
				1000–1460 Chimú Empire ◆ - - -
THE ISLAMIC WORLD				
SOUTH ASIA			Turkish invasions from Central Asia begin ◆	
EAST ASIA	794–1185 Heian period in Japan ◆ -			
			Song dynasty founded 960 ◆	
			918–1392 Koryo dynasty rules ◆ -	
			Gunpowder invented ◆	
SOUTHEAST ASIA				
		899–1431 Khmer kingdom ◆ -		
CHRISTIAN EUROPE				

STUDY QUESTIONS

1. List the four major cultural regions in Afro-Eurasia, and briefly explain the defining characteristics of each. What did the various people and groups in these geographic areas all have in common that distinguished them from others?

2. Explain the role of global commercial hubs in India, China, and Egypt in fostering commercial contacts across Afro-Eurasia. How did they reflect revolutions in maritime transportation?

3. Which areas of sub-Saharan Africa were parts of the larger Afro-Eurasian world by 1300? How did contact with other regions shape political and cultural developments in sub-Saharan Africa?

4. Describe the cultural diversity within the Islamic world during this era. How did diverse Islamic communities achieve a uniform regional identity?

5. Analyze the impact of Muslim Turkish invaders on India. To what extent did India remain distinct from the Islamic world in this era?

6. Describe how the Song dynasty reacted to the military strength of its nomadic pastoral neighbors. How did these relationships foster a distinct Chinese identity?

7. Compare and contrast cultural and political developments in Korea, Japan, and Southeast Asia during this era. How did other regional cultures influence these societies?

8. Describe how Christianity expanded its geographic reach during this era. How did this expansion affect Latin Christianity in western Europe and Orthodox Christianity in eastern Europe?

9. Analyze the extent to which peoples in the Americas established closer contact with each other. How extensive were these contacts compared with those in the Afro-Eurasian world?

10. Describe the empire that the Mongols created in the thirteenth century. How did their policies promote greater contact among the various regions of Afro-Eurasia?

1100 CE	1200 CE	1300 CE	1400 CE

◆ Kingdom of Mali emerges

◆ Swahili emerges as a distinct language linking the coast of East Africa

◆ Great Zimbabwe

1325–1326 King Mansa Musa of Mali (ruled 1312–1332) completes the hajj ◆

◆ 1071 Turkish forces defeat Byzantine armies at Manzikert

◆ 1258 Mongol forces sack Baghdad, end Abassid caliphate

1206–1526 Turkish warriors found Delhi Sultanate in northern India

◆ Buddhism loses almost all influence in India

◆→ 1274–1281 Japan fends off Mongol invasions

◆ 1279 Mongols conquer Southern Song dynasty

◆ 1127 Song dynasty loses North China to Jurchen Jin dynasty

1192–1333 Kamakura shogunate ◆

1280–1368 Yuan dynasty ◆

◆ Islamic influence increases in city-states

◆ Mongols invade southwestern China and Burma

1061–1492 Spanish Reconquista

1095–1272 Crusades

voyagers—became accidental conduits for deadly microbes. These germs devastated societies far more decisively than did Mongol warfare. They were the real "murderous hordes" of world history, infecting people from every community, class, and culture they encountered. So staggering was the Black Death's toll that population densities did not recover for 200 years. Most severely affected were regions that the Mongols had brought together: settlements and commercial hubs along the old Silk Road and around the Mediterranean Sea and the South China Sea. While segments of the Indian Ocean trading world experienced death and disruption, South Asian societies, which had escaped the Mongol conquest, also escaped the dying and political disruptions associated with the Black Death.

During the fourteenth and fifteenth centuries—following population loss, political crises, and social disorders—peoples struggled to remake their societies. This chapter explores the ways in which Afro-Eurasian peoples restored what they thought was valuable from the old while discarding what they felt had failed them, in favor of radically new institutions and ideas. Considering how grievously people suffered and how many had died, it is surprising that so much of the old (particularly religious beliefs and institutions) survived, though in modified forms. What was truly new and would prove enduring was a group of imperial dynasties that emerged all across Afro-Eurasia: national monarchies in Europe, Ottoman sultans in Anatolia, Safavids in Persia, Mughals in India, and Ming dynasts in China. The aftermath of Mongol rule and of the Black Death witnessed the transformation of the political setting in Afro-Eurasia. Focusing on the formation of new states with highly centralized forms of rulership, this chapter explores how societies coped with the long-term impact of the Mongol invasions and the Black Death.

COLLAPSE AND INTEGRATION

> → *Why was the plague so devastating, and what were the key factors in rebuilding societies after it subsided?*

Although the Mongol invasions overturned political systems, the plague devastated society itself. Rulers could explain to their people the assaults of "barbarians," but it was much harder to make sense of an invisible enemy. Many concluded that mass death was God's wish. However, the upheaval gave ruling groups the opportunity to consolidate power by making dynastic matches through marriage, establishing new armies and taxes, and creating new systems to administer their states.

THE BLACK DEATH

The spread of the Black Death out of inner Asia was the fourteenth century's most significant historical development (see Map 11-1). The disease stemmed from a combination of bubonic, pneumonic, and septicaemic plague strains, and it caused a staggering loss of life. Among infected populations, death rates ranged from 25 to 50 percent.

How did the **Black Death** spread so far? One explanation may lie in climatic changes. A drying up of the central Asian steppe borderlands, where bubonic plague had existed for centuries, may have forced rodents out of their usual dwelling places and pressed pastoral peoples, who carried the strains,

Focus Questions

🌐 WWNORTON.COM/STUDYSPACE

→ *Why was the plague so devastating, and what were the key factors in rebuilding societies after it subsided?*

→ *What were the major differences among the three Islamic dynasties?*

→ *How did the disasters of the fourteenth century change Western Christendom?*

→ *How did the Ming centralize their authority?*

to move closer to settled agricultural communities. So, it is thought, began the migration of microbes. But what spread the germs across Afro-Eurasia was the Mongols' trading network. The first outbreak in a heavily populated region occurred in the 1320s in southwestern China. From there, the disease spread through China and then took its death march along the major trade routes. The main avenue of transmission was across central Asia to the Crimea and the Black Sea, and from there by ship to the Mediterranean Sea and the Italian city-states. Secondary routes were by sea: one from China to the Red Sea, and another across the Indian Ocean, through the Persian Gulf, and into the Fertile Crescent and Iraq. All routes terminated at the Italian port cities, where ships with dead and dying men aboard arrived in 1347. From

Plague Victim. The plague was highly contagious and quickly led to death. Here the physician and his helper cover their noses to avoid the unbearable stench emanating from the patient; they can do little to help the victim as they do not understand what causes the boils, internal bleeding, or violent coughing that afflict him.

there, what Europeans called the Pestilence or the Great Mortality engulfed the western end of the landmass.

The Black Death struck an expanding Afro-Eurasian population, made vulnerable because its members had no immunities to the disease and because its major realms were thoroughly connected through trading networks. Rodents, mainly rats, carried the plague bacilli that caused the disease. Fleas transmitted the bacilli from rodent to rodent, as well as to humans. The epidemic was terrifying, for its causes were unknown at the time. Infected victims died quickly—sometimes overnight—and in great agony, coughing up blood and oozing pus and blood from ugly black sores the size of eggs. Some European sages attributed the ravaging of their societies to an unusual alignment of Saturn, Jupiter, and Mars. Many believed that God was angry with mankind. One Florentine historian compared the plague to the biblical Flood and believed that the end of mankind was imminent.

The Black Death wrought devastation throughout much of the landmass. The Chinese population plunged from around 120 million to 80 million over the course of a century. Europe saw its numbers shrink by one-third. When farmers were afflicted, food production collapsed. Famine then followed and killed off the weak survivors. Worst afflicted were the crowded cities, especially coastal ports. Some cities lost up to two-thirds of their population. Refugees from the cities fled their homes, seeking security and food in the countryside. The shortage of food and other necessities led to rapidly rising prices, work stoppages, and unrest. Political leaders added to their unpopularity by repressing the unrest. The great Arab historian Ibn Khaldun (1332–1406), who lost his mother and father and a number of his teachers to the Black Death in Tunis, underscored the sense of desolation: "Cities and buildings were laid waste, roads and way signs were obliterated, settlements and mansions became empty, dynasties and tribes grew weak," he wrote. "The entire world changed."

REBUILDING STATES

Starting in the late fourteenth century, Afro-Eurasians began the task of reconstructing both their political order and their trading networks. (By then the plague had died down, though it continued to afflict peoples for centuries.) However, the rebuilding of military and civil administrations—no easy task—also required political legitimacy. Rulers needed to revive confidence in themselves and their polities, which they did by fostering beliefs and rituals that confirmed their legitimacy and by increasing their control over subjects.

The basis for power was the **dynasty**—the hereditary ruling family that passed control from one generation to the next. Dynasties sought to establish their legitimacy in three ways. First, ruling families insisted that their power derived from a divine calling: Ming emperors in China claimed for

Progress of bubonic plague
Trade routes
Known areas of major outbreaks
Modern Chinese provincial names for regions affected by outbreak of plague

MAP 11-1   THE SPREAD OF THE BLACK DEATH

The Black Death was an Afro-Eurasian pandemic of the fourteenth century. What was the origin point of the Black Death? What were the main trade routes that allowed the Black Death to spread across Afro-Eurasia? Can you explain why certain parts of Afro-Eurasia were more severely affected than others?

MAIN THEMES

→ *The Black Death spreading out of Inner Asia brings a staggering loss of life, claiming one-third of the population.*

→ *Afro-Eurasians remake their societies in the wake of the plague's devastation.*

→ *Something old remains: religious beliefs and institutions. And something new appears: radically different imperial dynasties in Europe, Anatolia, Persia (Iran), India, and China.*

FOCUS ON *Rebuilding States*

Islamic Dynasties

+ Ottoman, Safavid, and Mughal empires replace the Mongols.
+ Ottomans overrun Constantinople and become the primary Sunni regime in the Islamic world.
+ Safavids come to power in Iran as a Shiite state less tolerant of diversity than the Ottomans.
+ Mughals replace the Delhi Sultanate in South Asia and continue to accommodate diverse religious beliefs.

China

+ The Ming dynasty replaces the Mongol Yuan dynasty and rebuilds a strong state from the ground up.
+ An elaborate, centralized bureaucracy oversees the revival of infrastructure and long-distance trade.

Western Christendom

+ Devastation from the Black Death provokes revolt and extremist religious movements.
+ New national monarchies appear in Portugal, Spain, France, and England.
+ A rebirth of classical learning (the Renaissance) originates in Italian city-states and spreads throughout western Europe.

---

themselves what previous dynasts had asserted—the "mandate of heaven"—while European monarchs claimed to rule by "divine right." Either way, ruling households asserted that they were closer to the gods than to commoners. Second, leaders squelched squabbling among potential heirs by establishing clear rules about succession to the throne. Many European nations tried to standardize succession by passing titles to the eldest male heir, but in practice there were countless complications and quarrels. In the Islamic world, successors could be designated by the incumbent or elected by the community; here, too, struggles over succession were frequent. Third, ruling families elevated their power through conquest or alliance—by ordering armies to forcibly extend their domains, or by marrying their royal offspring to rulers of other states or members of other elite households. Once it established legitimacy, the typical royal family would consolidate power by enacting coercive laws and punishments and sending emissaries to govern far-flung territories. It would also establish standing armies and new administrative structures to collect taxes and to oversee building projects that proclaimed royal power.

The innovative state-building that occurred in the wake of the plague's devastation would not have been as successful had it not drawn on older traditions. In China, the Ming renounced the Mongol legacy by emphasizing their role in restoring Han rulership and by rejecting the Mongol eagerness to expand. In Europe, a cultural flourishing based largely on ancient Greek and Roman models gave rise to thinkers who proposed novel views of governance. The peoples of the Islamic world held fiercely to their religion as two successor states—the Ottoman Empire and the Safavid state—absorbed numerous Turkish-speaking groups. A third Islamic state—the Mughal Empire—drew on local traditions of religious and cultural tolerance as it built a new regime on the foundations of the weakened Delhi Sultanate (see Chapter 10). Many of these regimes lasted for centuries, promoting political institutions and cultural values that became deeply embedded in the fabric of their societies.

ISLAMIC DYNASTIES

→ *What were the major differences among the three Islamic dynasties?*

The devastation of the Black Death following hard on the heels of the Mongol destruction of Islam's most important city and capital of the Abbasid Empire, Baghdad (see Chapter 10), eliminated Islam's old political order. Nonetheless, these two catastrophes prepared the way for new Islamic states to emerge. Of these, the Ottoman, the Safavid, and the Mughal dynasties ultimately grew powerful enough to become empires themselves.

THE MONGOL LEGACY AND THE RISE OF NEW ISLAMIC DYNASTIES

Rather than assimilate the peoples they defeated, the Mongols, whose numbers were always small, often assimilated themselves into the cultures they had conquered. For example, they adopted the Turkish language, and they converted to Islam. In addition, the Mongols fared better when they were closer to the steppe grasses, where their horses could graze. They had a harder time in urban centers. The Mongol Ilkhans in Persia made Maraghah in Azerbaijan their capital, even though it was little more than an enlarged military encampment, in preference to the great administrative center of Baghdad. Still, Mongol armies in Persia as well as China suffered a decline in prowess (Mongol rule in the southern Russian steppes lasted longer). Mongol rule had always had two components. One was an ability to terrorize opponents into voluntarily submitting by such tactics as parading the heads of resisters on pikes. But this strategy began to lose effectiveness and sometimes even backfired. The other Mongol tactic had involved borrowing skills from across the empire and promoting the exchange of technologies and knowledge. But new groups aspiring to rule could do this, too.

Muslim peoples had no respite following the Mongol conquests. The Black Death reached Baghdad by 1347, perhaps carried there by an Azerbaijani army that besieged the city. By the next year, the plague had overtaken Egypt, Syria, and Cyprus; one report from Tunis records the deaths of more than 1,000 people a day in that North African city. Animals, too, were afflicted. One Egyptian writer commented: "The country was not far from being ruined. . . . One found in the desert the bodies of savage animals with the bubos under their arms. It was the same with horses, camels, asses, and all the beasts in general, including birds, even the ostriches." In the eastern Mediterranean, the plague left much of the Islamic world in a state of near political and economic collapse.

As new polities emerged from this economic and demographic crisis, they had to build from the ground floor. Warrior chiefs and religious leaders vied to fill the political vacuum. After Mongol power waned, the new rulers—notably the Ottomans in Anatolia and the Safavids in western Persia—operated out of strategic locations in the Islamic heartland and gradually rebuilt state institutions.

Through migration, warfare, and the eventual consolidation of post-Mongol states, Islam's domain expanded. Prior to the Mongol invasions, the political, economic, and cultural centers of the Islamic world were in Egypt, Syria, and Iraq. Most of these territories' inhabitants spoke Arabic, the language of the Prophet Muhammad—hence the language of Islamic devotion and theology. These areas, along with the Arabian Peninsula, contained Islam's most holy cities: Mecca, Medina, Jerusalem, Damascus, Cairo, Baghdad, and various other cities in Iraq. Even before the Mongol invasions, Turks had migrated into these regions and Persian had become a rival language of Islamic poetry and philosophy. Yet it was the Mongol invasions, which brought devastation to Persia and Iraq and an influx of nomadic peoples, that enabled a new Islamic world to appear. (See Primary Source: Qalandar Dervishes in the Islamic World.)

THREE ISLAMIC EMPIRES This new Islamic world, now including large numbers of Turkish- and Persian-speaking populations, occupied a vast geographical triangle. It stretched from Anatolia in the west to Khurasan in the east and to the southern apex at Baghdad. Of course, the old Arabic-speaking Islamic world remained vital, still at the heart of Islam geographically, but it now had to cede authority to the new rulers and religious men.

The Ottomans, the Safavids, and the Mughals emerged as the dominant states in the old Islamic world in the early sixteenth century. They exploited the rich agrarian resources of the Indian Ocean regions and the Mediterranean Sea basin, and they benefited from a brisk seaborne and overland trade. By the mid-sixteenth century the Mughals controlled the northern Indus River valley; the Safavids occupied Persia; and the Ottomans ruled Anatolia, the Arab world, and much of southern and eastern Europe.

Despite sharing core Islamic beliefs, each empire had unique political features. The most powerful, the **Ottoman Empire,** occupied the pivotal area between Europe and Asia. The Ottomans embraced a Sunni view of Islam, while adopting traditional Byzantine ways of governance and trying new ways of integrating the diverse peoples of their expanding territories. The Safavids, though adherents of the Shiite vision of Islam, were at the same time ardently devoted to the pre-Islamic traditions of Persia (present-day Iran). An internally cohesive people, their rulers were not so effective at expanding

Primary Source

QALANDAR DERVISHES IN THE ISLAMIC WORLD

The Qalandar dervish order sprang up in Damascus, Syria, and Egypt in the thirteenth century and spread rapidly throughout the Islamic world. In reaction to the period's widespread unrest, its members renounced the world and engaged in highly individualistic practices as they moved from place to place. The educated elite, however, criticized them as ignorant hypocrites living on alms obtained from gullible common folk. One of their practices was chiromancy, or palm-reading. In this excerpt Giovan Antonio Manavino, a European observer of Ottoman society, gives an obviously biased account of the Qalandars, whom he called the torlaks.

Dressed in sheepskins, the *torlaks* [Qalandars] are otherwise naked, with no headgear. Their scalps are always clean-shaven and well rubbed with oil as a precaution against the cold. They burn their temples with an old rag so that their faces will not be damaged by sweat. Illiterate and unable to do anything manly, they live like beasts, surviving on alms only. For this reason, they are to be found around taverns and public kitchens in cities. If, while roaming the countryside, they come across a well-dressed person, they try to make him one of their own, stripping him naked. Like Gypsies in Europe, they practice chiromancy, especially for women who then provide them with bread, eggs, cheese, and other foods in return for their services.

Amongst them there is usually an old man whom they revere and worship like God. When they enter a town, they gather around the best house of the town and listen in great humility to the words of this old man, who, after a spell of ecstasy, foretells the descent of a great evil upon the town. His disciples then implore him to fend off the disaster through his good services. The old man accepts the plea of his followers, though not without an initial show of reluctance, and prays to God, asking him to spare the town the imminent danger awaiting it. This time-honored trick earns them considerable sums of alms from ignorant and credulous people.

→ *Describe the way the Qalandar dervishes dressed, where they congregated, and how they obtained food. How did their lifestyle reflect the turmoil of the times?*

→ *Why do you think the Qalandars chose individualistic practices rather than communal living?*

→ *Why do you think Manavino is so critical of the Qalandars?*

SOURCE: Ahmet T. Karamustafa, "Dervish Groups in the Ottoman Empire, 1450–1550" from *God's Unruly Friends: Dervish Groups in the Islamic Later Middle Period, 1200–1550*, pp. 6–7. Oneworld Publications, Oxford, 2006. Reprinted with the permission of Oneworld Publications.

---

beyond their Persian base. The Mughals ruled over the wealthy but divided realm that is much of today's India, Pakistan, and Bangladesh; here they carried even further the region's religious and political traditions of assimilating Islamic and pre-Islamic Indian ways. Their wealth and the decentralization of their domain made the Mughals constant targets for internal dissent and eventually for external aggression.

THE RISE OF THE OTTOMAN EMPIRE

Although the Mongols considered Anatolia to be a borderland region of little economic importance, their military forays against the Anatolian Seljuk Turkish state in the late thirteenth century opened up the region to new political forces. The ultimate victors here were the Ottoman Turks. They transformed themselves from warrior bands roaming the borderlands between Islamic and Christian worlds into rulers of a settled state and, finally, into sovereigns of a far-flung, highly bureaucratic empire (see Map 11-2).

Under their chief, Osman (r. 1299–1326), the Turkish Ottomans formalized a stern and disciplined warrior ethos, and they triumphed over their rivals by assimilating the techniques of settled administration from their neighbors. Other warrior bands, which lived off the land and fought for booty under charismatic military leaders, had little regard for artisans, merchants, bureaucrats, and clerics. By contrast, the

MAP 11-2   THE OTTOMAN EMPIRE, 1300–1566
This map charts the expansion of the Ottoman state from the time of its founder, Osman, through the reign of Suleiman, the empire's most illustrious ruler. Identify the earliest part of the empire under Osman. Then identify all the areas of conquest under Suleiman. Against whom did the Ottomans fight between the years 1326 and 1566? What were the geographic limits of the empire? According to your reading, how did Ottoman rulers promote unity among such a diverse population?

Ottomans realized that the consolidation of power depended on attracting just these groups. In time, not only did the Ottoman state (based in Bursa in western Anatolia) win the favor of Islamic clerics, but it also became the champion of Sunni Islam throughout the Islamic world.

By the mid-fourteenth century, the Ottomans had expanded into the Balkans, becoming the most powerful force in the eastern Mediterranean and western Asia. The state controlled a vast territory, stretching in the west to the Moroccan border, in the north to Hungary and Moldavia, in the south through the Arabian Peninsula, and in the east to the Iraqi-Persian border. At the top of the Ottomans' elaborate hierarchy stood the sultan. Below him was a military and civilian bureaucracy, whose task was to demand obedience

and revenue from subjects. The bureaucracy's vigilance enabled the sultan to expand his realm, which in turn forced him to invest in an even larger bureaucracy.

THE CONQUEST OF CONSTANTINOPLE   The empire's spectacular expansion was primarily a military affair. To recruit followers, the Ottomans promised wealth and glory to new subjects. This was an expensive undertaking, but territorial expansion generated vast financial and administrative rewards. Moreover, by spreading the spoils of conquest and lucrative administrative positions, rulers bought off potentially discontented subordinates. Still, without military might, the Ottomans would not have enjoyed the successes associated with the brilliant reigns of Murad II

The Conquest of Constantinople. In 1453, the Ottomans, led by Sultan Mehmed, later called the Conqueror, broke through the defenses of the city of Constantinople and incorporated this bastion of Byzantine Christian civilization into the Ottoman Empire. They changed the city's name to Istanbul and made it their own capital.

(r. 1421–1451) and his aptly named successor, Mehmed the Conqueror (r. 1451–1481).

Mehmed's most spectacular triumph was the conquest of Constantinople, an ambition for Muslim rulers ever since the birth of Islam. Mehmed left no doubt that this was his primary goal: shortly after his coronation he vowed to capture the capital of the Byzantine Empire, a city of immense strategic and commercial importance. He knew this feat would require a large and well-armed fighting force, for the heavily fortified city had kept Muslims at bay for almost a century. First he built a fortress of his own, on the European bank of the Bosporus strait, to prevent European vessels from reaching the capital. Then, by promising his soldiers free access to booty and portraying the city's conquest as a holy cause, he amassed a huge army that outnumbered the defending force of 7,000 by more than tenfold. For forty days his troops bombarded Constantinople's massive walls with artillery that included enormous cannons built by Hungarian and Italian engineers. On May 29, 1453, Ottoman troops overwhelmed the surviving soldiers and took the ancient Roman and Chris-

tian capital of Byzantium—which Mehmed promptly renamed Istanbul.

Although Christians generally portrayed the "fall" of Constantinople as an insult and a disaster, in fact the Muslim conquest had cultural benefits for western Europe. Many Christian survivors fled to ports in the west, bringing with them classical and Arabic manuscripts previously unknown in Europe. The well-educated, Greek-speaking émigrés generally became teachers and translators, thereby helping to revive Europeans' interest in classical antiquity and spreading knowledge of ancient Greek (which had virtually died out in medieval times). These manuscripts and teachers would play a vital role in Europe's Renaissance.

The Ottomans followed their capture of Constantinople with other military successes that put many of Christian Europe's great cities in peril. Their forces sacked Athens in 1458, then took Bosnia in 1463. In 1480 the Ottomans launched an invasion of Italy. They captured one port city; but Mehmed II's death, and fights between his sons for control of the empire, prevented further conquests in Italy. The

Ottomans then turned to the Balkans and central Europe, invading Hungary in 1492 and Croatia in 1493. Their inroads so frightened the French king that he decided to invade Italy himself in order to lead his own crusade against the Ottomans.

Meanwhile, Mehmed made Istanbul the Ottoman capital, adopting Byzantine administrative practices to unify his enlarged state and incorporating many of Byzantium's powerful families into it. From Istanbul, Mehmed and his successors would continue their expansion, eventually seizing all of Greece and the Balkan region. As a result, Ottoman navies increasingly controlled sea-lanes in the eastern Mediterranean, curtailing European access to the rich ports that handled the lucrative caravan trade. By the late fifteenth century, Ottoman forces menaced another of Christendom's great capitals, Vienna, and European merchants feared that never again would they obtain the riches of Asia via the traditional overland route.

THE TOOLS OF EMPIRE BUILDING Having penetrated the heartland of Christian Byzantium, under Selim (r. 1512–1520) and Suleiman (r. 1520–1566), the Ottomans turned their expansionist designs to the Arab world. During the latter's reign the Ottomans reached the height of their territorial expansion, with Suleiman himself leading thirteen major military campaigns and many minor engagements. An exceptional military leader, Suleiman was an equally gifted administrator. His subjects called him "the Lawgiver" and "the Magnificent" in recognition of his attention to civil bureaucratic efficiency and justice for his people. His fame spread to Europe, where he was known as "the Great Turk." Under Suleiman's administration, the Ottoman state ruled over 20 to 30 million people. By the time Suleiman died, the Ottoman Empire bridged Europe and the Arab world. Istanbul by then was a dynamic imperial hub, dispatching bureaucrats and military men to oversee a vast domain.

The Suleymaniye Mosque. Built by Sultan Suleiman to crown his achievements, the Suleymaniye Mosque was designed by the architect Sinan to dominate the city and to have four tall minarets from which the faithful were called to prayer.

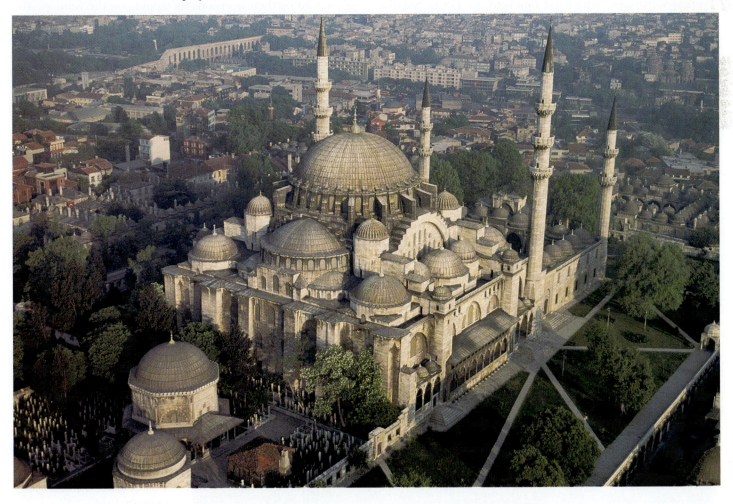

Ottoman dynastic power was, however, not only military; it also rested on a firm religious foundation. At the center of this empire were the sultans, who combined a warrior ethos with an unwavering devotion to Islam. Describing themselves as the "shadow of God" on earth, they claimed to be caretakers for the welfare of the Islamic faith. Throughout the empire, the sultans devoted substantial resources to the construction of elaborate mosques and to the support of Islamic schools. As self-appointed defenders of the faithful, the sultans assumed the role of protectors of the holy cities on the Arabian Peninsula and of Jerusalem, defending the realm's internal cohesion and constantly striving to extend the borders of Islam. Thus the Islamic faith helped to unite a diverse and sprawling imperial populace, with the sultan's power fusing the sacred and the secular.

ISTANBUL AND THE TOPKAPI PALACE   Istanbul reflected the splendor of this awesome empire. After the Ottoman conquest, the sultans' engineers rebuilt the city's crumbling walls, while their architects redesigned homes, public buildings, baths, inns, and marketplaces to display the majesty of Islam's new imperial center. To crown his achievements, Suleiman ordered the construction of the Suleymaniye Mosque, which sat opposite the Hagia Sophia. That domed Byzantine cathedral was formerly the most sacred of Christian cathedrals, the largest house of worship in all of Christendom, but Suleiman had it turned into a mosque. Moreover, the Ottoman dynasts welcomed (indeed, forcibly transported) thousands of Muslims and non-Muslims to the city and revived Istanbul as a major trading center. Within twenty-five years of its conquest, its population more than tripled; by the end of the sixteenth century, 400,000 people regularly swarmed through its streets and knelt in its mosques, making it the world's largest city outside China.

Istanbul's **Topkapi Palace** reflected the Ottomans' view of governance, the sultans' emphasis on religion, and the continuing influence of Ottoman familial traditions—even in the administration of a far-flung empire. Laid out by Mehmed II, the palace complex reflected a vision of Istanbul as the center of the world. As a way to exalt the sultan's magnificent power, architects designed the complex so that the buildings containing the imperial household nestled behind layers of outer courtyards, in a mosaic of mosques, courts, and special dwellings for the sultan's harem.

The growing importance of Topkapi Palace as the command post of empire represented a crucial transition in the history of Ottoman rulers. Not only was the palace the place where future bureaucrats received their training; it was also the place where the chief bureaucrat, the grand vizier, carried out the day-to-day running of the empire. Whereas the early sultans had led their soldiers into battle personally and had met face-to-face with their kinsmen, the later rulers withdrew into the sanctity of the palace, venturing out only occasionally for grand ceremonies. Still, every Friday, subjects queued up outside the palace to introduce their petitions, ask for favors, and seek justice. If they were lucky, the sultans would be there to greet them—but they did so behind grated glass, issuing their decisions by tapping on the window. The palace thus projected a sense of majestic, distant wonder, a home fit for semidivine rulers.

And Topkapi was indeed a home—for the increasingly sedentary sultan and his harem. Among his most cherished quarters were those set aside for women. At first, women's influence in the Ottoman polity was slight. But as the realm consolidated, women became a powerful political force. The harem, like the rest of Ottoman society, had its own hierarchy of rank and prestige. At the bottom were slave women; at the top were the sultan's mother and his favorite consorts. As many as 10,000 to 12,000 women inhabited the palace, often

The Topkapi Palace. A view of the inner courtyard of the seraglio, where the sultan and his harem lived.

in cramped quarters. Those who had the ruler's ear conspired to have him favor their own children, which made for widespread intrigue. When a sultan died, the entire retinue of women would be sent to a distant palace poignantly called the Palace of Tears, because the women who occupied it wept at the loss of the sultan and their own banishment from power.

DIVERSITY AND CONTROL   The fact that the Ottoman Empire endured into the twentieth century owed much to the ruling elite's ability to win the favor of exceedingly diverse populations. After all, neither conquest nor conversion eliminated cultural differences in the empire's distant provinces. Thus, for example, the Ottomans' language policy was one of flexibility and tolerance. Although Ottoman Turkish was the official language of administration, Arabic was the primary language of the Arab provinces, the common tongue of street life. Within the empire's European corner, the sounds and cadences of various languages continued to prevail. From the fifteenth century onward, the Ottoman Empire was more multilingual than any of its rivals.

In politics, as in language, the Ottomans showed flexibility and tolerance. The imperial bureaucracy permitted extensive regional autonomy. In fact, Ottoman military cadres perfected a technique for absorbing newly conquered territories into the empire by parceling them out as revenue-producing units among loyal followers and kin. Regional appointees could collect local taxes, part of which they earmarked for Istanbul and part of which they pocketed for themselves. (This was a common administrative device for many world dynasties ruling extensive domains.)

Like other empires, the Ottoman state was always in danger of losing control over its provincial rulers. Local rulers—the group that the imperial center allowed to rule locally—found that great distances enabled them to operate independently from central authority. These local authorities kept larger amounts of tax revenues than Istanbul deemed proper. So, to clip local autonomy, the Ottomans established a corps of infantry soldiers and bureaucrats (called janissaries) who owed direct allegiance to the sultan. The system at its high point involved a conscription of Christian youths from the empire's European lands. This conscription, called the *devshirme,* required each village to hand over a certain number of males between the ages of eight and eighteen. Uprooted from their families and villages, selected for their fine physiques and good looks, these young men were converted to Islam and sent to farms to build up their bodies and learn Turkish. A select few were moved on to Topkapi Palace to learn Ottoman military, religious, and administrative techniques. Some of these men later enjoyed exceptional careers in the arts and sciences—such as the architect Sinan, who designed the Suleymaniye Mosque. Recipients of the best education available in the Islamic world, trained in Ottoman ways, instructed in the use of modern weaponry, and shorn of all family connections, the *devshirme* recruits were prepared to serve the sultan (and the empire as a whole) rather than the interests of any particular locality or ethnic group.

The *Devshirme.* A miniature painting from 1558 depicts the *devshirme* system of taking non-Muslim children from their families in the Balkan Peninsula as a human tribute in place of cash taxes, which the poor region could not pay. The children were educated in Ottoman Muslim ways and prepared for service in the sultan's civil and military bureaucracy.

The Ottomans thus artfully balanced the decentralizing tendencies of the outlying regions with the centralizing forces of the imperial capital. Relying on a careful mixture of faith, patronage, and tolerance, the sultans curried loyalty and secured political stability. Indeed, so strong and stable was the polity that the Ottoman Empire dominated the coveted and highly contested crossroads between Europe and Asia for many centuries.

THE SAFAVID EMPIRE IN IRAN

The Ottoman dynasts were not the only rulers to extend Islam's political domain. In Persia, too, a new empire arose in the aftermath of the Mongols. The legitimacy of the Safavid Empire, like that of the Ottoman, rested on an Islamic foundation. But the Shiism espoused by Safavid rulers devotees preached the doctrine of divine love. In the Punjab, previously a core area of the Delhi Sultanate, a new religion known as Sikhism came into being. **Sikhism** largely followed the teachings of Nanak (1469–1539). Although born a Hindu, he was inspired by Islamic ideals and called on his followers to renounce the caste system and to treat all believers as equal before God. (See Primary Source: Nanak's Teachings in India.)

Following Timur's attack, rival kingdoms and sultanates asserted their independence, leaving the Delhi Sultanate a mere shadow of its former self. It became just one of several competing powers in northern India, ruled first by the Sayyids and then by the Afghan dynasty of the Lodis. Surrounded by resurgent Hindu and Islamic polities, the weakened sultanate experienced something of a revival in the Lodi era. But the attempt by the last Lodi sultan to consolidate power by clipping the wings of the Afghan nobility provoked the governor of the Punjab to invite the Turkish prince Babur (the "Tiger") to India in 1526. A great-grandson of Timur, Babur traced his lineage to both the Turks and the Mongols (he was said to be a descendant of Chinggis Khan). For years, Babur had longed to conquer India. Massing an army of Turks and Afghans armed with matchlock cannons, he easily breached the wall of elephants put together by defenders of the sultan. Delhi fell, and the sultanate came to an end. Babur proclaimed himself emperor and spent

MAP 11-4   THE MUGHAL EMPIRE, 1530

Compare the Mughal state with the other major Asian empires of this period, notably the Ottoman, Safavid, and Ming states (see Maps 11-2, 11-3, 11-6). What geographic characteristic distinguished the Mughal state at this time from the others? Where in the landmass did the new state arise, and what effect do you think its place of origin had on the nature of Mughal rule? Based on their geographic location, to what religious traditions did the Mughals need to be sensitive?

Primary Source

NANAK'S TEACHINGS IN INDIA

Nanak (1469–1539), generally recognized as the founder of Sikhism, lived in northern India and participated in the religious discussions that were prominent at the time. As in western Europe and Islamic Southwest Asia, this was a period of political turmoil and intense personal introspection. The following excerpts demonstrate Nanak's views on the failings of the age and his use of Islamic and Hindu ideas to elaborate a unique spiritual perspective. Nanak stressed the unity of God, an emphasis that reflected Islamic influences. Nonetheless, his insistence on the comparative unimportance of prophets ran counter to Islam, and his belief in rebirth was strictly Hindu.

There is but one God, whose name is true, the Creator,
    devoid of fear and enmity, immortal, unborn, self-
    existent; God the great and bountiful. Repeat His
    Name.

Numberless are the fools appallingly blind;
Numberless are the thieves and devourers of others'
    property;
Numberless are those who establish their sovereignty by
    force;
Numberless the cutthroats and murderers; Numberless
    the liars who roam about lying;
Numberless the filthy who enjoy filthy gain;
Numberless the slandered who carry loads of calumny
    on their heads;
Nanak thus described the degraded.
So lowly am I, I cannot even once be a sacrifice unto
    Thee. Whatever pleaseth Thee is good.
O Formless One, Thou art ever secure.

The Hindus have forgotten God, and are going the
    wrong way.
They worship according to the instruction of Narad.
They are blind and dumb, the blindest of the blind.
The ignorant fools take stones and worship them.
O Hindus, how shall the stone which itself sinketh carry
    you across?

What power hath caste? It is the reality that is tested.
Poison may be held in the hand, but man dieth if he eat it.
The sovereignty of the True One is known in every age.
    He who obeyeth God's order shall become a noble in
    His court.

Those who have meditated on God as the truest of the
    true have done real worship and are contented;
They have refrained from evil, done good deeds, and
    practiced honesty;
They have lived on a little corn and water, and burst the
    entanglements of the world.
Thou art the great Bestower; ever Thou givest gifts
    which increase a quarterfold.
Those who have magnified the great God have found
    Him.

→ *Identify all the "numberless" groups that Nanak lists. What range of social classes do they represent? How does this enumeration reflect the tumultuous times?*
→ *What criticisms of Hindu worship does Nanak raise?*
→ *What lines reveal his belief in rebirth?*
→ *How does Nanak expect true believers to behave?*

SOURCE: "Nanak's Teachings in India" from *Sources of Indian Tradition*, ed. William Theodore de Bary, © 1958 Columbia University Press. Reprinted with permission of the publisher.

the next few years snuffing out the remaining resistance to his rule (see Map 11-4). Thus he laid the foundation of the Mughal Empire, the third great Islamic dynasty (discussed in detail in Chapter 12).

By the sixteenth century, then, the Islamic heartland had seen the emergence of three new empires. Their differences were obvious, especially in the religious sphere. The Ottomans were Sunni Islam's most fervent champions, determined to eradicate the Shiite heresy on their border where an equally determined Persian Safavid dynasty sought to expand the realm of Shiism. In contrast to these dynasties' sectarian religious commitments, the Mughals of India, drawing on well-established Indian traditions of religious and cultural tolerance, were open-minded toward non-Muslim believers and sectarian groups within the Muslim community. Yet, the political similarities of these imperial dynasties were equally clear-cut. Although these states did not hesitate to go to war against each other, they shared similar styles of rule. All established their legitimacy via military prowess, religious backing, and a loyal bureaucracy. This combination of spiritual and military weaponry enabled emperors, espousing Muhammad's preachings, to claim vast domains. Islam also bound together rulers and those whom they ruled. Moreover, their religious differences did not prevent the movement of goods, ideas, merchants, and scholars across political and religious boundaries—even across the most divisive boundary of all, that between Sunni Iraq and Shiite Persia.

WESTERN CHRISTENDOM

> → *How did the disasters of the fourteenth century change Western Christendom?*

In western Afro-Eurasia, the period 1100–1300 was one of prosperity, population growth, and cultural flowering. Known as the High Middle Ages, this era saw spectacular advances in the arts, technology, learning, architecture, and banking. Expanding populations freed up laborers to move from the countryside to the cities. London, with a population of some 60,000 within its walls and 10,000 or more outside them, was only one city to experience a housing crunch; in some of its poorer sections, up to twelve people slept in a single room. Though excluded from many crafts and professions, women made gains in retail trades, weaving, and food production. Wives often supervised shops or took goods to local fairs, where producers met to exchange their wares.

During the High Middle Ages, Europe's 80 million inhabitants remained largely rooted to their local communities, but growing wealth allowed some to widen their horizons. Bologna, Paris, Oxford, and Cambridge had universities (with medical, law, and theology faculties), and a few scholars had begun to appreciate the learning of Arabs and earlier Greeks and Romans. Thomas Aquinas (1225–1274), a leading philosopher and theologian, had laid out the main tenets of western Christianity and resolved questions of faith and reason to the satisfaction of clerical and secular intellectuals. Florentine bankers opened establishments in commercial port cities, and Greek shipbuilders expanded their trade. New devices like mechanical clocks and the compass improved the accuracy of measurements on sea and on land, while spinning wheels increased the pace of cloth production. But all of this prosperity, population growth, and innovation would be halted by the tragedies of the fourteenth century.

REACTIONS, REVOLTS, AND RELIGION

Disastrous climatic changes struck first. Beginning around 1310, extremely harsh winters and rainy summers shortened the growing seasons and played havoc with harvests. Exhausted soils no longer supplied the resources to feed and clothe growing urban and rural populations. Nobles squeezed the peasantry hard in an effort to maintain their luxurious lifestyle. States raised taxes to balance their growing expenditures. In this context, Europe endured the first of several disasters: famine. It appeared in 1315 and did not let up for seven cruel years, by which time millions had died of starvation or of diseases against which the malnourished population had little resistance. But this was merely the prelude to a century and more of warfare, epidemic disease, famine, and social unrest.

THE PLAGUE IN EUROPE In the wake of famine came the Black Death, starting around 1347 and ravaging the Italian Peninsula; then it seized France, the Low Countries, (present-day Netherlands, Belgium, and Luxembourg), Germany, and England in its deathly grip. The overcrowded and unsanitary cities were particularly vulnerable. Bremen lost at least 8,000 souls, perhaps two-thirds of its population; Hamburg, another port city, at least as many. The poor, sleeping in crowded quarters, were especially at risk. But master bakers, bankers, and aristocrats died too, unless they were able to flee to the relatively safer countryside in time to escape infection. No one had seen dying on such a scale. Some 25 to 50 percent of Europe's total population perished between 1347 and 1351.

After 1352, the epidemic died down, having killed all those with no natural immunities and most of the original carriers of the disease, the European black rat. But the plague would return every seven years or so for the rest of the century, as well as sporadically through the entire fifteenth century, killing the young and those who had managed to escape exposure in the first epidemic. The European population continued to decline, until by 1450 many areas had only one-quarter the number of a century earlier. Indeed, it took three centuries to return to population levels that existed prior to the Black Death.

Disaster on this scale had enduring psychological, social, economic, and political effects. Many individuals turned to pleasure, even debauchery, determined to enjoy themselves before it came their turn to die. Others retreated into a personal spirituality, convinced that they needed to put their lives in order before passing on to the next life. Occasionally, eccentric groups took shape. The Beghards, or Brethren of the Free Speech, claimed to be in a state of grace that allowed them to do as they pleased—including adultery, free love, nudity, and murder. By contrast, the Flagellants were so sure that man had incurred God's wrath that they whipped them-

Primary Source

FLAGELLANTS IN ENGLAND

Like the Qalandar dervishes in the Islamic realm (see p. 000), European Flagellants renounced the world and engaged in public self-punishment in reaction to the warfare, famines, and plagues of the fourteenth century. The Flagellants carried whips (flagella) with metal pieces run through knotted thongs, which they used to beat and whip themselves until they were bruised, swollen, and bloody. Robert of Avesbury here describes the actions of Flagellants in England during the reign of King Edward III.

In that same year of 1349, about Michaelmas [29 September], more than 120 men, for the most part from Zeeland or Holland, arrived in London from Flanders. These went barefoot in procession twice a day in the sight of the people, sometimes in St Paul's church and sometimes elsewhere in the city, their bodies naked except for a linen cloth from loins to ankle. Each wore a hood painted with a red cross at front and back and carried in his right hand a whip with three thongs. Each thong had a knot in it, with something sharp, like a needle, stuck through the middle of the knot so that it stuck out on each side, and as they walked one after the other they struck themselves with these whips on their naked, bloody bodies; four of them singing in their own tongue and the rest answering in the manner of the Christian litany. Three times in each procession they would all prostrate themselves on the ground, with their arms outstretched in the shape of a cross. Still singing, and beginning with the man at the end, each in turn would step over the others, lashing the man beneath him once with his whip, until all of those lying down had gone through the same ritual. Then each one put on his usual clothes and, always with their hoods on their heads and carrying their whips, they departed to their lodgings. It was said that they performed a similar penance every night.

→ *Describe how the Flagellants dressed, and identify the languages they spoke. What elements of Christianity did these characteristics display?*
→ *Why do you think the Flagellants whipped themselves?*
→ *How did the Flagellants differ from the Qalanders?*

SOURCE: Robertus de Avesbury, "Flagellants in England" from *The Black Death*, Rosemary Horrox, trans./ed., pp. 153–54. Copyright © Rosemary Horrox 1994. Reprinted with permission of Manchester University Press.

selves to atone for human sin. They also bullied communities that they visited, demanding to be housed, clothed, and fed. (See Primary Source: Flagellants in England.)

For many who survived the plague, Thomas Aquinas's rational Christianity no longer appealed, and disappointment with the clergy smoldered. Famished peasants resented priests and monks for living lives of luxury in violation of church tenets. In addition, they despaired at the absence of clergy when they were so greatly needed. In fact, many clerics had perished while attending to their parishioners. Others had fled to rural retreats far from the ravages of the Black Death, leaving their followers to fend for themselves.

THE CHURCH'S RESPONSE   In the aftermath of famine and plague, religious authorities struggled to reclaim their power. The late medieval western church found itself divided at the top (at one point there were three popes) and challenged from below, both by individuals pursuing alternative kinds of spirituality and by increasing demands on the clergy and church administration. Facing challenges to its right to define religious doctrine and practices, the church identified all that was suspect and demanded strict obedience to the true faith. This entailed the persecution of heretics, Jews, Muslims, homosexuals, prostitutes, and "witches." But during this period the church also expanded its charitable and bureaucratic

Peasant Revolts. Long before the French Revolution, European peasants vented their anger against their noble masters. Lacking armaments and supplies, they usually lost—as this image of the brutal suppression of the French Jacquerie of 1358 depicts.

functions, providing alms to the urban poor and registering births, deaths, and economic transactions.

Persecution and administration cost money. Indeed, the needs as well as the extravagances of the clergy spurred certain questionable money-making tactics. One was the selling of indulgences (certificates that reduced one's time in purgatory, where souls continued the repentance that would eventually make them fit for heaven). This sort of unconventional fund raising, and the growing gap between the church's promises and its ability to bring Christianity into people's everyday lives, more than the persecutions, eventually sparked the Protestant Reformation (see Chapter 12).

A WEAKENING FEUDAL ORDER   Just as the mayhem of the fourteenth and fifteenth centuries unleashed hostility toward the church, it also undermined the feudal order. Since the Roman era, peasant uprisings had occasionally erupted. But now they escalated into large-scale insurrections. In France and England, massive revolts signaled the peasants' resentment against lords who failed to protect them from marauding military bands, as well as their exasperation with feudal restrictions that now seemed—for the few survivors of plague and famine—too much to bear. In 1358 the French revolt, or **Jacquerie**, broke out (the term derived from "Jacques Bonhomme," a name that contemptuous masters used for all peasants). Armed with only knives and staves, the peasantry went on a rampage, killing hated nobles and clergy and burning and looting all the property they could get their hands on. At issue was the peasants' insistence that they

should no longer be tied to their land or have to pay for the tools they used in farming.

A better-organized uprising took place in England in 1381. Although the **English Peasants' Revolt** began as a protest against a tax levied to raise money for a war on France, it was also fueled by post-plague labor shortages: serfs demanded the freedom to move about, and free farm workers called for higher wages and lower rents. When landlords balked at these demands, aggrieved peasants assembled at the gates of London. The protesters demanded abolition of the feudal order, but the king ruthlessly suppressed them. Nonetheless, in both France and England a free peasantry gradually emerged as labor shortages made it impossible to keep peasants bound to the soil.

STATE BUILDING AND ECONOMIC RECOVERY

In the wake of famine, plague, and peasant uprisings, Europe's rulers tried to rebuild their polities and consolidate their power. Although their efforts at state building pale in comparison with those of the empires rising in Asia, one family, the Habsburgs, established a powerful and long-lasting dynasty. They provided emperors for the Holy Roman Empire from 1440 to 1806. Yet the Habsburg monarchs never succeeded in restoring an integrated empire to western Europe (as Chinese dynasts had done by claiming the mandate of heaven).

Moreover, language did not unite Europeans. While the written literary Chinese script remained a key administrative tool for China's dynasts, and in the Islamic world Arabic was the common language of faith, Persian the language of poetry, and Turkish the language of administration, in Europe Latin lost ground as rulers chose various regional dialects to be their official state language. In 1450 Europe had no central government, no official tongue, and only a few successful commercial centers, mostly in the Mediterranean basin (see Map 11-5). Feudalism had left a legacy of political fragmentation and enshrined privileges, which made the consolidation of a unified Christian Europe even more difficult to achieve.

Those who sought to rule the emerging states faced numerous obstacles. For example, rival claimants to the throne financed threatening private armies. Also, the clergy demanded and received privileges and often meddled in politics themselves. The church's huge landholdings and exemptions from taxation made it, too, a formidable economic powerhouse. And once the printing press became available in the 1460s, printers circulated anonymous pamphlets criticizing the court and the clergy. Some states had consultative bodies—such as the Estates General in France, the Cortes in Spain, or Parliament in England—in which princes formally asked representatives of their people for advice and, in the case of the English

CENTRALIZATION UNDER THE MING

Zhu and successive Ming emperors had to rebuild a devastated society from the ground up. Although in the past China had experienced natural catastrophes, wars, and social dislocation, the plague's legacy was devastation on an unprecedented scale. It left the new rulers with the formidable challenge of rebuilding the great cities, restoring respect for ruling elites, and reconstructing the bureaucracy.

IMPERIAL GRANDEUR AND KINSHIP   The rebuilding began under Zhu, the Hongwu ("expansive and martial") Emperor, whose extravagant capital at Nanjing reflected imperial grandeur. When the dynasty's third emperor, the Yongle ("perpetual happiness") Emperor, relocated the capital to Beijing, he flaunted an even more grandiose style. Construction here mobilized around 100,000 artisans and 1 million laborers. The city had three separate walled enclosures. Inside the outer city walls sprawled the imperial city; within its walls lay the palace city, the Forbidden City. Traffic within the walled sections navigated through boulevards leading to the different gates, above which imposing towers soared. The palace compound, where the imperial family resided, had more than 9,000 rooms. Anyone standing in the front courts, which measured more than 400 yards on a side and boasted marble terraces and carved railings, would gasp at the sense of awesome power. That was precisely the effect the Ming emperors wanted (just as the Ottoman sultans did in building Topkapi Palace).

Marriage and kinship buttressed the power of the Ming imperial household. The dynasty's founder married the adopted daughter of a leading Red Turban rebel (her father, according to legend, was a convicted murderer), thereby consolidating his power and eliminating a threat. Empress Ma, as she was known, became Hongwu's principal wife and was praised for her compassion. Emerging as the kinder face of the regime, she tempered the harsh and sometimes cruel disposition of her spouse. He had numerous other consorts as well, including Korean and Mongol women, who bore him twenty-six sons and sixteen daughters.

BUILDING A BUREAUCRACY   Faced with the challenge of reestablishing order out of turmoil, Hongwu initially sought to rule through his many kinsmen—by giving imperial princes generous stipends, command of large garrisons, and significant autonomy in running their domains. However, when the princes' power began to threaten the court, Hongwu slashed their stipends, reduced their privileges, and took control of their garrisons. No longer dependent on these men, he established an imperial bureaucracy beholden only to him and to his successors. These officials won appointments through their outstanding performance on a reinstated civil service examination.

In addition, Hongwu took other steps to install a centralized system of rule. He assigned bureaucrats to oversee the manufacture of porcelain, cotton, and silk products, as well as tax collection. He reestablished the Confucian school system as a means of selecting a cadre of loyal officials (not unlike the Ottoman janissaries and administrators). He also set up local networks of villages to rebuild irrigation systems and to supervise reforestation projects to prevent flooding—with the astonishing result that the amount of land reclaimed nearly

The Forbidden City. The Yongle Emperor relocated the capital to Beijing, where he began the construction of the Forbidden City, or imperial palace. The palace was designed to inspire awe in all who saw it.

Lloyd, G. E. R., *Early Greek Science: Thales to Aristotle* (1970). An especially clear and concise introduction to the main developments and intellectuals that marked the emergence of critical secular thinking in the early Greek world.

Lloyd, G. E. R., and Nathan Sivin, *The Way and the Word: Science and Medicine in Early China and Greece* (2002). A comprehensive rethinking of the social and political settings in ancient China and city-state Greece that contributed to the different views of science and medicine that emerged in each place.

Murray, Oswyn, *Early Greece*, 2nd ed. (1993). One of the best introductions to the emergence of the Greek city-states down to the end of the archaic age.

Osborne, Robin, *Archaic and Classical Greek Art* (1998). An outstanding book that clearly explains the main innovations in Greek art, setting them in their historical context.

———, *Greece in the Making, 1200–479 BC* (1999). The standard history of the whole early period of the Greek city-states characterized by an especially fine and judicious mix of archaeological data and literary sources.

Pallottino, Massimo, *The Etruscans*, rev. ed., trans. J. Cremona (1975). A fairly traditional but still classic survey of all aspects of Etruscan history, political and social institutions.

Redford, Donald B., *From Slave to Pharaoh: The Black Experience of Ancient Egypt* (2004). A description of Egypt's twenty-fifth dynasty, which was made up of Sudanese conquerors.

Schaberg, David, *A Patterned Past: Form and Thought in Early Chinese Historiography* (2002). A comprehensive study of the intellectual content of historical anecdotes by the followers of Confucius collected around the fourth century BCE.

Schaps, David, *The Invention of Coinage and the Monetization of Ancient Greece* (2004). A new analysis that offers a broad overview of the emergence of coined money in the Near East and the eastern Mediterranean and its effects on the spread of money-based markets.

Sharma, J. P., *Republics in Ancient India, c. 1500 B.C.–500 B.C.* (1968). Relying on information from early Buddhist texts, this book first revealed that South Asia had not only monarchies but also alternative polities.

Shaw, Thurston, *Nigeria: Its Archaeology and Early History* (1978). An important introduction to the early history of Nigeria by one of that country's leading archaeologists.

Shinnie, P. L., *Ancient Nubia* (1996). An excellent account of the history of the ancient Nubians, who, we are discovering, had great influence on Egypt and on the rest of tropical Africa.

Snodgrass, Anthony, *Archaic Greece: The Age of Experiment* (1981). A good introduction to the archaeological evidence of archaic Greece.

Taylor, Christopher, Richard Hare, and Jonathan Barnes, *Greek Philosophers* (1999). A fine, succinct, one-volume introduction to the major aspects of the three big thinkers who dominated the high period of classical Greek philosophy: Socrates, Plato, and Aristotle.

Torok, Laszlo, *Meroe: Six Studies on the Cultural Identity of an Ancient African State* (1995). A good collection of essays on the most recent work on Meroe.

Welsby, Derek A., *The Kingdom of Kush: The Napatan and Meroitic Empires* (1996). A fine book on these two important Nubian kingdoms.

Chapter 6 Shrinking the Afro-Eurasian World, 350 BCE–250 CE

Bradley, Keith, *Slavery and Rebellion in the Roman World, 140 B.C.–70 B.C.* (1989). A description of the rise of large-scale plantation slavery in Sicily and Italy, and a detailed account of the three great slave wars.

Browning, Iain, *Palmyra* (1979). A narrative of the history of the important desert city that linked eastern and western trade routes.

Casson, Lionel, *The Periplus Maris Erythraei* (1989). An introduction to a typical ancient sailing manual, this one of the Red Sea and Indian Ocean.

———, *Ships and Seamanship in the Ancient World* (1995). The classic account of the ships and sailors that powered commerce and war on the high seas.

Colledge, Malcolm, *The Art of Palmyra* (1976). A well-illustrated introduction to the unusual art of Palmyra with its mixture of eastern and western elements.

Fowler, Barbara H., *The Hellenistic Aesthetic* (1989). How the artists in this new age saw and portrayed their world in new and different ways.

Green, Peter, *Alexander to Actium: The Historical Evolution of the Hellenistic Age* (1990). The best general guide to the whole period in all of its various aspects, and well illustrated.

Habicht, Christian, *Athens from Alexander to Antony*, trans. Deborah L. Schneider (1997). The authoritative account of what happened to the great city-state of Athens in this period.

Holt, Frank L., *Thundering Zeus: The Making of Hellenistic Bactria* (1999). A basic history of the most eastern of the kingdoms spawned by the conquests of Alexander the Great.

Hopkirk, Peter, *Foreign Devils on the Silk Road* (1984). A historiography of the explorations and researches on the central Asian Silk Road of the nineteenth and early twentieth centuries.

Juliano, Annette L., and Judith A. Lerner (eds.), *Nomads, Traders and Holy Men Along China's Silk Road* (2003). A description of the travelers along the Silk Road in human terms, focusing on warfare, markets, and religion.

Lane Fox, Robin, *Alexander the Great* (1973). Still the most readable and in many ways the sanest biography of the world conqueror.

Lewis, Naphtali, *Greeks in Ptolemaic Egypt* (1986). An account of the relationships between Greeks and Egyptians as seen through the lives of individual Greek settlers and colonists.

Liu, Xinru, *Ancient India and Ancient China* (1988). The first work to connect political and economic developments in India and China with the evolution and spread of Buddhism in the first half of the first millennium.

Long, Antony A., *Hellenistic Philosophy: Stoics, Epicureans, Sceptics*, 2nd ed. (1986). One of the clearest guides to the main new trends in Greek philosophical thinking in the period.

Martin, Luther H., *Hellenistic Religions: An Introduction* (1987). An introduction to the principal new Hellenistic religions and cults that emerged in this period.

Mendels, Doron, *The Rise and Fall of Jewish Nationalism* (1992). A sophisticated account of the various phases of Jewish resistance in Judah to foreign domination.

Miller, James Innes, *The Spice Trade of the Roman Empire, 29 B.C. to A.D. 641* (1969). A first-rate study of the spice trade in the Roman Empire.

Pomeroy, Sarah B., *Women in Hellenistic Egypt: From Alexander to Cleopatra* (1990). A highly readable investigation of women and family in the best-documented region of the Hellenistic world.

Ray, Himanshu P., *The Wind of Change, Buddhism and the Maritime Links of Early South Asia* (1994). Ray's study of Buddhism and maritime trade stretches from the Arabian Sea to the navigations between South Asia and Southeast Asia.

Rosenfield, John, *The Dynastic Art of the Kushans* (1967). Instead of focusing on the Gandharan Buddhist art itself, Rosenfield selects sculptures of Kushan royals and those representing nomadic populations in religious shrines to display the central Asian aspect of artworks of the period.

Rostovtzeff, Michael Ivanovich, *Caravan Cities*, trans. D. and T. Talbot Rice (1932). Though published more than seven decades ago, this small volume contains accurate descriptions of the ruins of many caravan cities in modern Jordan and Syria.

———, *The Social and Economic History of the Hellenistic World* (1941). A monumental achievement. One of the great works of history written in the twentieth century. An unsurpassed overview of all aspects of the politics and social and economic movements of the period. Despite its age, there is still nothing like it.

Schoff, Wilfred H. (ed. and trans.), *The Periplus of the Erythraean Sea* (1912). An invaluable tool for mapping the names and places from the Red Sea to Indian coastal areas during this period.

Shipley, Graham, *The Greek World after Alexander, 323–30 B.C.* (2000). A more up-to-date survey than Peter Green's work (above), with more emphasis on the historical detail in each period.

Tarn, W. W., *Greeks in Bactria and India* (1984). The most comprehensive coverage of Greek sources on Hellenistic states in Afghanistan and northwest India.

Thapar, Romila, *Ashoka and the Decline of the Mauryas* (1973). Using all available primary sources, including the edicts of Ashoka and Greek authors' accounts, Thapar gives the most authoritative analysis of the first and the most important empire in Indian history.

Vainker, Shelagh, *Chinese Silk: A Cultural History* (2004). A work that traces the cultural history of silk in China from its early origins to the twentieth century and considers its relationship to the other decorative arts. The author draws on the most recent archaeological evidence to emphasize the role of silk in Chinese history, trade, religion, and literature.

Wood, Francis, *The Silk Road: Two Thousand Years in the Heart of Asia* (2004). Illustrated with drawings, manuscripts, paintings, and artifacts to trace the Silk Road to its origins as far back as Alexander the Great, with an emphasis on its importance to cultural and religious movements.

Young, Gary K., *Rome's Eastern Trade: International Commerce and Imperial Policy, 31 BC–AD 305* (2001). This study examines the taxation and profits of eastern trade from the perspective of the Roman government.

Chapter 7 Han Dynasty China and Imperial Rome, 300 BCE–300 CE

Bodde, Derk, *China's First Unifier: A Study of the Ch'in Dynasty as Seen in the Life of Li Ssu (280?–208 B.C.)* (1938). A classic account of the key Legalist adviser, Li Si, who formulated the Qin policy to enhance its autocratic power.

Bowman, Alan K., *Life and Letters on the Roman Frontier: Vindolanda and Its Peoples* (1994). An introduction to the exciting discovery of writing tablets at a Roman army base in northern Britain.

Bradley, Keith, *Slavery and Society at Rome* (1994). The best single overview of the major aspects of the slave system in the Roman Empire.

Chevallier, Raymond, *Roman Roads*, trans. N. H. Field (1976). A guide to the fundamentals of the construction, maintenance, administration, and mapping of Roman roads.

Coarelli, Fillipo (ed.), *Pompeii*, trans. Patricia Cockram (2006). A lavishly illustrated large volume that allows the reader to sense some of the wondrous wealth of the buried city of Pompeii.

Colledge, Malcolm A. R., *The Parthians* (1967). A bit dated but still a fundamental introduction to the Parthians, the major power on the eastern frontier of the Roman Empire.

Cornell, Tim, *The Beginnings of Rome: Italy and Rome from the Bronze Age to the Punic Wars, c. 2000 to 264 B.C.* (1995). The single best one-volume history of Rome through its early history to the first war with Carthage.

Cornell, Tim, and John Matthews, *Atlas of the Roman World* (1982). A history of the Roman world; much more than simply an atlas. It is provided not only with good maps and a gazetteer but also with marvelous color illustrations and a text that guides the reader through the basics of Roman history.

Csikszentmihalyi, Mark, *Readings in Han Chinese Thought* (2006). A volume presenting a representative selection of primary sources to illustrate the growth of ideas in early imperial times; a useful introduction to the key strains of thought during this crucial period.

Dixon, Suzanne, *The Roman Family* (1992). The best one-volume guide to the nature of the Roman family and family relations.

Garnsey, Peter, and Richard Saller, *The Roman Empire: Economy, Society, and Culture* (1987). A perceptive and critical introduction to three basic aspects of social life in the empire.

Maalouf, Amin, *The Crusades through Arab Eyes*, trans. Jon Rothschild (1984). The European Crusaders as seen by the Muslim world.

Marcus, Harold G., *A History of Ethiopia* (2002). An authoritative overview of the history of this great culture.

Mass, Jeffrey, *Yoritomo and the Founding of the First Bakufu: The Origins of Dual Government in Japan* (1999). A revisionist account of how the Kamakura military leader Minamoto Yoritomo established the "dual polity" of court and warrior government in Japan.

McDermott, Joseph, *A Social History of the Chinese Book: Books and Literati Culture in Late Imperial China* (2006). The history of the book in China since the Song dynasty, with comparisons to the book's role in other civilizations, particularly the European.

McIntosh, Roderick, *The Peoples of the Middle Niger: The Island of Gold* (1998). A historical survey of an area often excluded from other textbooks.

Moore, Jerry D., *Cultural Landscapes in the Ancient Andes: Archaeologies of Place* (2005). The most recent and up-to-date analysis of findings based on recent archaeological evidence, emphasizing the importance of local cultures and diversity in the Andes.

Niane, D. T. (ed.), *Africa from the Twelfth to the Sixteenth Century*, vol. 4 of *General History of Africa* (1984). The general UNESCO

Tyerman, Christopher, *God's War: A New History of the Crusades* (2006). The balance of religious and nonreligious motivations in the Crusades.

Watson, Andrew, *Agricultural Innovation in the Early Islamic World: The Diffusion of Crops and Farming Techniques, 700–1100* (1983). An impressive study of the spread of new crops throughout the Muslim world.

Chapter 11 Crises and Recovery in Afro-Eurasia, 1300–1500

Brook, Timothy, *Praying for Power: Buddhism and the Formation of Gentry Society in Late Ming China* (1994). An analysis of the role of a significant religious force in the political and social developments of the Ming.

Glossary

Abd al-Rahman III Islamic ruler in Spain who held a countercaliphate and reigned from 912 to 961 CE.

aborigines Original, native inhabitants of a region, as opposed to invaders, colonizers, or later peoples of mixed ancestry.

absolute monarchy Form of government where one body, usually the monarch, controls the right to tax, judge, make war, and coin money. The term *enlightened absolutists* was often used to refer to state monarchies in seventeenth- and eighteenth-century Europe.

acid rain Precipitation containing large amounts of sulfur, mainly from coal-fired plants.

adaptation Ability to alter behavior and to innovate, finding new ways of doing things.

African National Congress (ANC) Multiracial organization founded in 1912 in an effort to end racial discrimination in South Africa.

Afrikaners Descendants of the original Dutch settlers of South Africa; formerly referred to as Boers.

Agones Athletic contests in ancient Greece.

Ahmosis Egyptian ruler in the southern part of the country who ruled from 1550 to 1525 BCE; Ahmosis used Hyksos weaponry—horse chariots in particular—to defeat the Hyksos themselves.

Ahura Mazda Supreme God of the Persians believed to have created the world and all that is good and to have appointed earthly kings.

AIDS (Acquired Immunodeficiency Syndrome) Virus that compromises the ability of the infected person's immune system to ward off disease. First detected in 1981, AIDS was initially stigmatized as a "gay cancer," but as it spread to heterosexuals, public awareness about it increased. In its first two decades, AIDS killed 12 million people.

Akbarnamah Mughal intellectual Abulfazl's *Book of Akbar*, which attempted to reconcile the traditional Sufi interest in the inner life within the worldly context of a great empire.

Alaric II Visigothic king who issued a simplified code of innovative imperial law.

Alexander the Great (356–323 BCE) Leader who used novel tactics and new kinds of armed forces to conquer the Persian Empire, which extended from Egypt and the Mediterranean Sea to the interior of what is now Afghanistan and as far as the Indus River valley. Alexander's conquests broke down barriers between the Mediterranean world and Southwest Asia and transferred massive amounts of wealth and power to the Mediterranean, transforming it into a more unified world of economic and cultural exchange.

Alexandria Port city in Egypt named after Alexander the Great. Alexandria was a model city in the Hellenistic world. It was built up by a multiethnic population from around the Mediterranean world.

Al-Khwarizmi Scientist and mathematician who lived from 780 to 850 CE and is known for having modified Indian digits into Arabic numerals.

Allied powers Name given to the alliance between Britain, France, Russia, and Italy, who fought against Germany and Austria-Hungary (the Central powers) in World War I. In World War II the name was used for the alliance between Britain, France, and America, who fought against the Axis powers (Germany, Italy, and Japan).

allomothering System by which mothers relied on other women, including their own mothers, daughters, sisters, and friends, to help in the nurturing and protecting of children.

alluvium Area of land created by river deposits.

American Railway Union Workers' union that initiated the Pullman Strike of 1894, which led to violence and ended in the leaders' arrest.

Amnesty International Non-governmental organization formed to defend "prisoners of conscience"—those detained for their beliefs, race, sex, ethnic origin, language, or religion.

Amorites Name that Mesopotamian urbanites called the transhumant herders from the Arabian desert. Around 2300 BCE, the Amorites, along with the Elamites, were at the center of newly formed dynasties in southern Mesopotamia.

Amun Once insignificant Egyptian god elevated to higher status by Amenemhet (1991–1962 BCE). *Amun* means "hidden" in Ancient Egyptian; the name was meant to convey the god's omnipresence.

Analects Texts that included the teachings and cultural ideals of Confucius.

anarchism Belief that society should be a free association of its members, not subject to government, laws, or police.

Anatolia Now mainly the area known as modern Turkey; in the sixth millennium BCE, people from Anatolia, Greece, and the Levant took to boats and populated the Aegean. Their small villages endured almost unchanged for two millennia.

Angkor Wat Magnificent Khmer Vaishnavite temple that crowned the royal palace in Angkor. It had statues representing the Hindu pantheon of gods.

Anglo-Boer War (1899–1902) Anticolonial struggle in South Africa between the British and the Afrikaners over the gold-rich Transvaal. In response to the Afrikaners' guerrilla tactics and in order to contain the local population, the British instituted the first concentration camps. Ultimately, Britain won the conflict.

animal domestication Gradual process that occurred simultaneously with or just before

G1

Five Pillars of Islam The five tenets, or main aspects, of Islamic practice: testification or bearing witness that there is no God other than God (Allah, in Arabic) and that Muhammad is the messenger of God; praying five times a day; fasting from sunup to sundown every day during Ramadan (a month on the Islamic calendar); giving alms; and making a pilgrimage to Mecca.

Five-Year Plan Soviet effort launched under Stalin in 1928 to replace the market with a state-owned and state-managed economy, to promote rapid economic development over a five-year period of time and thereby "catch and overtake" the leading capitalist countries. The First Five-Year Plan was followed by the Second Five-Year Plan (1933–1937), and so on, until the collapse of the Soviet Union in 1991.

Flagellants European social group that came into existence during the bubonic plague in the fourteenth century; they believed that the plague was the wrath of God.

floating population Poor migrant workers in China who supplied labor under Emperor Wu.

Fluitschips Dutch shipping vessels that could carry heavy bulky cargo with relatively small crews.

flying cash Letters of exchange—early predecessors of paper cash instead of coins—first developed by guilds in the northwestern Shanxi. By the thirteenth century, paper money had eclipsed coins.

Fondûqs Complexes in caravan cities that included hostels, storage houses, offices, and temples.

Forbidden City Palace city of the Ming and Qing dynasties.

Force Publique Colonial army used to maintain order in the Belgian Congo; during the early stages of King Leopold's rule, it was responsible for bullying local communities.

Fourierism Form of utopian socialism based on the ideas of Charles Fourier (1772–1837). Fourier envisioned communes where work was made enjoyable and systems of production and distribution were run without merchants. His ideas appealed to middle-class readers, especially women, as a higher form of Christian communalism.

free labor Wage-paying rather than slave labor.

free markets Unregulated markets.

Free Officers Movement Secret organization of Egyptian junior military officers who came to power in a coup d'état in 1952, forced King Faruq to abdicate, and consolidated their own control through dissolving the parliament, banning opposing parties, and rewriting the constitution.

free trade Domestic and international trade unencumbered by tariff barriers, quotas, and fees.

Front de Libération Nationale (FLN) Algerian anticolonial, nationalist party that waged an eight-year war against French troops, beginning in 1854, that forced nearly all of the 1,000,000 colonists to leave.

Fulani Muslim group in West Africa that carried out religious revolts at the end of the eighteenth and the beginning of the nineteenth centuries in an effort to return to the pure Islam of the past.

fur trade Trading of animal pelts (especially beaver skins) by Indians for European goods in North America.

Gandhi, Mohandhas Karamchand (Mahatma) (1869–1948) Indian leader who led a nonviolent struggle for India's independence from Britain.

garrison towns Stations for soldiers originally established in strategic locations to protect territorial acquisition. Eventually, they became towns. Alexander the Great's garrison towns evolved into cities that served as centers from which Hellenistic culture was spread to his easternmost territories.

garrisons Military bases inside cities; often used for political purposes, such as protecting rulers and putting down domestic revolts or enforcing colonial rule.

gauchos Argentine, Brazilian, and Uruguayan cowboys who wanted a decentralized federation, with autonomy for their provinces and respect for their way of life.

Gdansk shipyard Site of mass strikes in Poland that led in 1980 to the formation of the first independent trade union, Solidarity, in the communist bloc.

gendered relations A relatively recent development that implies roles emerged only with the appearance of modern humans and perhaps Neanderthals. When humans began to think imaginatively and in complex symbolic ways and give voice to their insights, perhaps around 150,000 years ago, gender categories began to crystallize.

genealogy History of the descent of a person or family from a distant ancestor.

Geneva Peace Conference (1954) International conference to restore peace in Korea and Indochina. The chief participants were the United States, the Soviet Union, Great Britain, France, the People's Republic of China, North Korea, South Korea, Vietnam, the Viet Minh party, Laos, and Cambodia. The conference resulted in the division of North and South Vietnam.

Genoa One of two Italian cities (the other was Venice) that linked Europe, Africa, and Asia as nodes of commerce in 1300 CE. Genoese ships linked the Mediterranean to the coast of Flanders through consistent routes along the Atlantic coasts of Spain, Portugal, and France.

German Democratic Republic Nation founded from the Soviet zone of occupation of Germany after World War II; also known as East Germany.

German Social Democratic Party Founded in 1875, the most powerful Socialist party in Europe before 1917.

Ghana The most celebrated medieval political kingdom in West Africa.

Ghost Dance American Indian ritual performed in the nineteenth century in the hope of restoring the world to precolonial conditions.

Gilgamesh Heroic narrative written in the Babylonian dialect of Semitic Akkadian. This story and others like it were meant to circulate and unify the kingdom.

Girondins Liberal revolutionary group that supported the creation of a constitutional monarchy during the early stages of the French Revolution.

global warming Release into the air of human-made carbons that contribute to rising temperatures worldwide.

globalization Development of integrated worldwide cultural and economic structures.

Gold Coast Name that European mariners and merchants gave to that part of West Africa from which gold was exported. This area was conquered by the British in the nineteenth century and became a British colony; upon independence, it became Ghana.

Goths One of the groups of "barbarian" migrants into Roman territory in the fourth century.

government schools Schools founded by the Han dynasty to provide an adequate number of officials to fill positions in the administrative bureaucracy. The Imperial University had 30,000 members by the second century BCE.

Gracchus brothers Two tribunes, the brothers Tiberius and Gaius Gracchus, who in 133 and 123–21 BCE attempted to institute land reforms that would guarantee all of Rome's poor citizens a basic amount of land that would qualify them for army service. Both men were assassinated.

Grand Canal Created in 486 BCE, a thousand-mile-long connector between the Yellow and Yangzi rivers, linking the north and south, respectively.

grand unity Guiding political idea embraced by Qin rulers and ministers, with an eye toward joining the states of the Central Plain into one empire and centralizing administration.

"Greased cartridge" controversy Controversy spawned by the rumor that cow and pig fat had been used to grease the shotguns of the sepoys in the British army in India. Believing that this was a British attempt to defile their religion and speed their conversion to Christianity, the sepoys mutinied against the British officers.

Great Depression Worldwide depression following the U.S. stock market crash on October 29, 1929.

great divide The division between economically developed nations and less developed nations.

Great East Asia Co-Prosperity Sphere Term used by the Japanese during the 1930s and 1940s to refer to Hong Kong, Singapore, Malaya, Burma, and other states that they seized during their run for expansion.

Great Flood One of many traditional Mesopotamian stories that were transmitted orally from one generation to another before being recorded. The Sumerian King List refers to this crucial event in Sumerian memory and identity. The Great Flood was assigned responsibility for Uruk's demise to the gods.

Great Game Competition over areas such as Turkistan, Persia (present-day Iran), and Afghanistan. The British (in India) and the Russians believed that controlling these areas was crucial to preventing their enemies' expansion.

Great League of Peace and Power Iroquois Indian alliance that united previously warring communities.

Great Leap Forward (1958–1961) Plan devised by Mao Zedong to achieve rapid agricultural and industrial growth in China. The plan failed miserably and more than 20 million people died.

Great Proletarian Cultural Revolution (1966–1976) Mass mobilization of urban Chinese youth inaugurated by Mao Zedong in an attempt to reinvigorate the Chinese revolution and to prevent the development of a bureaucratized Soviet style of communism; with this movement, Mao turned against his longtime associates in the communist party.

Great Trek Afrikaner migration to the interiors of Africa after the British abolished slavery in the empire in 1833.

Great War (August 1914–November 1918) A total war involving the armies of Britain, France, and Russia (the Allies) against those of Germany, Austria-Hungary, and the Ottoman Empire (the Central Powers). Italy joined the Allies in 1915, and the United States joined them in 1917, helping tip the balance in favor of the Allies, who also drew upon the populations and material of their colonial possessions. Also known as World War I.

Greek Orthodoxy Enduring form of Christianity that used the framework of the "Roman" state inherited from Constantine and Justinian to protect itself from Roman Catholicism and Muslim forces. The Greek Orthodox capital was Constantinople and its spiritual empire included the Russian peoples, Baltic Slavs, and peoples living in southwest Asia.

Greenbacks Members of the American political party of the late nineteenth century that worked to advance the interest of farmers by promoting cheap money.

griots Counselors and other officials to the royal family in African kingships. They were also responsible for the preservation and transmission of oral histories and repositories of knowledge.

Group Areas Act (1950) Act that divided South Africa into separate racial and tribal areas and required Africans to live in their own separate communities, including the "homelands."

guerrillas Portuguese and Spanish peasant bands who resisted the revolutionary and expansionist efforts of Napoleon; after the French word *guerre*.

guest workers Migrants looking for temporary employment abroad.

Gulag Administrative name for the vast system of forced labor camps under the Soviet regime; it originated in a small monastery near the Arctic Circle and spread throughout the Soviet Union and to other Soviet-style socialist countries. Penal labor was required of both ordinary criminals (rapists, murderers, thieves) and those accused of political crimes (counterrevolution, anti-Soviet agitation).

Gulf War (1991) Armed conflict between Iraq and a coalition of thirty-two nations, including the United States, Britain, Egypt, France, and Saudi Arabia. It was started by Iraq's invasion of Kuwait, which it had long claimed, on August 2, 1990.

gunpowder Explosive powder. By 1040, the first gunpowder recipes were being written down. Over the next 200 years, Song entrepreneurs invented several incendiary devices and techniques for controlling explosions.

gunpowder empires Muslim empires of the Ottomans, Safavids, and Mughals that used cannonry and gunpowder to advance their military causes.

Guomindang Nationalist party of China, founded just before World War I by Sun Yat-sen and later led by Chiang Kai-shek.

Habsburg Empire Ruling house of Austria, which once ruled both Spain and central Europe but came to settle in lands along the Danube River; it played a prominent role in European affairs for many centuries. In 1867, the Habsburg Empire was reorganized into the Austro-Hungarian Dual Monarchy, and in 1918 it collapsed.

Hadith Sayings attributed to the Prophet Muhammad and his early converts. Used to guide the behavior of Muslim peoples.

Hagia Sophia Enormous and impressive church sponsored by Justinian and built starting in 532 CE. At the time, it was the largest church in the world.

Hajj Pilgrimage to Mecca; an obligation for Muslims.

Hammurapi's Code Legal code created by Hammurapi, the most famous of the Mesopotamian rulers, who reigned from 1792 to 1750 BCE. Hammurapi sought to create social order by centralizing state authority and creating a grand legal structure that embodied paternal justice. The code was quite stratified, dividing society into three classes: free men, dependent men, and slaves, each with distinct rights and responsibilities.

Han agrarian ideal Guiding principle for the free peasantry that made up the base of Han society. In this system, peasants were honored for their labors, while merchants were subjected to a range of controls, including regulations on luxury consumption, and were belittled for not engaging in physical labor.

Han Chinese Inhabitants of China proper who considered others to be outsiders. They felt that they were the only authentic Chinese.

Han Fei Chinese state minister who lived from 280 to 223 BCE; he was a proponent and follower of Xunzi.

Han military Like its Roman counterpart, a ruthless military machine that expanded the empire and created stable conditions that permitted the safe transit of goods by caravans. Emperor Wu heavily influenced the transformation of the military forces and reinstituted a policy that made military service compulsory.

Hangzhou City and former provincial seaport that became the political center of the Chinese people in their ongoing struggles with northern steppe nomads. It was also one of China's gateways to the rest of the world by way of the South China Sea.

Hannibal Great Roman general from Carthage whose campaigns in the third century BCE swept from Spain toward the Italian peninsula. He crossed the Pyrenees and the Alps mountain ranges with war elephants. He was unable, however, to defeat the Romans in 217 BCE.

Harappa One of two cities that, by 2500 BCE, began to take the place of villages throughout the Indus River valley (the other was Mohenjo Daro). Each covered an area of about 250 acres and probably housed 35,000 residents.

harem Secluded women's quarters in Muslim households.

Harlem Renaissance Cultural movement in the 1920s that was based in Harlem, a part of New York City with a large African American population. The movement gave voice to black novelists, poets, painters, and musicians, many of whom used their art to protest racism; also referred to as the "New Negro movement."

harnesses Tools made from wood, bone, bronze, and iron for steering and controlling chariot horses. Harnesses discovered by archaeologists reveal the evolution of headgear from simple mouth bits to full bridles with headpiece, mouthpiece, and reins.

Hatshepsut Leader known as ancient Egypt's most powerful woman ruler. Hatshepsut served as regent for her young son, Thutmosis III, whose reign began in 1479 BCE. She remained co-regent until her death.

Haussmannization Redevelopment and beautification of urban centers; named after the city planner who "modernized" mid-nineteenth-century Paris.

Hegira "Emigration" of Muhammad and his followers out of a hostile Mecca to Yathrib, a city that was later called Medina. The year in which this journey took place, 622 CE, is also year 1 of the Islamic calendar.

Photo Credits

CHAPTER 1

Pages 2–3: Erich Lessing/Art Resource; p. 7: Volker Steger/Photo Researchers; p. 8: Robert Preston/Alamy; p. 11: Kenneth Garrett/National Geographic Image Collection; p. 12 (clockwise from top): Des Bartlett/Photo Researchers; John Reader/Photo Researchers; Staffan Widstrand/Corbis; p. 14: Pascal Goetgheluck/Photo Researchers; p. 15: Lionel Bret/Photo Researchers; p. 18: John Reader/Photo Researchers; p. 19: Images of Africa Photobank/Alamy; p. 21: Archivo Iconografico, S.A./Corbis p. 22 (both): French Ministry of Culture and Communication, Regional Direction for Cultural Affairs–Rhône-Alpes Region–Regional Department of Archaeology; p. 30 (top): Christie's Images/Corbis; (bottom): Lowell Georgia/Corbis; p. 32: Bruce Smith, *The Emergence of Agriculture* (New York: Diane Publishing Company, 1998), p. 104; p. 33: Boltin Picture Library/Bridgeman Art Library; p. 35: Erich Lessing/Art Resource.

CHAPTER 2

Pages 42–43: The Trustees of the British Museum/Bridgeman Art Library; p. 51: Granger Collection; p. 52: Peter Bull Art Studio; p. 53: Dean Conger/Corbis; p. 54 (left): HIP/Art Resource; (right): University of Pennsylvania, Museum of Archaeology and Anthropology, B16693; p. 55: The Trustees of the British Museum; p. 56: University of Pennsylvania Museum of Archaeology and Anthropology; p. 58: Scala/Art Resource; p. 61 (top): Diego Lezama Orezzoli/Corbis; (bottom): Réunion des Musées Nationaux/Art Resource; p. 62: Borromeo/Art Resource; p. 63: Roger Wood/Corbis; p. 66: Kenneth Garrett/National Geographic Image Collection; p. 67: (clockwise from top left): Gianni Dagli Orti/Corbis; Christine Osborne/Corbis; The Art Archive/Corbis; p. 69 (left): Scala/Art Resource; (right): Sandro Vannini/Corbis; p. 73 (top): HIP/Art Resource; (bottom): The Art Archive; p. 75 (bottom): The Museum of East Asian Art/Heritage Images/The Image Works; p. 78: Simon Norfolk/INSTITUTE; p. 80: Adam Woolfitt/Corbis; p. 81: Ashmolean Museum, University of Oxford.

CHAPTER 3

Pages 84–85: JTB Photo Communications/Alamy; p. 87 (clockwise from top left): Scala/Art Resource; JTB Photo Communications/Alamy; Art Resource; p. 94: Roger Wood/Corbis; p. 95: Sandro Vannini/Corbis; p. 97: Berlin Museum; p. 100: Eric Lessing/Art Resource; p. 101: Vanni/Art Resource; p. 106: National Museum of India, New Delhi; p. 109: Yale University Art Gallery/Art Resource; p. 111: from Luo, Zhenyu ji, Yin xu shu qi jing hua. China: Shangyu Luo shi, Minguo 3: 1914; p. 112: Albrecht G. Schaefer/Corbis; p. 114 (left): Gianni Dagli Orti/Corbis; (right): http://ina.tamu .edu/ub-ingots.htm, Institute of Nautical Archaeology, Bodrum, Turkey; p. 116: Erich Lessing/Art Resource; p. 117: The Art Archive/National Archaeological Museum, Athens/Dagli Orti; p. 118 (top): University of Cincinnati; (bottom): Peter Clayton; p. 119: Hermitage, St. Petersburg, Russia/The Bridgeman Art Library; p. 120: Giraudon/The Bridgeman Art Library.

CHAPTER 4

Pages 124–25: Dagli Orti/Louvre/Bridgeman Art Library; p. 127 (left): A. Paul Jenkin/Animals Animals; (right): S. Muller/Peter Arnold, Inc.; p. 132 (top): The Trustees of the British Museum; (bottom): Erich Lessing/Art Resource; p. 133: British Museum/Bridgeman Art Library; p. 135: SEF/Art Resource; p. 138: Alinari/Art Resource; p. 139 (top): Dagli Orti/Louvre/Bridgeman Art Library; (bottom): Erich Lessing/Art Resource, NY; p. 140 (top): Lloyd Cluff/Corbis; (bottom): The Art Archive/Dagli Orti; p. 142: Scala/Art Resource, NY; p. 144: AKG images/Peter Connolly; p. 145: Dagli Orti/Art Archive; p. 150: Oleksiy Maksymenko/All Canada Photos/Corbis; p. 151: The British Library/HIP/The Image Works; p. 152: Giraudon/Art Resource; p. 156 (left): Asia Society, New York: Mr. and Mrs. John D. Rockefeller 3rd Collection 1979, 100a,b. Photograph by Lynton Gardiner; (right): HIP/Art Resource.

CHAPTER 5

Page 160 (from left to right): National Library of China; Scala/Art Resource, NY; Erich Lessing/Art Resource, NY; p. 166: © Asian Art & Archaeology, Inc./Corbis; p. 168: Viktor Korotayev/Reuters/Corbis p. 171: Wikipedia; p. 172 (left): Erich Lessing/Art Resource, NY; (right): Smithsonian Freer Gallery of Art and Arthur M. Sackler Gallery; p. 173: British Library; p. 175: Borromeo/Art Resource, NY; p. 176 (left): Paul Almasy/Corbis; (right): Corbis; p. 180: Erich Lessing/Art Resource, NY; p. 181 (left): National Library of China; (right): Scala/Art Resource, NY; p. 183: (both): Gillett Griffin; p. 185: Princeton University Art Museum; p. 186: JTB Photo Communications, Inc./Alamy; p. 187: The Art Archive/ Xalapa Museum, Mexico/Gianni

Index